PENGUIN BOOK

THE FIRST HER

Craig Nelson is the author of three previous books; his writings have appeared in *Salon, Blender, Genre,* and a host of other publications. He was an editor at HarperCollins, Hyperion, and Random House for almost twenty years and has been profiled by *Variety, Interview, File, Manhattan, Inc.,* the *Daily News, Publishers Weekly,* and *Time Out.* He lives in New York City.

Praise for *The First Heroes*

"A riveting history . . . The author brings a passionately fresh perspective to this amazing story. . . . A gripping drama of WWII, retold with such freshness that it's nearly impossible to put down."
—*Kirkus Reviews* (starred review)

"The Doolittle Raid was Franklin Roosevelt's answer to Pearl Harbor. The gutsy mission shocked the Japanese, electrified America, and determined the shape and tenor of the entire Pacific War. If you want to read one book to understand how a humbled America rose to defeat mighty Japan, you hold that book in your hands. Read about the original 'Mission Impossible' of World War II. Read about the boys who flew off into history, believing they would never come back. Read about the boys who were the first heroes."
—James Bradley, author of *Flags of Our Fathers*

"*The First Heroes* is epic in sweep. The story of the Doolittle Raid lifts off the page, as rich and engrossing as any legend, and Craig Nelson proceeds to bring to vivid life the dramatic story behind the story. This is an astounding feat—the hours breathe with even the tiniest gesture of young men desperately fighting to stay alive against the panorama of modern war and a turbulent century in the making. Nelson is an amazing storyteller."
—Doug Stanton, author of *In Harm's Way*

"In this passionate and intimate history, Craig Nelson reminds us that America's first response to Pearl Harbor was neither tepid nor undramatic, but rather one of warfare's boldest chapters of righteous revenge."
—Hampton Sides, author of *Ghost Soldiers*

THE FIRST HEROES

★ ★ ★ ★ ★ ★ ★

The Extraordinary Story
of the Doolittle Raid—
America's First
World War II Victory

CRAIG NELSON

PENGUIN BOOKS

PENGUIN BOOKS

Published by the Penguin Group

Penguin Group (USA) Inc., 375 Hudson Street, New York, New York 10014, U.S.A.

Penguin Group (Canada), 90 Eglinton Avenue East, Suite 700, Toronto,
   Ontario, Canada M4P 2Y3 (a division of Pearson Penguin Canada Inc.)

Penguin Books Ltd, 80 Strand, London WC2R 0RL, England

Penguin Ireland, 25 St Stephen's Green, Dublin 2, Ireland (a division of Penguin Books Ltd)

Penguin Group (Australia), 250 Camberwell Road, Camberwell,
   Victoria 3124, Australia (a division of Pearson Australia Group Pty Ltd)

Penguin Books India Pvt Ltd, 11 Community Centre, Panchsheel Park, New Delhi – 110 017, India

Penguin Group (NZ), cnr Airborne and Rosedale Roads,
   Albany, Auckland 1310, New Zealand (a division of Pearson New Zealand Ltd)

Penguin Books (South Africa) (Pty) Ltd, 24 Sturdee Avenue,
   Rosebank, Johannesburg 2196, South Africa

Penguin Books Ltd, Registered Offices: 80 Strand, London WC2R 0RL, England

First published in the United States of America by Viking Penguin,
a member of Penguin Putnam Inc. 2002
Published in Penguin Books 2003

16   15   14   13   12   11   10   9

Map by Mark Stein Studio

Page 416 constitutes an extension of this copyright page.

Illustration insert credits: Bob Bell: page 2, top. Dick Knobloch: page 5, top; page 10, top. Bill
Birch: page 10, center, bottom; page 11, top left, top right, center, bottom. USS *Arizona*
Memorial: page 15, top right. Bill Aldrich (patiopan@aol.com): page 16. All others courtesy of
the National Archives and Records Administration, College Park, Maryland.

ISBN 978-0-670-03087-3 (hc.)
ISBN 978-0-14-200341-1 (pbk.)
CIP data available

Printed in the United States of America
Set in Adobe Garamond
Designed by Nancy Resnick
Map by Mark Stein Studios

For Mrs. Arlene B. "Tomi" Nelson,
Sgt. William D. "Bill" Nelson,
and Lt. Col. M. Thomas "Tom" Nelson

"Off we go, into the wild blue . . ."

CONTENTS

History Runs Away . . .   xi

Liftoff: April 18, 1942   xv

PART ONE   1

Volunteers   3

"The Man Who Can Never Stand Still"   32

Ship   50

Dai Nippon Teikoku   71

The Dreamer, Paralyzed   96

Liftoff   113

Bomb   131

Crash   161

PART TWO   189

Escape   191

Seized   235

Death   268

Metamorphosis   298

Peace   326

Coda   354

Acknowledgments   373

Notes   375

Sources   403

Index   417

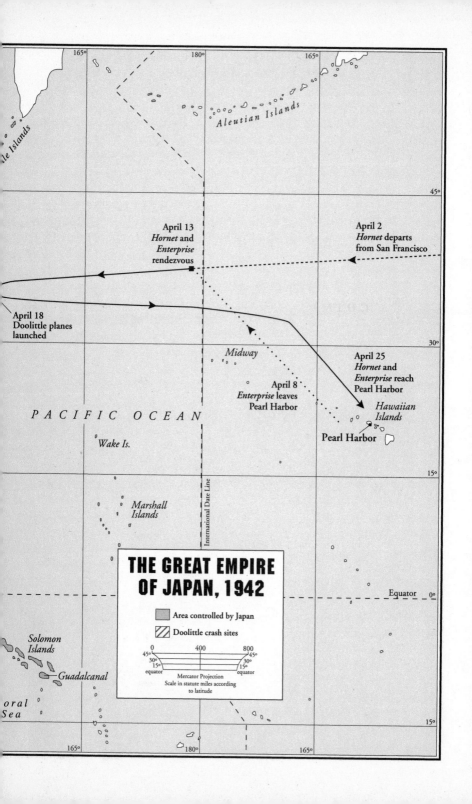

Aleutian Islands

le Islands

45°

April 13
Hornet and
Enterprise
rendezvous

April 2
Hornet departs
from San Francisco

April 18
Doolittle planes
launched

30°

Midway

April 25
Hornet and
Enterprise reach
Pearl Harbor

April 8
Enterprise leaves
Pearl Harbor

*Hawaiian
Islands*

PACIFIC OCEAN

Pearl Harbor

Wake Is.

15°

*Marshall
Islands*

International Date Line

THE GREAT EMPIRE
OF JAPAN, 1942

Equator   0°

Area controlled by Japan

Doolittle crash sites

*Solomon
Islands*

0   400   800
45°   45°
30°   30°
15°   15°
equator   Mercator Projection   equator
Scale in statute miles according
to latitude

Guadalcanal

*oral
Sea*

165°   180°   165°

HISTORY RUNS AWAY . . .

On October 14, 2000, I received a letter from an eighty-two-year-old man with the most distinctive handwriting I'd ever seen. Each stroke, a carved and italic spider line, looked as though it had been painfully chiseled into the page. The writer explained that "as a rural farmboy, I augmented my modest allowance by operating a trap line before catching the school bus. In skinning my catch, i.e., badgers, coyotes and skunk, I froze my fingers. Now, as an octogenarian, I'm paying for it with non-operative finger joints."

The letter was from Harry McCool, the navigator of plane four in the covert operation that became the first U.S. victory of World War II. Harry wrote me in answer to a questionnaire I had sent to every surviving member of his mission almost sixty years after it had taken place. I'd become convinced that their astounding story was one of the greatest moments in American history—a story that, until earlier that year, I'd never heard.

In World War II my father served with the Army Air Forces in New Guinea while my mother was an air traffic controller in Atlanta; later one of my uncles would become a career air force navigator. They filled my childhood with stories of daring raids, secret missions, and the astonishing bravery of what I learned, much later in life, were men barely out of their teens. Then Vietnam happened, and we no longer talked so much about my uncle's job or my parents' service years. It wasn't until I came across the story of Harry and his fellow airmen in an old issue of *American History* magazine that those tales from my childhood suddenly took on historical significance. That mission was the birth of the U.S. Air Force—a key part of my family's past—and I didn't know a thing about it.

Embarrassed and ashamed about my ignorance, I started asking around. It turned out that almost anyone who had been alive during World War II was as vividly aware of the story as Americans of my generation recall precisely where they were when John Kennedy was assassinated. Yet, with the exception of diehard World War II scholars and buffs, it seems to have completely escaped the attention of most other Americans today. Some areas of national amnesia deserve immediate attention, and I believe this is one of them.

I saw the story as one of ordinary people who became heroes, but in interviews, it became clear soon enough that more than a few of those involved believed otherwise. "None of us thought of ourselves as heroes," insisted co-pilot Dick Cole, while navigator Nolan Herndon had even stronger feelings: "To tell you the truth, I wish all of that would go away. We were just doing our job." Their job was an assignment many predicted would be a suicide mission, carried out by men with only rudimentary training. It would require, for the first time, the cooperation of thousands of recruits from both the army and the navy, as well as a new, frightening, and exhilarating method of flying bombers that no one had ever attempted before and no one would ever try again. Almost every man on the mission would be forced to abandon his plane as he ran out of gas in the middle of the night in a violent thunderstorm on the far side of the world. The men escaped from enemy-controlled territory by resourcefully managing to communicate with people who couldn't speak, read, or write their language.

Several of these boys, landing in a war zone, were captured, confined to years in solitary, tortured, forced to sign false confessions, tried as war criminals, and executed by firing squad. One flier was starved to death, while the survivors, rescued at war's end, had been reduced to living skeletons. One of them, tortured to the limits of human endurance, found God and subsequently returned to Japan on a campaign of forgiveness. Another was lost in a stateside limbo of army bureaucracy and mental illness. Still others were interned as enemy aliens by the Soviet Union, and had to be smuggled out into what is now Iran. One airman who began his military career on horseback would survive the mission, be captured by the Nazis, become part of the "Great Escape," and end his service years working with NASA and astronauts. Their raid, meanwhile, would lead directly to what every historian now believes was the turning point in the war against Japan.

As a child I was taught that history is made by kings and generals, popes and presidents, leading their secular and spiritual nations ever forward. As an adult I learned that often enough the polar opposite is true—that the big moments just as often depend on the actions of ordinary people in extraordinary times. In the last years of his life, Dwight D. Eisenhower told Stephen Ambrose that "Higgins was the man who won the war for us," Andrew Jackson Higgins being the New Orleans boatbuilder who invented and mass-produced thousands of plywood, flat-bottomed, ramp-fronted barges that floated American soldiers onto the beaches of Italy, Normandy, and the South Pacific. There were plenty of other unheralded men and women Ike could have mentioned, such as Robert Alexander Watson-Watt, the British physicist who developed enemy-aircraft-detecting radar; William M. Friedman of the U.S. Army Signal Intelligence Service and Alan M. Turing of the British Government Code and Cipher School, the American and English decrypters of Japanese and Nazi ciphers; the thousands of stateside Rosie and Ronnie the Riveters who built more tanks, planes, ships, guns, and bombs than any other country could ever hope to produce; and the men of this story, who convinced the American public in the war's first dark days that the Allies might ultimately triumph over what then seemed an invincible enemy. Today the United States is a global superpower, but at the dawn of World War II, the entire American coastline was under assault, and the nation was too weak to do much about it. It was an era when the United States and Britain had lost every single battle they'd entered, and had been beaten from all sides. It was a time when most Americans thought the war was over, that the Axis powers had already won.

In the early days of researching this book, my mother died, and when I came home for her funeral, there was one thing I especially wanted to see—her photo albums. Keeping these books, chronicling seven decades, had been one of her many hobbies, meticulously tipping in official pictures at family ceremonies as well as a barrage of casual snaps. During the war she escaped her hometown in rural Wisconsin to become an air traffic controller in Atlanta (where she found herself surrounded by interested servicemen), and the pictures from that time are astounding. Though the world may have been falling apart, a professional posed her in one of the classic looks of that era, the eyes focused ahead, the smile a determined glow of optimism for the future. Across the album's page were serrated Brownie shots my father had sent from New Guinea—in his khakis, as lean and slouching as Robert Mitchum. The pictures were mystifying. Neither was the mother and father I remembered, but both were people I'd like to know.

Research for the book led me to a newspaper archive and an article listing the survivors of this mission and the towns where they lived. Using an Internet white pages, I started dialing, in the order of what the article had implied was the importance of the men's standing in their Raiders' association. Twelve hundred World War II vets are dying every day, and the men I was trying to reach were no exception.

I called the first name on the list: deceased. The second: dead. The third had advanced Hodgkin's and could no longer talk on the phone. The fourth said it had been so long ago, he couldn't remember a thing. The fifth: dead.

On the sixth a daughter answered and very politely explained, "He can't come to the phone right now. He's out getting tested, since next week he's having brain surgery. Could you call back another time?" One airman was so active as a retired senior citizen that it took eleven phone calls to set up an interview. I called a few weeks later to double-check some facts, only to learn he'd suddenly passed away. Others wanted to participate as part of their last testament. These very sick men would recount events from sixty years past in faint, barely there voices, determined to have their stories told.

Around this time I had to make two business trips, one to Massachusetts and another to California. In both Nantucket and Yosemite, at opposite ends of the country and completely by chance, I wandered into local cemeteries. Their tombstones were blank. Though originally carved into marble to last for all eternity, the names and dates of the dead had been fully erased by two hundred years of history. The stones had forgotten, and were now rendered into rock-hard spots of amnesia.

Bill Birch, bombardier of plane eleven, said: "It is my hope that your book will acquaint future generations with the tenacious spirit America's men and women displayed those fifty-odd years ago . . . the aircraft and shipyard workers who built the necessary planes and ships needed to defeat a savage and ruthless enemy . . . the farm- and schoolboys who, in a few short weeks, learned to use the products of the factories and shipyards and then manned the ramparts of defense. . . . It was their determination and courage which ensured the final victory. This they did through personal sacrifice and in spite of facing an invader superior not only in numbers but in experience and equipment." It is my hope that *The First Heroes* has met Bill's challenge, and that it clearly demonstrates how the most ordinary men and women, "just doing their jobs," can change the course of the world.

PLANE ONE
Pilot—Lieutenant Colonel James H. Doolittle (45), b. Alameda, Calif.
Copilot—Lieutenant Richard E. Cole (26), Dayton, Ohio
Navigator—Lieutenant Henry A. Potter (23), Pierre, S.D.
Bombardier—Sergeant Fred Anthony Braemer (25), Seattle, Wash.
Engineer/Gunner—Sergeant Paul John Leonard (29), Roswell, N.Mex.

PLANE TWO
Pilot—Lieutenant Travis Hoover (24), Melrose, N.Mex.
Copilot—Lieutenant William N. Fitzhugh (27), Temple, Tex.
Navigator—Lieutenant Carl Richard Wildner (26), Holyoke, Mass.
Bombardier—Lieutenant Richard Ewing Miller (26), Fort Wayne, Ind.
Engineer/Gunner—Sergeant Douglas V. Radney (25), Mineola, Tex.

PLANE THREE *(WHISKEY PETE)*
Pilot—Lieutenant Robert Manning Gray (22), Killeen, Tex.
Copilot—Lieutenant Jacob Earle Manch (23), Staunton, Va.
Navigator—Lieutenant Charles John Ozuk, Jr. (25), Vesta Heights, Pa.
Bombardier—Sergeant Aden Earl Jones (21), Flint, Mich.
Engineer/Gunner—Corporal Leland D. Faktor (21), Plymouth, Iowa

PLANE FOUR
Pilot—Lieutenant Everett W. Holstrom (25), Cottage Grove, Oreg.
Copilot—Lieutenant Lucien Nevelson Youngblood (23), Pampa, Tex.
Navigator—Lieutenant Harry C. McCool (23), La Junta, Colo.
Bombardier—Sergeant Robert J. Stephens (27), Hobart, Okla.
Engineer/Gunner—Corporal Bert M. Jordan (22), Covington, Okla.

PLANE FIVE

Pilot—Captain David M. Jones (28), Marshfield, Oreg.
Copilot—Lieutenant Rodney R. Wilder (25), Taylor, Tex.
Navigator—Lieutenant Eugene Francis McGurl (25), Belmont, Mass.
Bombardier—Lieutenant Denver Vernon Truelove (22), Clermont, Ga.
Engineer/Gunner—Sergeant Joseph W. Manske (21), Gowanda, N.Y.

PLANE SIX *(GREEN HORNET)*

Pilot—Lieutenant Dean Edward Hallmark (28), Robert Lee, Tex.
Copilot—Lieutenant Robert John Meder (24), Cleveland, Ohio
Navigator—Lieutenant Chase Jay Nielsen (25), Hyrum, Utah
Bombardier—Sergeant William J. Dieter (29), Vail, Iowa
Engineer/Gunner—Sergeant Donald E. Fitzmaurice (23), Lincoln, Nebr.

PLANE SEVEN *(RUPTURED DUCK)*

Pilot—Lieutenant Ted W. Lawson (25), Fresno, Calif.
Copilot—Lieutenant Dean Davenport (23), Spokane, Wash.
Navigator—Lieutenant Charles L. McClure (25), St. Louis, Mo.
Bombardier—Lieutenant Robert Stevenson Clever (25), Portland, Oreg.
Engineer/Gunner—Sergeant David J. Thatcher (20), Bridger, Mont.

PLANE EIGHT

Pilot—Captain Edward J. York (29), Batavia, N.Y.
Copilot—Lieutenant Robert G. Emmens (27), Medford, Oreg.
Navigator/Bombardier—First Lieutenant Nolan A. Herndon (23), Green-
    ville, Tex.
Engineer—Staff Sergeant Theodore H. Laban (27), Kenosha, Wis.
Gunner—Sergeant David W. Pohl (20), Boston, Mass.

PLANE NINE *(WHIRLING DERVISH)*

Pilot—Lieutenant Harold Francis Watson (26), Buffalo, N.Y.
Copilot—Lieutenant James N. Parker (22), Houston, Tex.
Navigator—First Lieutenant Thomas Carson Griffin (24), Green Bay, Wis.
Bombardier—Sergeant Wayne Max Bissell (20), Walker, Minn.
Engineer/Gunner—Staff Sergeant Eldred V. Scott (34), Atlanta, Ga.

PLANE TEN
Pilot—Lieutenant Richard Outcalt Joyce (22), Lincoln, Nebr.
Copilot—Lieutenant J. Royden Stork (25), Frost, Minn.
Navigator/Bombardier—Lieutenant Horace Ellis Crouch (23), Columbia, S.C.
Bombardier—Sergeant George Elmer Larkin, Jr. (23), New Haven, Ky.
Engineer/Gunner—Staff Sergeant Edwin Weston Horton, Jr. (26), North Eastham, Mass.

PLANE ELEVEN *(HARI KARI-ER)*
Pilot—Captain Charles Ross Greening (27), Carroll, Iowa
Copilot—Lieutenant Kenneth E. Reddy (21), Bowie, Tex.
Navigator—Lieutenant Frank Albert Kappeler (28), San Francisco, Calif.
Bombardier—Staff Sergeant William L. Birch (24), Galexico, Calif.
Engineer/Gunner—Sergeant Melvin J. Gardner (22), Mesa, Ariz.

PLANE TWELVE *(FICKLE FINGER OF FATE)*
Pilot—Lieutenant William M. Bower (25), Ravenna, Ohio
Copilot—Lieutenant Thadd Harrison Blanton (23), Archer City, Tex.
Navigator—Lieutenant William R. Pound (23), Milford, Utah
Bombardier—Sergeant Waldo J. Bither (36), Houlton, Maine
Engineer/Gunner—Staff Sergeant Omer Adelard Duquette (26), West Warnick, R.I.

PLANE THIRTEEN
Pilot—Lieutenant Edgar E. McElroy (30), Ennis, Tex.
Copilot—Lieutenant Richard A. Knobloch (23), Milwaukee, Wis.
Navigator—Lieutenant Clayton J. Campbell (25), St. Maries, Idaho
Bombardier—Sergeant Robert C. Bourgeois (24), Lecompte, La.
Engineer/Gunner—Sergeant Adam Ray Williams (22), Gastonia, N.C.

PLANE FOURTEEN
Pilot—Major John A. Hilger (33), Sherman, Tex.
Copilot—Lieutenant Jack A. Sims (23), Kalamazoo, Mich.
Navigator/Bombardier—Lieutenant James Herbert Macia, Jr. (26), Tombstone, Ariz.
Engineer/Bombardier—Staff Sergeant Jacob Eierman (29), Baltimore, Md.
Gunner—Sergeant Edwin V. Bain (24), Greensboro, N.C.

PLANE FIFTEEN

Pilot—Lieutenant Donald G. Smith (24), Oldham, S.D.

Copilot—Lieutenant Griffith Paul Williams (21), Chicago, Ill.

Navigator/Bombardier—Lieutenant Howard Albert Sessler (24), Boston, Mass.

Engineer/Bombardier—Sergeant Edward Joseph Saylor (22), Brusett, Mont.

Gunner—Lieutenant Thomas Robert White (33), Haiku, Maui, Hawaii

PLANE SIXTEEN *(BAT OUT OF HELL)*

Pilot—Lieutenant William G. Farrow (23), Darlington, S.C.

Copilot—Lieutenant Robert L. Hite (22), Odell, Tex.

Navigator—Lieutenant George Barr (25), Brooklyn, N.Y.

Bombardier—Corporal Jacob Daniel DeShazer (29), West Stayton, Oreg.

Engineer/Gunner—Sergeant Harold A. Spatz (20), Lebo, Kans.

PART ONE

★

VOLUNTEERS

On January 21, 1942, the men of the Seventeenth Bombardment Group were ordered to transfer from their current base, an unnamed and still-under-construction airfield outside Pendleton, Oregon, to Lexington Field near Columbia, South Carolina. Though they were Army Air Corps men who followed orders and did what they were told, they couldn't help but have mixed feelings about this move. On the plus side they'd be getting out of the wet, frigid Northwest, where winter nights meant eighteen below, days were eternally overcast with soup (making landings consistently tough), and runways were clogged in half-melted slush. On the minus they were trading in antisub patrol across the Pacific for similarly worthless efforts over the Atlantic, a job one pilot derided as "stooging around, going from A to B, looking for things that weren't there."

Since the attack on Pearl Harbor six weeks earlier, the men of the Seventeenth had spent every daylight hour of permissible weather circling repeatedly over the same patches of coastline while searching with bare eyes and binoculars through endless coves and inlets for the speck-and-slash of an enemy conning tower or the slight break in the waves of a lurker, for the famed midget two-manners like the one that'd been captured off the coast of Oahu, or for a real prize, the eighty-five-crew giant, the biggest submarine Japan could sail. These airmen were trained and ready for war, but instead, after logging thousands of man-hours flying over their assigned grids, there had been only one engagement that could be considered a success—and it was hushed up by the brass.

"It was Christmas Eve 1941," remembered bombardier George Hammond. "We were on one of our first patrols. I was twenty-two years old. Brick Holstrom, the pilot, and the copilot, Hoss Wilder, were both second lieutenants; our navigator was a corporal; the radio operator, John O. Van Marter, a buck private; and I was a PFC, so we were a *very* high ranking crew.

"We'd taken off probably near noontime, and we'd been out flying repeatedly back and forth over the grid, approximately sixty-five miles west of the mouth of the Columbia River. We were flying quite low because the weather was not good, and we were staying below the clouds as much as possible."

"We went out over the ocean and went down to make contact with the water at about five hundred feet," said pilot Brick Holstrom, then twenty-five. "Our orders were: *If you see an unescorted submarine, attack!* Any American sub would be escorted by a surface vessel."

George Hammond: "There must have been several submarines operating out there, because there was a lot of lumber floating in the Pacific—quite a bit of debris bobbing around. We noticed that all day, and we guessed it came from where they had sunk some freighters, and that sort of thing. One or two times, we'd spot something, but they were far enough away they could escape with a quick dive. Suddenly Wilder shouted that he saw a submarine right next to us, and I looked out the right side and there was its nose coming out of the water—they were just surfacing.

"Wilder immediately made a very steep turn around to line up with it, but we were very close on it. At that distance you could set up a drop angle because the bomb, when it leaves the bomb bay of the aircraft and is suddenly out in the air and going forward, the two of you—the plane and the bomb—are going the same speed and the same direction. You'd take into account the wind and the airspeed, and use that to know when to flip the switch.

"As we rolled out, I dropped one bomb on it but it was over—a miss. So he made a quick turn around to come in the opposite direction across it for a second drop, which probably took eighty seconds—he brought it around very sharply. And I dropped two bombs at that time. One hit just by the stern of the submarine, and the second bomb hit right on deck, just forward of the conning tower.

"We got quite a concussion out of that drop; the plane shook like it broke. Holstrom banked so we could get a look. There was a lot of roiled water, the oil slick spreading out, and so forth. We only had four bombs, so we turned around once more and dropped the last bomb on the slick, because they leveled off and started the nose back down into their dive. That was about the extent of that. We circled the area a few times, and sent out a radio message about the strike."

It wouldn't be until August 1942—eight months later—that the five men aboard that B-25 would be awarded Air Medals for sinking the first enemy submarine in American coastal waters, as it took that long for the Army Air Corps to confirm and make public what had happened sixty-five miles off the coast of Washington. George Hammond explained: "We recovered into Boeing Field and were met by someone from the command of the West Coast area, and we were told that we couldn't speak of this at all. And we didn't, and it was kept very secret. The West Coast was in a turmoil anyway because of the attack in Hawaii just three weeks before. They had had sightings of offshore naval vessels and so forth, and it was all very sudden. They didn't want to give the people there more reason to worry, but I'm telling you, there were plenty of reasons."

The entire country was in fact already in a state of panic. As early as the night of December 7 three air-raid alerts had screamed through the streets of San Francisco, and the following morning the commander of defenses for the West Coast told reporters that enemy planes had been spotted overhead, that "they were tracked out to sea. Why bombs were not dropped, I do not know. . . . Death and destruction are likely to come to this city at any moment." Hollywood Hills residents insisted on installing their own battery of antiaircraft guns, while pitchfork-armed farmers walked the beaches of Puget Sound, looking for would-be invaders. Eventually the postattack trauma bloomed into mass hysteria: A Hawaiian dog was reported "barking in Morse code to Japanese subs offshore," and a Honolulu newspaper announced that enemy farmers on the islands were planting tomatoes in a secret method that would direct Axis planes to nearby military installations.

It was only the beginning of the dark days. On December 8 Librarian of Congress Archibald MacLeish shipped his institution's Declaration of Independence, Constitution, Bill of Rights, Gutenberg Bible, and Magna Carta to Fort Knox for safekeeping, while the Secret Service arranged for the president to use Al Capone's bulletproof limousine. Marine-manned machine-gun emplacements popped up overnight across the Federal District, and Treasury Secretary Henry Morgenthau urged FDR to have tanks standing by on Pennsylvania Avenue (Roosevelt declined). There were so many accounts of mob violence (both in physical attacks and in ransacking of homes and businesses) against anyone who looked Asian that eventually the first lady felt compelled to point out in her nationally syndicated newspaper column that not every person of Japanese descent living in the United States was a traitor or a spy. The *Los Angeles Times* replied: "When she starts bemoaning the plight of the treacherous snakes we call Japanese, with apologies to all snakes, she has reached the point where she should be forced to retire from public life." Later that same newspaper's headlines would scream: L.A. AREA RAIDED! JAP PLANES IMPERIL SANTA MONICA, SEAL BEACH, EL SEGUNDO, REDONDO, LONG BEACH, HERMOSA, SIGNAL HILL.

The most authoritative history of Pearl Harbor remains Gordon Prange's *At Dawn We Slept,* and its title sums up the mood of the entire country at that moment. The Seventeenth Bombardment Group's commanders were just as unprepared for the start of World War II as everyone else. Twenty-four-year-old bombardier Herb Macia remembered: "We got the call to report to base. Suddenly, within twenty-four hours, here were new aircraft flying in. The crews gathered that evening, and we were briefed that there was an aircraft carrier off the mouth of the Columbia River that had launched its aircraft to bomb San Francisco. We were to go out and attack it.

"Well, the group had just returned from maneuvers, and the navigators hadn't gone with them, nor had the bombardiers. None of us were familiar with the equipment. None of us knew how to even open the bomb bay doors. Ross Greening got up and explained exactly what we were to do. 'You go in,' and he drew a chart of it, 'and on your right-hand side you will see a toggle switch here, and you do something with that; and then you do this, and then you do that.' This was the degree that we were ready to go and attack this carrier."

Twenty-seven-year-old pilot Davey Jones remembered that moment as well: "We were at March Field in Riverside, California, on a maneuver involving the navy, on December 7. That's when it hit the fan. We all left in our airplanes, and off we went to Sacramento to get guns from the arsenal. The darn place was closed, and they had a hell of a time. Eventually we loaded some guns in the bomb bay, .50 caliber. Then off we went to Pendleton at night, and there must have been fifty or sixty of us. None of us were much at flying in formation at night.

"Some people were running around trying to load up with 250-pound bombs to repel the invasion. They were coming from Alaska, going to hit Seattle, and all that sort of business. During the night, two guys—two pilots—went in and said, 'Sir, I can't do it.' Colonel Otto Peck, our commander, said, 'If you are on this base at daybreak, I'll kill you.' I don't know whatever happened to those two guys. It was real, you know; we were all shaking in our boots."

At dawn we slept. The decade's first army recruits were armed with Springfield rifles designed in 1903 and outfitted in uniforms left over from 1917— tin hats and puttees (canvas strips for wrapping around the tops of shoes to keep them dry) and woolen pants reeking of mothballs. These novices were trained with cardboard weapons that fired flour instead of shells, and since the service didn't have enough tanks, it gave its new inductees trucks and told them to pretend. Recruits outfitted with American state-of-the-art had nothing to crow about, either—the U.S. Army Air Corps P-39 Airacobra fighters were notorious for suddenly tumbling out of the skies, their pilots completely losing control of the planes, the crew having to "get out or get dead." The P-38 Lightning, meanwhile, was designed to be used at high altitudes, but at those heights its oil would freeze, blowing out the engine, and its crew's hands and feet would get frostbitten.

Even the B-25s flown by the men of the Seventeenth Bomb Group were not exactly combat ready. Manufactured by North American Aviation and powered by twin Wright (as in brothers) R-2600-9 Double Cyclone fourteen-cylinder air-cooled radials (each rated at 1,700 horses for takeoff), the B-25 had a maximum speed of 300 mph at 15,000 feet, with a service ceiling of 27,000 feet and a range of 1,350 miles with a 3,000-pound load. Eventually North American would revise this model through a series culminating in the B-25J; it would become the world's most popular midrange bomber, selling tens of thousands of units to air forces domestic and foreign. The B-25Bs assigned to the Seventeenth were such a new design, however, that they were handed over in prototype for the men to test and work out any kinks. As the airmen found out soon enough, engine fires were so common that it became standard air corps procedure to have ground crew standing by with extinguishers every time the planes were started up, and the Wright Cyclones failed so often in the middle of cruising that cadets were taught to land on one engine before they learned how to do it on two.

The most glaring flaw of these early models was a profound lack of defense. While such big brothers as the B-17 Flying Fortress came with thirteen machine guns, the B-25B had only three. "These planes had absolutely nothing compared to what came later," ball gunner Chick Berger said. "These guys were flying on pure guts." In the nose the bombardier had to awkwardly slide a .30 caliber gun in and out of various ports to aim, but by the time he managed to get from one port to the next to repel any attacking fighters, it was too late. In Plexiglas bubbles at the aft, Bendix power-operated turrets housed twin .50 calibers armed by a full nine yards of ammo belt. The hydraulics powering these turrets, however, failed repeatedly, and the settings on the dorsal guns were such that low firing would tear the skin off the aircraft's fuselage. Even the targeting system didn't work past the first few seconds, as gunner Bert Jordan (a twenty-two-year-old from Oklahoma) found out: "Once you fired your guns, the sighting system would fog over. It was all mirrors and stuff in there. . . . After that you would just have to trace—every fifth bullet there was a tracer, and that was what you more or less aimed by, your tracer bullets."

It was the B-25 belly gunner, though, who found himself especially cursed. Cramped up and forced to his knees, he had to sight through a periscope of lenses and mirrors while using a dual hand control. He couldn't see either what his hands were doing or his barrels through the periscope, and the disjointed mechanism made most recruits too dizzy to fire. "The bottom turret was very complicated and worked 'backwards' to what was normal," their mission commander would complain. "It would have taken more time than we had available to master it; a man could learn to play the violin good enough for Carnegie Hall before he could learn to fire this thing."

In a B-25 the pilot and copilot sat side by side in a cockpit just barely big enough for two grown men; behind them, in a lowered cubbyhole, sat the navigator with a table full of charts and an array of instruments: a B-3 drift meter, A-12 and A-8 octants, and an aperiodic compass. Beneath the flight deck, crawlways led to the bombardier's station in the plane's ribbed, clear Plexiglas nose, and to the radioman-gunner's roof bubble and the engineer-gunner's belly ball. In an emergency the flight deck and tail gunners could pop out their own escape hatches, while the noseman would be forced to make his way back to the deck. Through that mullioned Plexiglas, he at least had the greatest view in the history of aviation—a real magic carpet ride. Since aerial combat often included enemy fighter and flak attacks, however, this amenity wasn't always appreciated.

Despite its flaws the B-25, which North American also named the "Billy Mitchell" in honor of the visionary brigadier general who had championed the combat use of air power, was such a dramatic improvement over the depression-impoverished air corps' prior craft that the men of the Seventeenth were thrilled to have them. "The B-25 was a really superior airplane, right on the cutting edge of technology for medium bombardment," said twenty-four-year-old pilot Trav Hoover. "We kind of fell in love with it." "You just had to stand there and look at them and breathe heavily," said another flier, also twenty-four at the time, Ted Lawson. "It's a grand ship, fast, hard-hitting, and full of fight. It is so much more than an inanimate mass of material, intricately geared and wired and riveted into a tight package. It's a good, trustworthy friend."

Moving a group the size of the Seventeenth from Oregon to South Carolina was a major headache, especially since the operation included several days of strange rumors and revised orders. While most flew directly south, one group was detoured. "We took about fifteen airplanes to Minneapolis by way of Cheyenne, for reasons unknown to us," said officer Davey Jones. "There several modifications were made.

"I got a call from Captain Ski York, who was Group Ops, to meet him at Wright-Patterson Airfield. So I went down to Dayton, and Ski and I climbed to the very top of one of the hangars there to get away from everybody else."

When he got back to Minneapolis, Jones called his men together in his hotel suite to announce: "There's been a change. We're not going to work out of Columbia. Captain York wanted me to talk to you and see how many of you would volunteer for a special mission. It's dangerous, important, and interesting."

Bombardier Bob Bourgeois, a twenty-four-year-old from Louisiana, remembered thinking: *Dangerous* is a pretty bad word when you're talking about airplanes.

"Well, what is it?" asked one lieutenant.

"I can't tell you," Jones said. "I don't even know myself. I've got a hunch, but no real information, and I'm not talking about my hunch. All I can tell you is that it's dangerous, and that it'll take you out of the country for maybe two or three months."

"Where?" someone wanted to know.

"I'm sorry, I can't tell you any more. You've heard all the particulars I can give you. So, who'll volunteer? It's perfectly all right if you don't. It's strictly up to you."

Here was a pack of good-looking young men, almost all just a few years out of high school, looking forward to trading the hell of rainy Oregon for those sultry Columbia weekends hunting for southern chippy and bearcat in their bomber jackets and khaki uniforms. Even so, they'd spent at least a year getting ready for combat, and few had second thoughts—pretty much every hand in that room shot up as fast as Jesse Owens. Almost exactly the same thing had happened a few days earlier with the rest of the boys already down in South Carolina.

Some of these airmen would be picked for the mission right off the beat, while others were forced to wheedle their way in. Before getting into the corps, twenty-three-year-old pilot Dick Knobloch was studying to be a veterinarian at the University of Wisconsin: "One day our ROTC group was about to have their spring formal, and I asked a friend if he could get me a date. He did, and I met the girl who turned out to be my wife . . . Rosemary Rice. We dated for about a year, and then, in 1940, I decided I had to 'do something' about the war situation, and so I got into my little Ford and drove down to San Antonio, Texas, to join the air cadet program at Kelly Air Force Base. Rosemary and I wrote letters and talked on the phone often . . . but my mind was on flying and getting into the thick of it.

"On graduation I was sent to the Seventeenth. When we were stationed at Pendleton and got the transfer to South Carolina with a layover in Minneapolis, I'd have a chance to visit Rosemary, who was living in Madison, Wisconsin. When I returned to the group, imagine my shock when I learned that there'd been a request for volunteers for a secret flight and I had missed it. To say I was brokenhearted would be putting it mildly! I went on with the group to South Carolina and began begging everyone I could find to please let me go along—in any capacity at all—even as the commander's bootblack. As it happened, one of the copilots was dismissed, and I got the job of flying copilot on plane thirteen—my favorite number."

Not everyone, however, jumped in with both feet flying. Bert Jordan (who'd eventually be Brick Holstrom's gunner on the mission) was already down at Columbia when the call for volunteers came: "One night I was on guard duty, and I got off at daylight. We had formation, and I was a little bit late getting in. People were holding up their hands. I said, 'What are you holding up your hands for?' They said, 'Well, they want somebody to go someplace.' I just wanted to get out of Columbia, so I held up my hand, and I was one of the fortunate or unfortunate, whichever the case may be. . . . I didn't know I was going for that, but I would have still volunteered, because I've got itchy feet and I like to travel."

One of the squadron's elder members was twenty-nine-year-old bombardier Jacob DeShazer, who was doing mechanic work in South Carolina at the time: "A sergeant called me while I was up in the hangar working and told me to get in the jeep and go see the captain. I'd never had any order like that before and wondered what I'd gotten into.

"I got into that room, and he had about fifteen or twenty of us there. He said, 'We're going to form a dangerous mission. Some of you fellows are going to get killed. How many of you will volunteer?' Well, I thought, Boy, I don't want to do that. We went around, and he said, 'Would you go? Would you go? Would you go?' And they all said yes. I was right down at the end of the line, so because all the others said they'd go, I said I would, too."

Out of these volunteers, the commanders selected 140—enough pilots, copilots, navigators, bombardiers, and gunners for twenty-five planes—and had them transferred to Eglin Field, the Air Corps Proving Ground just outside Pensacola. They arrived to find themselves not in the resort-beach Florida of their dreams, but instead in the northern Panhandle on the Gulf, and closer to Alabama than Miami. There weren't any orange or citrus groves, only loquats, and Eglin itself turned out to be a mosquito-infested palmetto swamp. "The reason Eglin was chosen," said ops officer Ski York, "was because it had about seven or eight satellite fields out in the swamps and the woods, and it was pretty secure from prying eyes." To men who'd spent months in the Northwest, however, the beaches on the other side of the highway stretched out white and inviting along the Gulf of Mexico, and even with a high in the low sixties and frequent drizzle, everyone went goose-bump swimming and boating when they could.

At Eglin they found they'd been quarantined away from everybody else on the base. "For secrecy's sake, we ate separately," said navigator Frank Kappeler, a twenty-eight-year-old from San Francisco, "and some of the waitresses referred to us as the 'Suicide Boys.'" When they then checked out their detoured-via-Minnesota B-25s, they discovered that odd changes had been made. The radios were missing; their commander would explain that "you won't need them where you're going." Instead of the nausea-inducing ball turrets, two broomsticks, painted black, stuck out from the tail to imitate .50 caliber guns. "In the 25, if an enemy fighter comes up at our same level he can make a pass at us on our tail and we can't shoot at him at all. At all," remembered noseman Sally Crouch, a twenty-three-year-old from South Carolina. "They took what looked to be something like two-by-sixes or two-by-eights and planed them up so that they looked like guns. They had to bore holes in the tail cone of the B-25 to put these wooden guns through them. Then they painted a black stripe on the cone to give the impression that they could elevate and depress the guns. But those guns were simply screwed down to support pieces inside." Copilot Robert Emmens, a twenty-seven-year-old from Oregon, looked at the broomsticks and thought: "I don't know whom they scared most, the Japs or us."

Deicer boots had been screwed into the wings, and a 160-gallon rubber fuel bag filled the tight crawlspace connecting the tail gunner to the cockpit. Ten 5-gallon cans of gas were locked down where the men usually stored their extra gear. The bomb bays themselves were stocked with a 225-gallon leakproof tank, along with, as their commander would report, a serious pile of ammo: "Special five-hundred-pound demolition bombs were provided by the Ordnance Department. These bombs were loaded with an explosive mixture containing 50 percent TNT and 50 percent Amatol. They were all armed with a one-tenth-of-a-second nose fuse and a one-fortieth-of-a-second specially prepared tail fuse. The one-tenth-of-a-second nose fuse was provided in case the tail fuse failed. Eleven-second-delay tail fuses were available to replace the one-fortieth-of-a-second tail fuse in case weather conditions made extremely low bombing necessary. The Chemical Warfare Service provided special five-hundred-pound incendiary clusters, each containing 128 incendiary bombs. A special load of .50-caliber ammunition was employed. This load carried groups of one tracer, two armor-piercing, and three explosive bullets."

These modifications, in total, gave the craft a 1,141-gallon fuel capacity (nearly double its usual 694), and overweighted it by three tons. Getting this all done in the four weeks of prep allowed for the mission was wildly difficult—just replacing the belly bubbles with the sticks was a bureaucratic headache. "We had Bendix turrets in the bottom of the airplane, which were not good," said Ski York. "To have those turrets removed was a hell of a job. You had opposition *(a)* from Bendix, *(b)* from the general in the Pentagon who was responsible for the procurement of the turrets, and so on. . . . Oh, there were just dozens of other jobs like this that had to be done all in thirty days and all not interfering with the training. Getting the bombs was not a small job. They had a full colonel in command of the Benicia Arsenal. He said he wasn't going to release any goddamn bombs to anybody without authority from Washington. It developed that we had three hundred bombs in the United States at the time, and that was one of the reasons he wasn't going to release any, war or no war. We had a lot of these tasks, and not everything went smoothly."

When the B-25 bombardiers went up to the nose to check on their Nordens, meanwhile, they had another shock. The Norden bombsight was America's biggest secret weapon in the early days of the war, and considered so important that it was loaded and removed by an armed guard. A Norden came equipped with its own emergency pistol for destroying it in case of a crash over enemy territory, and every man trained to drop American eggs had to first take the Bombardier's Oath:

> Mindful of the secret trust about to be placed in me by my Commander in Chief, the President of the United States, by whose direction I have been chosen for bombardier training . . . and mindful of the fact that I am to become guardian of one of my country's most priceless military assets, the American bombsight . . . I do here, in the presence of Almighty God, swear by the Bombardier's Code of Honor to keep inviolate the secrecy of any and all confidential information revealed to me, and further to uphold the honor and integrity of the Army Air Corps, if need be, with my life itself.

The bombardier keyed his altitude, crosswind, and airspeed readings into the Norden's analog computer, and sighted the target. The mechanism would then take control of the craft's autopilot, releasing its ordnance at exactly the right moment. This secret weapon was a key element in the AAC's strategy of high-altitude precision bombing, since, during its testing phase, well-trained crews had successfully used it to strike within fifty-five feet of a target from three miles up. Those tests, however, were conducted in excellent California weather, and when the Norden was employed in real-life combat with overcast, squalls, antiaircraft, and enemy fighter attack, its usefulness would be severely compromised. Still, for the men trained to use them, knowing how to operate the top-secret computer was a major part of their assignment, and the bombardiers of the Seventeenth were stunned that their Nordens were gone. Their commander explained that this modification was for security's sake, since "it's inevitable that some of the ships will fall into enemy hands."

In the computer's stead sat a cheap sliding gauge made from scrap Dural aluminum, modeled on a rifle sight and swiveling in sync with the cockpit's pilot direction indicator needle. Its designer, twenty-seven-year-old armament officer Capt. Charles Ross Greening, was also the man responsible for the broomstick tailguns. Ross called his sight the Mark Twain, and to make sure it worked, he and his mission commander took a few black-cat test flights with twenty-one-year-old Ken Reddy acting as noseman. Lieutenant Reddy would ultimately serve as Ross's copilot on the "interesting" operation, and before those tests he'd never dropped a bomb in his life. When Ken got three solid hits in a row over the Gulf of Mexico, the commander ordered all the mission's Nordens replaced with Twains.

The volunteers next discovered that the training for this mission would be even more peculiar than their rejiggered Mitchells. The man in charge, the man who would decide which sixteen of the twenty-four crews would actually go on this hush-hush operation and which would be left behind, wasn't even an army man but Lt. Henry Miller, USN. The day this navy pilot arrived at Eglin, he couldn't find the mission's commander or executive officer, so he fell into chatting with ops man Capt. Ski York, nav chief Capt. Davey Jones, and ordnance officer Capt. Ross Greening.

Miller explained that he was at Eglin to train them to take off from a five-hundred-foot taxi at a mere fifty miles an hour. The army pilots thought he'd lost his mind. It was the era of very long takeoffs—when flying boats, which floated in the water on their bellies, would use entire rivers and lakes to launch—and these men in particular had been trained to stay on the runway until they'd hit 110 mph before lifting up and away. They asked Miller if he had ever accomplished this five-hundred-foot stunt in a Mitchell, which, fully loaded, would normally take at least a thousand feet to launch. Hank admitted that, in fact, he'd never even seen a B-25 before.

The four men loaded up into a Billy. Greening sat in the nav well, observing, while Miller took the copilot chair. Carefully following Hank's instructions, Ski York lifted off . . . at fifty miles an hour. It was so impossible for the army men to believe that they were unanimously convinced that something had to be wrong with the airspeed indicator. Then Davey Jones had his turn with this crazy technique, and he got her up at sixty. It was a revelation.

The next day every crewman was taught what York, Jones, and Greening had just begun to believe was possible. Their Eglin runway had been narrowly outlined in white paint, and then flagged at 450-, 500-, 550-, 600-, 650-,

700-, 750-, and 800-foot points. A pilot had to get off by the 500 marker, always traveling within the very narrow lines, or his crew would be excused from the mission. It was a test not every man would pass.

Piloting a plane, like driving a car or riding a bike, becomes second nature, and for men used to thousands of feet of runway, taking off in a short burst meant fighting years of training and instinct. The technique itself was harrowing. They'd keep the wheel brakes on, with the elevator trim tabs set at three-fourths tail-heavy, and shove the throttle all the way forward, revving the engines to full bore. As the plane would shake violently on its tricycle struts, the wing flaps would be turned to down position and the brakes released. The plane would then tilt back, its tail scraping the ground and its wheels wobbling in every direction as it zigzagged haphazardly down the runway before lifting off. Keeping the wheels within the painted outlines was next to impossible—one pilot remembered it as "inducive to a short life." The taxiing looked so awful, in fact, that his buddies told Ted Lawson (whose Billy additionally had a left engine that kept cutting out) that he should call his plane the *Ruptured Duck,* which he did—even getting a gunner friend, Corporal Lovelace, to draw a sputtering, crutch-wielding, cartoon Donald on its side.

Miller's advice to the struggling fliers was to "drop the landing flaps and pour on the coal." They learned to pull the control yoke back gently, keeping the tail about six inches above the runway, which dramatically reduced the zigzagging skid. When the plane touched off, the yoke would slowly be eased up until cruising speed was hit, and the flaps then raised. Eventually the men grew to love this new technique. "At around four or five hundred feet, the airplane would leap in the air, and the copilot (who was in charge of the gear) pulled it up," said Brick Holstrom. "Actually it was stalling on and off and then recovering from the stall, that was the trouble [a stall being when the wind, speed, and position of an aircraft combine to make it suddenly falter in altitude; "like disconnecting a car's steering wheel at sixty-five miles an hour," as one pilot explained]. Getting past that, all we thought about at Eglin was returning back to the runway and doing it all over again." "You'd go to power and turn things loose," said Davey Jones. "We counted about three, pulled the stick back as far as it would go, and the airplane jumped up and you went forward with the yoke as far as you could go and held it there. Of course there are other factors that raised the level of your adrenaline pretty much." Before Florida no army airman could've imagined a B-25 lifting off in a mere 500 feet. Even with all their instructions, the pilots at first could barely get off before the 800 marker. By the end of a week, one hotshot—Don Smith—did it in 287.

The volunteers were next trained in hedgehopping—flying at extremely low levels to confuse radar installations and evade enemy fighters and antiaircraft guns—which involved tilting around buildings, grazing trees, skimming parallel to riverbanks, and inching under power lines with altimeters that read "0." The technique was hair-raising to those who'd never attempted it before, as it meant full concentration at every second on exactly what you and your plane were doing. Once they became adept at it, however, it was also the most fun the cockpit boys could ever possibly have.

In flier hierarchy fighters are the hotshot race-car jockeys, evading fire and coming in for the kill, while bombers are the truck drivers, with the just-as-dangerous but dramatically less glamorous job of making deliveries—one World War II bomber man even titled his memoirs *Milk Run*. American crews in particular, trained in high-altitude precision flying, commonly rose to between ten and twenty-five thousand feet, sighted their target, turned the plane over to the Norden, and returned to base for reloading to do the exact same thing all over again. For all the tough days of schooling they'd gone through to get these jobs, it didn't require an Eddie Rickenbacker to fly your basic American egg layer.

Now, in the skies of the Florida Panhandle and across the Gulf of Mexico to Houston (their regular 1,900-mile round trip), these bomber boys were flying as fighter Formula One as you could get. It's one thing to watch a sleek and nimble single-seater zoom, twist, and swoop its aerobatic way across the clouds—and quite another to see a bruising, portly Mitchell, with its crew of five and its ordnance of two thousand pounds, diving into plateaus a few feet overhead, those mighty Wright Cyclones screaming against the fields.

Whatever their initial misgivings, pilots and copilots especially thought this Eglin method of flying was the best thing that had ever happened to them: "In those days, we figured rules were only made to be broken," said Ross Greening. Navigators, bombardiers, and gunners—sitting more or less in the backseat, helpless—thought otherwise. Navigator Chuck Ozuk, a twenty-five-year-old from Pennsylvania, said, "Some pilots were doing a lot of crazy things against regulations, but they got all hepped up. They'd fly under those little bridges out where the plane could just about get through. It was a dangerous maneuver." Bombardier Jake DeShazer remembered, "We did low flying right down in the ditches sometimes. My pilot would get down in the ditch, for hiding, so he wouldn't be seen, I guess."

The low-altitude cruising also included experiments to see how far down they could get while still accurately dropping bombs. Using one-hundred-pound practice dummies, the pilots approached their targets from inches above the ground, pulling up to drop altitude, where the bombardiers would sight, open their doors, and release their loads. The Bombs Away signal light would blink in the cockpit, and the pilots would again dive back into a rooftop-skimming getaway. Their first drops were at the pre-Eglin standard of ten thousand feet, and then plunged far lower—Ted Lawson said he "laid one of the *Duck*'s one-hundred-pound eggs in practice one day from five hundred feet. The shock of the explosion on the ground threw me against the roof of the pilot's compartment and raised an egg on my head."

While navigators reviewed their celestial training, gunners began to learn how to shoot their .50 calibers in coordination with their Bendix-powered turrets. Almost every bubble boy was using each for the first time, as they'd been previously trained only with turretless .30s (in caliber, a .20 kills squirrels while a .50 pierces armor). Again and again their turret hydraulics would fail, but the problem couldn't be successfully fixed as it couldn't be consistently pinpointed. Sometimes a turret would work for a while and then stop for no reason; sometimes the plane had to be tilted up for the turrets to rotate fully, and sometimes down, and sometimes flat straight would be the only way to go. "A lot of the turret's electrical connections and brushes were exposed. Weather condensation would get on them and cause malfunctions, a salt atmosphere would disable them, and they frequently were out of commission, like so," explained Lt. Sally Crouch. "Our automatic pilots malfunctioned for the same reason, and our pilots would [eventually have] to hand-fly the airplane through some fourteen hours of mission." Their own commander added: "So much work had to be done on the turrets that few, if any, got the practice they needed in the air. The gunners had to get familiar with the .50s by ground-firing them on the firing range; none of them ever fired on a moving target from the B-25 in flight before we left Eglin." At one point a few of their practice misfires would almost bring down the plane carrying the base chief.

If the gunners finished their time at Eglin less than fully ready for combat, the bombardiers came away with the barest experience using the Mitchell's sole weapon of forward defense. "A certain amount of training was devoted to the firing of the .30 caliber nose gun," said armament officer Ross Greening. "It was realized that this gun would be ineffective, but the installation of .50 caliber guns in the nose did not seem possible in the time allowed. Practice strafing runs were made over sea slicks, but it was found [that] the mounts provided would not hold the gun firmly. This gun was mounted in such a fashion that it could be removed from one mount and placed in another, but the change could not be effected fast enough to warrant an attempt to change from one mount to another on any one pass at a target."

On top of everything else, each volunteer had to learn at least the basics of one other assignment. Navigators were schooled in the bombardiers' Mark Twains; pilots brushed up on their long-forgotten dead reckoning; copilots crash-coursed through the key mechanical operations. It was a bruising, around-the-clock schedule. "Our planes were in the air at 7 A.M. each morning and sometimes we'd still be at it at 10 P.M. . . . The officers in charge were always keeping after us to see that our ships were in tip-top shape," Ted Lawson said. "We had to be sure the life rafts worked. We had to check and recheck our instruments. We had to swing our compasses, for we had been warned that our mission would entail tricky navigation. Lifebuoys were placed three miles apart out in the Gulf, and we had to make many speed runs over them to test our airspeed indicators. One day we had to check the extra gas in the ships to test it for possible leaks. An extremely close record had to be kept of our gas consumption."

Between the quirks of their early-stage design and peculiar modifications, the Mitchells now seemed completely jinxed. The first 265-gallon tanks kept springing leaks, so they were replaced by 225-gallon self-sealers, but these eventually would be discovered leaking at their connectors. The engines would frequently refuse to crank over, the spark plugs were always fouling, the carburetors were constantly falling out of tune, and the racks kept refusing to release their ordnance. The boys were supposed to undergo fifty-five hours of flight training, but because of these mechanical troubles (and a few spells of heavy overcast), few even made it past twenty. Knowing the mission's secrets and considering its rudimentary training, Ross Greening said, "The record number of 'firsts' we were attempting quite chilled our blood."

The army doctors insisted everyone be fully immunized against pneumonia, typhoid, smallpox, tetanus, yellow fever, typhus, bubonic plague, and cholera. For most, that meant a course of eleven shots over a period of three weeks, and one sergeant complained that if anything happened to him, he'd bleed serum.

Eglin wasn't just an endless grind, however: "Most of the wives showed up and we lived it up, dancing and carousing most of the night and then up the next morning," said Davey Jones. "It got pretty wild. Of course when you're young, it doesn't really bother you." Many pilots, in fact, would finish their training days by giving the Valparaiso Inn, where the marrieds stayed, a nice buzz. Ted's wife, Ellen, was one of the women living there: "After everybody was transferred out of Oregon to Columbia, I drove cross-country in our Buick across Route 66 in tandem with Patty Gilbert, whose husband was in the group but not on the raid. We parted ways when it turned out she had to go to Columbia while I went on to Florida. I'd wear a rainhat—we were driving at night sometimes—and people would look and think it was a man driving.

"First night at Eglin, we had to go to a motel nearby, but then finally they arranged for the Valparaiso Inn to house us. They had meals and good food, and it was real fun. The inn had been a golf course resort for people from Chicago, and a bunch of us wives were there. We played golf once or twice, went boating, and Ted took me up in the B-25 on one of the practice runs, when he flew out over the Gulf of Mexico to drop his bombs. I was dressed like a guy, with my hair tucked under a cap. There were guards around, but Ted said we'd be okay, that we were supposed to do anything we wanted.

"The plane ride was really fantastic. Cold and noisy. Ted had to wear earplugs. I was three months expecting, and when he touched the ground, I got sick. McClure grabbed his cover for his navigational instrument. Bless him . . . he saved me."

At the last possible moment Hank Miller trained everyone in ship protocol—the proper way to board, how to salute the stern flag, how to take a shower with as little water as possible, how to man stations. Everyone finally realized that the navy would be ferrying them somewhere—but where? On a ridiculously speeded-up schedule 140 volunteers had learned a whole new way of flying, in bizarrely modified planes that seemed cursed for trouble, and still, only a few officers knew for certain what they were doing or where they were going.

Even though they were told not to discuss the mission, it couldn't be helped, and rumors swept from ear to ear. They were off to the Panama Canal, some insisted. No, it's the South Seas; nothing else makes sense. One looked at the deicers and was certain they'd end up on patrol in the Aleutians. Others tried guessing the destination from the contents of their first-aid kits: iodine, quinine, bandages, sulfa tablets, whiskey, morphine Syrettes, and condoms. "The biggest rumor I heard," said bombardier Bill Birch, a twenty-four-year-old from California, "was that we were going to help the French get planes off the Caribbean island of Martinique." Ted Lawson tried to keep from thinking about their future: "At night, back in barracks, it was tough to stay away from the subject. It helped a little to play hearts. . . . At least it kept us from thinking." Others tried to lose their worry with music: "The officers bunked in one giant room, and what I remember to this day about that is [Virginian] Shorty Manch and his record player," said navigator Frank Kappeler. "Shorty would be copilot for crew number three. His real name was Jacob, and he was six feet seven inches tall. Shorty had a record player and a collection, but it seemed like he owned only one record, 'Deep in the Heart of Texas.' He played 'Deep in the Heart of Texas' on getting up in the morning and three or four times prior to turning the lights out at night."

For most of the boys guessing about their destination was in fact more game than anything else. No matter how many times their superiors warned them how dangerous this mission was going to be, most couldn't help but feel devil-may-care. "We were young, and we didn't really give a damn," said bombardier Howard "Sess" Sessler, a twenty-four-year-old from Boston. "When they said, 'You're going to help the war effort,' all of us thought it was about time we did something. We weren't scared. Nobody knew what it was to be shot at. It was just like a sport. Like football or basketball."

The most senior officers had been informed—barely—about the mission's details. They knew its target, that it had originated with the ultimate higher-up, and that American military chiefs referred to it only as Special Aviation Project #1. Capt. Ski York, for one, did not think it would be like basketball: "I was fairly well convinced that none of us would come out of this thing alive. I was surprised that with such a conviction, my excitement and nervousness was replaced by a deep, and unusual for me, calm.

"My only real thought was that I had not been as good a husband as I could have been, and I blamed myself for being such a bastard at times."

The volunteers of the Seventeenth were like other World War II servicemen in that they came from every state in the Union, and from every background there was. On *Hari Kari-er*, for instance, bombardier Bill Birch had worked at his father's California meat market, navigator Frank Kappeler stevedored for the Southern Pacific Railroad, and pilot Ross Greening was an art student. Like other recruits they were mostly small-town boys still living at home with Mom and Dad when the army took them in and taught them how to fight: Before the war most had never been far from the house in which they were born; never been on a boat or a plane; and most of what they knew about Asia came from newsreel footage of Japanese bombing raids or from watching Paul Muni and Luise Rainer playing the parts of Chinese peasants in *The Good Earth*. The men of this mission were, however, very different from those who would follow, in that almost every one of them joined up well before the peacetime draft and the post–Pearl Harbor flood of inductees. They had gotten in during (and, in many cases, because of) the Great Depression, when Uncle Sam most definitely did *not* want you. The Army Air Corps especially did everything it could to deter recruits. When the war effort got under way in earnest later on, and the army faced heavy manpower shortages, the brass looked into the reasons why. As something of a joke, the president of MIT took a standard AAC entrance exam. He flunked.

The men of the Seventeenth had varied reasons for joining the corps when they did. Some had been in high school ROTC and were looking forward to a lifelong career in the service. Others were college kids who had run out of money, and some were sons being groomed to run the family business when the depression took its toll and destroyed that future. But no matter what the reason for their signing on, almost every man shared one powerful desire: to fly.

To be a little boy in the twenties and thirties, and to look up from your backyard to hear the roar of a man soaring through the clouds—well, it was so new, so exciting, and so exotic, that even Gen. Curtis "Iron Ass" LeMay would remember that moment: "Suddenly, in the air above me, appeared a flying machine. It came from nowhere. There it was, and I wanted to catch it. . . . Some day I'm going to go up in an airplane. . . . I'll be flying it. I'll just ride around wherever I want to go—fly wherever I want to, stay up as long as I please." Dick Knobloch, copilot of what its Raider crew would dub the *Lucky Thirteen,* had a similar memory: "My mother tells me that I was always building airplanes whenever I could get some pieces of wood, hammer, and nails together. I even tried to throw them off the top of the little barn we had in our backyard, where they used to keep the team of horses before people had cars. But the earliest thing I remember is after Lindbergh had flown the Atlantic in May 1927, he made a tour of the States. . . . I remember Charles Augustus Lindbergh looking directly at me, and waving."

Men who wanted to crew air for the United States at that time had to be in great physical condition with perfect, unaided eyesight; between the ages of eighteen and twenty-seven; and with a minimum of two years of college. They would have to ace the Army General Classification Test, and then be put through two weeks of the "classification battery"—mental and physical assignments that would judge "speed and accuracy of perception, ability to read and understand technical information, resourcefulness and judgment in problem solving, knowledge of math and mechanical principles, motor skills, coordination, finger dexterity, and reflexes." Their battery performance meant whether they'd train as pilots, copilots, navigators, engineers, radiomen, bombardiers, or gunners.

Those picked to be pilots then had to survive primary, which one instructor described as "learning how to handle a basic airplane; recover from stalls and spins; how to land, how to fly patterns, precision approaches, and landing techniques; and finally aerobatics like loops and snap rolls." Primary graduates (about half of those accepted) went on to ten weeks of basic, operating more complicated craft. Instructors drilled their cadets endlessly until they were able to run a cockpit completely on instinct, and then classified them for either single-engine (the road to fighters) or double-engine (bombers or transport). Everyone wanted to be a fighter, but few were chosen.

It wasn't all a grind, though, as Dick Knobloch remembered from his advanced training at San Antonio's Kelly Air Force Base: "I had one little girl that used to come out. I can still see her standing there in the farmyard, or ranch yard, I guess you'd call it in Texas, with the wind blowing and her dress pressed firmly against her budding body, and I'd come down and go right on by that little girl and wave my hand at her. I never met her, never saw her close up, but anytime I'd buzz that ranch, she'd come out of the house and stand there and wave at me."

Pilot Ted Lawson, with his classic, rangy GI good looks, would eventually become famous around the world in public appearances and with his best-selling memoir and MGM movie, *Thirty Seconds over Tokyo*. "In 1938 I was working at a little library at the LA City College," recalled his wife, Ellen. "Ted would come in there to sleep, because he worked at Douglas Aircraft nights till twelve while going to school in the day, and never got enough rest. He'd come into this little library and go to sleep, and I'd wake him up with the bell. That's how we met."

"I was chucking a thirty-six-dollar-a-week job with a company that was beginning to get big war orders from abroad for a seventy-five-dollar-a-month job that might break my neck," Ted remembered. "But I wanted experience. I wanted to get my fingers into different kinds of planes and see how they worked. The army had those planes.

"The training period did something to me spiritually. It gave me my first real feeling of belonging to something; of being proud of being a part of a team. I knew that for me there would now be more than just taking something the army was offering. I'd want to be giving, too."

"In 1940 he went to Randolph and Kelly for the nine-month course to get his wings, and while he was at Randolph he sent me a ring, a diamond ring of engagement, in the mail," said Ellen. "It fit. This was kind of a surprise, because they told him if he wanted to get into the regular air corps, he couldn't be married. Then he decided that, well, maybe he'd wait. The week he graduated, he had been saving his money, and he also bought us a second-hand car from an iceman. It was a beautiful 1939 Buick that he was just so proud of.

"When Ted was on maneuvers in Spokane, he called and said that if I wanted to get married, to come on up. He arranged a flight on United Airlines—a small plane from Portland to Spokane—and he and his pals from the Seventeenth Group met me at ten P.M. On September 5, 1941, two of them went with us to get married across the border in Coeur D'Alene, Idaho.

"On December 5, he came home to Los Angeles for a month's leave. We had plans to go up the Columbia River, we thought that would be fun, go out in nature and ride the river—we didn't know exactly what we were going to do. We were sitting outside three days later, listening to the president talk, when someone knocked on the door with the message: *All men return to your base.*

"I drove our car to McChord AFB to spend Christmas; then on New Year's Day the group was sent to Pendleton AFB for coast patrol. It was snowing and everything. It was terrible; they couldn't fly. But as we look back, it was just a perfect time for all of us to get acquainted. We were living in a motel, a little apartment, with a hotplate. I had all my sheets and Ted's radio-phonograph, the kind that let you play twelve records automatically. We'd go to the Saturday-night dances, and the guys went hunting by the bases—jackrabbits, mainly. They'd take them to the cook of the base, and he'd cook them. Big jackrabbits, almost like those in Texas."

One career army man, Edward "Ski" York, the only member of the team to have attended West Point, grew up thirty miles outside Buffalo: "Batavia is a very small town, and even at a young age, I knew I wasn't going to stay in Batavia, New York, all of my life. There was no opportunity there for anything, and anyone who wanted to get somewhere left Batavia as quickly as they could.

"I was not one of those born flyboys who tell you that ever since they were two years old they wanted to get in the air. As a matter of fact, I wanted to be a cavalry officer. The last year at West Point, they allowed us to train in the branch of the service that we intended to go into after graduation, which in my case was cavalry.

"About three months before graduation, they told us that anyone going into cavalry would have to buy two pairs of pink britches, two green blouses, two pairs of blue britches, two blue blouses, three pairs of brown boots, and two pairs of black boots. Good boots in those days cost $110 a pair, even during the depression. They read all this off for cavalry officers, and it all amounted to about two thousand dollars. At the end of all this, he said, 'Anyone going to flying school has to buy one shirt and one pair of slacks,' [and I said], 'Put me in, coach.'"

One of Ski's closest friends after the mission, pilot Davey Jones, has a service record that would make anyone want to sign up with the USAF right this minute: "I started out in horses and ended up Mach 2," he said. "You can't beat that! . . . I go back to the early days of flying, when you flew railroad tracks at night by the beacons. The old story of a few hours of boredom interspersed by moments of sheer terror is true. Why you didn't kill yourself, I don't know. I'll never know. How we fought the damn war, I'll never know. You think of thousands and thousands of decent people who didn't know what the hell they were doing . . . twenty-six-year-old colonels leading five hundred airplane raids and so on. . . . It tends to mature a person.

"At the University of Arizona I majored in JFA—just fooling around— and then went to active duty in the cavalry, which was one of the greatest years in my life. I was pretty tall at the time, a slim, dark-haired, dark-complected type. About ten of us went to Fort Bliss [Texas] and I was in E Troop of the Eighth Cavalry for a year, a very wonderful year. We had lots of night exercises. I can remember the Fifth and Sixth Cavalries came up in 1936, and I was on parade with fifteen thousand horses; four regiments of cavalry, two regiments of horse artillery, pack trains, mule trains—it was pretty thrilling. We had big trailers, and we could load eight horses in the trailer. The idea was that you went around the enemy in trucks, and then mounted up and rode into battle. Astonishing, isn't it? As late as 1937–38, we were thinking that way, or some people were thinking that way.

"However, I didn't get a commission. One day, I was walking across the parade field and ran into a friend. I said, 'Where are you going?' He said, 'I am going up to the hospital to take a physical.' I asked, 'What for?' 'Well,' he said, 'I'm going to the flying school to be a pilot.' I said, 'Huh, that sounds like a good idea.' So with my uniform, boots, spurs, and campaign hat, I went into an office, enlisted as a flying cadet, got into my car—a 1932 Chrysler Imperial roadster—and drove to Randolph.

"When we went onto Kelly, they divided us into pursuit, bombardment, observation, and attack; I was in the attack section. We had A-10s and A-17s, and we were the crème de la crème, the real thing. Then I was really in. I was assigned to the Thirty-fourth Attack Squadron, so I was happy as a fox. Things were cranking up, and they converted us; we became the Seventeenth Bomb Group, and they gave us B-18s. We'd load up with one-hundred-pound practice bombs, run these damn racetrack patterns or cloverleaf patterns, figure-eight patterns, dropping bombs for hours on end."

Pilots and copilots weren't the only crewmen who underwent heavy training. Bombardier school lasted from twelve to twenty-four weeks, mostly centered on the Norden, while navigators spent fifteen to twenty weeks learning dead-reckoning navigation (using ground features), celestial navigation (by the stars), and radio navigation (using signals received from ground stations). On this mission twenty-three-year-old Lt. Harry McCool would navigate for Brick Holstrom: "I grew up outside Beaver, Oklahoma, on a subsistence farm in the wheat belt that had been passed down, father to son, since the 1890s. It was the depression, and this was the Dust Bowl, so we went more than five years without a crop.

"I'd taken a flying course with the Civilian Aviation Program in '38–'39, training on Piper Cubs and Taylor Craft, and really got hooked. After graduating I got offers from both the Army Air Corps and the navy. Since the army acceptance letter had shown up three weeks before the navy, that's where I ended up.

"In primary, after you'd been there for three months, you'd have a check flight, a graduation flight, to see if you're ambidextrous enough to go onto the next phase. It turned out I had two left feet. I couldn't do the World War I combat maneuvers, which included an Immelman, a diving twist to get the enemy plane off your tail, and vertical reversement, for when you were being chased and you go through this violent gyration, and hopefully came out as the chaser. I wasn't that good, so they washed me out.

"At the time I was offered the choice of either bombardier or navigator training, or I could go home and take my chances with the draft board. It was now June 1940, and they had just started with the selective service. Well, I liked to fly, and the celestial navigation sounded like a nice, light-color version of being a specialist, so I was in the Army Air Corps' first class of navigators."

Quiet, small, shy, and something of a loner—but also direct and plainspoken—twenty-nine-year-old bombardier Cpl. Jacob DeShazer was born with neon blue eyes that would serve him well later in life. Jake's father, a farmer and minister in the Church of God, died when he was two years old; his mother remarried, and the family moved to Madras, Oregon, a town of less than three hundred, where his stepfather had a wheat farm and a dairy business, delivering milk. In high school Jake liked baseball, football, and math; smoked cigarettes; and sometimes played hooky: "When I got through high school in 1931, the depression was going real strong. I had a terrible time getting a job. I wanted to go on to school and get training; I signed up to go to a school down in Portland that trained you to be a diesel mechanic. But I couldn't even raise the fifty dollars I needed for that.

"I got a job as a camp tender over in Nevada for around three or four thousand sheep. I'd have to bake the bread out in the sagebrush, and had a string of mules and a bell mare saddle horse. I had a good time for about two years while I had that job.

"I thought if I had enough money, I'd go into business. I had a little place over near Medford, Oregon, and I had five hundred turkeys. I got them when they were a day old. I got those turkeys up in good shape by Thanksgiving time. They were so fat and good. The price had dropped from twenty-two cents a pound, had gone down to about thirteen or fourteen cents. I just came out even. I paid all the bills, but that was all I could do. That's when I got in the army, in 1940. I wanted to fly those airplanes and be a pilot. I didn't see any reason why I couldn't get in there and fly them. I guess I'd seen an advertisement or something."

Jake got his bombardier training at McChord Field after he'd been assigned to the Seventeenth as a mechanic from the Boeing School of Aeronautics: "I had been used to shooting jackrabbits over at Madras. My brother and I would go out in the old Model T and stand up. We didn't have any top on it. We'd see a rabbit running, or we could do that from the back of a horse, too, and get them on the run. We didn't think we were very good if we couldn't get them while they were running. So this sitting on the B-25 and just getting those crosshairs on that target down there at twenty thousand feet seemed like a pretty easy thing to me."

The bombardier for Ross Greening's *Hari Kari-er* would be the twenty-four-year-old, boyish, energetic, and meticulous Bill Birch: "My responsibility was to see that the bomb racks were in working order, and the bombs loaded correctly. I was charged with receiving, guarding, and installing the Norden in the bombardier's compartment, and returning it to the bombsight vault at the end of every mission. Since I'd passed the squadron exam for mechanic, I'd also assist our crew chief in inspecting and maintaining the plane.

"I'd arm the bombs, and from the nose, use a toggle to open and close the bomb bay doors, and release the load, either individually, in train, or in salvo. With the Norden, after the bombs dropped, the bay doors were closed, the AFCE [automatic flight control equipment, or autopilot] disengaged, and control of the aircraft was returned to the pilot.

"The bombardier's compartment was fitted with a bucket seat and safety belt; the backrest was armor plate. I talked to the rest of the crew with an interphone, which consisted of a handheld mike and an earphone headset. Besides the bombsight, the bomb bay door toggle, and the shackle toggles, I also had an altimeter and a magnetic compass. You'd get to the nose through a tunnel from the cockpit, which was both shallow and narrow and had to be traversed on hands and knees.

"Finally I manned the .30 caliber nose gun, which we learned soon enough was of little help in defense of the aircraft. There were three gunport positions from which it could be fired: above the bombsight and on each side of the compartment. These ports were a ball-and-socket joint attached to the Plexiglas, which could rotate through a certain degree of arc, both horizontal and vertical. The vertical and lateral movements were limited, and it was quite awkward and time-consuming to change position. There was a cocking or arming lever, which when pulled back advanced the ammunition belt, positioning a cartridge in the firing position. The twin handles containing the trigger mechanism were interconnected and could be activated by either of the gunner's hands."

Like military forces anywhere in the world, the Army Air Corps had hierarchy atop hierarchy, both a real-world chain of command and a de facto pecking order. This would operate even at crew level, where it was vital to pull together as a team. Throughout their careers navigators, bombardiers, radiomen, engineers, and gunners would often feel treated as second-class by the cockpit boys. "Today we're in a new level of civilization and regard for our fellow man, and we are not as stratified as we were back in those days when the class stratification by rank was rather strong," said navigator and bombardier Sally Crouch. "You associated only with your own kind, officers with officers, pilots with pilots, navigators with navigators, bombardiers with bombardiers. As a matter of fact, navigators looked down on bombardiers." Fellow nav/bomb man Herb Macia sensed this as well: "The feeling that we would never be accepted wholeheartedly by the pilots as fellow officers started growing. We tried to make friends among ourselves, particularly those of us who were married. In medium bombardment the navigation role was always questioned."

Even so one B-25 gunner would say: "You're flying with a crew, and you get very close. Sometimes it's better than brothers." In the latter years of the war, air force psychiatrists would study bomber crews to find out exactly what made the great majority of these men face the deadly skies of Europe in mission after mission. What they discovered was the Brotherhood of the Skies: Every airman felt he just couldn't let the rest of the guys down. One explained, "These men hung together like bananas on a bunch. We trembled together. We sorrowed together. We wept together."

"We were whipped into shape and we were good," remembers pilot Bill Bower about the men of the Seventeenth. "Oh, it was the greatest, wildest bunch of men that I have ever been associated with. There was just something about that Seventeenth Group, about the collection of people that were in it, that I have never experienced since. We played hard, we worked hard." The air corps' own report on the volunteers of this mission would say:

The men who were to compose the Expedition thus were not in any sense hand-picked. They were not the "cream of the crop," but average flying men of the United States Army Air Force. The gunners, almost without exception, had never fired a machine gun from an airplane. The navigators had had very little practical experience. None of those who had come forward was versed in combat or seasoned in any kind of action against an enemy. None of the crews had worked together as a group before they began their training.

While the volunteers of Special Aviation Project #1 trained away on the Florida Panhandle, the rest of the Seventeenth Bomb Group were assigned to counter a plague of attacks that would eventually kill twice as many seamen as had died at Pearl Harbor. The United States spent the first months of 1942 waiting daily for Japanese assaults on the mainland, assaults that would eventually come. In those early days of war, however, a far deadlier menace would arrive from the opposite front, and it would be as hushed up as the sub strike off the coast of Oregon had been.

"I was sent on down to Miami," said George Hammond. "We flew every day for about five months down there. Our ordinary route was from near Jacksonville all the way down past the Keys and out to the Dry Tortugas, southwest of Key West, and then back. I flew over five hundred hours, and all that time, we only saw one or two Nazi subs. We couldn't get to them in time. They were always able to dive out of sight before we could get a bead." With their six tubes shooting a mix of fifteen electric and steam-driven eels loaded with eleven hundred pounds of Torpex (a combination of cyclonite, TNT, and flakes of aluminum), and an array of deck-mounted 10.5 cm cannons, 3.7 cm guns, and twin 2 cm antiaircraft machine guns, squadrons of Nazi *Unterseeboote* had taken control of shipping lanes from Newfoundland to the Caribbean, devastating North American commerce and critically damming the flow of oil from Texas to the Northeast.

On December 12, 1941, the day after he declared war on the United States, Hitler decided that his country wasn't ready to launch a direct assault on New York, Boston, New London, Newport, and Hampton Roads, as the German navy had been planning for the past ten months. Instead he ordered a strike against U.S. merchant shipping. His U-boat chief, Adm. Karl Dönitz, would call this operation Paukenschlag (Drumbeat), and after taking a month to cross the Atlantic undetected and assume their positions, the

Drumbeat subs would be blindingly effective. Following their motto—
Angreifen! Ran! Versenken! (Attack! Advance! Sink!)—from January 11 to 31,
1942, Nazi U-boats would destroy fifteen ships in American coastal waters
between New England and the Carolina shoals, killing more than five hundred. By February 24 seventy-one ships would be lost.

The Nazi captains had no charts of American waters; instead they were
given tourist guides. At the start of the war, Japan, Germany, and England
had all blacked out their coasts, so that city lights couldn't be used at night
against their own ships. In the first three months after Pearl Harbor, the
United States refused to follow suit, and the U-boats had no trouble finding
their targets—the Nazi sub chiefs would in fact call Drumbeat "the Great
American Turkey Shoot." In his memoirs, U-boat 123 commander Reinhard
Hardegen recalled approaching New York City: "I cannot describe the feeling
with words, but it was unbelievably beautiful and great. I would have given
away a kingdom for this moment if I had one. We were the first to be here,
and for the first time in this war a German soldier looked upon the coast of
the U.S.A."

At dawn we slept. To protect the coastline from Calais, Maine, to Jacksonville, North Carolina (which the navy then called the Eastern Sea Frontier),
Rear Adm. Adolphus "Dolly" Andrews had twenty ships at his command.
In the winter of '41, between the weather and the fleet's age, only three
could be on station at any one time. None of them had a crew trained and
ready for antisub patrol, and none had the engine or gunpower to match German tin.

By March 4 twenty-seven tankers had been sunk from Maine to the
Caribbean, and at emergency meetings with the Navy and War Departments,
oil industry executives warned that if this destruction was not halted, the
domestic economy and the war effort would be fully derailed. Nothing
changed; in April the Eastern Sea Frontier war diary called the East Coast "the
most dangerous area for merchant shipping in the entire world," prompting
insurance companies to stop writing policies. A terrified oil industry committee now recommended arming all tankers with guns crewed by navy men,
bringing in the Civil Air Patrol to hunt for U-boats, and blacking out the
nighttime lights on the coast by which the Nazi subs clearly targeted their victims. Navy chief Ernest J. King rejected blackouts (he did, however, request a
"dim-out") and would have nothing to do with the Civil Air Patrol (though
the Army Air Corps would welcome it).

On March 15 King finally ordered all naval district commandants to have
the Coast Guard Auxiliary acquire or enlist small private vessels to be orga-

nized into coastal picket patrols on the Atlantic, in the Gulf of Mexico, and in the Caribbean. Their crews would include Comdr. Vincent Astor out of New York and Ernest Hemingway off the shores of Cuba. On March 19, Britain's First Sea Lord, Sir Dudley Pound, advised Admiral King that his coastal waters needed convoys as desperately as his Atlantic crossings did. The Royal Navy would end up transferring ten escort vessels, two dozen antisubmarine trawlers, and two squadrons of airplanes to guard English ships in American waters.

Few citizens at that time were even aware of this carnage, since the government was doing everything it could to keep Drumbeat a secret. On April 1 the Department of the Navy sent out a press release announcing that twenty-eight Nazi U-boats had been sunk off the coastal waters of the United States. In fact, by that date not one German submarine had been stopped. Instead, in its first six months of operation, Drumbeat would sink 397 American ships and kill more than five thousand civilians—America's worst-ever ocean defeat. The men of the Seventeenth would have even less success fighting subs in the Atlantic than they had in the Pacific—the AAC would not record one single strike against the U-boat armada.

Those living along the Eastern Sea Frontier, however, could see the truth for themselves—nighttime skies red from the fires of burning tankers; daytime beaches strewn with wreckage and human flotsam. On April 10, *U-123* would sink *Gulfamerica* so near Jacksonville that thousands swarmed to the beaches to watch the battle. Commander Hardegen remembered that triumph: "All the vacationers had seen an impressive special performance at Roosevelt's expense. A burning tanker, artillery fire, the silhouette of a U-boat—how often had all of that been seen in America?"

On February 23 at ten o'clock eastern time, sixty-one million American families dialed up their radio consoles to prepare for a special broadcast whose ratings would double those of the most popular show of the era, *Amos 'n' Andy.* Power stations would see their meters peak as the radio tubes warmed into gear; movie houses would watch their ticket sales for the night dwindle away. Washington had earlier announced that anyone listening to this particular broadcast might benefit from having a map of the world on hand to better understand what was being discussed. On February 21 one CS Hammond store in New York City sold more than two thousand maps.

Walking down a Chicago street, Saul Bellow reported that "drivers had pulled over, parking bumper to bumper, and turned on their radios to hear

Roosevelt. They had rolled down the windows and opened the car doors. Everywhere the same voice, its odd Eastern accent, which in anyone else would have irritated Midwesterners. You could follow without missing a single word as you strolled by. You felt joined to these unknown drivers, men and women smoking their cigarettes in silence, not so much considering the President's words as affirming the rightness of his tone and taking assurance from it":

> My fellow Americans. Washington's Birthday is a most appropriate occasion for us to talk with each other about things as they are today and things as we know they shall be in the future. . . . Washington's conduct in those hard times has provided the model for all Americans ever since—a model of moral stamina. He held to his course, as it had been charted in the Declaration of Independence. He and the brave men who served with him knew that no man's life or fortune was secure without freedom and free institutions.
>
> The present great struggle has taught us increasingly that freedom of person and security of property anywhere in the world depend upon the security of the rights and obligations of liberty and justice everywhere in the world.
>
> This war is a new kind of war. It is different from all other wars of the past, not only in its methods and weapons but also in its geography. It is warfare in terms of every continent, every island, every sea, every air-lane in the world. . . . Speaking for the United States of America, let me say once and for all to the people of the world: We Americans have been compelled to yield ground, but we will regain it. We and the other United Nations are committed to the destruction of the militarism of Japan and Germany. We are daily increasing our strength. Soon, we and not our enemies, will have the offensive; we, not they, will win the final battles; and we, not they, will make the final peace. . . .
>
> This generation of Americans has come to realize, with a present and personal realization, that there is something larger and more important than the life of any individual or of any individual group—something for which a man will sacrifice, and gladly sacrifice, not only his pleasures, not only his goods, not only his associations with those he loves, but his life itself. In time of crisis when the future is in the balance, we come to understand, with

full recognition and devotion, what this nation is and what we owe to it. . . .

The task that we Americans now face will test us to the uttermost. Never before have we been called upon for such a prodigious effort. Never before have we had so little time in which to do so much. These are the times that try men's souls. . . .

"THE MAN WHO CAN NEVER STAND STILL"

On Tuesday, March 3, the 140 Special Aviation Project #1 volunteers were called to the Eglin ops office for an introductory speech from their mission commander. The bare-bones room was much too small for that number and quickly turned packed and sweaty, with the late arrivals forced to lean on windowsills and against door frames. The atmosphere was especially tense as more than a few of the boys expected that now they'd finally be told the truth about where they were going and what they'd be doing. This day would, in fact, be the first time that many of them would learn who, exactly, their mission commander was. Those not in the know were shocked right out of their shoes when, exactly on time, the doors swung wide and in marched a hero from their childhood dreams.

Boys growing up between the wars had two kinds of men to look up to. There were the sports titans like Jack Dempsey, but looming much larger were those aces of the air, those awe-inspiring aviators who defied the laws of ordinary life, men like "Lucky Lindy" Lindbergh and World War I ace fighter Eddie Rickenbacker. For these Eglin volunteers, at that time, to learn that their mission leader was none other than the world-famous and notorious Lt. Col. James Harold Doolittle—well, it would be like being asked to join a secret new baseball team, and it just so happens the lead guy's Babe Ruth. They were completely stunned and excited.

Twenty-five-year-old Mac McClure, who would navigate *Ruptured Duck*, whispered to the men waiting near him: "We're in for something *really* big." Herb Macia said, "Of course he was a legend. Even then I would not have hesitated to call him America's greatest aviator. One thing was clear: This mission was very important if he was involved in it," and for Davey Jones, "It didn't take but two minutes, and you were under his spell. We were ready for anything."

The lieutenant colonel strode to the front of the room, faced his new men, and said:

> My name's Doolittle. I've been put in charge of the project that
> you men have volunteered for. This is the toughest training you'll

ever have. It will be the most dangerous thing any of you have ever done. It is inevitable that some of your planes will fall into the hands of the enemy.

The most important thing I have to tell you men today is that the lives of many are going to depend on how well you keep this project to yourselves. Not only your lives, but the lives of others will be endangered because there are a lot of people working on this thing. Don't talk about it with your wives, don't even discuss it among yourselves. If you think you've guessed this mission, you're wrong, but even so, don't share your guesses. Don't start any rumors and don't pass any along. If anybody outside this project gets nosy, get his name and give it to me. The FBI will find out all about him.

If you have any doubts, drop out now. Any man can drop out and nothing will ever be said about it. In fact, if there's any worry at all, if you've got a wife, or some kids, it would be your duty to drop out. No one will ask any questions; no one will think less of you for it.

None of the volunteers even considered taking Doolittle up on this offer. One airman said, "Within five minutes, we were his . . . we'd have followed him anywhere. . . . I don't think there was any doubt in anybody's mind that as long as he was with us, whatever he wanted to do, we'd go ahead and do it." Now, more than ever, no one wanted to miss out on this mission—whatever the hell it was.

Perhaps at that moment, though, if the volunteers had considered Jimmy Doolittle's professional history, they might have had second thoughts about that decision. After all, the flier chosen by the chief of the Army Air Corps to engineer and lead this attack force was at that time no one's idea of a sterling military commander, and no stranger to hopelessly daring causes. In an era known for its intensely complicated, internally contradictory, larger-than-life military leaders (Eisenhower, Patton, MacArthur, and Stilwell among them), Jimmy Doolittle was arguably the most dynamic, contradictory, and remarkable of them all. His character, from start to finish, was marked by a startling combination: a laser-sharp analytical intelligence and balls the size of your head. One look at the handwriting of this headline-grabbing daredevil with a Sc.D. from MIT defies expectations, as it so fully reveals someone methodical, intricate, and damned always to seek perfection—a john hancock as finely wrought as John Hancock's. At the same time, it was remarkable that this lieutenant colonel had survived to the year 1942 to be a middle-aged man of forty-five, since almost every one of his many professional colleagues had long since been killed in aerial crashes and explosions.

If a yearning for pulse-pounding, seat-of-your-pants action and adventure is genetic, then it's clear that James Harold Doolittle (he hated that "Harold") inherited quite a bit from father, Frank, who sailed around the Horn from Massachusetts to San Francisco in the early 1890s and then shipped out to Alaska, all to follow his gold rush dreams. If force of personality is equally hereditary, that must have come from his mother, Rosa Ceremah Shephard, a turn-of-the-century woman of strong opinion and indomitable will, who'd married Frank when he was doing carpentry work out of Alameda. Pictures of Jimmy's parents reveal their own contradiction: While Frank looks exactly of his era, with pomaded hair and handlebar mustache, Rosa seems timeless, with a charged presence that speaks eloquently of the much-remembered power of her will.

Within six months of Jimmy's birth in Alameda on December 14, 1896, Frank left to make a new life for the family in the Klondike mecca of Nome. He would have little success at mining or prospecting, but would earn enough making sleds and selling supplies to bring Rosa and Jimmy north three years later, when a major gold vein had been tapped just outside of town. That trip would be something Jimmy would never forget:

> We were just three of an estimated 25,000 people who landed on the Nome beach that summer. The scene that greeted my young eyes as we landed was chaotic. Everything one could imagine was being hauled in on barges from the ships: machines, mining equipment, lumber, sewing machines, mirrors, bar fixtures, tents, liquor, hardware, tools, food, clothing, small boats, furniture, wagons, horses, dogs, and everything else needed to make life as easy and "civilized" as possible. Along the beach as far as one could see were hundreds of people working almost shoulder to shoulder using the simplest hand tools, rocker boxes, and crude contraptions to look for those magic gold flecks among the sand grains. The streets were nothing but muddy trails winding around tents, cabins, and shacks that extended about two blocks wide and five miles long. Thousands of people slept outdoors in tents. Sewage and garbage were dumped into the Snake River; typhoid fever, dysentery, and pneumonia were common. Disputes were settled with guns, knives, or fists. The gold rush attracted not only optimistic adventurers, but also gamblers, thieves, confidence men, and prostitutes in droves. Years later, when I witnessed the hun-

dreds of vessels off-loading men and supplies for the invasion of
Normandy, it reminded me of that scene at Nome.

With his tiny physique and a face framed by corkscrew blond curls, Jimmy
would be regularly picked on in Alaska—one sadistic teacher even made him
write twenty-five times on the blackboard, "Jimmy Doolittle is the smallest
boy in the school"—and he grew up as he had to, becoming quite a scrapper.
"At the age of five I had my first fight," he said. "An Eskimo lad and I were
alone on the beach one day and we got into an argument. He pushed me and
I pushed back. He started to flail at me with his fists and I returned his blows.
One of my punches caught him on the nose and blood spurted all over his
parka. It scared us both. He began to cry and ran home to his mother. He
thought he was dying. I ran home to my mother, certain that I had killed an
Eskimo."

Many of Doolittle's other childhood memories, though, weren't so charming: "We had many dogs running loose in town all the time and some of them
were vicious, especially when they were hungry. There was a black lad in our
school named Phillip Goodwin. He was older than I but we were good
friends. One winter day when school let out and we were all running home,
Phillip tripped and fell. In an instant, a half dozen or more malamute sled
dogs jumped him. Many people came running but before the dogs could be
pulled off, they killed him. It was my first loss of a close friend." Nome win-
ters frequently saw epidemics of influenza that decimated the population, and
even the basic necessities didn't come easy. Since the Doolittle home had no
indoor plumbing, Jimmy had to take a dogsled four miles north every morning, chop through the ice of the nearest pond, and ferry home the family's
drinking and cooking water.

After eight years of this raw, harsh life, Rosa decided enough was enough.
She and Jimmy moved to Los Angeles, and though Frank showed up down
south from time to time and sent money from Alaska when he could afford
it, Rosa became her son's primary means of support and direction. She would
make sure that, no matter what, he would grow up to be a gentleman.

At the age of thirteen Jimmy attended an event he'd remember as the start
of his life's greatest passion. "In the winter of 1909–1910 the first air meet
was held on the West Coast at Dominguez Airfield, outside of Los Angeles,"
he said. "Dominguez was a pasture—there were no such things as airfields in
those days—and I had the chance as a youngster to go to this air meet and see
such aviators as Wright, and Curtiss and Hoxey, the old-timers of the day, flying their stick-and-wire airplanes. I can remember some of the pilots putting
their fingers in their mouth and holding it up to see if one side cooled faster

than the other, and if it did, there was too much breeze to fly." It was such an inspiration that for the next two years, the teenager would save up enough money to buy the materials to make his own hang glider, with instructions provided by a 1909 issue of *Popular Mechanics* magazine. His first flight, running off a cliff, ended in a crash and an almost-totaled flying machine. After months of repairs and rethinking, Jimmy decided he hadn't run fast enough to take off, and arranged for a car tow. He crashed again, the glider now destroyed beyond repair.

As a student at Los Angeles Manual Arts High School in 1910, he would meet the woman of his dreams, Josephine Daniels, but he didn't know that just yet. "Joe was a nice little girl," said Jimmy. "At that time, I was an ornery little boy, and I couldn't see any future in nice little girls." He did, however, see quite a future in the boxing ring, especially after winning twenty official bouts and becoming flyweight champion of the Pacific Coast. On weekends he was more than happy to jump in on a street brawl, and when an argument at a dance hall got seriously out of hand and he was one of those arrested, Jimmy called his mother to bail him out. Rosa said he could spend the night in the can. It was another turning point, as Doolittle vowed from then on to take control of himself, to leash his volatile emotions, and never again to get caught breaking the law. Jimmy would develop a remarkable sense of thinking things through in advance, detail by detail, honing an analytical mind-set that would become legendary in aviation science.

After high school Doolittle ceaselessly begged and wheedled Rosa to buy him a motorcycle. She offered a deal: If he'd give up boxing and flying for the rest of his life, he could have the bike. Jimmy quickly agreed, got his cycle, and just as quickly crashed and was hospitalized for six weeks. He then decided he would do what his father never could, and returned to Alaska to make a fortune in gold. His luck was even worse than Frank's, however, and he was forced to eat, meal after meal, the cheapest food in the state—fish. It would take twenty years before he could bring himself to look at a plate of salmon without having his stomach churn.

At the University of California (Berkeley) he studied mine engineering, even spending a few weeks working the Comstock Lode. As a sophomore he joined the tumbling team; one teammate, Frank Capra, would become a film director (and a 1942 Oscar winner for *Why We Fight*). Jimmy later believed that tumbling had grounded him with a sense of balance, while boxing had sharpened his reactions and forced him to think and act with renewed focus—all good qualities for a test pilot. At college he also developed a life-long taste for a glass of fine scotch.

After graduating, Jimmy found himself falling in love with Josephine Daniels, and he proposed. Joe, easily as strong willed as his mother, wasn't a bit interested in a husband with a future in pugilism. "I tried to think of any advantages she might want to consider in marrying me," Jimmy later remembered. "Actually they were hardly even measurable."

When war was declared Doolittle immediately signed up for the Aviation Section of the United States Signal Corps, the army division responsible for all areas of military communication from telegraph to radio to telephone, as well as for the creation of the national weather service, the transcontinental homing pigeon system, and what would in time be known as the United States Air Force. It was an era when planes were first being sent into battle— Germany's "Red Baron," Manfred von Richthofen, in his Fokker Dr-I triplane, was just starting to gain worldwide renown as a master of the dogfight (helped by a secret gear that enabled his machine gun to fire bullets between the propeller's blades). It was the most glamorous and exciting area of the service to be in, and it was also the one in which you were most likely to die.

Even those with broad piloting experience today can only vaguely imagine what it was like to go aloft in those early years, when balloons, dirigibles, and zeppelins were so common that the new craft were referred to as "heavier-than-air flying devices." The world's first flying man, civil engineer Otto Lilienthal, built himself a cone-shaped hill just outside Berlin to catch whatever wind might pass, and tried running down its sides cuffed to wings made from waxed cotton, willow, and bamboo. By 1891 he could glide for up to a thousand feet, but in 1896 Lilienthal's lack of control over his wings led to a fatal crash. In Washington, D.C., that same year, Samuel D. Langley made history with a powered machine, the *Aerodrome,* which flew 4,200 feet. It was unmanned, and when Langley tried the same design with a pilot seven years later, the *Aerodrome* crashed, twice. Luckily the pilot was fished out, more or less unharmed, from the Potomac.

Two months later, on December 17, 1903, two bicycle manufacturers stood on a beach and flipped a coin. The weather was terrible, with blustery, twenty-one-mile-per-hour winds, patches of frozen ground, and wet sand blowing in every direction, but the brothers just couldn't wait one more day. Orville Wright won the toss, climbed aboard, started the engine, double-checked the controls, and unhooked the wires that anchored the flimsy craft to a wooden track laid out in the sand. He began rolling forward while brother Wilbur ran alongside, and they "held onto each other's hand[s] . . . like two folks parting who weren't sure they'd ever see one another again," as one spectator recalled. The track ended, Wilbur let go, and Orville soared a wobbling 120 feet. Next came Wilbur's turn; he cleared 195 feet. Orville tried again, this time covering 200 feet; and Wilbur took a final spin, covering 852 feet in fifty-nine seconds (making the world's first flight shorter than the wingspan of a Boeing 747). A little boy, watching from the sidelines, ran all the way to Kitty Hawk screaming, "They done it! They done it! Damned if they ain't flew!" The brothers waited for five years until all their patents had been ratified before announcing their achievement to the world. After so many flying machines had so publicly failed, however, no one would believe them.

Has there ever been a pursuit more life threatening than being a pilot during the golden age of aviation? Anyone who's ever been on a sailboat knows you can be speeding along and then, for no good reason, stop dead—the mystery of the air. The first airplanes were as fragile as box kites (which they resembled), with spruce support bars; wings of stretched muslin; a four-cylinder, water-cooled engine; two rear-mounted eight-foot "pusher" propellers attached with bicycle chains; and a saddle. To fly, pilots lay facedown, turning and banking by twisting their hips in the saddle, which warped the shape of the wings in imitation of birds—the Wrights' breakthrough invention. In the first thirty years of flight, airplane engines had a regular tendency to stop working in the middle of a cruise. Newly designed craft were tested by being flown, and most of those experiments ended badly. None of the early craft could reach enough altitude even to make parachutes an option.

Between 1909 and 1913 twenty-four army officers learned to fly. By the end of those four years, eighteen would be dead from crashes and explosions. Of the first forty air mail pilots, thirty-one would die on the job. "Many thought air mail just next to suicide," one postal employee wrote. "I never worried, though, about being maimed or crippled, since air mailmen were always killed outright." One of the big attractions of the many flying shows of that time, on top of the planes canterwheeling inches over the heads of the spectators and rocketing around pylons in a perfect sideways bank, was the very real possibility of watching someone die.

With all the danger and excitement, the required stamina, and the daily broken records in speed and distance, it's no wonder these men—and a few women—were worldwide heroes. For those who loved it, flying was the most exciting thing you could ever possibly do, and well worth every risk. Besides the feelings of power at being above it all and the beauty of the world as seen from on high, there was always the pure sense of thrill. When you face death, your body reacts as it never has before. The adrenal gland pumps for all it's worth, and your brain supercharges into pinpoint focus. Time seems to collapse. When it's all over and it's absolutely clear you've beat the reaper, there is a vertiginous rush of euphoria, an overpowering lift of spiritual transcendence more addicting than any well-tuned drug. Test pilot Walt Noyes said, "When you're up there, you're God," while daredevil aviatrix Pancho Barnes claimed that flying made her feel "like a sex maniac in a whorehouse."

On his first day of cadet school in San Diego (a mere fourteen years after Kitty Hawk), Jimmy was taxiing to take off when, almost directly above his head, two Curtiss Jennys collided in midair. One pilot was killed outright; the other plane's student and teacher were seriously injured. Doolittle was shaken but knew from that very first day in the air that he loved to fly, and that he had the attitudes of a solid airman. "A poor pilot is not necessarily a danger- ous pilot as long as he remains within his limitations," Jimmy would come to believe. "And you find your limits in the air by getting closer and closer and closer and sometimes going beyond them and still getting out of it. If you go beyond and don't get out of it, you haven't learned your limitations, because you are dead." He also understood that if he wanted to live to see another day, he'd have to learn one thing immediately—how to crash: "A crack-up was not always serious, particularly if you could hook your wingtip on a tree or on anything that would cause the plane to break up gradually. Going in head- first or nose-first, of course, could be dangerous. But if you were able to break the initial impact, you could often walk away without a scratch."

At the dawn of World War I, planes were still manufactured from flimsy wood and easily ripped canvas (aviation giant Boeing, in fact, began life as a timber company). The pilot and passenger sat, with goggles, leather helmet, and seat belt, out in the open air, and flew with engines about as powerful as a lawnmower's. The controls were basic and simple: a stabilizer, a stick, a rud- der, a throttle, and a spark control. You just got in, and flew.

On Christmas break, between ground school training and reporting for active duty, Jimmy once again asked Joe for her hand. They'd now been dat- ing for almost seven years, and this time she said yes, even though both her mother and his tried to talk her out of it. They eloped, and were married on Christmas Eve 1917. Joe had to use a gift of holiday cash to pay for the license, which left them a nest egg of twenty bucks.

Doolittle now waited impatiently for the dream of every Signal Corps cadet, to be assigned to aerial combat over the skies of France. The Aviation Section, though, didn't have enough planes to go around, so instead he was transferred to Ohio's McCook, and then to Louisiana's Gerstner, and then back home to San Diego's Rockwell Field, test-piloting and learning a little about maintenance but, mostly, doing nothing but killing time along the way as a second lieutenant flight instructor. "I was pretty upset," he said. "My stu- dents were going overseas and becoming heroes. My job was to make more heroes. . . . I was then twenty-one, and it seemed to me a sad commentary on life that I should be sending other people over to be heroes, instead of going over myself." Doolittle would never see combat duty during the whole of World War I, a bitter disappointment he'd remember for the next twenty-five years.

Even so, the lieutenant didn't return to college for a mining degree but stayed in the service and became a notorious skylarker. His stunts had to be kept secret from Rockwell's disapproving base commander, Harvey Burwell, whose tight budget meant constant worry over downed planes. Doolittle paid no mind; he crashed one machine while chasing a duck, and another while trying to get a rise out of some navy pedestrians: "While I was hedge hopping, I saw two soldiers walking along a road and decided to give them a little scare. I buzzed a few feet over their heads, thinking they would be completely surprised. However, they just waved at me. I was indignant and came around for another pass, lower than before. I zoomed over them and felt my wheels hit a bump. I looked back and saw one of the soldiers lying prostrate on the ground. I was so shocked at my miscalculation that I didn't look where I was going and caught a barbed wire fence in my landing gear, and as I pulled up, the fence came along. The extra weight caused the plane to stall and smash on the ground. I wasn't hurt, and was consumed by the thought that I had killed someone because of my stupidity. I jumped out of the wreckage and rushed to the two boys, one of whom was rubbing his head. Amazingly, he wasn't hurt, but said he had a slight headache."

For a few weeks Cecil B. DeMille showed up at Rockwell to film airplanes taking off and landing as stock footage for his upcoming blockbuster. Every night the director invited Burwell to watch the footage with the crew, and at one screening the audience noticed something odd. Eventually DeMille realized that one of the planes was touching down with a man sitting in its landing gear, and immediately Burwell screamed: "Ground Doolittle for a month!" His subordinate, responsible for actually carrying out the order, asked how he could tell who the guilty airman was, and the colonel answered: "Who else but Doolittle?"

This was only the start of what would become a nationwide reputation. With a receding hairline and a chin so dimpled it would eventually cleft, Jimmy now stood five foot six in shoes, but height was the only thing that was small about him. A fireball of energy until his very final years—one biographer, C. V. Glines, would call him "the man who can never stand still"—he would inspire a tremendous following in the service with his commanding presence and his actions as an unremittingly loyal and fearless chief who'd never ask a subordinate to do anything he wouldn't do himself. "Doolittle was a great commander because he had just the right mix; he was both a forceful leader, and approachable as a man," said Bill Birch, while Dick Knobloch remembered the Old Man as "very astute. In meetings he'll sit there and listen and listen and listen and in a few short words he'll sum it all up and come up with a solution . . . an amazing grasp. He listens and then acts and that's it. Doesn't waste a lot of words. Yet he's a man's man. He's a hell of a guy to be with."

Despite the devotion he inspired in the corps, the number of records he would break, and the innumerable awards he would win, Doolittle could never feel truly satisfied with himself. At one point in his military career, he would even come to feel that the daredevil exploits of his salad years prejudiced certain brass against him. This personal dissatisfaction, however, would remain well hidden, and in every Doolittle photograph or newsreel appearance, he'd be immediately recognized by his outgoing persona, his endless optimism, and his now-famous grin.

In aviation history the post–World War I era was marked by barnstormers, airmen who crawled out onto the wings of biplanes and were twirled through the air as a gathering crowd cheered (and young boys dreamed of their own future in the clouds). Barnstormers started out by reenacting the acclaimed dogfights of Europe, and eventually developed more and more intricate, demanding, and dangerous maneuvers. It was not an easy life, and to make ends meet, they sold plane rides at five bucks a pop. One pilot of the time said that a barnstormer's biggest risk wasn't crashing or exploding, it was starving to death.

With air chief Gen. Billy Mitchell's encouragement, the corps sought to capitalize on the public's fascination. Doolittle approached Burwell with the idea of letting the local pilots organize air shows, and after receiving a grudging approval, he formed a five-man stunt team, the Five Daring Acrobats, who dazzled mere earthbound mortals with their multiple barrel rolls, tailspins, power spirals, and inverse flights, soaring "as if controlled by one hand," enthused the *Los Angeles Times*. Jimmy would spend hours sitting at a desk, figuring out the moves, and then more hours training until the five achieved complete aerial perfection. He next convinced his commander to let him and two other pilots try to be the first to fly from San Diego to Washington, D.C. By the second day his squadron had made it only as far as Needles, California, with two of the planes destroyed. They were ordered to give up and come home.

Doolittle couldn't give up. Pilots in that golden age saw aircraft as the future of the world, and they were determined to demonstrate to American businessmen, military chiefs, and civilians the glorious benefits that the shining tomorrow of global aviation would bring. Jimmy knew that long-distance flights would one day ferry cargo and passengers across the country, and he wanted to show the public exactly what it was missing. He decided he needed to make a successful transcontinental flight, no matter what it took.

The first person to fly coast to coast had been Calbraith Perry Rodgers. Deaf from a childhood attack of scarlet fever, Cal entered a contest sponsored by publishing magnate William Randolph Hearst to cross the country in less than thirty days in a Wright B, modified into a single-seater with a fifteen-gallon fuel tank. The Armour Company of Chicago paid him five dollars a mile to be the floating billboard for their new grape soft drink; his craft was named *Vin Fiz*.

Cal took off from Sheepshead Bay in Brooklyn on September 11, 1911, but couldn't reach Pasadena until November 5, and so failed to win the Hearst money. He'd crashed nineteen times along the way, and the only things that the *Vin Fiz* that departed from Brooklyn had in common with the *Vin Fiz* that landed in California were two wing struts and the vertical rudder; he'd gone through two engines, twenty skids, and multiple patches of wing fabric. Cal would touch down in the surf of Long Beach, California, on December 12 to lay clear claim to the coast-to-coast title, but four months later, on April 3, he crashed into a flock of seagulls and died.

A decade later Doolittle faced plenty of transcontinental competition. He decided to make his run in the De Havilland 4, a plane manufactured by actress Olivia's cousin Geoffrey, which was so notoriously fussy and difficult to handle that it was known as "the flaming coffin." He removed all its excess weight, replaced the passenger seat with an extra gas tank, and installed a new turn-and-bank indicator. Like all pre-1930 pilots, though, he had to settle for a barometric altimeter, which measured altitude from sea level rather than the actual height from the ground beneath one's wings. To solo over such distance, Jimmy himself would have to do some inventing: "As far as I know, I conceived the first little pilot dehydrator, a funnel and tube going out the bottom of the aircraft, facing aft. Unfortunately, occasionally the tube swiveled the wrong way so it blew instead of sucked. You can imagine what that did to the dignity of the pilot who wanted desperately to dehydrate in flight and couldn't turn that dehydrator around!"

On August 6, 1922, accompanied by a state-of-the-art coffee thermos with straw, Jimmy prepared to take off from Florida's Pablo Beach (a wide, flat expanse commonly used for car speed tests, that era's Bonneville Salt Flats). Word had gotten out, however, and a big crowd of fans and press had gathered. They watched as he and Joe fueled up, as Jimmy put on his goggles, waved farewell, and climbed into his De Havilland. He revved his engines, the plane taxied down the sand, and just as he was about to lift off, the left wheel caught in a soft patch of sand and the plane skewed toward the water.

Before he could right it, a wave broke against the landing gear, flipping the DH upside down and into the surf. "When I hit, my helmet and goggles slipped down over my eyes and nose and I was sure I was in water over my head," Doolittle remembered. "I held my breath, unbuckled my safety belt, dropped out, grabbed the side of the fuselage, and began to climb up. I was shocked to find out how heavy I was because I thought I would be more buoyant." Jimmy came out of the sea struggling and sputtering, only to hear the crowd laughing at him. He was standing in about ten inches of water.

Doolittle decided then and there he'd keep his future record-breaking attempts as much of a secret as possible—there was too much risk of humiliation for both himself and the Air Section, of which many now considered him a symbol. On September 4 he made another attempt. This time there were no crowds at Pablo Beach. He and some helpers set up lanterns down the strip to keep his takeoff path straight, and he made a test run to make sure that there were no soft spots. At 2152, he popped into the air without a hitch, hiked an arc over the ocean, and banked west: "A favoring wind was on my quarter. A severe thunder and lightning storm then came up. Some of those lightning strikes were so close that I could smell the ozone. I realized the storm area was too extensive to dodge, and plunged directly into it, trusting my compass to steer a straight course. At each flash of lightning I peeked over the side of the cockpit, saw familiar landmarks, and, after consulting the Rand-McNally road maps spread out before me, knew that I was flying high and free and true. . . . From Kelly to the Arizona border, nothing happened to disturb the serenity of the voyage. The desolate appearance of the country and the constant throb of the Liberty engine began to lull me to sleep. Despite the fact that sleep meant death, my head began to nod. But good fortune perched on the cowl. A light rain began falling. The raindrops, whipped back by the propeller, began eddying over the windshield and running in a tiny stream down my back. This made me angry, but was the stimulant I needed."

He touched down at Rockwell twenty-two hours and thirty minutes after taking off, a new world record. A thrilled U.S. Army awarded him the Distinguished Flying Cross for demonstrating "the possibility of moving Air Corps units to any portion of the United States in less than twenty-four hours." Overnight Doolittle became a tabloid sensation, known throughout the country as "the Lone Pilot."

The twenties had seen the nationwide spread of both motion picture theaters and the miracle of radio—the birth of mass media—and the two had created a new kind of celebrity. Before, the public might dream of Rudolph Valentino or Theda Bara, but wouldn't imagine having them over for dinner. Now millions could see national figures in real life via newsreels, as well as hearing, live, Jack Dempsey getting up from the canvas to throw a knockout. It was the beginning of a new kind of fame, and those the millions loved most, those whom every kid in the United States wanted to be, were the conquerors of the air, whose every record-breaking achievement was cause for national celebration. In the years between the wars, Jimmy Doolittle would become as famous and admired as any American alive.

To spur advances in aviation science, the army decided to enroll six of its pilots in the aeronautical engineering master's course at MIT, Doolittle included. At that time the institute had far more of an independent spirit than it does today, acting as a locus of entrepreneurial dreams that would lead to innumerable scientific breakthroughs and the founding of NASA—the perfect spot for a man ahead of his time. Jimmy's MIT thesis, "Accelerations in Flight," drew heavily on his own and his friends' personal experiences with blackout—losing consciousness during a sudden turn, or after pulling out of a dive. In 1925, at the age of twenty-eight, he was awarded a Sc.D., and that same year he got to achieve two aerial dreams. The first was to entertain the lunchtime crowds at the Pulitzer Trophy races in Manhattan. Doolittle and his partner played a game of tag between the skyscrapers of New York, winging close enough to the Woolworth tower to wave at the secretaries in the windows, zooming across the treetops of Central Park, and finally astounding the throngs at Manhattan's southern tip, where "the Lone Pilot" soloed across the Battery upside down, diving repeatedly at the crowd; for his finale, he chased balloons and popped them with his props.

For the international aviation races that year, the army and navy had joined resources by putting up five hundred thousand dollars to design and build four planes. One was destroyed in tests, two ended up in the navy, and the army's plane won that year's Pulitzer Trophy. A month later Doolittle replaced the craft's wheels with pontoons to enter the Schneider seaplane race in Baltimore, where his MIT education and outstanding skills as a pilot led him to average more than 232 mph, setting a new world record for seaplanes and winning the race. The next day, on a straight course, he topped 245, beating his own record. Americans were wildly excited that a countryman had won this prestigious honor, but navy pilots were more than annoyed that the champion turned out to be a landlubber who'd only recently trained himself in water takeoffs.

In 1926 Doolittle went to South America for six months to demonstrate and sell Curtiss P-1 Hawk fighters. His first stop was Santiago, Chile, at an international convocation of aeronauts. "On May 23, 1926, the Chilean pilots held a cocktail party in the officers' club in Santiago," he remembered.

I was introduced to a delightful, powerful drink called a pisco sour, a specialty of the fun-loving Chileans. During the course of the evening, the name of actor Douglas Fairbanks came up. Silent motion pictures had come to South America, and his legendary balcony-leaping, sword-playing, swashbuckling motion picture roles had captured the imagination of the Latins. . . . Feeling devilish, I said that Mr. Fairbanks wasn't so unusual. All American kids could do those things. When my poor Spanish was finally understood, my Chilean pilot friends raised their eyebrows in doubt and wanted proof.

With the utmost confidence, inspired by the pisco sours, I upended into a handstand and "walked" a few paces. The pilots clapped and yelled "Bravo!" and "Olé!" I did a couple of flips to more applause. This was encouraging. One of them said that he had seen Fairbanks do a handstand on a window ledge. That seemed reasonable, so I went to an open window, crawled out onto a two-foot ledge, and did a two-hand stand first, then a one-hand stand. . . . As I held there for a few seconds, I felt the sandstone ledge crumble and pull away. With practically all of my body hanging in midair it was inevitable: the law of gravity took over. I plunged about fifteen feet into the courtyard. I landed on my feet and felt sharp pains in both ankles. I knew I was in trouble.

Doolittle still had to fly across all of South America for his new job, now with two broken ankles. He solved the problem by attaching his boots to the rudders. Even in casts, however, the work his feet had to do in piloting made him almost black out a number of times from the pain. Ernst von Schoenbeck, a member of the Richthofen Flying Circus, was also in Chile at the time, as a sales demonstrator for Fokker. Doolittle challenged him to a dogfight and, even in casts with his feet glued to the pedals, won. He then had to cross the Andes without any chute since, with the boots and casts, there was no way to bail out.

When Jimmy returned to the United States and the doctors at Walter Reed took a look at his X rays, they insisted on complete immobilization; he'd so damaged his legs by flying and repeatedly breaking the casts that it would take him six months to recover fully. Doolittle spent that time contemplating the research he'd done at MIT about pilot blackouts. Talking with the other Signal Corps patients at Reed, he wondered if the fears of an outside loop were justified. Flying inside loops was a common show stunt, but as far as anyone knew, no one had successfully done an outsider. Would high G forces at the ebb point burst the pilot's blood cells, damage his internal organs, and lead to a blackout and a certain crash? The minute he was well enough to fly, Doolittle started testing the various elements of the outside loop, finally completing one, for the first time ever, in 1927, and emerging unharmed. Once again, "the Lone Pilot" was front-page news around the world.

At this time planes were flown pretty much the same way a car is driven, by looking out the window, pushing pedals, and turning a wheel. In a car, however, the driver doesn't have to clear mountaintops in the dark or make landings in heavy fog, both of which are very hard to do by looking out the window. For instruments, pilots only had a rudimentary compass, a speedometer, and that vague barometric altimeter. Doolittle was determined to find and develop proper tools to fly safely through any conditions whatsoever. In a lifetime marked by outrageous feats of courage, this would be the most remarkable achievement of them all.

Imagine driving down a highway at seventy miles an hour in a car that could use more than just a tune-up. The steering is erratic, and every so often, the brakes fail. All the windows have been blacked out, and only a few dials and audio beeps keep the vehicle from running off the road and crashing into whatever obstacles lie ahead. These dials and audio instruments, however, have never been used before, and no one is really certain whether or not they'll work.

On December 29, 1929, that was exactly what Jimmy did in the air—for fifteen minutes, he flew completely blind. Before the attempt, in Doolittle fashion, he'd made hundreds of practice runs. When the twenty-ninth arrived with zero-zero visibility, Jimmy decided it would be perfect for the test. "On the ground we had a small beacon on which we could home, and we had a fan beacon that indicated when we had passed the edge of the field," he reported.

> The small homing beacon, unlike today's varied, effective indicators, had an indicator that consisted of two vibrating reeds, which were painted white, and as they vibrated you had an indication as to whether you were right or left of your course in heading toward this beacon. You merely kept these reeds vibrating with the same amplitude, and then gradually as you approached the beacon turned down the volume, because otherwise they would go clean

off the scale. And then just as the edge of the field was passed, there was a little fan beacon, and it caused another reed to start to vibrate, and it vibrated to maximum amplitude as you went through the fan, and then tapered off after you had gone through. This indicated when the edge of the field was reached. . . . I came to the edge at 200 feet, and then upon passing through the beacon merely cut the throttle to a prearranged position that I had found through experimentation, and flew right into the ground, and with a little throttle the impact on the ground was so gentle that I made better landings this way than usually without the instrumentation. I worked on this for something over a year.

Out of this extraordinary effort would come the directional gyroscope (which functioned like a compass, but was more useful to a pilot), the artificial horizon (which showed exactly the plane's attitude in contrast to the ground), and the first altimeter sensitive enough to be genuinely useful—a revolution in aviation science. Today, in fact, almost every airline crash or collision takes place in skies of perfect visibility when the pilots aren't flying on instruments.

The blind flight also marked the beginning of a remarkable Doolittle custom: Everyone who worked on the experiment signed Joe Doolittle's damask tablecloth, signatures she then stitched over in black silk thread. Over the years the tablecloth would amass such a wealth of legendary names that today it hangs in the Smithsonian's National Air and Space Museum.

By now Joe herself was flying as a hobby, and trying to make a home for a husband who was constantly being reassigned all over the country and all over the world. She was taking care of their two sons, Jimmy Jr. and John, as well as hosting her husband's ever-growing horde of friends and flying buddies. "Her beer-making skills made our home an oasis for all and sundry," Jimmy marveled during Prohibition. "Almost every friend who cared to imbibe learned to fetch some hops so she could stay in production." If the years had hardly diminished Doolittle's reserves of energy, they had equally little effect on his wife's willpower. At one point Joe learned that Jimmy was cheating on her with a New York model. The young woman had demanded that Doolittle buy her a big fur coat, and when he demurred, she threatened to tell his wife. Instead he told Joe himself, and she let him have it with both barrels. She then calmly wrote the model a letter, explaining that she'd never gotten a fur coat either.

On September 4, 1932, Jimmy would attempt to win the $4,500 Thompson Trophy in one of the deadliest planes ever made—the Gee-Bee Sportster

R-1. Hand-built by the five Granville brothers in an abandoned dance hall near the Springfield, Massachusetts, city dump, the Gee-Bee looked like a giant barrel with tiny wings and fins tacked on as afterthoughts. Almost every pilot who'd tried it had either been killed outright or extensively injured. As one pilot observed, "Anything that stalls at a hundred knots and has the glide ratio of a manhole cover is not a safe airplane."

"Recognizing that this airplane would be extremely hot to handle, I knew I had to fly it delicately," Doolittle said. "I walked around it several times to try to predict what it would do in flight. I climbed in, had the hatch closed from the outside, and warmed up the engine. The engine was obviously extremely powerful and ready to go, so I blasted off and headed for Cleveland. . . . I didn't trust this little monster. It was fast, but flying it was like balancing a pencil or an ice cream cone on the tip of your finger. You couldn't let your hand off the stick for an instant. . . . I climbed up to 5,000 feet, and it's a good thing I did. It did two snap rolls before I could get it under control. If I hadn't had some altitude, I would have been dead. There was no doubt that I had to fly this thing every second I was in the air. . . . That airplane was the most dangerous airplane I have ever flown. I was asked many years later why I flew it if it was so dangerous, and the only answer I could think of was, 'Because it was the fastest airplane in the world at the time.'"

Doolittle would win the Thompson, but the experience would change his life. On landing in triumph, he discovered that a crowd of press photographers had formed around his wife and sons in the viewing stand, waiting to take their pictures the minute he did what so many previous fliers in the Gee-Bee had done—crashed and died. Jimmy immediately retired from racing, but not from record breaking. In 1934 he beat Eddie Rickenbacker's transcontinental speed in a passenger plane, getting from Burbank to Newark in twelve hours. "It was an uncomfortable flight," passenger/wife Joe told reporters, with characteristic Doolittle sangfroid. "I could hardly sleep."

Although her husband was now internationally famous, he was still making only two hundred dollars a month as a first lieutenant in the newly titled Army Air Corps. Through friends Doolittle got a job with Shell Oil, demonstrating aviation products with the new Curtiss-Wright Hawk across Europe. The army gave the bon voyage present of placing him on reserve status and double-promoting him to major. Jimmy used his usual bravado stunts to impress the foreign governments and their armed services (at one point flying under one of the Danube bridges connecting Buda with Pest), but he became more and more concerned after seeing the state of the art in European aviation, especially in Germany, and how far it surpassed U.S. efforts. When, two years later, Curtiss-Wright and Shell put together an around-the-world tour of Asia and Europe for Jimmy to show off their products (this time accompanied by his family), he was once again astonished by how common air transportation had become in Europe, while in the United States, it was still in its infancy.

On July 1, 1940, in the wake of Hitler's invading Poland, Belgium, the Netherlands, Luxembourg, and France, the forty-three-year-old Doolittle was recalled to active duty by a man he'd known since 1918, Army Air Corps chief Henry H. "Hap" Arnold. His first assignment was to troubleshoot the AAC's leap from producing two thousand planes a year to fifty thousand, practically overnight. "I was sent up to Detroit in charge of the Army air activities in connection with the conversion of the automobile industry from the manufacture of automobiles, trucks and so forth, to the manufacture of aircraft and aircraft engines," he said. "I was to act as midwife at a wedding that nobody wanted to take place. The automobile industry didn't want to build airplanes, and the aircraft industry didn't want the automobile industry to build airplanes, because they felt that at the end of the war they would have developed a strong competitor."

Ford would eventually produce a very fine bomber, the Consolidated B-24,while Jimmy would spend eighteen months at a desk job. He was not happy. After December 7, he began actively petitioning his superiors to be assigned to combat, determined to make up for what he'd missed twenty-five years ago in World War I. Just as he was flatly turned down by official channels in January 1942, the phone rang.

It was Hap Arnold. He needed a commander to organize a top-secret mission. Would the lieutenant colonel be interested?

SHIP

The Army Air Corps volunteers at Eglin Field needed many more weeks of training to get fully combat ready, but their time had run out. At three o'clock in the morning on Tuesday, March 24, telephones rang out across their quarantined sleeping quarters. Twenty-two plane crews were told to immediately get their gear, load their craft, and fly to McClellan Field, just outside Sacramento. The mission was on.

"They shook us out of the sack," Sally Crouch remembered, "and we had to leave our wives without much of a good-bye and get in our planes, like a police raid on a crack house." Maj. Harry Johnson, Jr., Doolittle's adjutant or administrative officer, remembered that while everyone selected got ready to go in the middle of the night, "those who were left behind at Eglin were heartbroken."

"When Ted took off for California he told me, 'Don't expect me for three months at least,'" said Ellen Lawson. "We both knew what he was going to do, and my lips were sealed, because lives depended on it. I didn't, in fact, think much about what might happen. He wanted to fly, and he was a capable, excellent flier. We always felt the Raiders were the only ones who were doing anything toward the war effort. They were in there in the beginning, while everyone else went on partying."

The volunteers were ordered to keep practicing their hedgehopping along the way, which was thrilling news—to the pilots. Ted zoomed "so low we could look up at the telegraph wires. All of us seemed to figure we might not be around very long, so we might as well do things we always wanted to do. It was the craziest flying I had ever done, and I had done some kid-stuff tricks, like banking a B-25 through a low, open drawbridge." Jake DeShazer watched the whole country go by from his first-class window seat in the nose: "When we got to Texas and New Mexico, we could see the cattle in the fields. Our pilots would fly low in order to frighten the animals. It was great sport to see them put their tails in the air and run for all they were worth. We thought that was lots of fun and were glad to be in the army and see something exciting." "We played funny little games like, *Can you race a dust cloud on the desert?* and all sorts of things like that," twenty-five-year-old Lt. Bill

Bower remembered. "I suppose you could say we were irresponsible, but it was a release." On his way to McClellan, Bob Gray took a pit stop with the crew of *Whirling Dervish* on a Texas highway to say farewell to his mom and dad, and as his Mitchell crossed Arizona, navigator Herb Macia pointed out a town racing past under their feet and mentioned, "That's where I was raised."

"What in the hell's the name of that place?" pilot Jack Hilger asked.

"Tombstone!" Herb said. His crew thought of their future and laughed like all get-out.

One of the mission's most-remembered insignias would be created at this moment. "On our flight from Eglin to Sacramento, we spent the night at Kelly Field in San Antonio because of weather conditions," said Bill Birch, bombardier of plane eleven. "Sergeant Gardner [the engineer-gunner] and I had become friends way back when we'd both started out with the Thirty-fourth at March Field, and the next morning, he and I were preflighting our B-25, and we decided her name should be *Hari Kari-er*. When Ross Greening arrived, we talked over the idea, which he liked; as pilot he had the final say. Knowing he was an art major, we asked if he wanted to do the appropriate illustration. So it was Ross who ended up drawing our insignia: a flying lady carrying a bomb."

The naming of planes in the Army Air Corps had an odd history. Every craft, just like every man and every object, was first assigned an army serial number—for Lawson's *Ruptured Duck,* it was 40-2261—and most pilots just left it at that, following the superstition that naming a plane would tempt the gods of weather and mechanics into throwing bad luck their way (on this mission, in fact, three of the planes with the worst hits of luck would all be named). After hearing all the various rumors and warnings about their assignment, however—perhaps the clearest being when their commander casually mentioned that some of them would come home as heroes, and others, as angels—plenty of crew decided their luck couldn't get any worse. Soon enough, the stolid Mitchells were transformed into *Whiskey Pete, Green Hornet, Anger Angel, Bat Out of Hell, Whirling Dervish,* and *Fickle Finger of Fate.*

Ironically, going to California would turn out to be one of the more dangerous moments in the entire operation. The United States had finally learned a lesson from its allies and had ordered blackouts along its coastal waters to deter sub attacks and nighttime bombing raids. The volunteers, however, now discovered that California had decided to black out not just its coast but most of the state, including the Central Valley and the landing lights of McClellan Field. After hitting bad weather all the way from El Paso to Sacramento, the airmen now had to guess their way to ground.

This pit stop turned out to be another round of tune-ups and modifications for the B-25s, similar to the detour in Minneapolis. Eglin airspeed indicator checks over the Gulf of Mexico revealed that the Mitchell propeller blades were so scratched and pitted from their first ten months of service that they reduced efficiency and top speed. At the McClellan maintenance depot, all the Bs had their props replaced with brand-new, fifteen-hundred-dollar three-bladers, and those with turret problems had their hydraulic valves redone. The local civilian mechanics, however, couldn't be told of the mission, and even though the base commander had been specifically ordered not to make any other changes, the mechanics routinely followed standard operating procedure, setting each craft back to the air corps' or the manufacturers' specs, undoing all the minute adjustments made in Minnesota and Florida.

"One incident was typical of several that happened," Doolittle said.

I was standing in base operations talking with a couple of pilots when I noticed a civilian worker trying to start one of our B-25s. He churned and churned the prop, but couldn't get the engine started. Then there was a loud bang and backfiring with black smoke and flames pouring out of the exhaust stacks. I ran out to the plane and shouted to the mechanic to shut the engine down, but he kept on turning the engine over and paid no attention to my arm waving. I crawled up into the cockpit and yelled in his ear to stop. I'm afraid I used some expletive I hadn't used before and probably haven't since. The man turned to me indignantly and said he was running up the engines as he was required to do whenever carburetors had been changed or adjusted. I was very, very angry. I had especially told the supervisors that no one was to touch the carburetors because they had all been bench-checked at Eglin and were adjusted just the way we wanted them.

"We're readjusting the carburetors," the man said. "They're all out of adjustment."

"What? Do you mean that somebody fooled around with these carburetors without my OK?"

"All I know is that they were checked, found way out of adjustment, and fixed up."

Some workers had unknowingly even replaced the mission's special carbs with standard models. "We just happened to find out by looking the engines over and checking the serial numbers, that they were different," said Ski York.

"No mention was made, nor notation made, to let us know that the carburetors had been changed." The discovery was made after it was too late to fix, and it's more than likely that this small matter led to Ski and his crew's years of imprisonment behind the Iron Curtain.

Again, as at Eglin, the men kept their distance from everyone else on base, giving them the reputation of being "a bunch of stuck-up SOBs." This only escalated the conflicts with the locals. Before leaving McClellan, Doolittle was supposed to fill out an interminable questionnaire summarizing the depot's work, one of those forms engineered by creative military bureaucrats. He took one look at it and scrawled one word across the entire page: *"Lousy!"* Seeing this, the field operations officer blew up: "Just a minute, Colonel. You will have to give us a detailed report. This will not do." Jimmy's response was to get into his plane and fly away. The commander turned to pilot John Hilger, standing nearby, and screamed, "Who is that guy? I can tell you, he is heading for a lot of trouble!"

Hilger, who knew exactly what Doolittle and his men were heading for, replied, "He sure is."

Jimmy was so fearful that his mission's secrecy might be compromised if he used a telephone that, apart from all his other responsibilities, he was regularly flying back to Washington to update Hap Arnold in person. At some point along the way, the forty-five-year-old commander decided that somehow he himself was going to lead his men into battle, even though this was just about the last thing his chief would have wanted. The newly minted air corps wasn't exactly filled with officers of Doolittle's talent and abilities, and chief Arnold could ill afford to lose one of his finest men and most trusted subordinates on what even the overdriven and optimistic general believed would be a suicide mission.

On his next trip to see Arnold, Jimmy told his boss: "General, it occurred to me that I'm the one guy on this project who knows more about it than anyone else. You asked me to get the planes modified and the crews trained and this is being done. They're the finest bunch of boys I've ever worked with. I'd like your authorization to lead this mission myself." As Doolittle wrote:

> Hap stared at me and his ever-present smile disappeared. He knew I had missed combat in World War One, that I didn't want to miss this war. He shook his head and said, "I'm sorry, Jim: I need you right here on my staff. I can't afford to let you go on every mission you might help to plan."

I thought he was going to say that and launched into a rapid-fire sales pitch I had mentally prepared beforehand. Finally, Hap gave in. He shrugged and said, "All right, Jim. It's all right with me provided it's all right with Miff Harmon." Miff was Brigadier General Millard F. Harmon, Jr., Hap's chief of staff.

I smelled a rat so I saluted, about-faced, and ran down the corridor to Miff's office. I knocked and opened his door.

"Miff," I said breathlessly, "I've just been to see Hap about that project I've been working on and said I wanted to lead the mission. Hap said it was okay with him if it's okay with you."

Miff was caught flat-footed, which was what I had intended. He replied, "Well, whatever is all right with Hap is certainly all right with me."

I thanked him and closed the door. Just as I did, I heard Hap's voice on Miff's squawk box. Miff said, plaintively, "But Hap, I told him he could go."

I didn't wait to hear any more.

On April 1, the volunteers were told to jump the hump from California's Central Valley to Alameda Naval Air Station, just outside San Francisco. Ted Lawson and his crew were still feeling their hedgehopping oats. "McClure had a movie camera along with a roll of color film," Lawson remembered. "He wanted to get some shots of the Bay Bridge. 'What about flying under the bridge?' Davenport asked me. 'The Pan American boys do it all the time in the Clippers. It would make a good shot for Mac.'

"Dean was at the controls. He put the nose down and we ran for the bridge. I hoped there weren't any cables hanging under the span. I was half tempted to take over and pull the *Ruptured Duck* up over the bridge at the last moment. But I knew what a nut McClure was about home movies, so we went underneath.

"Just as we did, Mac let out a yell. He couldn't get his camera working. He wanted us to do it again, but I said to hell with it. Some time later we came to the rendezvous.

"As I put the flaps down for the landing, we all let out a yell at the same time, and I guess we all got the same empty feeling in the stomach that I did.

"An American aircraft carrier was underneath us. Three of our B-25s were already on its deck.

"'Damn! Ain't she small!' somebody said on the interphone."

"Small" used to describe the navy's newest aircraft carrier could only be a comment made by an airman from up on high. The USS *Hornet's* deck was 809.5 feet long, 127 feet wide, lined with 20 mm and 1.1-inch light guns, and painted in "measure twelve camouflage"—streaks of navy blue and dark and light grays—that was supposed to make her harder for enemy ships and planes to target. Beneath the deck of the "Gray Ghost" was a 565-foot hangar bay enclosed by steel roller curtains, which could be raised to ventilate the fumes from the eighty planes warming up their engines before being lifted, by three elevators, onto the deck. Her forty-foot-high midship starboard island, meanwhile, held the navigation bridge, chat house, captain's deck, admiral's quarters, signal bridge, and flight control and gun director's platforms.

Fully loaded, a *Yorktown*-class carrier like *Hornet* displaced twenty-five thousand tons, was manned by a crew of three thousand, and cost thirty-two million dollars. Her nine Babcock & Wilcox boilers powered the turbines at 120,000 horsepower to attain top speeds of thirty-three knots (about 38 mph). She went through twenty tons of food every week, and came with her own bakery and a mechanical cow that churned ice cream from dehydrated milk for the "gedunk" bar, or soda fountain. Ships of the *Yorktown* class additionally carried three hundred tons of ship fuel, avgas (aviation fuel), bombs, torpedoes, and shells. While British and Japanese aircraft carriers had armored flight decks, American carriers did not, and as her crew would learn in a little over six months' time, *Hornet's* strongest plate, surrounding the engines, boilers, and fire rooms at the waterline, was only four inches thick—no match for state-of-the-art Japanese torpedoes.

Since carriers were so vulnerable, they traveled at the center of a task force, or task group, or multi-ship battle group armada. A standard TG was supposed to include state-of-the-art battleships with at least twelve inches of specially hardened steel belted around their hulls, each armed with a dozen guns ranging from 11-inch (firing 750-pound shells) to 18.1-inch (3,200-pound shells). After Pearl Harbor, however, the American navy had no spare battleships to protect *Hornet*. Instead she sailed with light cruisers (each loaded with six to a dozen five- or six-inch guns, one or two banks of torpedoes, and some antiaircraft armament) and heavy cruisers (six to ten guns of eight-inch caliber, and antiaircraft weapons). Surrounding this force would be the workhorses and bodyguards of the fleet, the torpedo-boat destroyers—small, cramped vessels that were so fast they usually ran out of fuel in four days. One bell-bottom joked that their real name should have been "destroyeds," since their mission was more often than not to be the first to reveal the enemy by taking a hit. By the end of the war, a common American task force would fall into a four-mile-wide circle of five carriers in the middle, closely accompanied by two or three destroyers, surrounded by cruisers and a picket line of more destroyers. For this mission, however, the navy had only two carrier groups to spare, one to pick up the men in Alameda, and the other to provide defense in enemy waters.

The West Coast group, known as Task Force Mike, included *Hornet,* cruisers *Nashville* and *Vincennes,* oiler *Cimarron,* and destroyers *Gwin, Meredith, Monssen,* and *Grayson,* which would eventually meet in the middle of the Pacific with Task Force Howe, departing from Pearl Harbor: carrier *Enterprise,* cruisers *Northampton* and *Salt Lake City,* oiler *Sabine,* and destroyers *Balch, Benham, Ellet,* and *Fanning.* Combined, the group would be known as Task Force 16. As Doolittle had warned the volunteers again and again, the lives of thousands of men depended on Japan's being kept from learning of this armada and its assignment—ferrying the bombers to their launch site. The secrecy had to be maintained at an extraordinary level, as with the cargo of army planes on deck forcing its own fighters to be stored below, the *Hornet* couldn't defend herself in an ocean teeming with Japanese cruisers, destroyers, carriers, and submarines. The four destroyers and two cruisers could put up a serious fight against an attack from enemy watercraft or subs, but if a Japanese carrier hove into range with its own planes ready to drop and strafe, the entire task force would be easy prey. There wasn't a navy man on board who didn't think, from time to time, of that moment when they'd unite with the other half of the TG, and then, at least, have defense supplied by Vice Adm. William F. "Bill" Halsey and the planes of the "Big *E*."

When it comes to ship names, the U.S. Navy believes in reincarnation—this wasn't the first *Hornet,* and she wouldn't be the last. The original, a ten-gun sloop, was commissioned in Baltimore in 1775 and destroyed by the British navy outside Philadelphia in 1777. The second took part in the war against Tripoli; the third was a hero of the War of 1812; the fourth was a schooner; the fifth a steamship taking part, for both sides, in the Civil War; and the sixth a yacht converted into a gunboat for the Spanish-American War. The seventh, officially known as CV-8 (as the eighth carrier of heavier-than-air planes in the U.S. Navy), was the one that would become so famous during World War II, not just for Special Aviation Project #1, but for the battle that Doolittle's men would directly provoke.

Schooled by the Great Lakes Naval Training Station just outside Chicago, *Hornet*'s crew was as raw as raw could be—soda jerks, schoolboys, and farmhands from Minnesota, Wisconsin, Iowa, and Michigan, many just the service legal age of eighteen years. Their leader—who'd had REMEMBER PEARL

HARBOR painted in huge white letters on the ship's stack—was fifty-four-year-old Capt. Marc Andrew "Pete" Mitscher, who'd piloted the first navy transatlantic plane in 1919, and who would come to be considered one of the great masters of carrier warfare in World War II (at the Battle of Truk, for example, Mitscher would lose around thirty planes, while the Japanese lost two light cruisers, four destroyers, two submarines, five auxiliaries, and twenty-four merchant ships). The chain-smoking, sunburned Mitscher was often described as Lincolnesque for his height and tight-lipped demeanor, though a truer mark of his character might be found in his pioneering of a captain's wearing a baseball cap, which quickly became a navy tradition.

CV-8 was built to carry 103 airplanes, but the navy could only afford to give her 80. Of these, just 48—fifteen fighters, twelve bombers, twelve scouts, and nine torpedo planes—were consistently flyable. The fighters were Grumman F4F-4 Wildcats, and during the war years the press would tout them stateside for their ingenious hand-operated folding wings. Compared to Japanese and German fighters, however, Wildcats were rugged in armor but turgid in speed and handling. The scout and bomber crews used the Douglas SBD-3 Dauntless, an excellent aircraft with a top speed of 250 mph, but the torpedo boys were stuck with Douglas Devastators from 1937, which could barely reach a top of 100, less than half that of Japanese Zeros (as Mitsubishi A6Ms were known to Americans). American torpedoes were just as outdated, crude, and more inaccurate than not; it would take until the end of 1943 before the Department of Ordnance could produce an eel that would consistently find its target. For the men of *Hornet*'s Torpedo Squadron Eight, that would be two years too late.

As the army bombers touched down in Alameda that April Fool's Day (the perfect moment for launching this mission, Sally Crouch would later come to believe), Ski York or Jimmy Doolittle would ask each pilot: "Is there anything wrong with your plane?" Anyone who said yes was sent to a hangar; the first sixteen who said no were directed to a wharf, only to have know-nothing navy grunts take control of their precious Mitchells. After their gas tanks were drained, a donkey pulled the planes to the end of the pier as their crews walked silently behind, carrying their B-4 canvas musette grips. Every flyboy knew that if the bell-bottoms damaged their plane in any way, it'd be their own bad luck, and they would be tossed off the mission. The Mitchells were winched aboard *Hornet* and tied down to the open deck with wheels chocked. All the airmen, even those whose planes didn't make the cut, were then ushered aboard this giant city of steel. The extras would serve as replacements in case of any last-minute emergencies, but, more important, giving them a *Hornet* cruise ensured there could be no loose lips.

Hank Miller had warned the army airmen not to discuss their business with the sailors, and their silence would lead to rumors flying across *Hornet:* They were off to Alaska . . . to Hawaii . . . to Australia . . . to the Dutch East Indies. The scuttlebutt got so serious that marine sergeant George Royce called his own detachment together in his office, closed the door, and told them that while he didn't know any more about all this than they did, if they were smart, they'd take out government life insurance immediately. When Cpl. Larry Bogart, orderly to Captain Mitscher, overheard that one of the army strangers was the infamous Jimmy Doolittle, he thought it over and paid out enough in premiums to quintuple his benefits.

Army Air Corps servicemen had always found themselves in an odd sort of limbo when it came to status. On the one hand it was almost impossible to get into the air in the first place. Pilots were the era's great heroes, after all, and who in his right mind wouldn't want to go to war soaring above the clouds instead of crawling through the mud? Corps school meant mind-numbing test after test, accompanied by training sessions lasting from dawn to midnight. At any point along the way, for whatever reason, a boy could be mustered out and sent back to the trenches. In the armed forces' overall ranking, though, the air corps was the poor half-brother of the army, just as marines were considered by navy men as would-be sailors who couldn't make the cut. Now the army volunteers would find out exactly where they stood in the military's hierarchy.

This was the first time since the Civil War that the army and the navy had coordinated a joint mission, and tensions ran high. The two forces were long-standing rivals, as anyone who's ever attended an Army/Navy Game well knows. Even the lowest-ranked sailor thought of himself as a great adventurer facing the vastness of the seas, having little in common with army grunts or full-of-themselves flyboys. The airmen, meanwhile, were fiercely proud of having reached their own positions in the world, and weren't about to accept any kind of attitude from coddled seamen who seemed to care more about glowing brass than beating Japs.

Navy intelligence officer Stephen Jurika took one look at the army fliers in their scuffed shoes, wrinkled caps, and open-collared, short-sleeved shirts, and was stunned that these servicemen could be so shoddy and ill-kempt. Ross Greening called the atmosphere "strained and defensive. There was no evidence of open dislikes, only a defensive aloofness," while Sally Crouch said that "the marine personnel in particular resented our being there and treated us with contempt. When they would see you in the passageways or otherwise like that, there was a very active minority group who made it very apparent that it was an insult for their ship to be used as a transport vehicle." When Mac McClure arrived for his first mess, he was told to sit at the end of the table and given no cutlery and no service.

The volunteers were shown to quarters inside this steel behemoth only to discover that, regardless of rank, they'd be sleeping on rickety cots while the sailors had berths. A spacious cabin, originally designed for the admiral's use, had even been turned into an army dormitory. "Old Bill Miles and I were assigned to share a stateroom with an Ensign Thumb," remembered Sally Crouch. "It was right up in the bow next to the anchor storage. When you're at sea, that bow is going to get it. It will oscillate. At night when you're sleeping there, your bed almost comes out from under you as the bow goes down and then as it comes up, you get buried in your mattress. You pull something like a tenth or two-tenths of a G."

Even with the less-than-welcoming reception, however, in some ways, being aboard *Hornet* was a big step up for the men of the AAC. At the Columbia and Portland bases, they'd slept out in tents and eaten chow-hall food, while *Hornet* had good cooks and its own ice cream machine. The Doolittle boys also hit it off immediately with their direct counterparts: "The navy fliers were very interested in the B-25s sprawled all over the deck. We took them all over our planes, bragging like kids about how fast and how far they could go," said Ted Lawson. "We were awful proud of our planes. The navy boys returned the favor by taking us below decks and showed us their dive bombers, torpedo planes, and fighters. Their wings were folded and naturally, they were cooped up because our ships took up all the space on the flight deck."

Once the men, planes, and gear were fully aboard that afternoon, tugs eased *Hornet* away from the docks, and she anchored in the middle of San Francisco Bay. With the rush to coordinate all hands, no time had been set aside for the placing of camouflage nets, and her precious cargo was exposed for all the world to see. That evening the commander called his men together and announced a surprise. After again emphasizing the need for complete secrecy, Doolittle was going to let them have one last night on the town.

Ferried back to San Francisco, the volunteers were determined to make this bon voyage something they'd remember forever (or be incapable of remembering, ever). "We were all drinking very freely, so anything could've happened," as Herb Macia put it. "I remember lots of things about San Francisco that night," said one pilot, "but they're not for publication." The red-light district beckoned, with its Liberty Follies burlesque house filled to bursting with strippers. Mac McClure had spent plenty of time in Northern California, and he'd fallen in love with the city: "More than once, it crossed my mind that this would be the last time I would see it." Many bar-hopped all the way uphill to the Top of the Mark and its stunning views, which included a dismayingly clear sight of their B-25s. Looking down, Tom Griffin was sure that every spy in San Francisco was making copious notes to forward on to Tokyo. One sailor on leave, in fact, told a reporter that for the right amount of cash, he could tell him all about a pending raid on Japan. The newspaperman patriotically turned down this scoop of a lifetime.

Jack Sims introduced Howard Sessler to the gorgeous Tutelee Rosenbaum and, accompanied by one of Tutelee's equally beautiful friends, they hit the famed Finocchio's nightclub. Men looking for a quieter time went to the movies; there was Paul Henreid in *Joan of Paris* at the Golden Gate and burlesque queen Ann Corio in *Swamp Woman*. Frank Kappeler, meanwhile, went alone to Alameda for one last night of pinochle with his mom and dad.

Jimmy Doolittle spent that night with his wife: "Next morning, I had an early breakfast with Joe and packed my B-4 bag. I told her, 'I'll be out of the country for a while. I'll be in touch as soon as I can.' We had had many separations before in our lives together, but I had the feeling she knew this departure was different. I kissed her tenderly. She held back her tears, but I'm sure she thought it was going to be a long time before she saw me again.

"I wondered if we would ever see each other again."

Doolittle arrived back on *Hornet* to find three classified messages waiting from Washington. The first was a relay from American forces in China, promising that their stopover's needed fuel and equipment had all been arranged. Another was from Hap Arnold: "May good luck and success be with you and each member of your command on the mission you are about to undertake." George Marshall himself had cabled, "As you embark on your expedition, please give each member of your command my deep appreciation of their services, and complete confidence in their ability and courage under your leadership to strike a mighty blow. You will be constantly in my mind, and may the good Lord watch over you." Navy head Ernest King, meanwhile, had radiogrammed Pete Mitscher: "I hope—and expect—that the first war operation of the *Hornet* will be a success. I am confident that it will be insofar as her officers and crew—under your able leadership—can make it so. Good luck and good hunting."

On April 2, 1942, at 1018, *Hornet, Vincennes, Nashville, Gwin, Grayson, Meredith, Monssen,* and *Cimarron* weighed anchor and set off under a heavy fog, *Hornet* destined never again to see the continental United States. Almost immediately a small ship appeared, pulled alongside, and announced that

Doolittle was to return to shore immediately for a call from Washington. The lieutenant colonel knew exactly what this meant:

> My heart sank. I was sure it would be Hap telling me I couldn't go. When I got to a phone onshore, the caller was General Marshall. If it had been Hap trying to cancel me out of the mission, I would have argued with him, but not with General Marshall.
> "Doolittle?" he said, sternly.
> "Yes, sir," I answered, expecting the bad news to follow.
> "I just called to personally wish you the best of luck," he said. "Our thoughts and our prayers will be with you. Goodbye, good luck, and come home safely."
> All I could think of to say was, "Thank you, sir. Thank you."

The minute he returned, Jimmy called his men together for the most important briefing of their lives. He explained, briskly, exactly where they were going to go and what they were going to do. Howard Sessler remembered him saying, "If there's any of you who don't want to go, just tell me. Because the chances of you making it back are pretty slim." One flier said, "When Doolittle revealed what the mission was, I was scared, but also impressed and fascinated by the audacity of this plan. Not volunteering was as unthinkable as not stepping over the line at the Alamo."

Two days after the task force cleared the Golden Gate Bridge, the bosun's whistle sounded. It was the moment every officer had been waiting for—the time to let the curtain rise. Captain Mitscher announced over *Hornet*'s loudspeakers, and simultaneously via semaphore to the other ships: *The target of this task force is Tokyo. The army is going to bomb Japan, and we're going to get them as close to the enemy as we can. This is a chance for all of us to give the Japs a dose of their own medicine.*

Cheers and screams of excitement broke out across the decks of every ship. Both services would now unite, at every level, to strike a blow of vengeance. "They told us over the loudspeaker and when they said it, it was like you were at a football game and somebody has just kicked a goal at the last second," Bob Bourgeois remembered. "People went wild. I rejoiced just like everyone else. I was glad to see somebody was going to retaliate for Pearl Harbor." Mac McClure said, "The sailors I saw were jumping up and down like small children." A ditty soon swept from man to man across the deck: "Heigh-ho! Heigh-ho! We're off to Tokyo! We'll bomb and blast and come back fast. Heigh-ho! Heigh-ho!"

"America had never seen darker days. Americans badly needed a morale boost," Doolittle noted. "I hoped we could give them that by a retaliatory surprise attack against the enemy's home islands launched from a carrier, precisely as the Japanese had done at Pearl Harbor. It would be the kind of touché the Japanese military would understand."

"From that time on, the navy could not do too much for us," Sally Crouch said. "Our engineers and gunners could not do their work alone, they had sailors assisting them, handing them tools and what have you. As you would go down the corridor, the navy personnel would stand back to let the army aviation people go past." Many of the army crew would begin lifelong friendships with their navy colleagues, including Davey Jones: "My roommate on the *Hornet,* Gus Widhelm, was a fighter pilot who became a good friend of mine. I saw him after the war several times; he had a great record."

The sailors so admired the flight crews for what they were about to attempt, in fact, that they even insisted on switching cabins. The army fliers could now have the comfortable bunks instead of the stiff, squealing cots. At the same time, the members of the stand-by crews started begging to go on the mission and, when that didn't work, even tried offering money—up to $150—to change places. Copilot Thadd Blanton remembered for the rest of his life how, at one time, men were willing to pay to die.

Not everyone behaved honorably. "There was a sergeant who liked the car that I owned," Dick Knobloch remembered. "It was a Pontiac. He said, 'I'll give you $50 for that. You're not coming back anyway. You're not going to live. Give me that car for $50.' . . . When you are young, however, you don't think about it. You know if you are going to have 50 percent losses, you look at the other guy and say, 'You poor devil, you aren't going to make it.'" And not everyone was overcome with feelings of joy at the mission. "As we passed under the great Golden Gate Bridge, we wondered if we would see it again," said bombardier George Larkin. "At that time you almost have to have lived it to realize how impossible this sounded," commented Ski York. "Japan was so far and so mighty and so well protected that it sounded impossible."

At the briefing Doolittle had told his men how the navy would carry them as far as it safely could but that—even under the best of circumstances and even with all the extra gas tanks—the operation would be very difficult to pull off. The goal was for Task Force 16 to get them within 450 miles of Japan. At 550 miles they could still make it, but with little margin for error, while at 650 miles they'd need every lucky break they could get to make it past Japanese defenses and on to the Kuomintang-controlled landing fields in eastern China. If the task force was attacked before getting within range, the crews would have to take off immediately and fly to either Hawaii or Midway. If the attack was sudden and their planes couldn't be launched, they'd be pushed overboard so *Hornet*'s own defense could be brought up and into play. But if they were within range, they were to get their planes into the air as quickly as possible, head for Japan, drop their eggs, follow the homing signals to the mainland, refuel immediately, and get as quickly as possible to the safe ground of the Nationalist capital, Chungking.

The commander then discussed the pros and cons of different approaches. The perfect scenario would be to take off a few hours before dawn, attack in the early morning, and land in China for refueling while it was still light. Unfortunately the navy would never risk illuminating the flight deck of one of its last remaining Pacific ships in the middle of enemy waters at night. The second strategy would be to launch at dawn and try to land by dusk, but that would put them over Tokyo in the middle of the day, when they would face the maximum risk of antiaircraft guns and enemy fighters. Loaded with ordnance, the Mitchells could never outrun squadrons of Japanese Zeros, as everyone well knew.

After hours of deliberation, Doolittle had come up with what he believed was the solution. On April 19 they would launch at dusk, arriving over Japan at night. He himself would fly three hours ahead of the rest, dropping incendiaries. Since the wood and paper cities of Japan were so extraordinarily flammable, the quickly spreading fires would serve to light up the targets, and the men could then see their way clearly.

The others disagreed vehemently with this strategy. It put Doolittle over Japan at sunset, easily visible to enemy defenses, and had him landing in China in darkness. It was too dangerous for the mission commander, they insisted; a different crew should take the lead. Doolittle, tight-lipped, refused. He would take the brunt of the danger, as he had so many times before.

The commander then outlined the industrial and military targets that American army intelligence had selected in Tokyo, Yokohama, Osaka, Kobe, and Nagoya, and the crews were allowed to pick their strikes. The first choice, to a man, was to take out Emperor Hirohito and the Imperial Palace, and they cut cards to see which lucky crew would claim the prize. Doolittle, however, had experienced firsthand how, after the Luftwaffe had struck Buckingham Palace during the Blitz, all of Britain had united in common cause against the Germans. He immediately vetoed an attempt on the palace, and later in life he'd consider this one of the best and most significant command decisions he'd ever made.

At dusk on that first day at sea, the army men were relaxing and getting ready for dinner when suddenly a klaxon horn screamed and loudspeakers everywhere shouted out: *"Man your battle stations!"* Lt. Hank Miller had coached the Doolittle boys on this routine. They scurried to their Bs (surrounded by two thousand sailors rushing to their own posts) and made ready to launch. Blue-shirted plane pushers, red-shirted bomb boys, and yellow-shirted aircraft directors helped get the craft ready. To the army group, it was an insane kind of chaos, and soon they'd learn that this would happen twice a day, every day. Afterward everyone would watch the gunners practice, as Ted Lawson remembered: "The *Hornet*'s 'Chicago pianos,' those multibar-reled pompoms, gave out with the darndest musical scale you ever heard—a grim broken chord of three or four sharp notes. *Hornet* gunners would pour a perfect curtain of fire into the sky. Other ships frequently tried their guns, too, to add to the growing tension."

A carrier's working hours started at 0400, when the officers awoke to bugles and the crew to a screaming whistle carried by loudspeakers through-out the ship. Everyone had fifteen minutes to shave, shower, dress, and be battle-station ready; the cooks, bakers, and messmen had already gotten up hours before to feed the pilots, mechanics, and ordnance men who had day-break search missions. The army air crews, however, wouldn't make it to every dry run, as Ted Lawson remembered: "The late call to stations was sounded one time just as a messboy was bringing two whole hot blueberry pies to Lt. Denver Truelove of Lula, Georgia, and me, at the long table where our bunch ate. Everybody else at the table made a beeline for the flight deck. I took one look at the pies that were coming in, and so did Truelove. We sat there and finished off both pies, though it was a kind of funny feeling, what with the navy bolting the bulkheads and locking us in.

"The pie was delicious."

Being on board an aircraft carrier was a very disorienting experience, as one crewman recalled: "We found out soon enough that you had to remem-ber exactly what you did to get to where you were, or you'd get lost in the halls. There was absolutely no privacy, and everything was done in whistle codes—when to get up, when to eat, when to not smoke because of refueling, when to bring bedding out to air—and it took us more than a few days to get used to it. We could never get used to the smell below, though, which was a mix of bilge water and unwashed sailors, bay rum and witch hazel, which the navy used for heat rash and fungus.

"So if the weather was okay, we slept on deck, next to the island, every chance we could."

Sgt. Joe Manske, Davey Jones's mechanic, was sleeping on the deck next to his Mitchell when a sailor came running in the dark, tripped, and kicked him in the face. The pain was bad, but what was even worse was that Manske's glasses were smashed, and he'd have to spend the rest of the mission in a myopic blur. Another night brought high seas, and, worried about his plane, Manske went out to check its ropes. The rough weather picked up, the deck was soon covered in water, and Joe knew that he'd be washed overboard at any minute if he tried to get back below on his own. "Fortunately, after about twenty minutes, I was able to get the attention of the navy men on watch during their rounds, and they helped me back inside," he said.

Navigator Chuck Ozuk spent his nights getting used to the new equipment: "They issued us sextants that we were unfamiliar with. It was like driving a new car; it took a while to get the knack of it. So we were out there practicing as much as we could."

Other guys remember different things about that particular boat ride. "Pork and beans," Bob Bourgeois said. "I never ate pork and beans for breakfast in my life. That's a favorite of theirs in the navy."

As the days passed, the thrill of their history-making endeavor and the visceral joy of giving payback for December 7 wore away, and serious thoughts about what they would be facing began to occupy many an airman's mind. They knew Japan was, at that moment, neck-and-neck with Germany as the world's greatest military power. They'd be striking at the very heart of its territory, and they'd be met with a barrage of instantly launched fighters on their tails and antiaircraft fire at their bellies. No one could imagine a more dangerous assignment. Doolittle had considered the odds, and come up with his own professional estimate of their chances: fifty-fifty.

Twenty-year-old gunner Harold Spatz remembered all the training that had led up to this—shooting skeet from the back of a pickup in Pendleton, targeting floating balloons from the *Bat*'s turret in Florida. It had all been like a game, like going to the county fair every spring as a kid. Now he'd be shooting at other men, and they'd be shooting back at him. "I began to wonder how many more days I was to spend in this world," Jake DeShazer recalled. "Maybe I wasn't so fortunate after all to get to go on this trip. I tried to comfort myself with statistics that I could recall. I reminded myself that only fifty thousand Americans had been killed in the First World War." He also tried to silence his worries by watching the seals and albatrosses that kept pace with *Hornet*. On April 5 the ship's chaplain held an Easter service, which filled immediately with pensive army airmen. Lawson remembered, "We couldn't convince ourselves that we were halfway around the world from home on our own with a one-way fare and that we were doing a dangerous thing. I felt the mission was well-planned, but certain that our losses would be necessarily high."

One afternoon Hank Miller walked the deck with Doolittle. They passed the sixteen big bombers patiently queued, their aluminum fuselages and Plex-iglas blinding glints in the sun. The distance from plane one—Jimmy's—to the front end of the deck was 495 feet. The last of the squadron, plane six-teen, had been so crowded to the rear that its tail hung over *Hornet's* stern. Two white guidelines had been painted down the length of the deck, just for the army. If the pilots kept their nose wheel on one and their left wheel on the other, it was guaranteed that their right wing would miss the island super-structure—by about six feet.

"Well, Hank, how does it look to you?" Doolittle asked, in a tone clearly less than his usual fireball of confidence.

"Oh, gee," Miller said. "This is a breeze." The two climbed into Jimmy's cockpit. Doolittle silently gauged the runway before him and then said, "This looks like a short distance."

"You see where that tool kit is way up the deck by that island structure?" Miller asked. "That's where I used to take off in fighters on the *Saratoga* and the *Lexington*."

Jimmy looked at him with a scowl. "Henry, what word do they use in the navy for 'bullshit'?"

Other pilots would pace off the deck from their own planes, and similarly worry about clearance. The Eglin tests they'd passed, after all, didn't include a bucking carrier in the middle of the ocean. They'd been told that two army pilots had succeeded in a test launch off the coast of Virginia, but those Mitchells hadn't been fully loaded with crew and ordnance. Hank Miller kept insisting it'd be easy, but then, he'd never done it in a B-25 himself, and he would in fact confide some nagging doubts to another navy officer: "I've done everything I can. They know how, it's just . . . will they? . . . there's nothing they don't know about short takeoffs. It's just that when that deck is moving and they're taking off, will they go through with it?"

On April 3 Jimmy introduced his men to Comdr. Apollo Soucek and Lt. Comdr. Stephen Jurika. Soucek, the carrier's air officer, would train them for everything Hank Miller hadn't covered—what the airdales did to prep the planes for takeoff, what the deckhand's signals for launch would be, and how to recognize Japanese planes from their silhouettes. Jurika, who'd spent years as the American naval attaché in Japan, would teach the men as much as he could about Asia; the volunteers called his lectures "How to Make Friends and Influence Japs." He told them to memorize the phrase *lushu hoo megwa fugi*, Chinese for "I am an American." He said there were many ways to dis-tinguish Japanese from Chinese, the best being "simply to look at the feet. The Chinese have all their toes together and the Japanese have the big toe sep-arated from the others because for years they've worn a thong between them."

Jurika came away from the experience extremely unimpressed with the men of the AAC: "I think our initial reaction—most of the officers on the ship and certainly the captain's and mine—was that an all-volunteer crew like this had to be special in ability to fly and desire to do something as a group together. But in looks, in appearance, and in demeanor, I would say that they appeared undisciplined. . . . Our initial impression was pretty well justified by their actions during the time there on the *Hornet*. Most of them were really fatalistic. It was a lark. They knew they'd get medals if they got through; they'd probably get promotions. They felt like this was a way to get back at the Japs. Everyone was very lighthearted, except for Doolittle, who was all seriousness.

"My briefing would be set up for 8:30 in the morning, after breakfast. They would saunter in, and the briefing scheduled for 8:30 wouldn't start before 9:15, sometimes as late as 9:30. And their attention span was very short, half an hour at the most. They would be interested up to a point, and yet, from my point of view, their lives were at stake. The success of the raid was at stake. I felt that they took it very, very casually, surprisingly so. . . . I felt that most of the pilots, with the exception of Colonel Doolittle, were far more interested in getting their aircraft off the flight deck of the *Hornet* than they were in any possible troubles they might encounter over Japan. There were very few questions during these briefings."

Frank Akers, *Hornet* navigator, agreed, saying that "the pilots were a care-free bunch, and seemed little concerned as to the danger of the mission or what might happen to them if they were shot down over Japan. A great many of them grew beards, and our suggestions that this was giving the Japanese an additional torture device in case they wished to pluck them out had no effect." Army airman Tom Griffin, however, thought otherwise: "I felt that if Lieutenant Jurika had given us a test after his lectures, he would've been surprised and pleased to find out how much we heard and retained. After all, Japan and the Japanese were very much on our minds. But we must remember this group of young men found themselves living under totally alien surroundings aboard an aircraft carrier, and they had on their minds their soon unpredictable rendezvous with the enemy over his territory. Their care-free facades undoubtedly covered many apprehensions—probably in a very healthy way."

Besides briefings, the crews had to undergo a significant amount of prep work for bombing alien territory and landing on the other side of the world. "At one point during Eglin, I had been dispatched with Tom Griffin, a navigator, to Washington, D.C., to get target and map material from the War Department," Davey Jones said. "We were assigned a little room where they brought the material we asked for: aviation charts—1:500,000 scale maps—for China and Japan. We'd get American maps, English, French, and Chinese versions, some from different eras, and compare them.

"We found that along the coastline, especially in China, everything jibed pretty much, but once you went 100 to 150 miles inland, mountain A would be five hundred meters on one map, and it would be one thousand meters on another, and fifteen hundred on another. The towns and the cities were maybe 30 to 40 miles different in location on these various issues of maps. Pretty inaccurate. So Tom and I studied all the options and, best we could, selected what we thought were the best of the four or five types.

"We didn't have time to have them duplicated in color, so they were printed in black and white. Tom and I then hand-colored an area that we were likely to be over, and that was what we used for the maps. After we got on the ship and the Old Man had announced the target, we issued these maps to everybody, and each crew colored their own.

This voyage was the first time most of the army crew had ever even been at sea, and more than a few passed their days green-gill sick. "I never got seasick on the *Hornet*," says *Hari Kari-er*'s Bill Birch, "but spent the whole eighteen days wondering if I would." Meanwhile, mechanical troubles with the B-25s were endless: Hydraulic lines clogged, fuel tanks leaked, an entire engine had to be overhauled. Some airmen were able to take their minds off the mission by compulsively checking their planes. Since the spark plugs, generators, and hydraulics failed repeatedly, this wasn't such a bad strategy. Meanwhile, the navigators shot the sun and compared their findings with the *Hornet*'s, while gunners tried to take down floating strings of balloons and red kites. The test-firing would reveal even more problems with the turrets, as Ski York's gunner, David Pohl, discovered: "We found that practically all of the machine guns, after we got aboard the ship, had these weak firing-pin springs—you fired three or four hundred rounds and they would lose all their punch and start misfiring all the time. We took as many as we could get from the crew on the *Hornet*, but we didn't have enough to go around. We took all the ones that hadn't fired, but we didn't get them all fixed. All that should've been done."

For fun in the evenings, the men would stop by the gedunk wagon for some ice cream; tour the ship to see its immense power plant, hangar elevators, or other state-of-the-art technology; play Benny Goodman, Guy Lombardo, Harry James, and Bing Crosby records; and gamble, usually at poker or craps. Gambling was so popular in the navy that Bob Hope would eventually define "aircraft carrier" as "a crap game with a flight deck over it," and

Davey Jones would say, "The navy was standing watch, but when they weren't standing watch, they were shooting craps." One army man remembered, "Believe it or not, there was a billiard table in the admiral's quarters on the *Hornet*. After sixty years, I have yet to find out from the navy what it was doing on the boat. How did they play, with the ship rolling and tossing and all? But it made a hell of a crap table." Doolittle was one of the few who passed: "Not being a gambler, I didn't take part. The odds in favor of winning any game of chance never seemed right to me."

At first the airmen won time and again, upping the ante to a month's pay. As the voyage continued, however, they lost every cent. Ted Lawson decided he'd make up for his deficits by buying cigarettes for five cents a pack on *Hornet* and then selling them in Chungking for what he'd heard was the going rate of seventy-five cents. That way he could afford gifts from the Orient for Ellen and his mom.

Every airman checked his own equipment: pistol, water canteen, field ration, ammo clip, knife, parachute, gas mask, and some et cetera items. "Doc White was putting out whiskey," remembered Bob Bourgeois. "He gave each of us two pints of rye whiskey to put on a snakebite or an infection. And if that didn't help, then just drink it." The lectures—which the boys called "skull practice"—continued daily, and now covered bombing runs, maintenance, guns, and medicine. They were told how the Chinese used night soil—human feces—to fertilize their rice fields, and were warned that Americans would have no immunity to its foreign microorganisms. The crews would have to take every nick and scratch seriously, as if their lives depended on it—since they would. Doolittle also reminded them again and again not to take any pieces of paper on the planes that might link them to *Hornet*. The one skull session that nobody included was one covering emergency bailouts and parachute technique—an omission that would turn out to have fatal consequences.

At one briefing Jurika told the men that military intelligence had determined they would be greeted over the skies of Tokyo by three hundred 75 mm antiaircraft guns and five hundred Japanese planes. These fighters usually flew in a three-unit V formation on an approach outside the range of Allied machine guns, and then broke off to attack simultaneously from above, below, and behind. Through newsreels and military reports coming back from China and the Philippines, the men knew full well how horribly the Japanese treated their POWs, and greatly feared being taken prisoner. Jurika confirmed that "if they were captured dropping bombs on Japan, the chances of their survival would be awfully slim; very, very slim. I figured they would be, first of all, paraded through the streets as Exhibit A, and then tried by some kind of kangaroo court and probably publicly beheaded. This seemed to settle them down quite a bit."

One of the men asked Jimmy what he planned to do if he crash-landed in Japan. The commander replied that, once they were off the carrier, each pilot would be responsible for and in command of his own crew. If they were separated for some reason, each man would then have to decide for himself what course of action to take.

Doolittle had already decided on the course he intended to follow. He announced that, no matter what, he would not be taken prisoner. If plane one was damaged beyond hope, he would order his men to bail out. Then he would drive it, full throttle, into the enemy target where he could do the most damage.

DAI NIPPON TEIKOKU

The target of what would one day be known as the Doolittle Raid was at that time the world's most astounding military power. After a string of decisive conquests in the space of a little over four months, the empire of the Land of the Rising Sun now extended across much of China, from Burma through Singapore, Hong Kong, Indonesia, and all the way to Polynesia, with no end in sight. *Dai Nippon Teikoku* (the empire of Japan) was a vast, mighty, and awe-inspiring nation, the ruler of all Pacific Asia; and its leader, Hirohito, descended directly from the goddess of the sun, seemed invincible.

The creation of a Japanese empire was in fact a dramatic about-face in the nation's history. Since the second century A.D., when the Yamatos arrived from Korea to decimate the native Ainu and begin what became the Kingdom of Japan, the island had isolated itself entirely from the rest of the world. In the 1600s, after Catholic missionaries had landed in search of new converts, the nation issued a decree: Any Japanese trying to leave and any foreigners trying to enter the country would be immediately executed. This would serve as the rule of law for two hundred years, until the arrival of Matthew Perry in 1853 in Tokyo Bay, aboard U.S. Navy steam-powered gunboats. The United States wanted to open Japanese ports for their whaling and import/export businesses, and Tokyo—after taking measure of Perry's craft, which could sail upwind, and his cannons, which could demolish anything in their path—agreed. As more and more examples of Western science, business, and culture appeared in Perry's wake, the Japanese underwent an extraordinary cultural upheaval: the Meiji Restoration. The kingdom that had so isolated itself from the rest of the world now sent its top-ranking students to study shipping in London, law in Paris, medicine in Germany, and business in the United States, while every Western innovation of the past three hundred years—from lightbulbs to hansom cabs—was systematically imported, including an abiding interest in the dominant political ideology of the late nineteenth century: empire.

By 1900 Japan had begun to perceive itself as hemmed in by foreign domains. Hong Kong, the Malay Peninsula, Singapore, and part of Shanghai belonged to the British; China's Shantung territory and the great island of

New Guinea were under German control; the Dutch had their vast East Indies holdings (now Indonesia); Hawaii, Midway, Guam, Samoa, and the Philippines belonged to the United States; and even the Russians were moving into Manchuria, China's northeastern province. When the 1930s global economic depression arrived—and with it many countries' remedy of stringent tariffs—Japan, which depended so greatly on trade, found itself in an especially difficult situation. It couldn't sell its luxury goods, and soon enough it wasn't able to buy foreign products. As the economy collapsed, the same *Lebensraum* solution that would so motivate the other Axis Powers found great and immediate favor with the Japanese, appearing first among an odd group of expatriates: the Kwangtung (Guangdong) Army, Japan's regional police force in China.

If World War II began for Europe with the invasion of Poland in 1939 and for the United States with the attack on Pearl Harbor in 1941, for Asia it started in 1931, with a railroad accident. On September 18 of that year, lower-level officers of the Kwangtung, which protected Japan's transportation and communication lines, farmers, miners, and businessmen in volatile, warlord-run northern China, blew up a train on the Japanese-owned South Manchuria Railway. Blaming the explosion on Chinese rebels, they amassed troops and occupied the town of Mukden. Within a few months the Kwangtung had seized the entire region, establishing the state of Manchukuo with Pu Yi—the last emperor of the Qing Dynasty—as its puppet governor. The Chinese were enraged; a mob attacked five Japanese Buddhist priests in Shanghai, killing one, and the Japanese retaliated by bombing the city, inflicting hundreds of thousands of casualties.

Over the next two years army and navy cadets in Tokyo assassinated the premier who had opposed the army's Chinese adventures; ultranationalists murdered the finance minister; and army officers killed his replacement, as well as the previous prime minister, and then took control of the major federal buildings, forcing civilian legislators to flee for their lives. The militarists justified their wave of terror by saying they were trying to rid the nation of corrupt influences in service to the emperor—a tradition known as *gekokujo*—and at the lengthy public trials where these views were elaborated, many Japanese came to side with the defendants. From then on, Japan's military chiefs would use the threat of right-wing chaos to make escalating demands on the government's civilian ministers. Inspired by their historic successes against China and Russia, these same chiefs were overcome with "winner's fever"—Japan's fighting forces, they now believed, could beat any foe. By the mid-thirties, almost half of the country's national budget was earmarked for its armed forces, and by the end of the decade, almost every politician with high government standing had arrived via a military career.

On July 7, 1937, Japanese and Chinese troops were practicing night maneuvers near the Marco Polo Bridge outside Peking. Bullets were fired; the next morning, a Japanese officer was missing. As the two sides were negotiating a truce and agreeing that the shooting had been just an accident, more shots were fired, by whom is uncertain. Japan retaliated by bombing three nearby cities and beginning a wide assault against Chinese troops. Franklin Roosevelt condemned Japan for this aggression, and the League of Nations voted censure, but now nothing could stand in its way. The country quit the League and, by 1937, its army had overcome Peking, Tientsin, and Shanghai.

It was the beginning of a Japanese reign of cruelty that today remains a permanent stain on the country's history: Locals were treated like slaves and animals; POWs were subjected to unspeakable brutality; and soldiers were allowed to run amok. Over the next eight years, more than two hundred thousand illiterate rural women in the conquered territories would be told that high-paying factory jobs were available in Japan. They were instead sent to "comfort stations" across the Chrysanthemum Empire, imprisoned for up to eight years, referred to as "public toilets," and required to sexually service up to fifty Japanese soldiers a day.

Manchukuo's 2nd Lt. Tominaga Shozo described what the Kwangtung Army did with its new recruits: "At the last stage of their training, we made them bayonet a living human. When I was a company commander, this was used as a finishing touch to training for the men and a trial of courage for the officers. Prisoners were blindfolded and tied to poles. The soldiers dashed forward to bayonet their target at the shout of 'Charge!' Some stopped on their way. We kicked them and made them do it. After that, a man could do anything easily. . . . Everyone became a demon within three months. Men were able to fight courageously only when their human characteristics were suppressed."

Throughout China, Japanese troops would follow *senko-saisaku*, the "Three All" policy: Burn All, Seize All, Kill All. They torched the town of Sungchiang, killing one hundred thousand civilians, and slaughtered nearly the entire population of 350,000 in the ancient city of Suzhou. When the Republic of China's capital city of Nanking fell on December 13, 1937, fifty thousand Japanese soldiers faced the task of subduing its five hundred thousand inhabitants. After going from neighborhood to neighborhood and tacking up posters on every street corner that urged TRUST OUR JAPANESE ARMY. THEY WILL PROTECT AND FEED YOU, the troops would methodically divide local men who had surrendered their arms into groups of around 150, promise the beleaguered, starving residents food and water, send them outside the town walls, and kill them.

During *Nanjin Datusha*—the Rape of Nanking—Japanese soldiers rampaged through the streets for months, eventually killing between 260,000 and 350,000 civilians; the exact number remains unknown. "Few know that soldiers impaled babies on bayonets and tossed them still alive into pots of boiling water," a Japanese eyewitness reported. "They gang-raped women from the ages of twelve to eighty and then killed them when they could no longer satisfy their sexual requirements. I beheaded people, starved them to death, burned them, and buried them alive, over two hundred in all. It is terrible that I could turn into an animal and do these things. There are really no words to explain what I was doing."

Nanking, however, was the last of Japan's "successes" in China. As the fighting with the armies of Chiang Kai-shek, Mao Zedong, and the various guerrilla warlords dragged on for four years and one million Japanese lives were lost, Tokyo's military leadership realized it had fallen into a quagmire. In 1940 they formulated plans for a withdrawal, but just as a retreat was being arranged, Hitler's own triumph of empire reignited Tokyo's colonial ambitions, and Tojo Hideki became minister of war.

At five feet two inches and weighing under 115 pounds, the man who would become prime minister of Japan and America's most hated foe of World War II was, in personality and demeanor, a by-the-books, ramrod-straight classic military man who gave orders and expected them to be followed, just as he followed the orders of his own commanders. Having served as Japan's military attaché in Berlin, Tojo would become an enthusiastic supporter of the Germans, and would use his positions in both the military and the government to move Japan toward aligning with the Axis Powers. In 1935 he became head of the Kwangtung Army and the Kempeitai (the Japanese Gestapo), before ascending up the ladder of Tokyo politics to become prime minister on October 16, 1941, pledging a "new order in Asia."

When Germany invaded the Soviet Union in June of that year, it inspired in Japan's leaders a new sense of global ambition. Just next door to their own limited natural resources were the invaluable rice paddies, rubber plantations, and oil fields of Southeast Asia (Burma, Cambodia, Laos, Vietnam), British Malaya, the Dutch East Indies, and the American Pacific colonies, not to mention the riches of British-held Hong Kong and Singapore. Victory in a new pan-Pacific campaign would accomplish many objectives simultaneously: It would isolate China from her allies; deliver Asia to Asians, casting out the Anglo-Saxon colonial rulers; and solve a number of Japan's most pressing economic problems.

With Britain and the Netherlands sidelined by the Nazis, the country would face only one potentially serious military foe in the Pacific: the United States. If they went to war, Japan believed that America, a nation governed of the rich, by the rich, and for the rich, would be fighting merely to protect its wealth, while the Japanese would be engaged in a more noble struggle for their very existence, as well as to liberate their Pacific neighbors from the tyranny of white rule. An overwhelming success, Tokyo believed, would stun the slothful, isolationist Americans into accepting Japan's new empire.

With so much national sentiment and moral authority on their side, and with their turn-of-the-century wins against the far greater foes of China and Russia, it seemed to Tokyo that victory was easily within reach. They would use this moment of international chaos to launch Operation Number One, the greatest military achievement of modern times, a small part of which would go down in history as America's greatest military loss: Operation Z.

Japan's attack on Pearl Harbor was, oddly enough, originally inspired by a novel, *The Great Pacific War,* written in 1925 by Hector E. Bywater, Far East correspondent for the *London Daily Telegraph.* Translated into Japanese, Bywater's tale of simultaneous attacks on Pearl Harbor, Guam, and the Philippines' Lingayen Gulf and Lamon Bay became extremely popular with the cadets at Etajima, Tokyo's Naval War College, where it was included in the curriculum. In 1936 Etajima published *Study of Strategy and Tactics in Operations Against the United States,* which said that "in case the enemy's main fleet is berthed at Pearl Harbor, the idea should be to open hostilities by surprise attacks from the air." All this made a lasting impression on Etajima student Yamamoto Isoroku, who in 1939 became the admiral in charge of the entire Japanese fleet. When, on November 11, 1940, biplanes flew from the British carrier *Illustrious* to bomb and cripple Italian warships at their base in the harbor of Taranto—the first use of an aircraft carrier in combat—Yamamoto decided a similar attack could be mounted against Hawaii. The Imperial Japanese Navy hadn't participated in the nation's many campaigns in China, and this would be a chance to restore the service to the preeminence it deserved.

Considered by both Japanese and Americans to be Japan's greatest military leader, Admiral Yamamoto always traveled with a Bible to consult, even though he wasn't Christian. An expert bridge, poker, and mah-jongg player, the admiral was five foot three, and, like American naval chief Ernest King, his gray hair was shorn into a crewcut, he was famous for temper tantrums that often ended with his stamping the floorboards until the flagship quarters shook, and he was viscerally convinced that the future of aquatic warfare lay with the aircraft carrier. Tokyo geishas nicknamed him "Eighty Sen," as he'd lost two fingers in the Russo-Japanese War—a manicure then cost one hundred sen—and they knew him well from his decade-long love affair with the remarkable temptress "Plum Dragon."

Vilified for decades in the United States as the demonic architect of the attack on Pearl Harbor, Yamamoto was in fact so fundamentally opposed to waging war that his most authoritative Japanese biography would be titled *The Reluctant Admiral.* He took such a public stand against his country's alliance with Nazi Germany and its fighting forces' plans for imperial expansion that in 1939 the minister of the navy made him commander of the Combined Fleet and shipped him off to sea to reduce his risk of assassination. A Harvard graduate, he described Japan's going to war with the United States as "a major calamity for the world" and wrote to a friend, "I find my present position extremely odd, [as I'm] obliged to make up my mind and pursue unswervingly a course that is precisely the opposite of my personal views."

Besides empire, the source of the depression-era conflict between Japan and the United States centered on one issue: oil. In response to Tokyo's attacks on China, the United States and Britain had turned a stopple in their pipelines, and since these two countries alone supplied almost 90 percent of Japan's petroleum, it presented a serious economic threat. The American secretary of state, Cordell Hull, demanded that Japan immediately withdraw from China, renounce the Tripartite Pact with Italy and Germany, and guarantee no further overseas engagements, or it would have to find another source of fuel. Tokyo and Washington would spend all of 1941 arguing about this issue, Japanese leaders believing that, without an immediate resumption of the flow, their country's tottering economy would collapse entirely.

The argument had grown so heated by the beginning of that year that on January 24, Secretary of the Navy Frank Knox would send a memo to Secretary of War Henry L. Stimson (with a copy sent to commander in chief of the Pacific Fleet [CINCPAC] in Hawaii, Adm. Husband "Mustapha" Kimmel): "If war eventuates with Japan, it is believed easily possible that hostilities would be initiated by a surprise attack upon the Fleet or the Naval Base at Pearl Harbor. In my opinion, the inherent possibilities of a major disaster to the fleet or naval base warrant taking every step, as rapidly as can be done, that will increase the joint readiness of the Army and Navy to withstand a raid. . . . [An] air bombing attack . . . and air torpedo attack . . . might be initiated without warning prior to a declaration of war."

March 1941: Yoshikawa Takeo sails to Honolulu to spy on American ships, airfields, and armories. Members of the Japanese consulate in Hawaii regularly take taxis down to Pearl Harbor, make careful observations, and radio back to Tokyo the ships' locations and their movements. The U.S. Pacific Fleet has fallen into such a regular and dependable pattern that the Japanese pilots in the attack will know exactly where each battleship lies.

As Yoshikawa begins surveillance in Hawaii, Asaeda Shigeharu does the same in Thailand, while Col. Tsuji Masanobu monitors the Malay Peninsula. Tsuji discovers that, while British Singapore is virtually impregnable to an attack from the sea, it is completely defenseless at its landed rear.

April 1941: Japanese navigators initiate a study of which ships have crossed the Pacific over the past ten years, learning that no boats travel during November and December at latitude 40 degrees north because the seas are so rough.

Summer 1941: After six months of exhaustive planning using information gathered by spies across the Pacific, Colonel Tsuji sends the master blueprint for the Japanese takeover of the Asian Pacific—Operation Number One—to General Staff Headquarters in Tokyo. Questioned carefully by the imperial army chief on this incredible, simultaneous invasion of Malaya, Singapore, Burma, the Philippines, Wake Island, Guam, Borneo, and Java, Tsuji predicts that "if we begin on November 3, we will be able to capture Manila by the New Year, Singapore by February 11, Java on March 10, and Rangoon on April 19." His words are almost exactly to the letter what will eventually happen.

As the Japanese army prepares for its invasions across Southeast Asia, its navy prepares for Hawaii. Yamamoto has his pilots practice bombing runs on target vessels in the port of Kagoshima on Japan's southernmost island of Kyushu, whose high peaks and narrow approach are similar in topography to that of Oahu. Ordnance engineers invent a new kind of winglet torpedo that will function in the shallow waters of Pearl Harbor, and convert sixteen-inch armor-piercing shells into bombs for the assault on Battleship Row. The torpedo pilots must learn a whole new style of flying—slowing their planes to a near-stall and dropping to a minimum altitude of twenty-five feet—to launch their torpedoes successfully.

The senior flight commander of the First Air Fleet, Fuchida Mitsuo, divides the men from carriers *Akagi, Kaga, Soryu,* and *Hiryu* into squadrons of five horizontal bombers and nine divers, each group traveling in an arrow formation. Japan's pilots were not yet using any kind of mechanical bomb-sight, and the strike record of their horizontals was historically poor. With his new squadron design and intense training, Fuchida raises it by 70 percent.

Nicknamed *Tako* (octopus) since he was so quick to blush (as the mollusk turns red when cooked), Operation Z's lead pilot grew up in the rural out-skirts of Kyoto, with a father who was a grammar school principal and a maternal grandfather who was a *samurai* chieftain. As a student at Etajima Naval College, he became friendly with both Prince Takamatsu, brother of Hirohito, and Genda Minoru, who'd be his commander on many a mission. When Japan allied with Germany, the naval airman was so pleased with his resemblance to Hitler that he trimmed his mustache into a similar shape.

Over Battleship Row, Nippon's pilots will follow a four-part approach: A squadron of B5N torpedo planes will take out the first ring of ships, followed by G4M high-flying bombers wreaking widescale havoc and D3A dive-bombers targeting key missed sites. Everywhere Mitsubishi A6Ms will strafe before and mop up after. Silhouette charts of the American fleet's principal ships are used to drill the bomber crews repeatedly to ensure they'll hit the most important targets—*Yorktown, Lexington,* and *Enterprise,* the American navy's three Pacific aircraft carriers.

July 1941: With Vichy approval, fifty thousand Japanese troops are sta-tioned in French Indochina, alongside warships anchored in Cam Ranh Bay, posing a direct threat to the Philippines, Malaya, and the Dutch East Indies. Learning of this, Roosevelt orders an embargo of all high-octane fuel to Japan. The subordinates actually in charge of carrying out the command, however, embargo all of Japan's oil instead.

August 1941: From Hawaii, the army's Lt. Gen. Walter Short sends Hap Arnold a report from a group of air officers, warning that "the Army Air Corps units are at present not charged with the reconnaissance mission for the defense of Oahu." Without such reconnaissance, it went on to say, a Japa-nese striking force of carriers could get within three hundred miles of the island, concluding that "the early morning attack is, therefore, the best plan of action open to the enemy." The navy is assigned responsibility for long-range scouting, but as they are also training the new Philippine air force, few spare planes are available. It is decided to send out long-range patrols only if an attack seems imminent.

That same month FDR tells Secretary of the Interior Harold Ickes that "it is terribly important . . . for us to keep peace in the Pacific . . . I simply have not got enough Navy to go around." The Japanese transfer their aircraft car-riers' radio call signals to destroyers stationed far from the path of attack, tricking U.S. Naval Intelligence as to the strike force's real location.

August 11: Dusko Popov, a Yugoslav working as a British double agent under the code name Tricycle while also employed as an Axis spy, appears in the New York City offices of the FBI. He hands the bureau's regional chief documents from his German superiors, ordering him to acquire specific information on ammo dumps, airfields, pier installations, anchorages, and the depth of water at Pearl Harbor. Tricycle is surprised at the American's dismissive attitude, and asks about it: "It all looks too precise, too complete, to be believed," the G-man replies. "If anything, it sounds like a trap." Tricycle explains his bona fides, as well as the high Nazi source of the materials, but the agent refuses to take him seriously. Popov then goes to J. Edgar Hoover himself, but Hoover is equally dismissive.

September: American naval intelligence decodes a cable from Tokyo to the Japanese consul in Hawaii, ordering him to report regularly on the specifics of type, number, and movement of ships in Pearl Harbor. Navy officials do not find this information significant.

September 2: At the Naval War College outside Tokyo, three teams of admirals, taking the roles of Japan, England, and the United States, conduct the same war game repeatedly—an attack and occupation of Malaya, Burma, Indonesia, the Philippines, the Solomons, the central Pacific Islands, and Hawaii. December 7 is chosen as the date to launch Operation Z, since the night before will be a full moon (making it easier for the carriers to launch), and that day would be a Sunday (when the Japanese have determined that most of the U.S. fleet would be at anchorage). They also decide on the final Operation Z armada: six carriers, two battleships with fourteen-inch guns, two heavy cruisers, a light cruiser, eight destroyers, three oilers, and a supply ship. The carriers ferry, in total, 350 planes: 81 fighters, 135 dive-bombers, 104 high bombers, and 40 torpedo bombers.

September 6: The Japanese cabinet and the chiefs of staff meet in the Imperial Conference Chamber in the Temple of Heaven, the Imperial Palace. Reclining on a platform far from the table where his ministers confer, the emperor listens, his divine and silent presence a blessing to their undertaking. As the leaders of Japan discuss "the purpose of a war with the United States, Great Britain, and the Netherlands to expel the influence of the three countries from East Asia, to establish a sphere for the self-defense and the self-preservation of our Empire, and to build a New Order in Greater East Asia," it becomes clear that the military chiefs are less than certain of victory. Despite their qualms, the discussion veers more and more toward an open declaration of war, until the meeting is interrupted for the first time in Japanese history by the shrill, reedy voice of the emperor declaiming a poem written by his grandfather, the great emperor Meiji:

All the seas everywhere are brothers to one another,
Why then do the winds and waves of strife
Rage so violently over the world?

HIM (His Imperial Majesty) Hirohito is the 124th ruler of Nippon, a descendant of the Yamato clan, which had established the kingdom two thousand years earlier with the first emperor, Jimmu. As the Nazis revered their supposed Aryan lineage, so too did the Japanese honor their "Yamato race," with *Yamato damashi* meaning "the spirit of Japan." Hirohito originally wanted to be a marine biologist, not a monarch; he preferred whiskey to saké, listened to Western classical music, and loved golf. Subordinates were forced to interpret his cryptic, expressionless utterances, which usually took the form of haiku or quotations from past leaders. Regardless of his eccentric, shambling ways, however, HIM relished victory. He knew from the military chiefs' tepid response that Japan was not ready, and his commentary put an end to the immediate move to war. Instead Tokyo's diplomatic negotiators in Washington were given a new deadline to arrive at an acceptable solution to the oil crisis: October 15.

October: The Japanese liner *Taiyo Maru* takes an extremely roundabout voyage from Tokyo to Honolulu, traveling far north of the common international shipping lanes and then turning due south for Oahu. The *Taiyo* radios back to the Japanese navy that, in the course of the journey, they had not made contact with a single other vessel of any nation at any time.

October 14: Facing in twenty-four hours the deadline that had been decided at the Imperial Palace meeting, Prime Minister Konoye sidesteps Cordell Hull to send a plea directly to Roosevelt, but is met with silence. On October 16 he is replaced by a new prime minister, Tojo Hideki, who tells an associate: "I'm praying to the gods that some way, we'll come to an agreement with America." The oil negotiations with Cordell Hull, however, make no significant progress.

November 3: The emperor formally approves Operation Z.

November 5: Navy cryptanalysts crack Japanese diplomatic codes to reveal instructions from the Tokyo Foreign Ministry to its ambassador in Washington that he has one last chance to negotiate, and if this fails, it will put the Pacific situation "on the brink of chaos." The American ambassador to Japan, Joseph Grew, who had sent warning after warning back to the State Department, each more urgent than the last, now cables Washington that a failure to come to terms will result in an "all out do-or-die attempt actually risking national Hara-Kiri to make Japan impervious to economic embargoes rather than yield to foreign pressure."

That same day, Army Chief of Staff Gen. George Marshall holds a secret press conference, informing *Time, Newsweek,* the *New York Times,* the *New York Herald Tribune,* and the three wire services that the United States is on the brink of war with Japan. He insists that by spring the United States will have so strong a force of bombers stationed in the Philippines that Japan will easily be destroyed: "Our aim is to blanket the whole area with air power. Our own fleet, meanwhile, will remain out of range of Japanese air power, at Hawaii. . . . The danger period is the first ten days of December." By this time three-quarters of Japan's foreign trade and 90 percent of its oil supplies have been cut off by the U.S./UK embargo. Japan's military leaders believe that the country, which uses twelve thousand tons of petroleum every twenty-four hours, will economically collapse within six months' time.

November 7: *Kido Butai,* the world's most powerful carrier strike force, under the command of Vice Adm. Nagumo Chuichi, holds its dress rehearsal: 350 planes launching from six carriers. The complicated operation is executed perfectly, and Admiral Yamamoto gives the final orders for Operation Z, bringing Hector Bywater's novel to life.

Late November: British, Dutch, and American consulates in Asia report Japanese troops marshaling in Formosa and Indochina. Learning this, FDR puts together a compromise plan for Tokyo, telling Cordell Hull to resume oil shipments to the Japanese "on a monthly basis for civilian needs." The secretary of state instead shelves the president's counterproposal and on November 26 presents Japan with a far harsher set of demands. The Tokyo Diet interprets Hull's position as an American declaration of war, and Prime Minister Tojo announces to his cabinet that there is "no glimmer for hope."

November 27: Hull notifies Secretary of War Stimson that he is giving up on trying to reach any agreement with Tokyo, and that the issue would now be "in the hands of you and Knox—the Army and Navy." In turn Marshall and Adm. Harold "Betty" Stark, chief of naval operations, memo the president: "Japan may attack the Burma Road, Thailand; Malaya; the Netherlands East Indies; the Philippines; the Russian Maritime Provinces. . . . The most essential thing now, from the United States viewpoint, is to gain time." Stark also sends a message to every commander in the Pacific, including Kimmel at Pearl Harbor: "This dispatch is to be considered a war warning. Negotiations with Japan . . . have ceased and an aggressive move by Japan is expected within the next few days."

November 28: Secretary of War Stimson receives information that a large Japanese flotilla has assembled and departed from Shanghai, heading south. Its destination is presumed to be Singapore, Hong Kong, the Dutch East Indies, or the Philippines. That same day, carrier *Enterprise* leaves Hawaii for

Wake Island, and on December 5 carrier *Lexington* takes off for Midway, both carrying fighters to help defend the outlying American territories.

Saturday, December 6: Most of the staff at the Naval Cryptographic Section in Washington have already left for the weekend. A new employee, Mrs. Dorothy Edgars, decides on her own to go through a backlog of untranslated decrypts. She comes across a flurry of messages between Tokyo and its Honolulu embassy concerning barrage balloons, airfield locations, ship movements, antitorpedo nets at Pearl Harbor, and even one report describing how a German spy in Oahu will transmit last-minute information. She shows the documents to Chief Ship's Clerk H. L. Bryant, but he says he doesn't have time to do a translation before leaving the office at noon, and Mrs. Edgars should just let the job wait for Monday. Mrs. Edgars thinks the material is so important, however, that she stays at the office and does the translating herself. At three o'clock Lt. Comdr. Alvin Kramer, chief of the Translation Branch, arrives, and Mrs. Edgars shows him her work. Kramer finds her efforts amateurish and begins editing the pages, but gives up, saying he has more important things to do, and urges her to go home.

That afternoon Roosevelt sends a telegram directly to Hirohito in response to reports of Japanese troop movements in Indochina. It concludes: "I address myself to Your Majesty at this moment in the fervent hope that Your Majesty may, as I am doing, give thought in this definite emergency to ways of dispelling the dark clouds." Held up for more than ten hours by Japanese post office censors, the message fails to arrive at Ambassador Grew's office until the next day. He immediately passes it on to Foreign Minister Togo Shigenori to present to the Son of Heaven.

As the *Kido Butai* armada turns south for the final run to Oahu, bombers and fighters in Formosa and Indochina are being loaded for attacks on the Philippines, Malaya, and Singapore, and small task forces are assembling to invade Guam and Wake. Twenty-five full-size Japanese submarines, along with five two-man midgets, arrive at Hawaii. The midgets are to sneak into the harbor, wait for the air attack to begin, and then fire their torpedoes at the most significant American ships.

At 9:30 P.M., Roosevelt and his special adviser Harry Hopkins are discussing the *Chicago Tribune*'s public release of secret War Department materials when the assistant to the president's naval aide arrives with a decrypted and translated intercept—the Japanese response to Hull's latest proposal, sent to its Washington ambassador, totaling fourteen parts, with the final section withheld. The cover sheet explains that this last point will arrive just in time for the ambassador's meeting with Hull at 1:00 P.M. on December 7. FDR reads the document, hands it to Hopkins, and when Harry finishes, the president gravely summarizes: "This means war." Hopkins agrees. Roosevelt tries to call navy chief Betty Stark, but he is out at the theater. When army head George Marshall sees the cover note from Tokyo, he and his aides also interpret it as meaning Japan will attack the United States, most likely in the Philippines or the Panama Canal.

That night, packed into the holds of transports on their way to landings across the Pacific, Imperial Japanese Army recruits browse through a pamphlet especially prepared for them, explaining how their efforts in the coming days will free "a hundred million Asians tyrannized by three hundred thousand whites." Many of the soldiers, especially the officers, consider themselves a new breed of warrior, and for inspiration they memorize Yamamoto Tsunetomo's *Hagakure (The Book of the Samurai):*

> Meditation on inevitable death should be performed daily. Every day when one's body and mind are at peace, one should meditate upon being ripped apart by arrows, rifles, spears, and swords, being carried away by surging waves, being thrown into the midst of a great fire, being struck by lightning, being shaken to death by a great earthquake, falling from a thousand-foot cliff, dying of disease, or committing *seppuku* [suicide by disembowelment] at the death of one's master. And every day without fail, one should consider himself as dead.

At 0330 on December 7, *Kido Butai* pilots and crews are roused from quarters. The previous day they had finished composing farewell letters to their families, enclosing locks of hair and fingernail clippings to be placed in Shinto altars of remembrance. Every airman believes that he will never see his country again. That morning, they dress in fresh loincloths and bandanas that read *Hissho* (certain victory). Many wear "thousand-stitch" belts, talismans created by wives, mothers, or sisters who stood at street curbs asking strangers to add a stitch, each symbolizing a prayer for luck and victory. Air chief Fuchida Mitsuo wears bright red undershirts and pants so that in case of injury, no blood will show to dishearten his men. The fliers have a ceremonial breakfast of rice and red snapper, and dress in dark green overalls, leather jackets, goggles, and—for the chill of high-altitude flying—leather caps with earflaps. The seas are so heavy that waves sweep across the great carriers' decks.

0400 (9:30 A.M. in Washington): Navy Translation Branch chief Kramer receives another decoded intercept from Tokyo to its Washington ambassador, telling him to deliver the fourteen-point message exactly at one o'clock Eastern Time to Cordell Hull, and then to destroy the embassy's code machines. Kramer had spent two years in Hawaii, and knows that 1:00 P.M. on the East Coast means dawn over Oahu. He hurries to Admiral Stark with the message and shares his concern, but Stark replies that the Pacific Fleet is already on full alert and doesn't need further warning.

0430: Two minesweepers let into Pearl Harbor are followed by a midget Japanese sub, which circles Ford Island, noting the position of each warship.

0500: *Kido Butai's* heavy cruisers *Chikuma* and *Tone,* the armada leaders, now 150 miles north of Hawaii, catapult four seaplanes to do a final scouting of local Hawaiian weather and the latest position of the American fleet.

0530 (11:00 A.M. in Washington): General Marshall returns from his morning horseback ride to read the message passed on by the navy's Kramer. He in turn sends an urgent cable to commanders in San Francisco, the Philippines, Panama, and Hawaii: "Just what significance the hour set may have we do not know, but be on the alert accordingly." The army's cable to Oahu is broken, however, so the message is sent via Western Union. General Short at Hawaii's Fort Shafter will receive it six hours later.

0545 (11:45 P.M. in Singapore): Four destroyers and a cruiser shell the Indian army pillboxes on the north coast of the Malay Peninsula as five thousand Japanese troops make their way ashore in heavy rain and crossfire.

0600: "In the predawn darkness of 7 December, Nagumo's carriers reached a point 200 miles north of Pearl Harbor," remembered pilot Fuchida.

> The zero hour had arrived! The carriers swung into the wind, and . . . the first wave of the 350-plane Attack Force, of which I was in overall command, took off. . . . One hour and forty minutes after leaving the carriers I knew that we should be nearing our goal. Small openings in the thick cloud cover afforded occasional glimpses of the ocean as I strained my eyes for the first sight of land. Suddenly a long white line of breaking surf appeared directly beneath my plane. It was the northern shore of Oahu.

0630: Skipper William Outerbridge of destroyer *Ward,* anchored at the entrance to Pearl Harbor, has just gotten out of bed and is still in his morning kimono when he sees a submarine conning tower following target ship *Antares* past the antitorpedo net. *Ward* fires its guns, hitting the tower, and drops four depth charges. Outerbridge radios Kimmel's office with the news, but when Kimmel's chief of staff and Adm. Claude C. Bloch receive it, they decide it is just another false alarm.

0706: Pvt. George Elliott, Jr., spots two huge blips on the primitive radar oscilloscope at Opana on Oahu's northern shore. He calls the Army Aircraft Warning Service Information Center to report a vast squadron of incoming planes 137 miles to the north. Kermit Tyler, the duty officer who answers his call, knows that some B-17s are about to arrive from the mainland, and so tells Opana "not to worry about it."

0730 (1:30 A.M. in Singapore): At Thailand's border with Malaya, the landing Japanese transports quickly overcome local resistance. One thousand recruits, camouflaged as Thai soldiers, round up dance-hall girls, get into thirty buses, drive to the Malay border, and—waving Thai and British flags while shouting "Hurrah for the English!"—are let into the country.

0735: Japanese scout planes report back to *Kido Butai* that the entire American Pacific Fleet is at port, and that the sky is absolutely clear.

0748: Three armadas of twenty ships approach the Malay coast and begin bombardment, unleashing twenty thousand Japanese troops, who roar down the peninsula's main highway in abandoned English trucks and on bicycles in the opening offensive of the campaign to capture Singapore. British fighter control operations try calling the Civil Air Raid Headquarters about unidentified aircraft heading for the city, but no one is there to answer the phone. When the raid begins, British expatriates in Singapore try to turn off the lights to make it harder for enemy bombers to target them, but the custodian with the keys to the master switch can't be found.

Nestled dead-center on Oahu's south coast is the bay known as Pearl Harbor, home to Pearl City and forty thousand servicemen of every stripe. At its center is Ford Island, which hangars the navy's planes and docks its carriers and battleships. Pearl is home to ninety-six warships: cruisers, like *Detroit, Baltimore,* and *Raleigh;* seaplane and aircraft tenders, like *Tangier, Swan,* and *Curtiss;* repair ships; minelayers; leftovers from Teddy Roosevelt's Great White Fleet; and of course, the queens of Oahu, the mighty tenants of Ford's Battleship Row: *Pennsylvania, Nevada, Arizona, Tennessee, West Virginia, Maryland, Oklahoma,* and *California.*

Even with such a force of men and matériel, on Sundays the harbor is remarkably quiet. This morning, Coxswain James Forbis is overseeing a crew rigging *Arizona*'s fantail for church service; Signalman John Blanken from *San Francisco* gets ready to go swimming at Waikiki; Ens. Thomas Taylor on *Nevada* has a tennis game scheduled; the marines of *Helena* have picked sides for a softball match; and a group of old navy hands on *St. Louis* plays a round of checkers. Other seamen are sitting around their cabins and bunk quarters in pajamas, robes, and kimonos, just starting the Sunday comics; far more are sleeping off a Saturday night tour of Honolulu's red-light Hotel Row. Hawaiian locals, meanwhile, are recovering from the thrill of their university's having beaten Willamette, 20–6, at the Shrine football game. Like every dawn of every day on every island in that part of the world, there is a cool wind, a hint of rain, and the empty, endless yaw of the electric blue Pacific.

0740: On reaching landfall, the Japanese torpedo planes fall to just above the treetops (they will strike first, before the smoke from the ensuing explosions masks their targets), while the divers climb to 12,000 feet and the horizontal bombers fall to 3,500. Misinterpreting a joke played by Fuchida and a fighter squadron leader, the fifty-one dive-bombers (who call themselves "hell divers" after the popular Clark Gable movie) believe they are to attack first, so all ninety-one craft begin their approach. Now they stream across the aqua hills of Kahuku Point, swoop past the ominous black tower of Diamond Head, and finally race toward the bottle green waters of Pearl Harbor. On this Sunday ninety-six American vessels lie below.

0749: "Presently the harbor itself became visible across the central Oahu plain, a film of morning mist hovering over it," Fuchida reported. "I peered intently through my binoculars at the ships riding peacefully at anchor. One by one I counted them. Yes, the battleships were there all right, eight of them!" Not a single American fighter appears, not one cloud of defensive ackack explodes, and Fuchida radios his men: *To To To!* (*Totsugeki* [Charge]!)

On the ground there is heard the vibrato roar of low-flying props and, on the horizon, there appears what resembles a cloud of bees. *Raleigh* Ens. Donald L. Korn sees one black stream coming in from the northwest. *Arizona* seaman Red Pressler notices another, crossing over the mountains to the east. Helm quartermaster Frank Handler watches a group coming in due south, flying directly into the harbor's entrance and heading up the channel a mere one hundred yards from where he stands. They are so close that one of the pilots gives Frank a wave, and he cheerfully waves back. *Helena* signalman Charles Flood thinks the approach is very strange, reminding him of when he was in Shanghai in 1932, during the Japanese invasion. Those planes had dived and glided in exactly the same formation.

Church bells strike across Honolulu as the *Nevada* band, on deck and halfway through their morning "Star-Spangled Banner," is strafed by machine-gun fire. The musicians are convinced it must be a drill . . . until they notice the deck, splintering into pieces. They finish the national anthem and run for cover.

On the marines' Ewa, the air corps's Hickam, and the navy's Kaneohe airfields of Oahu, almost four hundred planes are closely packed, wingtip to wingtip, with the antiaircraft battery ammunition locked away in the various compounds' central magazines, all to deter would-be saboteurs. The Nazis had commonly used the "fifth column," locals of German ancestry, to aid in their European campaigns, "fifth" in that they followed the infantry, cavalry, navy, and air forces, and the army's General Short was convinced that Tokyo would employ the 157,905 Hawaiians of Japanese descent in exactly the same way.

Hickam, the Army Air Corps field housing six B-17s, twelve A-20s, and thirty-three ancient B-18s, sits just down the road from Pearl on the way to Honolulu. Twelve new B-17s are due to land that morning, and some local air buffs have gathered to watch. Aircraft mechanics Jesse Gaines and Tod Conway see the formation of bombers, in a perfect V, begin to peel, and Conway says excitedly, "We're going to have an air show!" Then Gaines sees small black specks drifting from the leader's belly like rabbit droppings, and hears the crescendo whistle of falling ordnance. There is an explosion in the middle of the field of planes. The men look up to see bombs now falling straight at their heads and scramble away in zigzag terror. An oil tank explodes, as does the Hickam mess hall. Thirty-five men die instantly.

After a fourteen-hour nonstop flight from the mainland, those dozen B-17 Flying Fortresses are now coming in to land, only to find themselves under attack by Zeros. The pilots are able to evade the enemy fire, but the exhausted airmen inside are otherwise helpless. Their guns are stored in vats of Cosmoline, and the crews aren't personally armed. As they land in the chaos of the airfield, they are easy pickings for strafers.

At the Ewa marine base next door, by the time everyone realizes what is happening thirty-three of their forty-nine planes have already been destroyed.

At Oahu's central Wheeler Field, the army's brand-new P-40 fighters are guarded by Private First Class Fusco with a 1903 Springfield rifle. He immediately recognizes the red circles on the wings of the approaching planes and runs to the nearest hangar for a machine gun. The armament shack's door is locked, and Fusco can't break it open. Bombers strike the ordnance building, setting its million rounds of ammo on fire. Bugler Pvt. Frank Gobeo doesn't know how to play "To Arms," so he blows "Pay Call," and the men swarm from the barracks. Wheeler's antiaircraft units pull out their shells, only to find they are vintage 1918, the belts falling to pieces before they can be loaded.

Twelve miles away, on Oahu's windward coast at the Kaneohe Naval Air Station seaplane base, five pilots jump into a car to race to their planes, but are repeatedly strafed by a Zero's machine-gun fire. They arrive and jump out, their vehicle exploding a few seconds later. The navy pilots discover that all of Kaneohe's planes are already destroyed.

0810 (1:40 P.M. in Washington): The secretary of the navy is one of many who receives Admiral Kimmel's cable: AIR RAID PEARL HARBOR THIS IS NOT A DRILL. Frank Knox could only reply, "My God! This can't be true. This must mean the Philippines." The Asiatic Fleet headquarters in downtown Manila is sent the same message, and within an hour Gen. Douglas MacArthur and his commanders know that war has come. Immediately MacArthur is ordered by air corps chief Hap Arnold to send all his planes aloft. The B-17s at MacArthur's Clark Field, north of Manila, are the largest concentration of modern American bombers anywhere, but like the B-25s, they are sparse in defense, with squadron commander Rosie O'Donnell complaining that his pilots might as well "have been flying spotted ponies."

0820: "As we closed in, enemy aircraft fire began to concentrate on us," Fuchida Mitsuo remembered.

> Dark gray puffs burst all around. . . . Suddenly, my plane bounced as if struck by a club . . . the radioman said: "The fuse-lage is holed and the rudder wire damaged." [But] it was nearly time for "Ready to Release," and I concentrated my attention on the lead plane to note the instant his bomb was dropped. Sud-denly, a cloud came between the bomb sight and the target . . . we would have to try again. We were about to begin our second bombing run when there was a colossal explosion in Battleship Row. A huge column of dark red smoke rose to one thousand meters. It was a hateful, mean-looking red flame, the kind that powder produces, and I knew at once that a big magazine had exploded. [It was *Arizona*'s.] The shock wave was felt even in my plane, several miles away from the harbor. . . . This time our lead bomber was successful, and the other planes of the group followed suit promptly upon seeing the leader's bombs fall. I immediately lay flat on the cockpit floor and slid open a peephole cover in order to observe the fall of the bombs. I watched four bombs plummet toward the earth. The target—two battleships moored side by side—lay ahead. My four bombs in perfect formation plummeted like the devils of doom. The bombs became smaller and smaller and finally disappeared. I held my breath until two tiny puffs of smoke flashed suddenly on the ship to the left, and I shouted, "Two hits!"

Five bombs from the high levels tear into *Arizona*, one striking sixteen hundred pounds of black powder stored against regulations, and the ship explodes in fire like a volcano, spewing a five-hundred-foot ball of flame and leaping halfway out of the water, finally breaking in half. Fifteen hundred sailors are trapped below.

The men who can escape jump into the harbor and—clutching prized possessions: a carton of cigarettes; a pair of dress shoes; a canned ham—begin swimming to Ford Island. But leaking fuel from the damaged ships floats atop the waters and bursts into flame, killing almost every swimmer. *California*, with two torpedo hits, sinks in a matter of minutes. As bombs and torpedoes drive through hulls and decks, power systems fail, tanks explode, oil streams across the floors, and seawater pours in. Each strike on the gray queens, filled with ammo, shells, and fuel themselves, triggers a fireworks-factory bonfire, both above and below the waterline, commingling into a heavy black fog. Bombs that miss the ships ignite into escalating geysers of harbor water and steam, lit by exploding ordnance and framed in growing, bilious clouds, black and rising, as one fuel tank after another chain-reacts. On Ford Island, Chief Albert Molter watches as *Oklahoma*, hit by three torpedoes, gradually rolls completely over into the water, "slowly and stately . . . as if she were tired and wanted to rest." It is eight minutes after the first assault of torpedo planes, and now the once great ship is completely overturned, her mast dug into the mud. Four hundred die with her.

Nevada, saved by virtue of not being directly in the line of attack, heads out for sea, and the hell divers now come straight for her. Bombs that fall short throw up jetting columns of water on every side, while direct hits rain explosions across the front half of the decks. Six bombs ultimately strike *Nevada*.

In the dash to get topside on *Pennsylvania* someone has left a record player on; the lulls between bombs detonating and antiaircraft guns responding are filled with Glenn Miller's "Sunrise Serenade." The bodies catapulted by the force of the explosions remind Ens. David King of the circus, when cannon would propel clowns through the air. This time was different, he thought; no one would land, happily, in a net.

Of Pearl Harbor's 780 antiaircraft guns, three-quarters are unmanned, and only four of the thirty-one antiaircraft batteries are in position, with all ammo stored in depots far from the line of fire. One frustrated bosun's mate throws wrenches at the low-flying bombers. A master sergeant follows the enemy squadrons on his bicycle, shooting at them with a pistol. Comdr. Duncan Curry stands on the *Ramapo* bridge firing away with a .45 while sobbing uncontrollably. Antiaircraft shells with bad fuses or direct misses landed in Honolulu, causing forty explosions and killing an unknown number of civilians.

Seaman Leslie Vernon Short, in *Maryland*'s foretop, loads his machine gun and attacks the planes. In *Nevada*'s mainmast birdbath platform, one boy drops a torpedo plane using a .30 caliber gun. On the USS *West Virginia,* Mess Attendant First Class Doris Miller takes a machine gun, which he's never used before, and brings down several Japanese craft. But these moments of Americans fighting back are few, as so many servicemen are either away on this Sunday or trapped in the sinking holds below. A mere thirty Army Air Corps pilots are able to take to their fighters, ultimately bringing down eleven Japanese aircraft. Many American pilots are bombed out of their cockpits as they try to defend their country.

In Hawaii the military's upper echelon lives in suburbs terraced into the hills above Pearl City. Wives and children watch the attack from their front yards. With the black fog of smoke now completely obscuring the harbor and the airfields, Zeros turn their sights on this neighborhood. Mothers upend their sofas to create shelter for their young children.

At the very beginning of the attack, Hawaii's navy chief, Husband Kimmel, is leaving home, dressed in his admiral whites; his next-door neighbor notices his face "as white as his uniform." As he arrives at his Pearl Harbor office, an errant bullet ricochets from his chest and falls to the floor. Kimmel picks it up and says, "I wish it had killed me." When he returns outside, a yeoman notices that Kimmel has replaced his four-star shoulder boards with two stars, demoting himself.

In just minutes, the Kaneohe and Ford Island navy bases; the Ewa marine air base; and the Wheeler, Bellows, and Hickam Army Air Corps bases are fully crippled. *Arizona, Oklahoma,* and *West Virginia* have sunk; *California* is finished; *Maryland* and *Tennessee* are immobilized by the destroyed vessels surrounding them; *Nevada* is half-demolished from two bombs and one torpedo. Fuchida circles overhead, taking pictures of his achievement: "A warm feeling came with the realization that the reward of those efforts was unfolded before my eyes. I counted four battleships definitely sunk and three severely damaged, and extensive damage had also been inflicted upon other types of ships. The seaplane base at Ford Island was all in flames, as were the airfields, especially Wheeler Field."

0942: One false report after the next sends Adm. Bill Halsey rushing in all directions with his *Enterprise* carrier task force to hunt down *Kido Butai*. He never succeeds in finding the Operation Z armada, but this turns out for the best, since a confrontation with Nagumo could have ended only with the destruction of the American ships. When Halsey comes home that night to Pearl and sees the devastation, he announces: "Before we're through with 'em, the Japanese language will be spoken only in hell!" Meanwhile the Opana radar station, which had been first to detect the enemy planes, now carefully tracks their withdrawal to the north. Everyone ignores this information.

1000: The first Japanese crews return to their carriers in such bad weather and pitching seas that a number of the pilots crash while trying to land. When Fuchida touches down, he begs his commander to send out one final attack to destroy the American drydocks and fuel tanks. Nagumo, worried that his fleet has been detected, instead orders a withdrawal. In his estimation, Operation Z is already a complete success. In one hour and forty-five minutes, seven battleships, eleven support vessels, and 227 planes have been destroyed, and more than 2,400 Americans are dead.

The squadrons of enemy bombers and fighters attacking Hawaii are now replaced by panic spreading across the island, with servicemen and civilians passing on rumor after rumor: The Japs have overtaken Waikiki; they've landed at Diamond Head; forty enemy army transports are discharging hordes of troops along the western shores while thousands of paratroopers in blue coveralls are descending across the valleys. Spies are everywhere, landed by flotillas of sampans, disguised as an army of milkmen. None of this turns out to be true; instead Operation Z proves to be a mere overture to Operation Number One:

1030: Gen. Lewis Brereton, air commander of the Philippines, asks permission to send his B-17s on bombing runs against Japanese bases in nearby Formosa. MacArthur's chief of staff, Gen. Richard K. Sutherland, refuses to allow Brereton to speak with the commander.

1230: Brereton again tries to get permission from MacArthur to launch his planes, but is again turned down by Sutherland.

1257: From their Saipan base Japanese naval bombers attack the five hundred marines and sailors posted to Guam, who have no weapons beyond a few machine guns and pistols. After destroying the local barracks and the USS *Penguin,* the planes depart, to be succeeded by an invasion force of transports and destroyers.

1300: With only fifteen seconds of warning, the Americans on Wake atoll can't get their fighters into the air or their antiaircraft guns ready to defend against thirty-six Japanese bombers arriving from the Marshalls. Seven planes, just delivered by *Enterprise,* are destroyed, along with the island's fuel storage tank. As Pan Am's flying boat *Philippine Clipper* takes off with airline personnel and Allied wounded, the captain radios that he sees Japanese cruisers and destroyers heading for Wake.

1400: Thirty-five hell divers arrive over Hong Kong, destroying *Hong Kong Clipper* and the China National Aviation fleet, as ground forces advance on the British mainland territory of Kowloon. Allied defenses consist of a few Canadian and Indian infantry battalions, one antique destroyer, and eight PT boats.

At 7:00 A.M. in Tokyo, Foreign Minister Togo hands Ambassador Grew the thirteen-page, fourteen-section memorandum declaring that negotiations have terminated, and "said that he had already been in touch with the Emperor, who desired that the aforementioned Memorandum be regarded as his reply to the President's message." That afternoon Yamamoto's chief of staff writes in his diary: "It is almost certain that the U.S., after reorganizing their forces, will come against us in retaliation. . . . Tokyo should be protected from air raids; this is the most important thing to be borne in mind." (In 1939, Yamamoto had told a group of his fellow officers that "Japanese cities, being made of wood and paper, would burn very easily. The Army talks big, but if war came and there were large-scale air raids, there's no telling what would happen.") After Prime Minister Tojo reads the announcement of war over Tokyo radio, the government broadcasts the song "Umi Yukaba," which includes:

> *Across the sea, corpses in the water,*
> *Across the mountain, corpses in the field.*

1500 (2030 EST): The cabinet and leaders of Congress gather at the White House, with Secretary of Labor Frances Perkins noting, "It was obvious to me that Roosevelt was having a dreadful time just accepting the idea that the navy could be caught unaware." At the fences outside Pennsylvania Avenue, a crowd sings "God Bless America."

British agent Tricycle hears the news, assumes the FBI has passed along all his detailed intelligence, and is thrilled: "I was sure the American Fleet had scored a great victory over the Japanese. I was very, very proud that I had been able to give the warning to the Americans four months in advance. What a reception the Japanese must have had!"

1530: Brereton calls MacArthur again for permission to launch an assault, and again is told to wait. At some time between 10:00 and 11:00, Brereton receives approval, and by 11:20 orders for the attack are sent by teletype to Clark Field.

1730: The Philippines' Iba Field radar operator tries to send teletype, radio, and telephone warnings to Clark that he has detected two hundred Japanese warplanes heading straight toward them. The radio doesn't work, the Clark teletypist is out to lunch, and the lieutenant who answers the phone promises to spread word of the impending attack "at the earliest opportunity," but never does.

1750: Brereton's planes are still on the ground being fueled, checked, and loaded when fifty-four bombers and thirty-six Zeros from Formosa attack, destroying half of the American air forces in the Philippines on the first day of war and killing more than one hundred men. In less than an hour the Japanese have won the victory that will enable them to launch their ground assault. Hearing the news, MacArthur refuses to believe the attackers could be Japanese, insisting they must be German or Italian mercenaries.

The general's attitude underscores a key reason why the United States was caught so unaware on every front. Before Operation Number One, practically every American held a stereotypical vision of the Japanese as a dimwitted, irrational, primitive, grossly nearsighted, compulsive, and mechanically incompetent people. Roosevelt and Hull had dragged out their negotiations with Tokyo in large part because neither could take seriously the notion that the small, bowing, agreeable Asians they knew might pose a military threat.

December 18: The Japanese take Kowloon and begin their assault on the island of Hong Kong.

December 22: 109 Japanese transports launch almost 10,000 men in the Philippines, not at the heavily defended southern end of Lingayen Gulf, but miles up the coast near the town of Aganoo, and miles south in Lamon Bay. Almost immediately Manila is under attack.

MacArthur had long planned to defend the territory at the beaches, but the country's endless coastline makes this impossible, and the Philippine troops stationed there capitulate in two days. Instead the general is forced to abandon his Manila hotel suite for the northern peninsula of Bataan and the sheltered island of Corregidor. Seventy thousand American and Filipino troops, accompanied by twenty-six thousand civilians, now seek refuge in the peninsula as well, but the logistics of getting supplies, weapons, and food to them from the beaches and cities immediately falters into chaos. While MacArthur stays in the relative comfort of Corregidor's tunnel defense, where he will be known as "Dugout Doug," the nearly one hundred thousand on the peninsula run out of food, water, and medicine, falling prey to dysentery, scurvy, malaria, and beriberi.

December 23: The Japanese send two thousand men, four heavy cruisers, and the carriers *Soryu* and *Hiryu* to invade Wake Island. The marines surrender in twenty-four hours.

December 25: Hong Kong surrenders to the Japanese, whose airmen sink Britain's battleship *Prince of Wales* and cruiser *Repulse.*

December 28: Borneo surrenders, while off the coast of Java, the Japanese navy engages Dutch, British, and American forces, the Allies in ancient craft left over from World War I, the Japanese with state-of-the-art torpedoes with a range of thirty thousand feet and an oxygen propulsion system that makes them all but invisible.

January 22: Fuchida leads a squadron of ninety fighters and an equal number of bombers from *Akagi, Kaga, Shokaku,* and *Zuikaku* in an attack on Rabaul, the Australian air base on New Britain Island.

January 31: The Malay Peninsula is now under Japanese control, and the assault on Singapore has begun. Defended by eighty-eight thousand British, Australian, Indian, and Malay soldiers and volunteers, the city falls to the Japanese in two weeks. When Chinese and Indian civilians try to resist the Imperial Japanese Army, they are immediately executed, their heads left as warnings along the streets.

February 19: Fuchida and his squadron attack the harbor of Darwin, Australia, destroying dozens of Allied planes and ships and so obliterating the town that it has to be abandoned.

March 2: On Hirohito's forty-second birthday, the news of one military success after the next is so rapid and so astounding that he tells his closest adviser, "The fruits of victory are tumbling into our mouths too quickly."

March 4: A Japanese plane appears over Honolulu but misses the city with its bombs. Pilots of the Seventh Air Force give chase, but overcast skies allow the would-be attacker to escape.

March 8: Rangoon falls to Japanese ground troops, along with Sulawesi, the Celebes, Bali, and Sumatra. The news from the Philippines is so relentlessly negative, meanwhile, that George Marshall becomes convinced the Japanese will capture MacArthur, one of America's great World War I heroes, and parade him through the streets. On March 11, under orders from Washington, MacArthur, his wife, his son, and his officers are evacuated from Corregidor on PT-41, slipping through enemy lines to the Philippines' southernmost island of Mindanao. As he passes his men, now known as "the battling bastards of Bataan," "I could feel my face go white," MacArthur remembers later, "feel a sudden, convulsive twitch in the muscles of my face." After his safe arrival in Alice Springs, Australia, Roosevelt awards him with the Medal of Honor.

March 9: Java surrenders to the Japanese, who now control the entire Netherlands East Indies.

April 3: Fifty thousand Japanese troops with 150 guns, howitzers, and mortars arrive at Bataan to face 78,000 starving Americans and Filipinos, three-quarters of them only half alive from malaria. At 1000, a rain of bombs and shells explode against the Allied front lines. The jungle bursts into flame, and the defenders run pell-mell in retreat. Tanks and infantry pour through from all directions. The Japanese commander originally estimates it will take a month to win the territory; instead Bataan falls in six days.

Running out of water, food, and medicine, the Japanese force-march their captive POWs sixty-five miles through the jungle to prison camps at the peninsula's base. Ten thousand will die along the way, with thousands more subsequently perishing in the camps.

In a mere five months the entire Pacific Ocean west of a line drawn from the Aleutian Islands to Hawaii and Australia has come under the control of *Dai Nippon Teikoku*. The Japanese empire stretches six thousand miles from the home islands to Korea and eastern China, across today's Vietnam to Myanmar, down Malaysia to Taiwan, Hong Kong, and Singapore, and then across all of Indonesia to most of New Guinea. What Tokyo calls the Greater East Asia Coprosperity Sphere spells the end of Western control over Sarawak, Borneo, Sumatra, Java, the Celebes, the Moluccas, western New Guinea, the Solomons, the Philippines, Malaya, Indochina, the Andamans, Guam, Wake, the Gilbert and the Marshall Islands, and includes a vast amount of the world's oil, rice, tin, and rubber. The bucktoothed, nearsighted race of American cartoons had unceasingly defeated England, Australia, and the United States in battle after battle. The tally: 15,000 killed and wounded Japanese; 320,000 killed, wounded, and captured Allied soldiers.

THE DREAMER, PARALYZED

For thirteen years there was a very special room on the second floor of 1600 Pennsylvania Avenue. Every evening as twilight fell, the most important men and women in the world would gather there to drink cocktails mixed (badly) by the president himself, and to share in the latest gossip about everyone from Eva Braun to Clark Gable. At this predinner hour, no one was allowed to discuss politics, war, economics, or anything else remotely serious. Only if you had juicy news, a good joke, or a wonderful memory could you, at that moment, hold the ear of FDR.

By day this same room—Roosevelt's library-office, right next to the building's elevator—held an entirely different tone, since it was where American leaders would meet to discuss the nation's most overwhelming difficulties. Following December 7, 1941, it would serve as the staging ground from where the United States would fight its first battles of World War II. Except for one pivotal engagement, the country would lose every single one of them—months of loss after loss that Winston Churchill would call "a cataract of disaster."

During the day men and women would meet around a small table, their coffee cups refreshed and their cigarettes lit; a bell would chime, and the president would enter, his wheelchair pushed by a White House usher. Though his legs had been reduced, literally, to skin and bone, Roosevelt was a remarkably physical presence—bull-shaped head; powerful upper torso; giant, meaty hands; and that perfectly cadenced voice—the voice that, on the radio, had made a nation fall in love.

This second-floor room didn't add up to much: a portable wet bar; a table barely big enough to play Miss Millikin, the president's favorite solitaire game; shelving for Roosevelt's greatest love, his stamp collection; and a floor littered with tumbling piles of papers, always getting in the way. The room's most dramatic and distinctive element, though, would have to have been its decorations: an overflowing, Victorian-packrat deluge of paintings, photographs, and carved wooden models of ships and boats and vessels, of flattops and barques, of cruisers and dreadnoughts, steamboats, subs, and brigantines.

Franklin Roosevelt was a sailor, who spent many a vacation yachting the Potomac. At the age of fifteen his favorite Christmas present was Alfred Thayer Mahan's *The Influence of Sea Power upon History, 1660–1793,* and his first job on the national stage had been the seven years he'd spent as Woodrow Wilson's assistant secretary of the navy during World War I. Roosevelt was so taken with the service, in fact, that he wanted to resign from his civilian duties to become a commissioned officer. As president FDR would personally choose the navy's flag officers, and annually raise the service's budget year after year, even during the depression when the army and its air corps received no such treatment. He'd also refer to the navy as "us" and the army as "them" until, in February 1942, Army Chief of Staff George Catlett Marshall insisted he stop.

A scion of East Coast patricians who found public displays of emotion to be in exceedingly poor taste, the president never discussed with anyone his paralysis, his strange marital arrangement, or his numerous professional setbacks. Instead FDR would commonly tell his employees, "If you run into troubles, bring them to me; my shoulders are broad." Few would be aware of the desolate grief and rage he felt on hearing the news of Pearl Harbor, though the attack would in fact be the culmination of months of unrelenting failures, tragedies, and disappointments, both personal and professional. As biographer Kenneth S. Davis remarked, "At no time during his presidency was Roosevelt under greater, more various public pressures than during the long autumn of 1941, and in no other extended period . . . did he feel in general more helpless, less able to effect significant change in the course of onrushing events . . . his general experience was that of a man whose major effort and purpose are simply to keep his balance, a precarious balance, as he rides an all-too-flimsy raft down a narrowing turbulent river toward the roar of a rock-strewn rapids or, perhaps, of a death-dealing waterfall."

FDR had come into office nine years earlier on a great promise, launching over the course of his first term one creative and dynamic federal initiative after another, inspiring tremendous devotion across the country. That success would be short-lived. By the end of 1941, FDR's New Deal was generally thought to have been too little, too late, and though in general Americans were feeling more confident and hopeful about the future than during Hoover's presidency, the nation was still in turmoil after suffering more than a decade of economic catastrophe. For the past three years, ever since Wall Street had tumbled all over again in 1937, the economy was in a phase many called "the Roosevelt Recession"—17 percent of the nation (some ten million people) were out of work, and of those able to get jobs, half the men and two-thirds of the women scraped by, barely, on less than a thousand dollars a year.

Roosevelt was above all else a consummate politician who took care that his every word and deed were in tune with the public consensus. Yet, in the area of foreign affairs, he now found himself almost entirely alone. The president wanted more than anything to help England in its war against Germany, while the American people wanted their government to focus entirely on domestic concerns. They simply felt too poor and beaten down to wage war on behalf of distant continents, and in many minds the conflict had already been decided. A U.S. poll from the summer of 1940 revealed that two-thirds of the respondents were convinced that Germany would defeat Britain and Russia, eventually becoming the ruler of all Europe. After the fall of France (whose legendary fighting force capitulated in a mere six weeks), the American ambassador to England, Joseph Kennedy, General Marshall, and numerous D.C. strategists urged FDR to stop sending military supplies to the English, since the Germans were so certain to prevail. "It's a terrible thing," Roosevelt told an aide, "to look over your shoulder when you're trying to lead, and to find no one there."

At the same time, the most important person in FDR's life, his mother, Sara Delano Roosevelt, had fallen into a coma and died three months earlier, on September 7. Over the course of her last year, the president had commissioned a gigantic, larger-than-life-size portrait of "Mrs. James" (as she was known in the family), a painting that would dominate his home office at Hyde Park for the rest of his life. Roosevelt would wear a black armband in mourning for more than a year, and her funeral was the first occasion that anyone on his staff had ever seen him cry.

August 10, 1941, meanwhile, had been another milestone—the twentieth anniversary of his attack by poliomyelitis. Though he'd made some progress from the very first days of his diagnosis, when he'd been fully immobilized from the neck down, nothing seemed to bring his now completely withered legs back to life. He'd tried sunlamp treatments, harnesses, hundreds of massage techniques, electric belts, and just about every "cure" that the twenties and thirties had to offer, and he would keep trying them until the day he died.

The president's almost fanatical power of will was reflected in the way he'd spent most of his adult life publicly camouflaging the fact that he couldn't walk. With one hand atop a cane and the other gripping the tensed elbow of an aide or a son, FDR would tilt his rigidly steel-braced legs from side to side, inching forward like a contortionist on parallel bars, powered entirely by his arms and shoulders. Thanks to a gentleman's agreement with the press of that era, the American public knew next to nothing about his disability. Using only his hands, he drove a Ford convertible he designed himself, at maniacal speeds, and of the more than forty thousand photographs of Franklin D. Roosevelt at the Hyde Park library today, only two include a wheelchair.

At 1:40 P.M. on December 7, Navy Secretary Frank Knox telephoned the Oval Office to notify the president of the attack on Hawaii. As was commonly the case on a Sunday, he was at work that afternoon with his closest friend, Harry Hopkins. After receiving the news FDR hung up the phone and, with his head in his hands, murmured to Harry, "How did it happen? . . . how did it happen? . . . now I'll go down in history . . . disgraced." As assistant secretary of the navy, Roosevelt had overseen the bolting of the keel, at the Brooklyn Navy Yard, of what would be the country's thirty-ninth battleship: the USS *Arizona*. Now his beloved navy had been half destroyed, and the *Arizona* lay at the bottom of Pearl Harbor, a tomb to 1,103 fellow sailors.

Four days later Germany declared war on the United States, with Hitler reminding his subordinates of Japan's glorious military history: "Now it is impossible for us to lose the war; we now have an ally who has never been vanquished in three thousand years!" FDR would have to lead his country into battle in separate fronts on opposite sides of the world—a task for which Americans were wholly unprepared.

As of 1940 the United States stood fourteenth in global military power, trailing Germany, France, Britain, Russia, Italy, Japan, China, Belgium, the Netherlands, Portugal, Spain, Sweden, and Switzerland. While 6.8 million Germans were trained and ready for active duty, the United States could count 504,000 enlisted recruits. That year military professionals were still arguing in *Cavalry Journal* that men on horseback were a superior fighting force to men in tanks; while, after viewing war games in Louisiana, *Time* magazine bluntly reported that "against Europe's total war, the U.S. Army looked like a few nice boys with BB guns." In 1941 America had only a six-month supply of rubber, which in that preplastic era was a necessary ingredient of tires, rafts, gas masks, tape, stethoscopes, and high-altitude pilot suits. Ninety percent of American rubber came from the Dutch East Indies, territory now controlled by Japan. The export embargo so feared by Tokyo had now been perfectly reversed, and the United States would now starve for key raw materials.

In ocean warfare the Japanese had engineered in the 1930s a twenty-foot-long torpedo that could travel twenty-four miles; the best American torpedo had a range of 4,500 yards, and almost always missed. Pearl Harbor had left the navy with six operating battleships, but these were more or less obsolete, since they traveled ten knots slower than the navy's aircraft carriers and couldn't keep up with any modern battle group. When it came to air power, matters were no better. Japan's Zero fighter, which could take off from a carrier, was superior to any fighter that the United States could produce, even those that were land based. From August to November 1942, high-altitude B-17s—the mainstay of the air corps—would drop 828 bombs on sixty enemy ships, sinking only four of them. Defense contractors, meanwhile, were supplying equipment that they knew to be flawed. Curtiss-Wright was delivering airplane engines that weren't testing out, and in testimony before Sen. Harry S. Truman, Glenn Martin admitted his craft had wings that were too narrow. However, he had a federal contract, he said, and wasn't going to change a thing.

Along with Secretary of War Stimson and presidential aide Harry Hopkins, the men who met in the White House library office during the day, most of whom would eventually be known as the Joint Chiefs of Staff, included Roosevelt's military aide and appointments secretary, Gen. Edwin "Pa" Watson; Secretary of the Navy Knox; Chief of Naval Operations Stark; Commander in Chief U.S. Fleet King; Army Air Corps Chief of Staff Arnold; and Army Chief of Staff Marshall. A more disparate band of headstrong individuals could be found only in novels. Marshall would say of his relationship with the president, "He would talk over something informally at the dinner table, and you had trouble disagreeing without embarrassment. So I never went. I was in Hyde Park for the first time at his funeral." While Roosevelt was constantly laughing, bantering, joking, waving his cigarette holder in arcs of enthusiasm and declaiming, "I love it! I love it!" in agreement with your position no matter what (and no matter what he would say the minute you left the room), the general was notoriously without a sense of humor or even any visibly close friends. Stimson remarked that following FDR's thought process "was very much like chasing a vagrant beam of sunshine around an empty room," while almost every Marshall subordinate commented on the general's chilling blue eyes, his austere presence, and his constant drive to get to the point—which left more than a few officers tongue-tied in his presence.

Both the general and the president, however, shared a remarkable gift for spotting talent. In 1939 Roosevelt had passed over thirty-three others in line to give Marshall the top army job, while the general, for years, would keep a little black book with the names of junior officers he thought had leadership potential—names like Eisenhower, Patton, and Bradley. George Marshall would become such an effective leader himself, in fact, that Roosevelt felt he couldn't give him the one position the general really wanted: commander of Operation Overlord, the invasion of France. The president let Marshall make the choice, and the general, who would spend much of his life mulling the role of a soldier in a democratic society, replied that he would serve wherever the president wished. Explaining that "I didn't feel I could sleep at ease with you out of Washington," FDR gave the job instead to Eisenhower.

In the aftermath of Pearl Harbor, Chief of Naval Operations Stark would ship out to London in March, demoted to commander of U.S. naval forces in Europe. Stark's official biographer would insist that the admiral voluntarily offered his resignation and proposed this new assignment, while Stark's at-the-time underling, Ernest King, would just as fervently claim that the president fired Stark. King would additionally wonder why Roosevelt didn't demote Marshall as well: Hadn't the army been just as culpable as the navy for the disaster in Hawaii?

"Lord how I need him," wrote Navy Secretary Knox on December 23, 1941, the day he summoned King to become commander in chief of the U.S. Fleet (for which King, not liking the sound of CINCUS, came up with the acronym COMINCH). Navy historian Samuel Eliot Morison described the admiral as "tall, spare and taut, with piercing brown eyes, a powerful Roman nose and deeply cleft chin; a sailor's sailor who neither had nor wanted any life outside the Navy . . . more feared than loved . . . a hard, grim, determined man," while FDR commented: "[H]e shaves with a blowtorch," and one of King's daughters claimed, "He is one of the most even-tempered men in the Navy. He is always in a rage."

Coming up in the ranks, King regularly got written up for his drinking, tardiness, and insubordination, and an Annapolis professor wrote that "his weaknesses were other men's wives, alcohol, and intolerance." For all his personal flaws, however, the admiral could himself perform just about any naval assignment in existence, since he'd previously been a submariner, aviator, aircraft carrier captain, and fleet commander. While King had an astoundingly powerful memory and could recall the names of people he'd met only once, decades earlier, Marshall couldn't remember the names of his own secretaries, one of whose regular assignments was to replace the dime-store reading glasses the general was always losing. King felt he was the most astute military thinker of the group (as a strategist, he probably was), but he would typically defer to Marshall. He would not, however, in any way bow to Army Air Corps Chief Arnold, and the two were notorious antagonists. At meetings of the Joint Chiefs, whenever Arnold would address King, King would reply not to the inferior-in-rank Arnold, but to his equal in status, Marshall. Perhaps King felt too competitive with an army man responsible for controlling squadrons of pilots, since the admiral himself believed that air power would lead the war, especially in the Pacific—but it would be naval air power, launched from his mighty carriers.

No matter who attended these meetings of the chiefs, Marshall and King called the shots, with Arnold stepping forward on questions of air and Hopkins serving as peacemaker between admiral, general, and president. The last time that the U.S. army and navy had even tried to cooperate had been during the Civil War, and they'd been squabbling ever since. The *Washington Post*'s Raymond Clapper would get to the heart of this crucial American military conundrum in a piece on the Roberts Commission (created by a Roosevelt executive order and chaired by a Supreme Court Justice), which investigated what had gone wrong at Pearl Harbor: "The Army thought the Navy was patrolling. The Navy thought the Army had its detection service operating. Neither bothered to check with the other—or maybe they were not on speaking terms. . . . The two services were totally uncoordinated, and neither knew what the other was doing—or in this case, not doing. And the air force, so supremely important in the new warfare, apparently was regarded by both as a minor auxiliary."

Though the country and every branch of the service was then inspired by shouts of "Remember Pearl Harbor!" when it came to warfare in the Pacific, the American chiefs themselves would refuse to heed that catastrophic lesson, save for the one shining moment of Special Aviation Project #1. Again and again Marshall would propose that General MacArthur be named to the overall command of the fight against *Dai Nippon Teikoku,* while King would counter that, since there was more water than land on this particular field of combat, it should be a navy theater, with Adm. Chester Nimitz in command of everything and everyone, including General MacArthur. While Eisenhower would successfully unify squadrons of British, French, and Americans into a solid fighting force against Italy and Germany, King and Marshall could never resolve their Pacific conflict, finally making a Solomonic decision: General MacArthur would be given charge of Australia, the Philippines, the Solomons, New Guinea, the Bismarck Archipelago, and the Dutch East Indies, while Admiral Nimitz would oversee everything else, with no "unity of command" whatsoever. This novel antistrategy would require a vast number of minor decisions to be made by the Joint Chiefs in Washington, far from the fields of war. In his island-by-island drive from Australia to the Philippines, MacArthur would over time make so many demands (with an attitude suggesting that his were the only battles worthy of attention) that an exasperated Roosevelt finally erupted, complaining that MacArthur "seems to have forgotten that his record in Manila resembled that of [those] who faced court-martial on charges of laxity at Pearl Harbor."

The day after the Hawaiian attack (but before the United States was officially at war with Hitler), Winston Churchill made immediate plans to come to Washington. His foreign minister and chiefs of staff thought the visit too hasty and insisted that America needed time to catch its breath, but the prime minister overruled them, arguing, "That's the way we talked while we were wooing her; now that she's in the harem, we can talk to her quite differently." During that three-week series of Allied meetings beginning on December 22 (known as the Arcadia Conference), the British military, efficiently organized by the chiefs of staff committee and coordinated by daily meetings with the prime minister, was shocked to find that the American army and navy chiefs had been given complete autonomy and were often at loggerheads. The English had arrived in the United States thrilled that the country and its resources had finally been enlisted in the cause, convinced that victory would now most assuredly be won. At Arcadia's end, however, they sailed home despondent. Marshall's London counterpart, Field Marshal Sir John Dill, wrote of American military power that "the whole organization belongs to the days of George Washington, who was made Commander in Chief of all the forces and just did it. America had not, repeat not, the slightest conception of what the war means, and their armed forces are more unready than it is possible to imagine."

"More unready" would be true for every service. In September 1938 Roosevelt, who understood German, had listened to a radio broadcast of a Nazi party rally in Nuremberg. He became convinced that Germany would go to war, and immediately named Hap Arnold chief of the air corps, ordering that ten thousand planes be produced every year. Instead, by December 1941, between production and bureaucratic delays, Arnold had a mere eleven hundred combat-ready craft to defend the nation.

A graduate of West Point who had been rejected by the cavalry, Hap took his first flying lesson in 1911 from Al Welsh, one of the original members of the Wright exhibition team in Ohio. It lasted seven minutes, and it would take him ten days and twenty-seven more lessons to complete his training, since flights could only take place in the early mornings or late evenings when the wind was light. Every time they went out to the Wrights' airfield, Simms Station (a treeless, bushless cow pasture), they could see an old man in a horse-drawn carriage waiting by the side of the road: He was a Dayton undertaker, ready for new business. Hap became the first to pilot American airmail (delivered by throwing the bags out the window), and he made aviation history by winning a race with a flock of carrier pigeons (many of which had received distinguished combat records in World War I).

In 1912, by mere seconds, Arnold pulled out of a crash that was such a close call he would be afraid to fly for the next four years, though he would recover from that fear with a vengeance. The general was also famous for driving cars like a madman, terrifying his wife but thrilling his equally speed-addicted mother-in-law; after meeting Arnold one officer said that "he operates at 2,000 RPMs while everyone else is at one thousand." As a young man Hap was as handsome as any movie star, looking like a well-nourished Valentino, but a life plagued by ulcers, heart attacks, and spells of severe depression would age him before his time.

Arnold got his nickname from always having a smile on his face, though many of his professional colleagues would not remember him as especially lighthearted. When Hap had to tell someone bad news, his technique was to blurt it out as loudly and abruptly as possible, and if a subordinate protested that something couldn't be done, Arnold might well reply that "maybe you can't do it, but I can, and you're fired." Even his own biographer would call him "headstrong, often tactless, scornful of slow, conservative Army methods, critical of superiors, single-mindedly relentless in pushing his own beliefs, and impatient with those who failed to share his vision."

Though Marshall was Arnold's superior, the two men had known each other for thirty years, and Arnold ran his corps the way he wanted, with Marshall never once pulling rank. One senior staff officer said they "defied description by usual categories. There was no backslapping, no banter or chitchat that you'd expect between old pals. . . . Arnold was free to announce his intentions and plans. I never heard of him asking Marshall's permission." Marshall told his biographer, "I tried to give Arnold all the power I could. My main difficulties came from the fact that he had a very immature staff . . . not immature in years, because they were pretty old, but antique staff officers or passé fliers because they were not trained at that kind of staff work, as they were busy taking stands about promotions."

In fact Arnold bucked his superiors so often in his rise to chief that he was almost court-martialed. On March 5, 1940, he testified before Congress that the air corps was paying too much for its planes due to competition with the Allied Lend-Lease programs. When Roosevelt learned the details of his testimony, he told Arnold that if certain chiefs couldn't testify properly before Congress, their second or third in command would be sent instead, and that if members of the War Department weren't cooperative, there was a place they could be sent, called Guam. Even so, FDR most enjoyed Hap's company of all the Joint Chiefs, for they shared a boyish energy, a determined opti-

mism, great impulsiveness, and a can-do spirit. As much as the navy conde-
scended to the air corps, and as much as the president was a navy man, he
knew that planes were the future—that they could turn the tides of war.

Now there was a tide FDR himself wanted to turn. Even those who vilified him recognized that Roosevelt was one of the world's greatest politicians.
Time and again during the war, the commander in chief would override the
counsel of his military subordinates and follow his own intuition regarding
the will of the public. While bowing to the imminent danger of Hitler by following a "Europe first"strategy, FDR knew that the American people wanted
immediate revenge for Pearl Harbor. Although the country didn't have sufficient men and matériel to launch a major offensive in the Pacific, there was,
the president thought, an immediate and short-term solution to this problem:
The United States would, as soon as possible, bomb the home islands of Japan.

This was not an especially original idea since, at the time, every American
was looking for payback. Wealthy industrialists were taking out newspaper
ads, offering rewards for anyone who could deliver revenge, and the White
House, the War Department, the army, the navy, the air corps, and practically
every member of Congress were being deluged with telegrams and phone
calls suggesting just how such an operation could be arranged. One newspaper reporter suggested to the president that bombs be dropped into the
craters of some of Japan's nine hundred semiactive volcanoes, wondering if
"we could convince the mass of Japanese that their Gods were angry with
them by starting some local eruptions." What almost no one outside a select
inner circle knew at that time, however, was that Roosevelt personally loathed
the Japanese, believing their attacks on China to be immoral, and had spent
almost a year before Pearl Harbor fighting them secretly.

On December 23, 1940, the president had signed off on a covert operation sending 120 Curtiss P-40 fighters and three hundred men to Asia, all of
whom would outwardly appear to be volunteers training in Burma to help
the Chinese air force. Headed by Louisiana bayou–bred Claire Chennault,
the American Volunteer Group, or Flying Tigers, would become the country's
most famous overseas combat unit before the United States was officially in
the war. Funded and assisted by a secret government-supported private company using fighters subsidized by American foreign aid and pilots and ground
crews recruited from active-duty U.S. armed servicemen, "the Flying Tigers
were really a rough bunch," Herb Macia would remember; "the pilots were
paid on the basis of kills." They received three hundred dollars a week, and a
five-hundred-dollar bounty for every Japanese plane shot down.

Chennault had earlier tried to enlist support for providing the Kuomintang with planes to bomb Japan directly. The idea greatly excited Secretary

of State Cordell Hull, who told Treasury Secretary Morgenthau: "What we have got to do, Henry, is get 500 planes to start from the Aleutian islands and fly over Japan just once . . . that will teach them a lesson . . . if only we could find some way to have them drop some bombs on Tokyo." Stimson considered it and decided that the proposal was "rather half-baked," and Marshall said he just didn't have enough men and planes for the five-hundred-unit squad that Chiang Kai-shek and Chennault envisaged. Chennault then turned to Roosevelt, who agreed to an executive order. Obtaining men and equipment under those years of Lend-Lease and a depression-starved American military, however, wasn't a problem that even the president could solve. The Army Air Corps would only give Chennault obsolete aircraft that even the desperate English had turned down; planes whose forward .50 calibers frequently lost sync, shooting holes into their own propeller blades. The first Tiger candidates wouldn't ship out until the summer of 1941 (with passports reading "student," "artist," or "teacher"), and by the time they were trained and ready for war, the Tigers were so involved in defending China and Burma that they couldn't directly attack Japan.

On July 23, 1941, Roosevelt approved the Second American Volunteer Group, ordering sixty-six Lockheed Hudson and Douglas DB-7 bombers, marked with Chinese insignia, to transfer to Kuomintang China and from there to bomb Tokyo. Like the Tigers, the SAVG would be secretly financed by Washington and crewed surreptitiously by army and navy fliers. Production and bureaucratic delays, however, meant that on December 7, the SAVG ground defense forces were just out to sea, while the air crews and planes were still being assembled at Lockheed's Burbank field.

In the aftermath of Pearl Harbor, the president was determined to try yet again. "Immediately after the attack on Hawaii, on Monday morning, I began to work looking for a counterattack on the Japanese in their island," the secretary of war reported. "I sent . . . the Air Corps to work to find a route for our long range bombers, which could not be interrupted by the Japanese, and which could reach taking off places in China, from which we could reach Osaka and the industrial cities of Japan where munitions are made. I took steps also to see if we could make arrangements with Russia which would permit us to come down from Alaska." If a strike against Japan could be carried out with minimal loss of life, it would be a great blow to *Dai Nippon Teikoku* and a tremendous boost to U.S. morale—and, of course, to the president. At meeting after meeting of the Chiefs in that second-floor library-office, FDR would needle them about this idea, demanding that they "find ways and means of carrying home to Japan proper, in the form of a bombing raid, the real meaning of war."

Most were not enthusiastic. Stimson eventually came to believe that the idea was a waste of time, dismissively calling it FDR's "pet project." Marshall, as much as he wanted revenge, considered it an implausible (though crowd-pleasing) dream. Two of the Chiefs, however, shared their leader's commitment. No American wanted immediate revenge for Pearl so much as the men of the navy, particularly the service's newly appointed leader, Ernie King. His enthusiasm notwithstanding, the admiral couldn't imagine a feasible way to bring about the operation. Carrier air was made up of small bombers and close-range fighters, and the navy's ships would have to get so near Japan to launch that any U.S. armada could be easily destroyed by Japanese defense forces.

Another Chief, however, was so strongly supportive of this idea that he would try again and again to make Roosevelt's dream a reality. At that juncture in the history of warfare, it was still unclear to military strategists exactly what role airplanes would take in combat. Except for airmen themselves, most assumed they would repeat their World War I stints in minor-league reconnaissance and dogfights. For this and other reasons, the army regarded its air corps as something of a poor foster child, in much the same way that the navy thought of its marines. You had to be the best of the best to get into air, but once you were in, you couldn't get decent planes or decent pay, and there was little chance of promotion.

Hap Arnold was convinced that the future of war was written in his service and wanted to prove it immediately. The general had considered using his seventeen remaining B-17s at Mindanao, but losing Wake and Guam meant losing the refueling stops they'd need to make a round trip. He'd considered the planes they had in China, but those were so old they couldn't carry enough ordnance to do any meaningful damage. Arnold wanted, more than anything, to find a way to carry out the president's idea. Both he and the air corps needed a visible home run, and they needed it now.

FDR had urged his lieutenants to let their imaginations run wild when it came to envisaging an attack on Japan. At meeting after meeting the Chiefs explored potential approaches from every direction, but there were no solutions at hand, even after the idea had become a regular topic of conversation with their immediate subordinates. Somewhere there had to be an answer.

On Saturday, January 10, 1942, Ernie King's ops officer, Capt. Francis "Frog" Low, was in Norfolk, Virginia, inspecting the navy's eighth and latest aircraft carrier: USS *Hornet*. Low had good news to bring back to his boss—the virgin had successfully gone through her shakedown cruise, and *Hornet* was now ready to sail through the Panama Canal to join sister *Enterprise* in rebuilding the U.S. Pacific Fleet.

Frog was sitting in the plane for the trip back to D.C., looking out the window. One of the airfield's runways had the dimensions of an aircraft carrier's flight deck painted onto it, so the navy's pilots-in-training could safely learn to get into the air and return before the deck ran out. As Captain Low sat, not thinking of much, really, a little tired from the trip and ready to go home, two fat army bombers came in for a landing, their shadows falling across the phantom carrier.

Back in Washington, Low went to his commander's flagship, *Dauntless,* anchored in the Anacostia River. A mere three weeks into their new jobs running the service, Admiral King and his upper-echelon staff were spending every weeknight aboard this ship. Low approached King's cabin, knocked, and entered. Even though the two had a strong professional bond, both having served in the toughest, most elite naval service (submarines), and even though Low was aware of King's special interest in carrier tactics, it must've been a tough moment for the Frog. He was about to make a very unorthodox suggestion involving interservice cooperation to a man who never had a kind word for the Army Air Corps and who had a temper the size of General Motors. Low's notion was so peculiar, in fact, that he'd waited until King was alone before broaching the subject.

In King's quarters Low explained in detail what he'd seen down at Norfolk, but the admiral didn't understand where this story was heading. The captain finally blurted out his idea: "If the Army has some plane that could take off in that short distance, I mean a plane capable of carrying a bomb load, why couldn't we put a few of them on a carrier and bomb the mainland of Japan?"

The admiral tilted back in his chair, and sat in dead silence. Low couldn't guess what he was thinking, and he waited for an eruption. Instead King replied, "That might be a good idea. Discuss it with Duncan and tell him to report to me."

Capt. Donald "Wu" Duncan was a detail-oriented perfectionist, a Harvard-trained thinker who'd eventually become vice-chief of naval operations. If anyone in the navy could figure out whether Low's scheme was workable, it would be Duncan, and the fact that King had recommended this notion so far up the hierarchy indicated how seriously he took it. When first hearing Low's proposal at their meeting, however, Duncan posed an immediate objection: Army bombers could never return from a mission to land on a carrier's deck. Their approach speeds were too high, and their bellies were too weak to be modified with arrester hooks (which latched onto a carrier's taut steel cables). However, as they pondered this problem, the men thought that perhaps the bomber crews could land elsewhere, or simply ditch their planes into the sea and have destroyers pick them up. Could the rest of the idea actually work?

Duncan loved this kind of theoretical conceptualizing, looking over spec sheets and figuring out the physics of a problem: "I started right away, and made a preliminary survey of the situation, considering such factors as the availability of a carrier, the practicability of some takeoff trials, the performance data of the various Army aircraft which might be used, the weather, things the pilots might strike in Japan with the force that could be provided." It would take him five days to sort out every one of these parameters.

The key puzzle would involve the army's midrange bombers. The B-23 Dragon's ninety-two-foot wingspan meant it couldn't fit on any navy carrier. The B-26 Marauder couldn't take off in the five hundred feet available on a deck. But the B-25, with extensive modifications to its weight and fuel specs, and its crews trained in methods they'd never known before, might barely fit.

To chart weather patterns over Asia, Duncan would send two submarines, *Trout* and *Thresher*, from Midway across the Pacific to Japan's coastal waters, radioing back every step of the way all the data an airman would need to know about wind, rain, and cloud cover. The captain's preliminary research had already revealed that by the end of April, less than four months off, storms across the North Pacific and winds across eastern China would doom any attempt. They had no time at all for the thousands of steps the air corps and navy would need to get this in gear.

Duncan knew how secret he needed to keep even these theoretical considerations, and instead of having a yeoman type up his notes, he handwrote them himself. At the meeting with King and Low on the sixteenth, he went over every detail, point by point, recognizing that the plan had great potential, but also what a wild card it was. Theoretically it could all work—but would it? Could army fliers take off from a ship, bomb the heart of Nippon, get home in some way no one could yet figure out, and live to tell the tale?

As the meeting ended, King said: "Go see General Arnold about it, and if he agrees with you, ask him to get in touch with me. But don't mention this to another soul."

When Low and Duncan arrived at Arnold's office on the seventeenth and presented their strategy, Hap was immediately enthusiastic. On Christmas Eve the general had been chatting with his English counterpart, Air Chief Marshal Charles Portal, who reminded him of Britain's 1940 inventive offense against the Italian fleet at Taranto, when English torpedo planes, launched from a carrier, had sunk three battleships. On January 4 the Americans had been discussing the preliminaries for Operation Torch—the invasion of North Africa, another idea no American in the room thought much of, save Roosevelt—when King solved the army's transport problem by suggesting a group of carriers ferry the needed Army Air Corps planes across the Mediterranean. As soon as Low and Duncan mentioned army planes on a navy ship, it turned on a light in Arnold's mind.

The general greatly admired the detail work that Duncan had already done, and knew his AAC would need someone of equal caliber to work in tandem with the navy on planning and execution. What was called for was not exactly a combat leader, but another detail man, an inspiring commander forceful enough to get this done on the very short timetable allowed, a methodical thinker who could anticipate the various problems that might arise and prepare for them, an officer with the guts to go up against the army's slow-moving bureaucratic deadwood and whip this mission right out of it.

There was only one man in the AAC who could do all that. His name was Jimmy Doolittle, and he worked down the hall.

King, Arnold, Duncan, and Doolittle immediately gave the mission a need-to-know, top-secret classification. Almost half of King's remaining Pacific Fleet would be involved, and the entire wartime role of the Army Air Corps would be at stake. The operation was so intricate that even the slightest misstep could compromise it, and the American military could hardly afford another public catastrophe after Pearl Harbor, Guam, Wake, and, soon enough, the Philippines. Most crucially, the men of this mission would need every inch of surprise. If the powerful Japanese armed forces were alerted in any way, there was no question as to what the outcome would be.

"Need to know" meant not discussing the mission with the thousands of military bureaucrats who had to approve the release of matériel. As Doolittle and Duncan raced to get their enterprise in motion, time and again they would run up against an army and a navy refusing to bend the rules. Hap instructed every member of his senior staff that "anything that Doolittle wants, help him get," and Doolittle would modestly claim, "I was given by Hap Arnold complete carte blanche. I had first call on anything I wanted, on people, on supplies, and it was one of the most interesting and one of the, I think, easiest jobs I ever had. Because all I had to do was to go in and say: 'I want this,' and I got it. I had first priority on everything." Doolittle, however, was every inch a gentleman as well as a firm believer in the theory that if you don't have anything nice to say, say nothing; late in life, when pressed by air force historians for critical comments on his fellow World War II officers, he would respond with dead silence. This job, in fact, was impossibly difficult. Both Duncan and Doolittle would constantly have to appeal to Arnold or King, and the service chiefs would have to intervene personally with the bureaucrats. Even direct orders from on high, however, would often not be a sufficient goad.

On January 28 the American Chiefs were attending a White House meeting when the president again asked about the bombing of Japan. King and Arnold believed that many at the table did not have a legitimate need-to-know status, especially the voluble president and what the military brass considered an overly talkative White House staff. After taking a second, Arnold simply reported that they were looking into attacks from bases in Russia and China, but "it would take a few months to get the gasoline and fields available."

Roosevelt, thinking that Arnold was shirking, blew up. From Churchill he'd developed a passion for maps, and he felt that there were many, many locations from which the United States could launch a strike. What about the Aleutians? What about Mongolia? He wanted every possible strategy considered.

Arnold followed up with a memo to FDR that very day in which he was honest, if not completely forthcoming: "I feel that the plan which is now in progress, for carrying out an attack upon the Japanese enemy's center of gravity, by making use of facilities for which the Chinese Government can guarantee us a reasonable degree of security on the Eastern Asiatic mainland, is the logical and most effective plan."

On February 2, in a cold and foggy dawn, crewmen from foc's'le to fantail watched in astonishment as *Hornet*'s deck crane lifted aboard two fat B-25s from the docks of Norfolk. No official written navy record exists of this incident. At 0900 tugs pulled the "Gray Ghost" away from her berth, freed her lines, and watched as she roared down Hampton Roads.

It was snowing that day on the Atlantic. Airdales spotted the planes at two opposite positions, one in the normal takeoff spot well before the ship's island, the other far to the aft. Even with the Bs at such hard port that their left wings stuck out over the ship's edge, they would have only six feet of starboard clearance to keep their right wings from hitting the tower. As Wu Duncan observed, Captain Mitscher (who'd been briefed on the experiment about to take place, but not yet on the mission) ordered *Hornet* to hit full power into the wind, into launch position.

At that moment signal crew arrived in the cabin with distressing news:

Destroyers *Jones* and *Ludlow* had semaphored that they'd spotted an enemy sub. The two ships chased after the Nazi periscope, throwing cans of depth charges overboard, while *Hornet* opened fire on the target with her five-inchers. The sea churned, and oil bubbled up; they had made a strike. Then Mitscher, through his binoculars, sighted the periscope, still sitting there. More semaphores flashed from the destroyers: It was not a sub but a sunken merchant ship. Even so the captain was proud of how his brand-new sailors had reacted in their first "battle" and semaphored back: "Well done."

It was now time. Who aboard didn't hold his breath as army lieutenants John E. Fitzgerald and James F. McCarthy climbed into their planes and revved their engines? At the fore stood *Hornet*'s flagman, whipping his checkered banner in a frenzy, watching the rise and fall of the bow for the exact moment when he would drop his flag and instantly fall prone to the deck. Fitzgerald's Billy rumbled, shaking alive, wobbling down the runway on its tricycle struts. The navy men, especially the air wing, so used to their sleek, lightweight craft, had only one thought: He's a sinker. The Mitchell powered itself harder and faster, Fitzgerald barely missing the island with his right wing, and just before the end of the deck . . . he was airborne.

A few hours later McCarthy accomplished the same maneuver, and *Hornet* returned to her dock. Duncan prepared his reports; the tests had gone exactly as he had predicted. Facing a 20-knot (23-mph) wind, the Mitchell needed to hit a taxi speed of 10 knots to get enough lift—a total of 40 to 50 mph. Still, they hadn't loaded these trial planes with bombs, with weight to suggest the extra fuel required, or with the typical six-man crew, and they'd been flown by two of the army's finest pilots. There were so many questions left to answer, so many things that could go wrong, but Duncan knew they only had so much time. To get into the North Pacific before Asia's squalling May weather would ruin any chance of success, *Hornet* and her already-trained army crews with their fully modified planes would have to be ready and departing San Francisco, at the very latest, by April Fool's Day.

LIFTOFF

Six days after *Hornet* and her defense fleet left San Francisco on April 2, Vice Admiral William Halsey sailed from Pearl Harbor on carrier *Enterprise* with two cruisers, four destroyers, and one oiler in a battle group known as Task Force Howe. At 0630 on the tenth, he radioed Mitscher in anticipation of Howe and Mike's meeting in the middle of the Pacific—38° 00' N, 180° 00'—at dawn on April 13. *Hornet* bell-bottoms spent those days in a state of quiet anxiety, accustomed to having sharpshooting, high-flying navy pilots always ready for defense. In Pearl's aftermath any oceangoing American sailor could easily imagine, just over the horizon, a Japanese submarine, battleship, or carrier force lying in wait. At dawn and dusk, search planes were catapulted to scout two hundred miles ahead in a sixty-degree arc, but they couldn't be counted on to spot every danger. Until the two groups merged and the fliers of the "Big *E*" could be put into play, the sailors couldn't help but spend more than a few moments with loose nerves.

In fact the Americans were in more danger than anyone could have known. Halsey's transmission on the tenth had been intercepted by Japanese Combined Fleet radio scanners. Tokyo immediately determined the location of both convoys, and knew an American fleet was heading straight for them.

Instead of alarm the empire reacted with a sense of victorious anticipation. Japanese naval intelligence knew exactly the range of American carrier air; *Enterprise* and *Hornet* would have to get within three hundred miles of the home islands before they could even think of launching their strikes. Knowing this, Tokyo planned its defense. Combined Fleet would now radio-track Halsey and Mitscher, wait for just the right moment, and destroy the all-important carrier groups they had missed in Hawaii. When the Americans reached a point six hundred miles from Tokyo, Japanese long-range, shore-based bombers would attack, followed by torpedo planes mopping up. Afterward, carriers *Lexington* and *Yorktown,* a few cruisers and destroyers, and some obsolete battleships would be the only force standing in the way of a direct assault on the continental United States.

The Japanese have for centuries believed that their islands resemble a dragon facing down the entire Pacific Ocean. At the tip of its belly—Honshu's southeastern curve—is the Boso Peninsula, the entrance to Tokyo Bay marked by the lighthouse of Inubo Saki, sixty-three miles due east of the city. Just as Brick Holstrom had found a Japanese sub off the Pacific coast, so now were Tokyo sailors looking for American subs in their own waters. Two in particular, sent as advance patrol for Doolittle's men, were there, and they were running for their lives.

These U.S. submarines had launched three weeks earlier from their home base of Midway under secret orders from Wu Duncan and Bill Halsey, orders that couldn't be opened until they'd reached cruising depth. At that time both captains unsealed their envelopes to learn they were to hunt down and sink every enemy ship they could find, and especially to attack any Japanese vessels heading toward a certain area of the Pacific—the cruising lane of Task Force 16. If empire craft were spotted that couldn't be sunk, the subs were to notify Pearl Harbor naval intelligence immediately.

On April 10 American sub *Trout* was patrolling Japanese shipping lanes a few miles south of Tokyo Bay. At 1158 her captain, Lt. Comdr. F. W. Fenno, Jr., sighted a steamer through his periscope and ordered his men to fire. The American torpedo missed, but the steamer saw its wake, turned quickly, and blew up a smoke screen. In minutes a sub chaser appeared out of the smoke, looking to kill her some *Trout*. The Americans shot another missile, which also missed. The sub dived, and both the chaser and the steamer plowed over their heads, but no depth charges were dropped. The next morning Fenno and his men came across a fifteen-thousand-ton freighter, and fired. The torpedo struck but didn't damage the ship enough to stop her. *Trout* fired again, missed, and gave up the hunt.

U.S. sub *Thresher*, meanwhile, periscope-sighted a ten-thousand-ton Japanese freighter just off Inubo Saki and at 0806, 0808, and 0810, shot its eels. All missed. Two hours later she spotted a five-thousand-ton cargo ship. This time the American missiles struck, and the target sank in less than three minutes. The attacker, though, was quickly put on the defense as another sub chaser appeared, rolling depth charges. Lieutenant Commander Anderson, *Thresher*'s captain, ordered evasive maneuvers. The sub descended as far as she could, her crew all the while hearing the rumbling engines of the Japanese ships above, desperate to drown them in their own tin. For fifteen minutes solid the depth charges exploded all around them, shaking the sea.

Something somewhere inside *Thresher* broke, and the men could hear it, rattling away, fearful that the noise could only bring their attackers closer. Surface vessels at that time hunted for underwater enemies using a presonar listening device, the hydrophone, forcing sub crews to speak only in whispers and to walk on tiptoes. Anderson tried to raise her, but *Thresher* wouldn't budge. The sub's air started leaking, out and away. More charges exploded, getting closer and closer. Then—silence.

Thresher, now leaking severely, finally managed to surface to relieve her dwindling auxiliary charge, only to face a rough sea. Out of nowhere a rogue wave crested over the tower, dumping water into the hatch, flooding the ship, and shorting the main generator's cables, which would take two days, in enemy waters, to repair. She and *Trout,* however, were able to report back to Pearl that they saw no enemy ships in the path of Task Force 16.

On April 10, 1942, in the dead middle of the Pacific, Howe and Mike united, and the giant armada of carriers, cruisers, oilers, and destroyers sped rapidly due west, hoping to get to a launch position within four hundred miles of Tokyo. Everyone who knew (or knew of) him was relieved—if not thrilled—that Admiral Halsey was now in charge. An early newspaper typo would mistakenly call Bill—described by Doolittle as "an aggressive, feisty leader itching for combat"—"Bull," and this would be his nickname with the press and the stateside public for the rest of World War II. "Bull" certainly fit the admiral's face, with its beaked nose and jutting prow of a jaw, as well as the typical Halsey expression, which suggested a man who commonly ate snakes for breakfast. Halsey was such a masterful navy fighter that even the lead pilot in the attack on Pearl Harbor, Fuchida Mitsuo, would say, "If the Japanese navy had had a half-dozen Halseys throughout the war and just one at Pearl Harbor, the story of the war in the Pacific would have been entirely different. Defeat is not only a matter of economics and matériel; it is a question of aggressive leadership. This would have saved the situation for us many times during the war. What we needed was a Halsey."

The April 10 union meant Howe's men could now be told the secrets of Special Aviation Project #1. "We were tremendously excited, not only at the idea of hitting Tokyo itself but also at the danger of going so close to Japan," remembered *Enterprise* bluejacket Alvin Kernan. "But we were technicians, and it was the technical problems that really intrigued us. Could the heavy planes with a bomb load of two thousand pounds, even when stripped of guns and armor, get to Japan and then make it to the nearest safe landing point in China? Even before that, could such heavy planes designed for long landing strips get off a short carrier deck? Sailors, like stockbrokers, work everything out by betting, and there was soon heavy money down on both sides: Would they make it, would they not? . . . I put down ten dollars at even money that less than half of them would get off."

As the ships continued westward, the typical spring weather of the northern Pacific arose and turned against them. Heavy seas and torrential squalls struck the decks, making work hazardous. Many waves were strong enough to toss the carriers' entire bows out of the water. During one especially wild ride, an army pilot was sitting in his Mitchell, watching the altimeter. As *Hornet* rose and fell, the needle swung by two hundred feet.

Army planes weren't designed to withstand the corrosive salt spray of a turbulent ocean voyage, so the airmen double-checked everything exposed that might be affected, especially their control lines. Doolittle ran his own inspections, warning the crews that if he found anything significant that could not be immediately repaired or replaced, that plane would be off the mission. They anxiously followed his every move and facial expression.

The weather grew so terrible that during fuelings, the hoses connecting the oilers to the other ships would break loose and whiplash, sweeping crewmen overboard and leaking onto the decks. Even after the greasy floors were thoroughly cleaned, the sailors had to tie straw rope around their shoes to keep from sliding into the ocean. "We fueled at sea, and occasionally a big tanker, named after a faraway American river—the *Platte* or the *Cimarron*—would come alongside, some twenty-five to fifty feet away, and with both ships still under way, pitching and rolling toward each other, these thousands of tons of mass would send rubber hoses across and pump fuel and aviation gas out of the tanker into the carrier," said Alvin Kernan. "The waves between the ships in this operation were huge, and standing on the flight deck of the carrier, you could watch the great bulk of the tanker rise up above you, and then crash down. It was blue-water seamanship at its best, always pleasant to watch how smartly it was done." During one prep for refueling from *Cimarron,* Seaman First Class P. D. Williams was thrown overboard. The tanker signaled destroyer *Meredith,* which sped to the bobbing sailor and yanked him out of the water, safe and unharmed.

This terrible run of squalls was in fact a mixed blessing. While the Americans couldn't send out scouts in such zero-zero overcast, it in turn rendered TG 16 stealth, making it invisible to enemy forces. Every sailor in every navy around the world knew the defense a good squall could provide—in just a few months' time, such weather would in fact save the skin of *Enterprise.*

As the battle group headed west, the big-band, baseball, and Jack Benny radio shows faded away and staticky foreign-language broadcasts took their place. On April 16 servicemen monitoring the airwaves picked up an English-language broadcast from Radio Tokyo, saying that "Reuters, British news agency, has announced that three American bombers have dropped bombs on Tokyo. This is a most laughable story. They know it is absolutely impossible for enemy bombers to get within 500 miles of Tokyo. Instead of worrying about such foolish things, the Japanese people are enjoying the fine spring sunshine and the fragrance of cherry blossoms."

The news alarmed everyone aboard, Halsey in particular. If some unknown Allied force had attacked, and this report was the propagandized version, then the navy and the air corps were heading straight into a trap. Tokyo would be on full alert for another assault, and the element of surprise would be entirely lost. The AAC volunteers were also upset, believing that they'd missed their chance to be the first to strike back. Doolittle assured his boys that, had a similar mission been under way, he would have known about it. The broadcast just had to be false, he insisted. Still, many couldn't get it out of their minds.

Although the broadcast has never been explained to this day, in fact Hap Arnold did have two other missions in the works to bomb Japan, and it's doubtful that he would have considered Doolittle a need-to-know for either. The first was Task Force Aguila (since often called Aquila, Aquilla, or Aquinas), put together by a man who'd become a key Allied commander for Asia, Caleb V. Haynes, and including Robert Lee Scott, Jr., bestselling author of *God Is My Copilot,* and Merian C. Cooper, who would become Chennault's chief of staff and Arnold's executive intelligence officer. Haynes, his B-17s, and his men were all in India and ready to head to Kuomintang-held bases in China a week before Special Aviation Project #1, when they were ordered to hold. If Doolittle and his men failed, however, Haynes and his were now standing by, to be followed immediately by Project Halpro. A few weeks after the Doolittle group had finished its abrupt takeoff and hedgehopping practice at Eglin, Col. Harry E. Halverson, twenty-three B-24D Liberators, and 231 men began their own stateside training. They would, like Aguila, either substitute or follow up for Doolittle by bombing Japan from Allied bases in eastern China.

That afternoon Jimmy read aloud messages of hope and luck from Marshall, Arnold, and King; each of the crews posed for navy cameramen; and Pete Mitscher held a special ceremony. In 1908 a group of American ships had visited Tokyo Bay, and the Japanese had handed out medals commemorating the event. Three sailors who had been present—Vormstein, Laurey, and Quigley—had sent their awards to the Navy Department in the week following Pearl Harbor, asking they be returned to Japan in an appropriate manner. Now the planes of Special Aviation Project #1 would do just that. Navy Secretary Knox passed them on to Nimitz, who gave them to Halsey, who gave them to Mitscher, who gave them to Doolittle, who attached each to a bomb heading for Tokyo.

On April 17 Task Force 16 was one thousand miles east of Japan. The weather grew even more hostile, winds rising to a gale force of thirty-eight knots. The seasick army engineers and mechanics worked overtime against beating rain as the waves crested at thirty feet, soaking the decks. Halsey semaphored the two oilers, which moved into position to refuel both carriers and their cruisers one last time. The moment the hoses were disconnected, Halsey gave the second order: Head on 270 degrees, at twenty-five knots (if possible; in the bad weather the speed would more commonly be twenty knots). It would be a run straight at the enemy, the turbines blowing their hardest, the slow oilers and destroyers left behind to wait for the convoy's return. If the tight unit could maintain that cruise for the next twenty-four hours, they would arrive five hundred miles from Tokyo at dusk minus three hours the following day—just the right time for Doolittle to launch.

Supervised by Ross Greening, the deck and army crews filled the planes' tanks with gas, loaded the bombs into their bays, and crated in the machine-gun ammo. As the sun set the men gathered for one last briefing, and Doolittle gave them another chance to bow out. No one did.

That same day Admiral King paid a visit to the White House to notify the president that his greatest hope in those dark days was about to be realized. One historical mystery remains today: How much did FDR know about Special Aviation Project #1, and when did he know it? Questioned about this after the war, Hap Arnold would repeatedly state that the president was kept informed at every step, but the general's actions at various White House meetings, as well as his own series of memos to the commander in chief, do not concur. Ernie King, meanwhile, would assert that the president was kept in the dark on the details until his official visit and report on the sixteenth (meaning, considering the international date line, the seventeenth on *Hornet*), when there was no longer any risk of a security breach. King's memory, however, is contradicted by a memo written by an Arnold subordinate on that same day, informing the president of the various difficulties involved in getting landing fields for the Doolittle squadron. In the end there can be only conjecture that FDR knew the basic outlines of the plan but not all its specifics.

To avoid detection by Japanese subs Task Force 16 had taken a zigzag course across the Pacific. With the armada observing strict radio silence, no further messages were intercepted by Japanese naval intelligence, and the estimated arrival date that Tokyo had deduced from the radio intercept came and went. The empire decided that the Americans must have other targets in mind. In turn, what U.S. ships, subs, and military intelligence hadn't uncovered was that Japan had stationed a flotilla of fishing barges six hundred miles off its coastline, radio-equipped picket boats that were on a round-the-clock look-out for enemy forces. It would be Task Force 16, unfortunately, that discovered it.

On April 18, 1942, at 0310, the boys in the "Big *E*'s" radar room sighted a pair of blips: enemy vessels at 255 degrees. Island lookouts reported winks of light on the horizon, at the same course. The klaxon screamed out, and every man jumped to station. The fleet veered an immediate ninety degrees to avoid detection. At 0415, not having picked up any Japanese radio calls, Halsey assumed they'd passed unnoticed and resumed 270 degrees.

At dawn the sky was a dark gray murk, and the force was surrounded by thunderstorms. They were in such dangerous territory now that at 0508, eleven scout planes were launched from *Enterprise,* one of them a Dauntless piloted by Lt. O. B. Wiseman. The lieutenant was following the arc of his search plan when he came out of cloud cover directly above what looked like a small tugboat. It was an enemy ship, sitting forty-two miles directly ahead of the force. He banked immediately, hoping to avoid being spotted, but knew it was too late. The Dauntless returned over *Enterprise,* where Wiseman's rear gunner slid open the tail hatch and dropped a beanbag onto the deck, with a note detailing the enemy ship's position, and explaining that they'd been seen. Meanwhile, some fourteen thousand yards from TG 16, a Japanese "fisherman" was looking over his catch with binoculars, and describing what he saw to his radioman.

"Practically all our lookouts were youngsters, seamen second class, and our ship never having experienced actual combat action, it was difficult for them to conceive the gravity of our present situation," explained Hubert B. Gibbons, yeoman first class in charge of the lookout station on the USS *Vincennes.* "One lad, only a few months in service, was more prone to want to rest his eyes than the others. He had been warned twice for taking his eyes from his binoculars to rest, and upon the third occasion when he backed away and dropped his head down to rest his eyes, I became much concerned. I grasped him by the collar and belt, lifted him from his stool and shoved him back across the station and assumed his place.

"The first thing I saw, looking across to the port and across the bow of the *Hornet* and ahead of the cruiser stationed on her port bow, was the masthead and crossarm of a vessel, not a part of our task force. I immediately opened the circuit of my telephone and started talking, giving the sighting with relative bearing and approximate range. The flag bridge talker started repeating the alarm, and signalmen started running up a flag signal to our task force, giving the message. Almost immediately the cruiser on the *Hornet*'s port bow [*Nashville*] directed her guns on the bearing given and opened fire. The target just exploded."

In fact it took substantially more time and effort before the ship was effectively destroyed. The spying Japanese picket was the seventy-ton *Nitto Maru,* a key component of Japan's early-warning system of fishing boats armed with radios. When she was spotted by Gibbons and TG 16's other lookouts, navy officers knew immediately that if they could see her, then she could see their giant ships all too well.

In the *Enterprise* radio room, the scanners burst with static, coming to life. From the signal codes, the operators knew they were listening to a message being sent to Japan's Fifth Fleet: "Three enemy carriers sighted at our position 650 nautical miles east of Inubo Saki at 0630." It was possible that Tokyo hadn't received the message due to the overcast, and that the fisherman–radio operator would keep trying to warn his navy. TG 16's planes and guns would have to make sure that did not happen.

Halsey ordered *Nashville* into action. Her cannon, nine thousand yards from *Nitto,* opened fire. Jake DeShazer, who had come out on deck to watch, recalled: "This was real warfare. The big guns were booming, and it looked as though the whole side of the cruiser was on fire." "There were heavy swells, and the picket boat was going up, it would be on top of a swell and then it could be seen, then it would be down, and you couldn't see a thing except perhaps the top of its mast," said Stephen Jurika, posted on *Hornet*'s bridge. "The splashes were all around it, but it was still there." It was the first moment of combat for many of the Americans, including Seaman John Sutherland: "I remember thinking that it was a very curious way to watch my first active engagement. We stood on the flight deck watching the fire between our ship and the meager return from the Japs, much in the manner of a crowd watching a tennis match with their heads going back and forth."

The shooting from the American ships was furious, but every shot missed. Dive-bombers from *Enterprise* joined in, and finally, after twenty-nine minutes of attack and 924 six-inch shells fired, the Americans scored a hit. "*Nashville*'s gunnery was disgraceful, and she was afterwards dispatched back to the States with those ominous orders, 'For Further Training,' that every unit that fails to meet standards dreads," reported Alvin Kernan.

The *Nitto Maru* crew raised a white flag, and as American vessels approached to take prisoners, their boat sank beneath the waves. At least five of the eleven Japanese were rescued from the water and immediately taken to interrogation. There one explained how he had been the first to see the TG and had gone below to the captain's quarters to tell him that two beautiful Japanese carriers were in sight. The captain, who knew of no plans for carriers in his territory, raced up to the deck and looked to the horizon. He turned to the crewman, said, "Yes, they are beautiful, but they are not ours," returned to his cabin, and shot himself in the head.

The Japanese picket system, however, had worked exactly as intended. In Tokyo the message had been received, and Yamamoto's commander in chief of combined forces, Rear Adm. Ugaki Matome, ordered all ships within a day's run on a course to *Nitto Maru*'s last reported location. Five carriers, six cruisers, ten destroyers, nine submarines, ninety fighter planes, and 116 Japanese bombers immediately headed toward Task Force 16.

Radio traffic announcing the sudden movement of the Japanese fleet was in turn intercepted by *Enterprise*. With the task force 688 miles from Japan, more than 200 miles from the planned launch site, the mission had been detected by the enemy, and the Japanese knew exactly where they were.

The American commanders now faced a terrible dilemma. Their ships were well within range of land-based enemy bombing squadrons. At the same time, with Tokyo on alert and the element of surprise lost, it seemed certain that Doolittle and his men would be shot out of the sky. Even if they survived the defenses of Tokyo, the added distance they would have to cover ruled out their being able to reach the Allied airfields. "We knew that the pilots really didn't have a Chinaman's chance of getting to China," said Hank Miller.

There was, in the end, really no choice. At 0800 Halsey blinker-lit a message: LAUNCH PLANES. TO COL. DOOLITTLE AND GALLANT COMMAND: GOOD LUCK AND GOD BLESS YOU.

Aboard *Hornet* klaxons bellowed, and shipwide speakers announced: "Army pilots, man your planes!" Most of the aviators hadn't yet even been above deck that morning, and they were either just getting up or waiting patiently at mess tables for the stewards to bring their breakfast of powdered eggs, bacon, pancakes, strawberries, and coffee. They assumed at first that the announcement was just another practice drill. When Ross Greening realized that they were now not only on actual alert but were about to launch hundreds of miles from the expected position, "cold chills were running up and down my spine. . . . I don't think there was a man leaving who really believed he would complete the flight safely."

"Doolittle called us all on the deck," Sess Sessler remembered, "and said: 'If there's any of you who don't want to go, just tell me. Because the chances of you making it back are pretty slim.' And nobody batted an eye." The Old Man, as calmly as possible, ran through all the instructions one last time: the heading to Tokyo, the flight to the south of Honshu Island, the turn west for Chuchow, and finished with a promise: "When we get to Chungking, I'm going to give you all a party that you won't forget!"

"The night before, we pretty well understood that it was going to be tomorrow, but it was supposed to be a late-afternoon takeoff. The sudden announcement the next morning when they called us to battle stations was a shock," remembered navigator/bombardier Herb Macia. "I assumed quite early in the game that we would not survive the mission. First of all I thought if the Japanese had been tipped off that we were coming, and if they had the defenses they were supposed to, and if we were going to strike right in the middle of the day, then we were going to encounter a swarm of fighters coming out after us. . . . Second, if we got to the targets and got out, we could not make it past midpoint in the China Sea, so we were going to have to ditch our planes in a Japanese-controlled area. I thought the only thing short of being destroyed over the target area would be to end up as a prisoner of war.

"Oddly enough, that is not as uncomfortable a feeling as you might imagine. You conclude, 'This couldn't have happened to me but it's happening to me, so I'm going to go in and really do it right, and that's all I care about!' I had a sort of nostalgic feeling. I just wished I had said this or that to my dad, my mother, and my wife, Mary Alice, and that I had seen my little boy. Mary Alice was expecting; I assumed it would be a boy." Those who had time to think twice in the mad rush agreed with Macia. They'd be bombing the heart of Imperial Japan in broad daylight, and if they weren't shot out of the Tokyo skies, they'd surely be forced to land in the shark-infested, Japanese-patrolled waters of the China Sea.

Immediately *Hornet* turned directly into a twenty-seven-knot wind, pointing herself straight at the entrance to Tokyo Bay. On Mitscher's order Chief Engineer Pat Creehan pushed the carrier's turbines to their fullest.

The weather continued sour, the ship pitched and yawed, the deck became a slippery mess of sea- and rainwater. "This was zero weather conditions. Zero. *Zero!* That means you can't see across the table," recalled bombardier Bob Bourgeois. "Have you ever seen a thirty-foot sea? I never had. It's seventy feet from the water to the top of the ship. And the bow of the ship was going down and picking up water and throwing it over the deck. I have never been in worse weather in my life. The rain! Oh, the rain! I've been in a bunch of hurricanes right here in Louisiana. And they were tame compared to this thing. Hurricane Betsy was a piece of cake compared to this."

Navy boys had to help the airmen get their equipment and themselves aboard the Mitchells across the lurching deck. Many had to crawl on their hands and knees, pushing their B-4 bags through the water. "I had Mercator charts that I had prepared for the overall mission," said navigator Chuck Ozuk. "One of the navy men had my main chart, he was going to help me carry it out. He came to me with tears in his eyes: 'I dropped your charts and they flew overboard.' Boy, that was a blow to me."

Hearing about China's sanitary conditions, navigator Sally Crouch stuffed his bags with toilet paper. Shorty Manch found that, with his carbine and automatic and record player, he had no room for his fruitcake tin of records, so he went over to his friend, *Ruptured Duck* bombardier Bob Clever, and asked, "Will you-all do a fellow a big favor and carry my phonograph records under your seat? We'll meet in Chungking and have us some razz-ma-tazz." Plane sixteen's pilot, the six-foot six-inch Bill Farrow, checked at the last minute to make sure Jake, his bombardier, knew how to row a boat.

Airdales unslipped the ropes constraining the bombers to the deck, yanked the wooden chocks from the wheels, crewed a donkey to maneuver the 25s into position, and topped off the fuel tanks, rocking the planes wing by wing to break up any air bubbles and fill them to their absolute physical maximum. Bombardiers armed their explosives and loaded up their incendiaries. "We knew the odds against us and it seemed to me we were doing things without thinking—like automatons," said plane two navigator Carl Wildner.

"We were further away than we anticipated being, so we put some five-gallon cans of gas on board," remembered copilot Dick Knobloch. "Each airplane was allocated ten, as I recall. I think we got about six. That was because we gave a couple to Davey Jones, who claimed that he was having excessive fuel consumption in his engines. I think that was a story. I think he just wanted extra gas. I made sure our airplane got double lunches."

The *Hornet* navigation room passed out the latest weather information on Japan and China, which included more bad news: The Doolittle men would face a twenty-four-knot headwind all the way to Honshu. Flight ops at the control tower hung out white cards, visible to the waiting line of pilots, of the ship's compass heading and wind speed. "We had done a lot of preflighting—we'd go sit in the airplanes a lot of the time onboard—and one little item we discovered sitting on the ship was that our magnetic compasses would be way off by forty, fifty degrees, diverted by the metal in the ship," said pilot Davey Jones. "So we asked the navy people about it, and they had never thought about it and didn't pay any attention to it, but it concerned us. So we devised a plan: When you take off, make a 360 and fly down parallel to the deck, where one of the navy would hold up a card giving the ship's heading, so our navigators could check the compass. Not a very sophisticated way of doing it. As it turned out, we were in such a big rush, most crews did not bother to do it. They just took off and kept on going."

As Doolittle's men prepared for launch, so did the crew of Comdr. John Ford. The Oscar-winning director of *Stagecoach* and *The Grapes of Wrath*, operating from *Hornet*'s island, would capture the moment on celluloid. The navy wanted a movie for its archives, and if the mission was successful, the president and Joint Chiefs would want the footage for the nation's movie-house newsreels.

In the middle of the chaos, navy pilots and army replacement crews ran from plane to plane, offering $50, $100, even $150 to trade places with the assigned crews and take their own vengeance for Pearl Harbor. Two were desperate to join up with Doolittle, not for glory but to get off the damn *Hornet*—they'd spent the entire voyage out miserably seasick. Plane twelve copilot Thadd Blanton thought he'd never in his life see men willing to pay every cent they had to get a chance to die. Those not contemplating their reception over the skies of Tokyo—which American military intelligence estimated at five hundred combat planes—instead worried about gas. Ted Lawson quickly calculated the distance, the headwind, the cruising speed, and the fuel he had, concluding that "the sums I arrived at gave me a sudden emptiness in the stomach."

Copilots checked the tire pressure, fuel caps, and gauges, and looked over the outside of the plane for oil and gas leaks. They tested the emergency brake pressure and unlocked the three escape hatches in case of an emergency bailout. As airdales pulled the props through ten or twelve rotations by hand to make sure oil hadn't settled in the lower cylinders, other deckhands stood by with fire extinguishers in case of engine malfunction. The Mitchell crews set their fuel emergency shut-off valves and generator and active inverter switches on. They opened their cowl flaps and closed their oil shutters, turned off the autopilot and battery disconnect switches, moved their fuel mixture to takeoff rich, and ran the throttle to a thousand. With ignition switches and fuel booster pumps on and the starter energized, each pilot primed the right engine with five to seven shots and then mashed it. If she turned over and her oil pressure got to forty pounds in thirty seconds, he did the same to the left, checking the oil temp at idle to 140 degrees and the cylinder heads at 150. At the same time copilots were verifying that all the flying elements—elevators, rudders, flaps, and ailerons—responded correctly to their controls, and that suction was between 3.75 and 4.25, with hydraulic pressure in the range of eight hundred to eleven hundred pounds and the brake pressure sitting at a thousand to twelve hundred pounds. The pilot would lower flaps, set trim tabs, uncage the gyro instruments, check the responsiveness of his prop rpms, and check his magnetos.

They were as ready as they could possibly be—which was hardly ready at all.

The army pilots had been explicitly warned by Halsey himself that "if there are any problems with your craft, if you have any trouble starting up or revving to full bore, you're off the mission. To make way for the next crew, the navy has orders to push your craft overboard."

They had also been assured that their bombers could take off from a carrier, but none of them, until that moment, had actually done it. Now they'd find out whether or not Low's notion would actually work.

At 0815, Edgar G. "Ozzie" Osborne, flight deck signal officer of the USS *Hornet,* standing to port at bow, whirled a checkered flag in broader and broader, faster and faster arcs above his head. First in line, Lt. Col. James Harold Doolittle turned down his wing flaps and revved his throttles to full power. The heavy plane shook as the brakes strained to keep the craft from rushing forward. Jimmy had less than five hundred feet of taxi space before him, and only six feet of clearance between his right wing and the island tower. Even with all their Florida training, the runway looked ridiculously short to the army fliers, while the waves crashing over the flight deck, sixty feet above the waterline, seemed mountainous.

Hornet was still awash in choppy seas, with an on-and-off downpour, a deck rocking in every direction, and crosswinds that had turned bitter. It took all thirty-two Mitchell engines running up to full power to drown out the roar of the wind and rain. The eyes of every man aboard, army and navy alike, stared at the Old Man's stubby, glass-nosed craft. They would all remember this moment forever; Ross Greening watched that first attempt while lying facedown on the wet deck in the rain, holding tie-down plates to keep from being blown backwards by the gales of wind. Even with his own extraordinary balls of steel, Jimmy felt challenged: "A rough sea such as the one in front of us could ruin a pilot's day . . . it was like riding a seesaw that plunged deep into the water each time the bow dipped downward."

Osborne, waiting for exactly the right moment, felt in his bones the rising and falling of the ship. "You knew how long it would take them to run down the deck, and you wanted to start them as the bow started down because it would take them that length of time to get to within fifty or seventy-five feet of the bow, and then, as the deck started to come up, you'd actually launch them into the air, or at least horizontal but on the upswing, in fact giving them a boost," said Stephen Jurika. This meant that as the great ship's bow gravely tilted down and forward, the air crews would be spending quite a bit of their time taxiing straight at the ocean waves.

Osborne's flag shot down, Doolittle yanked his feet from the brakes, the carrier tilted harshly, and the lead B, filled with fuel and ordnance, began its slow shuffle down that short white line. A navy pilot shouted to anyone within earshot: "He won't make it! He can't make it!" Asked later how he felt at that very moment, however, Doolittle said, "Confident." His navigator, Hank Potter, agreed: "We were particularly confident since we had the best pilot in the Air Force flying us," but the man sitting number two to Doolittle, Dick Cole, remembered thinking something else: "It'd be a pretty bad feeling for everybody behind us if we took off and dropped into the water."

As the lead crew of plane one waited to learn their fate, as her commander pulled the yoke all the way back to his stomach, Lawson saw it all: "With full flaps, motors at full throttle and his left wing far over the port side of the *Hornet*, Doolittle's plane waddled and then lunged slowly into the teeth of the gale that swept down the deck. His left wheel stuck on the white line as if it were a track. His right wing, which had barely cleared the wall of the island as he taxied and was guided up to the starting line, extended nearly to the edge of the starboard side.

"We watched him like hawks, wondering what the wind would do to him, and whether he could take off in the little run toward the bow. If he couldn't, we couldn't. . . . Doolittle picked up more speed and held to his line, and, just as the *Hornet* lifted itself up on the top of a wave and cut through it at full speed, Doolittle's plane took off. He had yards to spare. He hung his ship almost straight up on its props until we could see the whole top of his B-25. Then he leveled off, and I watched him come around in a tight circle and shoot low over our heads—straight down the line painted on the deck."

The entire convoy shouted in a surge of relief, a cheer so loud and throaty and ecstatic that the fliers could even hear it above the roar of their props. Adj. Harry Johnson, though, remembered different feelings: "I doubt if one man expected to return alive. I felt so badly about what I thought was certain death that I could not say good-bye to anyone—just a thumbs-up as each took off."

Immediately Trav Hoover in plane two began his taxi. He also lifted away "with yards to spare," but his stabilizer wasn't set quite right, making the launch too sharp. The plane lost its air and seemed to collapse in flight. As Hoover described it: "A real strong gust of wind took us right over the bow of the carrier. I'd just pulled up real hard, and the blast of wind picked me up even more, so it was kind of testy there."

Hornet was running at full bore, and every man aboard knew that if a Mitchell fell before her, the plane immediately would be sliced in two by the onrushing hull. Suddenly Trav leveled, banking into a steep right turn, and plane two climbed away, aimed straight toward its target.

Every four minutes another Billy nosed into position, gunned its engines, and peeled from the runway. In plane five pilot Davey Jones checked his gauges only to discover that his left rear tank was short by thirty gallons. He yelled out for more fuel, but it was too late. The hose had been turned off, and he could either have his plane pushed overboard or get in line and join the mission. Jones got in line: "The weather was not good. We were getting water over the deck, but we had great wind. The carrier was probably making twenty-five knots, and with probably twenty to thirty knots of wind. So it was pretty easy to make it up. In fact one pilot forgot to put his flaps down and he *still* made it."

That pilot was Ted Lawson: "I was on the line now, my eyes glued on the man with the flag. He gave me the signal to put my flaps down. I reached down and drew the flap lever back and down. I checked the electrical instrument that indicates whether the flaps are working. They were. I could feel the plane quaking with the strain of having the flat surface of the flaps thrust against the gale and the blast from the props. I got a sudden fear they might blow off and cripple us, so I pulled up the flaps again, and I guess the navy man understood. He let it go and began giving me the signal to rev my engines. . . . After fifteen seconds of watching the man with the flag spinning his arms faster and faster, I began to worry again. He must know his stuff, I tried to tell myself, but when, for God's sake, would he let me go?

"After thirty blood-sweating seconds the navy man was satisfied with the sound of my engines. Our wheel blocks were jerked out, and when I released the brakes we quivered forward, the wind grabbing at the wings. We rambled dangerously close to the edge, but I braked in time, got the left wheel back on the white line, and picked up speed. The *Hornet*'s deck bucked wildly. A sheet of spray rushed back at us.

"I never felt the takeoff. One moment the end of the *Hornet*'s flight deck was rushing at us alarmingly fast; the next split second I glanced down hurriedly at what had been a white line, and it was water. There was no drop nor any surge into the air. I just went off at deck level and pulled in front of the great ship that had done its best to plant us in Japan's front yard.

"I banked now, gaining a little altitude, and instinctively reached down to pull up the flaps. With a start I realized that they were not down. I had taken off without using them."

Osborne, from his bow position, saw it all: "Imagine our feeling as we saw that plane going up the deck without flaps, drop over the ship's prow, and skim the tops of the waves for what seemed like an eternity before starting to climb."

After Trav and Ted, a sign was posted at the control tower with the recommendation: STABILIZER IN NEUTRAL. According to Pete Mitscher, however, few army fliers seemed to pay it any attention: "With only one exception, takeoffs were dangerous and improperly executed. Apparently full back stabilizer was used by the first few pilots. As each plane neared the bow with more than required speed, the pilot would pull up and climb in a dangerous near-stall, struggle wildly to nose down, then fight the controls for several miles trying to gain real flying speed and more than a hundred feet altitude. Lt. [Hank] Miller, USN, held up a blackboard of final instructions for the pilots, but few obeyed."

The crew of plane eight had the most reason to be nervous. Their pilot, Ski York, had been so overwhelmed by his officer's duties in helping Doolittle with the mission's behind-the-scenes prep work that he had missed out on the Eglin training, as had his copilot, Lt. Robert Emmens.

"The ship shuddered under the strain of both throttles thrown wide open; flaps were down; controls all the way back in our laps," Emmens remembered. "York released his brakes and we began to roll, left wheel on the white line, down the deck of the carrier, slowly at first—my God, how slowly! Then faster, faster—the island of the carrier was lost from sight as it passed a bare eight feet away from our right wingtip; and then, like a big living thing, our plane seemed to leap into the air just as the deck of the ship disappeared under us and was replaced by the frothing sea."

As he waited in line, *Hari Kari-er* copilot Ken Reddy could feel his heart pounding in his chest: "The sea was rough and the airplanes were pulling against their ropes like circus elephants against their chains. Everybody was anxious to get off when his turn came, but perhaps we all felt the same—that our chances of meeting again were very few. We were shoved off 808 miles from our target, at such an hour that we would arrive in Japan in the middle of the day, and if we had gas enough to get to our field in China, it would be pitch dark. We had no weather reports. Our refueling field in China had been bombed, and we were not certain who controlled it. Nothing was in our favor."

"You'd think the later airplanes [would have] had more space to take off in, but we all took off from the same mark on the deck," recalled plane thirteen copilot Dick Knobloch. "That was just a little aft of the midsection of the island, about 472 feet. The navy didn't want us to take off [below] that for fear if we'd blow a tire or lose an engine, that we'd swerve into the island or superstructure, and set the carrier on fire, and that would be the end. So we all taxied up to the same position to take off. . . . Brakes were released when the bow of the carrier was pointed toward the water . . . you got a little roll because it was downhill. Then, as you got to the end of the deck, the deck gradually had come up in the interim as you were rolling, so you were facing the sky. Here you are looking at this real rough water, but fortunately it finally comes up and you see the sky, and you are happy." As Dick felt smooth air replace the rumbling wheels, his man in the nose, Bob Bourgeois, was having very different thoughts: "When we left the ship, that's when it hit me: Where the heck are you going to be tonight?"

Plane fifteen pilot Don Smith went through a hair-raising moment after he'd gunned both engines and his baby wouldn't budge. Every instrument checked out fine, and nobody could find a reason for the problem. Would his crew be the only ones to get washed out of the mission? As Smith fumed, he looked out to see one of the deckhands waving—they'd forgotten to pull the chocks.

This wasn't the end of plane fifteen's *Hornet* mishaps, however. Don pulled off at Ozzie's flag, but just as his Billy reached the end of the deck, the bow was thrown back down by a rogue wave instead of continuing on its normal rise. Smith and his men found themselves, at the wrong moment, pointed directly at the water. Even so the speed and the wind were enough to lift him over and up, and Don was just barely able to make his bank.

The last of the sixteen Mitchells to launch was *Bat Out of Hell*. If it's possible for a craft to be jinxed, *Bat* suffered bad luck from the very start. With the tall and scarecrow-lean lieutenant from South Carolina, Bill Farrow, piloting the plane, her copilot was the Texas Panhandle–born Lt. Robert Hite, who'd hitchhiked a hundred miles to Lubbock to take the air corps entrance exams; her navigator was Brooklyn redhead Lt. George Barr; her bombardier was the in-a-prior-life Nevada shepherd and Oregon turkey farmer, Cpl. Jacob DeShazer; and her engineer-gunner was the blond, boyish, and energetic Sgt. Harold Spatz.

Even after tightly stagger-parking the Mitchells inches apart, *Hornet* airdales had run out of deck room. *Bat*, at the rear of the line, had been chocked with her tail hanging over the ship's stern, so far back that Spatz would have to wait for the other B-25s to move up before he could climb aboard through the rear hatch. As Farrow revved up to taxi, however, a blast of air swept from Don Smith's props in plane fifteen, throwing *Bat* into a full-out tilt, her tail now heading straight toward the sea. With any more force or an errant toss of the waves, the plane would slide right off the deck.

Sailors ran to the nose hooks, looping line, but the ropes snapped. In the commotion to save the Billy, one of the navy boys slipped. The *Bat* crew watched in horror as Machinist Mate Bob Wall was thrown into their own left propeller, slicing his arm half off and spraying a river of blood across the deck. He was carried away by his deckmates and Jake DeShazer; there was nothing more the army men could do. "We had blocks behind and in front of the wheels, and one of my jobs as bombardier was to take them out for takeoff," remembered DeShazer. "I'd taken those blocks out, and I turned around, and here that sailor was, laying right under where the propeller turned. His arm was laying out separate from the rest, had been cut off. He was gouged in the back, too, but he was conscious. I looked at him, and he said, 'Give them hell for me.'"

Wall would survive, but his arm would have to be amputated. "Psychologically that was a pretty big shock to us, to know that at the last minute this naval fellow had fallen into our prop," said copilot Hite. "We took off not knowing whether he was alive or dead." Many aboard the *Bat* would later consider this an omen of things to come.

Jake finally climbed in to take his position as bombardier, only to find that during the commotion, the Plexiglas nose had somehow cracked open into a jagged, foot-wide hole. Jake would now be facing 150-mile-an-hour drafts, creating an additional drag that would mean even more gas gulped. Jake: "I thought, 'Should I tell the pilot?' They'd said, 'If you can't get the motor started, we're going to shove them off in the ocean.' That's what came over the loudspeaker. And I could just see them shoving it off in the ocean, and I wanted to go, so I thought, 'I'm going to let him go. Take a chance on it.'"

Their launch, at least, went well. The moment *Bat* leaped into the air at 0919 and made its bank, Jake could see the deck elevators immediately starting to bring up the navy's own planes to scout, patrol, and defend. Simultaneously every ship in the armada instantly reversed course to head straight back to Oahu. This style of sailing—on full bore at twenty-five knots, fleeing what was sure to be an imminent Japanese attack—would one day become famous throughout the Pacific as "hauling ass with Halsey." The admiral, in turn, would call the Doolittle Raid "one of the most courageous deeds in military history."

BOMB

In the sky now hummed a thin black stream of B-25s. With the critical gas situation, no one could afford to wait to fly in standard formation (a box of four planes whose overlapping machine-gun fire provides solid defense), so the sixteen-craft, eighty-man squadron cruised due west in a random grouping 50 miles wide and 150 miles long. To save on gas the men hovered just above the endless Pacific on economy cruise between 150 and 166 mph— about as slow as a Mitchell could fly and still remain airborne. The squad leaders would reach the Japanese coastline, the first landmark being point Inubo Saki and its famous lighthouse, around noon.

For many this would easily be the worst part of the mission—the hours and hours of barely flying at all. The protection of the task force was now far behind them, and their targets, their escape route, and their safe landing in friendly territory lay far, far ahead. After the satisfying adrenal pump of every crew's successfully making liftoff, each man was now facing the consequences of having volunteered in Columbia and Minneapolis, so long ago.

Nobody spoke unless he absolutely had to. Even with the interphone, a man had to shout to be heard above the Cyclones' roar and the screaming wind coursing through the planes. Mitchells, like every other American aircraft of World War II, had engines loud enough to permanently damage their crews' ears; later in life many fliers would find themselves hard of hearing or outright deaf (Flying Tiger chief Claire Chennault had originally left the air corps partly because of disagreements with his superiors and partly because he'd become too deaf to fly).

In the nose, bombardiers silently made certain that their Mark Twains still slid back and forth, that their .30 calibers were armed and mounted and could be moved in and out of position in their various sockets, and that their bomb bay door and egg-drop toggles seemed functional. Some inched on their hands and knees through the four-foot-high crawlway to verify that their ordnance had been correctly fused.

On the flight deck pilots and copilots watched their dials and gauges, their knob and toggle positions, their lights, switches, rheostats, and hydraulic and power controls. As the belly tank, guarded by its broomsticks, emptied out, gunners would juice it back up with reserve from the cans, punch holes in the empties, and throw them out the window (the holes to prevent a floating, shining trail from leading enemy ships straight to Task Force 16). Many would check their turrets and .50s one last time, trying a quick rotation and popping off a few bursts. More than a few would discover that their turrets had died, leaving them defenseless.

"I kept the clean nose of the *Ruptured Duck* about twenty feet above the water and settled into the gas-saving groove," remembered Ted Lawson. "I pushed the button on the interphone and told [gunner Dave] Thatcher to give the turret one more test. He did, and said it was still on the blink. Then I switched on the emergency juice, but that wouldn't work either. Our two .50 caliber rear guns were pointing straight back between the twin rudders and would be unable to budge one way or the other in case of attack.

"'Damn, boy, this is serious,'" Davenport, the copilot, said into the phone.

"Suddenly a dazzling, twisting object rushed past our left wing. It was startling until I realized it was a five-gallon can discarded by one of the planes in front of me. The can would have downed us if it had hit a prop. What a climax that would have been!

"At our low level and sluggish speed, it was a job to fly the ship. I called Clever on the phone, out in the snout of the bombardier's section, and asked him to turn on our automatic pilot. He did, but when I took my hands off the controls, the *Ruptured Duck* slipped off dangerously to the left. The automatic pilot wasn't working."

The men of plane nine, *Whirling Dervish,* also had turret trouble with the hydraulics used to charge the tail's .50 calibers. Gunner Eldred Scott tested them out, pulled off the device, and learned to charge and fire instead by hand. While he was working, Scotty remembered the beautiful pictures of Japan he'd seen in geography schoolbooks as a kid. He just didn't want to think about how this was now the enemy. The sergeant then smelled even more gas than usual and went below, only to discover the belly tank now leaking from every corner.

Dervish wouldn't be the only plane to find itself losing avgas on the flight to Japan; almost every member of the squadron was severely affected. The U.S. Rubber Company of Indiana had done a miserable job in designing and manufacturing Special Aviation Project #1's spare tanks. The outer casings of the new rubber models were too small, causing leaks at just about every seam, while the tank connections were incorrectly calculated, resulting in leaks at almost every tube. For aviators desperate to conserve every drop of fuel they could, these malfunctions would prove mission-critical.

"We were over six hundred miles when we launched, so it was pretty obvious that it wasn't going to fit," said plane five pilot Davey Jones. "At the time we just accepted the fact that we weren't going to have enough juice to get to our destinations in China. Putting it in real terms to yourself, that was just a statement and knowledge, and you did your best anyway. It didn't really enter your mind. To me that's the only thing that distinguishes this trip from the thousand other sorties that were flown during the war.

"We knew when we started that it wasn't going to fit."

Twenty-six-year-old *Dervish* pilot Lt. Harold "Doc" Watson came up with an answer for his men: "I got the crew together and presented my plan, to which all agreed. After leaving Tokyo we would proceed on our planned course as long as our gas held. We would then strafe a small boat, ditch beside it, take it over, and try to make our way to China. All agreed also that, if we were seriously hit over Tokyo, we would crash into the Imperial Palace rather then attempt a bailout or crash landing in the Tokyo area."

Plane eight's gas, meanwhile, was running out faster than hell. "At about eleven o'clock we had been flying long enough to have a fairly definite check on the amount of gasoline we were burning," said copilot Bob Emmens. "I flew while York did some figuring on paper.

"'Hey, Bob, take a look at this. Am I screwy, or are we burning this much gas?'

"His figures showed we were burning more gas than we should have been at those power and rpm settings. York's figures were right. Maybe the gauge was inaccurate and would give the same reading after more time. Maybe we had developed a gas leak, letting pure gasoline spill into the Pacific Ocean.

"'Hell, Ski, if that's right we're not going to get near the Chinese coast.'

"Herndon, busy in the nose with his charts and sextant, came into the pilot's compartment now. He personally checked the reading on the bomb bay tank. Yes, there was no mistaking it. We were burning a hell of a lot of gasoline. [Their cruise burn should have been seventy-two to seventy-five gallons an hour. Instead they were blowing through ninety-eight.] Besides landing in Japan, which, of course, was out of the question, we had one alternative other than taking our originally planned course south around the lower end of Japan and then west across the China Sea. That was striking out across the northern Japan Sea to Soviet territory, to our allies, the Russians, who might or might not be depended on to give us gas so we could continue to China; who might or might not recognize us as friendly, when and if we approached their probably well-fortified eastern coast."

Navigators like Herndon kept studying the compass and drift meter, but since the squadron was proceeding under overcast skies with no way of using their celestial training, they were mostly just dead-reckoning—guessing—their way to Japan. They compared their targets' chart positions with their compasses repeatedly, and the especially cautious ones checked their compasses against their pilot's. Frequently one or the other would be off by enough degrees to mean, because of the gas situation, that they would fail their objective. Plane two navigator Wildner said that he'd never in his life ever felt so helpless; plane four navigator Harry McCool commented: "From the takeoff until I got to land, I was surprised to be alive the next day."

Others, even though they didn't consider the Russian port of Vladivostok, couldn't imagine how they would make it to China. "The navigator was now the key man, having to guide us over 645 miles instead of the proposed five hundred miles of water to our target, then guide us over at least 1,140 more miles of water and hitting the 10-mile-wide Strait of Formosa, at the end of Japan," said *Hari Kari-er* copilot Ken Reddy. "Then overland for 160 more miles to a small field, where we were supposed to have some gasoline spotted for refueling." One sailor helping load in the rush to lift off had put *Hari* navigator Frank Kappeler's bag in the wrong plane by mistake. During the endless cruise Frank opened up the one he got instead to discover a navigator's manual. For four hours he used it to practice celestial navigation problems so that, in the dark over China, he'd be ready.

There was a lot of time for a guy to think. John Steinbeck, author of *The Grapes of Wrath,* described the feelings of combat virgins heading into their first mission: "They lack only one thing to make them soldiers, enemy fire, and they will never be soldiers until they have it. No one, least of all themselves, knows what they will do when the terrible thing happens. No man there knows whether he can take it, whether he will run away or stick, or lose his nerve and go to pieces, or will be a good soldier. There is no way of knowing and probably that one thing bothers you more than anything else. Every man builds in his mind what it will be like, but it is never what he thought it would be." A bombardier put it this way: "Naturally, not knowing what it was going to be like, I didn't feel scared. A little sick, maybe, but not scared. That comes later, when you begin to understand what your chances of survival are."

Bob Gray had named plane three *Whiskey Pete* after the pinto close to his heart back home in Texas. He and copilot Shorty Manch had together figured on one thing: By the time they got to Tokyo, planes one and two would have already roused the enemy, and being third in line would mean a trip straight to ack-ack hell. Even though the entire cabin reeked of octane from the leaking connections and bladder tank seams, Bob and Shorty took out one of the four boxes of Robert Burns cigars that Shorty had thought essential to this mission (along with his jazz records and two cartons of Baby Ruth candy bars) and smoked one after the next, all the way to Tokyo.

Their navigator, Chuck Ozuk, was feeling completely useless, since his charts had blown overboard in the rush to launch: "I knew once I got to Tokyo that I could find my way to China, but it was just getting there. I tuned a Tokyo station and the radio compass came on, and it agreed with my headings. We just followed the station all the way in.

"The music wasn't very good."

In plane sixteen bombardier Jake DeShazer now decided to interphone Bill Farrow about the tremendous amount of air coming through the jagged hole in his nose. Copilot Hite crawled forward on hands and knees to see what could be done. He and Jake tried stuffing an overcoat into the gash, but the constant hard wind kept throwing it back in their faces. They couldn't think of any other solution; Jake would just have to live with the situation.

"The Boss and I took turns at flying," said plane one copilot Dick Cole. "When I wasn't flying, Hank Potter, Braemer, Leonard, and I were continually checking the gas or other things about the ship. No one slept or got sick. Everyone prayed but did so in an inward way. I guess we all wondered more than anything—trying to imagine what was in store for us. If anyone was scared it didn't show. I believe I can honestly say that no one was really scared. I don't say this in a bragging way, it's just that at least we had never faced danger and didn't have sense enough to be scared.

"One thing I remember clearly is that the tune 'Wabash Cannonball' kept running through my mind. One time I was singing and stamping my foot with such gusto that the boss looked at me in a very questioning manner like he thought I was going batty.

"We flew low and kept a sharp lookout for surface ships and other aircraft. We veered once or twice to miss some ships and flew directly under a Japanese flying boat, which didn't see us."

That flying boat, a Japanese patrol plane cruising six hundred miles from shore, did in fact spot them and immediately reported back to headquarters. The patrol was one of many on its way to investigate the disappearance of the *Nitto Maru,* heading straight toward Task Force 16. As a group of Mitchells then flew, one after the next, over a Japanese light cruiser, she also radioed the sighting back to naval headquarters.

Two hundred miles from Inubo the front receded, and the weather turned CAVU (ceiling and visibility unlimited)—a perfect, cloudless day, which would hold all the way to central Japan. As the Americans appeared over Tokyo Bay, there could be no doubt that, one after another, the hundreds of military watercraft anchored there were spotting the incoming fliers and radioing home their news, guaranteeing a hostile reception over Tokyo.

The full military power of Japan would be waiting for them. There would be no surprise, and the beautiful, crystal-clear noonday timing would make the American fliers perfect targets for Japanese batteries on the ground and attack fighters in the air.

Between compasses fouled from weeks on *Hornet*, a forty-knot headwind, and the hundreds of miles of overcast ruling out solid navigation checks, only two of the sixteen Billys made landfall where they originally intended. Every other crew got lost, forcing each navigator to scan desperately for expected landmarks that just were not there. Almost all would eventually recognize pieces of the coastline from their dated assignment folders and give their pilots a new course to the targets. Getting lost, however, meant using up even more fuel.

The torso of the Japanese dragon is the island of Honshu, with the belly of the beast the nation's 225-mile-long urban sprawl of Tokyo, Yokohama, Nagoya, Osaka, and Kobe. Ten Mitchells were slated to strike the capital, while the other six were to target war-industry compounds (steel mills, ammo stockades, aviation factories, shipyards, and fuel plants) elsewhere in urban Japan. Unfortunately for a key group of Doolittle's men, the Japanese followed no policy of urban zoning, meaning that military-industrial plants, such as gasoline refineries and storage facilities, were often directly adjacent to residential neighborhoods.

April 18, 1942—four months and ten days after December 7, 1941, in Hawaii—was a bright, hot Saturday across the western Pacific. Most Japanese were out enjoying the unseasonably warm afternoon: cycling, shopping downtown, watching a baseball game in the new stadium, or even tanning in the parks and along the coast.

The sunbathers on the beach were first to see the solid, snub-nosed planes. Painted OD (olive drab), they soared just over the city's buildings, seeming to barely miss the power lines and shining new radio towers. Everyone assumed they were Japan's famous navy fighters, showing off their great skill with the latest daredevil stunts. Many, especially the children, looked up and waved.

That U.S. Air Corps planes would be mistaken for those of the enemy would happen again and again in the early days of the Pacific war. The first USAAC insignia consisted of a red circle inside a white star inside a blue circle, the red from a distance looking much like Japan's rising sun. Spotting it from the ground, so many American gunners would eventually fire on their own planes by mistake that the red dot would have to be removed. Now, however, this misleading emblem would be almost as good as camouflage.

As Doolittle flew just above the treetops, he saw, dead ahead and one thousand feet above, a squadron of Japanese fighters. He dropped even lower, rising and falling with the hills, hoping his paint would do its job and blend him into the landscape. Two pursuits kept pace. Jimmy zigzagged across his course, finally discovering a valley of rice paddies where the paint took, and the Mitchell seemed to disappear. "I swung very quickly around the hills in an S curve," he said. "The fighters turned also, but apparently they didn't see the second half of my S. The last time I saw them, they were going off in the opposite direction from us." With no other enemy craft in sight, the lieutenant colonel resumed his heading.

Tokyo at that moment hardly seemed a capital of empire. Though it had a few grand buildings (such as Frank Lloyd Wright's Imperial Hotel), most of the city was a sprawl of districts lined with small, two-story homes and shops of black wood frames or red brick, dotted with white paper screens. Since it had just spent eight years rebuilding after being completely destroyed by earthquake and fire, the entire metropolis looked new, fresh, and clean.

In a bizarre coincidence that very morning the town had dress-rehearsed one of its rare air-raid drills—sirens wailing, barrage balloons (whose cables could drop an enemy plane right out of the sky) being raised and lowered, fighter planes practicing maneuvers, and fire engines racing across their districts—to ensure wartime defense was ready and alert. The citizens of Tokyo ignored the exercise entirely, convinced by the regular assurances of their military government that the island fortress of Japan could never be attacked by foreigners.

One businessman, waiting at a railway platform in central Tokyo, watched the American planes arrive, their bellies almost brushing the leaves from the trees. He turned to a fellow commuter and said, "It looks real, doesn't it? Just like a foreign aircraft breaking through Japanese air defenses. I guess the Imperial forces want to impress the people that they are fully prepared."

It was not until the Mitchells reached the city center and passed over the palace that Tokyo's citizenry could see the gleaming red, white, and blue emblem of stars at the wingtips—gleaming white stars, instead of the blood red suns of Japan. Just as they realized that these couldn't be their nation's planes, the ordnance began to fall.

Cruising at a mere 30 feet, Doolittle pulled up to 1,200 so bombardier Fred Braemer could get to work. At 1,215 a tiny red cockpit light blinked four times, confirming that all four bombs had left the B. It was odd that North American had thought to include this feature, as every man aboard could feel each egg snap from its shackles, not to mention the fact that, with all bombs dropped, a Mitchell was in seconds two to three thousand pounds lighter, suddenly jumping into the air like an uncontrollable stallion. Many remembered, at that moment, that it smelled just like the Fourth of July.

Jimmy threw his yoke forward to bring the nose back down to hedgehopping level for his getaway. Almost immediately he ran into a stream of small black clouds of exploding antiaircraft fire. The commander was on the interphone with Paul Leonard in the rear bubble, and both watched the soft puffs, knowing all too well what lay inside them—exploding shrapnel that could drop their B right out of the sky. "Flak is very deceptive," explained Herb Macia. "A puff of flak looks so harmless; yet, you get a burst of flak in close; first of all, it is a *clap!* It has this very unique sound. Second, you get the shatter of the shrapnel from around it."

"They're missing us by a mile, Paul," Doolittle said to his gunner just as a new shell burst, this one close enough to splatter the fuselage.

"Colonel," Leonard said, "that was no mile."

"I kept Paul Leonard advised of enemy aircraft and at one time counted more than eighty," remembered copilot Dick Cole. "We were not bothered by fighters; however, flak shook us up a little and left some holes in the tail."

Jimmy threw his yoke and throttles full bore, diving to hedgehop the roofs, and instantly found himself over a plane factory. Navigator Hank Potter: "They bothered us because we had dropped all our bombs and had nothing to use on them. They were nice red-and-silver training planes, lined up on a factory field. You didn't need any earphone connection with Jimmy to hear his roar of disappointment that a little 'made in America' heat couldn't be turned on."

Noseman Fred Braemer saw a tank or armored car out on the highway and wanted to strafe it with his .30, but Jimmy told him to take a pass: "They probably think we are a friendly aircraft. Let them keep on thinking that." He thought of the Mitchell crews following right behind. Perhaps keeping this first assault to a minimum would max their surprise.

Plane two's Trav Hoover had followed Jimmy all the way in since his navigator, Carl Wildner, couldn't get a fix on their position. The photos Carl had from army intelligence didn't match what they were flying over—a big Florida-type beach, with no lighthouse anywhere in sight—and he thought he was losing his mind. Finally, at the last minute, Carl recognized some checkpoints and could give Trav a course. When they arrived where they were supposed to be dropping eggs, bombardier Dick Miller's pictures didn't make any sense, either, and he couldn't spot his primary, a powder works. Dick saw a factory and warehouse that looked like a good substitute, and recommended they cabbage that instead.

The new target was coming up fast. To hit it and get away, Hoover could only make it up to 900. When their eggs cracked, they were so low that the explosion rocked the plane, and a huge column of smoke rose all around them. If they had taken on the gunpowder factories at that altitude, they would surely have been blown out of the sky. "The concussion was so hard, I was sure the airplane was damaged," Hoover remembered, "but as things turned out, I never got a chance to see if it was."

Without a tail or belly gunner, the only way the crews could judge the effects of their drops would be to hook and bank an instant U-turn. Between the enemy fighters and rounds of ack-ack now blooming around them in every direction, however, few could even dare the attempt. To have any chance of escape, the Mitchells would have to dive and skim just above the treeline at top speed.

Whiskey Pete reached Tokyo only to find it in full defense mode, AA guns blazing hard, throwing up a steaming wall of ack-ack. After Bob Gray and Shorty Manch got rid of their cigars and pulled up to an evasive 1,450, the pilot called for a crew vote. What did everybody want to do when the inevitable happened and they were shot down into the hands of the empire? The crew decided they'd take their chances as POWs, but not Bob Gray, who intended to follow Doolittle's plan: If *Pete* was disabled, he'd wait for everyone else to parachute away, and then kamikaze himself and his Mitchell in a blaze of glory straight into the perfect Japanese target.

Even from 1,450, the day was so clear that bombardier Aden Jones could tell exactly when they passed over the Temple of Heaven, and he easily struck the assigned steel, gas, and chemical plants nearby. Navigator Chuck Ozuk watched several buildings explode in flames, confirming they'd made at least two of their hits. Outbound, Aden Jones used his .30 to plow through a factory yard, and *Pete* came upon dozens of fighters and enemy warships equipped with good-size cannons firing at them. Gray turned due south, to trick the enemy into thinking they were headed for the Philippines.

As night fell Shorty looked out the window and spotted another B taking a very different course from theirs. Manch called out to his navigator for a double-check: Which plane was right? Chuck Ozuk insisted he knew what he was doing, and told Shorty and Gray to stick to the headings he'd given them.

As he watched the plane vanish from sight, though, Manch couldn't help but have second thoughts about whether their navigator knew what he was doing. Shorty would keep wondering this until he figured out, weeks later, that the other Mitchell was the ill-fated *Green Hornet*.

On their way across the Pacific, Brick Holstrom and copilot Lucien Youngblood noticed something odd. As their plane four neared a Japanese freighter, they could clearly see the boat taking evasive action, and knew their U.S. insignia couldn't possibly be visible from that altitude. There could be only one answer: Tokyo knew they were on their way.

Brick and Lucien talked it over and decided to approach their targets from the south, in the hope of surprising the enemy fighters and AA gunners who'd be looking for more American planes coming in due east. Navigator Harry McCool gave them a new course, and as he did, gunner Bert Jordan came forward with some bad news.

Bert had been trying to talk to his pilot on the interphone again and again, but something was wrong and they couldn't understand each other. Like all the gunners Jordan had been separated from the rest of the crew by the inflated spare tank blocking his crawlway, but now that it'd been used up and collapsed, he could finally come forward. They had a pretty serious leak around the cap on the left wing tank, he explained, and his turret was malfunctioning: Plane four's top gun could be aimed for defense only by maneuvering the plane to position it.

As it happened, almost every raid gunner would officially report his turret to be "entirely unsatisfactory. Operating the turret for twelve hours ... resulted in Azimuth motor failures. ... The system of relay switches and power transmitting relays was unsatisfactory due to arcing of the points. ... Many hydraulic charging failures occurred, caused by loss of fluid and pressure. ... The most frequent cause of trouble was breakdown of the hydraulic seal. ... After firing about twenty-five rounds, the sight fogged up and couldn't be seen through. The field of vision was too small. It made the sight look smaller and farther away than the eye showed it ... these defects reduced the effectiveness of fire by sixty percent. ... In a dive steep enough to lift the ammunition out of the cans, the gun belts would jam and in some cases the links would be broken." The bombardier's .30 in the nose had its own problems: "It is impossible to quickly shift from one position to another under actual combat conditions, particularly if the gun has been fired and the motor warmed up and expanded. The glass molding for the nose gun is not strong enough and cracks after a few rounds are fired."

At 1230 plane four reached landfall. While Doolittle had arrived fifty miles off course, McCool now discovered they were eighty miles from true. A fifteen-degree miscalibrated compass meant they'd now have 160 miles to make up in the strike and return. Even if they survived Tokyo, there was no way they could make it to the landing fields of China.

While plane four tried to get its bearings, Mitchells one, two, and three were heading straight at them in getaway, each chased by enemy fighters. Two pursuits swooped in dead ahead, and Brick saw their tracers fly just over his hatch. Two more came in at three o'clock, and Lucien watched as they prepared to dive. They were being attacked from all sides, and they hadn't even reached Tokyo Bay. The tracer bullets were coming in closer and closer, while their own guns remained silent.

Brick knew that, eggless, they could easily outrun the enemy, and though it was the decision no bomber pilot ever wants to make, he just couldn't see their surviving long enough to reach the targets. Just then, they were over the bay at seventy-five feet, so Brick ordered bombardier Bob Stephens to salvo. Throttling to the max of 270, Brick was finally able to outrun what the men now counted as six fighters directly upon them. When the pursuits, giving up, turned away and no more were sighted, they pulled south, toward China.

Now clear of imminent danger, the men stewed over not reaching their targets and fulfilling their mission.

★

There hadn't been time enough to top off plane five's gas tanks in the launch from *Hornet,* so Davey Jones knew he was already low on fuel when they arrived over Japan. He was additionally concerned that his bomb bay had been extensively repaired just before takeoff, and wondered if the doors and shackles would even open and release correctly.

It took twenty minutes before anyone aboard could recognize the landmarks from their target folders, wasting even more gas, but soon enough the men of plane five found themselves directly over Tokyo Bay. They headed for their assignment on the far side of the city, and quickly found themselves engulfed in machine-gun fire and ack-ack, with some puffs a full eight feet in diameter. Over the roar of the B, the men could clearly hear the deep rumblings and high-pitched cracks of the exploding shells. Noseman Denver Truelove watched hundreds of tracers arcing from the hills, aimed straight for them, following the plane as it raced across the horizon.

Davey knew they'd never make it to their assigned target, so he started scouting for other possibilities as they soared over the waterfront. It seemed as if they were passing by one after another military or industrial operation well worth cabbaging. Coming to a decision, Davey pulled up to 1,200. Denver

Truelove succeeded in targeting an oil storage facility and a power plant. "I made a turn so we could see the effect of the demolitions we dropped," Jones remembered. "As the bomb struck, the power plant assumed the shape of a barrel. The sides rounded out and the top became circular. Then, the 'barrel' burst. Smoke and dust and bricks were everywhere. . . . Intense antiaircraft fire started after the release of the first bomb. There were black puffs six to eight feet in diameter. Elevation was good. Most of the fire was just behind the plane and just to the side. Some machine-gun fire was seen by the gunner. Tracers were passing just over the plane, coming from the south. After the release of the bombs as we were descending, antiaircraft fire was from above the small hills to the southwest of Tokyo. No opportunity was had to observe landmarks or other targets because of the intensity of the antiaircraft fire."

Davey screamed into a turn and dived back to skimming the rooftops of old Tokyo. As the hillside antiaircraft gunners fired a barrage, Denver Truelove could see the tracers follow them all the way to the city's outskirts.

Green Hornet's Dean Hallmark, following right behind Davey, got just as lost, but soon enough his navigator, Chase Jay Nielsen, found his bearings and plane six headed straight toward the assignment. Even though the flak clouds were heavy, *Hornet* demolished its target, the Central Tokyo Steel Mills. When he didn't get it all on the first run, Dean circled and took a second aim; in the turn, Chase saw the bombs "blow all hell" out of that factory.

They escaped from Japan untouched.

As *Ruptured Duck* arrived on the outskirts of Tokyo, Ted Lawson "caught a fleeting glimpse of a playground—and then a sharp, quick look at a tall flagpole from which fluttered the Japanese flag. It was like getting hit in the chest very hard." His gunner, Dave Thatcher, still couldn't get the turret to work properly. He tried juicing from the emergency battery, but it was useless; the bubble was dead. Dave interphoned Lawson over his dilemma, and Ted had a thought. He tilted the plane's nose up, and the turret swung around, just as it was supposed to. Back to level, however, the bubble once again refused to budge. If they were attacked by fighters, Lawson would have to evade while taking that handicap into account. They would have no defense whatsoever if attacked from above.

Over Tokyo Bay, Thatcher sat in his worthless bubble and watched as six Japanese fighters soared over their heads. He recognized each pursuit as it went by, perfectly matching the silhouette cards he'd memorized, but there was nothing he could do. One dived, and Lawson waited to hear from Thatcher when he'd need to gyrate the juice for defense. He waited and waited, until Dave finally reported that the attacker had vanished.

Coming into the city outskirts, the *Duck* crew saw Davey Jones and his men barely avoid dozens of ack-ack attacks. Ted flew defensively, hedgehopping as tightly as he could, keeping very fast and very low. He even had to pull up to avoid slicing off the roof of a lipstick red Shinto temple. Their low altitude meant that he and his crew had an extremely limited view of what lay ahead and could not get a bearing on their assignment. Every time they pulled up to get a better perspective, streams of ack-ack would bully them back down. "I was almost on the first of our objectives before I saw it," Ted remembered.

> I gave the engines full throttle as Davenport adjusted the prop pitch to get a better grip on the air. We climbed as quickly as possible to fifteen hundred feet. . . . There was just time to get up there, level off, attend to the routine of opening the bomb bay, make a short run and let fly with the first bomb. . . . Just as the light blinked, a black cloud appeared about a hundred yards or so in front of us and rushed past us at great speed. Two more appeared ahead of us, on about the line of our wingtip, and they too swept past. They had our altitude perfectly, but they were leading us too much. . . .
>
> In the southern part of the city, the fourth light blinked. That was the incendiary, which I knew would separate as soon as it hit the wind and that dozens of small firebombs would molt from it.

To escape the clouds of flak, Lawson made a screaming dive and pushed the throttle to the metal. At more than 350 miles an hour, they outran the cannon fire. "It was just impossible for me to believe that we were going to get away from the raid as easily as this," Ted recalled. "Clever crawled up from his bombardier's nose and climbed into our compartment.

"'Were you scared?' he asked me.

"I told him I sure was.

"I guess we all wanted to be together now."

Plane eight, like so many others, used up too much fuel finding its way in. Over the countryside, navigator Nolan Herndon watched a farmer with a cow look up and wave at them with his walking stick. "Hell, I'd seen lots of Jap laundry calendars, and I thought old Fujiyama, snow covered and pink, would be looming up to meet us," said copilot Bob Emmens. "I must admit I was plenty tense about that time. I think we all were."

"After flying for about thirty minutes after our landfall was made, we still hadn't spotted Tokyo itself, so I started looking for any suitable target, something that was worthwhile bombing," said pilot Ski York. Emmens: "Suddenly Ski pulled up to about fifteen hundred feet. There was our target directly on our nose. It was a big factory installation with four puffing stacks; at least a three-story structure with a fair-sized river alongside and several railroad tracks entering its immediate area.

"'Open your bomb bay doors, Herndon.' And then to me, 'Jesus, that would be a fine thing at a time like this—to forget to open your bomb bay doors!'

"The plane gave its characteristic shudder as the bomb bay doors underneath opened. . . .

"Ski began ruddering the ship from right to left, keeping the needle on zero. Fifteen hundred feet was indicated on our altimeter, and our air speed was well above 200 miles an hour now. It looked good to see that speed after the morning hours of riding along at a sluggish 165 to 170 indicated. The target disappeared under our nose.

"'Bombs away!' A pause, and then, 'Bomb bay doors closed,' just as a slight jolt told us the 'eggs' had landed, the repercussion making the ship rock. It was twelve-fifteen." When they next passed over an airfield low enough for a good strafe, Herndon opened up with his machine gun: "I wasn't going through this thing without firing that gun."

As they treetopped their getaway, Ski and his men once again ran through all their options. They could land in Japan and be captured. They could try to get as close as possible to China, but since Ski had calculated they'd fall short of dry land by at least three hundred miles, that didn't seem a promising alternative. But, on the other side of the Japanese territory of Korea, six hundred miles away, was one last choice—the Union of Soviet Socialist Republics, Allied territory. Doolittle had ordered them not to land in Russia, but what choice did they have? Ski told navigator Nolan Herndon to give him a course to Vladivostok.

About this decision Emmens would later insist that "people would think there was some secret reason as to why we landed in Russia. We did not make the landing as a test case. We made it to save five necks." Navigator Nolan Herndon, however, would come to believe a very different story.

⭐

With so many of the Mitchell crews getting lost finding their way to their targets, the American stream of attack turned chaotic, leading to one outstanding benefit. As planes arrived from every compass point imaginable, Japanese defense forces could never prepare adequately for the next assault. A mistake caused by weather and inadequate prep was interpreted by those on the ground as a brilliant tactic, overwhelming their abilities.

Decorated with such messages as "I don't want to set the world on fire— just Tokyo!" and "You'll get a BANG out of this," the five-hundred-pound bombs and thousand-pound incendiaries, helped by clear weather, broad daylight, and low cruising altitudes, struck target after target with tremendous accuracy. Explosion after explosion rang out across the harbor, through the manufacturing districts, and across the fields of power plants. There was silence, and then the unmistakable ack-ack of antiaircraft fire, the roaring whine of defense fighters taking flight and the wail of air raid sirens. Black plumes of smoke rose in billowing columns across the city. Fire engines roared through the suburbs, and the deafening explosions from the bombs continued to shake the streets.

Plane nine, *Whirling Dervish,* came in right on target without a moment lost over enemy territory, flying, as one eyewitness reported, with "majestic deliberation." Unfortunately the Japanese were now fully prepared, and *Dervish*'s path was covered in exploding shells. Gunner Eldred Scott remembered it as "a nice sunshiny day with overcast antiaircraft fire," while navigator Tom Griffin said, "We were surprised and shocked to realize that those small black clouds we were seeing were flak. They were shooting at *us.*" Pilot Doc Watson felt inspired: "Come on you bastards, knock hell out of us if you can, for we sure are going to bomb hell out of you. Come on, hit us, bring us down if you can—if we are going to die, OK, but if this crate falls, I'm going to put it nose down, full throttle, and bend it around a street. I'll take plenty of you bastards with me when I hit." Even under such heavy attack, *Dervish* was able to strike her primary, the Kawasaki Truck and Tank plant (or so the crew believed; later they would learn that they had actually destroyed the Tokyo Gas and Electric Engineering Company).

As they turned for China, "what I saw was four streams of tracer bullets shooting out past us, real close," remembered gunner Scott. "I looked down and there he was, a pursuit plane, coming hard. I began firing at him and he winged off. I know he was hit. Maybe we got him. Anyway, he only made that one pass at us."

When another fighter came in, only a hundred yards away, Scott returned fire only to discover that his sight had fogged up. Using tracers to guide his aim, he got his bullets closer and closer, until suddenly the enemy fighter fell away. Scotty thought it was his doing once again, but he couldn't swear to it. *Dervish* took off, and soon enough no pursuits could touch it.

Navigator Sally Crouch brought plane ten in over the Inubo Saki lighthouse exactly as planned. An aircraft carrier in Tokyo Bay immediately began firing her .20 mm cannons at them, but the strikes fell short. Japan's defenses were now on full alert, but plane ten was able to score two direct hits on her primary, the Japan Special Steel Company, though she lost the last demolition and the incendiary in a mixed industrial/residential district. "I encountered heavy AA fire over my target," remembered pilot Dick Joyce. "By the time my bombs were out, I found myself in an AA bracket with the puffs and bursts coming very close, but generally behind me but catching up fast."

A group of interned Americans saw the steel company explode, and they watched plane ten zooming west over the Tamagawa River. The clouds of black flak were so close to the ship that the onlookers kept expecting to watch the B catch fire and crash. One reported the Japanese batteries as "laying an unbroken carpet of fire from the smoke of which one could trace the course taken by the bombers for some minutes after they had passed."

The AA cannon were trained on Joyce and his men, as were nine Nakajima pursuits. A shell ripped up seven inches of plane ten's fuselage just before the stabilizer, and her left wing was tatted by machine-gun fire coming from two of the Nakajimas right on her tail. There were fighters before them, below them, above them, and behind them.

"I increased power and went into a steep diving turn to the left to escape AA fire and pursuit," Joyce said. "The fighters peeled off in attack and followed me, but I dove underneath them. They did not seem too eager to come in too close, as my rear gunner was firing at them from time to time." Yet another fighter was now coming head-on. Sally Crouch tried to take her from the nose, and tail gunner Ed Horton fired straight, broadside, and at her retreating tail. The tracers seemed to be striking repeatedly, and Ed saw that pursuit burst into smoke.

"I had my machine gun in the lower nozzle with the idea of strafing on the ground," Sally Crouch said. "I was looking up ahead for something to shoot, and I saw a couple of Japanese in the rice paddy. But as we came upon them,

I could see that it was an old man and a boy. Despite the fact that I didn't give any orders to my hands not to shoot, my hands did not squeeze, did not shoot.

"The next thing I know, I'm looking at a Japanese fighter right out the front of our aircraft. It looks like I could touch him. I went up against the bulkhead just like somebody had shoved a shotgun in my stomach. I remember looking down to see how many holes he had shot in me. The next thing I remember, I am changing cans of ammunition. What I don't remember is that I took the gun out of the lower nozzle, put it out the side nozzle, and had fired some fifty, seventy-five rounds at him.

"The rear gunner was firing on this aircraft as well; I could see his tracers, and I could see mine. My tracers were going into his wing root, and he went down in a shallow glide with black smoke, and our rear gunner Sergeant Horton took credit for that kill. So we got away from him.

"Next we could hear the guns of a Jap fighter who had come up behind us there as we were climbing into the clouds. He shot the two copper wire antennas that were strung on top of our fuselage, the deicer boot on our left wing, and a vacuum cup, a cup that catches the slipstream and creates a vacuum on our relief tubes, into which the crew urinates. He came up very close and could've sat there all day long and shot us up, except that in my opinion he saw the wooden guns sticking out the tail and broke off the attack. Otherwise we could've been shot down right there."

"I heard the copilot's voice over the interphone saying there were pursuits over us," gunner George Larkin remembered. "I looked around for them, and all I could see was antiaircraft bursting all around us. In the meantime Lieutenant Crouch had dropped the bombs, and all I could see was dust and flying debris. The pursuit was getting rather close at this time, and the AA also had our range. Joyce then dived for the ground. We left the pursuit for a while, but as we had to turn they were soon on top of us again. They opened the throttles and really flew. The copilot, Lt. J. R. Stork, told me we were indicating 337 mph. Thank goodness for the speed, because when Lieutenant Joyce dived it caused the ammunition to come out of the can and tangle up, throwing both guns out of commission. I finally got one straightened out and used it. It seemed that when the Japs saw the tracers coming after them, they were afraid to come closer. We were finally able to climb to the clouds and lose them."

On their way out of Japanese airspace, one more interceptor honed in on them. Joyce went into a two-thousand-foot-per-minute climb, outran the enemy, and escaped across the China Sea.

✪

That afternoon in the Tokyo suburbs, a housewife by the name of Mrs. Iwata was having a friend over for lunch. They were just finishing their meal when, in the middle of a radio broadcast of "The Blue Danube Waltz," they heard the first bombs. The two women hurried outside as a Mitchell screamed overhead. "It came from Hawaii!" Mrs. Iwata yelled over the explosions. "More will follow!" As she urged her guest to hurry home to safety, Mrs. Iwata decided then and there that her husband, a plumbing executive, would immediately have to dig an air raid shelter in their backyard.

Iida Minoru was working at his father's grocery store when he heard the planes screaming just over the roofs. He ran outside and looked up to see black pellets trickling from their bellies. Immediately comprehending the situation, he ran down the street screaming, "Enemy plane! Enemy plane, this is an air raid!"

Next to a house in his neighborhood, Iida found a smoking black tube—one of the incendiary bomblets. He ran back to the grocery and returned with a bucket of sand (a standard piece of fire-prevention equipment found throughout Tokyo). After smothering the bomblet, he ran through the neighborhood with pail and shovel, looking for more.

Honjo Seikichi watched two bombs fall on his next-door neighbor's house. He climbed up on the roof and put the fires out with his shirt. Mrs. Dobashi Midori heard the air raid sirens and ran outside to discover her own home had been hit, as one of the incendiaries, still smoking, had crashed into her upper floor. She ran back inside and covered it with a water-soaked mat, and then found part of the ceiling on fire. Using a bamboo pole tipped in wet straw, like a mop, she was able to put it out.

Haberdasher Yoshida Katsuzo heard the roar of low-flying planes and went to investigate. He looked up just in time to see an incendiary drop on Okasaki Hospital. The building exploded in flames and smoke. Yoshida helped the orderlies and neighborhood volunteers move the patients out of harm's way, flabbergasted at the Americans' barbaric act.

Children were outside playing at the Waseda Middle School when they saw an object fall from the sky. It was an incendiary, and Suzuki Kikujiro would tell the Japanese newspapers that it hit one of his schoolmates, who fell over and stopped moving. Some American misses would be used several months later as a justification for violating the Geneva Conventions and would have grave consequences for eight Raiders. There is little doubt, however, that just as a few Doolittle Raid bombs inadvertently struck civilian neighborhoods in the zoning welter of Tokyo, so, too, did some Japanese gunners, aiming at the rooftop-skipping enemy, end up missing the Americans and firing into Japanese homes, shops, and factories instead. In another classroom, Yamaguchi Hiroichi and his friends watched the firing of the AA guns and the bombers swooping overhead, shouting with delight. "Most of the people did not believe it, thinking it was just another drill," Catholic priest Gustav Bitter remembered. "But when they learned it was a real raid, nobody could hold them back to go outside, to climb the roofs or the chimneys to get a better view. In other words, it was a thrill rather than a frightening event."

Many Japanese did, however, feel the horror of being under attack. One Tokyo resident wrote to his cousin, a fighter pilot stationed in New Guinea: "The bombing of Tokyo and several other cities has brought about a tremendous change in the attitude of our people toward the war. Now things are different. The bombs have dropped here on our homes. It does not seem any more that there is such a great difference between the battle front and the home front."

"We heard a lot of planes overhead and saw five or six large fires burning in different directions with great volumes of smoke," said Joseph Grew, the American ambassador to Japan. "To the east we saw a plane with the whole line of black puffs of smoke, indicating antiaircraft explosions just on its tail; it didn't look like a bomber and we were inclined to believe that the Japanese batteries lost their heads and fired on their own pursuit planes. All this was very exciting, but at the time it was hard to believe that it was more than a realistic practice by Japanese planes. We were all very happy and proud in the Embassy, and the British told us later that they drank toasts all day to the American fliers."

"Our fondest wish had come true," remembered British attaché Frank Moysey. "I saw a black cloud of smoke belch suddenly from behind a hill to the northwest. I ran into a building and climbed to the roof; it was a beautiful sight. There, surging up from Tokyo's heavy industrial district, were six enormous columns of smoke, dense and black. While we watched the smoke increase and spread with the wind, a big twin-engined bomber suddenly roared across the sky a half-mile away." A Japanese woman who worked for him as a servant said, "It is so unfair that you should bomb us. Our houses are only made of wood, while yours are of stone." Associated Press Tokyo bureau chief Max Hill was told by a Japanese friend that "many of the people were killed by machine gun bullets from our own planes. They were shooting at one of the bombers, and the bullets sprayed a schoolyard."

"When I heard the alarm I ran to the roof," Argentine commercial attaché

Ramon Muniz Lavalle reported. "All Tokyo seemed to be in panic. Japs were running everywhere, pushing, shouting, screaming. There were no air-raid shelters in the city. I could see fires starting near the port.

"Our two Japanese interpreters in the embassy were frightened out of their skins. I sent down to get them, but they wouldn't come up to the roof. After the raid, a Japanese scrubwoman who worked for us came up to me and said, 'If these raids go on, we'll all go mad.'

"It caught the Japs by surprise. Their unbounded confidence began to crack. The day after the raid, the Tokyo newspapers said nine planes were shot down. The people knew such statements were a lie. The officer in charge of anti-aircraft defenses was compelled to commit suicide."

By the time Tokyo defense was fully engaged to take on any more American bombers, it was too late; plane ten was the last to attack Tokyo. The rest were already heading for targets elsewhere.

The first Billy over Yokohama was *Hari Kari-er.* Pilot Ross Greening had picked the city for his crew's target since he'd visited it as a teenager, and thought he'd know his way around. When they reached Japan, however, Ross immediately realized he didn't recognize a thing. "Our targets were the docks, oil refineries, and warehouses between Tokyo and Yokohama," said *Hari* bombardier Bill Birch. "When we arrived over the coastline, it reminded me of Southern California. People on the ground waved at us."

"On the way to the target in Yokohama, we flew alongside some air-training fields and some trainers tried to fly formation with us," navigator Frank Kappeler remembered. "Shortly thereafter we were intercepted by some Japanese fighters, and they came so close in order to look us over that I could clearly see their faces. They were not sure of our identity, and the Tokyo area had just completed a practice air raid exercise. Our pilot and copilot had their eyes focused on two fighters on our left side, when I observed two others approaching us from the right. Our turret gunner started firing and he hit two of them. One wobbled away, and the other went into a steep climb and started smoking. The copilot reported that we had been hit, but nothing serious."

"After crossing Kasumigaura lake, we were attacked by four new-model fighters closely resembling Zeros except with inline engines," Greening said. "These ships mounted six machine guns in the wings and apparently had a top speed of 260 on the ground. I don't think I'd ever flown so low in my life, dodging down creek beds and ducking between trees rather than going over them. We hugged the ground as tightly as we could and even flew under some power lines in the hope that some of the ships might crash into them. They didn't. Two of these were shot down, one on fire; neither were seen to hit the ground."

Copilot Ken Reddy: "They were very trim, silver planes [Kawasaki Ki. 61 Type 3s]. Gardner was shooting at them before we knew they were on us. As soon as the guns started we opened up to 2,200 rpm which is a good way from the maximum, but is fast enough to drink the gas. We were afraid to use more power for fear of burning too much fuel. Two soon dropped out. Not long after that another dropped out; we think that it might have been hit. The fourth just kept hanging on. When it would pull out to climb, I would retard the rpm, slowing us down. I wasn't trying to coax him on but to conserve on fuel. Perhaps if I had seen the eight to fifteen small-caliber bullet holes that had crept up the trailing edge of the wing on my side along the engine nacelle toward the propellers, I would not have teased our antagonist so much."

As they headed toward the target, more Type 3s appeared, and the situation turned critical. As Greening anxiously weighed his course of action, a miracle occurred. Directly in front of him was what looked like an old-fashioned, thatch-roofed village, but on closer inspection turned out to be a gas farm. Greening thought: Why not forgo the primary and knock out what the Japanese themselves thought crucial enough to camouflage? He was under such concentrated attack, however, that he could only raise to six hundred, a daredevil move. "We were right on course toward a large refinery with fuel storage tanks, so I opened the bomb bay doors and salvoed everything we had," Bill Birch said. "The resulting explosion and fire was a thrill and gave all of us a sense of satisfaction for having accomplished our purpose."

"When our bombs dropped, there were great sheets of flame and a terrific explosion that threw the copilot and me right out of our seats, even though we were belted, and banged our heads against the top of the cockpit," recalled Greening. "My mind was intent on my job, of course, but I remember that I also kept thinking: Oh if my wife could see me now!"

After successfully knocking down his enemy pursuits, twenty-two-year-old gunner Mel Gardner now discovered that his .50 had jammed, and his turret motors had burned out entirely. Hearing Gardner's news over the interphone, Greening found he couldn't swallow the bite of sandwich he had taken to calm his nerves. The pilot would fly across all of Japan with that piece of sandwich tucked in his mouth.

In the middle of Tokyo Bay on their getaway, the *Hari* crew saw a dead man in a leather jacket hanging on to a log. They decided that this must be one of their own, that a fellow Raider been brought down. Greening told his noseman to look for revenge. "We sighted several small fishing craft about five miles offshore, so I machine-gunned them with the .30 caliber in the nose," Bill Birch said. "I had the gun in the forward position. We approached at an altitude of approximately fifty feet, from the right and slightly astern. The tracers put me on target, and I raked the length of the deck from stern to bow. The first one burst into flames, and the crew jumped overboard."

"Here I got what was perhaps my greatest scare," Ken Reddy remembered. "Just as Birch cut loose on it with his machine gun, our right engine began to cough and sputter, throwing flames clear out the front of the nacelle. Greening and I both hit the mixture control at the same time, and shoved it into automatic rich. It soon stopped, but none too soon to suit any of us. I'm sure that they would have [had] no mercy on us if we had gone down there."

When Bill Bower in plane twelve, *Fickle Finger,* hit landfall, he marveled at the country's beauty: "I remembered that I had the impression that, my gosh, what peaceful, pretty countryside that was . . . what do they want war with us for?" His left engine kept coughing out until he upped the mixture and it recovered. Arriving over his primary, the Yokohama dockyards, Bill found them defended with barrage balloons and went looking for other targets while under heavy assault from AA fire. Evading the ack-ack, the crew watched the balloons exploding on every side of them. They saw a huge fire to the far east of Tokyo; later they'd learn these were the camouflaged storage tanks taken out by the men of *Hari Kari-er.* At the height of the fire, *Fickle Finger* rose to eleven hundred to get past the balloons and AA, and targeted some factories. The crew was able to watch bombardier Waldo Bither detonate the Ogura Oil Refining Plant with two hits. Bower then saw a power plant, and flew so Waldo could strafe it with his .30, after which "sparks were seen to fly from the building and transformers."

Plane thirteen would arrive over the Japanese coast with Mitchells eleven and twelve still in view. Once again no one aboard could figure out where the hell they were. Finally navigator Clayton Campbell announced that he thought they had wandered far off course, maybe a hundred miles north. Pilot Lt. Edgar "Mac" McElroy took his word and jockeyed left, while copilot Dick Knobloch watched out the window as eleven's Ross Greening turned right and twelve's Bill Bower went straight. Which crew's navigator knew where he was going?

Trying to get past Tokyo, the men of thirteen were greeted by a mass of fighters and AA fire, and Mac decided to drop his bombs sooner rather than later. By now the Japanese guns had almost entirely taken down the barrage balloons, and the Americans were able to inflict quite a bit of damage on Yokohama. Although bombardier Bob Bourgeois missed the intended on his first strike, his demolition fell into drydock, where it set on fire a merchant ship being turned into an aircraft carrier. The *Lucky Thirteen* would also provide a historic service, as copilot Dick Knobloch explained: "I had a little camera that I had picked up in the exchange at the Sacramento Air Depot. . . . I took pictures out of the right side just as we were going over the target and pictures out of the left side. People say, 'How in the world can you be taking pictures when you are supposed to be bombing a target and so busy?' Well, a copilot is sort of useless many times. The bombardier is dropping the bombs, and the pilot is flying the airplane. About all the good I was [doing] there was to serve sandwiches."

Though every one of Doolittle's Mitchells had both movie and still cameras installed to record documentary proof of their strikes, because of what would happen to these men over China, Knobloch's would be the only combat photos that survived the mission.

Florence Wells, an American teacher, was on the interurban train when it stopped in the Yokohama station. A guard yelled from the platform: "Everybody out! Go down to the passage under the tracks."

"Why?" Miss Wells wanted to know.

"It's orders!"

The commuters, assuming there was merely something wrong with the train, patiently and quickly exited the cars and walked downstairs to a pedestrian underpass. They could hear the Billies overhead but thought nothing of it. After about fifteen minutes, the guard yelled, "All clear! All clear!"

Miss Wells's destination that afternoon was Yokohama's New Grand Hotel, where she spoke with the manager. "I see the Japanese fliers are practicing," she said, making conversation. "That wasn't Japanese practicing," Mr. Nomura explained. "It was the Americans. It was the real thing."

On its way in, plane fourteen's crew found that both its AFCE autopilot and .30 caliber nosegun were out of commission. Pilot Jack Hilger suddenly had to ratchet up to a thousand feet to get over a line of hills missing from their maps. Gunner Ed Bain wasn't so nervous as to lose his appetite; he had a peanut-butter-and-jelly sandwich that Dick Knobloch had given out, at the last minute, from the *Hornet* galley. They flew over a park where a crowd was watching a baseball game, and it reminded many of home. Hilger looked at all the little towns and the people going about their lives, and started having second thoughts: How could they bomb regular human beings? Then he remembered Pearl Harbor.

They were hit with plenty of ack-ack, but flew above it. At first they had trouble matching up what turned out to be the small town of Nagoya with the big city they were expecting from their target folder. Finally Hilger spotted two crucial landmarks, the local radio station tower and a huge cemetery, and took her right in. Bombardier Herb Macia had no trouble hitting his primaries: the Mitsubishi Aircraft Works, the Matsuhigecho oil warehouse, the Nagoya Castle military barracks, and the Nagoya arsenal.

After completing their run, Hilger spotted some oil tanks and took a power dive so Ed could give them a nice strafing. Engineer Jake Eierman watched a woman shake her mop at them, and couldn't help but notice Ed Bain's fists. They were clenched, and dripping with jelly.

Like Hilger, Don Smith and the crew of fifteen had to make a few unexpected detours along the way: "It became necessary to bear to the northwest to avoid a 2,500-foot mountain which was located about four miles northeast of the center of Osaka. This mountain was not located on the H.O. Chart used. At this point some doubt as to their position was felt by the crew." While getting their bearings, the men listened to an excellent radio station. From his compass indicators Smith knew it was broadcasting from Tokyo, but after an hour it suddenly stopped playing music and started up with a shrieking alarm. Then there was a shouting Japanese voice no one could understand, followed by forty-five seconds of alarm, and then dead silence.

Arriving over Kobe, gunner Doc White was surprised to find zero defense waiting for them. Everyone had assumed from the broadcast siren that the city would be up in arms, but the only other aircraft they saw the entire way in was a passenger plane. After bombardier Sess Sessler accurately got off his drops on the Kawasaki Aircraft Factory, the dockyards, the Electric Machinery Works, and the Uyenoshita Steel Works #2, some desultory AA fire opened up, but it didn't even come close.

From his seat in the nose, plane sixteen bombardier Jacob DeShazer had a clear view of all Japan. As *Bat Out of Hell* passed over the mountains on its way to Nagoya, Jake was amazed that people lived at such altitudes, and in such isolation. He watched a gray-bearded man, hearing the plane, throw himself to the road in terror.

Some enemy pursuits chased *Bat*, but Bill Farrow was able to evade them by flying into the clouds. Jake targeted and struck an oil tank and an aircraft factory: "We were making a complete turn, and I smelled smoke. I wanted to see how an oil refinery looked when it was on fire. To the left of us I saw where the first bombs had dropped. There was fire all over the tank, but it had not blown up yet. What I was smelling, however, was the powder of the shells that were being shot at us instead of the bombs I had dropped. I had noticed a little black smoke cloud right in front of us and evidently the hole in the nose of our airplane allowed the smoke to come inside."

Crouching in his dorsal bubble, Harold Spatz was the only *Bat* crewman to notice a squadron of eight Japanese pursuits now right on their tail. They came so close he could see the glints of their weapons being fired, and started sighting them in his own .50 caliber machine. But with its payload gone, *Bat* proved much faster than the fighters, and they soon fell from visual range.

"We skimmed along down a valley on our way to the ocean," Jake De-Shazer remembered. "I was getting ready to shoot. There is something about being shot at that makes you want to shoot back. I had read in the newspapers one time about a German aviator shooting at French people, and I thought it was a mean thing to do. I made up my mind while on the *Hornet* that I would not shoot at civilians. But after they shot at us, I changed my mind.

"I saw a man standing in a fishing boat, waving as we came along. He thought that we were Japanese. I thought that I would show him that we weren't. I shot a few shots near him, and the poor fellow stopped waving. I wasn't a very good shot, however, and therefore no harm was done."

In an amazing quid pro quo, Doolittle and his men had followed Admiral Yamamoto's December 7 game plan to the letter (even to the point of suffering through similarly rough weather during their carrier takeoffs). Special Aviation Project #1 turned out to be just as much of a surprise to *Dai Nippon Teikoku* as Operation Z had been to the United States. Tokyo military intelligence just could not imagine that the Allies were capable of attacking their homeland. When picket boat *Nitto Maru* failed to send a confirmation message, its initial broadcast was dismissed as a false alarm, as were all the various reports from the patrol planes and the ships of Tokyo harbor. The mild damage to the fuselage of Dick Joyce's plane ten was the only hit that all of Japan could muster. Just as had been the case on the other side of the Pacific a mere four months earlier, one warning after another had been ignored by a foe too arrogant to pay heed.

As the army airmen were bombing their way into history, the sailors of Task Force 16 were anxiously awaiting the empire's counterattack. Japan's home island defenses may have been lax and its army intelligence dismissive, but its navy responded immediately, and with full force. The Combined Fleet was at that moment ordering carriers *Akagi, Soryu, Hiryu, Zuikaku,* and *Shokaku;* heavy cruisers *Aito, Takao, Maya, Nachi, Haguro,* and *Myoko;* nine submarines; ten destroyers, and 208 attack planes directly east in pursuit of *Hornet, Enterprise,* and their battle group.

The heavy clouds and watery squalls that had made launching the Mitchells such a difficult enterprise, however, now served as a benevolent screen for Halsey, Mitscher, and their TG. *Enterprise* radar spotted aircraft en route to their position, which the Americans assumed were scout patrols, but all turned back due to poor visibility. Japan would send out fifty-two scout planes to look for Task Force 16, and all of them would return to base with nothing to report.

"The Japs chased us all the way home, of course," Halsey remembered. "Whenever we tracked their search planes with our radar, I was tempted to unleash our fighters, but I knew it was more important not to reveal our position than to shoot down a couple of scouts. They sent a task force after us; their submarines tried to intercept us; and even some of their carriers joined the hunt; but with the help of foul weather and a devious course, we eluded them." Ironically it was the encounter with the *Nitto Maru* that may in fact have saved Task Force 16. The War Department would later come to believe that if they'd followed the original plan, "an interception of [Doolittle's] pathfinding plane on its flight into Japan could have conceivably resulted in an attack force of Japanese bombers finding the *Hornet.*"

The TG's path home to Hawaii was littered with the small patrol boats of Japan's picket-line defense system, and Halsey wanted to make sure they would not survive to cause any more trouble. At 1130, *Enterprise* launched two three-plane scouting parties from Bomber Squadron 3. Twenty minutes later Ens. R. K. Campbell tracked down one picket boat outfitted with a huge radio antenna. He attacked three times, twice with bombs and once strafing with machine guns, but failed to inflict significant damage.

At 1152, Lt. R. W. Arndt discovered another enemy vessel. He dropped eight bombs on it, and missed every time. Ens. J. C. Butler discovered two more. He bombed and strafed both, and felt fairly certain he'd sunk at least one. Later that afternoon a small enemy sub was discovered and attacked, but it escaped. Thirteen more enemy craft would be detected that day by sight and radar, but these would not be pursued.

The race home, unfortunately, would include two deaths. Coming back from scouting, bomber pilot G. D. Randall and radioman T. A. Gallagher ran out of gas and crashed into the Pacific. They could not be found and were assumed to have drowned.

Besides an all-out Japanese reprisal, the other thing the TG men awaited that day was news from Tokyo. They knew the Doolittle boys would be striking steadily from around 1200 to 1400. The *Hornet* and *Enterprise* radio rooms constantly scanned the airwaves, frequently tuning in to Japan's propaganda station, JOAK. At 1345 one of JOAK's regular female announcers, nicknamed "Lady Haw Haw" (after a famed Nazi propagandist), interrupted her smooth commentary with a scream. Then: "A large fleet of enemy bombers appeared over Tokyo this afternoon [causing] much danger to non-military objectives and some damage to non-military objectives and some damage to factories. The known death toll is between three thousand and four thousand so far. No planes were reported shot down over Tokyo. Osaka was also bombed. Tokyo reports several large fires burning." Just as suddenly her broadcast stopped entirely.

When Stephen Jurika translated the announcement and gave it to Pete Mitscher, who in turn loudspeakered it across *Hornet* and semaphored it to the other ships, elated cheers and whoops erupted, roaring from deck to deck. Pearl Harbor had been avenged, and the navy had proved critical to the mission.

China was also listening to JOAK that day, and it was the best news the Chinese could ever hope to have. Chungking, the Kuomintang capital, had been bombed 107 times by Japanese air raids over the past ten years. Now invincible Japan, winner of every battle, had itself been bombed! The news was released through special printings of local papers and announcements throughout the country's movie theaters. Chiang Kai-shek's war minister declared: "The nightmare of the Japanese militarists can be shattered only by bombs. These raids on Japan proper are only the beginning." An army man stationed in Chungking, Lieutenant Miller, would cable Washington: "Chinese newspapers reported that 120,000 people had suffocated in Tokyo as a result of smoke and fumes caused by the fires there. The supposition is, if this is true, that possibly large masses of the populace rushed to underground railway stations and were trapped. This information supposedly came from Tokyo as it was reported under a Tokyo item in a Chinese newspaper. A Japanese broadcast was heard in China on Monday, April 20, to the effect that the fires in Tokyo were then under control. . . ."

The Task Force 16 radio operators picked up more broadcasts. These reports, which had obviously been cleared by the government, asserted that nine enemy planes had been shot down, and urged all Japanese citizens to pray for enough rain to put out the fires started by the Americans. In eight foreign languages JOAK issued a follow-up: "The cowardly raiders purposefully avoided industrial centers and the important military establishments, and blindly dumped their incendiaries on a few suburban districts, especially on schools and hospitals." Home Minister Yuzawa Michio insisted that "the damage caused was very slight and no confusion was seen in the affected areas," while Tokyo's Air Defense chief of staff dismissed the attack as merely a good training experience for his men. Later the *Nichi Nichi* newspaper said that "the enemy's daring enterprise failed to achieve any results worth mentioning," while the *Japan Advertiser* claimed: "The few enemy planes that did manage to slip through the defense cordon failed to get near any of the establishments of military importance, which were too well guarded. Hence the planes were forced to fly around aimlessly over the suburbs of Tokyo, dropping incendiary bombs on schools and hospitals, machine-gunning innocent civilians and hitting at least one elementary school pupil before being brought down or driven away."

After the war MacArthur's occupying forces would uncover Japanese documents itemizing the actual damage caused by the Doolittle Raid: fifty dead, 252 wounded, ninety buildings damaged or destroyed, including the Japanese Diesel Manufacturing Company, the Japanese Steel Corporation's Factory Number One, the Mitsubishi Heavy Industrial Corporation, the Communication Ministry's transformer station, the National Hemp and Dressing Company, the Yokohama Manufacturing Company warehouse, the Nagoya Aircraft Factory, an army arsenal, a naval laboratory, an airfield, an ammunitions dump, nine electric power buildings, six gas tanks, a garment factory, a food storage warehouse, a gas company, two miscellaneous factories, six wards of the Nagoya Second Temporary Army Hospital, six elementary or secondary schools, and innumerable nonmilitary residences. The U.S. Army's official report, on the other hand, would conclude that "the material loss to the United States was $3,200,000." The tally may not add up to an overwhelming achievement in and of itself, but over the course of the war, the raid would in fact have significant repercussions.

That night, the chief of *Hornet*'s air group, Stanhope Ring, composed a shanty:

> *Was the 18th of April in forty-two*
> *When we waited to hear what Jimmy would do.*

Little did Hiro think that night
The skies above Tokyo would be alight
With the fires Jimmy started in Tokyo's dives
To guide to their targets the B-25s.
One if by land and two if by sea
But if from the air the signal was three
When all of a sudden from out of the skies
Came a basket of eggs for the little slanteyes
So Hiro and Tojo just buried their hands
Under the carpets and under the beds
Their posteriors turned into rising suns
As bombs they fell by tons and tons
Then a stab of pain made Hiro shiver
Was it his kidney or was it his liver?
Or was it perhaps; alack, alas
A returned Jap medal was assaulting his
(Honorable self) . . .

The only remaining problem for the sailors now returning home was that their good *Hornet* food, which the AAC boys remembered so fondly, had run out, and the TG was stuck with sprouted potatoes and Spam. The sailors also had their pockets picked, as the air corps men who hadn't been selected for the mission would at least stand up for their own. "Aboard the carrier *Hornet*, Gus Widhelm, the CO of one of the flying squadrons, a veteran poker player along with other shipmates, engaged the Army Air Corps in some plain and fancy poker," said Ross Greening. "By the time the B-25s took off for Tokyo, most of the Army boys who played poker were broke, and Gus was rolling in wealth, to say nothing of prestige. He forgot one thing, however. There were still some Army crew who didn't go on the raid that were still aboard. By the time the task force reached Pearl Harbor, revenge had been won—the Army cleaned Gus for eleven hundred dollars and cleaned every other Navy poker player of every cent they started to sea with."

The armada reached Hawaii in seven days, and there it heard more good news. Reporting back at Pearl, U.S. submarine *Thresher* said it had sunk a three-thousand-ton freighter in Yokohama Harbor, while *Trout* sank a tanker, two freighters, and a patrol vessel.

★

The *New York Times* front-page lead story, April 18, 1942 (April 19 in Asia):

JAPAN REPORTS TOKYO, YOKOHAMA BOMBED BY "ENEMY PLANES" IN DAYLIGHT; CLAIMS NINE

[Citing Japanese sources] Enemy bombers appeared over Tokyo for the first time in the current war, inflicting damage on schools and hospitals. Invading planes failed to cause any damage on military establishments, although casualties in the schools and hospitals were as yet unknown. This inhuman attack on these cultural establishments and on residential districts is causing widespread indignation among the populace. . . . Nine of the attacking planes were shot down and the rest repulsed by heavy anti-aircraft fire.

Other papers, such as Ohio's *Columbus Evening Dispatch,* carried further details, citing eyewitnesses in Tokyo: US WARPLANES RAIN BOMBS ON LEADING CITIES OF JAP EMPIRE; YANK BOMBING PLANES CARRY WAR TO ENEMY; TOKYO, YOKOHAMA, KOBE AND NAGOYA HIT IN THREE-HOUR OFFENSIVE. Journalists besieged the War Department, which evaded their questions by declaring that the U.S. government had no knowledge of the attacks, and besides, airplanes could bomb Japan without direct orders from Washington, couldn't they? The reporters were confused. Everyone in the United States wanted to bomb the hell out of Japan. If someone had finally managed to do it, why wasn't the army or navy taking credit?

At that moment, in fact, neither Marshall, Arnold, nor King had heard a single word from Doolittle, or from his mission officers, or from Stilwell or Chiang Kai-shek. What if these reports weren't enemy propaganda? What if the eyewitness accounts were true? If the Raiders had missed every single target, if more than half the force had been downed by the Japanese, then even considering how daring and suicidal this mission was to begin with, that result would be about as terrible as anyone could imagine, an out-and-out catastrophe. Until they received an official report from someone, the War Department would keep silent. That report, unfortunately, would be long in coming.

CRASH

As the airmen headed over the island of Kyushu and then across the vast East China Sea, they couldn't help but feel emotions that had so far been kept at bay. They were elated at having met their objective, or despondent at having missed it; exhausted by the hours of flying, coupled with their surging and spent currents of adrenaline; astonished at having survived enemy skies; and brooding about the next bend in the river. Would they make it to dry land? If so, would it be Japanese-held? If not, could they be rescued from a crash at sea?

Every crewman had been stunned by the lack of defense over the Japanese home islands, and now another shock would come their way. "We turned west over the China Sea and encountered a headwind," Doolittle remembered. "Hank Potter estimated we would run out of gas about 135 miles from the Chinese coast. We began to make preparations for ditching. I saw sharks basking in the water below and didn't think ditching among them would be very appealing."

Prevailing winds in East Asia blow from west to east, just as they do across the continental United States. Yet, just after Doolittle considered the prospects of swimming with sharks, and bare seconds after the American planes had fully exited enemy territory, the air itself reversed course.

The only other time a foreign nation had attempted a direct attack on Japan was seven hundred years earlier, when warlord Kublai Khan had sent an armada from China. That great Mongol fleet was destroyed by a typhoon, and ever since the Japanese had believed that their homelands were protected by a supernatural force, a *kamikaze*—a divine wind. The American airmen, fleeing the enemy, however, would now get their own *kamikaze*—a thirty-mile-an-hour tailwind moving east to west, pushing them toward the safety of Allied China. This gave the men an extra 250 miles or so they thought they'd never have; an astounding gift just when they needed it most. "We had looked at the target and weather information for years and years back for that season, and we just hadn't expected it," remembered Davey Jones. "We picked up this tailwind for a good five, six hours, and that's the only reason we all made it to the Chinese mainland.

"I remember, two or so hours out of Tokyo, my navigator called on the interphone and said, 'Hey, we got maybe within 150 miles before we gotta swim!' By the time we reached the southern tip of Japan, he said, 'Believe it or not, we got enough juice to make land.'

"Obviously that was comforting."

The squadron now turned to the closest of the Kuomintang-held airfields, Chuchow (or Chuhsien, now Zhuzhou), which lay more than twelve hundred miles from Japan. At their gas-conscious cruising speed of 150 mph, it would take another eight hours to reach. When it came to luck, however, their *kamikaze* would turn out to be a mixed blessing. The bizarre turn of weather that had eased their way across the China Sea had in fact been undermining the efforts of everyone trying to engineer their ground support. The significant question that Wu Duncan and Frog Low had never originally answered—If the fliers couldn't come back to a carrier, where would they go?—was still, four months later, not fully solved. The "friendly territory" where the men of Special Aviation Project #1 were supposed to touch down was in fact far from friendly and, at the moment, one of the most chaotic places on earth. What the relieved airmen couldn't possibly have known was that, even with George Marshall and Hap Arnold personally and directly involved in the effort, they still didn't have a safe place to land.

At that time China was a country that no American who hadn't been there could ever possibly hope to understand. Captivated by coverage of Chinese resistance to Japan's brutal series of invasions (which often referred to the beautiful Madame Chiang as an Asian Joan of Arc), the epics of Nobel laureate Pearl S. Buck, and the grand PR efforts of Foreign Minister (and Madame Chiang's brother) T. V. Soong, Americans had developed fantastically romantic notions about the nation and its people. FDR, for example, had grown up surrounded by Chinese household items and family tales about the luxuries of Shanghai, as much of the Delano family fortune had been made trading silk and tea for opium, and his lifelong hobby of stamp collecting had begun when his mother gave him some Chinese postage. In 1937 the era's leading media mogul, Henry Luce, born of missionary parents in China, would cap years of printing dramatic accounts of Kuomintang resistance and its great similarities to the American Revolution by featuring the Generalissimo and Madame Chiang on the cover of *Time* as "Man and Woman of the Year." A poll at that time revealed that 80 percent of Americans considered the Chinese their natural allies in the fight against fascism, as opposed to 40 percent who saw the British in that role. Americans so loved China, in fact, that the first nationally distributed paperback book was Buck's romantic epic *The Good Earth*.

The reality was something else altogether. China in 1942 was an ever-changing balance of power between Mao Zedong, Chiang Kai-shek, one million Japanese troops, two distinct American forces, and various independent warlords, the latter feudal chiefs still leading their nomadic guerrillas into battles over territory. For more than a decade the nation had suffered through civil war, repeated Japanese attacks, and a constant state of anarchy. Most of the recruits in what China referred to as its army wore straw sandals, shared one blanket among five men, and after being press-ganged out of the villages into forced service, typically died of starvation. Those who survived tended to be loyal not to the Kuomintang or the Communists but to their local rural leaders. As early as October 1941, the American naval attaché in Chungking Capt. R. E. Schuirmann, reported to Washington that, as far as considering China a vital part of any fight against Japan, "if such conception is seriously held by those controlling high strategy, it is fatally defective."

After ten years of invasion the Japanese had taken control of all of China's major seaports, urban areas, and lines of communication and transportation, destroying the nation's economy in the process. Famine was widespread across the countryside, and the only Chinese truly flourishing were those at the top of the political heap, who stayed ahead of inflation by pilfering foreign handouts and American Lend-Lease. When the United States trucked supplies in to China via the 715-mile Burma Road, thievery and corruption were so extreme that of every fourteen thousand tons leaving Lashio in Burma, only five thousand eventually reached the Nationalist capital of Chungking. In November 1944 an Office of Strategic Services unit would discover twenty warehouses just inside Free China (at the time defended by troops with weapons so antique that they were worthless) holding fifty thousand tons of weapons and ammunition, which the Kuomintang authorities explained had been kept aside in case of an emergency. To the Americans eventually stationed there, it looked as if the Kuomintang was doing nothing whatsoever to fight the Japanese empire. Eric Sevareid, then working in Chungking as a reporter, remarked that he was used to the idea of dictatorships using censorship and police terrorism to cover up their criminal behavior, but that Chiang's was the first he knew of to use these techniques to cover up the fact that his government was doing absolutely nothing. In fact the Generalissimo was deliberately applying minimal efforts in the fight against Tokyo to reserve his men and matériel for someone he considered a more serious foe: Mao.

In Washington knowledge of this chaos was limited. Even so, following Doolittle's original plan, George Marshall and Hap Arnold had first tried to get permission for the Raiders at least to refuel in Russia. Stalin, however, was in the middle of losing the European third of his country to the Wehrmacht, and absolutely had to maintain neutrality with Japan to protect his Siberian flank. Allowing an American retaliatory strike force any concessions at all would violate that neutrality as surely as a direct USSR declaration of war. The Russians, as much as they would have liked the Raiders' sixteen B-25s as a form of Lend-Lease, emphatically had to refuse.

Marshall and Arnold then turned to Gen. Joe Stilwell, chief of the China-Burma-India command. Fluent in Chinese after having served in the U.S. Fifteenth Infantry Regiment out of Peking, the general had personally witnessed the overthrow of the Qing Dynasty, the creation of the Republic of China, and the election of the country's first president. Just as they would for every military leader, America's war journalists were inspired to give the general a nickname—"Vinegar Joe." The "Vinegar" was not particularly apt—Stilwell's own men called him "Uncle," and one military historian quipped that if Saint Francis of Assisi had been given the China-Burma-India command, he'd be known today as "Vinegar Frank." Most likely the "Vinegar" tag stuck to Stilwell in the wake of his bestselling and posthumously published *Stilwell Papers,* originally written as private diaries: "I am just scribbling to keep from biting the radiator," he would note in the margins.

Adding to the difficulties of the Americans and Chinese trying to get landing spots for the Raiders was the ongoing Japanese invasion of Burma, which, because of the empire's control of every Chinese eastern seaport, served as the last connection between Allied supplies and Chiang's capital. Stilwell was simultaneously trying to follow Marshall and Arnold's orders to secure the Doolittle landing fields (a task he was forced to delegate to his air adviser, Brig. Gen. Clayton Bissell) while defending (and losing, and then ultimately retaking) Burma.

Besides Chiang, Mao, the local warlords, Stilwell, Burma, and the Japanese army, there was yet another force that had to be taken into account: Claire Chennault and his Flying Tigers. By 1942 the Tigers were in the process of being officially absorbed into the Army Air Corps, a move against which Chennault lobbied with committed fervor (and with the help of Chiang). The U.S. Army, however, had no intention of supporting a private air force that functioned outside established military channels. In the course of the merger, all but six of the original Tiger pilots would quit the field, and Chennault would be ordered to serve under Bissell.

In their constant squabbles over American aid and military strategy, Chennault would commonly take sides with Chiang against Bissell and Stilwell, and since Chiang wanted to do as little as possible against the Japanese, this led to four years of stalemate. Chennault would later claim that if only he'd been told about the Doolittle Raid, his forces could easily have brought the boys in safely. Since Marshall and Arnold considered Chennault untrustworthy, he was left entirely out of the loop on Special Aviation Project #1, as was Chiang himself. Knowing of a history of leaks to the Japanese, Marshall and Arnold decided to share as few details as possible about the mission with the leaders of the Kuomintang. At first Chiang refused their vague requests for help, and even Marshall and Arnold's direct threats were evaded. Finally they had to force him into cooperating.

The Generalissimo's reluctance stemmed from the certainty (shared by Stalin) that providing military support to the Americans could only lead to a massive Japanese retaliation. The Chinese had already spent years battling Tokyo, and Chiang knew all too well the kind of blood-lust carnage the Chrysanthemum Empire could unleash. Even he, however, could not imagine just how vicious the actual Japanese response to Doolittle's Raid would be.

Though the eastern China bases where Doolittle's men were supposed to refuel on their way to Chungking had in fact originally been prepped by the Tigers to use in their own bombing runs against Tokyo, these were not the kind of airports anyone stateside would recognize. Barely paved runways in the middle of nowhere, almost all of them unmanned and unprotected, these strips didn't even regularly stock the high-octane aviation fuel that the army pilots would need—or any other kind of fuel, for that matter. As Gregory "Pappy" Boyington, onetime marine ace of the Black Sheep Squadron, would remember from his Tiger days: "We stayed in the worst shit-holes you could imagine. . . . We were lied to about everything. The aircraft were garbage, with spare parts a virtual unknown and the tired engines barely able to get us off the ground. Every takeoff—let alone flight—resulted in a serious pucker factor. The maps we were supposed to use were the worst I had ever seen. Whoever made the maps had either never even been to those places or was more drunk than I was when they sat down to create those worthless objects."

The mounting problems in obtaining refueling stops for the Raiders in Kuomintang China's eastern airfields (Lishui, Kweilin, Kian, Yushan, and Chuchow, the latter two hundred miles south of Shanghai) are reflected in the army's official papers:

> By 10 March, Rangoon had to be fired and evacuated. . . . There followed the futile campaign to save Upper Burma. General Stilwell took command of the Chinese force as it moved south against the Japanese advance. . . . It was while Chungking was coping

with this organizational problem and Stilwell was in the middle of the campaign to save Mandalay and Lashio that their cooperation was asked in establishing certain stores and installations at a number of air fields in eastern China. . . .

In the middle of March, plans were started for providing refueling facilities and landing fields in China for the B-25s after the completion of their bombing mission. On 16 March, General Arnold requested information on the progress of airports and supplies of fuel and ammunition at those airports in eastern China. Stilwell reported to Arnold that the Standard Oil Company of Calcutta had five hundred gallons of 100-octane gas. . . . Arnold specified that 10,000 gallons of gas and 100 gallons of oil were to be left at Kweilin, and 5,000 and 100 of each respectively at Chuchow (Lishui), Kian, Chu-Chow and Yushan. Twelve men, including one who could speak English, were needed at each airport, with everything set to go by midnight 9–10 April. Flares were to mark the airport two hours before daybreak, 10 April as follows: five on each side of runway and five at windward end of runway, using oil cans if necessary. . . .

Stilwell reported on 29 March that Kweilin and Chuchow were safe for only heavy bomber operation, according to Chinese opinion. The Chinese disapproved the use of Yushan, Kian, or Lishui by heavy bombers, unless inspection was made by an American officer. . . . Personal verification (the only reliable method) of progress at fields was delayed by the crash and death of Colonel Georges, whose papers were destroyed therein. . . .

On 1 April, Arnold inquired of Stilwell as to whether or not a transmitter with frequency between 200 and 1600 kilo could be made available for temporary operation at an East China airport. . . . In reply to this query, Stilwell reported on 4 April that Kweilin, Chuchow, and Kian could provide homing radio stations . . . the number 57 was to be used for identification. . . .

On 1 April, the two most easterly fields . . . were bombed twice by the Japanese with pursuit support in daylight raids. . . . On 2 April, the three most eastern fields were bombed. . . . Lishui was bombed the following day with unreported consequences. . . .

On April 6 ten Pan Am DC-3s hauled thirty thousand gallons of avgas and five hundred gallons of oil from Calcutta to Asansol to Dinjan, India, for the eventual passage to eastern China. On April 13 Maj. E. N. Backus and Lt. Col. E. H. Alexander flew from Chungking to verify that the gas and oil had arrived from India, that lights and landing flares were available, that the DF (direction-finding) signals would be transmitted according to plan, and that there was at least one English speaker to translate and help the men continue on, as quickly as possible, to the safety of Chungking.

Backus and Alexander, however, found themselves helpless in the face of the very *kamikaze* that would give the Doolittle volunteers a heaven-sent push across the China Sea. Leaving from Chengtu in Curtiss Hawk III fighters, Alexander and Backus made little headway in the face of raging storms. Each tried to return to Chungking, only to discover that the zero-zero cover made landings impossible. Finally Backus felt he had no choice but to bail out, while Alexander swooped low enough to find a spit of sand in a nearby river. By the time the Chinese rescued them and the men returned to Chungking, four critical days had been lost.

As Army Air Corps Intelligence would report: "On 18 April, Alexander made another attempt. . . . But he could not land because of weather conditions and failure to establish radio contact. . . . On the morning of 19 April he was ordered back to Chungking from Kunming with no part of his mission accomplished. . . . Through his futile eight-hour attempt to get into Kweilin, the westernmost of the fields, on 18 April, Alexander proved by personal trial with the Chinese weather that the Expedition's luck would run out upon reaching the Asiatic mainland."

This was not the end of the bad news for the arriving volunteers. In crossing the international dateline, Task Force 16 had lost a day, moving directly from April 13 to April 15. The navy planners in Washington, however, had not taken this into account, and everyone in China trying to arrange for landing fields thought the planes would be arriving on the morning of the twentieth, when in fact they would appear a day earlier.

By the time Task Force 16 commanders realized this error, it was too late; they were on radio silence. Doolittle arranged for Halsey to have his team back at Pearl radio D.C. and Chungking about the mix-up immediately after the army airmen had lifted off. In the heat of the skirmish with the *Nitto Maru,* however, Halsey never got around to ordering that message. Doolittle would later speculate that the admiral may have felt that any signal at that moment of discovery by the enemy might seriously endanger his fleet.

In the end the airfields were never arranged, inspected, or supplied as planned, and the boys, already flying on a prayer, would find that some prayers go unanswered.

★

As the fifteen Mitchells neared land and night descended, their beautiful weather and helpful *kamikaze* suddenly stopped. One after another the airmen flew directly into the broad, thick path of the coastal storm that had brought down Backus and Alexander. The Raiders pulled their way through the soup, all the while fighting shifting currents that threw them in every direction. They couldn't get enough visual bearings to land or even to hazard a guess as to where they might be. What was most likely, in fact, was that they were nowhere near Free China.

To get to Chuchow, they had to pass over Chekiang and Kiangsi Provinces, a coastal area south of Shanghai and west of Taiwan that, for almost a decade, had been a war zone ruled by Japan. Running out of gas here would be almost certainly fatal, but it was either bail into the countryside and hope for the best, or attempt an ocean landing. Doolittle was the only one of them ever to have parachuted out of a plane before, but in the gathering darkness and storm cover, trying to find a landing spot would be unimaginably difficult.

The navigators listened intently for their "57" signal, but there were no beacons to guide them home. The only response was a dead silence. "We tried to contact the field at Chuchow on 4495 kilocycles," Doolittle remembered. "No answer. This meant that the chances of any of our crews getting to the destination safely was just about nil. Chuchow was situated in a valley about two miles wide and twelve miles long. Without a ground radio station to home in on, there was no way we could find it. All we could do was fly a dead-reckoning course in the direction of Chuchow, abandon ship in midair, and hope that we came down in Chinese-held territory."

Even the army's official report would use poetry to describe their fate: "The signal for which they listened did not come. For want of it, they groped their way forward. They had not been able to recognize any landmark where they made entry into the Asian mainland and some did not see the coastline at all, being on instruments when they crossed it. . . . Yet if these circumstances laid extraordinary stresses on the morale of the crews, it did not reflect itself in the conduct of a single member. . . . They had no feeling of chagrin that the Chinese arrangements had failed them, but only a sense of bitter disappointment that they had to abandon the ships which had carried them through."

The volunteers continued on their dead-reckoned courses. Some, in fact, would fly directly over Chuchow, but the roar of their cloud-covered planes would trigger an air raid alert and every light in the town would be extinguished. With no idea they'd reached their destination, the airmen would continue on.

As the gas gauges fell to nothing, needles knocking against their "empty" pegs and the engines beginning their last-gasp sputter, one by one most of the pilots yoked their Billys up as high as they dared and the crews bailed out, pulling ripcords into the unknown. Instead of the clear dawn that the mission planners had expected, however, these helpless boys would now be falling at 180 miles an hour in the dead of the night, through heavy thunderstorms and dense fog, into enemy-held territory on the other side of the world.

The one plane that had decided not to try for the Kuomintang airfields would in fact be the first to land, touching down on the other side of the continent from Chuchow. "At about a quarter to five, land came slowly into view on the horizon—tall mountains looming dark out of the sea," remembered plane eight copilot Bob Emmens. "Lord, what a welcome sight! They weren't really so high, they only seemed so to us, flying so low. We started climbing some and corrected our course slightly to the right where a point of land extended a little out into the sea. About three miles out, we turned ninety degrees right and flew north along the coastline. We thought if there was any possibility of having hit the coast south of the big jut of land where Vladivostok lies, we'd rather know about it now than after we crossed the shoreline."

While Bob and pilot Ski York shared a candy bar, navigator Nolan Herndon kept looking out the window, vainly trying to match the landmarks he spotted with those on his Russian charts. If Nolan could not determine the right course from his vague maps and dead-reckoning guesses, the crew could easily end up, not in Allied Russia, but in the Japanese-ruled territory of Korea. Finally Nolan told Ski and Bob he was sure they were out of danger, that they'd made it into Soviet airspace.

"It didn't seem a good idea to round the end of the point and come sailing into the port of Vladivostok big as life," Emmens said. "It was undoubtedly well defended. So we cut inland. As we turned, we could see, off to the left, the fingerlike projection of land extending seaward.

"'Let's find us a spot to sit down, what do you say?' said Ski.

"'A good idea,' I said.

"We were both thinking the same thing. You can't fly around over the seaboard area of a country at war without someone in that country eventually doing something about it.

"We were losing altitude now and turned right up the valley. Ahead of us, in the center of the valley, stretched a large square field with some dirty, white, tumbling, rather large buildings on one side. I could see a couple of small buildings with a few men dressed in long black coats standing watching us. Just as I spotted a small airplane under a camouflage net not far from the building, Ski hit my arm and said, 'Hell, it's an airport!'

"With that we turned slightly and lowered the nose to pick up speed, just in case some Russian 'happened' to notice a two-engine bomber roaring over an aircraft base on that vulnerable east coast and decided to shoot it down first and investigate later."

The Mitchell came down on a beautiful day in a perfect landing. "At last," thought Emmens. "Dry, good ground. It was a wonderful feeling."

More than a dozen men came over to have a look at the mysterious B-25. Ski got out, alone, while his crew watched, their pistols cocked and ready. As they approached, the strangers were grinning, and then they began laughing out loud. Ski turned back to his crew and smiled, and his men put away their guns and climbed down.

They could hear Ski asking about fuel, and getting no answer. He tried French, but no one understood that either. Bob attempted German, but again no one comprehended it. One of the Russians, clearly the leader, started talking a jumble none of the fliers could make out, until they picked up the word: "Americanski." The Raiders immediately replied "Americanski!" again and again, and the Russians laughed with relief.

As the sun was now going down and the Siberian chill was picking up, the Americans were taken to a small building with no heat. It reminded Bob of some kind of jail. The leader picked up a phone, and screamed into it. There was a knock at the door, and another man yelled out something. After about thirty minutes, the group motioned for them to follow.

They were taken to a dirty, dilapidated cement structure, which turned out to be the airfield's headquarters, and once inside to a small room, where a more senior officer smiled, asked them to sit, and tried to communicate. Again, no one could make himself understood. The Americans discussed among themselves how much of their mission they should reveal, when another Russian walked in with a large map of the world, and nailed it to the wall. Using sign language, he explained to them that they'd landed in Primorski, thirty miles from Vladivostok.

The senior officer again tried speaking to them in Russian, and Ski came to understand that he wanted to know the route that had brought them to the USSR. York walked over to the map, pointed to Alaska, and then traced an arc across the North Pacific to the Kamchatka Peninsula. He'd decided to tell nothing until they'd seen someone from the American Embassy. "The door opened abruptly and in stalked a young, healthy-looking Russian officer, obviously a pilot," Emmens remembered. "He wore a fur cap and fur-lined jacket and trousers, which indicated he must have landed a short time before. He was smiling as he faced us and nodded politely. He and our host up to this time talked brusquely for a moment and then with a severe attitude, yet still keeping a smile on his face, he indicated that he wished Ski's story about from whence we'd come told to him.

"Ski muttered something about 'This guy's no dummy,' and went to the map again. As before, his finger started at Alaska. He looked at our new host, who showed no change of expression, but waited patiently while Ski went through our dreamed-up flight. . . . Our friend's eyes were waiting for Ski's when Ski turned around, and with a friendly smile and almost a twinkle in his eye, he slowly shook his head—and put his finger emphatically on Tokyo, Japan. Ski did as good a job as he could at keeping a poker face, and also shook his head and quickly traced from Alaska to Vladivostok without stopping. Our guest this time laughed out loud, but not sneeringly—more as if he were enjoying a good joke, and again put his finger on Tokyo, Japan. He nodded politely with his friendly smile at Ski, then at the rest of us, and turned on his heel and was gone."

When the men asked about a bathroom, they were taken to a little shack that had holes cut into a board over an open trough, a floor of bare ground, and no roof. In Siberia. The stench was astounding. When they finished Nolan Herndon joked: "Just like home!" They were next taken to a banquet. "The food, all except the meat and potatoes, was strange to us," Emmens said. "But it tasted wonderful. The vodka had quite an effect on us, with our not having eaten all day. And our hosts seemed genuinely hurt if we refused anything. We had more vodka and another kind of wine which smelled and tasted like ether to me. I stuck to vodka. During the meal we toasted Stalin, and the Russians toasted Roosevelt. We toasted the Soviet Air Force, and they toasted ours. We both toasted our inevitable victory over Germany and fascism. A couple of times we again brought up the subject of gasoline for our airplane and of our departure the following day. We didn't recognize the subtle Soviet brush-off we were getting each time we mentioned it, and after a few more vodkas, we didn't particularly care."

When Ski again asked for one-hundred-octane gas, and to be allowed to get in touch with the American Embassy, the colonel answered: "You must rest now. Everything will be taken care of in due time." York: "When we went to bed that night, we were fully confident we were going to leave the next morning. But the next morning a general showed up along with the divisional commissar—the equivalent-ranking civilian town official. Evidently they had communications from higher headquarters. It was during a five-hour breakfast with the general and the commissar that, when questioned specifically about Tokyo's having been bombed, we admitted that we had been part of that mission." After an afternoon nap, the men were brusquely awakened and told to hurry; their plane was ready and waiting. They rushed out to discover that the waiting craft wasn't their Mitchell but a DC-3.

As they took off, they looked out the windows for one last sight of their Billy. When they tried to ask, "Where are we going?" their interpreter replied, "You will learn everything in due time." Maybe, they thought, they were on their way to the American consulate? Perhaps they were even being transported to some base where planes would take them home? Then there was always the possibility they were being delivered to Korea or Manchuria, to be turned over to the Japanese.

When the DC-3 finally landed, the pilot pointed out the window and announced: "Khabarovsk!" which meant nothing to the airmen. They were driven to a building at the edge of the field, and taken inside. There, behind a huge desk, stood a short but enormous bald man, whom Bob remembered looking like a beady-eyed gorilla. His female translator introduced them to General Stern of the Far Eastern Red Army, and through her, they were interrogated. Stern then made a long statement in Russian, looking into the eyes of each member of the crew in turn. When he finished the translator stood up and said: "The general has asked me to tell you that according to a decision reached between our two governments and by direction of orders from Moscow, you will be interned in the Soviet Union until such a time as further decisions are made in your case. You will commence your internment immediately in quarters which have been prepared for you outside the city of Khabarovsk. You will be given proper protection and attempts will be made to make you comfortable. I must ask you to obey all orders from the officer who will be in charge. Do you have any requests to make at the present time?"

In plane one Doolittle circled twice over where he thought Chuchow must be, looking for a break in the clouds but finding nothing but soup. He waited until the last possible minute to casually announce over the interphone: "We'll have to bail out." Jimmy turned on his AFCE autopilot to keep the plane steady and shut off the gas cocks. The crew tugged on their harnesses and checked their musette bags.

Experienced skydivers are familiar with the pull of an opening chute and the tug of mile-high winds, so they attach their gear to their bodies as tightly as possible. They understand exactly when to pull a ripcord, how to tug at the wires to change the drop's speed and direction, and how to land as smoothly as possible, taking into account the wind and terrain. The volunteers had no experience with any of this. The only one of the eighty who'd jumped out of a plane before was their commander, who assumed that on this jump he was going to break his ankles all over again.

The Army Air Corps always bailed out in reverse order of rank, so plane one bombardier Fred Braemer would be first to learn these lessons. After he made a quick pull on the cord, the wind buffeted his chute. As Fred yanked his lines to try and get a more solid descent, the storming winds spun him further, unsnapping his gunbelt, which flew off into the wet darkness.

After everyone but the flight-deck men had evacuated, it was copilot Dick Cole's turn: "I dove out head first facing the rear of the ship. This caused me to scrape or drag on the sides of the hatch. Fortunately, it didn't affect the operation of the chute. . . . The descent seemed like ages. The clouds, rain, and fog were so thick nothing could be seen, so I just waited."

"We hit the China Coast just below Ningpo, and it was getting dark just about that time, and General Doolittle was still in view ahead; we had followed him all along," remembered plane two pilot Trav Hoover. "The weather was definitely bad; visibility was very poor and clouds came right down to the sea—the ceiling was zero at the coastline (it was impossible to tell whether they were islands or a peninsula). We were actually on the mainland, but we did not know that until the next morning." At the coast navigator Carl Wildner was able to get the briefest glimpse through the clouds, line up his charts, and figure out that they were directly over Japanese territory. Carl told Trav to head southwest, which led to a range of mountains not indicated on their hand-colored maps. Trav climbed to pass over them, only to have the left engine start coughing and stop dead. The Mitchell began to wobble and fall. Trav flicked open the fuel booster pump, but when nothing happened, he pushed his joystick forward, taking a chance with a dive. Gas in the rear of the plane flowed into the wing tanks; the engine caught and came back to life. He climbed again to cross the range, and the engine died once more. He dived, the engine coughed back to action, and he tried to climb again.

Three times Trav and his copilot, Lt. William "Foggy" Fitzhugh, attempted a pass over the mountains, and each time the engine stopped. Now they were really stuck. The plane couldn't clear, and it couldn't gain enough altitude to afford the men a safe bailout. "I started to look for a place to land along the coastline," Hoover remembered. "The gas gauge read ten gallons in each of the front tanks and forty gallons in the two rear tanks." Time was running out.

It had been an hour since Bob Gray and *Whiskey Pete* had crossed over the coast, and nobody could see a thing. Someone had the idea to throw out some chute flares for illumination, which they did, but there still was no sign of flat land. They knew their gas would run out at any moment, and their only recourse would be to jump. After navigator Chuck Ozuk and bombardier Aden Jones vanished through the forward hatch, copilot Shorty Manch checked with his flashlight to make sure that gunner Leland Faktor had made it out the rear, and then "grabbed a box of cigars and candy bars and stuffed them in my jacket. Then I bundled up my private arsenal, a 44-40 Winchester rifle, German Luger, two .45 automatics, and .22 automatic, and an ax and a Bowie knife and got ready to go.

"As I went out I watched the two exhaust stacks go over my head, then reached for the D-ring on my chute but couldn't find it. Scrambling frantically, I finally found it dangling at my side and pulled. Since I only had a twenty-four-foot chute, which was too small for my weight, the opening shock was something I wasn't ready for. I saw red, and the impact jerked my Bowie knife, ax, canteen, and all my guns away, except the one in my holster. The box of cigars disappeared out of my jacket and the Baby Ruths were shucked, leaving nothing but the wrappers.

"Coming down, I thought I heard waves breaking on a beach and the horrible thought came to me that I had sent the rest of the crew out without their Mae West life vests on. They would surely drown if we were over the ocean and not over land as we figured."

"Direct westerly course taken on 29th parallel. No landfall possible due to overcast," reported plane five navigator Gene McGurl. "Computed ETA at coast and checked same on arrival. Checked ground speed and figured ETA at Chuchow (Chuhsien). Overcast and zero visibility made visual location impossible. Computation alone gave the position and the ruggedness of surrounding country made knowledge of exact position of paramount importance."

His pilot, Davey Jones, climbed to get some visibility: "Our last fixed point was the southern tip of Kyushu, and it was seven hundred miles to the coast, so we'd gotten by entirely on dead reckoning. You didn't know where the hell you were. It became obvious we were getting pretty close to land because the color of the water changed. So I pulled up to about 5,000 feet to avoid the mountains and the bad weather.

"When we reached our ETA, we decided to put out a flare, to see what was below. At that time, planes carried two powerful parachute flares; they floated down with the big light, and we could see a river. We conferred as a crew, and we said, 'Let's try the river.' Then the flare got down below the cloud, and we realized we were in mountains and there was no way we could possibly land.

"We kept heading west, and decided to bail. On the B-25 there's a navigator well—a compartment—and there's a hatch on the floor there, and that's where you get in and out of the airplane."

"My bailout was a very frightening experience," said gunner Joe Manske. "We were out of gas in closed-in weather conditions. I was first out of our ship, and didn't realize how far each of us would be separated on the ground. After my chute opened, I panicked, being a small-frame person, weighing about 110 pounds. With the weather socked in, I had nothing to compare my descent with. Being so light, I thought I was suspended and not falling."

"You blow that hatch and you go out through that black hole, and that's pretty bad," Davey Jones said. "You don't have the vaguest idea where you are, it's ten o'clock at night, and black as hell. Everybody else went out first, and I'm in that damn airplane by myself, and you know you gotta go out that hole, and I'm just scared. Just scared! I never used a parachute before. So I went out the damn hatch, and you face the rear, and the air blew me against the fuselage. I'm hanging on with my arms stretched out, and my last fingernail broke, and I pull the ripcord."

"With no visibility downward or upward, we had to trust entirely on our watches and our compass to guess at our approximate position. As navigator I felt like excess baggage," said plane nine's Tom Griffin.

"However, hope springs eternal. It was at this moment that a rift appeared in the clouds overhead and a lone star shone through! Four sets of eyes were turned on me. 'Griffin! A star! Get a fix!' Their eyes told me that somehow this was to be our salvation—if I could produce.

"I did not point out the dubious value of a fix. Nor did I attempt to point out that in celestial navigation, at least two heavenly bodies must be used to obtain a fix, and that they must be charted navigational bodies known to the navigator and that they must be separated so as to produce two lines, the nearer to perpendicular to each other the better. With those four sets of eyes on me it did not seem the moment to start a class in elementary navigation.

"I stepped back and picked up my octant, wondering just what I was going to do. I started sighting our strange dim star. I could feel those eyes on me tensely. After several moments of sighting, the storm once more entirely engulfed the plane. The star appeared no more. I was off the hook and once more excess baggage.

"After fifteen and a half hours in the air, our motors gave the sputtering sound we had long been waiting for. The bottom hatch was opened, and one by one we eased down through the black hole into nothing.

"Jumping at night and in a storm is an experience one will never forget. There were times during that descent from ten thousand feet when I thought I had missed the earth. I seemed to be suspended in a blank, silent void with no feeling of movement.

"The wind currents at the time must have been violent because I remember just being able to see my chute. It seemed to have a life of its own. It would descend to a level with me and start to collapse—I was afraid it would spill all of its air—then it would fill and swing overhead and descend to the other side, where it would once again collapse. I was, of course, in a great pendulum with no feeling of movement at all. Then it would swing up over my head, fill up, and come down on the other side, once again spilling its air."

Like all the others who had come to the decision to abandon ship, the last to jump from *Whirling Dervish* was pilot Hal Watson. After everyone else had gone and the plane was on autopilot, Hal was just finishing up his packing when the left engine coughed and went dead. He started toward the forward hatch but was suddenly yanked back; his chute and belt were tangled in the cockpit armor plate.

As the right engine sputtered and stopped, Watson struggled with the lines and his belt, finally freeing himself. He raced to the hatch and jumped before the plane fell too low to be safe. He quickly pulled the chute cord, and screamed out in pain, for the lines had wrapped around his right arm, and when the chute opened, its force against his two-hundred-plus-pound body yanked his shoulder right out of its socket. As he fell he tried to untwist the injured arm from the lines, finally succeeding. It fell limply to his side, useless.

Hal crashed, on his back, into a stream. The force of the water's current and the excruciating pain in his arm left him paralyzed. He couldn't roll in either direction and couldn't escape from his harness with only one hand. He pulled out a morphine tube and, using his teeth, broke the seal, but the attempt snapped off the Syrette's needle. He pulled out the other, remaining ampoule, and this time managed it successfully.

Hal Watson jabbed the drug into his arm. The horrible pain fell away to nothing, and he passed out, just as he'd prayed.

★

"The weather was just stinking from the ground up," remembered plane ten's Sally Crouch. "With those red lights on and it dark like that, it looked like hell in there, red illumination, the mouth of hell, because you can't turn that red light off, it will be on until you either land or crash." Over the interphone, pilot Dick Joyce told his crew that he couldn't find a landing spot in the dark, and that when the clouds parted, all they could see was a mountain. He pulled up to 9,000, slowed to 125, and said: "I figure that we will be out of gas in less than fifteen minutes, so it looks like we will have to bail out. Horton, you first, then Larkin, then Sally, then Stork. Larkin, you wait till Horton is gone before you release the forward door—it might hit him. O.K. fellows, I'll see you in Chuchow."

Like every gunner, plane ten's Eddie Horton had spent almost the entire flight from *Hornet* to China entirely alone, cut off from the rest of the crew in his rear bubble. In the middle of this fearsome bailout, pilot Dick Joyce had to laugh out loud when the shy, taciturn Eddie said, just before jumping: "Thanks for a swell ride!"

"They simply told us back in those days that it don't mean a thing if you don't pull that string," Sally Crouch said. "One, two, three, four, I remember telling myself don't get excited. And then I said to hell with it, and I pulled my ripcord. The next thing, why, it was just like somebody hitting me in the face. The shock of the chute opening. We had some men in our organization actually have their GI shoes, fully laced up, jerked off their feet. I had on chukker boots which only have three eyes in them and lace up only to ankle height, but I did not lose my shoes.

"As I'm falling, I hear this noise, *whop whop,* like popping a wet towel. Lo and behold, as best as I could determine, those of us that had on these chest-type parachutes had only a single lead of shroud line instead of two on either side to help stabilize. I was swinging underneath the canopy, almost up equal, and as I would swing up in one direction, it would empty the air out of the top side of the parachute, and it would *whop* like popping a towel. In addition to that, the wind was rotating the canopy and it was winding the shroud lines up in front of me into a single cord. If that continued, it could reduce the size of my canopy and cause me to have a much higher rate of fall.

"I attempted to pull myself up, but the opening shock had been like somebody hitting you with their fist. It weakens you. So I then rotated my body in the opposite direction to unwind it, and got it down far enough to where I could stick my fingers in there to keep it from winding up any further."

"I left the engines of the ship running," Dick Joyce said. "I dropped clear of the ship and pulled the ripcord and the chute opened and functioned perfectly, except that the metal sheared on one of the leg strap buckles and the leg strap on my left leg parted, and almost dropped me out of the chute. I slid down and the chest strap came up and smacked me in the chin with a stunning blow and at the same time, jerked my pistol out of my shoulder holster and tossed it out into space.

"I estimate that I floated about one minute. I heard the plane below me, and it hit the side of a mountain and exploded and burst into flame.

"A few seconds later I hit the ground, which was quite a surprise to me."

Before reaching landfall Ross Greening threw *Hari* into a nosedive, draining the rear fuel into the wing tanks. He hoped that if he could then pull above the soup, Frank Kappeler might get a celestial fix off the nighttime sky. They rose, only to have ice begin forming rapidly on the wings, and realized the gambit wouldn't work. They descended and continued on instruments, Kappeler setting a course by dead reckoning.

Instead of a homing signal, the only radio broadcast they could get was a Russian playing the cello, which to Greening made "the situation seem even more ominous and unreal." Using their estimated location and the names of nearby towns from his charts, Frank drew maps for each of the men. They agreed, after bailing out, to follow whatever streams they could find to a river, and from there get to the nearest village. Before abandoning the plane, Mel Gardner suggested that if they could see a light below, it might mean a rice paddy was nearby, and they could then toss their flares and land in it. Everyone thought that landing was a better choice than bailing, and Ross agreed to give it a go. He dropped to 4,500 and turned on the lights. Immediately trees brushed against the wings, and a hill appeared, dead ahead. They climbed back to 10,000 and prepared for the inevitable. "All our reserve tanks were drained to the last drop," remembered copilot Ken Reddy, "and the main tanks were reading much lower than I had ever seen before, or hope to see again.

"I could not get my gun belt under my parachute so I held it in my mouth in order to have my hands free. The belt had my .45, a small first-aid kit, a canteen of water, and two sets of clips. I crawled down through the hole, dropping my legs out first, then I turned loose. I was out in the darkness; the plane roared away before you could say scat. I changed the belt to my left hand from my mouth, and pulled the ripcord. Nothing happened. I pulled it harder and damn near blacked out. The impact was so hard that it pulled the clip holders off my belt. The breast straps were loose enough that they caught me under the chin; the bruise was not bad. This could have been when I chipped a small piece off of my teeth.

"I shined my flashlight on the chute. It really looked tiny, oscillating back and forth in the wind. All was *very* quiet. About that time I saw a black space in the fog. Just as I was trying to ascertain whether it was an opening or a mountain, one hell of a big jar answered my question."

"We wished each other luck, and then came the most fearsome event of my life: I jumped out of the plane into the night," Bill Birch said. "The fact that we weren't absolutely certain as to what we were jumping into was a big worry. Would we land in the ocean, a river, a lake, flat or mountainous terrain, or onto some Japanese soldier's bayonet?

"As it turned out, we abandoned our plane approximately eighty miles inland from the coast, but still in Japanese-held territory. When I hit the ground I landed between two pine trees on about a thirty-degree slope. Unable to see more than a few feet, I covered up in my chute and slept until it started to get light."

"I was the third person to leave the plane," Frank Kappeler remembered. "When my chute opened, my flashlight, which was lit, fell off of my belt, and I watched it fall in a spiral down below me and disappear. My chute's shroud lines seemed to be twisted all the way up to the canopy. I got the thought that maybe the chute wasn't opened all the way. I extended my arms between the twisted lines trying to straighten them out and as a result, I started going around in circles. I started to feel dizzy and sick to my stomach when suddenly my chute caught in some high branches of some trees and I landed gently in a sitting position on a steep hillside. It was pitch black, and each time that I tried to stand up, I would slip down the hillside four or five feet. My canteen and revolver were under my back and because of the twisted shroud lines, I couldn't roll over, so I decided to stay put until daylight. I couldn't get comfortable, and a light rain fell on my face all night."

After everyone else had gone, Ross found himself with last-minute second thoughts: He just couldn't abandon *Hari*. One look at the gas gauges reading zero, however, changed his mind.

He got prepped, fast. Worrying that obtaining food might be a problem in China and wanting to make sure his men had enough to eat, Ross pulled together as many provisions as he could carry. As he was hurtling at 180 miles an hour straight down, he suddenly realized he had no free hand, and would have to let go of his supplies to pull the ripcord. Considering the physics of the situation as fast as he could, he decided that the cans would fall right alongside him; that he could just reach out and grab them back after pulling the cord.

The pilot let the food go, pulled, and watched as the wind scattered his supplies in every direction. Some of the cans even rose up and rained back down on top of his head. After reaching the ground safely, he'd spend hours looking for his lost food and find not a single bit of it.

Throughout the night Ross listened to a burbling stream, which seemed to be talking to him. At one point it stopped sounding like a creek and started sounding like enemy soldiers looking for Americans. He pulled out his .45, cocked it up, and waited to be taken prisoner.

Getting ready to go through the cabin in the dark plane twelve bombardier Waldo Bither's chute's ripcord got yanked somehow, and the silk popped open. Waldo asked navigator Bill Pound if he knew how to repack it, and Bill had to admit that he didn't. So Waldo did the best he could with what he had, and jumped.

Plane thirteen arrived over China at 6,300 feet. Looking at a map of the region sometime later, the crew realized that, in the dark, they'd narrowly missed a 20,000-foot-high mountain range through pure luck. "One engine was sputtering, and the other one was barely running," said bombardier Bob Bourgeois. "My God, we had the engines throttled back as lean as we could get them to save fuel. We ran on an empty gas tank for fifteen minutes. When the other engine sputtered, we had to bail out.

"It wasn't frightening. You just had a choice to make. Either you stay there and die, or you bail out and you got a chance to live. That's the two choices you had. Not a lot of choices, but that was the choices."

Copilot Dick Knobloch: "None of us had ever jumped from a plane. We didn't know where we were and couldn't see what we were jumping into. We pushed out the escape hatch and looked at that black hole, and the wind whistling around. It didn't last very long, but all I was thinking was, I was hungry, and hoping I'd find a hamburger stand to get myself a hamburger and a milkshake."

"I went third," said plane fourteen navigator Herb Macia. "I had a chest pack. Right before I went I sat down over the exit, and just to make sure I knew where this ripcord ring was, I reached up and took hold of it. Somehow just after clearing the airplane, I pulled the ripcord, which was far too soon, and I got caught in the prop wash.

"This is like the wind catching you, and the airplane is flying away from you. That is the other thing you don't expect: to hear an airplane that you have been in, listening to the motors for hours and hours, suddenly fly off into the distance. You think, 'Hey, that's the airplane I was in all that time.' There is a complete silence, and you are all alone. Anyhow, when I went out, the chute caught this prop wash, which caused it to be forced up; then I swung back through. When I came to the end of the swing, it was like hitting a wall. It took the whole shoulder out of the leather jacket because it had such force. I lost the musette bag, and I got a tremendous jolt. I was swinging back and forth in a tremendous arc. It was an unreal experience.

"It was dark. I was in the clouds. It was raining. The swinging slowed, and then I started spinning around. I was trying to hold it from doing that. I finally felt that I wasn't falling. It seemed as though I was suspended in a white mass. It was so unreal that I started wondering, 'Where am I, and what's happening?' I looked down, and it looked like I was being taken into a big hole. I was trying to react to that when suddenly I hit the ground, and it turned out I was falling at a very high speed."

When pilot Jack Hilger finished the last of his chores and headed for the hatch, he couldn't fit between the pilot's and copilot's seats without unhooking part of his harness. In the rush of getting out at the very last minute, Jack cleared the Mitchell's belly and pulled his cord before completely refastening every clip. The chute opened with such force that it knocked him unconscious. Coming to, he felt a horrible pain on one side of his groin. He felt around to discover that he was barely being held in by one strip of harness cotton—the one causing such pain. His nose was bleeding from being whipped by a loose strap.

Looking down, Jack saw a hole in the clouds. He pulled on his shroud lines to target it, and successfully hit it straight on. It was not a hole.

Plane two's Trav Hoover decided that his only option now was to attempt a crash landing. They were too low on gas to climb, and too low in altitude to jump. He'd found a rice paddy that looked flat and long enough. With the plane running on fumes, Trav circled back in the darkness to try to make sure it could handle his B.

He began the approach. Copilot Foggy Fitzhugh called out the airspeed numbers as the ship slowed and drifted. Navigator Carl Wildner put a seat cushion in front of his face to protect it from the armor plating, and waited for the crash. Trav adjusted his trim, turned off his ignition, and brought her down. The Mitchell landed as if she were born to it.

The crew pulled their gear together and piled out. They didn't know exactly where they were, but they were certain that the Japanese had to be very close. "After landing, we had to destroy the plane to make sure it didn't fall into enemy hands," Trav Hoover said, "but we discovered we didn't have anything to burn it up with. We just didn't have enough fuel at that point. We did everything we could—turned on the fuel pump on the ground, poured oil over the engine trying to set it on fire. Finally we were able to get a little fuel onto a dry piece of tarp, and it caught, and we kept feeding it, and finally the B-25 went up. The tanks caught and exploded."

The men watched forlornly as their Billy went up in flames. Over the noise, they could hear voices, and in the dark, they could see silhouettes of people in the distance, watching. "We saw people sticking their heads up over the dikes, and assumed they were Japs," Hoover said. "I figured there was one behind every bush. It was pretty hairy. A whole bunch came out to look at the plane. Even the tanks blowing up didn't scare them off.

"We traveled that night, holding on to each other to keep from being separated. We'd rotate so each person got his time at the front."

Using their dimestore compasses, the men walked due west, toward Free China. Climbing over a ridge, they turned back for one last look at their Mitchell and saw that they were being followed.

Plane fifteen had just reached the Chinese coast when pilot Don Smith and copilot Griffith "Griff" Williams checked the gauges, and decided they could go no further. The only choice they had would be to land in the ocean.

Griff opened the windows as Smitty coasted parallel to the line of breakers, four hundred feet away, slowing the plane down to ninety and looking for a soft spot. He found one about a half mile from shore, bringing her in so adeptly that not a single crewman was hurt. They would now have to hurry, though, to evacuate from the heavy bomber before it sank.

The men grabbed their guns, rations, bags, and chutes and began to prepare the life raft while gunner Thomas "Doc" White remained inside, groping through the rising seawater for his surgical instruments and medical kit. Just seconds after he climbed out, plane fifteen dropped entirely beneath the waves.

The men jumped into the raft with their gear, but it turned out to be so small that if anyone moved suddenly, another crewman would be thrown into the water. Everyone tried to coordinate their paddling toward shore, but it seemed as if they were making no progress. Cresting waves kept pulling men overboard, and their crewmates would have to hoist them in to safety. Then they were hit by a serious piece of bad luck: A rogue wave threw the raft back up against the sunken Mitchell, striking the sharp edge of a wing flap.

The left end of the raft began to collapse, but in the dark no one could find or stop the leak. After half its air had been lost, another rogue wave upended the raft entirely. The men of plane fifteen lost everything: their guns, their rations, and what would prove to be most crucial, Doc White's bandages and medicines.

Plane seven's pilot was able to get down low enough to also conclude that landing would be preferable to bailing. Ted Lawson passed over island after island, looking for any flat surface big enough to set down his *Duck*, but none of them was satisfactory: "It's hard and embarrassing to speak of love for a plane, but I loved that ship. To desert it in the air, coughing and preparing to nose over for its final plunge, was beyond endurance." Finally he found what looked like the perfect spot: "I dropped down low and dragged the beach, inspecting it for logs. The sand was wet from the rain that was pounding down, but it looked firm enough to support that touchy nose wheel of ours. It was by all means the best thing I had seen for twelve hours or more.

"The concave shape of the beach meant that I would have to come into it over water and make a slight turn before putting the plane down.

"Davenport was calling off the airspeed. He had just said, 'One hundred and ten,' when, for some reason I'll never understand, both engines coughed and lost their power.

"In the next split second my hands punched forward and with one motion I hit both throttles, trying to force life back into the engines. . . . I tried to pull back the stick to keep the nose up, so we could squash in.

"We were about a quarter of a mile offshore when we hit.

"The two main landing wheels caught the top of a wave as the plane sagged. And the curse of desperation and disappointment that I instinctively uttered was drowned out by the most terrifying noise I ever heard.

"It was as if some great hand had reached down through the storm, seized the plane, and crunched it in a closing fist.

"Then nothing. Nothing but peace. A strange, strange, peaceful feeling. There wasn't any pain. A great, restful quiet surrounded me."

A wave had caught the *Duck's* landing gear, and at one hundred miles an hour, she slammed to a dead stop. Ted, Dean, and navigator Mac McClure were hurled through the windshield as bombardier Robert Clever was tossed through the nose.

Gunner David Thatcher was knocked unconscious. He came to. Water was pouring into the plane. He put on his Mae West, inflated it, and started to climb out the hatch, but couldn't fit. The plane was filling with water, and sinking. Dave then realized the *Duck* was upside down, and that he had been trying to squeeze through his broken turret blister. He crawled up out of the hatch, and sat on the belly to get his bearings. The aircraft was completely destroyed. About one hundred feet away, the surf was breaking on the beach, and from time to time, he could catch glimpses of the vests and heads of three men, bobbing between the crests. He couldn't find the fourth.

"I must have swallowed some water, or perhaps the initial shock was wearing off, for I realized vaguely but inescapably that I was sitting in my pilot's seat on the sand, under water," Ted Lawson said. "I remember thinking: I'm dead. Then: No, I'm just hurt. Hurt bad. I couldn't move, but there was no feeling of being trapped, or of fighting for air.

"I thought of Ellen—strange thoughts filled with vague reasoning but little torment. I wished I had left Ellen some money. I thought of money for my mother, too, in those disembodied seconds that seemed to have no beginning or end.

"I guess I must have taken in more water, for suddenly I knew that the silence, the peace, and the reverie were things to fight against. I could not feel my arms, yet I knew I reached down and unbuckled the seat strap that was holding me to the chair. I told myself that my guts were loose.

"I drifted up off the seat and started to the surface. It was like a dream of trying to escape from something that moves very swiftly, while you move slowly. There was no power in my arms or legs, only an instinctive want to live—a want that I couldn't understand.

"I came up into the driving rain that beat down out of the blackening sky. I couldn't swim. I was paralyzed. I couldn't think clearly, but I undid my chute.

"The waves lifted me and dropped me. One wave washed me against a solid object, and after I had stared at it in the gloom for a while, I realized that it was one of the wings of the plane. Another wave took me away from the wing, and when it turned me around, I saw behind me the two tail rudders of the ship, sticking up out of the water, like twin tombstones."

Navigator Mac McClure was trying to swim to shore with arms that were swollen from the shoulders all the way to the wrists. His pain was so unbearable that he feared he could not make it, but he kicked and hurled himself forward through the waves. Finally he crawled up onto the beach. Out of the water the pain was even worse. Then he heard Bob Clever's voice: "Is that you, McClure?"

"Yes."

"Come help me."

"I'm not sure I can," Mac said. "I've got two broken arms."

"You son of a bitch! Help me," Bob screamed.

"When I came upon him," Mac said, "he was sitting with crossed legs and holding his head. I could see blood oozing down his forehead. He said something like, 'I'm bleeding to death.'"

Clever had been seriously gashed, with deep cuts all over his head. He was bleeding in buckets, and his eyes were swollen completely shut. Mac tried to help him, but as it would turn out, his shoulders had been yanked out of their sockets.

Dean Davenport had struggled to the beach as well, where he now discovered Ted Lawson, also in terrible shape. "Goddamn, you're really bashed open!" Dean couldn't stop himself from crying out. "Your whole face is pushed in!" Ted was so groggy and confused he couldn't even answer: "I vaguely reached up to my mouth and felt it. The bottom lip had been cut through and torn down to the cleft of my chin, so that the skin flapped over and down. My upper teeth were bent in. I reached into my mouth with both of my thumbs and put my thumbs behind the teeth and tried to push them out straight again. They bent out straight, then broke off in my hands. I did the same with the bottom teeth, and they broke off too, bringing with them pieces of my lower gum. I guess I must have been punch-drunk, because I remember saying to myself that now I'd have to go to a dentist.

"I went over to Clever. He was in the sand on his hands and knees with his head hanging down between his arms. He didn't crawl, and he couldn't speak. When the water was in you could hear the blood that was pouring from his face and head fall into the water.

"It was very dark now, and the rain was getting heavier. I kept trying to think straight, but all I could do was moan."

From the beach, in the dark, the men watched their beloved *Duck* sink beneath the waves.

"I was lucky," Dave Thatcher said. "The other four crew members were all thrown out when we hit. The pilot, copilot, and navigator were thrown up against the top of the cockpit and not straight forward. Lieutenant Clever in the nose was thrown through the Plexiglas headfirst. The injuries he received were cuts around both eyes, and the top of his head was so badly skinned that half his hair was gone. His hips and back were sprained so that he was unable to stand up and walk; all he could do was crawl on his hands and knees. His eyes were swollen shut so he couldn't see. His face was covered with blood, but I thought it would be better to leave it that way because of what Doc White had told us about infections. I knew infection would set in soon enough if we couldn't reach help; besides I had my hands full with the other members of the crew.

"Lieutenant Lawson was by far the most seriously injured. His worst injury was a long, deep gash just above his left knee. He had another deep cut on his left shin that left the bone exposed. His foot below the ankle was so badly bruised that it turned black within a few hours. He had other cuts on his left arm, head, and chin, and most of his teeth had been knocked out. He was in such intense pain and so weak from loss of blood that I was afraid he would die if we didn't reach a hospital.

"Lieutenant Davenport, the copilot, received severe cuts on his right leg between knee and ankle. He walked a little after the crash, but not afterward. Lieutenant McClure, the navigator, only received a few scratches on his right foot, but they got infected later. The serious injury was in his shoulders, which were swollen so badly clear down to his elbows that he could hardly move his hands. He was unable to lie down and had to try to sleep sitting up.

"My injuries were minor. I had a slight gash on the top of my head. If I hadn't had my flying helmet on, it would have been much worse. My back was badly bruised, and I had a few small cuts, which later became infected, but I was in the best shape to take care of the others." For his extraordinary actions over the next few days, twenty-year-old Dave Thatcher would be awarded the Silver Star.

Dave had been able to get ashore with a few things, including his .45, which he was particularly happy to have when he spotted, up on a ridge, two Japs looking at them. He pulled out his pistol and took aim.

"Don't shoot!" Mac yelled out. "They're Chinese fishermen."

"How you know?" Thatcher yelled back.

"Haven't you ever read *National Geographic*?" Mac had seen pictures in the magazine that looked exactly like these men, with their big black shirts and pants, and bamboo hats. After Dave put his gun away, eight of them came down to the beach. They didn't speak a word of English, and they didn't understand any of the Chinese phrases that the men had been taught by Steve Jurika on *Hornet*.

The Chinese peasants were eventually able to convey their concern about whether or not anyone else was in the plane or out in the water. After being assured that the entire crew had made it to shore, they led the men to a shack about a half mile from the beach. Mac had throttled out a scream of pain when the fishermen had tried to carry him under the arms, and Clever had to crawl to the shack on his hands and knees. Dean's leg was so cut up that he couldn't walk either.

Once in the shack Dave Thatcher took control, urging the men to lie down on some mud-encrusted bamboo mats that the Chinese brought in.

Mac couldn't even lie down, and instead had to sit up all night with his dislocated shoulders. Bob Clever, still gushing blood, passed out in the corner on a pile of human feces. Dave wanted to move him, but there was no more space; he thought about washing the crust of blood out of Bob's eyes, but considered the bacteria in rural China, and was afraid he'd cause more harm than good. He'd saved the *Duck*'s medical kit, and he tried using it, along with some old dirty rags, to shore up the worst.

Dave looked at Ted's coveralls, which were so torn up and bloodied that he couldn't distinguish where the cloth ended and the torn flesh began. He saw that Ted had lost nine of his front teeth, and that his left arm had been destroyed, but what was really frightening was the state of his left leg. It wasn't just shattered; the entire limb was sliced wide open. By this time Lawson was coming to his senses: "When I warmed up a bit, and I knew for sure that this was no frightening nightmare, I told myself that it was time to see just what had happened to me. I had no idea that there would be anything wrong with my left leg except a bruise. It was cut from my upper thigh to my knee, and cut so deeply that it lay wide open enough so that I looked into it and saw the gristle and muscle and bone.

"It wasn't bleeding badly—just oozing. My circulation probably had slowed down because of the shock and the cold. I just stared at it, hypnotized and detached. I had never seen anything like it.

"The Chinese men helping me let out a low hum. I looked up at them and saw one pointing to my left arm. The bicep, halfway between my elbow and shoulder, had been cut as cleanly as if by an ax. The bicep had ripped downward until it lay in the crook of my arm.

"Davenport kept looking at me, and finally he said, 'Jesus, Lawson, your face looks terrible! How do you feel?' There wasn't anything to say. The Chinese men and women kept moving among us, speaking softly. They kept saying, 'Hmmm.'"

In their wet clothes, the men started feeling the chill, so a woman brought in some quilts. Ted wanted to sew up his leg, but the Chinese refused, either because they knew it was a bad idea, or because they didn't have a needle and thread.

As the Americans were giving up all hope of rescue, a powerful man, obviously some kind of chieftain, came in and very closely looked over their clothes, their military insignia, and their wounds. Throughout this examination there was no sign of emotion on his face. Lawson could only think: He knows who we are, and he's going to sell us to the Japanese.

The man turned to Lawson and said, "Me—Charlie."

The fliers were stunned. Someone who could speak English? They all started talking at once, asking questions, but the man could only respond once more: "Me—Charlie." Then he gestured at them and said, "Melican."

He knew! Again they tried explaining their need for a doctor, and their hopes of getting to Chungking. After many hours of misunderstandings, Charlie (whose real name was Jai Fu Chang) was finally able to explain: "Chungking—many, many day. . . . Many. . . . Doctor . . . Japanee man. Japanee doctor." He then promised that he would come back for them, and he kept saying the word "boat."

That night the only sleeping member of the *Duck* crew was the unconscious Bob Clever, who'd at last been pulled off the dungheap and onto a mat on the floor. No matter what position he put himself in, Mac McClure's pain was too overwhelming to allow any rest. Besides his own horrible wounds, Ted Lawson, as pilot, felt responsible for the rest of the crew. They talked things over. Could they trust this Charlie? Ted thought they could. In their condition, there wasn't, after all, much else they could do.

The next morning came, wet and gray, the rain unceasing. Dave Thatcher rushed back to the beach, hoping to salvage their equipment, at the very least the rest of their medical kits; especially the morphine Syrettes. The low tide had brought the *Duck*'s tail out of the water, and he spent hours searching and diving around it. The only things worthwhile he could retrieve, however, were a lifebelt and a carton of cigarettes.

As he got ready to go back to the hut, Thatcher could hear the sounds of a motor. Off in the distance a patrol boat idled. He stared intently, not certain of what he'd seen, but then he knew: From the stern of the boat waved the blood-red flag of Japan.

PART TWO

★

ESCAPE

All night long across southeastern China, the farmers and fishermen, their wives and their children, would hear the explosions of crashing planes, see the breaking fires and plumes of smoke against their mountain peaks, and watch the broad, white-circle ghosts descending through the clouds.

Plane one gunner Paul Leonard landed on the side of a very steep embankment which, in the middle of nowhere at night in the rain, was black as hell: "Crawled about twenty feet downhill. Noplace. Went uphill twenty feet past chute. Got noplace. Came back to chute. Rolled up in it. Put arm around bamboo tree and went to sleep." This would be the smart move for many airmen: to try, as much as possible, to keep out the wet and keep in the warm with whatever they had.

"Suddenly a tree limb brushed my feet and I came to a stop," copilot Dick Cole said. "My chute had drifted over the top of a thirty-foot pine tree. I couldn't have landed easier if I had planned it. Except for a black eye, I was all in one scared piece . . . and I do mean scared.

"I climbed to the top of the tree and untangled my chute, then got down for a look around. I had landed on the top of a very steep mountain, and from what I could see with my flashlight, it looked treacherous. I decided to make a hammock from my chute and spend the night in the tree. This I did. It was quite comfortable and kept me dry, but I didn't sleep except for short dozes. My only visitor was a cottontail rabbit."

As Lieutenant Colonel Doolittle plummeted through the rain and clouds, he thought of the last time he'd done this and broken both ankles. A crash now would mean the possibility of being crippled for life. So Jimmy was especially grateful when he touched down in the fetid swamp of a rice paddy, even though it had recently and thoroughly been fertilized with night soil: "I stood up, unhurt and thoroughly disgusted with my situation and the smell, unhooked my parachute harness, and looked around. I saw a light and approached what looked like a small farmhouse. I knocked on the door and shouted, 'Lushu hoo megwa fugi' ('I am an American'). . . . I heard movement inside, then the sound of a bolt sliding into place. The light went out and there was dead silence.

"It was cold and I was shivering. I stumbled on in the darkness and came to a sort of warehouse. Inside, two sawhorses held a large box that was occupied by a very dead Chinese gentleman. It must have been the local morgue. I left and found a water mill, which got me out of the rain, but I was thoroughly chilled. I lay down but couldn't sleep, so spent most of the night doing light calisthenics to stave off the cold."

During that sleepless night Doolittle couldn't help but think of his men. He knew nothing of their fate, not even what had happened to the others from his own plane. It's likely, though, that his optimistic nature would have made him wonder if his own crew was the only one to have missed the homing signal—if, in fact, all of his other Raiders were warm, dry, and smelling just fine in Chuchow.

The rain finally stopped. In the new day, the Americans discovered that they had fallen into a rugged terrain that looked something like the pine-capped foothills of the Rockies. In between the mountains, however, were valleys of rice paddies and citrus groves, and they knew they'd landed on the other side of the world.

The people who grew the rice and fruit, or fished along the coast and in the rivers, had never before seen an Occidental, a bomber jacket, khaki pants, a parachute, or a Colt .45. When these strange creatures appeared as if from nowhere, the Chinese thought them too big for their own good, with skin as white as the ghost clouds they carried and faces as pale as the dead. The farmhouses, towns, and villages of southeastern China did not have telephones, or even radios, but these rural provinces were blessed with an extraordinary centuries-old word-of-mouth communications system. Quickly news of the hairy big-nosed people who had fallen out of the sky across a hundred-mile range of the kingdom traveled throughout the region.

Trav Hoover and the men of plane two hadn't been able to determine whether they'd landed in Free China or in Japanese-controlled territory. Since they'd come in along the coast, they'd assumed the worst and tried as much as possible to avoid any contact with the locals. For three days the five men lived off one canteen of water, one ration, and a few candy bars, walking through the mountains and paddy fields, sleeping in abandoned huts and lean-tos. Eventually, however, their provisions ran out and their canteen ran dry, and they needed help. "We contacted a Chinese farmer for food and water in the mountains," Hoover remembered. "He had a young son, and by drawing a Chinese map and a Japanese flag on the edge of our map and pointing to them, the boy was able to establish the Japanese line for us. We landed in occupied China, but the Japanese had moved out of this particular area just the week before. He indicated that we were now in free territory.

"So we started traveling down the road, which was really only a trail, and we were picked up by Chinese guerrilla soldiers. They took us into their headquarters at Sungyao, and we stayed there overnight.

"I had no idea how friendly they were. I couldn't get anyone to understand what I was saying, no matter what I did, beyond that we were from America. It was rough. Then this young man came in—Tung-Sheng Liu—and he could speak a little English, and he asked if he could be of some help? I said, 'Yes, you sure can. Help keep us away from the Japanese.' He said, 'I'll do my very best,' and with great disregard for his own safety, he stayed with us and directed us away from places that, if I had been on my own, we would have walked right in and wound up in the hands of the Japanese. I know it for a fact. So I believe to this day that he saved my life, my skin, and that of my crew, and I thank him for it every time I see him. He makes more modest assertions about it, but I can't say too much about him."

"In July 1937, I was attending university in Beijing when the Japanese took the city, and my family was forced to move west to the interior, to Kunming," Tung-Sheng Liu said. "After I graduated with a degree in aeronautical engineering, I had to go to Shanghai for my wedding and for my father-in-law's funeral. When we were ready to come back to Kunming, the British consulate wouldn't give us transit visas to go through Hong Kong or Burma, and we were stranded. The local people in Shanghai said there was a way to get through the front line. There wasn't really anything else I could do, so I followed their advice to leave my new bride with her mother and my parents, and set off with a group of others, mostly merchants, in this out-of-the-ordinary and out-of-the-way sort of travel. We could not take the steamships, many of the coastal railraods, or the highways, just the back roads, to avoid the Japanese.

"We are traveling, and it's April of '42, and we reach an area you might call a no-man's-land, because the Japanese would patrol in motorcars or boats during the daytime, then they would retreat to their barracks at night—so, many Chinese resistance activities were still going on.

"One night I stayed in a small hotel in Ninghai. We heard airplane noises in the sky, and then the local folks sounded their air raid alarm. At that time, in that location, they often heard Japanese airplanes passing through to bomb the Chinese interior; they rarely dropped any bombs there. The next day, some of the local folks came for me and asked if I could speak English. At college we used many English textbooks, so I said yes.

"They said to pack up my bags and come with them, and I followed them to a hall. It was about noontime, and they had three tables of good food ready. I was wondering what they were doing. Pretty soon some soldiers showed up. These were guerrillas, members of the former Chinese army, still allied with the Kuomintang and resisting the Japanese occupation.

"The guerrillas brought in five American fliers. They'd spent three days on the run, up in the mountain in the rain, so they were dirty, and hungry, and their uniform pants had shrunk three inches.

"I began to speak English. We asked them if they were American. 'Yes.' The guerrillas wanted to know if they took off from Australia. Hoover nodded his head. The most urgent question the guerrillas wanted answered was, where did the Americans want to go? Hoover took from his shirt a map. They wanted to go to Chuhsien. At that time, Chuhsien was for Free China the foremost airfield.

"Ninghai was not too far, maybe only a hundred miles, from Chuhsien, so I translated the whole thing to the locals, and they understood and began to make preparations to escort us. Like before, we should not travel during the day around the highways or waterways; we would just go through the trails, like the farmers use, mostly during the night. Doing this, we could not travel too fast, maybe ten to fifteen miles a day. The local guerrillas arranged housing for us to rest after we left from one point to another. Usually it was an old temple, a Buddhist temple, with food and simple bedding for us to rest during the day and portions of the night."

The Americans were amazed when, at one point in their journey, the small and lithe Chinese carried them up and down the mountains in sedan chairs. The bearers had a daily contest as to who would get the prize—the small, light navigator, Carl Wildner—and who would get the burden—bombardier Dick Miller, a two-hundred-pounder.

Tung-Sheng Liu: "After about a week we got to Chuhsien, which had a big airfield and a hostel. However, since it was a Chinese air force base, the Japanese came to drop bombs on the runway practically every day, so that no Chinese or American airplane considered it safe to land, and no airplanes could come to pick us up. Except for the bombs, though, we were now completely safe in Chinese hands.

"We were there for about a week; then two buses showed up and took us all to Hengyang. Even this far to the interior, the Japanese still dropped a couple of bombs on the runways in the afternoon. Every evening the Chinese worker coolies would immediately fill the craters back up so the field would be ready for use.

"In Hengyang we waited about a week. Then one morning the Chinese air base people told us to pack up and get ready because there were airplanes coming in to pick us up. Pretty soon an American C-47 appeared. They all got on the airplane and flew to Chungking."

Army law forbade foreign civilian Liu from joining them for the ride, even though everyone from plane two demanded he be included, especially Trav Hoover. As the men from opposite sides of the world made their farewells, the Americans promised Liu that they would help him in any way they could. Maybe he could work for Chennault or the army? They would all write about him in their afteraction reports, and see what they could do in return for his saving their lives.

As he promised, Charlie returned that morning to the hut where the horribly injured Ted Lawson and his fellow crewmen suffered. He brought with him around a dozen bedraggled young men, barefoot, with open shirts and hand-woven shorts, carrying bamboo poles, ropes, and strips of palm and bark, which they used to construct a series of litters. Of the five airmen, gunner Dave Thatcher was the only one who could walk unassisted. The assembling took three hours and, with each passing minute, the Americans could think only of the Japanese troops they knew were very close by. McClure, Clever, and Davenport were slowly helped into the slings, and carried off. At noon the peasants laid the strips on the floor, and Ted rolled himself into position, screaming in pain.

Accompanied by Dave Thatcher, Lawson held onto the back ropes as the Chinese carried him away from the fisherman's hut, away from the beach, away from the Japanese patrols. "I swung between them," he said, "like a butchered hog." Late that afternoon they arrived at a well-appointed home set in a lush meadow, with grazing cattle. The dirty bleeding men were laid down in the grass outdoors. "About two hundred tough-looking, sinister men stood here and there about the house, silently watching us come toward them," Ted Lawson said. "I could see even from a distance that they were well armed. I had to blink, it seemed so unreal.

"Charlie was obviously in charge here. All remaining doubt that he was a guerrilla began to flee my mind.

"He disappeared, and we were left with the staring circle of guerrillas. We studied their tough, weatherbeaten faces as intently as they studied our wounds. I wondered if all of them could resist the temptation to turn us over to the Japanese. The Japanese must want us badly enough to pay a lot, I thought.

"One of the toughest-looking men in the bunch now got up and advanced on me as I lay there. He reached down quickly toward my mouth and when he pulled his hand away I felt a lighted cigarette between that part of my lips that still met.

"I tried to smile back at him, but I felt more like crying. Maybe from relief. Maybe shock. I don't know. Anyway, I closed my eyes now and I thought that wherever I was I was among good men—men who were fighting for about the same thing I was fighting for. These men had us at their mercy, and showed us that mercy."

Ted passed out, and awoke to find himself again being carried, through villages where the residents stood to the side, murmuring, and across fields of rice and cows. That afternoon the party reached a small, muddy canal, where the injured Americans were lowered into the hull of a flat-bottomed boat. Accompanied by four of the armed guerrillas, the boatman poled through the narrow waterway, heading due south. The boat came to a stop, and eight new peasants arrived to hoist the men back along a hillside trail winding straight up. From its peak the men could see that all this time they'd been on an island, which they were told was Nantien. On the lapping beach of its western shore waited a red-sailed junk to take them to the mainland. "Suddenly we heard a sharp, clear 'Hi-hi!' Without a word our new coolies dumped us in the ditch," Lawson remembered. "When we cried out from the shock of the fall, the guerrillas who had flattened out next to us held up their fingers for silence.

"I raised my head so I could see a little. A Japanese gunboat was coming around a promontory off the beach. With sick, mingled fears I watched it come up briskly to the side of the junk. I could hear the Japanese questioning the men on the junk. It was torture to lie there in the ditch, waiting. Physical and mental torture. The Japanese must have spotted us, I reasoned. They must be wild to catch us, for certainly they had been informed of the raid and our route to China. They surely had found the plane by now. They would make one of the men on the junk tell. . . ."

Ted wasn't the only American wondering about his fate. In the bailout, plane three navigator Chuck Ozuk's chute had caught in a pine tree, and the force of the landing threw him against a ledge, its rock cutting his left leg wide open and tangling him up in the lines. He tried bandaging his leg, only to have pieces of shinbone fall out. Then he tried cutting himself out of the lines and harness, but in the dark and wet it was impossible. "I was pretty high up in the mountains," he recalled. "There [were] clouds blowing, and a beautiful sun above me. So I said, I must be with Saint Peter. But I can't be with Saint Peter, but I can't be. I had that feeling: Where am I?"

In the morning he found he couldn't walk, so Chuck made himself a crutch from a tree limb, and continued west. He spent two days in the mountains, completely alone, unable to find help.

After having all his equipment and weapons yanked away during the free fall, Chuck's copilot, Shorty Manch, hit the ground hard, rolling seventy feet down the side of a steep hill. He got up bruised, shaken, and wondering what had happened to everyone else. Shorty decided it was too dark and too steep to go wandering around, so he cleared off a long patch of ground with his boots, wrapped himself in the silk chute, and went to sleep.

When daylight came Shorty began hiking in ever-widening circles, searching for all the things he'd lost when his chute popped. Giving up, he climbed a hill to have a look around, spotted a village, and walked toward it, eventually running into an old lady carrying firewood. He tried talking to her, but she took one look at the giant foreigner and ran off into one of the nearby houses, shutting the door behind her. Shorty followed her and knocked, and after getting no answer, he opened the door and looked around, but the room was empty. He came out the back way and between the thick stalks of rustling bamboo, caught glimpses of the villagers, fleeing for their lives.

Shorty walked, dead tired, until he found a nice creek with clear water running, and since he was hot, he stepped in up to the waist and rinsed off his hair and face, wondering what to do next: "About this time the brush parted and a Chinese with a big smile on his face stuck out his hand to help me out of the creek. Several more Chinese then came out of the brush and tried to push and carry me up to a little trail on the mountainside. They were armed with old seventeenth-century flintlock muskets. I was so tired that I couldn't walk over one hundred yards without rest. One of the Chinese, about five foot four, offered to carry me on his back. I laughed at him because I thought I would be too heavy for him. He insisted and when I did, he threw it into high blower and went up and down those hills for two miles like a billygoat and like I wasn't even on his back. As we approached his village at dark, I became embarrassed because he was carrying me, a supposedly great aviator. I tapped him on the head several times, indicating that I could walk. I said to myself, 'I'm going to walk into this damn village if it takes me all night. I won't come in with this little five-foot-four Chinaman carrying me.'"

The man took Lieutenant Manch into his home, where it quickly became clear that he and his family just could not understand what the American was trying to communicate. The farmer then took a stick and began drawing on the dirt floor. Shorty: "First he drew a Japanese flag and pointed at that. I didn't know whether he wanted to know if I'd bombed Japan or was a Jap myself. I decided the last was the idea, so I held my nose and waved the picture away. The Chinese grinned and then brought out a clipping of an old Blenheim [a British plane] and pointed at the English insignia. I shook my head again. Then he brought out a copy of the *Saturday Evening Post,* about four years old. On the cover was a picture of President Roosevelt. I grinned and pointed to Roosevelt, then to me. He got the idea and everybody in the room laughed, and we shook hands."

The family got Manch some dinner and gave him a place to sleep for the night. The next morning a crowd of villagers arrived, and some began making airplane noises. After breakfast they led Shorty to the next village, and along the way he spied pieces of the destroyed *Whiskey Pete.* In the village, they showed him the American clothes they had found, some pieces of equipment from the navigator's deck, and the body of twenty-one-year-old Cpl. Leland D. Faktor of Plymouth, Iowa.

Whiskey Pete's gunner was the first of the airmen to die. His chute may have failed or he may have been unable to jump—the Chinese eyewitness reports are in conflict. One who discovered the wreckage said that the corporal's body was found inside the plane; another said it was nearby, with a chute that hadn't fully opened. Doolittle would conclude that "he landed on extremely rough terrain and was killed in the secondary fall." Leland Faktor's burial, however, would be properly attended to, and it would be arranged by one of the most famous Americans of the 1950s.

Waking up in the morning after his bailout, plane four's Brick Holstrom followed a stream to a small group of huts, when he was suddenly surrounded by Chinese bandits. They took him inside one of the shacks at gunpoint, and made him hand over all his possessions. As Brick removed one item after the next—his knife, his money, his hat, his jacket, his scarf, his billfold, his compass, and his first-aid kit—they were passed down a line of guerrillas and carefully inspected by each in turn. After Brick was completely naked, they gave back his clothes, shoes, and canteen, and took off with the rest.

"The next morning, April nineteenth, was my twenty-fourth birthday," Holstrom's navigator, Harry McCool, remembered. "I had bailed out and landed on the top of a mountain in East China. I had toffee candy and rainwater for a birthday dinner, and more of the same for the next three days.

"It just steadily rained. My back hurt, and later I found out that in the jump I'd broken a vertebra in my spine. As soon as I was free of the airplane, I had jerked my ripcord and oscillated two or three times before I hit a tree. The speed of opening the cord decelerated me, hard, cracking a corner of one of the vertebrae in my back. I'd find this out, of course, later, when they X-rayed me, and as a result I'd have to sleep on a board most of the following year.

"For three days I kept walking, and finally I was down far enough from the craggy peaks to find a Chinese woodcutter's hut. Using a straw mattress for kindling, I started a fire to dry my clothes. Countless fleas jumped out of the mattress in the fire pit, and I had to go out into the rain again to find comfort and security from the parasites.

"That afternoon I found a family farm with twenty to thirty Chinese, who I think had never seen a white man before. But they were kind and could see I was hungry. They gave me some boiled, unhusked rice, and a poached goose egg sweetened with honey. In return, they indicated my parachute fabric would be very nice, so I gave them a piece.

"Unknown to me, they'd sent out a runner to the local government head-quarters, and two soldiers met us as the Chinese walked with me. I'd worn nonregulation shoes on the mission, and nails had come through the soles, puncturing my heels. They got infected, and I was limping from that and with the spine and all, so the soldiers made the farmers carry me on a litter—to a jail. The jail was all made of bamboo, and the toilet was a cage of bamboo. In that kind of situation, you lose all modesty despite five hundred pairs of eyes watching."

That afternoon the soldiers took Harry to a different town, where he was reunited with another American prisoner: his gunner, Bert Jordan. "When they searched Lieutenant McCool and found his .45, they got really shook up and I thought we had had it," Bert said. "They threw me up against the wall and put a gun in my belly; they also roughed up Lieutenant McCool a little. Things finally cooled down, and we slept on boards that night.

"Next day some big wheels came and apparently figured out what we had done and really treated us nice from that time on. As we were leaving, a bunch of firecrackers went off under my feet, and I thought it was the end. I went about two feet in the air. They told me that was the way they treated their VIPs."

"Soon after, Brick Holstrom and Lucien Youngblood arrived, and after several days, they put us in a truck fueled by charcoal-generated gas," Harry McCool said. "It coasted down hills, but we all had to get out and push to make it uphill. Then we met a train on tracks to a river, were ferried across by boat, put back on a train, and eventually arrived in Chungking."

Almost every volunteer would remember for the rest of his life how well the Chinese had treated him, what an extraordinary effort these "backward" people made to help alien creatures who didn't even know how to read or write. From a decade of war, the rural Chinese were intimately familiar with Japanese cruelty, and were well aware what would befall anyone caught helping Allied soldiers. Even so they bravely hid and transported the Americans to safety, and from their own meager provisions, they fed, sheltered, and clothed the airmen as well as they could. The Raiders would also learn from these peasants how vigorous and widespread the Chinese resistance to Japan remained, even after so many years of invasion and conquest.

There was one recruit who was especially well treated. He was discovered by a man and wife who, though they couldn't understand a word he said, took him into their home, gave him dinner, and let him sleep in their bed—with them. The American was so relieved to be safe and snug that he fell directly asleep, but not fast enough to miss the rock of the bed as the couple charged forward in connubial bliss.

"At first light it wasn't raining, just misty. I started west," remembered plane five pilot Davey Jones. "I had the musette bag I had held onto, with cigarettes and a pistol and a pint of whiskey. It was Old Overholt, I'll never forget that, and by golly I still have the label.

"By noon I heard bells, and saw cattle and some people. The first group I saw just smiled at me and at each other. I very cleverly got out my little notebook and I drew a map of China. They obviously hadn't the vaguest idea what I meant. And then I got very smart and I drew a little locomotive and then I went *choo-choo-choo,* and I got a good response; I got lots of smiles. I offered them cigarettes. They all took cigarettes. So I just left and went down the trail until I found a railroad. And after a quarter of a mile, I found a small stationhouse.

"There was one young man there, and he could print a little English, and I could print in our language 'Yushan,' the name of the town we were supposed to go to. My copilot Hoss Wilder walked in about that time. This young Chinese man had a handcar, and he pumped us up the road about three miles to another station, where there was a locomotive and a boxcar, with about twenty or thirty soldiers in khaki-type uniforms. We ascertained they were Chinese, not Japanese, thankfully. So Hoss and I got on the boxcar and we went up the road about fifteen miles, and came to this town, Yushan, and pulled into the railroad yard.

"The doors of the boxcar were opened, and we were standing there, facing this huge crowd. There must have been ten thousand people if there was one. The streets were hung in banners which said: WELCOME BRAVE HEROES! YOU'VE STRUCK A BLOW FOR US. A gentleman in Western clothes came up to the car and said, 'Hi. I'm Dani-Yang. I'm the mayor of Yushan, and these people are going to welcome you.'

"This is five o'clock in the afternoon on the nineteenth in the middle of nowhere in China, a little over twenty-four hours after we'd bombed Tokyo, and they knew all about it! Isn't that something?"

Whirling Dervish gunner Eldred Scott jumped out of his Billy headfirst and, before he even had time to get frightened, he bounced to a stop, his chute caught in a tree. His lines swung into a perfect landing, so Scotty decided to have a smoke and a drink and plan his next moves. Finishing the cigarette, he tossed it and watched the ember fall . . . and fall . . . and fall. Now, he was scared. He tugged on the lines. They were firm and secure. The sergeant finished his drink, tossed the bottle, and went to sleep.

In the morning navigator Tom Griffin almost immediately ran into his copilot, Jim Parker. They followed a path through the hills and tried talking to a Chinese man, but couldn't make themselves understood. Eventually they ran into Scotty, and together the three arrived at a farmhouse, whose owner let them take off their soaked clothes and dry out by a fire. While undressing, they put their guns on a table. "Suddenly a Chinese officer appeared in the doorway holding a scroll in one hand and a pistol in the other," Parker said. "Turning around, we saw that our pistols had disappeared from the table and that other Chinese were covering us with rifles from every window and door."

The farmhouse was turned into a prison. The next morning two bilingual Catholic missionaries arrived, talked to the fliers, and then explained to the villagers that these men were part of a group of Americans who'd bombed what the locals called "the land of the dwarfs." The explanation transformed the captives from interlopers into celebrities, and they were taken to the next town and given a hero's welcome.

A few days later their pilot, Hal Watson, was carried in. His right shoulder, which had been caught in his chute's lines when it yanked open, was dislocated, and he was in a lot of pain. They didn't have any anesthetic, but one of the missionaries had an idea: They gave Hal plenty to drink, and when he seemed sufficiently ripped, asked him to change seats. As he dropped to the other chair, one of the missionaries grabbed his arm and pulled up, hoping to pop it back into the socket. Instead Hal fainted dead away from the pain.

The next day bombardier Wayne Bissell showed up, and the crew was reunited. Sergeant Bissell had shown up a day late since he'd been held hostage by guerrilla Chinese bandits who didn't take too kindly to foreigners. At one point they were distracted, so he ran away.

The townspeople took the Americans to see the wreckage of the *Dervish*. That baby would never fly again, but at least her insides hadn't yet been completely scavenged. Griffin was able to retrieve his musette bag and dress uniform, which he has to this day.

"I came out of the clouds, and almost instantaneously I hit the ground on the side of a steep slope," plane ten's Sally Crouch remembered. "I couldn't stand up. I hadn't eaten for fourteen hours, and I'd just been flying for fourteen hours, and I'd just come off a ship—I have sea legs, like so. It turned out my feet were black from being bruised by the impact.

"I unbuckled and stepped out of the harness. I had to crawl up about fifty feet to a little saddle in there. I wanted to get the canopy and use it for cover, but I wasn't able to, it was entangled in the bushes. We had our Mae Wests on, and I made a little mattress out of it. That's one advantage of being small, because I was able to curl up my entire body on top of my Mae West and cover myself with my jacket there.

"It was rainy and cold as all get out. I didn't sleep much. I was able to get short naps and woke up shaking like crazy.

"On the ground I ran into a village, and they took me to the head man. I took out my map and told him where I wanted to go, and he gave me a guide and we took off. As we started to go past another village, a Chinaman came running out, and they took us to a school building where there was an American aviator looking at a book. It turned out to be Horton.

"Eventually these people put together some sedan chairs, stored in this little teahouse. They got them out and put them together like you would an Erector set, with little blue cloth curtains on the front. We each had four coolies carrying our chairs, and whenever they got tired, the soldiers would simply stop, go out in the fields, and recruit fresh manpower."

"My stiffness and soreness had intensified during the night, so I made a cane from dried bamboo stalk to aid me in walking. I planned to follow the streams until they led me to someone, friendly or otherwise," said *Hari Kari-er* copilot Ken Reddy.

"After walking about thirty minutes I was surprised by what I thought was a human voice—but I wasn't going to be optimistic. However, I answered it.

"'Is that you, Reddy?' was the reply.

"I guess everyone is proud of their name, but mine never struck me as being beautiful until then. Was I ever so glad to see anybody! I had given up finding any of the crew because the terrain and underbrush were so thick and the airplane had dispersed us fairly far apart. Greening came down to me as I could not climb up. I was so happy that when he tumbled about twenty feet once, I broke out laughing.

"Greening inquired about the extent of my head injury first, for I had dried blood all over my face. I told him that it was just a scalp wound."

Ken had hit his head on a rock, triggering a gush of blood, and then sprained his knee, which swelled up like a watermelon. Ross made him a crutch from a piece of bamboo, and tied up his scalp with some parachute. Soon enough the twenty-one-year-old lieutenant's right brow was so swollen he could see only out of the other eye. Ken would have to walk like this for the next forty miles, sometimes hopping as fast as he could on his crutch for fear of being discovered by Japanese patrols.

"As we made our way down the mountain, some cultivated land came into view," Reddy said. "There was an old man and a girl at the first house we came to. After drawing pictures and everything, we finally gave up, as we could not get any directions out of them. We followed trails through the winding canyons, asking questions in sign language of everyone we met, always with the same results. Finally, we quit stopping people as it was just a waste of time.

"At about 8:30 A.M. we found a village. Apparently no one had paid us any attention during that time, yet this village was either aware of our coming or some fifteen people had just gathered at its entrance for some unknown reason. We marveled at the Chinese communication system. One is not aware of anything but its results.

"The dried blood on my face caused them to bring me the filthiest wet rag I have ever seen to wipe it off with. Everyone seemed to be eating a large mealy fried pie, about twice as big as a good pancake. They brought us one each, and upon biting into it, we found that the filling was some kind of green weeds. There was absolutely no seasoning; it was the most horrible combination ever to be called food. I nearly gagged."

The *Hari* bombardier and gunner had a similar experience: "I cut a scarf out of my chute for a souvenir (along with a few shroud lines), climbed to the top of the ridge, and, with the aid of my compass, started walking due east," Bill Birch said. "We had been flying west when we bailed out, so I knew Sergeant Gardner, having jumped just before, was somewhere to the east of me. I whistled and yelled a few times, and finally heard an answering shout and a pistol shot. We kept calling to each other, and I finally located him on the other side of a mountain about a half mile away. Gardner had fallen head-over-heels on landing and had sprained both ankles, but, walking slowly and with the help of a stick, we started westward.

"We walked about three miles up a narrow valley when we saw a group of houses. We didn't know whether the people would be friendly or not, so we made sure our sidearms were in working order with a ready slug in the chamber. The people we met, however, seemed more afraid of us than anything else.

"After an additional five miles or so, we came to another village. The people here had evidently heard we were coming, since they were all lined up and waiting for us. They took us into one of the houses and motioned for us to sit down. About fifty of them gathered around, everyone talking all at the same time. A few minutes later a soldier came in carrying a parachute. We looked at the name; it was our navigator's—Frank Kappeler. The soldier motioned for us to follow, so with about two hundred people taking up the rear, we started out again. About two miles down the trail we arrived at another village, and there was Frank. We were all really happy to see one another." Frank was especially happy, since he'd wandered around for hours, alone, thirsty, and hungry, wondering if he'd spend the rest of his life in China.

"On the way we walked through many small villages. In many of these there were outdoor places where people were cooking strange-looking foods for sale," Frank said. "Originally I had refused all food, but after a while we were offered some Chinese wine and after several drinks the food looked pretty good, and we sampled all of it. About ten P.M. we arrived in a larger town and were taken to a small hotel."

They had made it to the city of Weichowfu, where some Raiders were already bunked out and sound asleep. The next morning Ross Greening woke up with a terrible fever—and to see Mel Gardner, Bill Birch, and Frank Kappeler standing in his doorway. The *Hari* crew had been completely reunited. They went outside town to take a celebratory picture at a historic stone bridge, and then went back to their hotel for a fine home-cooked breakfast of ham, eggs, beer, and fried snake.

"We then all loaded into the back of a GMC truck, rode until late at night and arrived at Chuhsien," Frank said. There they met a very strange-looking man wearing a Chinese robe that came only to his knees and sporting a Fu Manchu mustache. It was Davey Jones, whose own uniform had been ripped to shreds. Greening had by now torn completely open the back of his own pants, which he patched together with a piece of chute.

★

"When I bailed out in China, I landed in a pond fertilized with human waste, a rice paddy," plane thirteen bombardier Bob Bourgeois remembered. "Oh, horrible. And cold and wet. Raining like hell, and I'm in it up to my neck. It sounds funny now, but it ain't funny out there, I can tell you. I crawled up on the side of the hill and sat there in the rain all night. Very cold."

The sergeant couldn't sleep and hadn't eaten since the *Hornet* pork-and-bean breakfast, so long ago. He spent the night listening to a barking dog, while lightning flashes revealed thatched huts nearby. The next morning he decided to see if their inhabitants were friendly. It was a village of pigs roaming around on the paths, children covered in sores, and girls using coffee cans to boil fish over some fires.

"When I walked in, they had told me how to say, 'I'm an American,' but I found out that each province has a different dialect, and you could learn to say one thing, say, in New York, and you'd go over to New Jersey and they wouldn't know what the hell you were talking about. They told me if you smile at the Chinese, they'll give you a smile back and the Japanese wouldn't. Well, when I walked into this opium field I saw a Chinese, and I went in there laughing, and he smiled back because if he hadn't, he'd a been dead. I had my .45 with me and a bullet in the chamber. Then I walked into the village, and they were cooking some fish—looked like porgies to me. They eat the head, scales, everything; I couldn't eat that. But they gave me some tea, and I tried to talk to them by making signs in the mud, but I couldn't make sense.

"Then they pushed me into a shack they had there, and I had never seen such filth and mud. They had pigs in there, and they sleep on boards, and I stayed in there for a while. And there was a big commotion outside. I couldn't figure out what it was. And finally the door opened, and it was my navigator, Clayton Campbell. Found the same village that I did.

"We could understand that if we stayed there we were going to be shot—the Japanese were looking for us. So we walked and walked up through the mountains."

One of Bob's crew would have exactly the same landing in the bailout, but would feel completely the opposite about it. "I came down in a rice paddy, a nice soft landing," said copilot Dick Knobloch. "Of course, it was full of night soil. But it was nice. If I have to bail out again, I hope it will be a rice paddy." Dick ran into pilot Mac McElroy, and the two came up with a plan. Since they couldn't tell if they were in Chinese or Japanese territory, while Knobloch walked into the next village, Mac, hidden, looked on and gave cover. The villagers came out of their huts to touch Knobloch's clothes and his face. He smiled, and each of them smiled and bowed. The fliers were tremendously relieved. Then Dick brought out his Zippo and fired it up, only to see the Chinese run for cover.

Dick and Mac gave up on these villagers and started making their way again, following a river, when a young boy ran out, grabbed Dick's arm, and shook his head no. He made a gun with his hand, shouted, "Bang! Bang!" and pretended to die. The Americans figured that Japanese troops were marching through, just minutes away. The boy led them across the fields to a Chinese army contingent, whose Captain Wong could speak a little English. They were, it turned out, a hundred miles west of Chuchow. "They didn't have lines like they did in France or other battles that you read about," Dick explained. "The Japanese moved in platoon size or company size through the countryside. It was a very fluid sort of situation."

The pilot and copilot were eager to get on their way the next morning, but Captain Wong told them to wait. Bob Bourgeois, Adam "Hillbilly" Williams, and Clayton Campbell then appeared, and the entire crew was together again. On ponies so tiny the Americans' feet dragged along the ground, and then in sedan chairs carried by farmers, the fliers were carted to the closest enemy-free city, Poyang.

They arrived on the outskirts of town late in the afternoon. Again Wong told them to wait, and for more than an hour, they just sat there without any explanation. Then, from far off in the distance, came a noise, which grew louder, and closer, until the Americans found themselves in the middle of a glorious and enthusiastic parade, led by an eight-piece marching band. "There was this Chinese band who'd stayed up all night long, learning to play 'The Star-Spangled Banner,'" said Bob Bourgeois. "There was an American flag, and I tell you, there were five guys from crew thirteen, listening to them play 'The Star-Spangled Banner,' well, we had tears running down our faces." In the middle of the parade, they were carried through the city of three hundred thousand, where every house had a banner: WELCOME BRAVE AMERICAN FLYERS. FIRST TO BOMB TOKYO. UNITED STATES AND CHINA RULE THE PACIFIC! For hours they marched, as the citizens threw firecrackers and cheered. That night, the Poyang Catholic Mission home-cooked them a feast of mashed potatoes, pie, and wine, and the next morning they were taken to have hot baths, in a real tub.

The men of plane fourteen would have their own dicey moments in China. "Eventually I came across Staff Sgt. Jake Eierman, [our] engineer," Herb

Dawn on Battleship Row, Pearl Harbor, December 7, 1941, as photographed from Japanese planes.

In one of the few pictures capturing the actual attack on Hawaii, destroyer USS *Shaw* explodes.

Admiral Yamamoto Isoroku, chief of the Imperial Japanese Navy and the architect of the December 7 military assault.

"I am looking forward to dictating peace to the United States in the White House at Washington"
— ADMIRAL YAMAMOTO

What do YOU say, AMERICA?

Jimmy Doolittle, age twelve, with parents Rosa and Frank, in 1908.

Doolittle, world famous as "the Lone Pilot," in the wake of another triumph—winning the 1925 Schneider Cup seaplane race.

The brigadier general.

The U.S. Joint Chiefs of Staff in World War II. *Left to right:* Gen. Henry Arnold (air forces), Adm. William Leahy (navy), Adm. Ernest King (navy), and Gen. George Marshall (army).

Capt. Francis "Frog" Low, who conceived of the Doolittle mission's unique army-navy coordinated strategy.

USS *Hornet* skipper Marc Andrew "Pete" Mitscher, who would carry the men of Special Aviation Project #1 across the Pacific.

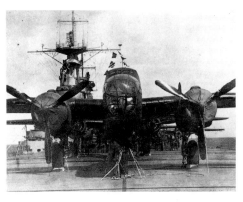

Above: A B-25, lashed to *Hornet*'s deck and heading straight for Japan.

Right: The legendary *Hari Kari-er*, its insignia drawn by pilot Ross Greening.

A lineup of bombers . . .

. . . and their eggs.

During *Hornet*'s voyage a ceremony was held symbolically returning Japanese commemorative medals that had been given to American sailors in 1908. *Left to right, front:* Doolittle, Adm. William Halsey, Youngblood, Reddy, Fitzhugh, Gray, Knobloch, Potter. *Rear:* Herndon, Joyce, Emmens, Watson, Greening, Cole, Farrow, Macia, Davenport, Griffin, Bourgeois, Sessler, Nielsen.

Above: The crew of plane two, on the deck of *Hornet* on the afternoon of April 16, 1942: Wildner, Hoover, Miller, Fitzhugh, Radney.

Left: Plane three: Ozuk, Gray, Aden Jones, Manch, Faktor.

Four: McCool, Jordan, Holstrom, Stephens, Youngblood.

Five: McGurl, David Jones, Truelove, Wilder, Manske.

Six: Nielsen, Hallmark, Fitzmaurice, Meder, Dieter.

Seven: McClure, Lawson, Clever, Davenport, Thatcher.

Eight: Herndon, York, Laban, Emmens, Pohl.

Nine: Griffin, Watson, Scott, Parker, Bissell.

Ten: Crouch, Joyce, Horton, Stork, Larkin.

Twelve: Pound, Bower, Duquette, Blanton, Bither.

Thirteen: Campbell, McElroy, Williams, Knobloch, Bourgeois.

Fourteen: Macia, Hilger, Eierman, Sims, Bain.

Fifteen: Sessler, Smith, White, Williams, Saylor.

Sixteen: Barr, Farrow, Spatz, Hite, DeShazer.

Liftoff: April 18, 1942.

Yokosuka Naval Base in Tokyo Bay, as photographed by Dick Knobloch from the flight deck of the *Lucky Thirteen*.

The men of plane one, reunited in western China: Braemer, Leonard, Cole, Doolittle, Potter.

Doolittle, feeling "lower than a frog's posterior," with the wreckage of his B-25.

Evading Japanese patrols, Chinese peasants ferried the Raiders across the country to safety in every form of transportation imaginable.

Jack Hilger *(top left)* at the bed of his injured bombardier, Jake Eierman.

The men of *Hari Kari-er*, together again and on their way to a fried snake breakfast: Birch, Kappeler, Greening, Reddy, Gardner.

The Raiders take cover, along with Chinese soldiers and civilians, from Japanese bombing raids in a limestone air raid shelter outside Chuchow (Chuhsien).

Robert Hite, prisoner of the Japanese.

As Doolittle looks on, Madame Chiang Kai-shek awards Jack Hilger the Order of the Cloud in Chungking.

At the White House, Hap Arnold, Joe Doolittle, and George Marshall bear witness to FDR's presentation of the Medal of Honor to Jimmy.

Doolittle would spend the summer of 1942 as the public face of the air corps, both in promotional shots . . .

. . . and in guest appearances. Here he speaks to North American Aviation's Inglewood, California, B-25 assembly line workers.

The ceremony awarding the Doolittle Raiders their promotions, stars, and Purple Hearts at Bolling Air Force Base, June 27, 1942.

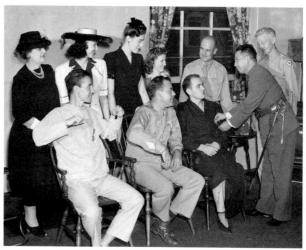

Left to right: Charles McClure, his mother, and his fiancée, LaVerne Rosegrant; Harold Watson and his wife; Ted and Ellen Lawson; Doolittle; General Chu Shi Ming; and the chief of Walter Reed Hospital, at a presentation of Chinese medals on July 25, 1942.

News of the Raiders' executions helped sell more bonds than any other event in the history of the war.

April 18, 1943: Hoover, Bower, Doolittle, Griffin, Pound, Wilder, Parker, Greening, Williams, and the men of Operation Torch salute the raid's first anniversary in a North African barn.

At the battle of Santa Cruz: the end of *Hornet*.

The lead pilot in the Pearl Harbor attack, Fuchida Mitsuo, would struggle as a humble farmer in postwar Japan.

Attendees of the notorious 1947 Raider reunion in Miami included Bither, Joyce, Stork, Knobloch, Blanton, Bower, Greening, Doolittle, and Hilger.

The Raiders at their fifty-seventh-anniversary reunion in 1999.

THE DOOLITTLE RAIDERS
57th Reunion – 17 April 1999
U.S.A.F. Museum – Dayton, Ohio

PANAVIEW
937-434 9287

Macia said. "As we walked through the countryside, we were passed from person to person and began to feel as if we were captives. Others have told me they had the same experience of feeling at times that they were possibly prisoners of war. I think it was sort of an attitude, a sense of proprietorship, that each would take, of assuming the authority over the previous person to take over these people who had fallen into their hands."

Herb and Jake were walking by the side of the road when "we looked across two hundred yards or so and saw a flatbed truck with soldiers in the back. They stopped, jumped down, and a young officer obviously took command. They started coming toward us, double time. . . . One of the things we were told in our briefings was the way to tell the difference between the Japanese and the Chinese military. The Japanese would be wearing uniforms, but for the most part the Chinese would not. These men were all in uniform. . . .

"Just as I was about to execute some of them, a young officer called out, 'American soldiers! We are your friends!' He told us that he had a friend of ours in the truck. We looked, and here was Jack Hilger."

Hilger had discovered, too late, that the hole in the clouds he thought he was heading for was in fact the peak of a mountain. Jack slammed into it so hard that for the second time in his jump, he was knocked completely unconscious. When he came to, he discovered that his lines were caught in the branches of a tree. This was Hilger's one piece of good luck, as he was hanging off the side of a cliff. With a left hand sprained and swollen from the fall, and a back wrenched hard from the untied harness and the pop of the chute, the major crawled up its branches, cut his silk free, and found his way to a slightly flat area. There, he stretched pieces of the chute across the branches to make a tent against the rain and crawled underneath, grateful to sleep, grateful to at least be alive.

In the morning Hilger walked past farmers with wooden plows hauled by buffalo and men wearing cone-shaped hats, and then into a village whose white-bearded mayor wore a long black robe and a skullcap. He felt as if he'd stepped into the China of two thousand years ago.

One boy decided to lead him to safety, but as they were traveling down a road, a truck filled with soldiers appeared. Men jumped out, pointed their machine guns at Jack, and began screaming. He had no idea what to do. The boy screamed back, but the gunmen didn't seem to understand or believe him. Finally one of the more senior men recognized the American symbols on Jack's uniform. They sent out searchers for the rest of his crew and drove him back to their barracks, where they gave him a savory pastry to eat (Jack later found out the filling was dog meat). When the major was reunited with the rest of his crew, he said: "I was never so glad to see anyone in my life. It was like a homecoming, and we were all as happy as kids. There's nothing like a familiar face in a foreign country."

"The Chinese took us up to Chuhsien," Herb Macia said. "The little place where we were staying was an air base, designed to accommodate some American or Western air force people. Almost every day the Japanese would send over a bombing mission; they knew we were at this place. The Chinese had dug a shelter into a limestone bluff, and they insisted that we go up there. The intelligence they had was fantastic because they would come in at nine and say, 'At ten-thirty there will be four Japanese aircraft over here dropping bombs; they have just taken off.' This obviously had been passed on by some Chinese working right at the airfield where the Japanese airplanes were operating. How their communications worked I never knew, but the word would come through.

"At a quarter after ten, the Chinese would insist we go up to the shelter. We would all wander up to the shelter, which was about a mile away and looked down over the airfield. Pretty soon four aircraft would come, just exactly as reported. They would come over, look around, circle, come back, maybe drop one bomb, circle a few more times. The Chinese had no air defenses. If we went out in front of the shelter to get a better view, our hosts would have all kinds of problems. I imagine they had been told that they were in charge of our safety and nothing had better happen to us.

"We all became fairly adept at chopsticks. If you got into something like a fried egg, then you were in trouble."

When he awoke in the morning, Jimmy Doolittle found a trail and followed its winding path. Eventually he came across a peasant, and tried again with *Lushu hoo megwa fugi,* but the man didn't understand a word. Jimmy couldn't imagine what to do to get his identity across, but then he had an idea. Using a stick, in the dirt, he drew a train, and the man's face immediately brightened.

They set off together, arriving at a group of buildings. Jimmy saw nothing to make him think this was a train station, and in fact, it was the local headquarters of the Chinese army. The man in charge seemed to understand a little English, so Jimmy tried to explain what had happened, while Chinese recruits kept their tommy guns pointed right at him. The officer didn't believe any of Jimmy's wild story, but finally he agreed to escort Doolittle back to where he'd crashed, so he could prove he was who he said he was:

> The officer, surrounded by about a dozen armed soldiers, escorted
> me to the rice paddy where I had landed, but the chute was gone.

I said the people in the house must have heard our plane and could verify that I had knocked on their door the night before. However, when the farmer, his wife, and two children were questioned, they denied everything. The major said, "They say they heard no noise during the night. They say they heard no plane. They say you lie."

The soldiers started toward me to relieve me of the .45. It was not a comfortable situation. I protested and was saved from having to tussle with them when two soldiers emerged from the house with the parachute. The major smiled and extended his hand in friendship, and I was thus admitted officially to China. He led me back to his headquarters for a warm meal and a much-needed bath. I dried out my uniform, but the stench remained intact.

Almost immediately he was reunited with the rest of plane one. "I was taken to the place where the boss was located," said copilot Dick Cole. "He appeared none the worse for his experience except that he had landed in the middle of a rice paddy and was still damp. Later Potter, Leonard, and Braemer were brought in. They had been picked up by a roving band of renegade guerrillas."

"I encountered four Chinese men armed with rifles," Leonard recalled. "One motioned to me to raise my hand while the other three proceeded to cock their rifles. One took aim. At the same moment I pulled out my .45. The one who was aiming fired, so I fired twice. All four of them turned tail and ran, so I turned and climbed back to the mountaintop. After about an hour and a half, I saw a crowd of people down the valley. In front I could see Lieutenant Potter and Sergeant Braemer. I reloaded my clip because I figured they were captured. I started yelling and ran down the mountain, but found they were in good company."

"Paul Leonard and I went to the crash site to see what we could salvage," Doolittle remembered.

There is no worse sight to an aviator than to see his plane smashed to bits. Ours was spread out over several acres of mountaintop. . . . I sat down beside a wing and looked around at the thousands of pieces of shattered metal that had once been a beautiful airplane. I felt lower than a frog's posterior. This was my first combat mission. I had planned it from the beginning and led it. I was sure it was my last. As far as I was concerned, it was a failure, and

I felt there could be no future for me in uniform now. . . . My main concern was for my men. . . . How many had survived? Had any been taken prisoner by the Japanese? Did any have to ditch in the China Sea?

As I sat there, Paul Leonard took my picture and then, seeing how badly I felt, tried to cheer me up. He asked, "What do you think will happen when you get home, Colonel?"

I answered, "Well, I guess they'll court-martial me and send me to prison at Fort Leavenworth."

Paul said, "No, sir. I'll tell you what will happen. They're going to make you a general."

I smiled weakly and he tried again. "And they're going to give you the Congressional Medal of Honor."

I smiled again and he made a final effort. "Colonel, I know they're going to give you another airplane and when they do, I'd like to fly with you as your crew chief."

It was then that tears came to my eyes. It was the supreme compliment that a mechanic could give a pilot. It meant he was so sure of the skills of the pilot that he would fly anywhere with him under any circumstances. I thanked him and said that if I ever had another airplane and he wanted to be my crew chief, he surely could.

While I deeply appreciated Paul's supportive remarks, I was sure that when the outcome of this mission was known back home, either I would be court-martialed or the military powers that be would see to it that I would sit out the war flying a desk. I had never felt lower in my life.

Bailing out of their useless raft, Don Smith, Griff Williams, and the rest of plane fifteen had to claw their way through crashing waves of surf before finally reaching the shore. They arrived to find a rocky beach faced by a high, solid line of cliffs. They climbed up and at the top saw rolling hills and, far off in the distance, a light. Armed with two little knives, they went to find out whether the light meant friend or foe.

They arrived at a small house, with a covered pen for goats. As they approached, the light was extinguished. The men knocked on the door, yelling the Chinese phrases they'd been taught on *Hornet,* but there was no answer. Finally giving up, they decided to spend the night with the goats. It was shelter from the rain, even though the floor was covered in dung.

As they were trying to figure out how to get some sleep, the light came back on, the door opened, and the man of the house stepped out. He peered at them, swinging a lantern, ignored their attempts at Chinese, and ushered them inside. The family had started a smoky fire, from straw. The men dried themselves and tried to keep from suffocating as the farmer's wife and mother gave them some hot rice, with bits of vegetable and some kind of meat. Doc White: "I'm sure he had never seen a white man before. I'd like to think that if I were called out in the middle of the night and met four giants (we were two feet taller than he was) in strange uniforms, speaking a strange language, and obviously in trouble, I'd like to think I would have the courage to ask them into my house. That's what that little man did."

They finished eating to find dozens of Chinese pushing their way inside to get a good look at these visitors. The fliers tried, through hand gestures and sketching pictures on the dirt floor, to explain themselves. Each peasant in turn tried to understand, but no one could.

In the back of the crowd was a group of children in raggedy clothes with dripping noses and a paperback book. They showed the men their precious volume, an almanac with maps and some English translations. Here was the key: Using it, the Americans could explain who they were and what they'd done. They asked where they'd landed, and how they could get to Free China. With the almanac's maps, the farmers showed the fliers that they were on an island, and explained that this island was the only one in the region that didn't house its own patrol of Japanese soldiers. The Chinese also said, using the English translations, that they would help the Americans get to friendly territory. They then made arrangements for the men to sleep in the beds, while the owner of the house and his family went out to spend the night with the goats.

The guerrillas and peasants accompanying the crew of *Ruptured Duck* waited until the Japanese patrol boat motored from sight. Then, at an unspoken signal, the injured men found themselves lurching back into the air, the bearers running with their charges as fast as they could down to the beach and to the sides of the junk, where they were roughly loaded into the hold. The guerrillas scanned the horizon, their guns at the ready, while one of the boat's crew covered the fliers with sheets of bamboo lattice. When torrential rains began soon afterward, the guards set out bowls to catch it, and the Americans drank the water in huge gulps.

Lawson fell asleep, only to be shaken awake by Dean Davenport, who explained: "You were having a nightmare. You kept hollering, 'Don't let them cut my leg off!' " At midnight the junk came to a rest, and the Chinese leaped ashore, pointing to their mouths. They came back with food, but Lawson's mouth didn't work well enough to get down anything but a boiled egg. He was hopeful at the sight of wine, which he thought could kill the pain, but instead "it was like raw, uncut alcohol. It burned my busted mouth and torn gums like lye."

The next morning, they sailed to a mainland town in Chekiang Province, where a new group of laborers carried them on bamboo poles to a China Relief station. There they were met by a Doctor Chen and his workers, who'd run all night from their hospital in Linhai, twenty-six miles away, with sedan chairs, ready to immediately carry the Americans back to relative safety. As they were lofted out, the town's contingent of Chinese army, Boy Scouts, and Girl Scouts, standing in formation, saluted them.

Even as Ted was trundled in a sedan chair, his pain was unremitting: "There were times when I thought I could not stand one more jolting bounce. When I felt I'd have to cry out and ask them to leave me behind, I'd suck on the bitter, tiny Chinese oranges and try to concentrate on the way the juice burned my mouth, the number of seeds the oranges had, and other things, so I wouldn't think about the leg and arm and hands."

They arrived at the Linhai hospital, run by Doctor Chen's father and staffed by volunteer nurses. One was a young Australian woman named Mary Andrews, who said, "The survivors from those planes looked like wild, wooly men from Borneo when they came to the hospital." Also working at Linhai was an English missionary couple, Frank and Bessie England. Mr. England explained, "We have an antiseptic fluid, a little chloroform, and bandage. Nothing else."

"My left ankle, near the scratch I had gotten on the junk, was the size of a football when I woke up in the early morning of the twenty-second," Ted remembered. "[Mary] told us she had come from Taichow, also in Chekiang Province, just ahead of the Japanese. She said it noncommittally, but a wave of helpless despair passed over me. . . .

"I thought night and day of sedatives. The anesthesia of shock was all gone."

When Miss Andrews first dressed his wounds, Lawson told her, "I knew I was not going to die when my plane crashed as my mother back in the States was praying for me." One night it began to storm, and Lawson woke up. He turned to Mary, keeping watch, and said, "Nurse, please get me some of that rain from heaven." She ran outside with a bowl to catch the water, which Lawson sucked down through his slash of a mouth.

As much as he couldn't stand the thought of losing it, his leg had now swollen from the ankles all the way up to his groin, and the entire limb had turned every shade of horrible color. As Ted's hope vanished completely, April 24 arrived with astonishing news, when Mr. England announced: "We've just received word that another crew whose plane crashed is coming here. One of them is a doctor. Is that possible?"

The next day, the entire crew of plane fifteen, including gunner Doc White, showed up. When their raft had sunk, they'd lost nearly everything. Doc had been able to salvage two tubes of morphine. They—and he—would save Ted Lawson's life.

Friends of the Chinese family with the goats had sailed the crew to the neighboring island, which turned out to be Nantien, where they were handed over to the local authorities, meaning the guerrilla band led by Charlie, who was once again tremendously helpful. Mary Andrews told everyone that they'd been awfully lucky to run into him, as Charlie was precisely the man to help the Americans evade the hundred-member Japanese search party now scouring the island for the bombers of Tokyo. Only the guerrillas knew every hiding place and secret trail, with a system of codes and signals that could be passed across the mountains and between the valleys.

On Nantien, Charlie explained to the men of plane fifteen that the Japanese had discovered the wreck of the *Duck,* and were searching furiously for the Americans they knew still had to be hiding on the island. The guerrillas were no match for such a force; they'd have to lie low for a while. This meant traveling only at night through the same circuitous routes, eventually hiding in the cellar of a Taoist temple.

The temple's priest, wearing a black silk robe and using his long pipe as a cane, threw joss sticks and prayed for their future. In the dark they could hear shouting voices and the sound of boots running on a stone path. Finally, after four hours, the Americans were led to the priest's home, where he slid aside a panel in the wall, and ushered them through, into a tunnel. The fliers and a few of the guerrillas crawled into a wet, smoky cave and waited. After half an hour, they could hear more shouts, the thud of rifle butts against bodies, and screams. The Japanese were interrogating the local Chinese, just outside the secret cave.

The guerrillas cocked their pistols. For two hours they waited, expecting at every minute to be discovered. Then, there came a yell: the all-clear sign. Pistols were uncocked, and everyone headed back up to the house. There, waiting, was the priest who'd helped them. His temple had been destroyed, and he had been beaten.

The fliers were taken to a boat, made to lie down in the bilge, and covered with mats. Fishermen poled them across the inlet, but halfway to safety they spotted the lights of a Japanese patrol boat. The Chinese pulled behind an island and waited. Finally, with no moon rising, they were able to reach the mainland unnoticed, where they were taken to the nearest village for a dinner of shrimp, eggs, rice, and a 180-proof rice liquor that tasted like gasoline. From there a group of Chinese carrying paper lanterns on long, hanging poles took them to the hospital in Linhai.

Doc White asked Ted how he felt, and Lawson replied, " 'Pretty good.' He poked around my lower leg with the blunt edge of the scissors. The leg was pulpy. Finally Doc picked a spot near the bottom of my calf and pressed the point of the scissors harder and harder against it until it punctured the skin.

"The stuff jumped out suddenly, and just kept spurting. It wasn't sickening. It was like water. Doc kneaded my leg and got a lot out. Some of the swelling went down, and I felt better. . . ."

The American doctor found nothing at Linhai that could help Ted. He kept giving him transfusions from Clever and McClure, and sprinkling sulfa powder directly into the wounds, hoping for a miracle. One night he doped up Lawson with chloroform and did some extra cutting to help with the drainage, but the anesthetic nearly killed the patient. Ted's options were quickly running out.

Missionary Frank England held a church service one afternoon on the hospital's porch, and invited crippled navigator Mac McClure to attend. McClure didn't want to be bothered, but then he reconsidered. Two men carried him to rest in a wicker chaise longue, and it turned out to be a service that McClure would never forget: "During the first song I halfheartedly mumbled the words. I remember thinking, 'That's over. How many more?' As I began to say the words for the next song, I noticed a very strange feeling coming over me. From that moment to the time the service was over, my aches and pains and my mind cleared to where I felt wonderful. It was such a change that I could not believe it.

"At the close of the service, without saying a word, I threw my legs over the edge of the lounge and popped up to a standing position. Mr. England looked at me in amazement. I explained what had happened during the service, that my mind had cleared, I felt good and the tension had eased. All he could say was, 'I believe you have received the hand of God.' I agreed."

Day after day alarms would scream through the streets of Linhai, announcing the bombing of the airfield nearby. The Japanese were getting closer, and soon it would be too dangerous for the Americans, as sick as they were, to remain. All of Smitty's crew, accompanied by Dave Thatcher, took off for Chungking, leaving behind only Doc White and the men too injured to be transported.

★

That the one medically trained American showed up entirely by chance at Linhai when he was critically needed wasn't the only remarkable coincidence striking the airmen as they were smuggled across China. "While we were hiding in the cabin of a boat, a Caucasian man in civilian clothes came aboard," Jimmy Doolittle remembered.

> He had been told there were Americans inside. Suspicious, he hesitated, but finally banged on the door. He called out in a strong southern drawl, "Are there any Americans in there?"
>
> We tensed and stayed quiet. The question was repeated.
>
> The voice was convincingly American, so Paul Leonard finally said, "Hell, no Japanese can talk American like that," and opened the door.
>
> Outside was a tall, gaunt white man with a several-days' growth of beard. He told us his name was John M. Birch, age 27, an American missionary based in Hangchow. After December 7, when the Japanese began to round up all Caucasians, he had fled to Shangjao, 250 miles to the southwest. He was returning on foot to Shangjao from a trip downriver when he stopped at a small Chinese inn and met a man who told him to go to the dock. There the man pointed to the riverboat and said, "Americans."
>
> Birch was as delighted to see us as we were to see him. He obviously knew his way around and could speak the language. I briefed him on our predicament and he agreed to join us, translate for us, and help us get on our way to Chuchow.
>
> En route, Birch told me he had been living off the cuff and was having a rough go of it. Having seen what the occupying Japanese were doing to his beloved Chinese, he wanted to join the American forces in some capacity, preferably as a chaplain. I promised to put in a good word for him. . . .
>
> On April 27, Birch met Davey Jones and other crew members at Chuchow and acted as their interpreter. It was there we learned that Corporal Leland D. Faktor, a gunner, had died bailing out. Birch was given the $2,000 in Chinese money I had left for ran-

som and was asked to buy a burial plot, bury Faktor, obtain as much information as possible about the others still missing, and then proceed with the last group to Chungking. . . .

Birch was killed on August 25, 1945, by Chinese communists—10 days after World War II was officially over. He had no way of knowing that the John Birch Society, a highly vocal postwar anticommunist organization, would be named after him because its founders believed him to be the "first casualty of World War III." I feel sure he would not have approved.

On Saturday, April 18, in Hyde Park, New York (April 19 in the Asian Pacific), Franklin Roosevelt was working in his home office—a room decorated with brass sculptures of Scottie dogs, paintings of ships throughout history, and, on an easel dead center in the room, that enormous portrait of Sara Delano Roosevelt—with secretary Grace Tully and speechwriter Sam Rosenman. They were developing ideas for a new "fireside chat" about inflation when an urgent phone call was patched through from the White House. It was the news FDR had been waiting for—Radio Japan had announced that American bombers were attacking Tokyo.

Smiling broadly and chain-smoking, the very excited president told Tully and Rosenman the entire story, only to be interrupted constantly by more calls with news of attacks on Osaka, Kobe, and Nagoya. As word spread throughout the executive branch, some of Roosevelt's staff, knowing how tightly Tokyo guarded its sea lanes, predicted that the more sophisticated newspaper reporters would hound the president to reveal the mission's launch site. They recommended he be prepared with an answer.

Sam Rosenman had a thought: "Mr. President, you remember the novel of James Hilton, *Lost Horizon,* telling of that wonderful, timeless place known as Shangri-La? It was located in the trackless wastes of Tibet. Why not tell them that that's where the planes came from? If you use a fictional place like that, it's a polite way of saying that you did not intend to tell the enemy or anybody else where the planes really came from."

Even though Washington still had no official word from Doolittle, Stilwell, Bissell, or anyone else in China, the president (who considered it his professional duty to appear publicly hopeful whatever his private thoughts might be) called a White House press conference on April 21 and made an extremely cryptic announcement. No mention was made of *Hornet* or Task Force 16, no concrete details were offered, and almost every follow-up question was ignored. The president confirmed the basics of what the newspapers had been reporting about bombs raining down on Japan, and added the official word that United States Army Air Corps planes had very successfully attacked "from our new base in Shangri-La." (FDR would become so enamored of this whole notion that one of the new aircraft carriers having its keel laid the following year would be christened *Shangri-La,* as would the president's country getaway in the Maryland hills. Today it is known as Camp David.)

The vagueness and opacity of Roosevelt's comments, especially the mention of Shangri-La, did not give reporters or the public pause. On the contrary, the fact that he refused to say much at all made the whole announcement even more romantic, exciting, and mysterious. News of the air corps victory spread rapidly across the country all over again through radio, newsreels, and newspapers.

It was the first time in many years that Americans had something to be proud of as a nation. Not only was the Doolittle Raid the first U.S. victory of World War II, but after month after month of defeat and humiliation in Europe, North Africa, and the Pacific, it was also the first solid win for the Allies as a whole. Many can recall to this day where they were at the moment they heard that our boys had successfully bombed Tokyo, especially that majority of citizens who felt certain that the fascists would eventually triumph over Europe, Asia, and perhaps the United States as well. The raid proved, at a crucial moment, that the Axis Powers weren't invincible after all.

While the president was holding his celebratory conference with the fourth estate, China's minister of foreign affairs was delivering some very bad news to Hap Arnold. Two days earlier a telegraph had been sent from the governor of Chekiang Province through the Chinese system to T. V. Soong's office in Washington. It was the first news from Doolittle: "Mission to bomb Tokyo has been accomplished. On entering China we ran into bad weather and it is feared that all planes crashed. Up to the present already five fliers are safe."

Arnold read this cable and thought: Out of eighty men, five were accounted for? It was too awful to contemplate. He shared the news with Marshall but wasn't quite as forthcoming with the president: "From the standpoint of damage to enemy installations and property, and the tremendous effect had upon our Allies," he wrote, "as well as the demoralizing effect upon our enemies, the raid was undoubtedly highly successful. However, from the viewpoint of an Air Force operation the raid was not a success, for no raid is a success in which losses exceed 10 percent and it now appears that probably all of the airplanes were lost."

Another very big question loomed in the minds of American leaders:

How, in the wake of the Tokyo bombings, would Japan react? Radio stations across California were ordered off the air so their signals couldn't be used as targets by vengeful enemy bombers, and San Francisco's bridges were shut down. The army, theorizing that Japan would immediately send planes to drop poison, shipped six hundred thousand gas masks to the Western Defense Command.

The deputy chief of staff for the Pacific and Far East, at that time Ike Eisenhower, asked army intelligence for their predictions. In Asia, and most especially Japan, honor and saving face were paramount, he was told. They would almost certainly retaliate, upping the ante significantly. They would destroy Washington, D.C., the Panama Canal, and military installations across the Pacific. Seattle, Portland, San Francisco, Los Angeles, and San Diego would become a string of Pearl Harbors. Clearly the worst was yet to come.

★

In the Soviet Union, meanwhile, the men of plane eight were taken to an army *dacha* out in the countryside on the banks of the Amur River, across from Manchuria, with military beds and angora blankets, and introduced to their five "companions"—one guard for each American. The fliers soon came to realize that their companions' major duty was to keep them at all times as drunk as possible. At least one of them, Mikhail Constantinovich Schmaring (nicknamed Mike), could speak a little English. He translated the questions that the companions had: Were the internees personally acquainted with Henry Ford, John D. Rockefeller, or J. P. Morgan? Is it true that "they have thousands and thousands of workers under them, over whom they have complete control, even jurisdiction over life and death?"

"We hadn't noticed a loudspeaker sitting on the table in the corner with an electric cord attached to it," Bob Emmens said. "Mike stood up and said that at midnight the news would be on. We were at once delighted to think we had a radio. But our delight was short-lived. The end of the electric cord fitted into a plug into the wall and you either plugged it in or you didn't, depending on whether you wanted to listen to Moscow or you didn't.

"Mike's translating from Russian to English was slow, and you had to gather pretty closely around the 'reproducer,' as it is called in Russia, in order to be able to hear it. So we sat in silence for the fifteen minutes of news from Moscow. At the very end, we heard the word *Tokyo* mentioned several times. When the news was over, Mike told us that all the news except the last report was about the marvelous advances the Red Army was making against the Germans, and that at the very last they had announced that a Tokyo radio had stated that eleven of the ships which had bombed that city and others in Japan had been shot down over Japanese territory. That was all—just that single statement.

"I'll never forget the shock of that moment. My God, there had been only sixteen airplanes on the whole raid, and if eleven had been shot down over Japan, we were one of five surviving aircraft! I can tell you we felt pretty sad that night as we turned in—our first night as internees in the Soviet Union. . . .

"Each day was almost exactly the same. We got up at about nine-thirty, had breakfast at ten, lunch at one, supper at seven, and rounded up each day with the news and tea at midnight. The drinks of vodka were beginning to be looked forward to as a relief from boredom, but the gaps of time in between were pretty hard to fill up. We slept quite a bit, whittled wood, and attempted now and then to get a start on the language. . . .

"'How would you like to look forward to spending a couple of months doing this?' asked Ski casually.

"We all laughed. That was unimaginable. After all, we were just waiting until a 'further decision' should be reached between the American Embassy and the Soviet government in Moscow. It might take a week or two to arrange it, but not longer, and then we would probably be taken out via Alaska."

On April 22 the American ambassador to the Soviet Union, William Standley, cabled Washington that a U.S. bomber crew had landed on Russian territory, and that Moscow had announced the internment of the crew and its equipment. Eisenhower and Arnold drafted a reply, asking if the Soviets would allow Americans to remove the crew and plane from eastern Siberia as quickly as possible, wondering whether the crew members might be attached to the U.S. Embassy for a time, and offering to give the B-25 to the Russians. If there was an official Soviet response, this writer could not uncover it.

After ten days the American fliers were driven to a train station, where they were padlocked into a third-class sleeper car hooked to a freight train on the Trans-Siberian Express. It would take twenty-one days to cross to western Russia, since they were constantly set onto siding tracks to let Soviet troop transports, and boxcars filled with men, women, and horses pass by. Each day brought the same meal: black bread, salmon caviar, bologna-type sausage, tea, vodka.

They arrived at a *dacha* in the village of Okhuna, three hundred miles south of Moscow, their new home even including a bathhouse out in the yard behind the kitchen. For a special treat, they went to town to see the most popular movie in the Soviet Union, *One Hundred Men and a Girl,* starring Deanna Durbin.

On May 25 Ambassador Standley would report to Washington:

> All [of the interned Americans] have received courteous and gen-
> erous treatment. After a number of delays, they are now housed in
> a spacious, clean bungalow in a village about ten miles from
> Penza; a second house near-by contains dining and recreation
> rooms and three Soviet companions, one of them being an inter-
> preter. The crew members are provided with recreation facilities;
> athletic equipment, books, billiards; etc. The men receive food
> which is better than that provided the diplomatic corps . . . and
> are allowed the freedom of movement given to chiefs of mis-
> sion. . . . A Soviet physician is always available. Immediate needs
> of the men: American toilet articles, cigarettes, and reading mat-
> ter, all of which the Embassy has tried to provide. The men are in
> excellent mental and physical condition. The only complaint:
> they are urged to eat and drink too much.

Though no one from the State Department had yet paid the airmen a
visit, the embassy assumed that, since the United States was getting billed
thirty thousand rubles a month for the cost of internment, the aviators were
being treated as hospitably as was possible in wartime Russia. In spite of the
free-flowing vodka and caviar, however, the men of plane eight were growing
more and more worried as the weeks dragged on. Why wouldn't the State
Department send over anyone to check up on them? And, regardless of the
endless optimism of the midnight reproductor, they could tell from a map
that the Wehrmacht was moving in closer and closer to Moscow. Okhuna
itself, as far as they could tell, was just a few days' march from the front lines
of the Eastern Campaign.

Ted Lawson's condition, meanwhile, was deteriorating:

> Doc was scissoring dead flesh off my lower leg each day. Twice a
> day, he'd clip flesh away, mostly around the ankle. Often I felt
> nothing. Doc would ask me to tell him when he touched live
> flesh, but he'd know, for I'd scream when he did cut living flesh.
> He'd give me a shot of morphine afterward, sometimes.
>
> It got to be more than I could stand, so one day I broke down
> and blurted that I couldn't take it twice a day.

Doc kept clipping away. "You'll either take it or you'll lose the leg," he said.

I told him for Christ's sake, take the leg.

Doc stopped when I said that. He gave me a pep talk, but it didn't do much good, I guess. . . .

The big day came toward the end of the first week in May. I don't even know what day it was. But in the middle of that day, Doc came into my room. He was very clean-looking in his uniform. But he was uncomfortable. Neither of us said anything for a little while.

I looked at him and asked him if he was going to take the leg.

"Yeah—I think so," he said.

Doc didn't ask me how I felt about it. So, after a bit, I said I wished he'd get started. All I could think of now was getting rid of that damned thing. I said to him that I guessed it wouldn't be so bad, with it off. It would be something like wearing a shoe with a high instep.

Doc didn't answer, and for the first time I knew that he was going to take more than my foot and ankle. I told him now, after I swallowed, that I wanted to be sure that he took it off well below the knee.

Doc was busy thinking about something else. He didn't answer, so I had to come out and ask him where he'd take it off.

"Well," Doc said, "above the knee. I'll leave you as much as I can."

It was hard to take that. Awful hard.

For the surgery Mrs. England baked linen bandages in an oven for an hour to sterilize them, while Mary Andrews did the same with their very limited instruments in an iron wok. Doctor Chen told White that "Before we operate in this hospital, we always ask God for his blessing," and White answered: "Please do. We sure need it today." As the men and missionaries prayed, they heard the sounds of Japanese bombers coming closer and closer. Mary thought: What would happen if the Japanese found these Americans?

"The anesthetic was a spinal shot," Ted remembered.

Dr. C explained that you stick an empty hypo in the lower spine and draw off the spinal fluid secreted at that point. Then shoot the same cc volume of the anesthetic into the same spot. It paralyzes everything from there down.

Doc took his time. He wanted to be sure. But at last he came over to the table with a scalpel in his hand. I cocked an eye down, and he started.

I couldn't see any blood, or feel anything. But I knew he was cutting. I could see his arm moving and see him lift my leg up so he could cut underneath. He cut around once, rolling back that layer and tied the blood vessels off. Then again and tied. Then again. Then again. Four times around.

Now I felt that I could move the toes on my good right leg, and it vaguely worried me. I thought the anesthetic was wearing off. There wasn't any more of the stuff, of course. I told Doc I could move my toes.

Doc hurried. I could move my whole ankle now. I told Doc this, and the two Chinese nurses came up on either side of the table and held my wrists.

Doc stepped away and walked back quickly with a silver saw. It made a strange, faraway soggy sound as he sawed through the bone. Except for the tugging fear that I was coming back too soon, the actual amputation was almost as impersonal to me as watching a log being sawed. I could hear the different sounds of the saw as Doc's elbow bent and straightened, bent and straightened, and the teeth went through thicker and thinner sections.

Then there was an almost musical twink, and deep, deep silence inside me as Doc laid aside the saw. The Chinese nurses let go of my wrists. The nurse on the right walked around to the left side of the table. She picked up the leg by the ankle. The other nurse picked up the other, thicker end.

I watched the two nurses carry it out the door.

The diary of *Hari Kari-er* copilot Ken Reddy describes the the following days for the other Americans smuggled across China:

4/20/42: We got to Chuchow (Chuhsien) to find three complete crews safe and sound. Our stories were very similar, all of us landing on a mountain of some sorts, with one exception. Lt. McGurl landed in a rice paddy on his head. For an unknown reason he had, upon freeing himself, started running as fast as he could. Anyone who knows China knows you can't run far in a rice paddy without hitting a terrace. He did. But one didn't stop him, and it took several to bring him to his senses.

4/21/42: I arose early in order to eat before the air raid sounded. After breakfast all of us piled into some station wagons and were rushed through Chuchow with horns blasting all the way. People on all sides of us were rushing to the outskirts of the city. We drove across a pontoon bridge to some hills in the country. Here we took refuge in a handmade cave. After the all clear sounded, we were shown to our new home, which was a part of an army post within walking distance of the cave.

Two more air raids sounded during the afternoon. The Japanese bombers were old; they took their time in bombing the airport as they had no opposition whatsoever. We called our home the Chuchow bombing range for that is all it amounted to—practice for the Japanese.

Lt. Ozuk had perhaps the roughest time of any of us present. He hung in his chute on a cliff all night with a very deep gash in his leg. He had made a tourniquet out of his scarf. The next morning he had just enough strength to pull himself up his chute to the top of the cliff. The knee of his other leg was also hurt. For two days, without food or water, he pulled himself through the bush. His hands were one solid scratch.

General T. T. Tong entertained us with an elaborate feed. He drove many miles to be present for the affair. A band opened the occasion with the Chinese national anthem, and then played what they thought was ours. They had signs up about the Americans, Roosevelt, and made many speeches to the same effect. They told us we were the first foreign power to strike a blow at Japan proper in its 2600 years of existence. They told us of the panic we caused, the greatest since the big earthquake of 1922.

4/29/42: In Hengyang the hotel was excellent and the food was the best we had had, perhaps because the chef had spent nine years running a chop suey joint in New York.

At 1500 on April 29, a C-47 appeared in the skies, landed, and sat with its engines running. "When it flew over with our insignia on the side we all shouted with joy," Ken Reddy remembered. "It was the most beautiful sight we had witnessed in China." Clayton Bissell rushed everyone aboard as quickly as possible for the flight to Chungking, where the Doolittle boys were bedded at the American Embassy.

The four-thousand-year-old capital of Free China stands on a promontory over the gorge where the Yangtze and Chialing Rivers meet; it is a steep and rocky town, carved into the hills. The Raiders arrived just in time, as in May the city wasn't yet beset by the summer's wet and torpid heat, or still suffering through winter's rain-drenched mud falls, though it was being bombed constantly by marauding Japanese squadrons.

Even with daily attacks, however, the volunteers arrived in Chungking to witness what could only be considered a miracle. Eighty men had bombed the heart of the empire, seventy-five of them landing in enemy-controlled territory and then smuggled across the whole of China. One had perished; five were in Russia; five were healing in Linhai; ten were MIA. Everyone else had survived this crazy suicide mission, and they were now safe, and together, in Allied territory. Considering the history of Special Aviation Project #1, it defied belief. The men weren't just thrilled to be alive, relieved to see one another, and proud of a job well-done; they were stunned by their unfathomable run of good fortune.

Ken Reddy's diary continues their story:

> We were all called together about nine o'clock in the morning [on the thirtieth] to receive from General Bissell what was the biggest shock of my life. The President, General Marshall and General Arnold all sent their personal congratulations, along with an award of the Distinguished Flying Cross for each of the twenty of us present. None of us had expected such an honor, so we were all astounded.
>
> The Crosses were not available of course.
>
> All of the higher-ups of the post came by and gave us their own congratulations, and we were invited over to celebrate at their house. Scotch is $75 a quart (our money) here, so they use a bathtub gin. It served its purpose well.
>
> They all said that when they found out we hadn't made our field that they were really worried about us. They had been unable to tell the Chinese people that there would be some American fliers coming over. They could not let it be known even after we had bombed Tokyo. Some Russians who landed in China had been shot. Many Chinese pilots had been shot when forced down because the people of that locality could not understand their dialect.
>
> These officers had mixed opinions of China and the war, but I do not wish to express any of them as that is their business.

5/1/42: We were invited to dine with the Generalissimo. His home was very lovely inside, having indirect lighting of a Chinese design, soft modernistic chairs with heavy padded cushions without backs to sit on, individual silver ashtrays, herringbone hardwood floors, and a soft glowing fireplace. One of the many items served at this banquet was a jam made from "flowers of the moon." No one could figure out what this was, but it was delicious. Later the Madame [Chiang] came in. That was when the party picked up. She got things going surprisingly quick.

The Madame is the most impressive character I have ever had the privilege to meet. She speaks excellent English, and better still she has control of the American slang. She's brilliant, witty and *beautiful.*

She is officially the Vice-Commander of the Chinese Air Force. In this capacity she awarded us [with the Order of the Clouds, the Chinese Air Force's highest medal]. We were all very thrilled and proud to receive such an honor. The awarding went off fine with one exception, and as usual I was involved. When the Madame came to me she dropped the medal, and about four men tangled up trying to recover it for her.

After we had finished we were lined up for a few group pictures. Fortunately when the Madame joined us, she stood right in front of me. I mumbled to the fellow next to me: "This should make my girl at home jealous." The Madame caught it and said, "Blonde or brunette?"

Chiang Kai-shek made a lengthy speech without a translator, so none of the Americans understood a word. The Generalissimo then handed out more decorations to every flier, and had just finished the ceremony when Doolittle arrived. Embarrassed at having run out of awards, Chiang went over to one of his own heavily decorated men, removed a medal, and bestowed it on Doolittle. The Chiangs were pleased; the donating Chinese general somewhat less so.

In Chungking, Bissell had the pleasure of informing Doolittle he'd been awarded a double promotion and was now a brigadier general. As there were no extra medals, stars, or insignia available, Bissell, who'd himself just been promoted to the same rank, took the stars off his own shirt to give to Jimmy.

Ken Reddy:

5/9/42: General Doolittle left today. As a general, we will lose him as our commander. We all hated this, but he is much too valuable

a man to allow to go on combat missions. I imagine he had to put
up a big fight to get to come with us.

Last night we had a little farewell party for him in our room.
He said he was slated for an office job at home, but would much
rather be in the field—and this wasn't just talk, for he meant it.

The General is a [short] man, but he's all there when it comes
to brains. I wish we had more like him.

The enraged Japanese did exact vengeance for the raid, although not so much
on the continental United States as army intelligence had warned Eisenhower, but on the Chinese who'd helped Doolittle and his men. On April 20
Emperor Hirohito signed an order for his army in China "to destroy the air
bases from which the enemy might conduct air raids on the Japanese homeland. The captured areas will be occupied for a period estimated at approximately one month. Air fields, military installations, and important lines of
communication will be totally destroyed . . . the Commander in Chief of the
China Expeditionary Army will begin the operation as soon as possible."

For the next three months Japanese army troops went far beyond even
these harsh orders, obliterating everything in their path across all of Chekiang
and Kiangsi Provinces. They demolished American church missions, dese-
crated Christian graveyards, strafed the region with more than six hundred
bombing runs, and ultimately slaughtered an estimated 250,000 Chinese
people.

Stilwell would report that "the Japanese began their advance upon Chuchow from out of the Hangchow area on 15 May. . . . [T]he plan for the
defense of Chuchow fell apart, and after the loss of that city, the Chinese
apparently abandoned all idea of blocking the Japanese advance in Chekiang
and Kiangsi." The Japanese gave special attention to what they considered the
gravest threat to their security, the airfields at Chuchow, Yushan, and Lishui.
At Chuchow armed soldiers compelled four thousand locals at gunpoint into
slave labor, carving eight-foot-wide, three-foot-deep trenches to permanently
destroy the runways so they could never be used by enemy bombers again.
They would wreck eastern China so thoroughly that the Doolittle Raid fol-
low-ups, Aguila and Halpro, would have to be canceled, and Chennault's
Chinese air force would be almost entirely crippled.

Marauding forces of more than one hundred thousand soldiers in fifty-
three battalions attacked every town with a link to Doolittle's crew. The trin-
kets and gifts from the crashed Mitchells that the fliers had given to those
who helped them now became evidence of perfidy. A Chinese schoolteacher

said, "We fed the Americans and carried them to safety so that they could bomb Tokyo again. Then, the dwarf-invaders came. They killed my three sons; they killed my wife, Angling; they set fire to my school; they burned my books; they drowned my grandchildren in the well. And I crawled out of the well at night, when they were drunk, and killed them with my own hands—one for every member of my family they had slaughtered." Discovering a farmer who'd helped *Whirling Dervish*'s Doc Watson, soldiers wrapped him in a blanket, soaked it in kerosene, and forced his wife to set her husband on fire. The Chinese fishermen of one village were lined up and shot, their town—and many more—reduced to ash. Women and babies were beheaded. One Chinese man told the *New York Times*, "From some of the villagers who had managed to escape death we heard stories far too brutal and savage to relate. Just one charge was not heard—cannibalism. But outside of that, take your choice and you can't miss the savage nature of the Japanese army."

Chiang Kai-shek, who was born in Chekiang, cabled Roosevelt on April 28, 1942: "These Japanese troops slaughtered every man, woman and child in those areas—let me repeat—these Japanese troops slaughtered every man, woman and child in those areas." The Chiangs would in fact become terribly bitter over the repercussions of the Doolittle Raid. The Japanese eventually extended their path of vengeance across the country, reaching to just a few days' march from Chungking itself, and the entire Kuomintang felt threatened. Simultaneously Stilwell and the British had been driven from Burma, losing the Burma Road, which supplied the Nationalists with foreign aid. From then on Chiang would only fight to keep Lend-Lease supplies and American foreign aid coming in through airlifts, and would repeatedly threaten Allied command with negotiation feelers sent to the Japanese.

But the slaughter was not the end of the empire's vengeance. In 1935 the Japanese had constructed what they called the Epidemic Prevention and Water Purification Department of the Shantung Army outside the city of Harbin, Manchuria. This was in fact a testing ground for bacterial warfare, using captured human beings as living guinea pigs to be infected with bubonic plague, pneumonia, epidemic hemorrhagic fever, typhoid, and syphilis. Founded by army medical lieutenant general Ishii Shiro and staffed by three thousand, this department was officially known as Unit 731.

As early as 1940, Unit 731 had turned loose its specially bred fleas and rats to spread bubonic plague among the people of Changde and Ningbo in central China, while dropping another of its inventions, anthrax-bacillus bombs, on the town of Anta. In September 1940 Japanese troops terrorizing Nanking were equipped with typhoid, paratyphoid, cholera, and plague bacteria.

In June and July 1942 Japanese forces sprayed cholera, typhoid, plague, and dysentery across southeastern China in retaliation for the Doolittle Raid. The casualties from this biological warfare have never been determined. A report stated that during one assault, a last-minute change in the wind led to the death of seventeen hundred Japanese soldiers and the injury of ten thousand more. We now know that if Allied forces in the Philippines had not surrendered when they did, the Japanese planned to spray them with a thousand kilograms of bubonic-plague-infected fleas, and if the United States hadn't quickly won the battle over the island of Saipan in July 1944, they would've been attacked with Japan's full arsenal of bacteriological weaponry.

These attacks against rural, civilian Chinese, however, would turn out to be only one part of Tokyo's reaction. The Doolittle Raid would antagonize the empire into launching assaults against the continental United States, and into a military campaign that would reverse the course of war in the Pacific. As Pearl Harbor lead pilot Fuchida Mitsuo explained:

> Headquarters spokesmen sarcastically pooh-poohed the attack as not even a "do-little" but rather a "do-nothing" raid. In point of physical damage inflicted, it was true enough that the raid did not accomplish a great deal. But the same could not be said of its impact on the minds of Japan's naval leaders and its consequent influence on the course of the war at sea.
>
> The fighting services, especially, were imbued with the idea that their foremost duty was to protect the Emperor from danger. Naturally they felt that it would be a grave dereliction of this duty if the Emperor's safety were jeopardized by even a single enemy raid on Tokyo. . . . In Admiral Yamamoto's mind, the idea that Tokyo, the seat of the Emperor, must be kept absolutely safe from air attack amounted almost to an obsession. . . . [L]ater, when he was directing operations in the distant southwest Pacific area, he never failed, before giving his attention to anything else, to ask for the latest Tokyo weather report. If the reports were bad, he felt relieved, because they gave added assurance that the capital was safe.

The Doolittle Raid had a more profound effect on the admiral than even Fuchida realized. When he first heard that Tokyo had been bombed, Admiral Yamamoto was so filled with shame and horror at the danger to which he had exposed his emperor that he went into quarters aboard the battleship *Nagato* and refused to come out. Day after day he ignored his staff's pleas, crippled by anxiety and depression. When finally Yamamoto emerged, it was with a determination that such a violation of his beloved country could never happen again.

When Doolittle and his men attacked, the American military had no idea that the Japanese navy was in the middle of a bitter strategic conflict in the wake of Operation Number One. The general staff logically wanted to consolidate and expand their Pacific conquests, solidifying their outlying bases in New Guinea and the Solomons, and then pushing on to New Caledonia, Fiji, and Samoa, cutting off Australia's sea lanes to the United States.

Yamamoto and his Combined Fleet officers, however, wanted to finish the job they'd started at Pearl Harbor by destroying what remained of America's Pacific Fleet, most crucially its aircraft carriers. They recognized that the Doolittle assault could only have been delivered by a carrier sailing near Midway, an American-controlled mid-Pacific atoll eleven hundred miles northwest of Oahu. By occupying Midway, the Japanese could ensure that no future American strike forces could ever approach the home islands again. Additionally, attacking Midway could draw the U.S. Navy into a battle that, dwarfed by Japan's vastly superior power, it was guaranteed to lose.

Faced with the possibility of further bombings of the homeland and direct assaults on their emperor, the general staff could no longer justify its position, and Yamamoto's strategy was approved. Midway would be taken, and the American navy's Pacific Fleet completely annihilated.

Roosevelt enjoyed weeks of goodwill from the announcement of the attack on Tokyo—the first public acclaim he had had in a very long time and, more seriously, his first obvious victory as the armed forces' commander in chief. Now the president wanted to extend that moment of triumph for both himself and the nation. Though weeks had passed, he felt that an announcement of further details on the raid could lift the country's spirits all over again, and consequently began to develop a "welcome home" plan that one airman—and the nation—would never forget.

At that time planes could not fly nonstop around the globe, and the international conflict had forced even the long-range Pan Am Clippers into serving as local puddle jumpers. It would take two weeks for Brigadier General Doolittle to travel from China to Burma, India, Iran, Egypt, Sudan, West Africa, South America, Puerto Rico, and finally back to Washington. In Calcutta, Doolittle had traded in his uniform, still smelling of Chinese night soil, for the only clothing available—a raj outfit of bush jacket, shorts, kneesocks, and pith helmet—which he wore all the way around the world. He got home, anxious for the company of Joe and the boys, only to have Hap order him instead not to tell a soul he was back, even his own family, who'd spent months with no news of his fate.

On his first morning stateside, Doolittle went to a little store to stock up on a few necessities. He was shocked by the higher prices brought on by war taxes, and didn't know that under rationing Americans had to turn in an empty tube of toothpaste in order to buy a new one. When he complained about all this to the man behind the cash register, the druggist took offense at what he felt were unpatriotic comments, and bitingly said, "Don't take it out on me. Don't you know there's a war on?"

Jimmy could only mumble in reply: "Sorry . . . I've been away."

Weeks passed, with the War Department still unsure of what more to say publicly beyond the president's cryptic Shangri-La announcement. Lawson and the other injured men were still caught in eastern China, and the release of any detailed information might endanger them. Besides, how would the public react to the news that all sixteen planes had been lost? Wouldn't that undermine support for the war?

By mid-May, after an entire month had gone by, Roosevelt decided to put his plan into action. "Completely unknown to me, Hap had called Joe and asked her to come to Washington, without telling her why," Jimmy recalled.

> He arranged a reservation for her on a commercial airliner and she left promptly that afternoon. She flew all night.
>
> Meanwhile, I had received a telephone call from Hap at our apartment. He told me he would drop by in a few minutes to pick me up, but didn't say where we were going. When his staff car arrived, Hap was sitting in the rear to the left of General Marshall. Surprised, I saluted them and climbed in the front seat beside the driver.
>
> There was silence as we drove off. Finally, I asked where we were going. "Jim, we're going to the White House," Hap replied.
>
> I thought about this for a minute, then said, "Well, I'm not a very smart fellow and I don't want to embarrass anyone. What are we going to do there?"
>
> General Marshall answered, "The president is going to give you the Medal of Honor."
>
> I was shocked and quickly said, "General, that award should be reserved for those who risk their lives trying to save someone else. Every man on our mission took the same risk I did. I don't think I'm entitled to the Medal of Honor."
>
> Hap flushed and I could see he was angry. General Marshall,

obviously displeased at my remark, scowled and said, "I happen to think you do."

There was no further discussion. In all our later association, this was the only time Hap ever got mad at me and General Marshall ever spoke sternly to me. The highest-ranking man in army uniform had made his decision. It was neither the time nor the place for me to argue.

We arrived at the White House and were ushered into the anteroom where Joe was waiting. We were both startled and immensely pleased. Hap beamed happily as the two of us embraced; General Marshall managed a smile. I wanted desperately to hear about Jim, Jr., and John and catch up on what she had been doing, but we were quickly led into the Oval Office where a beaming President greeted us warmly. He was in a jovial mood and shook my hand long and hard. He said our raid on Japan had had the precise favorable effect on American morale that he had hoped for.

General Marshall read the citation for the award and handed it to Joe. Nervous at her sudden appearance in the office of our country's leader, a place she never imagined she would ever visit in her entire life, she began twisting the citation scroll. Marshall told her later he was tempted to take it away from her before she ruined it.

The citation read: "To Brigadier General James H. Doolittle, United States Army, for conspicuous leadership above and beyond the call of duty, involving personal valor and intrepidity at an extreme hazard to life. With the apparent certainty of being forced to land in enemy territory or to perish at sea, General Doolittle personally led a squadron of Army bombers manned by volunteer crews in a highly destructive raid on the Japanese mainland."

"The President pinned the medal on my shirt and asked me to tell him about the raid, which I did," Jimmy continued. "I thanked him for the award and we were ushered out. On the way through the door, Hap congratulated me. I couldn't resist telling him that while I was grateful, I would spend the rest of my life trying to earn it. I felt then and always will that I accepted the award on behalf of all the boys who were with me on the raid. I have always felt that the Medal of Honor should be reserved for men who risk their lives in combat to save others, not for individual feats like shooting down a number of enemy planes or bombing enemy targets."

Roosevelt, Marshall, Arnold, Doolittle, and Joe then walked from that quiet, private ceremony into the White House press room, where reporters rumbled with excitement and flashbulbs exploded in that era's blinding lights. Everyone in the room knew Jimmy; FDR, clearly thrilled that no American journalist had figured out that it was this great, legendary pilot who had commanded the raid, introduced him as "just back from our base in Shangri-La." Before making his comments, Doolittle had been thoroughly briefed about the situation, so he carefully told the press that none of his planes had been shot down and that "none was damaged to an extent that precluded its proceeding to its destination."

Reading the papers the following morning, Americans were as astounded and thrilled at these new revelations as they had been with the original "Shangri-La" press conference. Doolittle, already a national hero, had now achieved an even warmer spot in the public's hearts, as Roosevelt Library files so clearly demonstrate. A letter to the president from Mrs. T. J. Dykema, Pittsburgh, says, "It certainly was fine for you to decorate James H. Doolittle with the Congressional Medal of Honor. However I think you should have gone a little farther by giving him the privilege of having his name changed to Doobig. I hope my two boys in the Army have a similar opportunity." From M. Sumner, San Diego: "Tell Doolittle we will do more buying war bonds if he will do less ordering his men not to bomb imperial palace." Glenn McKinney of Corry, Pennsylvania, sent the president a portrait of Jimmy made from "inlaid natural wood," while ten-year-old Evelyn Spencer of Raleigh, North Carolina, sent him the just-published comic book "*A Nation's Hero!*—a complete bio of Doolittle in eight full-color pages." Meanwhile, Alaskan newspaper headlines trumpeted: NOME TOWN BOY MAKES GOOD!

The day after his visit to the White House, Jimmy faced one of the hardest assignments of his professional life—writing letters to the Raider next of kin. Some were easy, like the one to copilot Dick Cole's mother: "I am pleased to report that Dick is well and happy, although a bit homesick. . . ." Others were more of a challenge, such as the one to Ted Lawson's mom: "Your son was wounded in action. We have been unable to ascertain the exact extent of the wounds. . . ." The final ten were the most difficult. To Dean Hallmark's mother: "Your son, according to the most reliable information that we are able to obtain, landed in Japanese-occupied territory in China and has been taken prisoner. Every effort was and still is being made to extricate him from Japanese hands, but to date we have not been successful. You may depend on everything possible being done in this direction."

Even after being awarded the nation's highest honor, traveling across the country selling War Bonds and seeing, firsthand, the crowds who showed up to cheer him with a nationwide flood of love and respect, Brigadier General

Doolittle could never come to think of his raid as a triumph—military, morale-building, or otherwise. When, some years later, he was asked for his thoughts, his feelings were muted, to say the least:

> The raid had three advantages, really. The first advantage was to give the people at that time a little fillip. The news had all been bad until then. The second advantage was to cause the Japanese to worry and feel that they were vulnerable, and the third and most useful part of the raid was that it caused a diversion of aircraft and equipment to the defense of the home islands which the Japanese badly needed in the theatres where the war was actually going on.
>
> The actual damage done was minimal. When you think that we had sixteen airplanes with one ton of bombs each—sixteen tons of bombs—and in the late raids they were dropping 5,000 tons of bombs in one raid, 16 against 5,000 is pretty puny.
>
> It, for me, was a very sad occasion because, while we had accomplished the first part of our mission, we had lost all of our aircraft, and no commander feels happy when he loses all of his aircraft. And of course, we lost some of the boys.

On April 23 and 24 Stilwell reported to Arnold the news of Allied rescue attempts: "One airplane, badly crashed, and three bodies were found near Yushan at about 9:25. One airplane was found badly crashed near Wuyan . . . one airplane landed at Kiu Kiang on the Yellow River, the information being received from the Japanese radio. . . . The crewmen were said to have been captured. . . . The Chinese Air Force further reported three crewmen killed (names and places unknown)."

Later Chungking's Lieutenant Miller would cable Washington:

> Hallmark's crew bailed out near the coast and not near Lake Poyang as previously reported. Lts. Hallmark, Meder, and Neilson [sic] were captured by a small Japanese land force. Lt. Neilson was reported to have been bayoneted resisting capture, but is still alive. Sergeant Deiter [sic] and Corporal [sic] Fitzmaurice are reported to have drowned. Presumably they bailed out first and landed in the ocean and their bodies were said to have washed ashore.
>
> Lt. Farrow's crew bailed out near Lake Poyang instead of on the coast as reported. Lts. Farrow, Hite, and Barr were said to have been captured and Corporal Deshazer and Sergeant Spatz were reported to have landed in Lake Poyang and drowned. The above

information came from Chinese Intelligence sources based on rumors which came through from the occupied areas.

On June 8 Stilwell reported: "Attempts to ransom prisoners or to effect their escape through guerrillas had been unsuccessful, though efforts were being continued by agencies under the Generalissimo. There seemed to be little reason to hope for success."

SEIZED

The extraordinary chain of good fortune that had carried the young volunteers from the deck of *Hornet* across the skies of Japan to safety in Chungking had unfortunately run out for a number of the boys.

When plane six, *Green Hornet,* arrived over China, her crew did not even have the option of bailing out; they had run out of gas four minutes before making landfall and were at an altitude of only a hundred feet—too low for chutes. Pilot Dean Hallmark prepared to bring her down in the water. He called out over the interphone for his crew to get on their Mae Wests and strap themselves in, anticipating a tough jolt.

It was tougher than anyone could have imagined. *Green Hornet* slammed against the waves with such force that it was thrown fully back up into the air and then crashed into the ocean in a direct nosedive. The cabin crew could hear bombardier William Dieter in the nose, screaming. The craft exploded into pieces when it hit the water, one wing shearing away, the cabin cracking open, the sea rushing in.

Navigator Chase Nielsen was thrown around his well and then knocked out. When he came to, his nose was broken, he was bleeding all over, and the water was already up to his chest. Chase pulled himself out onto the wreckage to find copilot Bob Meder, who'd miraculously come out more or less intact. Hallmark then appeared, hoisting himself onto the floating wreckage, his legs gashed wide open. Gunner Don Fitzmaurice had hit something in the turret, and now had a deep hole in his forehead. Bombardier Bill Dieter, having taken the full force of the crash in the nose, seemed the worst off. He had obviously suffered some kind of brain injury and was now incoherent.

The plane was sinking in the darkness as fifteen-foot waves crashed over the men. When Bob pulled the CO_2 lanyard to inflate their raft, the cord broke, and he, Dean, and Chase began looking for the hand pump. Dieter slipped and fell off his perch on the wing, and though Dean reached for him, he couldn't catch the sinking, damaged boy. A giant wave drew up and over, washing the rest of the crew from the plane. Fitz was clearly not going to make it on his own to shore, so Meder grabbed him.

Each of the men dog-paddled, shouting out in the dark to remain together as a team. The combination of the night, the storm, and their injuries soon derailed those efforts. In minutes, each of them was alone, facing the dangers of an unknown shore.

Plane sixteen, *Bat Out of Hell*, had arrived with fuel to spare, circling over Chinese territory for over an hour, desperately hunting for the "57" homing signal. Pilot Bill Farrow decided to try a due-west course; maybe they could break out of the thunderheads and find a place to land. Navigator George Barr recommended a turn to the south to make sure they were well away from Japanese territory, but copilot Bob Hite disagreed. Farrow went with Hite's call.

At 2345 the fuel warning lights blinked on. There was a break in the overcast, and Bill could see a spray of light, which was clearly a city. George said he was sure it was Nanchang, and that it was Japanese-held.

"Farrow said over the interphone, 'We're out of gas, we'll have to jump,'" remembered bombardier Jake DeShazer. "I said, 'Are we in Free China or in occupied China?' and he said, 'I don't know.' I had a parachute up there with me, and you have to crawl in under where the pilot and copilot sit, and the navigator. When I got back there, they had kicked that door out on the bottom of the fuselage, and I could look down there. I looked at the altimeter before I left the nose, and it said 3,000 feet.

"As soon as I got back there, Bobby Hite said, 'Jake, you're first!' and I thought, 'Boy, I'd like to see somebody else go.' But I had the parachute on, and I had stuck my feet out down through that hole. It wasn't exactly a jump. The wind just hit, hit my legs, and knocked me right back against the fuselage. It was awful strong. I think it was 160. That isn't awful fast, but it sure makes a lot of wind. I had to grab hold of the bottom and push, because it held me right up against it. I pushed real hard, gave a shove, and then watched the plane go over my head. I lost my hat as the wind was shrieking over me.

"They told us to count to ten before you pull the ripcord, so when the plane had gone beyond me, I did that, and was given a hard but welcome jerk as the parachute immediately opened. I watched the light go out of sight from the opening in the fuselage of the plane. Soon the sound of the motors died out. Everywhere I looked it was dark. The fog was thick around me, and I felt a strange sensation of loneliness.

"I didn't feel like I was coming down. It felt like I was just sitting there, up in the air. But after I got close to the ground, I could see it was coming up pretty fast.

"Suddenly I hit the earth with an awful jolt. . . . I threw my arms around a mound of dirt and gave it a big hug. I was glad to be back on the ground even if it was a good long way from the U.S.A. I saw several mounds of dirt and noticed that I was on a knoll. Then I realized, it was a Chinese graveyard."

"There seemed to be the quietest quiet coming down," copilot Bob Hite said. "You could hear the swish of the cords as you were falling. Then that sudden halt on the ground *is* sudden. I landed in a rice paddy and hit my right ankle on a rock . . . hurt it pretty bad. I was in the paddy right up to my waist, in the mud, slime, and so forth.

"I could hear the water running and tinkling, and it was still very, very dark. I had my flashlight. I was standing there and thinking of a little song that I had heard as a boy, 10,000 miles away from home and sitting in the rain. It was kind of a lonely, eerie feeling."

It took a long four hours for the *Green Hornet* crew to swim to dry land, Bob Meder tugging Don Fitzmaurice along by the straps of his Mae West. In the attempt Fitz blacked out, and Bob struggled ashore with the body to find Bill Dieter also unconscious, rolling back and forth in the breaking waves. He brought both men up to dry land, and alternated between them with the life-saving methods he'd been taught: mouth-to-mouth, and pounds to the chest.

Chase Nielsen, alone, scrambled up a different part of the shore. He came across a ditch where he felt safe enough, and fell asleep, but soon woke to a pair of vultures eyeing him with interest. Chase cautiously raised himself up to see where he'd landed. Below, on the beach, he saw a group of fishermen and soldiers surrounding two bodies lying in the sand. As he inched over to see what was going on, a voice said: "Stand up, or me shoot!"

Chase looked up to see a young, smiling man, wearing the same cap as the other soldiers on the beach, holding an ancient gun pointed at Nielsen's stomach. Chase said, "You Japanese?"

The man replied, "Me China. You American? You Japanee?"

Chase stood, fully relieved. "Me American," he said, and looked once more at the men in the sand. He could tell, now, that they were Fitz and Bill. The soldier followed his glance. "They dead. Bury them in one hour. You go with me."

Dean Hallmark had escaped being seen by the various men along the shore that morning and had walked into a village, where he was immediately surrounded by curious Chinese. Nothing could be communicated, so he was led to a mud hut and given some tea. One fisherman indicated that someone was coming, and Hallmark thought he meant Japanese troops. Dean took a club, and stationed himself next to the door, ready to knock unconscious the next person who came in. Thankfully he paused before striking, since it was Chase who stepped through.

They were, they discovered, in a Chinese guerrilla camp, and eventually Bob Meder was brought in as well. He explained how he'd tried to revive Fitzmaurice and Dieter, but there was nothing that could be done for them. The Chinese told the *Green Hornet* survivors they would smuggle them to safety, but it would be extremely difficult.

That night, the guerrillas led the men to where the bodies had been hidden. Coffins had been built, and twenty-nine-year-old Sgt. William J. Dieter of Vail, Iowa, and twenty-three-year-old Sgt. Donald E. Fitzmaurice, of Lincoln, Nebraska, were placed inside, carried to a high spot in the sand, and buried. The Americans prayed, remembering what Doolittle had said: Some will come home as heroes. Others, as angels.

Too deep in shock to realize that a few of his ribs had been broken, *Bat Out of Hell*'s Jake DeShazer walked until he came to a small brick building. Inside were platforms that had obviously been used in burning incense. It was a shrine, but shelter from the rain, so Jake fell dead asleep and awoke with first light.

Near the shrine was a path, which he followed. The people he met along the way were completely uninterested in him: "I could see inside their mud houses. Chickens, pigs, and children were wading around together in filthy mud inside the house. The people had heads about the size of a four-year-old child in America. The skin on their faces was wrinkled and old looking."

Jake walked into a store and wrote some words on a pad but couldn't communicate at all with the man behind the counter. He continued down the path, coming across a group of buildings. Outside, bent over a ditch, were some soldiers washing their clothes, but since he couldn't tell if they were Chinese or Japanese, he kept walking. Along the way a bit was another building, where soldiers were playing with children, which made him feel a little safer—but not safe enough that he didn't have his pistol ready, with a bullet chambered and the hammer cocked.

He pointed to himself, said "America," and then pointed to the Asians and asked, "China or Japan?"

"China," they said immediately. Even so, Jake felt something was wrong, and turned to leave. Ten soldiers were now blocking the doorway, armed with bayonets, pistols, rifles, and swords. One took his gun away, and then the group took him to a camp.

Led into the main building, he was seated at a table, where an officer began asking him questions, in fairly good English, and it was at that moment that Jake knew these men were not Chinese. He felt lower than a snake's belly. After letting him have some hotcakes with apple butter, the officer announced: "You are in the hands of the Japanese. Aren't you afraid?"

Jake said, "Why should I be afraid?"

The morning after the funeral of William Dieter and Donald Fitzmaurice, Captain Ling, head of the local guerrillas, arranged for a Chinese sampan, crowded with travelers and soldiers, to ferry away the *Green Hornet* survivors. Within hours of its departure, a Japanese patrol boat was spotted, and the Americans were hidden below. The patrol came abreast, halting the sampan at gunpoint. A boarding party began to search the boat, inch by inch, and in the darkness of the hold, one soldier poked the bags with a stick, hitting Chase right in the gut.

The next day they docked at the city of Wenchow. Everyone waited until nightfall, and then the Americans were led to the middle of town and hidden with an elderly man named Wong. Ling warned them that Japanese troops were out in full force, with dozens of search parties looking for the Americans who had bombed Tokyo. Wong was a man they could trust.

Their new benefactor could speak excellent English, having been educated in London. He served the men a wonderful dinner, and told them of the horrors of the war with Japan. Just as they finished, a young boy rushed in and talked to Wong hurriedly. He left, and the old man explained that the Japanese were searching that part of the city, and they would have to sneak out somehow. If they could get to the river, there were many boats to hide in, and they would be safe.

Dozens of Japanese soldiers with machine guns on tripods were already out on the street. Wong assembled a group of his neighbors, who surrounded the Americans, camouflaging them with their long robes. The party walked down the road and into another building. They were told to wait as the elderly gentleman went out to survey the situation. He came back a few minutes later to report that thirty Japanese soldiers were right on their trail and there was nowhere else to go. They would have to hide, somehow, right where they were.

The more seriously injured Dean Hallmark covered himself under a pile of sacks, blankets, and mats in the corner, while Bob Meder and Chase Nielsen climbed up into the ceiling's rafters. Wong started up a brazier in the middle of the room to create a distraction. They could hear the crack of the soldiers' boots on the cobblestone streets coming closer, and one Japanese came inside, looked around, and left.

Just as the Americans thought they were free and clear, Captain Ling returned, accompanied by a Japanese officer and two soldiers. Ling asked Wong a question, and when the older man shrugged, he slapped him hard across the face. One soldier ran to the corner and began kicking at the pile of blankets and sacks, uncovering Hallmark, who was ordered to stand. "Where are the other two men?" the officer demanded, in English. "What other men?" Dean asked.

The officer pulled out his pistol, turned to Wong, and began berating and pistol-whipping him. As Wong tried to defend himself, the officer pursued him into a corner and swung back to hit him with full force. As he did he looked up into the rafters, and directly into the face of Chase Nielsen.

Navigator George Barr's worries that his *Bat Out of Hell* crew had bailed into enemy-controlled territory were now coming all too true. "In the morning when the chickens were crowing and the daylight was breaking, I started wandering around from house to house to see if I could find a friendly Chinese," said *Bat* copilot Bob Hite. "As I approached some of these houses prior to daylight, the Chinese dogs were vociferous and barking. So the first two or three houses I tried, I backed off. . . . I found a house later in the morning that sort of accepted me. There were no dogs. It was a man and his wife, and I think they had three or four children. I had a pocketful of Lucky Strike cigarettes and Mounds candy bars and about $5 in silver. They ate my candy. I didn't know the Chinese women would smoke, but this Chinese lady was smoking those Lucky Strike cigarettes like they were going out of style.

"The man put on a little shawl and a big flat hat and his little wooden shoes and motioned for me to follow him, and I did. He led me through the rice paddies and dikes for about thirty minutes, but he led me to a house. In front of this was a soldier walking, a Chinese soldier without saber or rifle, or any armament. He spoke English. The soldier asked me who I was and I said that I was an American and that I was here to help Chiang Kai-shek. He was very friendly and he said, 'Well, let's get something to eat.' We went toward this little cluster of houses . . . as we approached . . . about fifteen Japanese soldiers came running out with bayoneted rifles and surrounded me. The first thing they did was search me and they found that I had a .45 in my knee pocket. They kept me surrounded with their rifles and then they put me in a 1938 Ford truck—that galled me a little bit—and carried me about a mile and a half into a little town with a building with a Japanese flag over the door.

"They had maps, and they were trying to get me to say where I had come from. I told them that I was just going to Chungking. There was a ranking Japanese officer that came in, and through an interpreter, told me directly that I was a prisoner of war of the Japanese, and that I should make no attempt to escape, and so on and so forth."

George Barr had also landed in a rice paddy, and though he had a sprain and a bruised knee, he felt okay and started walking. Suddenly he heard a shout and could feel the muzzle of a rifle against his back. A group appeared and searched him head to toe. The men tied his wrists in front of him and the crooks of his elbows behind, and took him at gunpoint to a nearby town. It was Nanchang.

Barr was led to a large room where between ten and fifteen Japanese officers, in full military dress, held court. The table in front of them was crowded with wine, whiskey, candy, and cigarettes. George was interrogated but refused to say anything beyond his name, rank, and serial number. He explained that he'd jumped out of an airplane, landed on his head, and couldn't remember a thing.

Eventually he was taken to a different room and told to go to sleep. Just as he was drifting off the door opened, and another man was shoved inside. It was Bobby Hite: "They put us into cells. Then they took us out, and they interrogated us one at a time to try to find out where we had come from. I was spat on. I guess the one thing that any human being despises would be for somebody to spit on them in the face."

Americans who signed up to serve in World War II believed that getting captured by the enemy was the worst thing that could happen to them. "Everyone going out swore they'd rather die in battle than be taken as a POW," one captive remembered. "When the Japs got us, I thought we were losers. I thought if I get out of this and get home, everyone will think I'm just a failure.

"Emotionally it was the worst thing that ever happened in my life. For the first time, I was completely out of control. Everybody felt that. Even in solitary you could hear some of the others crying late at night."

The Japanese themselves believed that *horyo,* soldiers who allowed themselves to be captured, were pathetic and subhuman. The nation's field manual, issued to all its army recruits, clearly ordered: "Bear in mind the fact that to be captured means not only that you disgrace yourself, but your parents and family will never be able to hold up their heads again. Always save the last bullet for yourself," while the army criminal code warned its officers: "A com-mander who allows his unit to surrender to the enemy without fighting to the last man . . . shall be punishable by death."

When it came to their new POWs, however, the Japanese had even greater antipathy. They judged Allied airmen as the lowest of the low, especially bomber crews. One B-29 group shot down over Singapore would be marched through the city naked and then, in a public ceremony, beheaded. At Han-kow three airmen would be tortured and then set on fire. One B-29 pilot would be locked up in the Tokyo Zoo monkey cage, naked and on display for public amusement. Though Doolittle had explicitly ordered his men not to bomb the Temple of Heaven, their attack on the homelands was nevertheless viewed by many Japanese as an attack on the holy father of the nation. The eight captive Doolittle Raiders would be dealt with accordingly.

At 0100 Pfc. Kumano Tatsuo was woken up and told to report to head-quarters, where he found army intelligence officers questioning captured *Bat* gunner Harold Spatz. Spatz refused to say anything, and finally the officers gave up, but Kumano, who understood English reasonably well, remained behind to chat. He and Spatz talked about Kansas, and the American's fam-ily, and eventually the gunner confessed: They'd shipped out from San Diego, loaded into bombers stationed on a makeshift island runway in the Pacific, and flown due south for seven hours to reach China.

In the morning George Barr and Bob Hite looked out the window to see the Japanese taking photographs of DeShazer, Farrow, and Spatz. At least they weren't alone. That afternoon all five were blindfolded, handcuffed, and leg cuffed; loaded into a plane; and flown to a military prison. Their new cells had wooden bars, like a cage, with dirt floors and nothing but a wooden-box toilet for furniture. Outside a parade of guards marched back and forth, back and forth.

That night each American was once again taken in for questioning. The officer interrogating Hite spoke perfect English and handed him a piece of paper. It was the roster of every man who'd taken part in the raid. "One of the officers, using lots of slang, said that I had better talk," Jake DeShazer remem-bered. "He said that these were mean people, and they would torture me until I did talk. I was still blindfolded, as I had been most of the time for over twelve hours, and hadn't eaten all day. I had been asked questions at every opportunity, but I would always tell them that I wouldn't talk. . . .

"I was then led into a room, and the blindfold was removed. A little Japa-nese of stocky build was standing behind a table, smoking a cigar, rubbing his hands together, and talking really fast in Japanese. . . . Through the inter-preter, he said: 'I am the kindest judge in all China. You're very fortunate to be questioned by me. You just tell us what the truth is, and we'll give you a nice glass of warm, sweet milk."

JUDGE: "Doolittle was your commanding officer, was that true?"
DESHAZER: "I won't talk."
JUDGE: "How do you pronounce H-O-R-N-E-T?"
DESHAZER: "Hornet."
JUDGE: "And this is the aircraft carrier you flew off to bomb Japan, isn't it?"
DESHAZER: "I won't talk."
JUDGE: "Colonel Doolittle was your commanding officer, wasn't he?"
DESHAZER: "I won't talk."

The judge "got madder and madder, and finally he yanked that sword out. He had that sword on the side, and he just pulled it out like that. He held it up, and it was a shining, bright steel sword. He said, 'Tomorrow morning when the sun comes up, I'm going to have the honor of cutting your head off.'"

DeShazer considered this. "I told him I thought it would be a great honor to me if the kindest judge in China cut my head off. The judge and the others laughed for the first time, and a little later I was taken to my cell. They gave me a glass of warm milk, and I remember drinking that nice, sweet milk.

"I lay in the cell all night, blindfolded, handcuffed, without blankets. They let me lie down, but, boy, the lice were just crawling all over me that night. There's a lot of lice in China, seems like. The next morning at sunrise, I was led out of my cell. I had no breakfast. The blindfold was taken off, the handcuffs were removed. I looked around for the judge with his weapon of execution, but I saw a fellow with a camera, and everyone was smiling. After the picture was taken, I was loaded onto a Japanese two-motor transport. Again I was blindfolded, handcuffed, tied with ropes. I could hear some of my companions talking, but I was not able to say anything to them."

The Japanese had first taken their prisoners to the local garrison offices, and then flown them up the chain of command to Shanghai. Now they were sent on another long flight. From time to time, Jake was able to peek out of his blindfold. At one point, he saw a snow-covered volcano, a mountain every American schoolboy knew well—Mount Fuji.

Arriving in Tokyo, the *Bat Out of Hell* crew was taken to a prison run by the Kempeitai, the Japanese military police force similar to Germany's Gestapo. The Kempeitai had refined the art and science of extracting confessions to the point where they knew exactly how far to take a man until he was as near to death as possible, without killing him completely. The most senior, most experienced, and most educated of the Kempeitai were stationed in

Tokyo. "I personally severed more than forty heads," said Kempeitai officer Cpl. Uno Shintaro. "Today I no longer remember each of them well. It might sound extreme, but I can almost say that if more than two weeks went by without my taking a head, I didn't feel right. Physically I needed to be refreshed. I would go to the stockade and bring someone out, one who looked as if he wouldn't live long. I'd do it on the riverbank, by the regimental headquarters, or by the side of the road. . . . A good sword could cause a head to drop with just an easy motion. But even I sometimes botched the job. . . . Sometimes I'd hit the shoulder. Once a lung popped out, almost like a balloon. I was shocked. All I could do was hit the base of the neck with my full strength. Blood spurted out. Arteries were cut, you see. The man fell immediately, but it wasn't a water faucet, so it soon stopped. Looking at that, I felt ecstasy. . . . It was almost like being addicted to murder. When I met people, I often looked at their necks and made a judgment. Is this an easy neck, or hard to cut?"

Every two to three hours, the Kempeitai brought each captive in for questioning. The interpreter at these sessions began every sentence with, "Well, well," which became his nickname to the Americans. Well-Well told them that all they had to do was cooperate. Why, he wondered, had they claimed they'd taken off from Midway or the Aleutians when everyone knew a B-25 couldn't fly that far? They were shown papers with details of the mission—mention of *Hornet,* the number of planes involved, the names of the crews—and it was clear that these had been found on one of the downed Mitchells.

"I'd sit there, cold, and my knees would be shaking," Jake DeShazer said. "I don't know whether it was the food or what made my knees shake. I tried to stop them from shaking, but I couldn't seem to stop them. I didn't like that. It looked like I was scared. I guess I was."

When the men wouldn't respond or would give false answers, they would be slapped and punched in the head. The Japanese had never before seen a redhead like the six-foot-two New Yorker George Barr. They asked George what he ate or drank to make his hair that color, and treated him like a monkey in a cage. George would eventually become deaf in one ear after being repeatedly hit in the head with a rifle butt.

The prisoners were given daily rations of watery rice and tea, and if they were ever discovered sleeping, the guards would scream them awake or poke them with sticks. The beatings escalated into kicks in the groin and punches to the face.

The Kempeitai then turned to even crueler strategies. Sticks would be placed between the captive's fingers, which would be tied up tight. As one guard crushed the hand as hard as he physically could, another yanked the sticks back and forth, popping out the knuckles. Some POWs were forced to drink gallons of water and then lie on the floor as five guards took turns jumping on their stomachs. Whenever a captive lost consciousness or the Kempeitai knew he was minutes from death, they would stop and resuscitate, beginning the tortures all over again.

On April 24 the Shanghai Kempeitai took the three *Green Hornet* captives into their custody. "My arms were bound to the back of a chair, and my legs to the chair," Chase Nielsen would remember. "I was slapped on my head and face and was kicked on my leg. A Japanese military police kicked me so hard that he even left a scar. They slapped my head and face and kicked my legs so hard that the wound which was received at the Shanghai prison reopened and bled. I was almost continuously beaten and kicked until four o'clock in the morning. . . .

"I was given what they call the water cure. . . . I was put on my back on the floor with my arms and legs stretched out, one guard holding each limb. A towel was wrapped around my face and put across my face and water was poured on. They poured water on this towel until I was almost unconscious from strangulation, then they would let up until I'd get my breath, then they'd start all over again. I felt more or less like I was drowning, just gasping between life and death. . . .

"The guard then brought in a large bamboo pole about three inches in diameter. This was placed directly behind my knees. I was then made to squat on the floor in this position like a kneel. One guard had hold of each of my arms, one other guard then placed his foot on my thigh and would jump up and down causing severe pain in my knees. . . . I felt that my joints were coming apart, but after about five minutes of that my knees were so numb I couldn't feel anything else."

The twenty-five-year-old lieutenant from Utah would additionally suffer through two varieties of rack torture. One held him horizontally with leather straps and winches above a table, pulling his head away from his ankles and wrists. Another time he was hung by his handcuffs high up on a wall, so that his toes just barely touched the floor. The pain traveling from his wrists through his entire body was so severe that he passed out within minutes. For that he was grateful.

Even though the Japanese had already retrieved enough documents to tell them everything they needed to know about the Doolittle Raid, they simply could not believe that American bombers had successfully launched from an aircraft carrier, and were determined to beat the truth out of their captives. As the questioning continued, the prisoners were not allowed to bathe, forcing the Kempeitai officers to wear stronger and stronger perfumes to mask their victims' odors. To all questions, the men answered: "Lt. Robert J. Meder, serial # 0-421280," "Lt. Dean E. Hallmark, # 0-421081," "Lt. Chase J. Nielsen, # 0-419938." Eventually the fliers learned what answers especially enraged the Kempeitai—such as insisting they'd never been to a particular city, even if it was true—and what responses seemed to please them, such as making up stories that were plausible to those who'd never been to the United States.

Thoughts of suicide naturally occurred to these young prisoners. The Americans would think, What could be worse than this? Why not end it now? Then they would remember they had no means; they didn't even have the power to kill themselves.

One evening their interrogator sadly explained to each of the *Green Hornet* crewmen in turn that, since he had not been cooperative and since the Japanese had tried everything they could think of, there was only one solution. At dusk the men were blindfolded and led outside. They could feel the heat of the sun, and could hear the boots and sounds of what must have been their firing squad. The POWs knew from moviehouse newsreel accounts that the Japanese frequently executed their prisoners, but they hadn't really believed that this might actually happen to them.

Their march came to a halt, and the men were swung to an about-face. They could hear a shouted order, and the racket of rifles being jerked into position and cocked. Sweat poured down their faces. There was another shouted order, followed by the sound of feet, this time marching off into the distance. Then the men heard their interpreter, laughing. "We are the Knights of *Bushido,* of the Order of the Rising Sun," he explained. "We don't execute at sundown; we execute at sunrise."

The next day the men of *Green Hornet* were leg cuffed, handcuffed, and flown to Japan. Being assembled for the trip brought them out of solitary for the first time since capture, and now they had the chance to see one another. Each was grateful for the knowledge that he wasn't alone in this, and, at the same time, shocked at the condition of his crewmates. They were taken to the same prison as the *Bat* aviators but kept in solitary, so none of the Americans had any idea that they were now eight in number. For two months their tortures and interrogations would continue.

As the crewmen of *Bat Out of Hell* and *Green Hornet* were being moved up the hierarchy of Japanese military torture, the empire's army in southeastern China was drawing closer and closer to the injured Americans stranded in Linhai. Frank England, the hospital missionary, had a short-wave radio powered by a windmill that mostly broadcast Chinese music not exactly soothing to American ears (as Ted Lawson noted, "Their scale has five notes, but there seems to be some ban against using more than three of them"). In the middle of May, however, the radio picked up a San Francisco station broadcasting news of American jubilation over the bombing of Japan and Doolittle's Medal of Honor. Mac, Dean, and Ted were thrilled to hear of the raid's success, yet terribly discouraged to learn, as the broadcast implied, that they were the only men of the mission in any real danger.

After three weeks in China, Ted had lost eighty pounds. He could see each of his ribs, and the kneecap of his remaining leg "looked like a turret." He tried shaving for the first time only to discover that his beard was matted with blood and covered in lice, and "what hurt most now were my arms. They were full of lumps and bruises from the needles. I couldn't sleep much because my back was now filled with bedsores."

Slowly Ted got stronger, however, and one afternoon, the missionaries came in with presents for him: a fork, created by a local silversmith, and a pair of crutches. Through runners Charlie sent his regards, as well as the news that some of the peasants who'd helped Ted and his crew on Nantien had been captured by the Japanese and tortured. At the same time the Chinese underground issued a warning: For the residents of Linhai, it was escape now or never. "We stayed at the hospital until the Japanese started the offensive against Xinhwa, at which time it looked like we might be cut off, so even though some of the men were not in as good condition as I would like to have them to travel, we started anyway," Doc White said.

May 18, the one-month anniversary of the bombing of Tokyo, was another day of torrential rains in Chekiang Province. Ted Lawson, Mac McClure, Dean Davenport, Bob Clever, Doc White, and the young Dr. Chen, with sedan chairs and bearers, began to make their way west. "Before we left the grounds of the little hospital, Dr. C came to my chair, smiling blandly," Ted remembered. "'I want to show you something,' he said, and ordered my coolies to carry me around to the other side of the hospital. They set me down beside a coffin. It was a new one, made by the same Chinese carpenter who had made my crutches. It was to have been mine."

They traveled all day, the bearers racing one another, encouraged by the offer of cigarette butts and sometimes spilling their human loads onto the cold, wet ground. That night they stayed in a missionary family's home and ate dove eggs sauced with peanut oil and brown sugar. "After I was in bed, I asked myself out loud why it was that every bed I slept in had the same overpowering smell," Lawson recalled. "It must be some sort of national disinfectant the Chinese use, I said to myself.

"Doc came in and gave me more morphine. Then I could say the truth. It was my leg, not any disinfectant. I had been trying to kid myself. . . .

"It was tough that night, trying to sleep. When I finally did doze off, I was promptly awakened by the sound of a gong in the street and the voice of a Chinese calling out something I couldn't understand.

"Mrs. Smyth came in early the next morning with a breakfast of English muffins and tea. 'Did the noise wake you up last night?' she asked, cheerfully.

"I said it did, and asked what it was.

"She laughed. 'Oh, it was just our town crier. He was telling the people to leave the village because the Japanese are getting closer.'"

The caravan started up again at dawn, climbing mountains along such rocky trails that Ted was certain if a Japanese sniper didn't kill them, a tripping bearer would. As they reached the top of a ridge, a plane soared overhead, its wings clearly marked with red suns.

That evening they reached a village and picked up a Ford station wagon and a charcoal-engine truck, so Ted could lie down: "The springs of that truck just weren't springs. Every time we'd hit a bump, and we must have hit a million, I'd leave the floor. The next bump would get me coming down. I used both my hands to keep what was left of my leg from banging. That didn't help much. It just thumped and bled and throbbed.

"Behind us I heard one explosion after another, regularly paced. I asked Dr. C what they were.

"'Japanese too close,' he said, sad and placid. 'So Chinese blow up road behind us, just after we pass. . . . I didn't want to tell you.'"

The group arrived in Chuchow, and the Americans couldn't help but be excited. This had been their original destination, and surely the Chinese air force could take over from here. But they were too late. The enemy was now so close that the Chinese had already destroyed the airfield to keep it from being useful to the enemy. The group hurried on.

Coming over the crest of a hill, the refugees paused to take a breath. In the valley below was a river filled with boats of fleeing Chinese. The only ones left behind were those with nowhere to go. "As we went down the road, they blew up the bridge in back of us and tore the road out," Doc White said. "We were the last car to get out. We traveled two days by bus and two days by station wagon to Hengyang, and then we took the train from Hengyang to Kweilin."

Here at last was an airfield from which they could be taken to Chungking, as well as an American Volunteers Group (Flying Tigers) hostel, and a great treat for the men: real coffee. Their plane was promised to arrive the following day. That afternoon they watched as a squadron of Japanese bombers attacked the city. "In their bewilderingly casual way the Chinese have an amazing system of air raid alarms," Lawson said. "We were having breakfast in Kweilin when the first warning sounded. The noise was made by a Chinese hitting an old automobile brake drum with a spike. As soon as we found out what it meant, we started to get up from the table.

"'Keep your seats,' the AVG man said, continuing his breakfast, pretty bored by the whole thing. 'The planes have just taken off. You'll know when the planes get closer. He'll start beating faster and faster.' And he went back to his food while we picked at ours and listened to the brake drum.

"The man was beating the brake drum a little faster now; then much faster. We looked at the AVG man lingering over his coffee . . . finally, he got up and stretched. We jumped up and followed him to a nearby cave that was the hostel's shelter.

"The planes were over the city and the field a few minutes later, giving both of them hell.

"Some terribly long time after that—maybe half an hour—we heard the jeep coming. And then saw it. The AVG man was driving; with him were Ed McElroy, who was on the raid, and Davey Jones—with a medical kit.

"I knew I'd start crying as soon as I heard Davey's voice, and damned if I didn't. You see, Dave was the first one of the boys I had heard from. The never explainable Chinese grapevine brought him word, after he reached Chuchow Lishui, that Doc was going to take my leg. Davey sent me a letter by a series of runners. It meant a lot to me. Davey never mentioned the leg in the letter, but I knew he knew."

That night Davey was able to fill Doc, Ted, and the other men from the *Duck* in on what had happened to the rest of the guys. As good as it was for them all to be together, and to be in a nice comfortable place, and to have coffee, these men desperately needed to get to a hospital. But day after day passed with no plane coming for them from Chungking. Their hopes began to fade, until finally, on the morning of June 4, the plane appeared, and they were rushed aboard. Within an hour of takeoff, the AVG man who'd been so unconcerned about getting to the shelter radioed: The Japanese were once again bombing the strip; they'd gotten out just in time.

"'You think it was worthwhile?' one of the boys asked me before we went to sleep that early morning," Ted remembered. "I thought it over for a while, trying to see the whole thing objectively. When I finally said that I did, I meant it. We'll probably never know just how much damage we caused. The important thing, I figured, was that our people got a lift out of it. It made them sure that we could go to work on the Japs, no matter how far away they were.

"I hadn't thought much about our people, before that night. A fellow doesn't volunteer for something like the Japan raid, bomb the place, try to get away, and, in my case, lose a leg and say, 'This is for the dear people.' You just don't say or openly feel those things. You think about yourself most of the time; whether you'll have guts enough to go through with the thing, and whether you'll get away with it. It's only later, when you add up things and get the sum, that you think of the people. And the cause. And then you hope you've done both of them some good."

If this story had been a typical movie of its era, all the Raiders who hadn't been captured by the Japanese, interned by the Russians, or were too sick to get out of China would by now have been stateside, paraded through the streets of small-town America by hordes of jubilant citizens. In fact the depression-stunted air corps now suffered from a serious shortage of qualified crewmen, and for every other Doolittle volunteer, the world was at war and the show must go on.

Many Raiders would spend the rest of the conflict stuck in CBI/SEAC hell (China-Burma-India/Southeast Asia Command, known to wags as "Confused Bastards in India" and "Saving England's Asian Colonies"). For an Allied command dedicated first to stopping Hitler and then to supporting the efforts of Nimitz and MacArthur, this theater was not a priority. "We were sort of orphans for a while," remembered plane thirteen copilot Dick Knobloch. "We didn't have airplanes. We sat around in Allahabad . . . living in barracks provided by the English and the Indian army. . . . The war in Europe was number one, and we were the end of the world so far as everything was concerned, matériel, few airplanes came over, equipment and spare parts, bombs. . . . I ended up in upper Assam, near the border with Burma, and then flew fifty-some missions out of there against the Japanese."

"With a bunch of the other guys, I was flown to India, and waiting for another flight back to the U.S.," said plane four navigator Harry McCool. "We had several days in Calcutta. The Allies were setting up an air force in India, and its commanding general needed fliers, so he canceled my orders home. He put me on a B-25 to Allahabad air base for training, and eventually I returned to China to help Chiang Kai-shek.

"A request for three B-25 crews to go to Calcutta and fly reconnaissance over Burma was announced. Due to my experience in China, I appealed to my crew members: 'Let's go down and fight the Japs in Burma instead of going to China.' And that's what ended up happening.

"The pilot of my thirteenth mission was a Texan called 'Singing Boy'

Johnson. It was his last mission, and he had never fired a single shot at the enemy (none of us had). We saw a Japanese ship anchored at the little port of Akyab, Burma, so he took the plane down to make a strafing attack. As we came around a second time, that ship fired on us. Our bombardier was killed, an engine damaged, and we had to ditch into the Indian Ocean, fifty miles offshore (a Japanese-controlled shore).

"We took out the two lifeboats, and found one had a broken inflator. We were six injured men, one dead, with the aircraft sinking and boats for only half of us. Somehow both rafts were inflated, tied together, and we climbed in and started drifting. We landed on what turned out to be Oyster Island off the Burmese coast, where we stayed two or three days. There was plenty of water, but we couldn't find anything to eat, so we filled up some cans with drinking water and got back in the rafts. One of the guys had used fabric from the lighthouse to make a sail, but it wasn't big enough to counter the winds and current. For six days we drifted north, and that night a typhoon wind came up and threw us ashore. We fell asleep on the beach and when we woke up, about twenty-five Burmese were watching us.

"Three of us stayed on the beach, and the other three went into the brush and rice paddy area, where we met a troop of Gurkhas. They doctored our wounds, and notified Calcutta we were safe. Our commanding officer flew a DC-2 down, landed on the sandy beach, and welcomed us aboard with a quart of Scotch. I had lost twenty pounds, and the others were equally weakened. After a two-hour flight back, the air force had six roaring drunks deplaning into India."

When Japan took full control of Burma and its famous Road, supporting China became terribly dangerous for the Allied transport crews. The only way to supply Chungking now was to fly over the Himalayas. "Jumping the Hump" from India's Assam or Ledo to China's Kunming meant raising a plane to twice its manufacturer-specified altitude until ice coated the wings, clearing 29,000 feet in 100-mph winds that could tear a craft apart at the seams, making their way through air pockets that could raise or drop a plane thousands of feet instantly, and then flying forty-five minutes over Japanese-held territory. The ATC (Air Transport Command) lost an average of thirteen planes a month in its three years of operation, or a total of 468. Morale soured, as many fliers soon came to believe they were risking their lives not to fight the Japs, but for the continuing prosperity of the Kuomintang elite. Even so, eventually these crews learned to do the impossible, and in the war's closing days, FDR would insist they receive a Presidential Unit Citation.

Too many Doolittle Raiders, however, would become part of the terrible Hump statistics. "On the sixteenth [of May 1942], Sergeant Larkin and I received orders for New Delhi," said *Hari Kari-er* bombardier Bill Birch. "There I saw Captain Greening, who told me that the detachment had been split up, with some of the officers heading for the States and the rest of us being absorbed into other squadrons as needed. For me that meant Karachi and then Allahabad, where I met up with Sergeant Gardner again." Clayton Bissell ordered a sortie of six B-25s from India to bomb Lashio, Burma, and then land in Kunming. Claire Chennault argued that, given the weather conditions and the poor charts for the area, this was a dangerous undertaking, but Bissell ignored the advice.

After the six Billys dropped their loads, they were immediately attacked by Japanese planes and ducked into the clouds to evade, but weren't familiar with the area's mountainous terrain. "Six ships left on June second, with Gardner flying as upper gunner for a Major Leiland in his B-25," Bill Birch said. "I was to go five days later. On the fifth, we learned that only one of the six ships made it to China, and it was all shot to hell. The others crashed either in Burma or somewhere nearby, trying to cross the Hump at too low an altitude." *Hari* navigator Frank Kappeler survived to land in Kunming. Twenty-five-year-old Lt. Gene McGurl of Belmont, Massachusetts, navigator for plane five; twenty-six-year-old Staff Sgt. Omer Duquette of West Warnick, Rhode Island, gunner for plane twelve; and twenty-two-year-old Sgt. Melvin J. Gardner of Mesa, Arizona, engineer/gunner for *Hari Kari-er*, were killed in those crashes on June 3, 1942.

As the Doolittle Raiders were thrown by war across the globe, another group of men, also not as well remembered as they deserve, would spend their combat years in Hawaii as self-confined prisoners of the windowless basement in Pearl Harbor's Naval District Administration Building. The Japanese attackers missed the building entirely on December 7, an oversight that would turn out to be one of their greatest strategic errors.

The men in that basement made up Hypo, the local branch office of Op-20-G, the Communications Security Section of the Office of Naval Communications. Their chief came to work in a scarlet quilted smoking jacket and bedroom slippers, an outfit designed not for relaxation but because he felt so responsible for December 7 that he rarely left the basement and he almost never slept. Joseph J. Rochefort, Jr., and his Hypo staff were responsible for decoding Imperial Japanese codes, a cracking known as Magic, which exposed a solid percentage of the thousands of messages pouring out from Tokyo daily to its foreign embassies and to all its ships at sea. The commander using Magic to its greatest advantage would turn out to be blue-eyed, silver-haired Adm. Chester Nimitz. When he first arrived in Hawaii to assume the post of Commander-in-Chief, Pacific Fleet (CINCPAC) on Christmas morning of '41, the boat ferrying Nimitz from the seaplane to the Pearl Harbor docks had to make its way between rescue workers still fishing out corpses from sunken battleships. From that moment, the admiral burned for revenge.

Just as the Nazis had no idea London was deciphering all their messages through Enigma, the Japanese were convinced that slothful Americans would never be able to crack their ingenious codes. This arrogance would give the United States an advantage in one crucial battle, the engagement that Yamamoto was next engineering, the decisive confrontation between the American and Japanese navies triggered by the Doolittle Raid. If it weren't for Rochefort, Hypo, a series of Japanese missteps, and the profound bravery of certain navy airmen in this battle, it's not unlikely that Tokyo's dreams of Operation Number One—and the vast Asian empire of *Dai Nippon Teikoku*—would remain intact to this day.

On May 5, 1942, Hypo intercepted an order to the Combined Fleet to strike the Aleutian Islands of Attu and Kiska on June 3, as well as a secret location known only as "AH" on June 4. Rochefort believed that "AH" might refer to the tiny American marine and Army Air Force garrison of Midway Island, a notion his superiors dismissed as ridiculous. Why would Tokyo want to strike at opposite ends of the Pacific simultaneously, and why would the Japanese use almost their entire navy in pursuit of two negligible specks of atoll? In fact, were Japan to seize Midway, it would have a solid ribbon of defense across the Pacific, keeping the home islands safe from the sea-lane used by Task Force 16; it could drive the Americans entirely out of its Asian sphere; it would get a key stepping-stone for the eventual conquest of Hawaii; and it could use Midway as the base for a full retaliatory strike against the North American continent.

Even though they couldn't discern Yamamoto's strategy, Rochefort's superiors gave him the go-ahead to plot a trick. Using the navy's undersea cable so that no Japanese listeners could overhear, Rochefort told Midway officers to openly broadcast a false distress call that their distillation plant was malfunctioning. Almost immediately Japanese forces on Wake reported back to Tokyo that "AH" had problems with its water.

Hypo then uncovered more details of Yamamoto's plan: "AH" would be attacked by a group of four carriers led by Nagumo Chuichi, the hero of Pearl Harbor, followed by an invasion from a second force. A third armada, which included three of Japan's finest battleships, would meanwhile wait nearby for the American navy to rush to Midway's defense.

This last piece of strategy was almost as important to Admiral Yamamoto as defending his emperor from further Doolittle raids, since it would realize a fifty-year-old dream of naval warriors from around the world. In *The Influence of Sea Power upon History, 1660–1783* (the teenage FDR's favorite Christmas present), Alfred Thayer Mahan theorized that command of the oceans was the key to success in any war, and that the way to secure the sea was to engage the enemy's main force and destroy it in what the Japanese called the *kantai kessen* (the decisive battle). After the enemy's fleet was vanquished, its coast and ports would be subjected to blockade and invasion—with the victor's army coming in, as a subsidiary force, to mop up. For Annapolis the War of 1812 had proved Mahan's strategies absolutely valid, and for the Japanese naval academy at Etajima, the great naval defeat of Russia in 1905 had done the same. At Midway, Yamamoto would exact revenge for the Doolittle attack as well as completely destroy America's Pacific Fleet in one gigantic and decisive battle of the sea.

As Yamamoto began to assemble his mission, Hypo was able to decrypt the date, location, time, and ships assigned to "AH." On May 24, Rochefort was able to hand the exact Japanese battle plans to Ed Layton, CINCPAC's intelligence officer, who studied the transcriptions, the Pacific charts, tides, winds, and weather, and informed Nimitz that the Japanese would "come in from the northwest on bearing 325 degrees and they will be sighted at about 175 miles from Midway, and the time will be about 0600." It was, point by point, exactly what would happen.

Even with this key knowledge, Nimitz only had three TGs to send against Yamamoto's ten battleships, twenty-four cruisers, seventy destroyers, eighteen tankers, fifteen submarines, eight aircraft carriers, and assorted transports—185 ships in all. The Japanese carriers were armed with 261 planes, outnumbering the Americans by around 40 craft, all manned by far-better-trained and far-more-combat-ready pilots. *Yamato* and *Musashi,* the most remarkable ships ever built by Japan and the largest battleships ever built anywhere, would also take part, each of them armed with nine eighteen-inch guns throwing 3,200-pound shells a distance of twenty-five miles. To compound Nimitz's difficulties, one of the greatest U.S. admirals had been sidelined; the stress and exhaustion of the first months of war had finally caught up with Bill Halsey, who succumbed to an attack of eczema that sent him to the hospital. In his stead, Rear Adm. Ray Spruance became temporary head of *Enterprise,* joined by Rear Adm. Frank "Jack" Fletcher on *Yorktown,* and Pete Mitscher on *Hornet.* Spruance's sole prior combat experience lay in overseeing the escort ships for the Doolittle battle group. Now, for the first and only time, all three flattops of the *Yorktown* era would go to war together, ordered by Nimitz to meet at a spot in the Pacific 325 miles northeast of Midway, a location the men nicknamed "Point Luck."

June 4 turned out to be a typical South Pacific summer day, with flat water, a few scattered white clouds, and wind so mild a carrier would need full-out turbines to launch its air. At 0534 scout planes radioed back to *Enterprise* that enemy ships had been spotted, and at 0603 Midway sent detailed information on the Japanese position: 150–175 miles to the west-southwest, precisely as Hypo had predicted. For the voracious fuel needs of the American fighters, this was very much at the limit for distance, but surprise was on the American side. Ray Spruance ordered his air to attack.

At 0615 Vice Admiral Nagumo ordered seventy-two bombers and thirty-six fighters to strike the Americans on the twin atolls of Midway. They were met by twenty-five obsolete fighter planes, which they downed instantly. In the twenty minutes between 0630 and 0650, the Japanese destroyed Midway's hospital, fuel tanks, and marine command post, killing another twenty men. They were met by heavy antiaircraft fire, however, so the attack was not fully successful. Thirty-six Japanese planes were downed, and thirty more made it back to their carriers so damaged that they couldn't fly again.

At 0702 *Enterprise* and *Hornet* together launched twenty Wildcat fighters, sixty-seven Dauntless dive-bombers, and twenty-nine Devastator torpedo planes, keeping behind only the air needed for bare-minimum ship defense. At 0838 *Yorktown* sent out seventeen Dauntlesses, twelve Devastators, and six Wildcats. It was pretty much everything the American navy had to throw.

One squadron taking off and making its way across an empty Pacific to attack the invincible, all-powerful Japanese fleet was *Hornet's* Torpedo Squadron 8, the airmen who'd spent so many hours showing off, palling around, and playing acey-deucey with Doolittle's army volunteers. Their chief was Lt. Comdr. John C. Waldron of Fort Pierre, South Dakota, and June 4 was the first time any of them had taken off from a carrier deck with live torpedoes in their bellies. Pilot George Gay admitted that he and the others were nervous beforehand, but after all, they'd seen every one of Doolittle's men take off, and "we figured by golly if they could do it, well we could too."

After thirty minutes of flying, Waldron followed a hunch and led Torpedo 8 off to the southwest, while the fighters and bombers continued 265 degrees true. *Hornet's* Bombing 8 would search in vain for its targets, Nagumo having withdrawn to exchange bombs for torpedoes to prepare for an attack on ships instead of on land, as Yamamoto had instructed. This change in Japanese position was never passed on to the American aviators, however, the *Hornet* battle report commenting: "[A]bout one hour after the planes had departed, the enemy reversed his course and started his retirement. We did not break radio silence to report this to the planes."

At 0705 ten Devastators from Midway attacked the *Kido Butai*. All of their torpedoes missed, and seven were shot down. Since by that time the Japanese hadn't yet vanquished the atoll and their patrol planes hadn't detected any sign of the expected American fleet, Nagumo changed strategy against Yamamoto's plans, and ordered another assault on Midway. This meant over an hour of lowering planes below, having their torpedoes replaced by bombs, and raising them back to the deck.

At 0728, the very last of Nagumo's patrol planes sent a message: "Sight what appears to be ten enemy surface ships . . . 240 miles from Midway." The reported position established that they were well within carrier air range, so Nagumo reversed direction again, ordering that all planes that hadn't yet been switched to bombs should now retain their torpedoes. Yamamoto's double-edged strategy of invading Midway while simultaneously destroying the American fleet was now compromising Nagumo's command. As all his fighters were deployed in strafing the marines on their island, none were available to accompany a squadron attack on American ships. His decks were full of land bombers and a few dive-bombers, not the right equipment for a naval aerial assault, and he had planes returning from Midway unable to land, since the decks were too crowded. In their haste to follow the change of plans, Japanese deckhands left unused ordnance sitting out on deck instead of returning it below to the magazines. This would prove to be a fatal error.

Almost immediately, twenty-seven dive-bombers and fifteen B-17 Flying Fortresses attacked from Midway, dropping 322 bombs—more than 120,000 pounds of explosives—all of which missed. Ten of these planes were shot down. The lead pilot in the attack on Pearl Harbor, Fuchida Mitsuo, watching on deck while recovering from the appendectomy that would sideline him from fighting, recalled: "We had by this time undergone every kind of attack by shore-based planes—torpedo, level bombing, dive-bombing—but were still unscathed. Frankly, it was my judgment that the enemy fliers were not displaying a very high level of ability. It was our general conclusion that we had little to fear from the enemy's offensive tactics."

Hornet's Torpedo Squadron 8 followed John Waldron's hunch straight to the Japanese fleet. At 0918, they were spotted by a cruiser, *Chikuma,* who signaled her closest destroyer. The two opened fire and blew out smoke screens. One by one Zero attackers appeared in the sky above the American fliers, quickly swooping down to maul the slow-moving Devastators. Of the fifteen planes of Torpedo Squadron 8, fourteen caught enemy fire, burst into flames, and fell into the sea.

The sole survivor was Ens. George Gay. During the assault the electric release for his torpedo jammed, so he had to do it manually. His target, the carrier *Soryu*, saw his missile's wake, moved, and the American torpedo missed entirely. Ensign Gay then tried strafing the carrier's deck with his guns, but they didn't work either.

Now five Zeros were after him. They disintegrated his rudder. They killed his crewman. They shot off one of his wings. His plane fell into the ocean, but the ensign, though hit in the leg and seriously wounded, was still alive. George grabbed his seat cushion and rubber life raft out of the cockpit, and hid under the floats from Japanese patrols.

The rest of *Hornet*'s air returned to their ship, never having found *Kido Butai*. Bombing 8 ran out of gas before they could get all the way home, and instead headed for emergency landings at Midway. The same insignia that had confused the Japanese during the Doolittle Raid now confounded the marines, and they opened fire. They missed every plane, and the navy pilots landed without injury. Other airmen couldn't make it back to *Hornet* before their tanks ran dry, however. They crashed into the Pacific and were lost.

At 0920 Wade McCluskey and his *Enterprise* dive-bombers arrived at the last reported Japanese position before the withdrawal. At an altitude of 20,000 feet, McCluskey could see for sixty miles or so, and there were no ships to be found in any direction. His gas gauge gave him two choices. Everyone in his squadron could give up, salvo into the water, and return to *Enterprise,* or they could immediately fly in exactly the right direction and just as immediately uncover the Japanese. Wade was a fighter pilot who'd never dropped a bomb before, and his decision was to begin a box search starting in the most likely direction he thought *Kido Butai* might have taken: the northeast.

At 0940 fourteen *Enterprise* torpedo planes found and attacked *Kaga*. Eleven were downed, and all the torpedoes missed. The American sub *Nautilus* launched three torpedoes against *Kaga*. Two missed, and the third struck but didn't explode. Another U.S. sub in the area, *Grayling*, was mistakenly attacked by Midway's B-17s, and had to crash-dive to escape.

At 0955 McCluskey sighted a Japanese destroyer—*Arashi*, which had been unsuccessfully chasing and rolling depth-charges against *Nautilus*—and quickly decided it was heading toward the fleet. Bombing 6 followed it.

At 1000 fifteen *Yorktown* planes attacked *Soryu*. Thirteen were downed, and all of the American torpedoes missed.

At 1005 pilots in McCluskey's squadron reported seeing "curved white slashes on a blue carpet"—the wakes of more ships than any U.S. naval airman had ever seen before.

At 1020 all four Japanese carriers turned into the wind, to begin a devastating assault on the American fleet. Simultaneously, McCluskey's force of thirty-seven dive-bombers met up with *Yorktown's* remaining fighters and torpedo planes directly over *Kido Butai.* The Japanese had no radar to warn them, and most of their air was either chasing *Yorktown* planes or on the way home from another round of attacking Midway. The Americans rose to position and began their screaming assaults.

In the air was the dance of planes twisting and spinning to avoid the firecracker pops of one another's machine guns; the climbing, back flip, and dropping into a straight 180 to max speed for attack; the coordinated geometric swoops of solid formation piloting; and, in the end, the shiny pricks of aircraft suddenly sprouting a ball of fire and plummeting into the ocean, leaving behind soaring black-and-white trails of smoke that rise and fade to nothing. "Zeros were coming in on us in a stream from astern," remembered James E. Thach, leader of the *Yorktown* fighters. "Then I saw a second large group streaming right past us on to the torpedo planes. The air was just like a beehive. . . . Then I saw this glint in the sun and it looked just like a beautiful silver waterfall; these dive bombers coming down. I could see them very well because that was the direction of the Zeros too. They weren't anywhere near the altitude the dive bombers were. I'd never seen such superb dive-bombing."

The first three bombs aimed at *Kaga* missed, but the fourth struck directly in the middle of her launch line. Two more missed, but the seventh and eighth struck forward, exploding on the hangar deck below. *Kaga* burst repeatedly into flames; even her paint caught fire. Three bombs then hit their mark on *Soryu;* its fire was so intense that the hangar doors warped. By 1915 both had sunk.

Akagi avoided bomb one, only to be hit by two and three. A Zero on deck caught fire and erupted, triggering a chain of explosions that led across the deck and into the hangar, setting off every piece of ordnance stored below. "At that instant a lookout screamed: 'Hell divers!' I looked up to see three black enemy planes plummeting toward our ship," Fuchida Mitsuo remembered. "Some of our machine guns managed to fire a few frantic bursts at them, but it was too late. The plump silhouettes of the American 'Dauntless' dive bombers quickly grew larger, and then a number of black objects suddenly floated eerily from their wings. Bombs! Down they came straight toward me! . . . The terrifying scream of the dive bombers reached me first, followed by the crashing explosion of a direct hit. There was a blinding flash and then a second explosion, much louder than the first. . . . Looking about, I was horrified at the destruction that had been wrought in a matter of seconds. There was a huge hole in the flight deck just behind the midship elevator. The elevator itself, twisted like molten glass, was drooping into the hangar. Deck plates reeled upward in grotesque configurations. Planes stood tail up, belching livid flame and jet-black smoke. Reluctant tears streamed down my cheeks as I watched the fires spread. . . ." *Akagi,* the lead flattop of what was once the world's mightiest naval force, was scuttled by destroyers on June 5 at 0330. Jumping into an escape boat, pilot Fuchida would break both his legs.

At 1040 eighteen dive-bombers and six fighters launched from *Hiryu* immediately found *Yorktown.* She was hit on the flight deck, down the smokestack, and four decks below by an armor piercer, as well as by two Japanese eels. Dead in the water, she was abandoned at 1458 but stayed afloat for two more days until she was sunk by torpedoes from a Japanese sub.

Shortly after 1600 *Enterprise* and *Hornet* sent out the rest of their air to mop up what remained of the Japanese navy. At around 1700 twenty-four *Yorktown* Dauntlesses scored four hits on *Hiryu;* she sank on June 5.

Yamamoto's airmen reported sinking three American carriers, and he ordered a pursuit, thinking he could incite a night battle, at which the Japanese excelled. But as time went on and more reports came in, he began to realize that his pilots' first calls were exaggerated, and that he could be heading into a dawn attack. At 0815 on June 5 the order was given to withdraw back to Tokyo. That night George Gay, sole survivor of *Hornet's* Torpedo Squadron 8, was found by an American flying boat, rescued, and returned to Oahu.

The Americans knew they had repelled a great force, but it was a long time before anyone understood that this was the turning point of the Pacific War. Roosevelt had sent the Doolittle Raiders as vengeance for Pearl Harbor; Yamamoto responded by attacking Midway; and the American triumph in that battle, using the secrets of Magic, would serve as the ultimate in revenge. At "AH," the Japanese lost four carriers, 322 planes, and seven hundred pilots, crewmen, and schooled naval officers. Their feared *Kido Butai* would never strike forcefully again, and the Japanese would from now on be on the defense against a stronger American naval power in the Pacific. Months after, George Marshall would honor the navy's success by calling this battle "the closest squeak and the greatest victory." For Tokyo the war was irrevocably lost.

Even after their defeat at Midway, however, the Japanese longing for vengeance against Doolittle did not abate. In June 1942 Imperial Japanese Navy *I-25,* a submarine manned by a crew of ninety-seven and with a cruising range of more than fourteen thousand miles, tried to terrorize the United States by shelling Fort Stevens in northwestern Oregon. Three months later she returned to the West Coast with a special accessory. Just fore of her conning tower now arched a waterproof hangar, and inside—its wings and horizontal tailplane folded, its wings, fins, and floats removed—was a Uokosuka E14Y1 floatplane, which could be launched from the sub by a catapult of compressed air.

On September 9 and 29, Warrant Flying Officer Fujita Nobuo, carrying two 170-pound thermite incendiary bombs, was catapulted toward Oregon's Cape Blanco lighthouse. He dropped his incendiaries over the forests of the Pacific Northwest. The Japanese expected that these dense woods would erupt in flames, causing great damage to America's timber industries and renewing the West Coast hysteria they'd been so successful at inciting with Pearl Harbor.

By that time, however, the lesson of Operation Drumbeat had been learned, and U.S. coastal areas were banned from broadcasting weather forecasts. This one piece of strategy kept the Japanese from knowing that the Northwest had spent weeks in unseasonable rain and fog. The fires did not engulf Oregon and Washington as expected but were quickly put out. Pilot Fujita, however, came home a national hero. According to the navy, he'd accomplished a quid pro quo for the Doolittle Raid, bombing the continental United States for the first time in its history.

The Japanese retaliatory assault on China, meanwhile, had reached such a fever pitch that the army gave up on trying to get Ted Lawson and the other severely injured *Ruptured Duck* aviators to Chungking, flying them instead directly to India. On June 5, as they cleared the Himalayas at nineteen thousand feet, Lawson passed out from lack of oxygen, but he was still in such pain that he welcomed it. In New Delhi they caught up with Bob Gray and Dick Joyce, now Hump jumpers running transports, and in Karachi, the passenger list would include Ross Greening, Jack Hilger, Brick Holstrom, Hoss Wilder, and Don Smith, all taking the Stratoliner back to the States.

At almost every stop along the way, Ted thought of sending a letter to his wife, Ellen, explaining what had happened, but then he would think of all the times they had gone dancing, or skiing, and he just couldn't bring himself to do it. Filled with guilt, love, and foreboding, he thought of her constantly, and wondered how she would react to the news that her husband was now less than a whole man, that her marriage vows would now mean a lifetime of caring for a permanent invalid. "I had talked to some of the boys about Ellen, especially to Hilger, Greening, and Jones—for the wives of Hilger and Greening were with Ellen," Ted remembered. "I asked them for advice. I told them

I had been thinking about this for a long time and that it was making me very nervous. But I couldn't bring myself to tell her. . . . I told them I had a plan that I had thought of suddenly: I'd just stay in Walter Reed Hospital until I had all the work done on my leg and face and learned to use the artificial leg. Ellen could think that I was still in China or India. Then, when I was right, I could walk up to her and tell her all the things that had happened."

As they waited at the Cairo airport, "[O]ne of the boys let out a surprised sound as he thumbed through a magazine. A June 1 copy of *Life* had been flown in and left there. It had all our pictures.

"'Golly, somebody does care,' one of the fellows said.

"I looked at the picture and then at myself in the mirror. Different fellows. . . .

"When everyone was asleep that night on the Stratoliner, I made my way up the aisle on the crutches and stood behind Niswander, the big plane's pilot. The copilot, Kratovil, was away from his seat. Niswander motioned to it, and after a little trouble, I got into the seat and leaned back, looking at the stars in the black sky.

"Niswander could read my thoughts, I guess, for I was just thinking how much I wanted to feel the ship's controls in my hands when he said, 'I know how you feel. Take it for a while.'

"He took it off the automatic pilot. I flew the Stratoliner for an hour. It helped. . . ."

On June 11, after seven weeks without contact, the Raiders interned in the Soviet Union finally received a visit from American officials when the Moscow embassy's secretary and military attaché appeared for an inspection tour of Okhuna. The boys were terribly excited, thinking that they would finally be sent home, until the attaché told them, "This is better than Moscow. In Moscow we have practically no freedom at all. I imagine you will be allowed to go out in the woods here. And food shouldn't be hard to get, because this is an agricultural area."

"We learned from the attaché that [the Russians] were going to allow us to leave the country and not make a statement publicly until an incident arose which prevented that," Ski York said. "The incident being a newspaper conference in Moscow [where] an American newspaperman, in discussing the raid, asked what the Russians would do if one of the planes involved in the raid landed in Russia. He insisted so much on an answer that they thought he must have some information on our being there, and our presence was announced."

Ski asked the attaché, "What about the rest of the boys on the Tokyo raid?"

"We have no detailed news on that," was the reply. "It is being kept very quiet in the States. We do know that the Japanese reports were greatly exaggerated—the ones we all heard at first. But we have no news from the States about the results nor what did happen to all the members of the raid."

"How about news from home?" Bob Emmens asked. "Do you have any mail for us?"

"Didn't you get the message from your family, Emmens?"

"No!"

"I brought a copy of the one we received and which we forwarded to you. Congratulations! You have a son!"

"He handed me a telegram in the Russian language," Bob Emmens remembered. "'You have a small, redheaded son. Everyone well including grandmothers. Wish you were here. Love, Justine.'"

The officials agreed to send telegrams to the aviators' families in the United States, gave them a small Russian-English dictionary, and then opened two cartons they'd brought, filled with cigarettes, shirts, socks, soap, two *Collier's,* three *Saturday Evening Post*s, and two *Life*s. "It seemed like Christmas to us," Emmens said. "I remember so well the number of magazines because I read them all at least five times from cover to cover."

The attaché did not keep in touch weekly, and the Russians, crippled by war, would not continue their generosity, even though they were billing Washington for every ruble of care. "Food and cigarette shortages were quite common now," Bob Emmens said. "We would go for days without meat or vegetables, or sometimes both. The vodka disappeared from the table and only occasionally, maybe once a week, would Mike return from his daily visits to Penza [the nearest city] with a small bottle of it. We didn't mind that so much, but the food shortage worried us considerably. Some days we had only rice and cabbage."

By the end of July even their allotment of vegetables turned erratic, and for weeks the men survived on cabbage, rice, black bread, tea "and that damned red caviar." Cigarettes stopped being supplied, and the men had to roll their own, using Russian newspaper. No one from the American Embassy visited or made any contact whatsoever. York and Emmens started thinking of ways to escape, but just as they began to make plans, Mike announced that they were leaving—that they must be ready and packed by eight o'clock.

That night the internees were put on a train heading northeast. The men hoped they were going to Moscow to be turned over to the American Embassy, or to Murmansk or Archangel, ports on the North Sea from which they could sail home. Instead, they got off the train at the Kama River and boarded a flat-bottomed paddle wheeler. After days of slow progress and nights of accordion duets, the boat pulled up to a dock in what seemed like the middle of nowhere. Mike announced: "We are here!"

The Germans had advanced so far east that for their safety, the Americans had been moved to Okhansk, in the foothills of the Urals, on the western edge of Siberia. The men were stunned at how poor and dirty everyone and everything was: babies covered in filth; children clearly suffering from malnutrition and lice infestation; old women, barefoot or in gunnysack socks even in winter, their dresses in rags. That night Mike took them to the People's Auditorium for a movie. It was Deanna Durbin in *One Hundred Men and a Girl.*

A few days later the attaché and secretary reappeared, this time accompanied by Adm. William Standley, the American ambassador to the Soviet Union. The airmen were certain that such a powerful statesman could pull strings to get them out of Russia. Instead Standley announced he could do nothing for them other than send up a medical officer and buy them some clothes on the next supply run from Persia. Wishing the airmen all the best, the State employees hurried back to Moscow.

"Our November food ration was even worse than our October issue had been," Bob Emmens remembered. "It seemed that nearly all shortages were made up by supplying the equivalent weight in a cereal similar to barley. It was called *kroopa* [buckwheat]. The women in the kitchen boiled it, fried it, and baked it. We ate it hot, cold, and in between. We had plenty of bread and tea, and our supply of cabbage was still lasting, although it was becoming quite obvious that it would not last many more weeks." One of their new rations was pure pork fat: "We ate it, uncooked as it was. They cut it into slices about an inch thick. There was no meat to it at all; it was plain white fat. We found it a bit more palatable with a little salt on it. . . .

"We spent the next seven months in Okhansk. They were the worst seven months I have ever spent in my life."

On April 28 Prime Minister Tojo called a special conference to resolve the question of what Japan should do with its eight captured Raiders. At this meeting the chief of the Imperial General Staff, Sugiyama Hajime, declared that the only way to send a warning to other Allied pilots intending to attack Japan would be to issue sentences of death by firing squad. Tojo himself, however, felt ambivalent; he considered the American bombing "contrary to international law. It was not against troops but against noncombatants, primary school students . . . since this was not permitted by international law, it was homicide." The prime minister also feared, however, that other countries would regard executions as barbarous, and that such a measure might endanger Japanese POWs held in Allied hands. Finally, Japanese law did not specify the death penalty for such a crime. This last point needed to be addressed before all else, and in the Japanese manner, doing so would require fourteen weeks.

By June the Kempeitai realized that they were making no progress in extracting worthwhile confessions from the Doolittle Raiders. Instead they would now try a "good cop" strategy. All eight captives from *Bat Out of Hell* and *Green Hornet* were joined together in a section of the prison by themselves, with George Barr and Bob Hite in cell one, Chase Nielsen and Bill Farrow in two, Dean Hallmark and Bob Meder in three, and Harold Spatz and Jake DeShazer in four. The beatings, tortures, solitary confinement, lack of sleep, and weeks of malnourishment had taken their toll, however. For days the reunited fliers refused to speak to one another, assuming the other Raiders had been turned into spies. They instead kept to opposite corners of their cells, crowded with suspicion.

All eight were overcome by dysentery, barely subsisting on "war criminal" rations of three cups of tea and six pieces of bread a day. They hadn't bathed or changed clothes since being captured, and the filth of their bodies and the odor of the toilet hole suffused the damp, stifling air. Their cells were concrete and steel, and they slept on tatami mats, woven from straw, on the floor, but even under such conditions all eight captured Doolittle Raiders were together for the first time. Eventually they accepted one another again, and began to tell their stories. Since the guards wouldn't allow them to speak openly, they whispered when they thought no one was nearby, wrote notes into the floor, and scratched comments on the cement walls. All eight men had one question on their minds: Would they be executed, or would they die a slow death in prison?

The interrogation sessions now took a new form. Pages in Japanese were handed to the men, and they were told to sign their names. Of course they couldn't read the words, so they asked what these documents were. "Confession," they were told. If they didn't sign, they were informed, they would be shot. After rounds of more beatings, each man came to the same conclusion: They were going to die one way or another, sooner or later. What did it matter what the confessions said? They signed:

> BILL FARROW: After leaving Nagoya, I do not quite remember the place, there was a place which looked like a school, with many people there. As a parting shot, with a feeling of "damn these Japs," I

made a power dive and carried out some strafing. There was absolutely no defensive fire from below.

BOB HITE: We saw in the distance what looked like an elementary school with many children at play. The pilot steadily dropped altitude and ordered the gunmen to their stations. When the plane was at an oblique angle, the skipper gave firing orders, and bursts of machine-gun fire sprayed the ground.

HAROLD SPATZ: I aimed at the children in the school yard and fired only one burst before we headed out to sea.

DEAN HALLMARK: We also bombed residential homes, killing and wounding many people.

JAKE DESHAZER: Since in this type of bombing it is inevitable that the bombs will scatter to the residential areas, from the beginning I expected such an eventuality and acted accordingly. As far as we were concerned, the quicker we discharged our bombs and caused a lot of casualties and escaped, the better it was for us.

The Kempeitai had completed its work. On June 15 the men were handcuffed and leg cuffed, posed for photographs in the courtyard, and put aboard a train to Nagasaki. They still had not been allowed to shave or bathe, and "the coal soot from the train ride made us look as though we had been living in a pigsty," DeShazer said. They were then put on a freighter for another journey, which at least included decent food. The men prayed an American sub would find the ship and torpedo it. That, at least, would give them a chance to escape or put an end to their misery.

On June 19 the prisoners were led into Shanghai's Bridge House. Previously an English hotel, under the Japanese, it had become one of Asia's most notorious prisons. "In the bottom part of the hotel they had made bamboo cells raised off the floor about two feet . . . about twenty feet long by about six or seven feet deep, from front to rear," Bob Hite said. "In the corner of the cell was a barrel with a board across it. That was our so-called toilet. The stink was almost unbearable.

"They put us in this cell with about thirty Chinese and some Japanese and foreigners. There were two women in the cell, and one of the women died the first night. Then there was a man that died the second night. They hauled them out the next day. People had dysentery and all that sort of thing. It was a horrible mess. I think we were sort of horror stricken to know that we had been exposed to we knew not what.

"At night we would hear this beautiful, beautiful American music with all of the popular tunes that we had heard in the States. That was hard to understand. . . . After a week or two, we didn't hear it anymore. They shut it out. It would drift in from outside, from the other areas of the city. One of the tunes they played when I think we all kind of wanted to cry a little bit was, 'Smoke Gets in Your Eyes.'

"It was hard to take and think that here we were, we could hear music like that, and then to realize where we were, and what had happened to us."

With almost thirty people in the cell, the prisoners had to take turns sitting and lying down. Each day they were given a daily bare subsistence of two quarts of water, eight ounces of bread, and a cup of "rice soup" made from the leftovers of the prison staff's meals, filled with maggots and dirt. Japanese POW bread was made with so much wood fiber and sawdust that when it was toasted, it burst into flames. After a few days of passing this food over to their cellmates, the Americans forced themselves to eat, determined to survive long enough to tell the world how the empire had treated them.

Eventually the civilians were taken elsewhere, and the fliers were left to themselves. After four months, they were allowed a bath in one of the hotel's rooms that hadn't yet been converted into a cell. Even though Bob Hite spent hours soaping and changing the tub's water, when he finished there was still a scum of filth floating on top of the final soak, and the water was brackish with dead lice. This would be their last happy memory of China.

The empire's long-term treatment of its captives would turn out to be far more barbaric than the tortures of the Kempeitai. The Americans were starved, dehydrated, and refused medical attention, and their bodies, minds, spirits, and emotions steadily deteriorated. "The way you determine that [you had] beriberi, you could mash in on your shinbone or just on about any part of your body, and push in, and the indentation would stay in right on your bone," Bob Hite said. Eventually a beriberi victim's lungs would fill with fluid, and the sufferer would drown. Another POW remembered that, "Everyone could tell when they were going to die by the choked noise that came out of them—it was called 'the beriberi song.'"

In the four months since his capture, pilot Dean Hallmark had lost more than sixty pounds. They were all terribly ill, but he was by far the worst off. The fliers made a bed for him from their jackets, and tried to keep him conscious. "One day Lieutenant Hallmark passed out," Jacob DeShazer remembered. "He was very sick after that. We had to carry him to the toilet. He had dysentery, and we had to take him about every fifteen minutes. We had regular shifts, but it was too hard on us; finally all of us gave out. We were all lying flat on our backs from exhaustion and practically ready to give up."

"I helped Dean Hallmark. He wanted me to sing songs to him," Bob Hite said. "But you know, he was in bad, bad shape. So I held Hallmark's head in my lap. He said, 'This is the hardest'—we didn't have anything to sleep on. We were just on the boards of this platform. So our bodies—we had boils on our hips. Our hips were skinned where we had tried to lay on our side. We were getting kind of bony and were laying on these plain boards. With all of the fever and the hurting that Hallmark had internally, he was wanting a little help. So we sort of took turns holding his head in our laps."

On August 13, 1942, the supreme commander of Japanese forces in China, Hata Shunroku, signed Military Ordinance Number Four, which stated: "Any individual who commits any or all of the following acts shall be subject to military punishment: . . . the bombing, strafing or otherwise attacking of civilians . . . private properties . . . [and] objectives other than those of military nature . . . [in] Japan proper, Manchukuo and the Japanese zones of military operation. . . . Military punishment shall be the death penalty, provided, however, should the circumstances warrant, this sentence may be commuted to life imprisonment. . . . This military law shall be applicable to all acts committed prior to the date of its approval."

The Japanese now had both the law and the "confessions" they needed to execute every captured Doolittle Raider.

DEATH

Back home in the United States, the prisoners' families and those of the men still left behind in China had received no further news. "Ross Greening's wife, Dot, and I moved to Myrtle Beach," Ellen Lawson remembered. "Jack Hilger's wife and their year-old daughter came down a little later. We rented a beach cabin, and there was a blackout since we were on the coast, with the shades drawn at night. I still had my radio and my Victrola, the coffeepot and the toaster. We of course watched the news, waiting. We waited and waited.

"I wrote to Ted every day. I told him I couldn't send the letters, but at least I was going to talk to him every night, so I wrote the letters. Then we got anxious, and figured there had been time enough for them to do what they had to do. We didn't talk about it, even though I knew."

On June 16 the seriously injured men from Linhai finally arrived in Washington, Lawson and Jack Hilger celebrating with a stateside breakfast of bacon and eggs, two quarts of milk, two chocolate milkshakes, and too many hamburgers to remember. "On my way to Walter Reed," Lawson said, "my main thought, aside from the feeling of relief that Ellen hadn't been tipped off, was the wonderful springs of the ambulance. Whoever designed them did a great job." After China's and India's medical facilities, they were relieved to find themselves in the army's state-of-the-art D.C. hospital, with its clean, antiseptic rooms, the latest drugs and equipment, and a staff of doctors and nurses who obviously knew what they were doing. For the first time in more than two months, constant thoughts of death stopped flickering in the backs of their minds.

Waiting for them at Reed was Hal Watson, who'd had an operation for his broken, dislocated shoulder. There was also bad news. Mayme, Ted's mother, had suffered a severe stroke. Even so, he couldn't bring himself to call home to Los Angeles, since Ellen would be there.

That night, while the men were eating dinner, they had a surprise guest. "Doolittle came in," Lawson said. "He didn't have to go to that trouble. He had to leave his office and his work, but it shows you what kind of guy he is. He said he'd see to it that we got the best possible care. He's kind of like a father, I guess.

"We talked awhile about the raid and the trip home, then he asked me if there was anything bothering me. I said that if I could get a good night's sleep I believe I could think better.

" 'How about the family situation?'

"I said I'd like a good night's sleep before I did anything about that. . . .

" 'What do you want to do about your wife?'

"I told him that I wanted to stay at Walter Reed until I was all right, and I asked him if he could fix it so Ellen would think I was still abroad.

" 'That would be a good idea, except that I've already written your wife and told her you were injured and on the way back,' Doolittle said, 'but that I didn't know the extent of your injuries. That's all I told her. You'd better do something about it.' "

"Because of Ted's mother being sick, I had to go back to L.A.," Ellen Lawson remembered. "I sold the Buick to pay for my airline ticket home, and got a job at Sears as a salesperson in radio. I worked as much as I could, but I kept in touch with the girls in Myrtle Beach. They phoned and told me that the guys had flown over and waved their wings on their way to Washington.

"Finally I got a call from Doolittle and he said, 'Do you want to come and see Ted?' And I said of course." She immediately wrote Ted a letter:

> You'll never know how relieved I am to know you're back. I'm coming to Washington just as soon as I can. At least I can see you every day.
>
> They wouldn't tell me what happened to you, yet, but I can't imagine your being sick very long.
>
> There isn't much to tell about your Mom just now. After she had the stroke on May 21st, she lost her speech. She is gradually getting it back, but it will take a long time.
>
> I'd love to talk to you on the phone, but since I am going to see you, I'll try and wait. I can start practicing my patience now on you, and then I'll make a better mommie.

While Ted still continued to fret over how his pregnant wife might react to his condition, the man who could never stand still stepped in to intercede. On June 17, Doolittle wrote Ellen:

> Ted arrived today and I have had a long talk with him. He is in good health but quite depressed. The depression results from the fact that a deep cut in his left leg became infected and it was nec-

essary that the leg be amputated. He also lost some teeth and
received a cut on his face.

He is receiving the best medical attention that it is possible to
obtain, here at Walter Reed Hospital, but I feel that his recovery is
being retarded by a fear of how his misfortune is going to affect
you and his mother. Ted will probably be hospitalized here for
some time and it is my personal belief that his recovery would be
expedited through your presence.

Knowing Ted as well as she did, Ellen understood immediately why he
couldn't have delivered this news himself. She again wrote to her husband:

I'm glad to know the truth. My imagination has been running
away with me. Darling, it could be so much worse. I've had so
many nightmarish dreams that you didn't come back at all, and
others in which you completely lost your memory and refused to
believe I was your wife. Those were horrible.

There is no reason in the world why we can't lead a perfectly
normal life and do the things we've planned.

The minute Ted finished reading Ellen's letter, he wheeled himself down
the hall to a pay phone. He told Ellen how much her letter had meant, but
insisted that it was a terrible idea for her to come to Washington. It was too
arduous a trip for a woman in her condition, and besides, they didn't know a
soul in the city. She should have the baby where her friends and family could
be with her. He was, of course, still hoping to mend as much as possible
before facing his wife in person.

As their three minutes drew to an end, Ellen (a woman with willpower to
spare) told Ted in no uncertain terms that she was coming east, period. Her
next letter to him ended:

What if you aren't in top condition—all prettily shaved and
combed? Do you think a wife minds that?

When I do see you, I'll do my best to control my tears. But
should there be any, please don't misinterpret them. Because
they'll be tears of happiness and joy.

The day Ted had dreaded for so many months finally arrived: "I was sitting in my room a day or two later, looking out the window and thinking of

her, and what would become of us, when the door opened and she stood there.

"I had thought so many times of what I'd say and what I'd do, but now all I could think was that Ellen was there, there in my room. Nothing mattered except that.

"I jumped up to go to the door, forgetting everything. Forgetting the crutches. And when I took a step toward her, I fell on my face in front of her."

His wife remembers that day just as vividly: "He was thin. He'd gotten down to eighty pounds. You know, the leg is about thirty pounds. He wasn't able to eat for about three weeks. He couldn't sleep. His face was still thin, with many cuts, and of course the teeth were knocked out. They'd all had their heads shaved in Cairo because of lice. Even so, he looked good to me."

The couple spent their time together catching up, Ted reading all of the letters his wife had written to him that she couldn't mail. As thrilled as Ellen was to be reunited with her husband, however, some of his worries proved to be well founded—it was difficult being a six months' expectant mother in a strange city, when your only relative, friend, and acquaintance lay hospitalized, and your life revolved around Walter Reed. "McClure was there, and also Hal Watson," Ellen said. "They all played cards in the sunroom. They were allowed a little rum that they kept in a medicine cabinet, so we had rum and Cokes. But they didn't want you to have any glasses or anything. The roaches were so bad, they sprayed every day. And the humidity there was terrible."

After a few weeks, when Lawson had gotten some of his strength back, the army decided it was time for a proper surgery. "The second amputation was as bad as the first one," Ted remembered. "The spinal anesthetic didn't seem to work as well as it worked in China. There was another operation after that on the leg, a trimming job.

"The doctors did a great job on my mouth and jaw. X-rays showed that the shock of going through the windshield had shoved one of my teeth up through my gums into a section of my sinus. They got that out, along with some broken-off nubs left in the gums, then went to work on the job of reshaping my mouth and chin. The doctors spoke only once. One of them said, 'Jesus! He's still got some of that beach sand in there.'"

On June 15 Jimmy Doolittle ordered "all officers and men with me at Shangri-La" to report to Washington. Given the state of the world, however, only twenty-three of the original eighty could assemble at Bolling Field on the twenty-seventh, accompanied by the Air Force Band and columns of soldiers at rigid attention. Before a parade of B-18s, Generals Hap Arnold and

Jimmy Doolittle pinned each volunteer with a Distinguished Flying Cross. Ten days later, those in Washington still too injured to attend were similarly honored at Walter Reed. While Ellen Lawson, Mac McClure's mother and fiancée, and Hal Watson's father, mother, and wife looked on, Doolittle awarded DFC's, Purple Hearts, and Chinese Orders of the Clouds to Ted in his wheelchair and to Mac and Hal in their braces and casts.

A few days later Ted would learn that a piece of the *Duck's* fuselage, the section that included Sergeant Lovelace's painting of a squawking Donald on crutches, had been found. It was, along with wreckage from *Bat Out of Hell,* featured in a display about war criminals at Yasukuni, Tokyo's Shinto shrine to soldiers killed in the line of duty. Two million Japanese visited the exhibit to see exactly what would happen to enemy airmen who dared attack their country.

Brigadier General Doolittle spent the rest of the summer of 1942 touring the country on War Bond drives and morale-boosting public appearances. All the while, he was anxious to get back into combat. Arnold wanted to land him a post that would be worthy of his various talents, but the chief found himself running into one obstacle after another. Hap called MacArthur about his air slot, but the general immediately demurred, which was just as well since, in so many respects, MacArthur and Doolittle were polar opposites. Arnold then turned to Eisenhower, now in London and needing a commander for his Twelfth AF. From Washington the match looked ideal, but the Ike-Jimmy working relationship would begin on a contentious note.

"General Arnold called me to his office and said, 'We are going to have an invasion of North Africa, and Gen. Patton has been recommended as the ground commander, and I am recommending you as the air commander,'" Doolittle remembered.

> Gen. Eisenhower immediately was pleased with Gen. Patton. I made a horrible mistake. [Eisenhower] made the statement, which was quite correct, that it would be necessary for us to acquire airfields in North Africa . . . and instead of saying, "[Y]essir, that's exactly what we'll do, and it's possible to do so, we will bring in supplies, we will bring oil, gasoline, bombs, ammunition, food, and all of the things that we need to operate,"—instead of saying that, which was what I should have said, I very stupidly said, "The fields will be of no value to us, General, until we have supplies, ammunition, troops to support them, and so forth."

I saw his face change, and I knew that I had blown it. It was just a stupid thing to say. Here was a one-star general telling a three-star general that he didn't know what he was talking about. . . . Once again, I had the uncomfortable feeling of being an illegitimate offspring at a family reunion. Ike knew of my reputation as a racing pilot through the press and had probably translated that to mean that I would be too reckless to command an air force. . . . I spent the next year selling myself to Gen. Eisenhower.

There was likely more to Eisenhower's antipathy toward Jimmy than his image as a daredevil, since many career army men held it against Doolittle for dropping out of the service between the wars to earn a decent wage as a salesman along with serious prize money at air shows, and then returning to the AAC and quickly getting jumped up the hierarchy by Arnold. Regardless of Doolittle's obvious talents, it smacked of favoritism, something Eisenhower hated completely. Additionally Jimmy was probably unaware of the many misgivings that Ike himself had at that moment regarding the North African campaign.

Two years before Overlord, Eisenhower had sketched out an invasion of France called Sledgehammer, to be immediately followed by an all-out assault known as Roundup. Though Marshall approved the strategy, the British insisted that both were hopelessly optimistic, and refused to cooperate. They wanted instead to invade French Africa, an operation Winston Churchill called Torch. When FDR sided with the English, Marshall and Eisenhower were devastated, Ike telling his deputy Mark Clark that the decision was "the blackest day in history." Three days later, when the Combined Chiefs discussed who should lead the assault, Ernest King said there was only one man for the job: Eisenhower. The commander who'd done all he could to stop Torch would now have to do everything in his power to make it succeed.

It would turn out to be a mission of enormous difficulty. The geography, with its endless miles of desert, was daunting; the main D-day ports, Casablanca and Algiers, were eight hundred miles apart; and the latter was in turn four hundred miles from Tunis, the ultimate target. Compounding these troubles was the territory's massive internal strife: The Free French loyal to Charles de Gaulle were openly fighting the Vichy French loyal to Marshal Henri Pétain, intermixed with French and Arab businessmen whose own loyalties shifted with every passing hour. Even though the Allies expected a majority of French locals to support their cause, nothing was certain.

"I was assigned to a new squadron of B-25s—young, untrained guys—and I was told to take them out and train them to be combat ready," Trav

Hoover said. "I started on that, but before they got to be anywhere near combat ready, they said 'It's time for you to go.' So we flew across the North Atlantic and landed in England, and then went from England to North Africa to start bombing the German tank forces under Rommel.

"A lot of Raiders were in North Africa—Doolittle of course; Davey Jones, Ross Greening—and we got together whenever we could. Some of the guys were getting shot down. I was very fortunate. . . . I made quite a few missions, and had some losses from formation; they were probably shooting at me but I was in high gear by that time."

"The next thing I knew, four or five of us got orders to participate in the invasion of North Africa," Davey Jones recalled. "In a B-26 I led a dozen P-38s [fighters]. We landed in Oran while the fighting was going on, into Sfax. Christ, there were bomb craters and wrecked airplanes here and there and all sorts of junk on the airfield, and so on, and it was a mess, a big mess. That's when we landed in all directions, straddling bomb holes and God knows what else. We must have ended up with almost two or three hundred airplanes on the field. No organization, no nothing, we just lived by our airplanes. In the morning we'd get up real early and you'd see hundreds of little fires; everybody was cooking.

"We were there a few days, and then all moved with the B-26s up to Algiers in November '42, where the Twelfth Air Force was operating out of downtown. Doolittle was there by then; I'd see the Old Man and brief him a couple of times as we ran our bombing raids. All we had was the flight crew and flight engineers—the ground crews hadn't yet gotten there—and we had to refuel the craft out of a five-gallon tin. It'd take you all day just to refuel! We had to muscle the bombs in, and we were using 250-pound bombs."

In North Africa, Doolittle would suffer the worst experience of the war with the Raider who'd supported him at his lowest moment in China, the man who'd predicted he'd win the Medal of Honor, and who had offered to crew with him wherever his orders might lead. "I had to go into Youks-les-Bains, Algeria, to attend to some business with the ground commanders there," Jimmy remembered.

I left Paul Leonard to take care of the airplane. About midnight that night the Germans came over and bombed the airfield. . . . I found that Paul had manned the top turret machine gun in the plane as long as the batteries held out and had shot back at the German planes that were bombing and strafing the field. . . . [He] had fought the attackers as long as he could, and then leaped into a nearby bomb crater for protection. But another bomb, aimed at the plane, had missed its mark and had hit the old bomb crater instead.

I found what was left of Paul. It was his left hand off at the wrist, with a wristwatch still in place. This was all that remained of the wonderful boy who had tried to cheer me up in China in my saddest moment. . . .

His loss was my greatest personal tragedy of the war.

Sgt. Paul J. Leonard would not be the only Raider to perish during that time. "There were six of us from the Doolittle group who were assigned to the 320th, five to the 319th, and three to the 17th," Herb Macia said. "I would like to mention their experience because the Doolittle Raid was considered a very hazardous mission. However, most of us survived it. Of the five fellows [in the 319th], Don Smith was killed in an accident in England. Davey Jones was shot down over Bizerte around early December 1942. Dick Miller, a bombardier, was killed on a low-level attack when his forty mm exploded in the bombardier's compartment. Tom Griffin was shot down [on the Fourth of July, 1943] on a mission over Sicily and taken prisoner of war. Griff Williams, copilot, was shot down on the same mission [and sent to Stalag Luft III for twenty-two months]. Out of the five guys that went into the 319th, two were killed and three ended up prisoners of war.

"In the 17th Group, Bob Clever, bombardier on Lawson's aircraft that crashed, was killed in an accident the day we were departing Fort Wayne, Indiana, when the airplane spun out climbing up through the clouds [on November 20, 1942]. Ross Greening was shot down over Naples in July 1943 and was a prisoner for the rest of the war. . . . Ed Bain was killed on the mission on Rome [on July 19, 1943]. Chuck Ozuk was in a crash on takeoff and had his tour curtailed. Dave Thatcher was in a takeoff crash and had his tour curtailed. . . .

"They decided forty missions was a tour. I was two or three missions ahead of [fellow Raider Jack Sims], so he said, 'Herb, why don't you wait for me. You stand down a few missions, and I will catch up, then we will fly the last one together.' When he said that, it went through my mind that it wasn't a good idea because usually something happened, but I agreed to do it, passing up two or three pretty routine missions. . . .

"Our fortieth mission was to support the troops who had landed in Salerno. They were having a tough time hanging on at the moment. . . . The Germans were pulling out of southern Italy at the time, and we would surprise them by coming up the valley behind the coastal mountain range and bomb them on the way out. . . . Our intelligence reports had never reported any flak in this area. . . . Suddenly, they opened up on us; we were in the lead aircraft. They got some real close hits on us; knocked out an engine. We dropped out of formation and tried to salvo the bombs. . . . We were on one engine, dropping out. . . . We headed for Sicily, hoping that we could make it. . . . We kept losing altitude all the way down, and finally when we got down to Catania where there were some fields, Jack had just enough altitude to be able to let them know that we were coming in for a landing. . . .

"Jack Sims and I were the first in the 320th to complete a tour."

There was even more bad news for the Raiders. On September 3, 1942, Lt. Kenneth Reddy, copilot on *Hari Kari-er,* was killed in an airplane accident in Little Rock, Arkansas, and on October 18, two days after getting the news he'd been promoted to captain, Bob Gray was flying from India to China when his plane crashed, killing Bob as well as Raider Sgt. George E. Larkin, Jr.

On November 11, Eisenhower began the campaign against Tunis, heavily reinforced and defended by thirty thousand German troops, starting at the port of Bizerte, twenty miles to the north. "I led five raids, the last on Bizerte," Davey Jones said. "It was the fourth of December. We were bombing at about twelve hundred feet because we didn't have any bombsights. Whappo knocked out my left engine and all the trim and the engine instruments, the bloody works are gone. I am cranking all the rudder and all the wheel I can get into it and didn't have any airspeed and I couldn't advance the throttle. I headed north to the coast, afraid the thing would snap on me.

"The terrain is sort of like it is around El Paso, just a bunch of little sandy nob hills, so I went down in a kind of a clear area between two little sand mounds and sort of took the wings off and then slid forward. We hadn't walked two hundred yards before running into a whole line of skirmishers, Germans. I pointed at my pistol; a German took it out and said, 'For you, the war is over.' They took me and one other guy to the fighter headquarters, to the command post. The commander was a lieutenant colonel, blond, Aryan-type, nice-looking guy, could speak reasonable English, wore the Iron Cross and the desert boots and so forth. He gave me a deck chair, and some cheese and wine. That night he said, 'OK, you sleep here. Please don't run away.' Or words to that effect.

"We ended up in Sicily, then they flew me to Rome for interrogation. I was in solitary I guess two weeks. You'd give them your name, rank, and number, and refuse to say anything more. They'd all laugh and tell you what squadron you were with and who your group commander was. You were apprehensive, 'cause you don't know if they were going to pull your fingernails out. But instead the guy gives you a cigarette. What you say and what he heard is between you and the Lord.

"They put me with a group on a train to Stalag Luft III in Silesia, now a part of Poland, 125 miles southeast of Berlin, and I got there on my birthday, December eighteenth. This was a huge, permanent camp run by the Luftwaffe instead of the SS or Gestapo, and there were maybe a thousand or more POWs, all RAF types, in the East camp alone. They'd been there for years. [From his Raider experience, Davey would be known in camp as "Tokyo" Jones; eventually the Germans would build six Stalag Lufts, each holding around ten thousand captive Allied aviators.]

"The POWs put you to work building things or hiding things or 'working to escape'-type things. You read or saw *The Great Escape*? So you know. In the spring of '43 we moved to the north camp and that's where the big tunnel effort went on. Pretty extensive organization, and we were mixed up in everything. The tunnel went down to about thirty feet, full of sand, just like Florida. You used your hands or a little trowel to dig your space and you had to shore everything up with bedboards or the sand would collapse on you. You'd be buried halfway and the guy behind you would have to pull you out. You're thirty feet under and you're in darkness.

"We were using oil, just a little tin with margarine for a lamp, and the lamp would go out. I would send it back up on this string and they would light it and send it back down, and every time I would take hold of it, it would go out. I thought, 'Boy, I'm really clumsy.' We finally realized that there wasn't enough oxygen to support the damn thing.

"After we got out a hundred feet, we put in two wooden rails and we had a little cart about two feet long and fifteen inches wide, and that's what we hauled the sand in from. You could ride it out to the face. We took cans and cut the tops and bottoms out, and stacked them in the back. We'd have a guy work a pump to bring air into the tunnel with big bellows, and eventually we ran electric lights. But the dispersal system was very complicated. We'd move tons of sand a day in two-pound lots. You'd have little bags you'd wear inside your pants leg, and you'd pull a little pin and the sand would trickle out."

In its outcome the Great Escape would be less than great. If everyone who'd worked on the three tunnels had gotten out, more than 250 POWs would have been freed. Instead the operation was uncovered after seventy-six had fled. Of those, seventy-three were recaptured and fifty were immediately executed, leaving three to make their way successfully to Allied territory. The rapid growth of the number of Allied airmen captured by the Germans meant a dramatic spurt in Nazi prison building; at the last minute the Americans of Luft III were moved to a new compound far from the Great Escape operation. Getting moved and kept from running out of that tunnel, however, very likely saved Davey Jones's life.

278 THE FIRST HEROES

★

On July 17, 1943, Col. Ross Greening, based in Marrakech, had completed 125 hours of combat and was taking part in a five-hundred-craft run on the Naples railyards. Everything went smoothly cruising over the Mediterranean, so Ross turned on his AFCE, lit up a stogie, and read a V-mail from his wife, Dot, which mentioned a fortune-teller predicting "exciting news" from her husband on July 21.

South of Naples the crew banked to get a fine view of Mount Vesuvius, which that day was surrounded by clouds of flak. Just minutes before reaching their target, bursts from antiaircraft guns hit right under the tail, destroying their control wires.

Ross continued flying, on trim tabs. He was able to drop his eggs and begin the turn to head home. Another burst took a direct hit off the right engine, crashing open the cockpit, and pieces of the plane started falling away.

As Greening ordered his men to hit the silk, an explosion ripped apart the fuselage, and the Marauder burst into flames. The crew hurried below to the bomb bay. One final burst threw the plane sideways, tossing the men into the air.

As Ross fell, the B-26's wreckage plummeted right beside him, until, at ten thousand feet, he felt he had to rip to avoid being struck by debris. He gently floated below, right into the line of fire. One bucket of artillery chewed holes out of his chute, while machine-gun bullets raked the lines, hitting him in the knee. He yanked his cords in every direction to try to get away, finally dropping directly into the smoking crater of Mount Vesuvius. Crashing against the inner wall of the volcano, he was knocked out cold.

Greening came to, mystified. His legs were terribly damaged in some way, his face was covered in blood, he was surrounded by a strange, black landscape, and he couldn't remember where he was or how he got there. A red-faced man in a weird helmet stood inches away, pointing a cocked pistol at his face. Behind him ashy smoke drifted up. When the stranger yelled some gibberish, Ross pointed down to his legs. Other men in strange helmets appeared. One sat on his knee, while another put a rifle between his legs and pushed. There was a horrible cracking sound as his hip popped back into its joint. One helmet man then made Ross climb on and carried him piggyback out of the volcano.

Using a motorcycle and sidecar, they took him to a house in town, where they gave him a beer and wiped his gashes with alcohol. Both his ankles were sprained, one leg was fully twisted, there was a slice wound from a bullet grazing his knee, and he was cut up all over from crashing into the volcano's gravelly tuff. As night fell, a crowd of Neapolitans gathered outside the house, screaming for vengeance against the airmen who'd bombed their city. The Nazis loaded their captives into a truck and took them to a jail, surrounded by another angry mob. The MPs insisted Ross get to his cell on his own power, so he crawled on his hands and knees from the truck to the prison, while the Italians spat and threw stones.

The captured Americans were sent to a prison in Chieti. On September 8, 1943, Italy surrendered, the *comandante* turned the prison over to the prisoners, and, for two glorious weeks, the POWs assumed they would be freed at any moment. Instead, on the twenty-third, a Wehrmacht detachment entered the camp and arranged for an immediate mass embarkation to Germany. On the northbound train, prisoners tried jumping off at every opportunity, but most were recaptured, and more than a few were shot. In the northern town of Bolzano, the train stopped in the marshaling yards for a new engine, only to come under attack by Allied bombers.

Ross was blown out of the carriage by a direct hit, and in the chaos he took off. Mobs were rushing in the streets; he followed one group to a wine cellar being used as an air raid shelter, now filled with German and Italian soldiers and civilians. Greening waited until the bombing ended and everyone else went home. It was October 3, 1943, and he was a free man.

After a few days' wandering across the mountains, Greening sneaked onto a train, hiding all the way to Verona, where he jumped off and met some Italians who had lived in the United States for many years. They gave him food, clothes, a bath, and a place to sleep. When the family grew nervous about his being there, he was passed from one relative's home to the next, until German patrols became so numerous and pervasive that the Italians could no longer help him. Ross joined up with two escaped POWs from New Zealand to hide out in a cave overlooking the Po Valley near Venice.

On March 23, 1944, the three were awakened by an explosion. They went outside to find a German patrol armed with machine guns and hand grenades, who'd stumbled onto their hideaway by accident; they were looking for partisans. As the Allied soldiers were marched, captives once again, through the town of Valle, all the villagers who'd helped them stood by, sobbing uncontrollably.

On April 18 Ross found himself 125 miles north of Berlin in Stalag Luft I, home to nine thousand POW aviators. Ross gave the prisoners art lessons and taught them to make their own supplies: brushes of human hair (preferably brunette) with handles from melted phonograph records; burned tree twigs turned into charcoal; paste made from boiled potato leftovers. One student, Lt. Claire Cline, decided he wanted to learn to play the violin, and made his own instrument from bed slats, a chair leg, and horsehair. By war's end, the Luft I arts and crafts collection would total five thousand pounds, and Ross would be CO of North Compound One. When the Red Army finally liberated the camp in 1945, the Nazi prison chief surrendered to Greening to spare himself the Soviets' known brutality.

After learning of Greening's and Jones's captures in December 1942, U.S. Army officials became concerned that the Nazis might turn over anyone who'd attacked Japan to the empire for torture and execution. "Word came out that we were evadees . . . not supposed to fly against the enemy in the theater of operations," Dick Knobloch said. "So they stopped the Tokyo Raiders from flying and said, 'Go on home.'" Dick found himself reassigned back to Florida's Eglin Field, where he became engineering and then flight test officer at the Twenty-seventh Sub Depot. The recall wouldn't reach every Raider, though; Herb Macia kept flying, eventually amassing more World War II combat missions than any other Raider. He would crew on more than seventy sorties, fighting all the way through to April 1945, supporting the landings in southern France, the operations in the Po Valley, and the Battle of the Bulge, getting awarded the Silver Star, the DFC, the Legion of Merit, and the croix de guerre.

Another Raider who for some reason missed the recall was Trav Hoover: "After some missions over Sicily and Italy, they needed a new group commander, so I volunteered to go for the B-24s, doing runs on Romania's Ploesti oil fields, which were the major source of fuel for the Nazis. After I'd done about fifty missions, they were going to be sending me home, but I'd always wanted to be a fighter pilot. So I talked to the general about it to see if I could stay on. He said, 'After flying those bombers, it would be a piece of cake, so go ahead.'"

On August 28, 1942, Bill Farrow and Bob Hite carried the emaciated Dean Hallmark on a litter into a truck, and the American captives were transferred from Bridge House to Kiangwan military prison, a compound of low-slung wooden buildings just outside Shanghai. There the eight fliers were each sent into solitary confinement (their cells measuring nine by five feet), were allowed no Red Cross assistance, and could not send or receive mail. Each morning they were taken out, alone, to wash their hands and brush their teeth, and were given a few minutes of exercise.

Having specifically passed a new law to mandate execution for these "war criminals," the empire was now ready to move forward. Each day the captives were bound and escorted to the Thirteenth Army Military Court for their trial. High above them sat a panel of three Japanese magistrates, wearing English barrister wigs, who listened impassively to the lengthy monologue of the prosecutor, Maj. Hata Itsura. The judges posed no questions; nothing was translated for the POWs, who were denied any manner of defense—no lawyers, no witnesses, no evidence. They were allowed to give only a brief personal history, which was translated for the judges but not transcribed.

On the first day in the courtroom George Barr fainted, and was allowed a chair; Dean Hallmark had to be brought into court on a stretcher, half dead and delirious; the remaining six were forced to stand at all times. For weeks Hallmark had lain in a fetal state next to the toilet in his cell, having lost all control over his bowels. The onetime 200-pounder now weighed about 120, and the always clean-shaven Jungle Jim had a black beard hanging down to his sternum. Flies were always on him, searching, but he was too weak to brush them away.

The proceedings were over in a matter of days. "They announced, in Japanese, our so-called sentence," Bob Hite said. "We didn't really know what it was. The interpreter said, 'They asked me not to tell you.' With that, they dismissed us."

In the first week of October both Prime Minister Tojo and Army Chief of General Staff Sugiyama met at the Imperial Palace with the Lord Privy Seal, who would convey their recommendations to the emperor for his final decision about the Doolittle Raiders. Sugiyama wanted all of them shot immediately, while Tojo urged leniency, believing that only those guilty of slaughtering innocent civilians should be executed, such guilt to be determined by the "confessions." Questioned after war's end by the International Military Tribunal, the former prime minister testified: "Since I had known of the humane nature of the Emperor, it would be to his wish that the death penalty be applied to the smallest possible number of prisoners. For this reason, only the three who had killed a schoolchild were to receive the death sentence. I consulted the Emperor regarding this matter, for he was the only authority who could issue the reduction of the sentence. . . . He was very generous." Sugiyama then wired prosecutor Hata on October 10: "I believe the verdict issued by the chief prosecutor at the military tribunal was fair. However, I am convinced that the sentence for the fliers should be commuted, except for three fliers."

On October 14 twenty-eight-year-old Lt. Dean Hallmark of Robert Lee, Texas; twenty-three-year-old Lt. William Farrow of Darlington, South Carolina; and twenty-one-year-old Sgt. Harold Spatz, of Lebo, Kansas, were informed that they had been found guilty of war crimes and were sentenced to execution by firing squad. Their deaths were scheduled for the following day. The men were allowed to write letters home to their families, which the Japanese promised would be delivered by the Red Cross. With his last strength, Dean Hallmark wrote to his mother in Dallas: "I hardly know what to say. They have just told me that I am liable to execution. I can hardly believe it. . . . I am a prisoner of war and I thought I would be taken care of until the end of the war. . . . I did everything that the Japanese have asked me to do and tried to cooperate with them because I knew that my part in the war was over." Bill Farrow urged his mother: "Don't let this get you down. Remember God will make everything right and that I will see you all again in the hereafter." Harold Spatz told his widowed father that "if I have inherited anything since I became of age, I will give it to you, and Dad, I want you to know that I love you and may God bless you. I want you to know that I died fighting for my country like a soldier."

That night Japanese carpenters fitted together three wooden crosses and three boxes. The following morning the airmen were handcuffed and taken to Shanghai's Public Cemetery Number One. The crosses had been sunk into the turf of a newly mown field, and each condemned man was forced to kneel before one of them. Twenty feet away a six-man firing squad assembled in front of a Shinto altar of burning incense.

In attendance were the prison warden, prosecutor Hata, the clerk of the court, staff of the Kempeitai, and an interpreter. Warden Tatsuta announced: "Your lives were very short, but your names will remain everlastingly. . . . [W]hen you die on the cross, you will be honored as gods." He asked the men if they had anything to say. They did not.

The prisoners' wrists were tied behind them to the crosses. White cloths were draped over their faces, and then black marks were etched onto them, at the center of each man's forehead.

The first line of Japanese riflemen was ordered to fire.

Each shot was accurate. The second line of riflemen was not required to assist.

Blood soaked into the new-mown grass.

The bodies were taken to the Japanese Residents' Association Crematorium and, after a brief moment of silent respect, were rendered into ash. The executed men had been told their cremains would be sent to their families, but this was not done. The boxes of ashes, deliberately mislabeled to cover up the wrongful deaths, were discovered in Shanghai's International Funeral Parlor at the end of the war.

Today, Harold Spatz is buried in Hawaii's National Memorial Cemetery of the Pacific, Bill Farrow is buried in Darlington, South Carolina, and Dean Hallmark is interred at Arlington National Cemetery outside Washington.

After two months of shore leave, the men of *Hornet,* outfitted with new guns and new fighter planes, again set sail that fall of 1942 with faithful sister *Enterprise.* Pete Mitscher had been promoted; the new *Hornet* captain was Rear Adm. Charles P. Mason, while *Enterprise* was now headed by Rear Adm. Thomas Kinkaid, Bill Halsey having become naval commander for the entire southern Pacific, stationed at Nouméa. Admiral Halsey had ordered the group—Task Force 17—to journey from Pearl that fall to provide offshore support for the horror show known as Guadalcanal.

As they did on most of their newly conquered Pacific islands, the Japanese defended Guadalcanal from a series of coral caves and tunnels, inspired by the slogan: "Duty is a heavy burden, but death is light as a feather." The U.S. Marine Corps would eventually learn to use grenades and flamethrowers (blasting a stream of two-thousand-degrees-Fahrenheit oil) to force the enemy out of these otherwise-impregnable bunkers, but at Guadalcanal this strategy hadn't yet evolved, and the first assault took three days of cave-by-cave, hand-to-hand combat. Over the full six-month campaign for this one island, the United States would lose around 6,000 killed and wounded, while for the Japanese, the total would exceed 24,000.

When *Hornet* and *Enterprise* sailed into battle, the Japanese navy still had four carriers, five battleships, fourteen cruisers, and forty-four destroyers in its Combined Fleet and had prepared for another *kantai kessen.* On October 25, 1942, a scout messaged *Enterprise* that they'd spotted Nagumo Chuichi and his carriers two hundred miles north of Task Force 17's position just off the Santa Cruz Islands; it took only three minutes for Admiral Halsey to order: ATTACK REPEAT ATTACK. *Enterprise* sent her air group into battle, but Nagumo had pulled farther north since the sighting, and the planes returned without having found the enemy.

The next morning a Japanese scout reported back to Nagumo that two U.S. carriers lay two hundred miles to his east-southeast. From *Shokaku, Zuikaku,* and *Zuiho,* he ordered dive-bombers, torpedo planes, and Zeros to attack. In turn Americans had uncovered the new Japanese position, and at 0832 *Hornet* launched fifteen Dauntlesses, eight Wildcats, and six Avengers, followed by the ragtag, ten-days-out-of-school replacement air group of *Enterprise.* While *Hornet* airmen maintained formation and downed every Zero that came after them, the *Enterprise* novices collapsed, losing a number of crew and craft. The fighting ended up directly over the Combined Fleet, where the new *Hornet* dive-bombers helped sink *Shokaku* and *Zuiho* in a matter of minutes. At 1000 the American TG spotted new squadrons of incoming Japanese planes, and immediately launched a wing of fighters in defense. While *Enterprise* then found a squall to hide under for twenty minutes, *Hornet* was left out in the bright, clear tropical sun.

The time for her decisive battle had come. A river of enemy torpedo planes and a cascade of dive-bombers gathered against the "Gray Ghost" from every direction. The ship's 20 mm, .30 caliber, pompom, 1.1-inch, and 5-inch guns raised a curtain of smoke and fire in defense, but it wasn't enough. Japanese forces were so overwhelming there was no direction in which Charlie Mason could turn to avoid their bombs or outrun their torpedoes. One gunner remembered it as "pitiless, . . . amalgamated hell. . . . It seemed to me those Japs would never stop coming in." The sky above, once clear with light cirrus to the horizon, was now a wall of black ack-ack.

The first Japanese strike would be a suicide bomber crashing himself straight into *Hornet*'s funnel. The wreckage of his fuselage fell onto the signal bridge, killing three, as a waterfall of fuel threw fire over twenty others, killing four. Another bomber scored two hits, one falling to the deck and detonating, while the other crashed into the ready room. Two minutes later, a pair of five-hundred-pounders hit just behind the island, one tumbling all the way through to the fourth deck before detonating, killing many on its way and igniting fires across the supply department. The second struck the flight deck, killing thirty starboard gunners with shrapnel, and an unknown number on the hangar deck below. Another bomb then crashed four decks down, exploding in the forward mess hall, turning its lockers, ladders, and tables into burning shrapnel that killed a number of officers and destroyed the forward generator switchboard, terminating electric power across the ship's bow. When the waterpower failed and the fire hoses went dry, sailors formed bucket brigades, passing seawater and Foamite in an attempt to save *Hornet*. In the terrible heat junior recruits passed out tomato sandwiches and melting ice cream from the ravaged galleys.

Hornet was now running full out at thirty-one knots to escape an assault by eels, but that just wasn't fast enough. "I remember [the torpedo planes] coming in . . . they were so low over the water they had to jump over the masts of the destroyers in the screen," Lt. Comdr. Francis Drake Foley said. "They came over the horizon so you couldn't see them, and came in full bore." Two Japanese torpedoes ripped through the starboard hull and detonated with a concussion that nearly threw the floating city completely out of the water. Stephen Jurika "felt as though the ship was a rat being shaken by a bull terrier, just literally shaken. My teeth rattled." One missile opened a hole four feet in diameter across the bulkhead and into the forward engine room, sending water and oil rushing over the crew. On their way to escape, the chief engineer was able to intercom the bridge to say that he and his staff were having to abandon quarters. The bridge replied to abandon ship. Francis Foley got on the horn to the men of *Hornet*'s Air Group 8, ordering them to head for *Enterprise*. The airmen landed, in shock, to be further stunned by *Enterprise*'s flight deck blackboard: "Proceed without *Hornet*."

Her death had taken all of five minutes. *Hornet*'s four gigantic props were silent, her engines dead. She could not be steered. Flooding seawater left her with a ten-degree list to starboard. Cruisers and destroyers tried to tow her from the line of attack, but she was too damaged to make the effort worthwhile.

At 1650 on October 26, 1942, a mere six months after entering history with the launch of the Doolittle Raid, the "Gray Ghost" received her final orders: CV-8 would sail no more, and she must be kept from Japanese hands. Guns and torpedo tubes from *Anderson* and *Mustin* fired on one of their own, until the great carrier was fully ablaze and clearly worthless. She'd withstood seven bombs, three aerial torpedoes, and two suicide crashes by damaged Japanese fighters, three hundred rounds of five-inch shells, and nine torpedoes from American destroyers, but still *Hornet* refused to sink. Japanese ships, arriving the next day, would have to finish her off with four long-lance torpedoes.

In death, she again made history, as the last American heavy carrier ever lost at war; 133 of her crew had perished in that final battle.

While the struggle against Japan dragged on across the jungles of the South Pacific, Ski York and his crew were wondering if they could survive the pitiless cold of the Soviet Union. "It was the middle of winter. We had seen the thermometer hit bottom for a three-day period, around fifty degrees below zero. That, however, had been a cold snap. The thermometer usually stayed around thirty-five to forty below now," Bob Emmens remembered.

"Time seemed to be standing still. The days and nights ran together and repeated themselves with an awful monotony. It was becoming an effort to study or take an interest in anything. Often we would sleep during the day and stay up at night. . . .

"We were beginning to notice ill effects from our diet of *kroopa*, bread, and tea. Our gums were bleeding whenever we brushed our teeth. We found that we could even spit blood just by sucking on our gums. Our skin was dry and flaky. We were all losing weight. And our morale was pretty well shot.

"It was January 6, 1943, and the men were especially dispirited. 'I've been thinking,' Ski said. 'It's a shot in the dark, I know, but it's just an idea I had. I thought of writing a letter to Stalin.' . . .

"We wrote the letter. First we congratulated the Red Army on its great feats in its struggle with the Germans. Then we told of our 'wonderful' treatment, but wished to point out that we were a liability to them, doing ourselves no good, and would very much like to be allowed to join American forces and continue the struggle against our common enemy. We likened our case to a hypothetical case of a German pilot bombing Russia and landing in Japan. We indicated that his probable treatment would be a dinner party given him by the Japs, and that he would probably be returned to Germany within forty-eight hours. We pointed out that we were familiar with international law, which technically bound us to internment, since the Soviet Union was not at war with Japan. But we stated that we felt that because of the length of time since the incident which landed us in the Soviet Union, our departure could be managed with a fair assurance of secrecy. Then we told him that in the event a clear way for our departure could not be seen, we would like to be moved to a warmer climate; that none of us had ever experienced such weather as the fifty below we had seen there in Okhansk, and that we desired to be put to work. We stated that we would prefer some kind of work where our training as a B-25 crew could be utilized, but that we were willing to do anything. Between Mike and the dictionary, we finally came out with what we considered a fairly literal translation of the letter. Ski copied it in his own handwriting, and we put copies of the English and the Russian together in the envelope."

After some months' waiting, the internees decided that nothing had come of this effort, and that only one option remained. Every night, after the English-comprehending Mike had gone off with his Gypsy girlfriend, the Americans planned an escape. Their only remote chance might come in the spring, after the ice had melted and the country's truck gardens were beginning to ripen, around the end of April. They took encouragement from the fact that a neighbor commonly left laundry out to dry—clothes the men could wear. They would split into two groups, take the laundry, steal food from the house, and try to seize a boat on the river.

"It was the twenty-fifth of March," Bob Emmens remembered. "The back door opened, and in walked two well-dressed, smart-looking Russian officers. One was a captain and the other a major. The cut of their coats and the smartness of their appearance definitely placed them out of the Okhansk class. The major opened his briefcase and said, 'This letter was received in Moscow a short time ago. Did you write it?'

"'Yes, sir,' said Ski. 'We wrote that letter.' His voice was a little shaky. His heart must have done a flip, as mine did.

"The major was smiling. 'The letter was given to the High Command of the Red Army in Moscow. We are here to tell you that the first of your requests cannot be granted. That is the request to be released from the Soviet Union. But our government has decided to grant you the second two requests. You will be moved to a warmer climate, and you will be allowed to work.'

"His words were unbelievable. Ski translated them into English for Herndon, Laban, and Pohl. For a moment the words didn't sink in. Even Ski blinked his eyes, trying to take in their full meaning. . . .

"Ski asked the major, 'Where are we going?'

"The major smiled. 'In due time, you will know everything.' . . ."

They piled into a four-car cavalcade and drove for twelve hours to the city of Molotov, where the major took their measurements and had them completely outfitted in breeches, blouses with hammer-and-sickle buttons, knee-high black boots, and wide leather belts, all topped by fur caps decorated with red stars. The next night they were taken to a performance of *Swan Lake,* and the night after to see a movie: Deanna Durbin in *One Hundred Men and a Girl.*

The following day they were put on a plane and knew they were heading south, since at one break in the clouds, Bob could see a camel pulling a sleigh through the snow. They landed in Chkalov (now Oranburg), which had the first flush toilet the men had ever seen in Russia (an especially pleasant discovery for Herndon, afflicted again with the GIs), and were then placed on a train to go even farther south. Their sleeping compartments were divvied up: The major would sleep with the food; the men were split into pairs; and the odd man out, York, found himself bunking with a stranger.

Immediately York called Bob into his room and shut the door. "The other occupant of Ski's compartment had already been there, apparently, and was off the train for the time being," Emmens remembered. "On the floor, directly in front of me, was an open leather satchel. Inside, I could see a book on top of some clothing. The book was a novel in English!

"On the table was some food. Its owner appeared to have eaten before he got off the train. There was a can of butter and some other items. The can was marked 'Maxwell House Coffee'! Next to the coffee can was an unopened can of Spam! I picked it up. It was real American Spam.

"'Well I'll be damned!' I said. 'What do you think?'

"'I haven't any idea. This is all part of the deal, or it's a coincidence,' said Ski. 'But keep it to yourself, and when the guy gets back here we'll see what it's all about.'

"That night Ski and I went back to his compartment. I was introduced to a short, stocky Russian who called himself Kolya. He was a man about thirty-two years old and spoke a little English, which was about the equivalent of our Russian. He had come all the way from Moscow on the train, and since one does not travel in the Soviet Union without taking food, he had brought along bread and butter, caviar and vodka, cheese and bologna. He was very friendly. We learned later that he was connected with the shipment of imports entering the Soviet Union from the countries to the south—India, Afghanistan, Iraq, and Persia. He had to make the trip to Moscow from his headquarters, Ashkhabad [now Ashgabat], the capital of the Soviet Turkmenistan Republic, about once every six weeks. Our trip lasted eight days. We saw a lot of Kolya during that time.

"'Yes,' said Kolya, 'I remember when Tokyo was bombed. It was a great feat; you were members of a great mission.'

"'But we are no longer members of a great mission, Kolya,' said Ski. 'We are no good to your country, or to ours, or to ourselves, in our present situation.'

"'You must be patient,' said Kolya. 'You will fight again.'

"'We've been patient for a year now, Kolya,' I said. 'We don't see why your government wants to keep us. We are a burden to them. I should think they would be glad to get rid of us.'

"'If it were right for you to leave, you would leave. If my government keeps you, there must be a good reason for it,' he said.

"'But we are soldiers, Kolya. There is a war going on. We are a trained crew of an airplane that is being used in the war. Don't you see?' Ski went on.

"'Yes,' he said, 'I can see, and I understand how you must feel. But you must not question orders when you are soldiers. Come now, do not be sad! We will have a drink of vodka to the day when you will again fight for your country.'"

Later Ski told Bob that "last night we sat up until after midnight, talking. He got out his vodka and we had quite a few drinks. I decided that I would stay with him and just see if I could get anything out of him after he got drunk. Well, he didn't get drunk, but neither did I. We got awfully serious in our talk, though. He is crazy about the United States. He said he would like to go there sometime. But he never missed a chance to say that his first duty was to his government. But, just the same, he said enough to make me think that if the guy is in a position to help us, I think we can talk him into it. It may take some time, but eventually, I think he'll do it."

"Bob Emmens and I differ on this," Ski York would later report. "He thinks we did it all on our own, and I am convinced we didn't. When we first got on a train . . . [t]hey put me in with a total stranger. This was against all their practices. Immediately I said, 'Oh oh, something is wrong.'

"We traveled for nine days together. I ate every meal out of stuff he had in big pieces of luggage kept under the bottom bunk. He had pickled sturgeon; he had caviar; he had all kinds of meats; he had bread; he had vodka—enough for the whole trip. This was no peasant. I told him who we were. He professed to believe that we were actually Russians. You know damn well, even if my Russian was perfect, the accent would give me away. It just didn't smack right. . . . He was there for a purpose. I wasn't put into that compartment by accident, and he wasn't either. He was doing his job."

The POWs remaining in Shanghai, whose sentences had been commuted, were now being held in full solitary, with no contact allowed between them. They had no idea that Dean Hallmark, Bill Farrow, and Harold Spatz had been executed by firing squad. At a date none of them remembers, they were marched back into the courtroom. They could see that only five were now in attendance, but had no idea what this might mean. Surrounded by Japanese army officers, the lead judge announced through the interpreter, "The tribunal finds the defendants guilty. . . . The tribunal, acting under the law . . . hereby sentences the defendants to death . . . but, through the graciousness of His Majesty the Emperor, your sentences are hereby commuted to life imprisonment . . . with special treatment."

The hearing had taken all of five minutes, and the men were marched back to their cells. "I had expected to be executed, from the way the Japanese had acted," Jake DeShazer said. "It was really a relief to know that they were now planning to let us remain alive. I could not help feeling a strange sense of joy, even though solitary confinement and a long war awaited any possible chance of freedom. At the same time, it seemed almost helpless to think of ever being free again, since the most probable thing would be that we would be executed when America did win the war."

Two days later Warden Tatsuta let the men return to the courtroom to claim their personal effects. Again there were only five of them. The belongings of Dean Hallmark, Bill Farrow, and Harold Spatz lay on the table, untouched. Each man knew, now, what had happened, but they couldn't bring themselves to talk about any of it.

The winter of 1942 came, and with it, a harsh freeze that never lifted. The prison was unheated, and though the men were given a few extra clothes, these were hardly sufficient. The only way they could warm up was with exercise, of which they were allowed only a few minutes each day. Additionally the endless hours of solitary confinement now began to take their mental toll. The men knew they could be driven stir-crazy, and they tried to come up with preventives. For a while they would yell to one another in their separate cells, but the guards soon put a stop to that.

One of their fellow inmates, Caesar Luis dos Remedios, a man of Portuguese and Japanese descent accused of spying (or drug dealing—prison rumor claimed both), was considered harmless by the staff. Since he spoke four languages and proved himself useful, he was made a trusty. Through dos Remedios, the guys would learn news of the war and of one another. When he brought the Americans their rations, he would hide notes inside. He explained their verdict's "special treatment" this way: "If the Americans win the war you are to be shot, and if the Japanese win the war, you are to be kept as slave labor."

Dos Remedios was finally able to convince the warden that they would very likely die from the cold and the treatment. He got them more blankets, and the solitary rescinded. The men were together again. In the years to come he would also help to bring them justice.

The POWs continued to suffer from dysentery and beriberi. Their vitamin deficiencies, now in advanced stages, had triggered various neurological disorders. They couldn't concentrate or sustain a thought, and they became touchy and irritable. They lost coordination and developed pains all over their bodies, horrible electric pains that moved from spot to spot and never went away.

Bob Hite was the worst affected. He became extremely ill over a period of three months, behaving strangely until the early spring. With a temper always at the brink, Bob would explode at the slightest provocation. The other men didn't have the strength to withstand his tirades, and were concerned that his actions would lead to punishments, but the guards seemed to understand his craziness and let him be.

Finally Bob Meder came to understand what was happening to them. To try to counteract the mental debilitation, he led the group in a series of intellectual calisthenics. They would name the presidents, the state capitals, facts of geography and history, and even started playing a lottery game with their food. They'd draw numbers, or see who could catch and kill the most lice and fleas, keeping score on the prison walls with marks from their calcium shirt buttons. At the end of each week one American would receive an extra half bowl of rice or soup from each of the others. Additionally, however, each aviator had to come up with an elaborate mental exercise to pass away the countless thousands of hours spent alone. Chase Nielsen built a house, from scratch, in his head, while Bob Hite designed a working ranch; George Barr manufactured a flowing and convoluted neon sign; Bob Meder wrote essays in philosophy; and Jake DeShazer composed poetry. As the months passed, however, the malnutrition, lack of exercise, and lack of stimulation overwhelmed even the most imaginative of their efforts, and their physical and mental conditions dramatically worsened.

On April 17, 1943, the Shanghai captives were roped, blindfolded, cuffed, and chained, flown to Nanking, and again put in solitary confinement. Their new prison was wood framed, with solid doors and walls, and air that never circulated in the summer. The cells were about ten feet square each, with only a small opening at the top of one wall for a vent.

Since Jake DeShazer was the smallest of the surviving POWs, he got the smallest cell. He wasn't too unhappy about this, though, since when no one was looking, he could climb the walls. His cell was only five feet wide, so with his hands on one side and his feet stretched to the other, Jake would inch himself twelve feet to the top. There, he'd look out of the vent at the Chinese countryside.

Since the Nanking military prison was a new building, it wasn't infested, like all the others, with lice, but the captives were ambivalent about this. As disgusting as lice might be, finding them and killing them with their fingernails gave them something to do. Eventually the Japanese brought in a desk and a chair for each cell, both of which were nailed in place. The men found it a great luxury to sit in their new furniture, even though they still had to sleep on the floor. Bobby Hite would later joke that moving from Shanghai to Nanking was like going from the worst slum you could ever imagine to a luxury residence out of *House & Garden*. They would be prisoners in Nanking for the next twenty-five months.

Their food was reduced to only one small bowl of rice and one of soup each day, but they were allowed fifteen minutes of exercise. Walking the courtyard gave them the chance to see one another, though the only communication they could manage was a whispered hello. Besides their gauntness and lethargy, the men noticed that their eyes had become very, very white.

The new prison guards were more talkative than the ones in Shanghai, and from their remarks the men were able to piece together what was happening in the outside world, especially the progress of the war. The guards would tell them that Tokyo was winning every battle (and in this they were being honest, since that was the truth as they knew it), but even with such limited information, the fliers could figure out from what little Asian geography they knew that Allied forces were moving in closer and closer. The guards would always end this discussion with the same comment: If the United States won the war, the prisoners wouldn't be freed. They would be executed.

Eventually the guards grew so friendly with their charges that they invited them to *sumo*—wrestle. Even though the Americans had been starved and suffered from months of dysentery, they were still bigger than the Japanese, and frequently won. When the guards employed novel rules and tripped and kicked their charges into submission, they would yell, *"Nippon banzai!"* (Japan wins). Every time Japan won, the Americans' meals would improve slightly, so the POWs learned to make sure that Japan won as often as possible.

Besides the other effects of beriberi, the men now found themselves regularly hallucinating. Astounding visions of home-cooked, all-American meals would appear on the walls. The loving faces of mothers, fathers, and girlfriends would materialize on the ceiling. These mirages made them so happy that, when the guards delivered food or checked up on them and interrupted their reveries, the men would seethe with anger.

By the fall of 1943 Bob Meder's constant dysentery, which had left him weak and thin for months, took a severe turn for the worse. His GIs ran from three a day to five times a day, and there was no letting up. He was weekly getting more and more emaciated, and his legs were swelling up. "I believe it was in the month of November," Bob Hite said. "Bob Meder had had dysentery very, very bad. He was losing weight like crazy, getting weaker and weaker. One of the things that happened—we were going outside and one of the guards pushed Meder. With his bravado, he said, 'Well, you little so-and-so, as sick as I am, I could still whip you.' He took a swing and he fell down. It was sort of sad, but it was sort of good to see that even in as bad a shape that he was in, that the spirit was still willing. Bob knew that he was in bad shape. He was just sort of a skeleton. I had melted down to practically about eighty pounds. We tried to find out if there was anything we could do and he said, 'Just pray.'"

Starving to death is, at the end, the human body eating itself. As fat vanishes and muscles thin into nothing, the skin becomes clammy, dry, and inelastic, while hair falls out in clumps across the body. The liver and intestines are the first organs to deteriorate, and then the heart itself begins to shrink. At a certain point the victim of starvation stops caring entirely whether or not he lives or dies. Some survivors have reported that they were overwhelmed, in the very last moments, by feelings of euphoria, of hope. Their relentless fatigue and brain fog of malnutrition evaporated, lifting into a luminous mental clarity.

Bob Meder didn't want to be a burden on the others, so he tried covering up how seriously ill he was. Everyone noticed when, out for their exercise, he was too weak to get up and come over for the daily whispered gossip. When Chase Nielsen went over to ask about his condition, Meder again asked Nielsen to pray for him. Chase knew this meant something far more serious than Bob could admit.

When Nielsen tried to find out in more detail how serious Meder's condition was, one of the attending guards ordered him to be quiet. Chase ignored him, and as he passed in the corridor on the way back to the cells, the chief guard punched him in the face. Whether it was the mental stress, or the beriberi, or seeing Meder at the end of his rope, Nielsen had taken all he could take. He hauled back and popped the guard right in the jaw. The enraged Japanese tried to retaliate by hitting Chase with his steel scabbard, but Nielsen was able to dodge out of the way.

The men went back to their cells, wondering what punishment would be inflicted. Chase could easily be shot in the head for what he'd done. But in fact nothing happened, and the men wondered why.

There was a kinder guard looking in on them later that afternoon, and Meder, using some of the Japanese he'd learned after nineteen months in prison, asked if the new man could make certain that his things would be returned to his family when he died. Hite could hear these goings-on and yelled out, again and again, to get Meder a doctor immediately. A few hours later, a medic appeared, and gave the lieutenant a vitamin shot.

It was too late. One day there was a big racket in the courtyard, and DeShazer crawled up his walls to have a look. There he saw prison workers building a coffin.

On December 1, 1943, Lt. Robert J. Meder of Cleveland, Ohio, died at the age of twenty-six. He had been starved to death. On the floor of his cell, he'd carved his epitaph: LIEUT. R. J. MEDER, USAF, O-421280, B-25 BOMBER COMMAND DETAIL PLANE NO. 2298. PLEASE NOTIFY U.S. ARMY LIFE IMPRISONMENT.

The one crewman who always had hope in his heart, who was always so confident they would get out of this all right in the end, was gone. "They opened all our cell doors and they took us one at a time and let us go in the cell and see him," Bob Hite said. "They had covered him all up from about his chest to his head. He was in that box, and they had a little cotton in his mouth. . . . Needless to say, we were very, very sad and quite disturbed. We thought, 'Well, any of us can die at any time. We could all die, and they could do away with us, and nobody would ever know the difference.' No one knew we were there. It was sort of an eerie feeling."

Chase Nielsen was now the only surviving crewman of *Green Hornet*.

★

By March 1943, when the North African takeover was in its final stages, plans were begun to invade Sicily and everyone was reorged. Tooey Spaatz became head of the Northwest African Air Force—the Twelfth—and under him, Jimmy Doolittle would command the Strategic Air Force, attacking German convoys trying to resupply Tunisia, destroying Axis air forces on the ground in Sicily, and "softening up" Italy. On April 18 thirteen Raiders assigned to the Twelfth had an anniversary party, which included French champagne, in an old North African barn. "We toasted those who couldn't be with us . . . and those who would never be with us," Doolittle said. The anniversary was the occasion for American newspapers to write up the story of the Tokyo Raid all over again. Even though, over the course of the year, the Allies had achieved a number of solid campaign victories—Torch included—Americans still looked back with particular pride on that first triumph. A group of civilians wanted to rename the Los Angeles airport in Jimmy's honor, and the fervor became so great that LA's mayor sent General Doolittle a letter, asking for his opinion. Doolittle replied that airports were named for people after they were dead, and he wasn't yet ready to make that sacrifice on behalf of the good people of Los Angeles. LAX's USO lounge is named for him today.

That same Doolittle Raid anniversary would bring startling news from the other side of the world. In the opening months of 1943 Admiral Yamamoto had sent three hundred planes to attack Allied positions at Guadalcanal and New Guinea. By now he'd lost almost every ace pilot, and his new air crews were combat virgins whose strikes accomplished little, even though the novices, in their zeal, reported one great victory after the next back to Tokyo. In April of that year the admiral flew to Bougainville (a Solomon island in the north fork of what is now Papua New Guinea) to congratulate them on these great achievements in person. Radio messages from nearby Japanese bases carried details of his travel plans, which were intercepted by the basement men of Hypo, and within twenty-four hours, the American navy knew the exact future whereabouts of the architect of Pearl Harbor.

On the morning of April 18, 1943, the admiral's plane approached southern Bougainville, escorted by nine Zeros. Eighteen P-38 Lightnings swooped in to ambush. Fourteen took on the Zeros; the other four attacked the bomber ferrying Yamamoto. Capt. Thomas Lanphier, Jr., and his wingman, Rex T. Barber, both strafed the craft with twenty-millimeter cannon and machine guns. The plane exploded in flames and crashed into the jungle.

Admiral Yamamoto's ashes were interred in a state ceremony on June 5.

His death shook every member of the Combined Fleet, many of whom saw this as an omen, even the always optimistic Fuchida Mitsuo: "I believed now that the war was entirely lost." Lanphier and Barber would spend the rest of their lives confronting each other in federal court over who deserved credit for the kill.

Two months later General Sugiyama had to tell his emperor that those same positions in the Solomons were now imperiled. Hirohito replied, "Isn't there someplace where we can strike the United States? . . . When and where on earth are you ever going to put up a good fight? And when are you ever going to fight a decisive battle? . . . after suffering all these defeats, why don't you study how not to let the Americans keep saying, 'We won! We won!'"

On April 20, 1943, the War Department finally issued its official communiqué on the Doolittle Raid. A testament to the fog of war, this eleven-page press release described the training at Eglin; revealed that Shangri-La was in fact the USS *Hornet;* listed the names of the men known and presumed to be prisoners of war; the deaths of Leland Faktor, Gene McGurl, Mel Gardner, Ken Reddy, Bob Clever, Bob Gray, Dick Miller, Don Smith, and Paul Leonard; the MIAs of Bill Dieter, Donald Fitzmaurice, and Omer Duquette; the imprisonment of Davey Jones; the heroism of Doc White and Dave Thatcher; and the name of every volunteer. It explained that one crew had been interned in the Soviet Union while eight other fliers had been captured by the Japanese, and told the American people that they'd been kept in the dark about so much of the mission in order to keep the Japanese as ignorant about its details as possible. The communiqué listed only Leland Faktor as a direct casualty, since even at that late date, the chaos in China and Tokyo's refusal to release concrete information about its captives prevented the War Department from knowing the truth.

The following day Roosevelt announced in a radio broadcast, "It is with a feeling of deepest horror, which I know will be shared by all civilized peoples, that I have to announce the barbarous execution by the Japanese Government of some of the members of this country's armed forces who fell into Japanese hands as an incident of warfare." Two days later, the *New York Times* headlined: JAPAN'S BARBAROUS ACT HAS NO PARALLEL IN WAR: TOKYO STANDS ALONE AS A CRUEL CAPTOR IN DEFIANCE OF GENEVA CONVENTION.

In the days following the executions of Hallmark, Farrow, and Spatz, the only information that Washington could uncover was a Japanese radio broadcast of October 19, 1942: "the cruel, inhuman and beastlike American pilots who . . . dropped incendiaries and bombs on non-military hospitals, schools and private houses and even dive-strafed playing schoolchildren, were captured and court-martialed and severely punished according to military law." U.S. State Department officials requested the Swiss Embassy in Tokyo to try to mediate, as well as to uncover precisely what "severely punished" meant in Japan. On February 17, 1943, Tokyo informed the Swiss that all of the American POWs had received death sentences for their crimes but that some lives had been spared. They declined to release the names of the executed or details of where the surviving POWs were being held, and refused to allow either the Swiss or the Red Cross to see the "war criminals." Roosevelt had waited two months before taking the issue public, as he worried any direct criticism might jeopardize the treatment of the seventeen thousand other Americans held captive by the empire.

Hap Arnold immediately sent a memo to every member of his Army Air Forces: "In violation of every rule of military procedure and of every concept of human decency, the Japanese have executed several of your brave comrades who took part in the first Tokyo raid. These men died as heroes. We must not rest—we must redouble our efforts—until the inhuman warlords who committed this crime have been utterly destroyed. Remember those comrades when you get a Zero in your sites—have their sacrifice before you when you line up your bombsights on a Japanese base." From North Africa, Doolittle announced that he and his Raiders were ready to go back and bomb hell out of Japan all over again, to finish up the job they started until "she crumbled and begged for mercy."

The American public reacted with overwhelming support. On the day following FDR's announcement of the executions, more War Bonds were sold—eleven billion dollars' worth—than in any other twenty-four-hour period of the war.

Several days after, the *New York Times* contacted Chase Nielsen's mother, who said, "I wonder if, and hope and pray, that it is propaganda. I don't see how anyone who professes to be of the human race can be so cruel and inhuman. We have had no word from Chase since he left the United States. This is terrible, sitting here helpless and not being able to do anything." Mrs. Nielsen would continue to write to everyone in Washington, including the president, to try to get stronger efforts made to release her son. Mrs. William F. Fitzmaurice of Lincoln, Nebraska, said that she believed her Donald was fighting with Chinese guerrillas. Mrs. John J. Meder of Lakewood, Ohio, commented, "The Japanese just can't be so heartless and inhuman as all that. They just couldn't resort to such vile and insane acts with our boys. I won't believe that my son was executed."

Tokyo would broadcast a radio message, in English, in response. It confirmed the execution of

> some of Doolittle's companions. . . . [We] were perfectly justified
> in severely punishing American fliers who were found guilty of
> purposely carrying out wanton attacks on innocent civilians, hos-
> pitals and schools. . . . This same policy will continue to be
> enforced in the future. General Doolittle has assumed the false
> colors of a hero in a conspiracy with President Roosevelt. Doolit-
> tle, commander of the raid on Japan one year ago, failed to do
> anything, so we have the pleasure of offering him the title of
> "Did-little." . . . Two can play at the same game of bombing. You
> know, you raid us and we raid you. It's all part of the war. . . . And
> by the way, don't forget America, [you can be] sure that every flier
> that comes here has a special pass to hell. Rest assured, it's strictly
> a one-way ticket.

METAMORPHOSIS

As their train arrived in the capital of Soviet Turkmenistan, the interned Raiders made their farewells to Kolya and took a good look at where their letter to Stalin had taken them. Lying in a barely green oasis situated between a vast desert and a forbidding mountain range, Ashkhabad was an arid, dusty Muslim town not so very different from the villages of its Central Asian neighbors: Iraq, Afghanistan, and, fifteen miles to the south, Persia. The streets were filled with chickens and goats, pomegranates and potatoes, women in paisley silk blouses and turbans, and men who looked as if they spent every day with nothing much to do.

The Russian major drove his American charges down a long, flat street to where the town stopped entirely on its southern fringe. Having left behind the lively bazaars and delicate mosques of the city, they now found themselves in an endless ghetto of hovels, each surrounded by a six-foot-high mud wall. "Our hearts sank as we slowed to a stop in front of one such abode," Bob Emmens said. "Even the major's face bore an expression of disbelief. The house was constructed entirely of mud, and contained two rooms. The larger room had two beds in it, a table, and five wooden chairs. This room was about eight by twelve feet. Off this was a small room, about six feet square. There were three beds in it. On each bed was a folded blanket. There were no sheets, no pillows, no mattresses. Immediately to the right, inside the fence, was a tiny house, about five feet square. Inside, in one corner, was a metal topping with a grate underneath. This was our stove. Across the back wall was a wooden bed, and against the wall on our left was a wooden table about two feet square. An old, old man lay on the bare wooden bed, snoring. Halfway back in the lot, a water faucet stuck up out of the ground. There was no handle on it, and it leaked a steady drip all the time. This was our water supply. At the back of the lot was a three-sided board screening with one plain two-by-eight board over a pit. There was no roof over the three walls—this was our toilet."

On April 10, 1943, they were photographed and issued identification passes. Every morning at eight o'clock, a bus met them at the town's main square to take them to their factory, an overhaul shop for small trainer biplanes. "Ski and I were assigned to the job of dismantling the fuselage, tearing away the fabric and removing screws and placing them in little bins of other screws the same size," Emmens remembered. "Herndon and Pohl were to clean instruments in a small instrument shop located in a lean-to on the side of the main building. Laban was to help clean up the small engines in the engine shop located in another small building. During smoking breaks, the other workers eyed us quizzically, but we were never asked who we were or why we were there." During the next ten days, all the Americans got the worst case of dysentery they'd ever had. For toilet paper they used *Pravda*.

Each night an officer from the local Soviet command came to check up on them, but left soon after a head count. On April 11 at around 2100, there was a knock at the gate, and Kolya appeared. He made sure they were alone since, as he explained, "I think it is best if I am not seen too much with you." He told them he would come back the next night to escort them to his house for dinner. "All our meetings with Kolya were clandestine," Bob Emmens remembered. "He would come to our house only after dark, and our visits to his house could be accomplished only at night, and behind secured shutters. . . . Finally, at the end of about the third week, and after some very special pleading on the part of Ski and myself together with solemn promises of secrecy, Kolya said, 'Very well, I can help you and I will. You must place yourselves completely in my hands. You must act entirely according to my instructions and do nothing until I tell you the plans are complete. Above all, you must not, under any circumstances, try to escape on your own. It is absolutely impossible. The mountains are very high and very rough. They are for the most part inhabited by unfriendly tribes. The border is manned by Russian troops, dogs, mines, and barbed wire. You cannot do it alone. Do not try!'"

The men assumed it would take a few days for these plans to be worked out; instead weeks passed, with no signs of progress. Ski finally lost his patience, confronted Kolya alone, and learned that everything had in fact been made ready, but that the scheme had fallen apart at the last minute. More dreary weeks went by in Soviet Ashkhabad. Finally York returned from a visit with Kolya to announce: "He has actually been in contact with a guy who does smuggling across the border into Persia! And he is making arrangements for me to talk to the guy about getting us out. Kolya says he can't take the chance of talking to the guy himself, that I will have to do that. He says the guy is not a Russian but knows a little Russian, and that he thinks I will be able to talk to him with what little Russian I know. He says that the only way we can get in touch with him is for Kolya and me just to pick a good spot on a bench in the square downtown some evening and wait for him to come along. When he spots the guy he will point him out to me, and it would be up to me to do all the rest."

On May 20, 1943, at 2000, Ski met Kolya on the bench when the square was at its most crowded. Kolya explained that he had never personally spoken with this man, a Persian named Abdul Arram, but knew that he regularly smuggled people, drugs, and jewels between Persia and Turkmenistan. After a long wait Kolya tapped Ski's arm and said, "There he is," pointing out a disheveled Arab making his way slowly down one street. The businessman wished his American friend good luck and took off, while Ski started toward Abdul Arram. For the first few minutes York kept his distance, not sure of what approach to make. Then "he increased his gait until he was right behind him," Emmens remembered. "'You're Abdul Arram, aren't you?' asked Ski from behind as he came within an arm's distance of the man. There was no response from Arram. Ski's heart skipped a beat. Then he came abreast of the man.

"'You're Abdul Arram. I know you are!'

"Again there was no sign of response, and again Ski's heart missed a couple of beats as he thought, 'Jesus, what if this isn't the right guy?' Ski watched the furtive eyes, which never rested. It was a continuous series of glances—behind him, to the right, to the left. And the man smoked, in chain style, Persian cigarettes, which gave Ski a fairly positive indication that he had the right man after all.

"Suddenly he said, 'And if I am Abdul Arram?'

"'I want you to do some work for me,' ventured Ski.

"'What kind of work?' the little man snapped back.

"'I want you to take something out of Russia into Persia for me,' said Ski.

"'That's impossible! Why do you bother me with such a thing?' And with that he spat, turned on his heel, and walked away. Ski was so startled that not until the little man had disappeared as he turned the corner back onto the square did Ski realize that if he let him go now, maybe he was letting our chance of departure go with him. So he started after him again.

"It took a minute or two for Ski to close the gap between them, and he wondered just what his approach should be this time. He tried to put himself in the other's place, in his mind. Naturally the little man would not admit immediately and readily that he was a smuggler. And if he were, he would not even admit readily that he was Abdul Arram. Money! That would naturally be the next question to discuss. Kolya had said that American money was very little known here but that it was like magic. But he had advised using rubles, if possible, since it would naturally be cheaper for us. We had, thanks to Ski's luck at winning in a poker game aboard the *Hornet* on our last night before the raid, about $380 among the five of us. Ski came abreast of the man for the second time, and for a few paces they walked along in silence, until Ski noticed that there were few people around them.

"He said, 'I can pay.'

"The little man stopped again. 'What's to be taken out?' he asked, apparently ignoring the subject of money.

"'Five people.' Ski swallowed hard. That would be a hard job in any man's language. The little man evidently thought so, too.

"'No!' was his only word. And with that, again he turned and started off down the street.

"This time his gait was faster, and Ski's heart sank as he started after him. Again they were retracing their steps. Ski caught up with Arram and watched him as he lighted another Persian cigarette off the butt of the previous one.

"'I repeat that we can pay,' started Ski.

"'How much?' he asked, glancing at Ski in between glances behind them, in front, and down the street to the right and left.

"Ski thought of Kolya's advice, and of the paychecks we had just received from the Russians, totaling among the five of us approximately seven hundred rubles.

"'Five hundred rubles—' said Ski.

"The little man's eyes came to rest on Ski's.

"'Impossible! Do not speak to me any more. I can do nothing for you.' His answer was hissed rather than spoken.

"'—or in dollars!' added Ski as Arram brushed past him.

"The little man walked about fifteen paces as hope slowly drained from Ski's heart with each step. Then Arram stopped and lighted a cigarette. And then he turned slowly and looked back at Ski, who stood his ground on the corner. The little man started slowly back to Ski and, opening his cigarette box, offered Ski one. The word 'dollar' had been as magic as Kolya had stated.

"'How much can you pay?' asked Arram.

"'What's your price?' countered Ski.

"'Five people?' said Arram to himself. 'Baggage?'

"'Yes,' said Ski, 'a little.'

"'To Meshed?' Meshed [now Mashhad] is the first town in Persia south of the Russian-Persian border at Ashkhabad.

"'Yes,' said Ski.

"They walked along in silence. Arram was evidently thinking the whole thing over carefully.

"'Eight hundred dollars.' The words struck Ski like a bolt of lightning.

" 'One hundred dollars,' he said.

" 'Seven hundred—it's very dangerous crossing the border.'

" 'One hundred and fifty dollars,' Ski answered.

" 'Six hundred—and no less!'

" 'We don't have that much,' Ski told him truthfully.

" 'What is the total amount you have?'

" 'Maybe I can borrow enough to make two hundred.'

" 'Four hundred, or no.'

" 'We don't have it, and I can't get that much.'

" 'Three hundred.'

" 'Two hundred fifty.'

" 'Three hundred.'

" 'Two hundred fifty is all we have,' said Ski.

" 'Done!' "

The death of Bob Meder had a terrible effect on the prisoners of Nanking. If he hadn't survived, many now came to believe, how could they? Each, alone in his cell, couldn't help but think that he was next in line to die, but mixed with these fears was rage at what the Japanese had allowed to happen. "I asked to write a letter to the prison governor, and told them that their so-called treatment of prisoners was against all Geneva conference rules that I had ever known, that our rations were outrageous or inadequate," Bob Hite said. "It was a complaint letter, I guess, but I did ask, 'If you can't do anything useful, will you please give us the Holy Bible to read?' . . . I had been sort of raised and brought up in the Baptist church. Jay Nielsen was a Mormon coming from Utah. . . . Jake's family had been very Christian, but up until that time Jake had proclaimed to be an atheist. His father was a preacher. He said he just didn't believe in all that stuff. He didn't see any fruits of so-called Christianity."

"I don't know—what an atheist is, a fellow that doesn't believe in God at all—I don't think I was like that," Jake DeShazer said. "An atheist says there isn't anything; it all just happened. That's terrible. I don't see how a fellow can say that. . . . There had to be something, and I didn't know which one was right. That's the way I felt. How can you tell? If you're born a Buddhist or a Muslim or a Jew, which one is right? It says that darkness will come over your mind, and that's what had happened to me. I was walking in sin and darkness, and you can't think of the truth."

Apparently Meder's death and Hite's angry letter caused trouble all the way up the Nanking penal hierarchy. The captives would later come to believe that the Japanese knew the war was already lost, and were worried about Allied retaliation if they allowed any more POWs to die. Whatever the reasons the prison captain made an appearance and asked the Americans what they would like to eat. They replied with the food they'd be getting at any half-decent army mess: chicken, steak, eggs, milk, vegetables, and chocolate. Within days their rations were changed, and they were now fed soup or rice three times a day, along with pieces of bread. They were also allowed to share a few English books, one being the Bible that Hite had requested. They decided to let each man read it for three weeks before having to pass it on to the next in line.

"It was the first time that I had ever—I think any of us—the first time any of us had really read the Bible from cover to cover," Bob Hite said. "I was sort of like a man being in the desert and finding a cool pool. . . . Instead of hating this enemy that we had such hate for, we began to feel sorry for them. . . . It was almost a miracle to realize the sort of thing that happened to us . . . we were no longer afraid to the extent that we had been . . . we no longer had the hatred."

The captives had been prisoners for two long years. They were lonely, homesick, starving, and ready to give up all hope. Bob Meder had, however, left them with one important legacy—using taps and scratches on the wall to signify dots and dashes, so the men could communicate with one another in Morse code. Now they used it extensively to make sure that no one else was falling apart.

One day they were cleaning their cells when a guard looked in and yelled *"Hayaku!"* (hurry up). Jake DeShazer had been festering with rage, and he yelled back, "Go jump in the lake." Jake: "Before I knew what was going to happen, the door was unlocked, and the guard hit me on the head with his fist. I immediately kicked him in the stomach with my bare foot, and he hit me with his steel scabbard. I had been using some water on the floor to mop up my cell. I picked up the dirty mop water and threw it on the guard. It cooled him off enough so that he didn't do any more than swear at me. But it is strange that he didn't cut off my head."

Immediately after this incident Jake had his turn with the Bible, and it proved to be an experience that would turn his life upside-down. The only light in his cell was a dim winking through the vent at the top of one wall, and like many Bibles, the one they had been given was set in very small type. Yet Jacob started reading, and the words on the page came to life. It seemed as though they were written just for him.

What DeShazer needed more than anything else at that moment was some sign of God's existence. In the revelations of the Old Testament and in the story of Christ's suffering in the New, he felt that God was indeed present, reaching out for someone as abandoned, as mistreated, as hopeless as he was. Since he could only have the Bible for three weeks, Jake wanted to spend every minute reading and rereading, memorizing by heart all the important passages. He ate and exercised as quickly as possible. He hardly slept.

On June 8, 1944, Jake read for a second time Romans 10:9: "That if thou shalt confess with thy mouth the Lord Jesus, and shalt believe in thine heart that God hath raised him from the dead, thou shalt be saved." Jake prayed: "Lord, though I am far from home and though I am in prison, I must have forgiveness." As he prayed constantly, thinking deeply about the message of the Bible, he was overcome with a tremendous sensation: "My heart was filled with joy. I wouldn't have traded places with anyone at that time. Oh, what a great joy it was to know that I was saved, that God had forgiven me my sins. . . . Hunger, starvation, and a freezing cold prison cell no longer had horrors for me. They would only be for a passing moment. Even death could hold no threat when I knew that God had saved me. Death is just one more trial that I must go through before I can enjoy the pleasures of eternal life. There will be no pain, no suffering, no loneliness in heaven. Everything will be perfect with joy forever."

The more he read, the more he realized how much he had to change deep down inside. He especially memorized I Corinthians 13, which he felt offered a goal to achieve: "Love is very patient, very kind. Love knows no jealousy; love makes no parade, gives itself no airs, is never rude, never selfish, never irritated, never resentful; love is never glad when others go wrong; love is gladdened by goodness, always slow to expose, always eager to believe the best, always hopeful, always patient. Love never disappears."

Jake felt that, through Jesus, his sins had been forgiven and that, as a Christian, he, too, would have to forgive. One day, as the corporal was being taken back to his cell from exercise, the guard slapped his back and yelled, "*Hayaku, hayaku!*" He shoved Jake inside, slamming the door on the prisoner's foot. Screaming, the guard kicked DeShazer's bare heel with his hobnailed boot, until eventually Jake was able to wrench himself free: "The pain in my foot was severe, and I thought some bones were broken. But as I sat on my stool in great pain, I felt as if God were testing me somehow."

As the guard came on duty the next morning, the corporal at first considered revenge. Then he remembered his lesson and instead called out: "*Ohayo gozaimasu!*" (good morning). The guard looked at him strangely, and Jake figured he thought he'd lost his mind. No matter. Morning after morning Jake tried the same polite and friendly greeting, until finally the guard came over and spoke with him through the door. In the limited amount of Japanese

DeShazer had picked up in prison, he asked the man about his family. The guard smiled.

A few mornings later he saw the guard pacing, his head bowed, his hands folded in prayer. The man later explained he was talking to his mother, who had died when he was a little boy. From that moment on he treated Jake well, never shouting, never kicking or beating: "One morning he opened the slot and handed in a boiled sweet potato. I was surprised, and thanked him profusely. Later he gave me some batter-fried fish and candy. I knew then that God's way will work if we really try, no matter what the circumstances. . . . How easy it was to make a friend out of an enemy because I had just tried."

During that summer Bob Hite's health took a turn for the worse. His body temperature spiked, and he remained feverish. Remembering the death of Meder, prison officials removed his solid door and replaced it with a screen to allow at least a small flow of air. This wasn't sufficient, and the captives were astonished to learn that a doctor had been summoned. They could hear him ordering ice brought in to cool off the fevers, but Hite's condition grew so severe that the doctor moved into the prison to take care of him night and day.

Finally, with constant attention and fall's cooler weather, the crisis passed and Hite recovered.

Over their endless days of illness and confinement, the POWs were completely unaware that there was a new reason for hope; that a secret group of heroes was now turning the tide of war. The most brilliant of generals, the most inspiring of admirals, and the greatest of battlefield troops paled in significance at that moment to the thousands of stateside Rosie and Ronnie the Riveters who had outproduced both the Axis and the other Allied powers combined, contributing nearly three hundred thousand planes, two million trucks, eighty-seven thousand warships, and one hundred thousand tanks to Roosevelt's arsenal of democracy in 1943. Over the last two years of war, Japanese shipyards would assemble six new fleet carriers, while the United States would produce seventeen fleet, ten medium, and eighty-six escort carriers. *Wasp, Hornet, Yorktown,* and *Lexington* were all reincarnated, joining *Enterprise, Essex, Intrepid,* and *Bunker Hill* in the Pacific, each bristling with 5-inch, 40 mm and 20 mm guns while carrying almost a hundred planes, most crucially a new fighter specifically engineered to beat Zeros: the F6F Hellcat. The Department of Ordnance was finally manufacturing torpedoes that could hit something, and these new eels allowed American subs to launch obliterating assaults on the Japanese merchant marine. Just as Nazi U-boats had crippled Atlantic shipping at the start of the war, now Chester Nimitz's 150 Pacific subs destroyed the economy of an island nation by making it incapable of importing or exporting anything at all.

After a year of waiting for his legs to mend from jumping into the lifeboat at Midway, Fuchida Mitsuo was appointed air operations officer of the Combined Fleet on April 20, 1944, just in time for the devastating losses at what Americans called "the Marianas Turkey Shoot." In the Philippine Sea, 395 of the Combined Fleet's 430 planes were taken down, along with the carriers *Taiho, Shokaku,* and *Hiyo.* Many of Fuchida's friends from his naval academy days, from Operation Z, and from Midway were killed that month, along with every member of the First Air Fleet, either by enemy fire or by suicide.

As 1944 drew to its close, Fuchida would become the only surviving Japanese airman from the attack on Pearl Harbor.

In the decades between the wars, military chiefs like Yamamoto, Mitchell, Arnold, and King had spent a great deal of time with their fellow officers theorizing about tactics and strategy, while working for organizations that couldn't afford to test any of their ideas. World War II would allow these military chiefs to put into practice their long-argued and much-discussed abstract concepts of battle. It could be argued that the war, from on high, was a series of military experiments, and that few of these produced their intended results. The Imperial Japanese Navy would fail again and again with its twin-edged *kantai kessen*s, while Europe would provide the staging ground for the Army Air Force's greatest experiment, which likewise would end with entirely unexpected consequences.

From Italy's Giulio Douhet to America's Billy Mitchell and AAF Chief Hap Arnold, air-power acolytes around the world believed in the tactic of high-altitude strategic bombing as ardently as any sailor subscribed to Mahan's "decisive battle." By relentlessly egging an enemy's cities and factories, they were convinced, the ability to produce weapons would be halted and the civilian population would quickly surrender. Arnold, especially, believed that his fliers, armed with their Nordens, could bring this long-discussed strategy to dramatic life with daylight raids over Nazi Germany.

In late 1939 Britain's Royal Air Force had tried its own daytime attacks, but losses had been so enormous they were soon abandoned for nighttime sorties, resulting in a large percentage of missed targets. In the summer of 1942 Arnold sent Maj. Gen. Ira Eaker to England as head of the Eighth Air Force—soon to be the largest air force in world history—to complement the British efforts with American daylight runs. Eaker, however, immediately ran into exactly the same problem that had afflicted the RAF. Since the Allies didn't have a fighter with sufficient range to accompany these raids, Eaker's daylight squadrons suffered an average loss of 7 percent, meaning a bomber crew could expect to survive between fourteen and fifteen missions. The standard tour of the Eighth AF, however, was twenty-five missions.

These were massive strikes involving six hundred to eight hundred planes crewed by six thousand to eight thousand men, and the mortality rate clearly had to be brought under control. On January 6, 1944, Hap Arnold replaced Eaker with Doolittle. As a result of his Torch experience, Jimmy immediately added fighter escorts by inventing a tag-team system that combined RAF Spitfires with American P-47 Thunderbolts and P-38 Lightnings. The results were remarkable: American losses immediately fell, while Nazi aviator mortality dramatically rose. In February 1944 alone, the Luftwaffe lost a third of its fighters and a fifth of its pilots to Doolittle's squadrons.

With tag-team pursuits keeping his bomber crews alive, however, Jimmy soon ran into a surprising logjam. Stateside pilot training wasn't churning out the numbers he needed to keep the Eighth going, and he couldn't afford to send his airmen home after a mere twenty-five missions. The decision to up that number would be the least popular idea he'd ever have as a commander in World War II. "We were told that after twenty-five we would probably be sent home for a rest, so that was how we kept figuring things—so many missions accomplished, so many missions still to go," said twenty-two-year-old 1st Lt. Ted Hallock, a B-17 bombardier who'd be awarded the Purple Heart, Air Medal, and Distinguished Flying Cross. "Then at about the halfway mark, the number of missions we would have to make was raised from twenty-five to thirty. That was one hell of a heartbreaker. Those five extra raids might as well have been fifty. . . . I knew then, even when I was most scared, that fliers have to be expendable, that's what Eaker and Doolittle had us trained for. That's what war is. The hell with pampering us. We were supposed to be used up."

The Eighth was a great military success, although high-altitude strategic bombing did not work at all as Douhet, Mitchell, and Arnold had theorized. Instead the Allies discovered that when civilians are ceaselessly pounded, they get used to it, and if a nation is determined to keep its military and industrial production going under heavy assault, it can and will. The Nazis' largest synthetic oil plant, just outside Leipzig, was defended by 437 88 mm antiaircraft cannons. It was attacked eleven times by the Eighth, with production halted five times. No matter—the Germans sent in thousands of workers to get the plant up and running all over again. Allied air raids would eventually damage the German petroleum industry, but at an astounding cost in men and machines. An unexpected side effect of the Eighth's runs, however, would make, in the most important moment of the European theater, an immense contribution.

On June 6, 1944, General Doolittle flew a P-38 for a ringside seat to watch the five thousand ships and 176,000 troops of Operation Overlord invade Normandy. In their ceaseless battles with the Eighth, the Nazis had lost more pilots than their schools could replace, and the quality of their aircrews had steadily deteriorated. By Overlord, the once-invincible Luftwaffe had been reduced to eighty fighters making 250 sorties, in comparison with an Allied total of 8,722 missions. The ratios had been fully reversed, with Axis pilots now battling an Allied air power of almost unlimited men and matériel, and for his great success over Europe, Brigadier General Doolittle would be knighted by King George VI.

After more than a year of internment, the day the Soviet-held captives had been waiting for finally arrived on May 26, 1943, when Ski York announced: "Abdul says that we are to be ready to go at five minutes before twelve midnight, with the lights off at that time. At twelve o'clock sharp, we will hear the truck coming down our street. We are to wait until we hear it stop and shut off its motor, and then we are to come out as quietly as possible, go straight to the back of the truck, climb in and lie down flat on the bottom. He will have a tarpaulin to cover us up. He wanted his money when we got in the truck, but I told him we would give him some of it then and the rest of it when he got us into Persia."

Kolya came to breakfast that morning to hear their plans, and was stunned to learn the fee was $250. Still he warned them to be careful: "If he says he will take you out, he will keep his word. But all the same, I would not let him see that you have any more money or other valuables on you." He then drew a map of how to get to the safety of the British Consulate in Meshed.

They spent the day, as always, working at the airplane repair factory, "experiencing an exhilaration which I found difficult to conceal," Bob Emmens remembered. "Somehow, it didn't seem so bad putting on our grimy coveralls. It would be the last time. Finally, after an eternity, it was five-fifteen. We walked normally out of the place to the bus instead of racing out as we felt like doing. The anticipation of the night's coming activity was almost overwhelming.

"At our house the old man was out. We decided that if he returned before twelve o'clock we would use one of our morphine syrettes on him. They were the only weapons we had. . . ."

At ten-thirty Kolya showed up with provisions for their journey: a loaf of black bread, a small can of caviar, and five half-liter bottles of vodka. In return the aviators gave him the things they wouldn't be needing, as well as some money and an alarm clock. At 2345 the vodka was finished and the lights turned out. The men waited in darkness. The night was clear and still. At five of midnight, everyone grew silent, straining to hear the truck's arrival. Twelve o'clock came—nothing. Then everyone heard all at once the shifting of a motor from high to second gear to make it down their pothole-filled mud track of a street. The vehicle stopped at their gate, and there was quiet.

Kolya whispered good-bye. Ski paid Arram one hundred of the $250, and the men crawled into the back of the truck, lay down flat, and covered themselves with a tarp. Arram had brought a driver he didn't introduce, who turned the key. There was a choking sound. He tried again. Arram finally came to the back and explained that the man would have to walk to town for a part.

More than half an hour went by. The driver returned and fiddled with something under the dashboard, and the engine turned over immediately. The Americans climbed back in and covered themselves, Arram muttering, "*Nee-soo! Nee-soo!*" (stay down). After an hour the truck left the highway and bounced onto a dirt road, where it came to a halt. The fliers suddenly realized just what a serious predicament they were in. Couldn't these Arabs have a change of heart and decide to rob them of everything? What if Kolya was in on the whole scheme? They could all be shot and buried up in the mountains, and who would ever know? Eventually, from the jiggling of the truck and the sound of scraping metal, they understood what Arram and the driver were up to: switching the license plates.

After traveling for another hour, the driver pulled over and turned off his lights. Arram told them to get out. "A third individual appeared out of the darkness as if he had been waiting there for us," Bob Emmens said. "Apparently he had been doing just that. Without a moment's wait he beckoned for us to follow him as he started away from the road. We followed after him in single file, stumbling in the darkness over the rocks and uneven earth. We heard the truck start, move ahead, and quickly fade out of hearing in the distance. We were going at a terrific pace, and the way was mostly upward. The ground seemed to be shale, loose rock, and gravel. The pace didn't slacken, nor did the climb become any less steep.

"Our guide certainly must have been a marathon runner. Our conversation had died out after the first few minutes. After fifteen I was gasping for breath, and my lungs felt as if they were on fire. I couldn't seem to get enough air into them. I couldn't seem to get a second wind. We were all coughing with about every third or fourth breath. We would hear a '*Psst!*' from our guide now and then to indicate that we must be as quiet as possible. I heard someone vomit. We stopped then, deciding that the guy could go no faster than we went, and set our own pace.

"As we started up again, my legs felt as if they were made of lead. The climb was steeper than ever. The boulders were more frequent now. There were no handholds. It seemed that we would take one step and slide back two. Once we heard a rifle shot echo and reecho through the hills. At about four o'clock, our guide turned and hissed, 'Nee-soo!' So down we went.

"We crawled on our hands and knees for several minutes. Finally our guide stopped among some huge boulders, ten or more feet high. He turned to the south, facing downhill, opened his arms and said very softly, in Russian, 'My Iran!' It was about 4:20 A.M. on the morning of the twenty-seventh of May, 1943.

"After everyone had a cigarette, we started off again. This time the going was downhill and, therefore, easier. In fact, it was almost too easy. Pohl went past me once; unable to stop, he fell and rolled some way down the hill before he was able to check himself. He lost the heel off his shoe. I banged my leg against a sharp rock and tore my pants leg. Then my hands hit a perpendicular wall. To our surprise, as we hoisted ourselves over it, it turned out to be a retaining wall on the precipitous outer edge of the road. We lay down in a ditch, single file. The guide disappeared.

"Ten minutes later, the truck appeared, coming slowly down the road. It came to a stop, with the lights out, close to where we lay in the ditch. We hoisted ourselves over the back of the truck and were glad enough to lie down again." While the truck had gone through the checkpoint border crossing, empty, the men had been led across the mountains into Persia. The Soviets, however, were occupying a swath of this territory, so the fliers weren't yet in the clear.

Emmens arranged the tarp so he could look out a bit. The truck came to a stop, and Bob could see a rough wooden arch, topped with a red star and a picture of Stalin—another roadblock. "There was animated conversation between the driver, Abdul, and at least two other persons outside the truck," he remembered. "They were yelling at each other in typical Russian fashion. It was difficult to tell whether they were mad at each other or not. Then I heard footsteps coming around toward the back. I wished that I had covered my head entirely with the tarpaulin. But it was too late then. We didn't stir, and scarcely breathed. Certainly the edge of the tarpaulin meeting a perfectly obvious cap with a bill on it would be a dead giveaway if anybody looked back there. All of a sudden I heard someone grab the edge of the truck close to my head. Almost immediately I was staring directly into a face a bare twelve inches above mine. There was a growth of stubble on the face, and a fur cap with a red star on it above the face. I closed my eyes and stopped breathing. Another movement outside—I opened my eyes again, and the head was gone. I exhaled and drew in another breath and held it.

"At about a quarter to twelve the truck stopped. Abdul got out and pointed straight ahead of us. The horizon to the south was smooth except for the outline of a small town. We judged it to be about four miles away. In the center of the rough spot on the horizon that indicated the town was what appeared to be a golden ball. It glistened in the sun.

"Abdul motioned for us to get out of the truck. We did so. Our bags were tossed out to the ground beside us.

"'Meshed!' said Abdul, pointing again at the break in the smooth horizon.

"The truck started, swung off the road on the right side, and then made a turn around, facing back toward the north.

"'But you promised to take us into Meshed,' said Ski.

"'No—impossible—guards—Russians,' answered Abdul. 'Now—give—money!'

"There wasn't much else to do. Although we hadn't seen a gun, I am sure Abdul, and probably his driver, were armed. Ski had prepared the balance of the sum in one roll, which he handed over. The remainder, which amounted to about fifty dollars, he kept hidden. Abdul took the roll of bills, grunted, and, without counting them, crossed the road to the truck, climbed in, and they started away to the north."

The Americans walked to the outskirts of Meshed, unsure of what to do next. Abdul had told them that the bridge, crossing a small stream just before the city gates, was commandeered by Russian sentries. How could they get past those soldiers and into the British Consulate unnoticed? Then they saw, a hundred feet away from the road, a series of bomb craters, six feet wide and about five feet deep. Climbing into one, now hidden from passersby, they ate the food and drank the vodka that Kolya had given them. They talked strategy over and decided that traveling together was just too conspicuous. Bob and Ski would first attempt to get past the sentries, with the others waiting in the crater for two hours. Emmens and York would then either come back for them, send someone to retrieve them, or get word to them, and if not . . . it would be every man for himself.

Bob Emmens: "It was about twelve-thirty when we started. We pulled our hats down low over our eyes and put our watches and rings out of sight. We tried to saunter along and not look as if we were actually headed somewhere. An old, dilapidated truck rattled by us, and we drew no more than a passing glance from the driver. We passed natives walking along the road and noticed that they, too, did not seem surprised. We felt more confident as we saw the bridge up ahead of us with the tall, square sentry house at one end of it.

"'Let's stop here to see what happens when people or trucks or carts come across the bridge,' Ski suggested.

"We watched a cart crossing, going in the same direction as we were going. The Russian guard gave the driver a quick inspection and the cart was allowed to pass.

"We watched several natives walking across the bridge, and they were not stopped. The outlying houses, all made of mud brick, seemed to be fairly continuous starting on the other side of the bridge. Natives coming from the town were not stopped either. In the distance, coming from the town, we saw another truck headed our way.

"'Now's our chance! The bastard might not stop us anyway, but just to make sure let's arrive at the bridge at the same time as the truck,' said Ski.

"We had timed our walking fairly well. The truck was pulling to a stop at the sentry house as we started across the other end of the bridge. It wasn't more than fifty feet across the thing. The temptation to break into a run was almost irresistible as we were even with the truck. The Russian was inspecting the documents of the driver, we observed, but since the guard had walked around to the driver's side, he had his back to us as we passed a bare few feet from him. We didn't look back after we had passed, but we did increase the speed of our steps somewhat.

"As we started down the street our hearts skipped a beat as we saw two armed Russians coming toward us. They did not seem to have their attention particularly upon us during the second or two in which we both saw them. We turned abruptly and looked intently—ever so intently—in a glass-fronted store. We saw them pass by the reflection in the glass, holding their slow and casual gait. Then we turned and headed again down the street."

Bob and Ski made their way through the city from the map Kolya had drawn, which they had earlier memorized and destroyed. One hour had already gone by since they'd left the others waiting behind in the crater. They tried to walk as quickly as possible, but not so fast as to arouse suspicion. Then, directly in front of them, curved the driveway and the whitewashed walls and the coat of arms of the British Consulate.

"We made a quick turn into the place and were about ten feet inside before the surprised guards rushed at us and stopped us," Emmens said. "There was an exchange of words we did not understand. Immediately, out of the sentry house just inside the entrance, came a turbaned officer.

"'We want to see the British Consul,' Ski snapped at him before he could say anything. Several people had started to gather at the entrance to see what was going on.

" 'British Consul—no—here!' said the Persian officer, in just those words. *That's the pay-off,* I thought to myself. 'Vice—Consul—here,' he finished.

"We breathed a sigh of relief as the Persian clapped his hands, summoning another turbaned individual whom he instructed to take us someplace farther inside the grounds. For the first time, we looked around us. The contrast to the town and to the surrounding land was amazing. We were being taken down a sandy path lined with shrubbery and flowers under a green arbor of vines. The path seemed to surround a rolling stretch of green lawn, beautifully kept. At the far end of the lawn was a swimming pool, and in its center, a gazelle played at the end of a long rope. It looked like a Garden of Eden."

They were told to sit on a bench outside and wait. It was now an hour and twenty minutes since they'd left the others. Ten more minutes passed. Ski realized they had to do something to get word back to their men in time. He got the guard to bring them a pencil and a piece of paper, and wrote out their names, titles, and that they were with the Air Corps. Almost immediately the guard reappeared, and took them into one of the houses circling the lawn. A young Englishman inside shook their hands in amazement. He'd been on the staff of the British Embassy in Moscow in 1942, and knew exactly who they were.

Ski explained that three others were waiting, and asked if they could send a truck to sneak them into town. The vice consul said yes, but how would the men be found? Ski explained that the driver would just have to look for a bomb crater marked with five half-pint bottles of vodka.

An hour later Herndon, Laban, and Pohl were delivered, and the men were shown to their rooms in the British consul's home, where they could take a bath, have a drink, and rest up for the flight back to India, and then to the United States. When Ski York launched from *Hornet,* he had weighed 180 pounds. At the British Consulate, he weighed himself to see the effects of a year in the Soviet Union. The scale read 135.

"I lay down on a real bed, complete with springs and mattress, sheets, and a pillow," Emmens said. "I closed my eyes. It was hard to realize that yesterday we were in the Soviet Union pulling rusty nuts and bolts out of old rotten, wooden airplane frames. Abdul, Kolya, all of them seemed far away. They seemed unreal, like characters out of a fiction book."

That fiction book would in fact be subject to interpretation, as the crew of plane eight would come to have different conclusions about what exactly had happened to them. Ski York and Bob Emmens would disagree about Kolya's role—had they really managed a daring escape from Russia, or was it all a setup arranged from on high? Navigator Nolan Herndon, meanwhile, would have second thoughts about why they ended up in the Soviet Union in the first place. Herndon would come to believe, and would maintain for the rest of his life, that the only way to make sense of their mission was that the crew had been deliberately sent to Russia. His suspicions began the very moment when York and Emmens were selected—out of all the men who'd wanted to volunteer, this particular pilot and copilot were signed on with no Eglin training whatsoever. Both, after the war, would go on to high-level jobs in military intelligence.

Nolan directly confronted Doolittle with his thoughts, and Jimmy replied, "I'll tell you one thing, Herndon. I didn't send you there." Ski York, Bob Emmens, Hap Arnold, and Brig. Gen. Merian C. Cooper (Arnold's executive intelligence officer at the time) were explicitly questioned about this matter long after the war was over, and all insisted that the plane was not covertly sent to scout Soviet airfields for future bombings of Japan. However, considering Arnold's persistent desire to wreak vengeance for Pearl Harbor (and the numerous AAF operations dedicated to just such a purpose), the question lingers.

The closer American forces got to the Japanese home islands, the more appalling was the carnage. On Iwo Jima alone almost the entire Japanese force of nearly 20,000 men fought to their deaths, while just under 7,000 Americans were killed and 19,000 wounded. On Okinawa around 300,000 Japanese soldiers and civilians died, while 12,500 Americans (7,000 of them sailors attacked by kamikazes) perished. Civilians on Saipan and Okinawa—told that American GIs routinely raped and murdered Asian women and that if any American wanted to become a marine, he had first to murder his parents—committed suicide by the tens of thousands.

It had taken almost three years since the Doolittle Raid for Nimitz and MacArthur to fight their way close enough to again directly bomb the enemy's home islands. The task would be assigned to B-29s based in the Marianas under Curtis LeMay. For these crews, a round trip to Tokyo ran three thousand miles, meaning fuel could run out on the way home, forcing the planes to ditch into the ocean. If LeMay failed, however, and Japan had to be invaded by land forces, military intelligence estimated that five hundred thousand Americans would die.

Over Nazi Germany the air forces had learned to come in at extremely high altitude, in formation, with guns and fighters blazing, to precisely bomb specific targets in daylight. This technique hadn't worked at all in the Pacific war, and LeMay was ordered to craft a solution. *Dai Nippon Teikoku* by this point had few fighters trained in nighttime operations, no more barrage balloons, and few antiaircraft guns aimed at low-altitude targets. So "Iron Ass" LeMay (a nickname inspired by both the Bell's palsy that kept him from being physically able to smile, and his bellicose demeanor) went with the opposite of everything that had been tried and refined so far: His B-29s sortied at night, at a mere five thousand feet, one at a time. Instead of demolitions, their bays were filled with napalm and phosphorus.

On the nights of March 9–10, 1945, 334 B-29s firebombed the capital of Japan with two thousand tons of incendiaries. Fourteen of those planes were lost at sea; five of the fourteen were rescued by the navy. At midnight on the eleventh, reconnaissance photographs were finally printed, and what they revealed stunned the American air force chiefs. More than sixteen square miles of Tokyo had been destroyed, a greater area of damage than what nuclear weapons would inflict on Hiroshima and Nagasaki combined. The fires produced with this early form of napalm were so hot that window glass melted, and victims trying to escape the conflagration by jumping into canals, sewers, and streams were instead boiled alive. One-quarter of the capital was gone, with 267,171 buildings demolished and more than one million left homeless. It would take almost a month to dig out the dead—almost 84,000 men, women, and children.

"I heard the huzzle-huzzle of something falling, and I ducked and crouched in a corner," Gustav Bitter, a priest living in Tokyo, remembered:

> It struck beside me, with a noise like a house falling, and I leaped a fine leap into the air. I must have shut my eyes, for when I opened them again I was in a world of fairyland. On every tree in the garden below, and on every tree so far as the eyes could see, some sort of blazing oil had fallen, and it was dancing on the twigs and branches with a million little red and yellow candle-flames. On the ground in between the trees and in all the open spaces, white balls of fire had fallen, and these were bouncing like tennis balls. . . . [Watching the firebombs from a distance] was like a silver curtain falling, like . . . the silver tinsel we hung from Christmas trees in Germany long ago. And where these silver streamers would touch the earth, red fires would spring up . . . and the big fire in the center sent up a rising column of air which drew in toward the center the outer circle of flame, and a hot, swift wind began to blow from the rim toward the center, a twisting wind which spread the flames between all the ribs of the fan, very

quickly. Thus, everywhere the people ran there was fire, in front of them and in back of them, and closing in on them from the sides. So that there were only a very few who escaped.

The Japanese would call these attacks the Raid of the Fire Wind and the Raid of the Dancing Flames. On the twelfth LeMay used the same weapons on Nagoya, on the thirteenth on Osaka, on the sixteenth, on Kobe; and on the nineteenth, again on Nagoya. By mid-June the urban industrial center of Japan had been completely annihilated. The summer would bring mop-up operations, with certain key targets precision-bombed beyond recognition, sixty smaller cities firebombed into oblivion, and the Japanese coastal waters so extensively filled with mines dropped by LeMay's B-29s that its naval traffic was entirely halted.

One ship that took its place at the forefront of this assault was the new USS *Hornet*. For fifteen continuous months, she served in the forward combat zone, often a mere forty miles from Japan. Fifty-nine empire planes attacked her, but those undertrained novice pilots had little of the skills of their predecessors. *Hornet's* remarkable new flyboys, meanwhile, knocked out 1,410 Japanese planes, a World War II record, with 72 destroyed in one day, a U.S. Navy record.

After their cities were destroyed and their sea-lanes shut down, military and government leaders in Tokyo met to discuss their next course of action. None of them could even consider the possibility of surrender. Instead they decided to inspire every man, woman, and child in Japan to resist to the very end, to fight to the last survivor of Yamato blood.

Newspapers and radio stations announced this new policy on a regular basis. Planes dropped leaflets over rural areas promoting it. The horrors of an American invasion were described in lurid detail, and the leaders of what was left of *Dai Nippon Teikoku* asked every Japanese citizen, "the hundred million," to die "like shattered jewels."

The winter of 1944–45 would turn out to be an unforgiving hell for the POWs of Nanking. The first of December brought the beginnings of a record snowfall to China, which would coat the prison yard every day until March. The weather was so unbearable that worried officials sent in extra clothes, even the Americans' original uniforms, to supplement their tattered, pajama-like prison garb. For shoes, however, they still had only their loose Japanese slippers. It was impossible to run outside to get warm (the only way in this weather they could get warm) without the slippers falling off. The guards warned them not to go outside barefoot, but the men couldn't run otherwise, and finally the need for heat won out. One day they took off their shoes and ran through the snow.

The guards called a halt, and sent them back to their unheated cells. On the way the prisoners stopped to wash their dirty feet at the courtyard hydrant. The guards, as punishment, insisted they clean their feet instead with ice. New Yorker George Barr refused, and when one guard grabbed his arm to force him to the snowbank, George elbowed the man in the stomach.

The other Americans were sent to their cells while ten guards gathered around Lieutenant Barr and beat him to the ground. They shoved him back into his cell and put him into a straitjacket. His arms were tied behind his back as far as they could go, and the restraints were so tight that he could barely take in breath.

George screamed so loud that the other fliers feared he was being tortured to death. For an hour the prison officials left him bound in pain, and for an hour he screamed and screamed.

Every prisoner, during that long cold winter, got sick. Jake broke out in terribly painful, infected boils that appeared everywhere on his body. To pass the time, he monitored how they appeared, rose, fell, and then came back to life.

On Christmas Day of 1944, the prisoners could hear planes going by overhead, and they sounded strange. Jake DeShazer inched himself up the walls of his cell, and looked out the vent. Year after year, the guards had been telling their prisoners that Japan was winning the war, that New York had fallen, that Japan was now running the United States. But what Jake saw out of his vent were American planes, deep in the heart of China.

That day during exercise, the fliers watched as American hell divers swooped right over the horizon, strafing and dropping eggs. They saw puffs of ack-ack, and then heard a huge explosion, followed by black clouds of rising smoke. The guards later explained that the United States had bombed a river, and some fish were killed. For the first time in as long as they could remember, the captives felt a tiny speck of hope.

"Before he got out of the hospital, Ted had decided he wanted to write a book, mostly as a way to have people know how wonderful the Chinese were," Ellen Lawson said. "He'd wake up at night and say, 'I'm gonna call Cecil B. DeMille—he's going to hear about this!' And I said, 'Let's try and get the number.' We tried writing it ourselves, we started a couple of notebooks, but just didn't get going, really.

"In our same apartment building, there was a man who recommended [writer] Bob Considine, and he and Ted met and hit it right off. They did the whole first draft over four days and nights, while everything was still fresh in Ted's mind. They didn't hardly sleep, and then Bob went back to New York with his typewriter in his lap, and started writing it."

Given the tremendous public interest in the Doolittle Raid, every publisher in New York knew immediately that *Thirty Seconds over Tokyo* was a potentially hot property. The winner of the prize would be another American celebrity of the time, Bennett Cerf, founder of Random House. MGM immediately bought the movie rights, and both publisher and studio moved forward as quickly as possible with the project.

"*Thirty Seconds over Tokyo* came out on the raid's anniversary in '43, and was a hit right away," Ellen Lawson said. "It was printed in Canada, Australia, Mexico, Finland, Denmark, New Zealand, and Italy, along with magazine excerpts and even a comic strip. It was a big selection for the Book-of-the-Month Club, and ten years later the children's Landmark edition was on the bestseller list."

At the same time, in the wake of the War Department's official raid communiqué, MGM's competitors were trying to beat it to the punch with a film version of the story. On March 22, 1943, Howard Hawks at Universal wrote Hap Arnold about a raid movie; Arnold replied, "Not yet." On April 23, Jack Warner of Warner Bros. offered a guarantee of one hundred thousand dollars and 10 percent of the gross, payable to any organization Arnold might designate. On May 4 Arnold responded by saying that General Doolittle was unwilling to have a picture portraying him or using his name be produced before the war ended, that his wishes should be respected, and that "no efforts to persuade him to the contrary should be attempted or countenanced."

"Ted decided he next wanted to get out of the country and do something for the service, so he got assigned to do undercover work with the air mission in Santiago, Chile," Ellen Lawson said. "Hollywood had seen the book in galleys and bid on it early, so that was already under way. We made a couple of trips to New York for the book, then we were transferred to LA, to work with MGM and Loew's Incorporated. Ted had told Loew's he could only stay for three months because we were due to leave for South America and had to get our shots. I took a Berlitz course in Spanish, and we went out and bought a whole houseful of furniture that we had shipped down via the Panama Canal.

"Ted was helping with translating the book to the screen with writer Dalton Trumbo, working with producer Sam Zimbalist on production planning, and meeting with lots and lots of people. Sam's the one who helped select Phyllis Thaxter; he wanted someone who was unknown and reminded him of me, and it worked out fine. We selected Robert Walker; we had seen him in *Bataan,* and we thought that he should play Thatcher. We didn't have much to say with the others, but Ted was there to stand over and keep things in line, to keep it all accurate."

The movie would turn out to be much harder to produce than anyone in Hollywood could have anticipated. Though the project was sanctioned by the Office of War Information, and though the army loaned Metro a dozen B-25s and the AAF crews to fly them, the war meant that the military didn't have enough spare resources available, even though everyone knew how useful the right picture would be for the nation's morale. Screenwriter Trumbo (who'd be blacklisted in the 1950s as a suspected Communist) and director Mervyn LeRoy (who'd become famous for *Mr. Roberts* and *The Bad Seed*) were determined to make *Thirty Seconds over Tokyo* as realistic as possible, since so much of the public already knew the story in detail. For a wartime production, they did a remarkable job. Though the *Hornet* deck had been re-created on a Hollywood sound stage, and an East Oakland oil refinery fire stood in for the bombing of Tokyo, many scenes were filmed on location at Eglin. In fact, preview audiences found the first cut of the film a little too realistic—they became so upset at a scene of the Chinese nurses carrying off Ted's amputated leg that it was not included in the final release.

"By March, Ted had to return to the hospital at Walter Reed," Ellen said. "He had a spur growing, and he couldn't wear his leg. He was in a lot of pain, and decided he wasn't really performing what he was trained to do in Chile, so he asked for a change. I'd been left behind to sell the furniture, and I couldn't get a priority to get home. I was writing him every other day, and about this time he met Mrs. Roosevelt. She had seen his picture in the paper and she invited him over to the White House for supper. He stayed over there a couple of nights, slept in Lincoln's bed, and he told her he wasn't getting any letters. Well, eventually we heard on the grapevine that they wanted him back in Chile, and they were holding out on my letters at the Pentagon. Mrs. Roosevelt called, found out what was wrong, that I was being held down there sort of as a hostage. So the next day he got five letters all at once, and she sent me a White House priority to fly on the airlines. The military transportation people called and said, 'Mrs. Lawson, when would you like to go home?' Well, I was six months pregnant, and our little girl, Ann, was now a year and a half, and I was doing everything by myself in Chile, so I said: 'The sooner the better!' I think it's a wonderful thing for young people to have that experience out of the country, but there's no place like home.

"In September 1944 MGM had the premiere of *Thirty Seconds* in Glendale, California, and Ted had his picture taken with Hedy Lamarr to help sell savings bonds." The movie would turn out to be one of MGM's biggest hits of that era, becoming a long-running favorite with audiences and winning an Oscar for best special effects. It would feature Van Johnson's breakout starring role, another triumph for Robert Walker as Dave Thatcher, a Spencer Tracy cameo as Doolittle, and one of Robert Mitchum's earliest appearances, as plane three pilot Bob Gray.

A great deal of the movie's success was its appeal to women, romance being the one area in which Hollywood didn't hew too faithfully to Lawson's book. In the *New York Times,* Bosley Crowther noticed: "[E]xcept for a thoroughly tactful and touching romance woven through the film, representing the abiding attachment between Captain Lawson and his wife, the story is taken almost from the record as it was set down." Ellen Lawson herself would say, "We were in love, but I don't know if we were in *that* kind of love." The Hollywood pros, though, knew what they were doing. "Not only is it a timely saga of our war in the Pacific but it's a thoroughly romantic tale which will get the *femmes,*" *Variety* predicted. "For once, here's a war picture eclipsed by its romantic components."

Thirty Seconds was not the only movie about the Doolittle Raid, though it would be by far the most accurate. Building upon vague reports of submarines *Thresher* and *Trout*'s role in the story, in 1943 MGM had released *Destination Tokyo,* starring Cary Grant, John Garfield, Alan Hale, and John Forsythe as a submarine crew ordered to sail to Japan to get information on "the weather, shore installations, barrage balloon positions, and the number and location of Japanese ships in the bay. We'll get that information back to them by radio!" The crew know they've reached their target when their periscope reveals a picture postcard view of Mount Fuji, and after fulfilling their espionage mission, they return to watch the launch from *Hornet.* When a nearby Japanese flattop tries to bring down Jimmy's B-25, Cary Grant torpedoes it.

The most unfortunate of the Doolittle Raid pictures, though, would have to be the one based on the experiences of the POWs. Released in 1944 by Twentieth Century–Fox, *The Purple Heart* featured empire judges who look just like Confucius and Kempeitai torture involving off-camera screams, a bandaged hand, a man carried by on a stretcher, and another POW rendered into a zombie. At the stirring finale the captives march to their deaths to a chorus of "Off we go! Into the wild blue yonder."

Besides being one of the more realistic war pictures released in its era, *Thirty Seconds over Tokyo* was the first major Hollywood production to deal with a pressing social problem: vet amputees. Ted Lawson was the first serviceman with a high public profile to come home severely injured, and long before *The Best Years of Our Lives,* recruits and their loved ones wondered about the potential ramifications of such a handicap. Using the euphemisms of its era, *Thirty Seconds* did not flinch at covering those issues:

> TED: I guess Ellen and I aren't going to [slight pause] ski anymore. That's too bad. I was going to teach her some fancy stuff.
>
> COPILOT DEAN DAVENPORT: Now don't start talking like that. You're going to pull through all right.
>
> TED: What do you think a girl would do? I mean, say Ellen and I like to ski. Be kinda funny if they cut my leg off, wouldn't it?
>
> DEAN: Why don't you try to go to sleep, Lawson?
>
> TED: Yeah, it'd be kinda funny all right. Marry a guy, he's got two arms and two legs. Then he comes back and he hasn't any . . .

One month after the Glendale premiere of *Thirty Seconds,* Japanese forces tried all over again to directly attack the North American continent in revenge for the Doolittle Raid. From November 1, 1944, until April 1945, an army team led by electrical engineer Takada Teruhiki launched from the eastern shores of Honshu more than nine thousand balloons crafted out of mulberry paper or rubberized silk, filled to a thirty-two-foot diameter with nineteen thousand cubic feet of hydrogen, armed with four incendiary and two antipersonnel bombs, and controlled by a barometer releasing a series of sandbags. It is estimated that about a thousand of these Japanese fire balloons (or *fugos*) completed a seventy-hour, six-thousand-mile drift across the Pacific to make it to their target—with 285 reported incidents from San Pedro to Saskatchewan. On May 5, 1945, a teacher and four children came upon one of the balloons while picnicking in the Oregon woods. It exploded and killed them all. Under Project Firefly, both AAF and Navy crews were assigned to spot and intercept *fugos* before they could cause any further damage. The U.S. government did such a good job of hushing up this assault, however, that the Japanese soon quit their campaign, and its history is little known today.

In June 1945 the prisoners of Nanking were assembled, tied up, hooded, handcuffed, and covered in green raincoats, their faces masked. Under individual armed guard, they were placed on a train for forty hours, finally arriving in Peiping (Beijing). There they were taken to a military prison holding more than a thousand others, and again placed in solitary. The informal guards of Nanking were replaced by tight-lipped, by-the-book MPs. In their cells they were made to sit on a bench, facing the wall, and remain that way, immobile (though Jake DeShazer soon discovered that, when no one was looking, he could still climb the walls). Every night they could hear beatings and torture and the screams of the other captives. There was no daily exercise, but once a week they were allowed to bathe and to see each other.

One morning Chase Nielsen had finished his breakfast soup and was looking at the light reflecting off of an aluminum teacup. Underneath he could barely make out a scratched marking that seemed to read "US Marines." At washing-up time he told the others about his discovery, and everyone decided that maybe they, too, could communicate with the rest of the prison in the same way. The men picked up nails in the hallways on the way back to their cells, and scratched the cups at every meal. It gave them something to do, and of course they had no idea that this primitive message system would save their lives.

The sickest of the four was now Brooklyn-born George Barr. The Kempeitai considered the tall, pale, freckled redhead an especially barbaric example of the white race, and treated the lieutenant even more inhumanely than everyone else. George spent most of his days in Peiping unconscious, too weak to stand or even to eat solid food. He was withered and emaciated, and in those periods when he was awake and logical, his thoughts turned to Bob Meder and the certainty that he would be the next to die.

The neurological disorders of starvation were now peaking. George couldn't understand what to do with the bowls of food that appeared through his door slit, and it took him hours, even in the tiny cell, to drag himself in a half stupor to the toilet box. Many times he thought he was already dead, in an afterlife that was an eternity of barely conscious moments of stench and filth, inching around on the floor, wanting to scream but not being capable of making a sound, and no one coming to help.

Jake DeShazer's health had also rapidly deteriorated. The dysentery that had struck periodically now seemed constant, and the plague of boils had returned with even greater virulence. At one point Jake decided to make a tally of them but had to stop when he got to seventy-five, for without a mirror he couldn't include the ones between the shoulder blades, where his hands couldn't reach. He, too, came to believe he would die at any moment: "I still kept going over the verses in the Bible that I had memorized. I thought it wouldn't be so long before I would be in heaven with Lieutenant Meder. My heart was hurting, and I could remember how Lieutenant Meder said his heart had hurt before he died. Several of the Nanking prison guards had told me the reason Meder died was that his heart had stopped. I thought I would probably die for the same reason. . . .

"I got out of bed and sat on the little bench one morning after I had prayed it all out with God. I was so weak that my heart could have stopped very easily. . . . I didn't know what to expect. I just prayed that God would make me better. I made up my mind to sit there until I either passed out or God healed me. It was not long before the voice of God broke into my thoughts. This was different from anything I had experienced before. . . .

" 'It is the Holy Spirit who is speaking to you,' the mysterious voice said. 'The Holy Spirit has made you free!' I immediately began to wonder if I was going to get out of prison. The voice said, 'You are free to do as you please. You can go through the wall or jump over the wall. You are free.' I couldn't figure that out. . . .

"I found out that I could ask questions and I could receive answers right away. This was a big help to me in connection with my food. I was always hungry, but often if I ate the food, I would become very sick. When the food came to the door, I would pray and ask if I should eat the food, or if I should send it back. If the voice said, 'Yes, yes,' I would eat; but if the answer was, 'No, no,' I would send the food back. For two days I was not given permission to eat or drink. I was weak, but the sickness was leaving me. . . .

"As I was sitting on this little seat facing the wall, I wondered if there wasn't some way that I could let the guards know about the wonderful spirit of Jesus which was so present with me. . . . There didn't seem to be much that I could do, but I remembered the story about Daniel. I went down on my knees in front of the door, folded my hands to pray, and I really did pray. The first guard came by, beat on the door with his sword and hollered at me to get back on my bench. It was against the rules for any prisoner to even look at the door. Japanese prisoners received a beating for such audacity, but I did not move when the guard shouted. I felt no fear, since God had shown me what to do. I felt a great weight of joy. . . .

"In a very short time the guard returned with several other guards. The door opened and the guards walked into my cell. They never hit me nor hollered at me. They acted a little awed. A medical man came to my cell, and I was picked up and laid down on a straw mat. The medical man rolled up my shirtsleeve and shot some medicine into my arm, after which I was left alone in my cell to thank Jesus, who was close by my side.

"When mealtime came, I was surprised to receive a nice pint of milk, boiled eggs, some good, well-made bread, and some nice, nourishing soup. I couldn't help crying and laughing when I thought how beautifully and wonderfully God had worked all this out for me. From that time, I received milk, eggs, bread, and good nourishing food. . . ."

On August 10, 1945, Jacob DeShazer woke up and was told by the mysterious voice to "start praying. . . . I asked, 'What shall I pray about?' 'Pray for peace, and pray without ceasing,' I was told. I had prayed for peace but very little, if at all, before that time, as it seemed useless. I thought God could stop the war at any time. . . . But God was now teaching me the lesson of cooperation. . . .

"About seven o'clock in the morning, I began to pray. It seemed very easy to pray on the subject of peace. I prayed that God would put a great desire in the hearts of the Japanese leaders for peace. I thought about the days of peace that would follow.

"At two o'clock in the afternoon, the Holy Spirit told me, 'You don't need to pray anymore. The victory is won.' I was amazed. I thought this was quicker and better than the regular method of receiving world news. . . ."

"We had a little signal," Bob Hite said. "We knocked on the walls between the cells, 'shave and a haircut, two bits.' This meant everything was all right. Well, I had knocked this morning, and Jake had not knocked back. . . . I didn't know what was going on. . . . I had knocked on the wall 'shave and a haircut' all morning, and I hadn't had any answers. So I was afraid that Jake might really be about to die because he had been ill, he had dysentery. Anyhow, about 12:30 . . . I heard this 'shave and a haircut, two bits' on the wall, and I knocked back.

"If we had anything to say to one another, we went to our *benjo* [toilet]. . . . His opening went into the same receptacle that mine went into, and we could talk through that opening back and forth. I ran to the *benjo,* and I lifted the lid off and said, 'Jake, what happened?' He said, 'I can't tell you everything, but I was praying, and it was revealed to me that the war is over today, and that we are victorious.'"

On that same August 10 that Jacob DeShazer was told the war had ended, Bill Laurence was part of a crew flying over the city of Nagasaki:

> Despite the fact that it was broad daylight in our cabin, all of us became aware of a giant flash that broke through the dark barrier of our arc-welder's lenses and flooded our cabin with intense light.
>
> Observers in the tail of our ship saw a giant ball of fire rise as though from the bowels of the earth, belching forth enormous, white smoke rings. Next they saw a giant pillar of purple fire, 10,000 feet high, shooting skyward with enormous speed.

Awe-struck, we watched it shoot upward like a meteor coming from the earth instead of from outer space, becoming ever more alive as it climbed skyward through the white clouds. It was no longer smoke, or dust, or even a cloud of fire. It was a living thing, a new species of being, born right before our incredulous eyes.

At one stage of its evolution, the entity assumed the form of a giant square totem pole, with its base about three miles long, tapering off to about a mile at the top. Its bottom was brown, its center was amber, its top white. Then, just when it appeared as though the thing has settled down into a state of permanence, there came shooting out of the top a giant mushroom that increased the height of the pillar to a total of 45,000 feet. The mushroom top was even more alive than the pillar, seething and boiling in a white fury of creamy foam, sizzling upward and then descending earthward, a thousand Old Faithful geysers rolled into one.

It kept struggling in an elemental fury, like a creature in the act of breaking the bonds that held it down. In a few seconds it had freed itself from its gigantic stem, and floated upward with tremendous speed. But no sooner did this happen when another mushroom, smaller in size than the first one, began emerging out of the pillar. It was as though the decapitated monster was growing a new head.

As the first mushroom floated off into the blue, it changed its shape into a flowerlike form, its giant petal curving downward, white outside, rose-colored inside. It still retained that shape when we last gazed at it from a distance of about 200 miles.

PEACE

A few days after the mysterious voice told him the war was over, Cpl. Jacob DeShazer crawled up the walls of his cell to look out the vent at first light, just as he'd done every dawn of every day for so many months. That morning, however, the fresh smell of the fields was replaced by a different odor, and Jake saw smoke and pieces of paper, feathery and smoldering, rising up into the sky. Paper was in short supply and never wasted in Japanese-held China, so it meant something that prison officers were burning documents. Later that morning the guards showed up dressed in crisp new uniforms. Change was coming.

Jake felt a stab of hope, but almost immediately his thoughts turned to the enemy . . . to the tormentors who had caught him, imprisoned him, starved him, and beaten him: "I could not help wondering what would happen to Japan now. Their hopes had been set on victory. It would be an awful blow to suffer defeat. But, if the Japanese found out about Jesus, the military defeat to them would in reality be a great victory. At this time the voice of the Holy Spirit spoke to me clearly: 'You are called to go and teach the Japanese people and to go wherever I send you.'"

Jake was frightened by this idea. He had no talent or skills as a public speaker; he couldn't even tell a joke all that well. He was small in stature, lacked a commanding, inspiring presence, and had no training as a theologian or education as a preacher. Yet he had promised God to do his will, and now he would keep that promise.

On the morning of August 15, 1945, the entire population of Japan, including the farmers laboring in distant fields and citizens living overseas, were told that at noon they must stop whatever they were doing and listen to the radio. Though everyone hurried to make ready for this once-in-a-lifetime event, most already knew what the announcement would be. The great empire that *Dai Nippon Teikoku* had won for itself in the first half of the twentieth century was now entirely gone, and the foreign barbarian hordes would be invading the home islands at any minute. The broadcast would give instruction and inspiration so that all civilians could sacrifice their lives fighting against the incoming wave of Americans.

What the people of Japan heard that day at noon was not just unexpected, it was unimaginable. First the national anthem played. Then a voice spoke—a voice they'd never heard before. The voice was strange, high-pitched, thin, and nasal, and it spoke an odd form of Japanese, a dialect hundreds of years old that very few could understand clearly. For the first time in the history of the Chrysanthemum Throne, the emperor was speaking directly to his subjects.

The voice told them: *senso owari,* the war is over. It said that the emperor was no longer the Son of Heaven, but an ordinary man. It said that events "did not turn in Japan's favor, and trends of the world were not advantageous to us. . . . The enemy has for the first time used cruel bombs to kill and maim extremely large numbers of the innocent, and the heavy casualties are beyond measure. To continue the war further could lead in the end not only to the extermination of our race but also to the destruction of all human civilization. . . . [M]y vital organs are torn asunder." The voice said it was time for the Yamato race to "endure the unendurable, and bear the unbearable."

Five days after the announcement an urgent Japanese army telegram was sent to all camps and bases recommending that anyone who had mistreated prisoners or local populations immediately vanish into anonymity. Over the next four weeks 1,066 Allied planes would fly more than nine hundred sorties, dropping 4,500 tons of supplies over 150 POW camps across Japan and East Asia. Along with medicine, food, cigarettes, magazines, chocolate, and chewing gum, the bursting canisters included leaflets that implored: "Do Not Overeat."

On September 2, Gen. Douglas MacArthur, accompanied by 260 Allied warships, arrived in Tokyo Bay on the last of the great dreadnoughts, the USS *Missouri*—Admiral Halsey's flagship—to accept the empire's surrender. The general had postponed the ceremony so that official delegations from China, Russia, England, the Philippines, and other countries involved in the Pacific conflict could attend. On *Missouri* waved two flags: one that had been flying at the White House on December 7, 1941; the other used in 1853 on Commodore Matthew Perry's gunboat *Powhatten.* Since the onetime greatest naval power in all the world no longer had a single seaworthy vessel, the destroyer *Landsdowne* had to ferry the Tokyo delegation to *Missouri.*

Attending the ceremony were Fuchida Mitsuo, Joseph Stilwell, James Doolittle, and Japanese Foreign Office member Kase Toshikazu, who had been assigned to prepare a report on the surrender for his emperor. What would the Americans do now? everyone in Japan wondered. Of the seven million Tokyo residents who'd survived the Raid of the Dancing Flames, five million were so overcome by fears of Allied vengeance that they'd fled to the country to hide.

MacArthur announced that "it is my earnest hope and indeed the hope of all mankind that from this solemn occasion a better world shall emerge out of the blood and carnage of the past—a world founded upon faith and understanding—a world dedicated to the dignity of man and the fulfillment of his most cherished wish—for freedom, tolerance, and justice." About this speech Kase wrote Hirohito: "Here is the victor announcing the verdict to the prostrate enemy. He can exact his pound of flesh if he so chooses. He can impose a humiliating penalty if he so desires. And yet he pleads for freedom, tolerance, and justice. For me, who expected the worst humiliation, this was a complete surprise. . . . [W]ould it have been possible for us, had we been victorious, to embrace the vanquished with a similar magnanimity? . . . We were defeated in the spiritual contest by a nobler ideal." That same week Hirohito would tell his twelve-year-old son, Crown Prince Akihito, that *Dai Nippon Teikoku* had lost because "Our people . . . knew how to advance, but they didn't know how to retreat." On the day of surrender, meanwhile, General Sugiyama, who had done everything he could to have all the captive Doolittle Raiders executed, would commit suicide.

As the signatures across the official documents dried, four hundred B-29 bombers and fifteen hundred navy fighters roared across the sky. The Pacific war had endured just under four years; the American occupation of Japan would last almost seven.

In the spring of 1941, when his thoughts were turning from one black-cat scenario to the next, Franklin Roosevelt initiated what would be the most enduring clandestine operation of them all—one that, during World War II, would produce legions of now-forgotten heroes. Foreign intelligence in the years between the wars was collected by American military attachés, overseas diplomats, and separate army and navy intercepts (like Hypo), but there was no central U.S. agency that collated and analyzed the material as a whole. In fact, after seemingly endless military, civilian, executive, and congressional investigations, Harry Truman would come to believe that this lack of a single coordinating body had been the defining issue leading to the deaths at Pearl Harbor.

In that spring of 1941, FDR appointed New York lawyer and Medal of Honor winner William J. Donovan to the post of Coordinator of Information, a civilian office under the aegis of the White House. When, as part of their standard operating procedure, the State, Army, Navy, and War Departments refused to cooperate by sharing their secrets, Wild Bill was forced to set up his entire operation from scratch. One area in which the military was more than happy to let him have carte blanche was espionage—Marshall and Stimson found such work unseemly. When his department was reincarnated as the Office of Strategic Services (OSS), Donovan sent a dozen operatives into North Africa to establish networks and monitor German troop, ship, and plane movements in advance of Torch. On D-day OSS agents led arriving Allied soldiers through the minefields to their objectives so successfully that their division was rethought into a long-term, widely ranging branch known as Special Ops (SO), with Donovan now reporting directly to the Joint Chiefs and overseeing an OSS staff of thirteen thousand.

Special Ops men would parachute behind enemy lines, aid whatever resistance might be in place, coordinate airdrops of arms and supplies, engage in sabotage and guerrilla tactics, and send home any useful information. MacArthur and Nimitz refused to have anything to do with spies, so China-Burma-India would be the only Pacific theater employing the OSS. Besides providing target intelligence for Chennault, OSS teams aided the Thai underground and helped anti-empire freedom fighters across Southeast Asia, including Indochina's Ho Chi Minh. At war's end, with surrender imminent, the men of Special Ops assumed they'd be queued to fly stateside immediately. They were instead given one last assignment.

The Japanese had regularly and publicly announced that, if they lost the war, they would kill every Allied POW under their control. Two days before American troops landed on Luzon with Douglas MacArthur in the campaign to retake the Philippines, Allied intelligence uncovered information that the Japanese had in fact massacred every captive on Palawan Island. Consequently Special Ops was given the task of hurrying behind enemy lines three months before the emperor's announced surrender, to ensure that no more Allied captives could be summarily executed.

In the first part of this mission OSS men throughout Japanese-held Asia tracked down exactly where POWs were being held. One of the surprises they uncovered was that Comdr. William S. Cunningham, who had been captured at the fall of Wake on December 23, 1941, was imprisoned in the old Chinese military jail of Fengtai at the center of Peiping. The Japanese had been in control of that part of the country for many, many years, and if any force would be loath to surrender, it would be the Imperial Expeditionary Army.

"Both of my parents were born in Hiroshima, Japan," Special Ops agent Dick Hamada remembered. "My father came to Hawaii as a contract worker, building homes for plantation laborers on the Big Island. I was born there in

1922. My brother too was a carpenter, and eventually he and I got jobs with the Pacific Construction Company, building barracks for the navy at Pearl Harbor.

"On December 7, 1941, I was at home in Honolulu, asleep. I heard a lot of noise—thundering explosions, and the sound of planes. I went outside with my telescope and could see they were not ours, since they were marked with *Hinomaru,* the Rising Sun. There was a lot of smoke rising from the harbor, and the sky was filled with antiaircraft shells exploding.

"I enlisted, and was assigned to the 442nd at Camp Shelby, Mississippi. In July 1943 Dr. Daniel Buchanan, head of the OSS Japan Desk, came down from Washington and asked for volunteers. In the interviews he told us that this mission would be more hazardous than combat, requiring the volunteers to live off the land—a one-way ticket that many might not survive. More than a hundred Nisei [American-born children of Japanese immigrants] volunteered, but only twenty-three were selected. Originally we were assigned to Australia, to infiltrate the home islands from a submarine. General MacArthur decided this was too risky, and instead we were shipped out to CBI.

"I arrived in Burma in November 1944 to translate captured documents, assist the radio operator in sending and receiving coded messages, and engage in guerrilla combat missions with the Second Battalion—two hundred Kachin [a hill tribe from northern Burma] Rangers. When Burma was retaken, all Detachment 101 personnel were reassigned to Kunming, China. There I became part of the seven-man Operation Magpie, assigned to Peiping and made up of Maj. Ray Nichols, the team leader; Capt. Edmund Carpenter; Lt. Fontaine Jarman, Jr., a doctor; Lt. Mahlon Perkins, Jr.; T/5 Nestor Jacot, the radio operator; Cpl. Melvin Richter, the Chinese interpreter; and Staff Sgt. Dick Hamada, the Japanese interpreter."

On August 17, 1945 (two days after Hirohito's broadcast), at three o'clock in the afternoon, Magpie flew a B-24 bomber from Hsian to an airfield outside Peiping. It was the peak of summer in China, a time of hot, dusty winds blowing in straight from the Gobi Desert. The team first circled the field, tossing out leaflets warning the Japanese not to harm the Allied soldiers and civilians coming in the name of peace. It was anyone's guess as to whether or not these would be heeded.

As each American jumped, he knew that hundreds of eyes were watching and waiting. It was impossible for the Magpie team to keep from fearing that at least one enemy soldier would attempt a final kill for the honor of his country. These thoughts were only confirmed as they lowered and saw the field surrounded by Japanese troops, with arms locked and loaded.

The plane made one more pass to chute out a crate of medical supplies, cigarettes, and blankets, and then took off for Kunming, leaving behind and completely alone the seven Americans in the middle of what had been, two days earlier, the heart of enemy territory. Each carried cash, arms, and a letter confirming that the bearer represented the United States government. The cash, however, was American, and the letter was in English.

Dick Hamada: "Several enemy fighter planes taxied but made no attempt to intercept. I could clearly see enemy soldiers running around, attempting to encircle the team. A shot was fired, but we sustained no injury. A flatbed truck with six Japanese soldiers, armed with bayonets and guns and led by an officer, approached us. The soldiers dismounted and surrounded our team.

"Major Nichols told the lieutenant, 'The war is over and we are here to get the prisoners.' I interpreted. The lieutenant stated emphatically, 'The war is not over yet,' and ordered Major Nichols, Lieutenant Perkins, and me to mount the truck to take us to his HQ. On the way, Major Nichols asked if his soldiers would give us assistance with the cargo. The lieutenant said, 'Japanese soldiers do not work for the Americans.'

"When we got to the headquarters, we were greeted by the officer of the day. Major Nichols stated that the war was over, and we would like to see the prisoners. This officer said the war was not over, and for us to wait for General Takahashi, commander of the Peiping area, who was on his way. The general arrived and begged us to be patient, saying that in a day or two we would be able to see the prisoners, and that hotel arrangements had been made for us at the Wagons-Lits. A limousine was provided. It was getting dark.

"As we were leaving the airfield, a shot rang out. The general jumped out of his limo and looked around. As far as my eyes could see, I saw soldiers standing at attention. The general said that had we jumped at about this hour, we would have all been killed."

The next day brought more conversation between the Americans and the Japanese, with nothing to show for it. Finally, on the twentieth, Ray Nichols declared that the American team would go to the POW camps with Japanese consent and support or without it. His men left for their rooms to prepare their weapons, med kits, and supplies.

Faced with the major's unshakable determination, the Japanese capitulated. By early that afternoon, hundreds of POWs, both military and civilian, were released from their cells and carried by bus to the hotels of Peiping. One of the first to arrive and be debriefed by Major Nichols was Wake Island's Bill Cunningham. The commander informed the major that the Japanese hadn't released a very special set of prisoners still being held at Fengtai. In fact, Cunningham was sure they would never be released, since they weren't considered POWs but convicted war criminals. The commander knew this, he said, because he had read it on the bottom of an aluminum teacup.

In the afternoon Major Nichols showed Japanese officials the results of his POW debriefings. He demanded they confess fully to their crimes of torturing, starving, and killing their captives. After confronting them again and again with evidence of their inhuman behavior, he demanded that they release the "war criminals" at once.

On the evening of August 20, 1945, guards opened the cell doors of Jacob DeShazer, Chase Nielsen, George Barr, and Robert Hite. They were taken to shave and wash with hot water, which shocked them, since it was the first hot water they'd had in three years and four months. They were given back the clothes they'd been wearing when they landed in China. George was too weak to do much for himself—he couldn't even walk—and had to be helped at every step along the way by two guards. The four were then brought together to hear a prison official announce: "The war is over. You can go home now."

Three of the men were stunned with relief. George, on his stretcher, grappled with the news. That he'd made it alive to war's end was a miracle, but he just couldn't understand what was happening. For days he had thought he was dead, but now, suddenly, here were all his pals. Only one thing made sense: They were all dead, but they were all together. George saw everyone smiling, excited, and happy. Clearly they had been reunited in heaven.

A truck appeared to escort them to the Grand Hotel des Wagons-Lits. The men looked out the windows along the way at the chaos, at the streets filled with delirious crowds, at the countless Asians, armed and in uniform. They'd just spent over three years with minimal human contact, and George wasn't the only one at a mental loss. It was unbearable, incomprehensible. What, really, was happening to them?

"Everyone came to look at us, and some people tried to tell us the news," Jake DeShazer said. "So many things were happening so fast. I couldn't seem to keep up with everything. After someone talked, I couldn't remember what he had said. My mind wasn't working right. . . ." The minute they arrived at the hotel, Nestor Jacot and Dick Hamada cranked their radio transmitter to tell Kunming that the Doolittle captives had been found, and the army immediately released the news to the press.

George Barr had to be stretchered all the way to his hotel room, where he was given a blood transfusion along with something to help him sleep. When he woke up and saw the plasma apparatus and Chinese nurse, the terrifying paranoia that often comes with starvation reignited. The others came in to check up on him, and he recovered a little, but suspicion lurked in all the captives' minds. Even Chase Nielsen, the heartiest of the group, kept thinking that at any moment, they would all be cuffed and sent back to solitary confinement.

"We were in that hotel I don't know how many days," DeShazer said. "I'd eaten all I wanted and was hiding some of the C rations in my clothes, and this banker living there saw me. He said, 'From now on you don't have to worry. You'll get enough to eat.' I said, 'What did you say?' I'd been in solitary so long, I couldn't even pick it up. He talked to me real slow. Finally, I caught ahold of what he said, and it made sense to me. But it took quite a while for me to get normal."

Three days later Doctor Jarman approved everyone but Lieutenant Barr to fly on to Chungking. When the three dropped by his room to say farewell, George couldn't understand why they were free, yet he was still a captive. When he awoke the next morning, all alone, he forgot what had happened over the past few days, and grew even more confused.

In the Kuomintang capital, DeShazer, Hite, and Nielsen underwent more medical checks, and were debriefed by G-2 intelligence to determine which Japanese had been responsible for their mistreatment and for the three Raiders' executions. They were put up for the night at one of the country's grandest residences, the home of T. V. Soong, where they were served American-style sandwiches and ice-cold beer, and were given pants, towels, razors, toothbrushes, and brand-new Army Air Forces patches for their uniforms. It was all as shocking as having been captured so many years earlier.

The three Raiders and their army doctors appeared at a press conference for Allied reporters on the twenty-fifth. The men were obviously exhausted and malnourished, but already a bit of color had returned to their cheeks. When one journalist criticized the OSS for chuting in before the official surrender had been signed, Chase Nielsen replied that in another month, they would've all been dead.

After a week George Barr could walk using a cane, but his mind was not healing. His recovery had caused the neurological disorders triggered by starvation, solitary confinement, and years of vitamin deficiency to return in full force, and relentless suspicions overwhelmed him. George couldn't really tell the difference between Chinese and Japanese people, so when he looked out the window, all he could see were armed Japanese everywhere. Even though the medical staff and other GIs at the hotel kept assuring him that he was free and no longer had anything to worry about, they wouldn't let him go home. The lieutenant became convinced that he was still a prisoner, and that the enemy was playing a trick—some new brand of torture.

His paranoia increased to the point that other Allied POWs began looking Japanese as well. He would wake up constantly from screaming nightmares of the hours being confined in a straitjacket, those hours when he couldn't breathe. On September 12 he was flown to Kunming, and placed in a bare room. He refused to allow the nurses to give him transfusions or even a thermometer, convinced that they were in league with the enemy and trying to take over his brain. He finally accepted some vitamins and sleeping pills, but in the middle of the night, George had another nightmare, fell out of bed, and became visibly unhinged.

Three orderlies transferred him to the psychiatric ward, where he awoke alone, in a room with padded walls and a barred window. A face would occasionally appear at the slit in the door, looking at him, saying nothing. It all added up: He was still a prisoner of Japan, and the changes in his treatment were their attempts to brainwash him. He decided he would pretend to be meek and docile, to go along with whatever these people wanted, until the opportunity arose when he could make his escape.

Most American POWs of that time came home to find no cheering crowds, no military or government support, no one sympathetic to the sacrifices they had made during the war. Too often girlfriends had met someone else and forgotten them, or wives had gotten divorces and were now married to new husbands. Some long-term captives who returned to women who'd waited, patient and determined, only to find that now they were strangers with nothing in common, and with children who didn't remember them and wanted nothing to do with them. Old friends were gone, or their lives had changed. They couldn't, or wouldn't, understand.

Some POWs couldn't break their years of prison habits. They would surreptitiously steal meals in restaurants, or get arrested for compulsively shoplifting a bag of socks. Others turned to liquor, to drugs, to whores, to suicide. Many saw only one solution: to run away from their lives.

The army at that time simply did not understand the special care that long-term POWs might need; it would take another forty years and the trauma of Vietnam before such issues were studied and professionalized. "I guess our people learned a lot about prisoners of war through the experience of working with us," Bob Hite said. "I didn't get any rehabilitation at all. After thirty-six months in a solitary cell and forty months as a prisoner, you need a kind of special 'rehabbing' and you need a friend. You need somebody that can maybe guide you a little bit.

"I had a pretty rough time [adjusting]. . . . [T]hese people were coming in my house ten and fifteen at a time for days. Lord, I was nervous and I kind of wanted to be alone. I think I was just sort of frightened of people. We had been in that solitary confinement so long that I don't know whether we wanted to see anybody or not. It had almost grown on us. . . .

"I think maybe where we missed the boat was that there might have been too much alcohol. It certainly wasn't good for me at the time, but on the other hand, it numbed all of my fears and that sort of thing. So maybe it had its place, too."

Even soldiers who hadn't been incarcerated had difficulty coming home at war's end. "I was in uniform, wearing my wings, my sergeant's stripes, my Purple Heart, my Distinguished Flying Cross, but nobody gave me a second look," remembered waist gunner Jack Novey. "I don't know what I expected. I guess I wanted people to acknowledge me in some way, even to come up and shake my hand and thank me. But they looked right through me." One Raider's wife said, "After the war ended, these men had time to think. The fact that they killed other human beings started to prey on their minds. My husband said again and again, 'I pushed that lever. What if the bomb killed some kids? They had nothing to do with the war. I can't stop thinking about it. I couldn't forgive myself if it were true.'"

One army psychiatrist who spent his entire professional life studying the effects of combat explained:

> One thing I've noticed in the interviews I've done is that these men cut off their feelings, and they almost were aware of it. They couldn't feel anything after a certain point. And yet they did have feelings. If a friend was killed, they would still be overwhelmed, but in order to go on, they would see things, and it would almost be like looking at a photograph. It's called emotional numbing, and it's a very common feature of PTSD [posttraumatic stress disorder]. . . . Often the only feelings they can feel are more intense feelings of rage, and when they're very stimulated, like a lot of vets who are numb are drawn to more daredevil activities as a way of feeling something. . . . [W]e don't know whether that numbing is due to a natural occurring opiate which is released in the body . . . but the fact is that this is a very common complaint, and it's a common complaint of the families, that these men are cut off from their feelings. They say that they just can't feel closeness for

anyone, they can't really be touched, although when they talk about World War II vets and losses there, they get very flooded emotionally. Somehow that overwhelms them.

War is one of those experiences that most people, unless you've been in war, you don't have a parallel experience to relate to, and a lot of combat vets, whether it's World War II or Korea or Vietnam, they feel that either there's not going to be an interest in what they have to say, or they'll be judged by their activities, or they're just simply not going to be understood, so there is a lot of withholding. I think as the World War II vets are aging and they're becoming more aware of their mortality as they see their numbers decrease, I see them reaching out more and feeling a need to talk more about their experiences with their families.

On September 5 Jacob DeShazer, Robert Hite, and Chase Nielsen arrived in Washington, where they were each given a full checkup at Walter Reed, and appeared once again before reporters. The public reaction was astonishing. A newspaper syndicate paid DeShazer $2,250 for his story, and a radio show paid him $400 for reading one sentence.

The corporal was finally reunited with his mother, stepfather, and sister, Helen, who'd since become a student at Seattle Pacific College. Jake told them of his future plans: He wanted to go to a university to get an education in religion and public speaking, and then return to Japan as a missionary. He explained his thinking: "How was the best way to let God use me? Was it to be a farmer? They had so many farmers they didn't know what to do with them. So many people that were unemployed and everything. The best thing I could do was tell the Japanese about Jesus. They didn't know anything about him, and there was a great need there. It just looked like the right thing."

More than a few of Jake's friends and relatives thought he was out of his mind, but his sister supported his plan immediately. Helen got him enrolled at Seattle Pacific, where he began an accelerated program of nonstop schooling so he could get his four-year degree in three: "I was in an awful hurry to get back to Japan, and boy, it was just right."

Soon after starting college, Jake met Florence Matheny. After they had dated seriously for months, he asked for her hand: "She was the most attractive young lady I had ever met, and she wanted to go into full-time work for the Lord. We both felt a oneness of purpose, and when I asked Miss Matheny if she would marry me, she said that she would. When we prayed to Jesus, we felt that he would be pleased to give us a life together." They were married the following year and, a year after that, were blessed with a baby boy. They named him for the first Christian missionary, the apostle Paul.

Still confined to a Kunming psychiatric ward, Lt. George Barr tried to appear as normal as possible, but couldn't cover up his confusion and fears, and the staff kept him in a bare cell. When he tried to tell the nurses that he was one of the famed Doolittle Raiders, they assumed he was suffering from delusions. One doctor, Capt. Werner Tuteur, however, believed him. When George told the doctor of his belief that he was being brainwashed, Tuteur did everything he could to convince him otherwise and to bring him back to reality. When George said he knew he was a prisoner since there were bars on the window, they were removed. When he asked why he wasn't allowed to leave the room, Tuteur opened the door and said he could. When he asked why he wasn't allowed to see other patients, he was taken to a dayroom and told he could talk to anyone he pleased.

The treatment worked for a week, but then George relapsed. When he demanded the nurses just kill him immediately, the hospital chiefs decided he would need extensive hospitalization. On October 9 he and an orderly were sent to the airport to board a C-47.

As they walked to the plane, George realized that here was his chance, and he began running as fast as he could. Then something happened, and he fell unconscious. He came to on a stretcher, in a straitjacket. He was surrounded by other men on stretchers, and they were in a plane, flying somewhere. George asked a man passing through where they were going, and the man smiled but wouldn't answer.

The plane landed in Calcutta, where George was first housed in a room with many others. That night, however, a nightmare of screaming terrified the nurses, and he was confined once again in a solitary padded cell. Three days later, he was given travel priority back to the United States. In fellow officers' bags on the plane home, the lieutenant saw Japanese swords. On a stopover in Hawaii, he saw the streets, filled with thousands who looked Japanese.

On October 12 the group arrived in San Francisco, and George was sent, alone, to Hamilton Field Hospital, where triage didn't know what to make of him—he arrived with no baggage, no records, no identification, and no money. When they asked George about his last assignment, he told them a ridiculous story of having been part of the Doolittle Raid on Tokyo.

He was given a pair of pajamas and led to a room, where he sat down on the bed and looked around. There on a table was the answer—his roommate had gone out, leaving behind a penknife. Finally everything that had happened to him over the past few weeks made perfect sense: The Japanese were clearly setting everything up so that he would, and could, kill himself. George grabbed the knife and drove it into his chest. Nothing happened; he didn't even bleed. They wouldn't even let him commit suicide.

The lieutenant looked around the room, determined to take control of his life for the first time in so many years. He found a lamp, ripped the electric cord out of its base, fashioned a noose around his neck, stepped up onto a chair, and after tying the other end to a chandelier hanging from the ceiling, he jumped.

The light fixture exploded, and Barr fell to the floor in a heap. The medical officer came running, and orderlies dragged George away. He was placed in a padded, empty cell, its door having a barred window and a slit at the floor for food. George screamed out; he only wanted to die.

On October 19 Barr and five other patients were secured in straitjackets and trundled aboard a train. At night he was forced to sleep in a berth under a restraining sheet. At one point in the trip he asked to look out the window, and the orderlies agreed. They opened the blind, and he saw a strip of snowy mountains that looked just like China.

George had signed up for the Flying Cadets while attending Northland College in Ashland, Wisconsin, and service records now mistakenly listed this as his home. According to regulations he was sent to Wisconsin's closest army hospital—Schick General, in Clinton, Iowa, where he was locked up with seven extremely disturbed vets. Except for a brief, cryptic note that George had been talked into sending during his first days in the Grand Hotel in Peiping, none of his family had any idea what had happened to him. This wasn't the first time in his life that George Barr had been abandoned as General Doolittle recounted:

> George had been orphaned at six months of age when his father drowned in a boating accident. When his mother couldn't support him, George spent the years from age nine through high school in a boys' foster home in Yonkers, New York. His sister, four years older, became the special interest of Mrs. Charles A. Towns, a social worker, who had taken her into their home. Mrs. Towns and her husband, themselves childless, "adopted" the Barr children in fact but not legally. They were determined to do what they could to see that these two luckless children were not set adrift without a proper sense of values.
>
> After the raid, when the names of the eight prisoners were known, Mrs. Towns communicated with the other families frequently and became the go-between to relay any information she

had that might give them some hope. She continually sought information from the International Red Cross, the Federal Bureau of Investigation, Army Intelligence, and the repatriated Americans from Japan who had been returned to the States in June 1942. The Townses were overjoyed when it was announced that George was one of the survivors. They met Nielsen, Hite, and DeShazer and sought news about George, but none of the three knew anything about what had happened to him since they had bid him good-bye in China. . . .

Mrs. Towns wrote to or called everyone she could think of to find out George's whereabouts. I was on the road giving speeches at that time, but there were telephone call slips and a distraught letter from her waiting for me when I returned to the Pentagon. I dropped everything and started an official search. In my reply I assured Mrs. Towns that "we who love George Barr will do everything we can for him. Our objective, however, is not to reform the Army but to find him and help him recover."

With her tremendous energy and determination, Mrs. Towns was the first to discover the lieutenant's stateside location. Since his sister, Grace, was pregnant and felt she shouldn't make the trip, her husband, Bill, was the first member of the family to arrive in Iowa.

George showed no happiness at seeing Bill, who seemed so much older than the man he remembered. Couldn't the Japanese use plastic surgery to make spies look like one of his relatives? Mrs. Towns herself then came to visit, but the same doubts remained. When, thought George, would this charade ever end?

Doolittle:

I immediately flew out to Clinton when the Army sleuths located him. Not knowing George's true condition, I had to be cautious because I knew he would be surprised to see me. I greeted him like an old friend and George immediately broke into tears. I was the first military person he had seen that he knew since his buddies had left him in China. He seemed very normal to me, so we went for a walk and he tried to tell me everything he could. He was hesitant at first, but then the tears flowed and the words began to pour out. Catharsis was obviously what he needed. I was shocked and found it difficult to believe that he had not seen a doctor and had no money, no clothes, and no military status except that of "patient." The last of my Tokyo Raiders to come home needed help, and I was going to see that he got it.

I can say unreservedly that I have never been so angry in my life as I was when George told me what had happened to him. I walked with him back to the ward and went immediately to the hospital commander's office, where I unloaded Doolittle's worst verbal fury on his head. I won't repeat what I said because it would burn a hole in this page. I will say that George was quickly outfitted in a new uniform, complete with the ribbons he didn't know he had earned, and was given a check for over $7,000 in back pay, and orders promoting him to first lieutenant. Best of all, he was seen immediately by a psychiatrist and began the slow road back to recovery.

Before I left, I asked George if he remembered that before we left the *Hornet* I had promised the fellows a party in Chungking. He said, "Yes, sir, I do."

"Well George, we never had that party because you and the rest of the fellows couldn't make it. But I'm going to keep that promise. The whole gang is invited to be my guests in Miami on my birthday on December 14. I want you to come. I'll send an airplane for you."

My visit, George told me later, was a turning point in his recovery.

Barr's full recuperation would take over two years. He was eventually transferred to Mitchel Field on Long Island to be near the Townses, and with the help of fellow ex-captive Bob Hite, Barr recovered enough to be promoted to captain, and to fall in love. By the end of 1946, he was married, but he still had never received the Purple Heart he was due for injuries suffered as a POW. It wasn't until the Doolittle Raider reunion of 1965 that the general was finally able to present him with his Heart.

In 1967, at the too-young age of fifty, Capt. George Barr died of cardiac arrest.

On March 18, 1946, at 9:00 A.M., another trial began in Shanghai at the Ward Road jail. The defendants were Kiangwan prison warden Tatsuta Sotojiro, prosecutor Wako Yusei, judge Okada Ryuhei, and Lt. Gen. Sawada Shigeru, at one time the commander of Japan's Imperial Expeditionary Army in China. Allied investigators had tracked down everyone who could provide firsthand testimony, such as Caesar dos Remedios, that would bring the empire's torturers and executioners of the Doolittle Raiders to justice. The others who were responsible, they discovered, were either dead, had escaped into anonymity, or had fallen under another country's jurisdiction.

When the American captives were shipped from Shanghai to Nanking, Caesar had promised them that, if the Allies won, he would bear witness to their suffering. Hired as a translator and deputy investigator, it was dos Remedios who ultimately uncovered the deliberately mislabeled Raider cremains at Shanghai's International Funeral Parlor.

At this new trial the proceedings were fully interpreted in Japanese, and the defendants were allowed to have both American and Japanese attorneys and as much time as they needed to prepare a defense. Chase Nielsen, who had willed himself to survive in order to give evidence to the enemy's brutality, flew back to China, scene of so many horrible memories, to testify. Statements from George Barr, Bob Hite, and Jake DeShazer were entered into the record, as well as testimony from other prisoners of Bridge House, Japanese guards who had witnessed the executions, and a doctor who discussed the starving to death of Bob Meder. The prosecutor asked that all four defendants be given the death penalty.

On April 14 the five-member military commission released its decision. The judges rejected the death penalty, as the accused had been following orders and took no personal initiative in the executions. Instead Warden Tatsuta, Judge Okada, and Lieutenant General Sawada were sentenced to five years' imprisonment, while prosecutor Wako received ten. The commission was heavily criticized for the leniency of these sentences by the public, by the parents of the executed Raiders, and by its army superiors, but its decision was allowed to stand.

The Shanghai trial was one of over 2,200 legal proceedings that Allied military courts would hold to prosecute an estimated 5,600 Japanese, convicting 4,400 and executing close to 1,000, the main venue being Tokyo's International Military Tribunal for the Far East. Unlike the attempts at Nuremberg to prove commission, these trials sought to show that Japan's military leaders were guilty of omission in allowing their troops to rampage through Asia and their POWs to die by the thousands. The tribunals uncovered the fact that, while 4 percent of Allied POWs held by Germany and Italy had died during their imprisonment, for those held by the Japanese, the mortality rate was a shocking 38 percent.

One conspicuously missing defendant was Hirohito, MacArthur having publicly explained that he had been just a figurehead, manipulated by military leaders, and had little to do with the war. Army intelligence officers had in fact convinced the supreme commander that prosecuting the emperor would undermine American attempts to rehabilitate the country. At one point in the tribunals, Tojo was asked about the Son of Heaven's role in war-mongering. He admitted that nothing could be done, by either the government or the military, without Hirohito's wishes. That afternoon, army officers sent Japanese workers to the onetime prime minister's cell to make sure he corrected this testimony the very next day.

Other significant defendants not summoned to the tribunals were officers of the Kempeitai, and the "purification" staff of Unit 731. When Japan fell, unit chiefs offered to share their research findings in exchange for release from prosecution, and MacArthur agreed. The Soviets later uncovered information on Unit 731 from captured Japanese in Manchuria, and proposed a joint investigation. The United States demurred, and refused to share the scientists' data with the other Allied powers.

One serviceman forced to testify against many of his navy colleagues was Fuchida Mitsuo. During reconstruction the hero of Pearl Harbor had bought land just outside Osaka from his father-in-law to became a farmer, raising wheat, rice, vegetables, fruit, grapes, chickens, rabbits, and ducks. This new life wasn't going well; his only success was in selling eggs to a nearby American artillery camp.

In wartime Fuchida had been nationally famous, regularly speaking to crowds of cheering countrymen. Now they treated him like a leper. The one-time hero grew disgusted by the Allied trials, especially the hangings of those convicted of mistreating POWs. This, he thought, was an entirely trumped-up charge; weren't all POWs treated horribly around the world?

Wanting to learn the truth for himself, Fuchida soon discovered that a sublieutenant who'd served with him at Midway, a serviceman the Japanese had officially determined KIA, had instead spent the remainder of the war as a POW in Colorado. There he'd met an American teenager, volunteer Peggy Covell, who did everything she could for the captive Japanese. When asked why, Peggy said: "Because Japanese soldiers killed my parents."

Miss Covell explained that her parents had been missionaries in Yokohama when war broke out. The local Japanese army decided that their radio was some kind of communications device, convicted them as spies, and cut off their heads. When Peggy learned how she was orphaned, the young girl was filled with hatred. Then she remembered her parents' spiritual beliefs, and knew that they must have forgiven their killers. She could do no less.

This philosophy baffled the Japanese POWs, who believed it a child's duty to avenge the death of a parent, even if it took generations to accomplish. It especially shocked Fuchida. As he thought the story over, though, he came to realize that Peggy Covell was right: The only way to end hate and war and the human race's natural inclination for an endless cycle of retribution was to personally achieve a level of forgiveness he himself could not even begin to comprehend.

Alone, working with his crops and his animals, Fuchida brooded over his miserable life. One night as he was out in the fields, he looked up at the sky and saw the North Star, a beacon to any navigator. He thought, "How steady, so beautiful, and so useful it was. . . . That night, there on my farm, God began to come into my heart. . . . I began to realize slowly that all things were dependent upon a divine Creator, and that I was living under the grace of God. I could sow the seeds, I could plant the saplings, I could draw water with my hands. But they all came from the benevolence of a kind and far-seeing Creator."

After graduating from college, Jacob and Florence DeShazer were accepted by the Free Methodist Church's missionary board for service. On December 14, 1948, the young family sailed from San Francisco to Honolulu and then to Japan, docking on the twenty-eighth. As they approached Honshu Island, they found it impossible to believe that, only a few years earlier, this had been the center of Asia's greatest empire, but this wouldn't be the last of their surprises. "We got in to Yokohama," Jake said, "and they said over the loudspeaker as we were going down the gangplank, 'Is Jacob DeShazer here?' I hollered back, 'I'm here!' They said, 'Will you please go back inside? We want to talk to you.' It was cold outside. So my wife and I and our little fourteen-month-old boy went down in the hold, and here come those newspapermen, a big crowd of them, I think maybe forty. They said, 'Now what happened to you? You were in that Japanese prison, and they kicked you and they spit on you, and the lice and bedbugs, the rats. Why did you come back to Japan?' So I told them. I don't know what they put in the newspapers, but they questioned me quite a bit."

While Jake had been finishing up his college work, he wrote an essay explaining what had happened to him during the war, which was printed in both English and Japanese, and given away throughout the home islands. It is called "I Was a Prisoner of Japan":

I was a prisoner of Japan for forty long months, thirty-four of them in solitary confinement.

When I flew as a member of General Jimmy Doolittle's squadron on the first raid over Japan on April 18th, 1942, my heart was filled with bitter hatred for the people of that nation. When our plane ran out of gas, and the members of the crew of my plane had to parachute down into Japanese-held territory in China and were captured by the enemy, the bitterness of my heart against my captors seemed more than I could bear.

Taken to Tokyo with the survivors of another of our planes, we were imprisoned and beaten, half-starved, and denied by solitary confinement even the comfort of association with one another, these terrible tortures taking place at Tokyo, Shanghai, Nanking and Peiping. Three of my buddies, Dean Hallmark, Bill Farrow and Harold Spatz, were executed by a firing squad about six months after our capture, and fourteen months later another of them, Bob Meder, died of slow starvation. My hatred for the Japanese people nearly drove me crazy.

It was soon after Meder's death that I began to ponder the cause of such hatred between members of the human race. I wondered what it was that made the Japanese hate the Americans, and what made me hate the Japanese. My thoughts turned toward what I had heard about Christianity changing hatred between human beings into real brotherly love, and I was gripped with a strange longing to examine the Christians' Bible to see if I could find the secret. I begged my captors to get a Bible for me. At last, in the month of May, 1944, a guard brought the Book. . . .

I eagerly began to read its pages. Chapter after chapter gripped my heart. . . . [S]uddenly I discovered that God had given me new spiritual eyes, and that when I looked at the Japanese officers and guards who had starved and beaten me and my companions so cruelly, I found my bitter hatred for them changed to loving pity.

Army chaplains and Christian organizations had distributed more than a million copies of this pamphlet, so that when his boat docked in Yokohama, the reverend was shocked to learn he was a national celebrity. Japanese newspapers and radio spread the news of his story, and heavily promoted his speaking engagements. Everywhere Jake went to preach, the churches and lecture halls were filled to overflowing.

One Japanese man donated a home for the DeShazer family in Osaka, but the reverend's celebrity was so powerful—attracting both would-be disciples and those who hated him for his comments about the Japanese and his proselytizing of Christianity to a Shinto/Buddhist nation—that a police box had to be installed next to its gate. Prince Takamatsu invited him to the Temple of Heaven. Besides explaining the teachings of Christ, Jake was able to thank the prince for the emperor's sparing his life.

While Florence held Bible classes in the family's living room, Jake traveled the country, preaching with a translator. During one rally he couldn't help but notice a young woman in the front rows, staring directly up at him. At the next meeting there she was again, and when, the following week, he had a class at his home, she was in the audience. Eventually, the woman confessed—her fiancé had been killed during the war, and she'd first gone to the rally for revenge. She was going to assassinate him. His words, remarkably, had touched her deeply, and her heart was changed. Now she was a Christian.

Jake worked hard to learn Japanese, but the difficult language didn't come naturally to him. One afternoon he was trying to talk to a group of high school boys without an interpreter; they couldn't understand a word. Then he gently placed a hand on their shoulders, and, seeing the love in his penetrating, ice blue eyes, the boys felt his conviction so powerfully that they burst into tears.

The DeShazer family would remain in Japan for the next thirty years, founding twenty-three new churches. They would be helped in part by a Japanese celebrity who would become a Christian because of Jake's mission, and whose conversion would be the subject of headlines around the world.

The other Raiders made new postwar lives for themselves as well. "I stayed in the service, going to training command and a staff job, and in 1951 got orders to the Forty-seventh Bomb Group in Langley Field, Virginia, equipped with a B-45, the air force's first four-engine jet," Davey Jones said. "In spring of 1952 I took the whole group to RAF Sculport in the UK for three years. We were part of the Forty-ninth Air Division, assigned to the United States Third Air Force in support of NATO, equipped with Mark 5 atomic weapons. Of course that's right in the middle of the old cold war, and we worked hard. Hell of an experience. The best damn assignment I ever had.

"I came home in 1955 and got orders up to Carswell AFB at Fort Worth to run the B-58 Test Force, a four-engine delta-wing bomber. It was the first Mach-2 bomber; the first supersonic, and top secret; the plant where they built the aircraft was right across the runway. The aircraft was one big, huge fuel tank aerodynamically formed into a flying wing—sort of like a giant boomerang on wheels—and the atomic weapon was tucked inside that. It was my last flying assignment. That was a super job."

"I received orders to go to Tampa to create a new bombardment group equipped with B-26s with Col. Jack Hilger, who was the second in command at the Tokyo Raid," said Harry McCool. "I got to Europe in January '44 and flew my B-26 missions out of England and France, finishing at the time of the Battle of the Bulge, in December '44.

"When nuclear weapons were dropped in August, I got on a B-17 and flew back to Wright-Patterson with a ton of V2 and V1 blueprints. After three months I was transferred to the Special Staff School in Orlando as an instructor in map reading, guided missiles, and joint operations. With flying models of the V1 and V2, along with various glide bombs, rockets, and radio-controlled bombs, we were teaching the officers what guided missiles had been built up to then, and what we were going to build in the next twenty years."

"There was a lot of Lend-Lease money appropriated to China left over when the war ended too soon," Tung-Sheng Liu remembered. "So the Congress decided that this money—part of it—could be used to help young Chinese students who wanted to come to the U.S. to study. Under that regulation I obtained a passport and visa to come to America in 1946.

"I knew from reading the newspapers that General Doolittle was in Miami, so I wrote him a letter. He kindly wrote back to me, telling me where Colonel Hoover and each of his crew were at that time. So I was happy to know that."

On December 14, 1945, General Doolittle was finally able to keep the promise he'd made to all the boys moments before takeoff from *Hornet*. Military planes picked up every available Raider from across the country and brought them to Miami's MacFadden-Deauville Hotel. Jimmy would spend two thousand dollars of his own money to make sure this event was more than memorable, and according to those able to recall the celebration, he succeeded in fine fashion. Ski York: "Ted Laban came. Before he even showed up at the hotel, he had been arrested. I said, 'Laban, what in the world did they arrest you for?' 'Walking while drunk.' I had never heard of that. He paid a $35 fine, and they let him go." Jimmy Doolittle:

> Some would say we raised hell at that Miami reunion. I wouldn't quarrel with that assessment. When several suggested we have a reunion like that every year, I told them I'd like that, but the party had cost me $2,000 and I couldn't afford it every year. We had shared an unusual life-threatening situation and had formed an unusual bonding relationship. It was understood that we would

meet again annually if we could. We didn't have a reunion in 1946 but met again in Miami in 1947. It could be said that we raised more hell. So much, in fact, that the hotel's night watchman made a report to the hotel manager. It said: "The Doolittle boys added some gray hairs to my head. This has been the worst night since I worked here. They were completely out of my control. I let them make a lot of noise, but when about 15 of them went into the pool at 1:00 A.M., including Doolittle, I told them there was no swimming allowed there at night. They were in the pool until 2:30 A.M. I went up twice more without results. They were running around the halls in their bathing suits and were noisy until 5 A.M. Yes, it was a rough night."

When we checked out, the manager showed us the report and asked us all to autograph it. He said as far as he was concerned, we had earned the right to make all the noise we wanted to in his hotel.

On September 21, 1947, after completing ten thousand hours of piloting over three decades and in 265 different types of craft, Gen. James Doolittle laid down his wings. Before quitting, however, he went through a burst of flying just about every state-of-the-art plane he could get his hands on, from the supersonic F-100 fighter to the Boeing 707 airliner and the B-52 bomber. He expected to be miserable in retirement but—"I never missed it a speck!"

In October 1948 Fuchida Mitsuo came to Tokyo to visit his mistress, Kimi, and their daughter. He had been consumed with thoughts about the path of his life. Once it had been filled with promise, but now it had become a debased meaningless struggle for existence. After running some errands, Mitsuo came out of the Shibuya subway station and saw, between the frenetic Tokyo crowds, an American giving away pamphlets next to the bronze statue of a dog. When Fuchida learned that these were written by an airman like himself and heard the title—*Watakushi wa Nippon no Horyo*—he took one and immediately read its four pages. Like Peggy Covell's story, the pamphlet told of spiritual love overcoming hatred, and to Fuchida the coincidence was overwhelming.

After rereading "I Was a Prisoner of Japan" a few more times, Fuchida bought a New Testament. Though raised a Buddhist, the airman/farmer decided he should immediately go to the source to see for himself if this kind of human forgiveness was plausible. Making his way through the Bible turned out to be a tough assignment—the language was archaic, the stories were hard to follow, the teachings didn't make any sense, and there were all those miracles that couldn't possibly ever have happened. He kept putting it aside and then forcing himself to keep reading. Finally he got to the end of chapter three, the Gospel of Saint Luke, and found himself riveted. In the final moments of the most terrible death any man could endure, Jesus said: "Father, forgive them, for they know not what they do." Fuchida found himself barely able to breathe. Here was the message of Peggy and Jacob DeShazer. Christ had prayed for his tormentors and for all humanity . . . including the onetime hero of Pearl Harbor. "It was," Fuchida said, "like having the sun come up."

Fuchida decided he wanted to become a Christian, but he didn't know any, and he wasn't sure how to go about it. He remembered that there was an address on DeShazer's pamphlet, so he wrote to its distributor, the Pocket Testament League. The letter made its way into the hands of PTL's leader, Glenn Wagner, who was astounded. He immediately wrote back to the great Japanese war hero, offering to get together with him on April 14, when the league would be holding services in Osaka.

At their meeting Wagner explained the key practices every Christian must perform for his faith—reading the Bible and praying every day (which Fuchida said he was doing already)—and bearing witness, which Fuchida insisted he could never do. As their conversation continued and deepened, the farmer came to realize that it was cowardly of him to pursue these profound spiritual beliefs in secret. He would have to try.

A PTL group drove to a major intersection in the Osaka business district in its Chevy truck, which was outfitted with a loudspeaker and podium in the back. After a very small number of curious passersby had gathered, the once-revered soldier stepped up to the podium and announced: "I am Fuchida Mitsuo, a former navy captain who commanded the air attacking forces against Pearl Harbor on 8 December 1941. But now I'm a Christian, and I want to let you know how I became one. All Japanese want peace, I'm sure of that. No one wants war again, no one less than I, who engaged in war as a naval officer for almost four years. I know the brutality and the cruelties of war better than many people. Now I want to work for peace. But how can mankind achieve a lasting peace?"

More and more pedestrians stopped to listen, amazed and fascinated. As Fuchida described his awakening, a large crowd gathered, quiet and attentive. It was his first experience in the role of a preacher, and the onetime admirer of Hitler was thrilled at his life's new purpose.

In the spring of 1949 Reverend Jacob DeShazer was speaking in a huge theater in Osaka, when two men stepped forward to tell him they had accepted Christ in their lives. They knew Jake already, since they'd guarded him in prison in Nanking. One year later Jake was again speaking in the great theater in Osaka, when Fuchida came up to him, explained his wartime history, and how he had become a Christian on April 14, 1950, because of Jacob's teachings. DeShazer explained that since the Japanese weren't receiving Christ's message, a miracle was needed, so he was going on a forty-day fast, taking nothing but water. Though meeting Jake was a highlight of his life, the new convert found DeShazer's face thin and wild, and his eyes piercing. Fuchida also disagreed about the worth of fasting, which seemed more a Buddhist idea than a Christian one. Despite these differences, the two preached together at a rally in Osaka that had been heavily promoted. Almost five hundred Japanese converted to the faith at that event, a remarkable achievement. Every major newspaper in Japan carried the story.

The strength of his newfound faith notwithstanding, Fuchida would have some difficulties adjusting to the tenets of Christianity. "Fuchida had two women; one was his concubine and one was his wife," Reverend DeShazer said. "Some of the fellows didn't think he was much of a Christian that he didn't start straightening out and become a moral man. 'You've got to get rid of one of those women.' But it was a big problem for Fuchida. I guess eventually he realized it was wrong, and he got so he only had one wife, or one woman. I think he took the best-looking one."

"In 1948, the Raiders decided to have a reunion in Minneapolis," Tung-Sheng Liu said. "I did not know beforehand where, just that they were having a reunion. I opened up a newspaper and read that Doolittle Raiders were having a reunion at so-and-so hotel! I was overjoyed. So I went to the hotel and saw Colonel Hoover again, with two other members of his crew, Bill Fitzhugh and Carl Wildner. I invited them to a Chinese restaurant to have dinner, and to visit my home and meet my wife.

"When the situation in China greatly changed and the Communists took over, I could not go back. I found a job as a teaching assistant and lecturer in engineering at the University of Minnesota. After ten years there was an opportunity at Wright-Patterson AFB working for the USAF as an engineer.

"Colonel Hoover and his crew were so happy with what happened in China that they elected me to be an honorary Raider, to be in the group. So I was able to attend the Raiders' reunions whenever I could, and I've gone almost every year."

General Doolittle: "We have held a reunion every year since, except one year during the Korean War and one year during the Vietnam War. Of all the men who served with me during World War II, I have been closest to my Tokyo Raiders and treasure the days we have spent together at reunions over the years. I know a commander is not supposed to have any favorites, but these men are mine. I care deeply for them and have always considered them part of my family."

At these annual get-togethers, the boys have been entertained by a host of show-biz luminaries including actor Bob Cummings and comedians Joe E. Brown, George Jessel, and Bob Hope. Today the Doolittle Raiders Association Scholarship Fund (begun on the twentieth anniversary in 1962) makes a grant to a high school senior in the city hosting that year's reunion planning on a career in aerospace science.

The 1955 reunion was to be held in Los Angeles, and a number of the Raiders were getting there on a C-47 out of Atlanta. Just minutes after take-off the left prop developed serious trouble, and the plane began to fall. The copilot had all the baggage thrown out, but the plane kept losing altitude. He then ordered the passengers to jump. They couldn't believe their ears; Bill Bower said he'd stay on board, thanks very much. The plane just barely made it back to a little airstrip. Bower leaped out, found a helicopter pilot warming up his engines, and explained what had happened. The rotorman picked up the ten Raiders who'd been forced to jump, and soon the guys were back on their way to LA . . . without their luggage.

In 1958 North American Aviation gave the group a B-25B, which today is part of a Raiders' Memorial at the Wright-Patterson Air Force Museum outside Dayton, Ohio.

"In 1959, the reunion was held in Tucson," Herb Macia said. "A friend of mine, Chuck Arnold, was in charge of preparations. He and I got together to talk about the arrangements. Chuck was speculating on what they might do that would be unusual and lasting. Suddenly the idea of the city of Tucson's giving a set of silver goblets occurred to him. They were presented to us at our reunion in Tucson. Then, in October, Chuck brought them to the football game between the Air Force Academy and the University of Colorado. At halftime they had a ceremony where Doolittle presented the case and goblets to the superintendent of the Air Force Academy for safekeeping. Each year the goblets, escorted by cadets, appear at the reunion of Doolittle's Raiders and are used to toast departed comrades. The goblet of any Raider who has died is turned upside down in the case. The last two Raiders will open a bottle of cognac—vintage 1896, the year of Doolittle's birth—and once again toast departed comrades."

Drinking that brandy may be the bravest thing any Raider will ever have to do.

After the war ended a great many of the Raiders who'd fallen into the Corps because they had no other options or because they couldn't think of where else to turn would in fact stay on for a full haul of thirty years. They had found a home in the world. For all its faults, they loved the U.S. Air Force, though there was one fault that no one could fix and no one could reconcile: the military's system of forced retirement. It might have made sense in 1812 to think that a fifty-year-old man could no longer be of use to the armed forces, but today that policy is nonsense.

Most, when the time came, just were not ready to start their lives all over again. What jobs could there possibly be for a pack of fifty-year-olds whose major experience was crewing bombers? Just as so many of these men had fallen into the service, now they fell into civilian life, into the only kind of jobs they could get. It was, said one, like getting demoted in the hierarchy of the world. In the air force, they'd been like CEOs and vice presidents. Now they were salesmen, contractors, and laborers, and most civilians couldn't have cared less that, once upon a time, they'd been war heroes.

One of the most poignant retirement stories of them all would have to be that of marine pilot Pappy Boyington, hero of the Black Sheep Squadron. After winning the Medal of Honor, he would spend decades broke and drunk: "I think that the only reason the Corps released all the glowing heroic junk about me was because they thought I was dead. It took a few weeks after I returned for anything to be forwarded or for any of the public relations brass to get in touch with me. But, as I have been quoted as saying, '[S]how me a hero and I will show you a bum.' I was retired due to wounds. I could not find a job until I began working as a wrestling referee part time. Later I was a beer salesman for a few years; it seemed like poetic justice in a way."

Eventually most Raiders, like most other servicemen, would struggle back into decent livelihoods. They would build homes, manage hotels, sell insurance, join up with their buddies, and do whatever they could to establish a civilian life. This was, after all, a very special group of men who'd already proved their mettle by surviving about the worst that life could throw at them.

The week after a *New York Times* columnist declared World War II passé, I went to Fresno, California, for the May 18, 2001, Doolittle Raiders' Reunion, Airshow, and Dinner-Dance. Tickets sold out in a few days' time, and our VIP parking passes were rendered worthless when more than ten thousand jammed the show's airfield, even though the temperature had been forecast in triple digits. Hank Potter took one look at this mob and asked, "I wonder why the hell they're all out here on an afternoon like this?" Vets, their grown children, and their grandkids swarmed past book signings, souvenir stands, and more than a dozen fighters. Teenage girls had themselves photographed in WAC outfits while "Boogie-Woogie Bugle Boy" played over the public-address system. As the Raiders passed by, the crowd buzzed in a rising wave, many commenting how thrilled they were that these heroes were getting the attention they deserved.

The organizers had hoped that sixteen B-25s would be able to take part. Thirteen made it, all Js (eight generations beyond the B), sprouting machine guns in porcupine fashion. That eleven were in flying condition was real testimony to the loving care of their hobbyist owners, who started their engines up with a deafening roar, clouds of oily gasoline smoke spreading across the entire field, the prop wash kicking up dust and stones into our faces. They buzzed the field twice in formation, thrilling the ten thousand into awed silence.

In its first years the reunion was very much a boys' night out, but eventually Joe Doolittle convinced the general that wives and girlfriends should be included. Today these events are full-out family affairs, the hotel pool filled with the screams of grandchildren, the daughters-in-law helping their Raider dads through the conference rooms and banquet halls. In 2001, against all expectations, Mrs. Hattie Holstrom, who'd just lost her husband, Brick, came, and the other women wrapped around her in a crowd of support and serious affection. Hank Potter also made a showing, a mere four months after undergoing brain surgery. Since for a while there it had been iffy whether or not Hank would survive, it was especially heartening to see him.

The reunions' tone was set down by General Doolittle from the very beginning: "They are like sons to me, that group of boys, and I'm very grateful, very grateful indeed, that the good Lord gave me this family." Gunner Adam Williams thought that the men were especially close because they did something everyone said couldn't be done. Bob Hite, who's been through about everything a human being can take, teared up when he remembered: "The guys that I have known on the Doolittle Raiders are some of the finest guys I know. Jim was a very, very special man. I doubt that there is anyone else as a leader who developed the comradeship that we have. 'Of all the people I've commanded, I love you the best.' He said that."

Chatting with the guys means being interrupted every five minutes by buffs armed with books, prints, photos, brochures, and miscellaneous mementos, which they desperately want autographed. On the one hand it is something of a circus, and on the other the Raiders are getting treated like celebrities, just as they deserve. The men even have a special group of hardcore fans who come to reunion after reunion to swap stories and enjoy the company of vets.

That evening more than three thousand took their seats at the sixty-dollars-a-head dinner dance—endless rows of folding tables and chairs that filled an entire airplane hangar. The sound boomed around the ceiling with such reverberations that we couldn't really understand what any of the speakers was saying, but there was plenty of musical atmosphere to make up for it from the big-band Rhythm Aires. College boys appeared in khakis, leather jackets, and envelope caps, escorting girls in Crawford wigs, Davis eyes, and Lamour lips.

The Raiders appeared in their association's blue blazers and matching ties, both embroidered with their insignia: soaring Mitchells, streams of chevrons, crests of Mercury's cap, Navajo thunderbirds, roaring tigers, kicking donkeys, and the motto, *Toujours au Danger*. Accompanied by wives, children, grandchildren, and the widows of fallen comrades, the men walked through the dining mob exactly the way any honest-to-God American celebrity appears at a charity event, in a parade-and-wave. Even as octogenarians most of the boys remain sharp as steak knives, and it's regrettable that the public at these events never gets to experience how intelligent, charming, and funny so many of these men really are. The guys have terrific stories to tell that few have heard, and soon enough those stories will never be told. Still the parade marches on.

Every year more than a few Raiders announce that this reunion will be their last. Even with all the drawbacks, though, it's hard to keep from coming. These men and women have now known one another, through times flush and tragic, through weddings, births, and deaths, for sixty years. Like any group of such size, factions, rivalries, and feuds rise and fade with time—but who alive wouldn't wish for exactly what the Raiders have? After one's family, isn't a band of brothers and sisters, friends forever no matter what, pretty much the best life has to offer?

CODA

THE B-25 MITCHELL would become the Allies' most popular medium-range, twin-engine bomber, going through a dozen generations, used for low-level, torpedo, and long-range attacks, and selling almost ten thousand units to twenty air forces around the world.

Retired real-estate appraiser Richard Kurilchyk has made it his life mission to track down the Mitchell left behind in Russia by Ski York, Bob Emmens, and their crew, while others are convinced that another Raider plane, in fine fettle, could be salvaged from its resting place in the South China Sea.

On July 28, 1945, one last B-25 made history. Lt. Col. William F. Smith, Jr., was flying a Billy from his home in Bedford, Massachusetts, to Newark, New Jersey, when a dense fog moved across the metropolitan region. The pilot became disoriented, and at 9:40 A.M. that Saturday, he smashed into the seventy-ninth floor of the Empire State Building. Historian John Tauranac: "The building shuddered, realigned itself, and settled. Probably instantly, although several witnesses said there seemed to be a moment's interval, came the explosion, and the top of the fog-shrouded Empire State Building was briefly seen in a bright orange glow. High-octane airplane fuel spewed out of the ruptured tanks and sprayed the building. . . . The heat was so intense that partition frames within offices disappeared, and the shattered glass from windows and lamp fixtures melted and fused into stalactites. . . . One engine, part of the fuselage, and a landing gear tore through the internal office walls, through two fire walls and across a stairway, through another office wall and out of the south wall of the building. . . ." Fourteen were killed and twenty-five injured.

NORTH AMERICAN AVIATION would eventually design and produce World War II's greatest fighter: the P-51 Mustang. In the 1950s the company would create the state-of-the art, rocket-powered X-15, which set the still-unbeaten altitude and world speed records (354,200 feet and Mach 6.7) for a winged flying machine. Today North American is part of Rockwell International, creator of the B-1 supersonic bomber. In 2001 Rockwell split itself into

Rockwell Automation and Rockwell Collins, the latter a manufacturer of communication and aviation electronics (or avionics).

EGLIN FIELD is today no longer a muddy, mosquito-infected palmetto swamp, but split between the Eglin Air Force Base and the Sarasota-Bradenton International Airport, while the LEXINGTON COUNTY [COLUMBIA] ARMY AIR BASE has become the Columbia Metropolitan Airport.

In 1969, the USS HORNET (CVS-12), daughter of the ship that carried the Raiders, recovered the Apollo 11 astronauts—the first men to walk on the moon. Hornet was designated a National Historic Landmark in 1998 and returned to the docks of Alameda, California, where she is berthed today as a floating museum.

In April 1997 the navy shut down the ALAMEDA NAVAL AIR STATION, ending a sixty-year lease. The yards now house Manex Entertainment, creator of special effects for such films as The Matrix.

The United States Navy reincarnated the USS ENTERPRISE on November 25, 1961, as the service's first nuclear-powered carrier. As of this writing she is on active duty in the northern Indian Ocean with 3,350 crewmen, 2,480 airmen, eight nuclear reactors, and eighty-five warplanes striking Afghanistan with two-thousand-pound laser-guided GBU-20 bombs.

In World War II, it took an average of five thousand UNITED STATES AIR FORCE bombs to demolish a target. By the Vietnam era that number would drop to five hundred, while the 1990–91 Gulf War's "smart bombs" would bring it down to ten. Soon enough it will only take one "brilliant bomb" to destroy a target, but according to the service's plans, the plane that lays such an egg will fly itself. Just as there are no more horses in the nation's cavalry, soon enough there will be no more pilots, copilots, navigators, bombardiers, or engineers/gunners in the USAF. In its Strategic Master Plan the service considers itself to be in a "transition from a cold-war garrison force to an expeditionary aerospace force" that will train and educate "21st century aerospace warriors." On August 24, 2001, President George Bush named Vietnam fighter pilot and former head of the Air Force Space Command, Gen. Richard Myers, as chairman of the Joint Chiefs of Staff.

On March 1, 1945, FRANKLIN D. ROOSEVELT took a seat while giving a speech to a joint session of Congress, explaining that it was fatiguing to carry ten pounds of steel on his legs—his first public mention of polio. Six weeks later, on April 12, he died of a cerebral hemorrhage at Warm Springs, Georgia, at the age of sixty-three. Though he did not survive to see the victories over Germany and Japan, Roosevelt had come into office at one of America's weakest moments. By the time of his death, FDR's leadership had transformed his country into the strongest nation in the world.

In 1938, when GEN. HAP ARNOLD became head of the Army Air Corps, he oversaw twenty thousand men and a few hundred planes, most of them so old they could be used only for training. By 1944 the United States Army Air Forces would number 2.4 million airmen and eighty thousand state-of-the-art craft. From 1943 to 1944, over a period of fourteen months, Hap suffered three heart attacks. After the war the general had two more, and the fifth, on January 15, 1950, killed him, but not before Hap got to see Congress pass the National Security Act on July 25, 1947, which created the Department of Defense, the Central Intelligence Agency, and the United States Air Force as a separate and independent service.

ADM. ERNEST KING resigned as COMINCH and CNO on December 15, 1945, to be replaced by Fleet Adm. Chester Nimitz. He died in 1956 at the age of seventy-eight.

In May 1943, King organized all of his antisubmarine units into the Tenth Fleet, with REAR ADM. FRANCIS "FROG" LOW as chief of staff. With the cooperation of the Royal Navy, this fleet would thoroughly scour the *Unterseeboote* from the entire Atlantic Ocean.

COL. JOHN E. "JACK" FITZGERALD, JR., the first pilot to launch a B-25 from an aircraft carrier and developer of the technique used by the Raiders from *Hornet,* would eventually be awarded three Distinguished Flying Crosses, two Legions of Merit, and eight Air Medals and would end his Air Force career as vice commander of Wheeler AFB on Oahu.

At a Pentagon ceremony on May 15, 1995, Navy Secretary John Dalton presented the surviving members of TASK FORCE 16 with navy citations for their bravery in carrying the Doolittle Raiders.

In the final days of 1945, Harry Truman sent GEN. GEORGE MARSHALL to China to try to settle the civil war between the Kuomintang and the Communists. The two sides refused to come to terms, and four years later the Communists would emerge victorious.

The European Recovery Program of 1947 became known as the Marshall Plan, and for it, he would receive the Nobel Peace Prize in 1953. Six years later the general died in Washington, D.C., at the age of seventy-nine.

When CHIANG KAI-SHEK refused to fight the Japanese, he lost the support of the Chinese people, along with every battle in the civil war with Mao Zedong. The Kuomintang eventually fled to Taiwan in 1949 to establish the Republic of China, and after thirty years and four billion dollars in foreign aid, the United States withdrew diplomatic ties with the republic, and Taiwan's UN seat was given to the mainland. In 1975 Chiang passed away at the age of eighty-eight.

Until 1967, the name of MADAME CHIANG KAI-SHEK regularly appeared as one of the world's ten most admired women in American polls. Today, she is 105 years old and lives in New York City.

CHUNGKING (now transliterated Chongqing) has become the world's largest metropolitan area, with a population of seventeen million.

On May 30, 1976, FUCHIDA MITSUO died of complications from diabetes at the age of seventy-three. Attending his funeral was Reverend Jacob De-Shazer.

Before he died this great Japanese hero of World War II had become an American citizen, and today his children and grandchildren live in the United States; his son, Joe, is an architect in New York City.

In 1959, Gen. Paul Tibbets, who'd piloted *Enola Gay*, which dropped the atomic bomb on Hiroshima, was giving a tour of U.S. Air Force equipment to a group of visiting Japanese. One of them was Fuchida, who introduced himself and then told Tibbets: "You did the right thing. You know the Japanese attitude at that time, how fanatic they were, they'd die for the Emperor. . . . Every man, woman, and child would have resisted that invasion with sticks and stones if necessary. . . . Can you imagine what a slaughter it would be to invade Japan? It would have been terrible. The Japanese people know more about that than the American public will ever know."

ADM. MARC ANDREW "PETE" MITSCHER was promoted to commander, Fast Carrier Task Force 58 in 1944, and participated in every major naval engagement of the Pacific war: the Marshall Islands, Leyte Gulf, Iwo Jima, Okinawa, and the Marianas Turkey Shoot. He turned down an offer of the post of chief of naval operations to command instead the Eighth Fleet and then become commander in chief, Atlantic Fleet, the position he held when a heart attack killed him in 1947 at the age of sixty.

Two destroyers have subsequently been named for him, and USS *Mitscher* (DDG 57) sails today from her home port of Norfolk, Virginia.

FLEET ADM. WILLIAM FREDERICK "BILL" HALSEY, JR., left the navy in 1946 to serve on the board of directors of ITT. He died in 1959 at the age of seventy-six.

After training the Doolittle Raiders in aircraft carrier launches, REAR ADM. HANK MILLER served as Pacific theater and Vietnam War commander for air wings aboard *Princeton, Ranger, Coral Sea,* and *Hancock,* retiring from the service in 1971.

Chester Nimitz recommended JOSEPH J. ROCHEFORT for the Distinguished Service Medal for his work in decrypting Japanese codes. Navy intelligence brass in Washington, however, had fought with Rochefort constantly, and kept it from the Hypo leader's chest. On October 8, 1985, Rochefort was awarded his medal posthumously.

MIDWAY is now a National Wildlife Refuge administered by the U.S. Fish and Wildlife Service. Since the service refuses to allow fishing or hunting anywhere near the atoll, it has become, like the Galápagos, a haven for rare wildlife (including spinner dolphins, Hawaiian monk seals, and green turtles) that shows no fear of human beings. Up to one hundred visitors are allowed at a time, and accommodations are in renovated naval officer quarters. To arrange for your Midway vacation, call (808) 245-4718 or (888) 643-9291.

In the 1950s members of the FLYING TIGERS would start the Hell's Angels motorcycle club. In 1991 the U.S. Army granted them veterans' status.

CLARK AIR BASE, MacArthur's Army Air Corps stronghold in the Philippines, is now an America Online member service center employing nine hundred Filipinos, who handle 90 percent of the six hundred thousand online questions AOL receives every month.

ASHKHABAD, Turkmenistan, last stop of the Soviet-interned Raiders, was entirely destroyed by an earthquake in 1948.

•

In the closing days of 1945, President Harry Truman would dismantle the OFFICE OF STRATEGIC SERVICES, replacing it with an almost identical operation (and including much of the staff, but not William Donovan) that would become known two years later as the Central Intelligence Agency.

The U.S. Department of Defense used the captured UNIT 731 Japanese biological warfare research in its own efforts. By 1969 the army had succeeded in engineering and stockpiling more than two million bombs and other types of munitions made from anthrax, tularemia, and the most deadly biotoxin of them all, botulinum (it takes five grams of botulinum to kill a million people). Three years later seventy-one nations jointly agreed to outlaw biological warfare, and President Richard Nixon ordered the weapons destroyed.

On October 30, 2000, as part of a defense appropriations bill, Congress requested that the president clear the names of Adm. Husband Kimmel and Gen. Walter Short for their responsibility in the attack on PEARL HARBOR. The bill stated that the two men "were not provided necessary and critical intelligence that would have alerted them to prepare for the attack," and requested the commander in chief posthumously to restore their wartime ranks. Sponsored by Senators Joe Biden and William Roth from Delaware, the measure is another effort by Kimmel's son, Edward, to clear his father's name, even though, as late as 1995, a Pentagon investigation (undertaken primarily through Edward Kimmel's efforts) had refused to do so, concluding: "the intelligence available to Admiral Kimmel and General Short was sufficient to justify a higher level of vigilance than they had chosen to maintain."

This bill is only the most recent manifestation of what has become a popular conspiracy theory—"the back door to war"—which posits that FDR, his advisers, the U.S. Army, the U.S. Navy, and a cast of thousands secretly colluded to instigate the attack on Pearl Harbor in order to provoke an outraged American public into fighting World War II. Most back-door conspiracy theorists believe Kimmel and Short to be scapegoats, deliberately kept in the dark by Washington so that they could do nothing to defend Hawaii. Comdr. Chihaya Masataka of the Japanese Imperial Navy put his finger on the key weakness of this theory: "Even if one admits . . . that President Roosevelt wanted to have Japan strike first, there would have been no need to have all the major ships of the U.S. Fleet sit idly in the harbor to be mercilessly destroyed and many killed."

The case has also been made that if Kimmel, Short, and Harold Stark took career hits for Pearl, Douglas MacArthur deserved similar treatment for his behavior in the Philippines, as did Ernest King for doing too little, too late against Operation Drumbeat. Otherwise "the back door to war" has been so repeatedly debunked that no serious historian gives it credence today, though it continues to retain a powerful hold on the public's imagination. Considering that December 7, 1941, is arguably the most investigated moment in American history, the theorists must defend their contentions against staggering piles of evidence produced, in turn, by civilians, the army, the navy, the executive branch, and Congress.

On January 24, 1942, the first investigation (the Roberts Commission) released its findings:

> The Commission examined 127 witnesses and received a large number of documents. All . . . who were thought to have knowledge of facts pertinent to the inquiry were summoned and examined under oath. . . . The oral evidence received amounts to 1887 typewritten pages, and the records and documents examined exceed 3000 printed pages in number. . . .
>
> The Commanding General, Hawaiian Department [Short], the Commander in Chief of the Fleet [Kimmel], and the Commandant 14th Naval District, their senior subordinate, and their principal staff officers, considered the possibility of air raids. Without exception they believed that the chances of such a raid while the Pacific Fleet was based upon Pearl Harbor were practically nil. . . . On November 27 each responsible commander was warned that hostilities were momentarily possible. The warnings indicated war, and war only. Both of these messages contained orders. The Commanding General was ordered to undertake such reconnaissance and other measures as he deemed necessary. The Commander in Chief of the Fleet was ordered to execute a defensive deployment in preparation for carrying out war tasks.
>
> Other significant messages followed on succeeding days. These emphasized the impending danger and the need for war readiness. In this situation, during a period of ten days preceding the Japanese attack, the responsible commanders held no conference directed to a discussion of the meaning of the warnings and orders sent them, and failed to collaborate and to coordinate defensive measures which should be taken pursuant to the orders received. . . . Had orders issued by the Chief of Staff and the Chief of Naval Operations on November 27, 1941, been complied with,

the aircraft warning system of the Army should have been operating; the distant reconnaissance of the Navy, and the inshore air patrol of the Army, should have been maintained; the anti-aircraft batteries of the Army and similar shore batteries of the Navy, as well as additional anti-aircraft artillery located on vessels of the fleet in Pearl Harbor, should have been manned and supplied with ammunition; and a high state of readiness of aircraft should have been in effect. None of these conditions was in fact inaugurated or maintained for the reason that the responsible commanders failed to consult and cooperate as to necessary action based upon the warnings and to adopt measures enjoined by the orders given them by the chiefs of the Army and Navy commands in Washington.

Follow-up investigations by the army and navy concluded that Kimmel and Short were responsible for errors of omission rather than commission, and declined to pursue courts-martial. In 1945 Congress organized the Joint Committee on the Investigation of the Pearl Harbor Attack, which found that the Army War Plans Division had not warned Hawaii to the fullest extent, but that there was no evidence to support charges that FDR, Hull, Stimson, or Knox "tricked, provoked, incited, cajoled, or coerced Japan into attacking this Nation."

Even sixty years later the memory of Pearl Harbor lingers over the halls of the Pentagon, with the deep and pervasive fear of unpreparedness that American military chiefs seem cursed to bear for the rest of time. Whether or not the separate armed forces and intelligence agencies have ever learned to work together fruitfully—the true lesson of Pearl Harbor and the Doolittle Raid— is still, six decades later, to be determined.

The faded white memorial hovering over the sunken USS *Arizona* and its bodies of 1,177 servicemen (including twenty-two sets of brothers), meanwhile, has become the most popular tourist attraction in all of Hawaii. A very large percentage of the tourists who daily come to visit and take pictures at Pearl Harbor are Japanese.

Any tourist visiting JAPAN today is almost guaranteed to encounter a very unusual group of young men. Dressed in ersatz military outfits and practicing marches in public parks, this cult (the *uyoku*) is also commonly heard roaring through the major cities in black armored buses, vans, and jeeps, festooned with flags and slogans and carrying loudspeakers connected to state-of-the-art, thousand-watt sound systems blasting nationalist hymns.

The *uyoku* is huge and powerful—estimated at more than a thousand units with more than a hundred thousand members—and has clear ties both to *yakuza* gangsters and to higher-ups in the nation's government and business circles. A group of fanatical race purists who target media companies with violence and demonstrations, the *uyoku* has attacked anyone trying to discuss publicly Japan's Pacific war history, or even anyone who doesn't believe in the emperor's divinity. In 1989 the *uyoku* tried to assassinate the mayor of Nagasaki after he publicly conceded that Emperor Hirohito had "some responsibility" for the events leading to World War II. After the mayor was shot in the back, not one politician came to his defense, and he was ousted from the Liberal Democratic Party.

One of the island nation's biggest recent bestsellers is Kobayashi Yoshinori's *On War,* a *manga* comic book that calls the Great East Asian War a force of liberation, dismisses as fiction the Rape of Nanking and the existence of the two hundred thousand "comfort women" sex slaves, and finally concludes: "There was justice in Japan's war! We must protect our grandfathers' legacy!" *On War* has sold almost one million copies.

At the very center of Tokyo, surrounded by parkland, stands the low-slung Temple of Heaven, home of the emperor, and just up the street on a small hill overlooking the palace can be found a very different kind of building. Overseen by dozens of busy Shinto priests and virgins dressed in stark red skirts and billowing white blouses, its grounds dotted by the brilliant white of its specially bred doves, Yasukuni Jinja (the Empire at Peace Shrine) is perhaps the most controversial site in all Japan. Fronted by two rows of ginkgo and cherry trees, the wooden entryway is draped in purple curtains marked in the facet emblem of the Chrysanthemum Throne—the emblem for which the two million soldier-gods memorialized there sacrificed their lives. Many Japanese believe that the world's most beautiful *sakura* (cherry blossoms, whose brief and vivid blooms are symbols of fallen warriors) are found there. Supplicants appear before the cedar altar and summon the deities of departed soldiers by clapping their hands. In 1978 the urn of Tojo's ashes, along with the remains of other Pacific war leaders hanged as war criminals, were clandestinely brought to Yasukuni to be housed in its inner sanctum.

Next door to the shrine stands the Hall for Communing with Noble Souls, a museum surveying the country's entire history of warfare, concluding with the Great East Asian War. Inside are swords, maps, medals, an *Oka kamikaze* cherry blossom attack glider, memorabilia of Admiral Yamamoto, a carrier minibomber, a light tank, field guns, antiaircraft guns, naval shells, and the statue of a young, vigorous airman whose inscription reads "To the Brave Men Who Made the Special Attacks" (meaning the six thousand kamikaze suicide pilots who killed over five thousand U.S. Navy men in the battles for Okinawa). As they boarded their one-way flights, the kamikazes promised each other to meet again, when the cherry trees bloomed at Yasukuni.

EMPEROR HIROHITO would remain on the Chrysanthemum Throne for sixty-three years, the longest reign in all of Japanese history, until his death in 1989.

Of the eighty men who dedicated their lives to this mission, twenty-one are alive today.

In 1993, JAMES HAROLD DOOLITTLE's own silver Raider cup was turned over. The daredevil-may-care flying ace, known for his risky, outrageous stunts, a man who called himself "a crackpot pilot," had lived to the ripe old age of ninety-six, passing away at his son John's beautiful home in Pebble Beach, California. Just before he died, even after all his achievements and acclaim, the general told a reporter, "There has never been a time when I've been completely satisfied with myself." In 1989 he was awarded the Presidential Medal of Freedom.

General Doolittle's son John himself would serve in the air force, retiring as a colonel, while grandson James H. Doolittle III would become vice commander of the Air Force Flight Test Center at Edwards AFB in California. The general's private papers were bequeathed to the University of Texas at Dallas to serve as the keystone for the James H. Doolittle Military Aviation Library.

Jimmy and his wife, Joe (who died in 1988 after the couple had celebrated their seventy-first wedding anniversary), are buried side by side in Section 7-A of Arlington National Cemetery.

After leaving the service in 1946, Flight Officer ROBERT C. BOURGEOIS returned to his native Louisiana, and for many years ran a pest-control business. He and his wife, Betty, remained in their home state after they retired, and Bob died in November 2001.

After the raid, COL. WILLIAM BOWER served for three years out of England with the Eighth Air Force, retiring to Colorado with his wife, Lorraine.

LT. COL. CLAYTON CAMPBELL served with China-Burma-India before returning to his native Idaho with his wife, Mary.

•

LT. COL. HORACE "SALLY" CROUCH was in the reserves when Korea brought him back to serve in the Strategic Air Command. He left the service to come home to Columbia, South Carolina, where he taught high school math for nineteen years. Sally became such close friends with fellow Raider Herb that he named his daughter Macia.

When MGM approached the War Department for a stunt pilot on the picture *A Guy Named Joe,* the army recommended COL. DEAN DAVENPORT. During the filming at Columbia AFB, South Carolina, he met Mary—to whom he'd be married for the next fifty-seven years. When MGM produced *Thirty Seconds over Tokyo,* the department again sent him in, as technical adviser. In the 1950s and '60s, he became a jet fighter pilot in the F-84, 86, 94, 101, 102, 106, and his "true love," the 100. He finished his military career as head of Semi-Automatic Ground Environment at Hancock Field, part of NORAD (North American Air Defense Command), which monitored enemy planes and missiles over the entire mid-Atlantic region, and as wing commander of Tyndall Air Defense Wing.

In 1978 Florence and STAFF SGT. JACOB DESHAZER retired from missionary service and returned to Oregon. More than thirty million copies (in more than twenty languages) of "I Was a Prisoner of Japan" have been distributed around the world.

In 1961, Justine and ROBERT EMMENS returned to their hometown of Medford, Oregon, known for its vast pear orchards. In 1992 Bob died of cancer at the age of seventy-seven.

After the war ROSS GREENING put together an exhibit of arts and crafts made by Nazi-held POWs, which traveled to seventeen American cities. He held various air force positions as a fighter pilot, in the Pentagon, and as air attaché in Australia and New Zealand.

Before his untimely death on March 29, 1957, as a result of an infection he acquired during his two years as a POW, Ross Greening recorded his memoirs on Dictaphone cylinders. His widow, Dot, spent a year transcribing them, and the next four decades trying to get them published. In 2001 Ross Greening's memoirs were released by Washington State University Press under the title *Not As Briefed.*

•

DICK HAMADA: "After the war, the CIA requested my services, but my wife, Irene, and I were expecting our first child, so I declined the offer. I worked for the Federal Civil Service at Hickam AFB and Pearl Harbor naval shipyard as supervisor-planner-estimator, Electronics and Fire Control.

"Today I'm a retired grandfather still living in Honolulu, and one of the great highlights of my life was when I was invited to the fifty-ninth Doolittle Raiders' Reunion. There they were—Jacob DeShazer, Bob Hite, and Chase Nielsen—and we saw each other again for the first time in fifty-six years."

After the war, MAJ. NOLAN HERNDON moved to South Carolina with his wife, Julia, to raise cattle and distribute groceries wholesale.

After recovering from his ordeal as a POW, LT. COL. ROBERT HITE retired from the USAF in 1955 to operate hotels in Camden, Arkansas, and Enid, Oklahoma, with his wife, Portia. After many decades together, Portia died, and Bobby was alone. He kept coming to the Raider reunions, however, and it was at one of those events that he would fall in love all over again, with the widow of Foggy, Trav Hoover's mission copilot. Dottie Fitzhugh would return those feelings, and today they are husband and wife.

BERT JORDAN crew-chiefed on the Berlin airlift, worked for R&D command at Alamogordo, and ended up at Da Nang, where he put in for retirement at the age of fifty-one.

LT. COL. FRANK KAPPELER flew fifty-three combat missions in Martin Marauders and B-26s out of England, France, and Belgium, as well as twenty-six more in B-29s out of Japan for the Korean War, retiring from the service in 1966. He spent a few years driving a school bus before getting certified in real estate, and became a broker for the next eighteen years. He and his wife, Betty, live today in Northern California.

After the war, DICK KNOBLOCH was accepted into an exchange program and attended England's RAF Flying College. During the Korean War, he set up Ninth Air Force bases with matériel, and in the 1950s, became air attaché in Italy under Ambassador Clare Boothe Luce, an assignment arranged through Ski York. He finished his career with jobs at the Pentagon and Randolph and Andrews AFBs, "where the president's plane flies out of, and where most of the foreign dignitaries visiting D.C. come in and leave from. After serving thirty years in the air force and making it to brigadier general, I became a VP with United Technologies [owner of Sikorsky, Norden, and Otis Elevator, among others], served on the board of Barclays Bank, was a trustee of the College of Aeronautics, president of the Wings Club, and chairman of the Doolittle Tokyo Raiders Group for about fifteen years."

One day Brigadier General Knobloch was piloting a C-47 from the Pentagon to Colorado Springs when he mentioned to his copilot that he'd like to drop by and have a look at "our cups." Dick took the officer to the Air Force Academy Museum and, in front of the display, explained the Raider silver chalices, and the significance of the upturned cups for those who were gone.

The copilot, Col. Carroll V. Glines, was so moved by this story that, when he retired from the service to begin a career as an author, five of his more than thirty books would cover the Doolittle story. For recording their memories, the airmen made him an honorary Raider and their official historian.

"Rosemary and I are still together—fifty-eight years later—and still in love," Dick wrote, shortly before he passed away on August 13, 2001.

TUNG-SHENG LIU: "I retired in 1978. My wife and I had three children born in the U.S., with one left in China. In the 1980s I was able to get our oldest son and family also to come to America, so now we are pretty much all together. I won't be able to go to the Raiders' Reunion this time, because I'm recuperating from a hospital stay. I had to have a heart valve replaced. With four kids and the grandchildren, I stay pretty busy!"

The air force sent LT. COL. EDGAR "MAC" MCELROY from China-Burma-India to the Marianas, England, Germany, and Laos before his service retirement in 1962. He and his wife, Agnes, live in Texas.

After retiring from the air force in 1962, LT. COL. CHASE JAY NIELSEN worked as an engineer in missile production, eventually moving back to his home state of Utah. His wife, Phyllis, made her living as a landscape designer, and her own retirement has meant that their home has one of the most beautiful gardens in the state.

After many years as an engineer with Motorola, CAPT. CHUCK OZUK retired with his wife, Georgian, to Air Force Village in San Antonio.

After the raid COL. HENRY "HANK" POTTER took stateside assignments in Michigan, Washington, Florida, and California before serving in Germany during the 1950s and then retiring to Texas. Hank died on May 26, 2002.

•

LT. COL. EDWARD JOSEPH SAYLOR held posts in Iowa, Labrador, and England before leaving the service to move to Washington State with his wife, Lorraine.

After serving in China-Burma-India, Europe, and the Mediterranean, MAJ. HOWARD "SESS" SESSLER went back to school, getting his civil engineering degree from the University of Southern California, and becoming president of a construction firm, retiring with his wife, Anna Bell, to the San Fernando Valley.

After escaping from Russia, SKI YORK was assigned to Italy's Foggia Plain, where he ran thirty-one B-17 missions into Ploesti, Hungary, Austria, Bulgaria, and southern Germany. In 1945 he was sent to Warsaw, Poland, and Copenhagen, Denmark, as air attaché, returning to the States to be commandant of the Air Force Officer Candidate School; chief of staff of the Attaché Branch of the Pentagon; and chief of staff of the USAF Security Service in San Antonio. He retired from the service in 1966 to become city manager of Olmos Park, a San Diego suburb, and died in August 1984. His widow, M. E., continues to be a notable presence at every Raider get-together.

MAJ. THOMAS GRIFFIN: "After the raid, five of us reported to a B-26 Group starting in Harding Field, Louisiana, in July '42. By July '43 two of the five had been killed and the other three were in Nazi prison camps, including myself. . . .

"I believe all the Raiders thank their lucky stars that they were at the right place at the right time to be chosen for this mission. You might say it was our 'Saint Crispin's Day,' and it certainly changed all our lives."

Tom and his wife, Esther, live in Ohio.

BRIG. GEN. EVERETT "BRICK" HOLSTROM: "After the war, I continued on in the service for a total of thirty years, and my proudest moment besides the raid was getting the Convair B-58, our first supersonic bomb wing, combat ready in the SAC inventory. In retirement, my wife, Hattie, and I were lucky to have enough assets to do a lot of traveling. We went back to Europe about fifteen times, and traveled over South America and the Far East, including China. I think the 'been there, done that' thing pretty well describes us."

On December 1, 2000, Brick passed away at the age of eighty-four.

•

LT. COL. DICK COLE: "After Chungking, I was one of the fourteen sent to another assignment in Asia, so I didn't get back home for over a year. Then from October of '43 to July of '44, I returned to China-Burma-India with the First Air Commando Group, and finished out the war as a test pilot with the Douglas Aircraft Plant. I stayed in the service a total of twenty-six years, and when I got out, I raised citrus and farmed for another fourteen. I raised five kids and built five houses.

"I was a 'bit player' who did what was expected of him for his country in its time of need. The war years were nothing compared to having one son, an F-15 pilot, survive a midair collision, and another survive a severe attack of spinal meningitis." Dick and his wife, Martha, live in Texas.

COL. TRAVIS HOOVER: "After the war was over I was sent to be executive officer for the operation in Okinawa. It was pretty quiet. Primarily rather than being in the action part it was support and logistics, making sure you took care of everyone in the home base, being ready and raring to go. I got to fly the airplanes, but didn't get tied up in any of the missions because I was too busy running the base. I came back to the States after that and went to the Armed Forces Staff College, then got assigned for a while in Turkey, then back to the States to be commander of the pilot training group in Lubbock, and then commander of the technical training school at Kessler AFB. These, too, were interesting assignments, but kind of quiet compared to the places I'd been.

"In '69, I retired from the service, and got together with some friends to build apartments in San Antonio. I'd been buying acres of citrus fruit in the Rio Grande Valley, and eventually had enough to be a fruit farmer. Eventually I had to stop that to take care of my wife, who had Parkinson's.

"When my wife realized she was terminally ill, she decided she wanted to spend the last days with her grandchildren. So I said if that's what you want, that's what you'll get, we'll sell the house tomorrow. She had about three good years with the grandkids after we moved from San Antonio to Joplin, Missouri, before she passed on.

"I like it here in Joplin, and I still have some grandkids—my whole family is here. Including my dachshund. He's a professional beggar, fully retired . . . he's the pro in the family!"

LT. COL. HARRY McCOOL: "I got 'bit by the education bug' and tired of teaching, so I applied for graduate training. I was selected to go to the Institute of Technology at Wright-Patterson, a two-year course, and just when I graduated in '49, the cold war was getting up to a pretty high tempo. General

Curtis LeMay was having a hard time getting enough crews to man the Strategic Air Command, so he put out a freeze, air force–wide, transferring all unassigned bombardiers and navigators to the SAC. I then spent the next twelve years on assignment with SAC, the CIA, and the Joint Chiefs of Staff in Washington. When I officially retired from the service in 1966, I was offered a job at Pearl Harbor, working for the navy as a civilian in Logistic Planning—creating a computer-based plan to control the bits and pieces from the factory to the base to the carrier or the other ships.

"Working for the navy was a breeze. When the Vietnamese War cropped up, they didn't have time to finish up this fine-tuned logistics program, so they went back to just brute effort. They just loaded up everything they thought they might need onto transport ships, hauled them out there, and anchored them offshore, and when you needed something, why, you pulled up to one of these ships with your shopping list and got what you needed. I was involved in that until '82 or 3, when I retired the second time. Since we loved Hawaii, I became a beachcomber, living as a 'lotus eater' while traveling the South Pacific, the United States, and Europe.

"One thing I'll never forget from that time was when *Tora! Tora! Tora!* was filmed. We lived in a little home on one of the mountains that looked out over Pearl Harbor. It was real eerie to sit up over there and watch those blasted planes fly by our house in formation and go down and make these runs on these barges that were simulating Battleship Row.

"In '88 we found out that I was developing skin cancers from spending so much time on the beach, and my wife's friends started losing their husbands to heart attack, stroke, and cancer, and we decided that Hawaii was a wonderful place to be as long as you were hale and hearty, but when you became handicapped, it was a prison. So we started looking for a place that we would operate out of in the States, and they had started building this Air Force Retirement Village here in San Antonio, so after twenty years in Hawaii we came back here. And that's where we are today, with a number of the other Tokyo Raiders. As career officers, we didn't have any roots. No one wanted, really, to go back to their childhood home. You come here and you're taken care of—if you want to go on a trip, you lock the front door and put a hold on your mail at the front desk, and take off. And then, San Antonio is an air force service town, with four or five golf courses, three or four clubs, and four or five bases, terrific medical care. It is a fine place for a retired military man to live."

SECOND LT. BILL BIRCH: "In Los Angeles they gave me a decoration ceremony for my Distinguished Flying Cross, and I joined in some War

Bond–selling drives. Afterwards I reported to Barksdale Field, applied to flight training, was accepted as a cadet and sent for preflight at San Antonio, primary at Sweetwater, basic at Dennison, and advanced at Lubbock, finally graduating in the summer of '43. Assigned to a B-24 group, we right away had an accident, so I spent almost two years in a hospital. The war ended before I could get to flying, so I went back to civilian life.

"After a number of years in the machinist trade, I returned to flying in the '60s by getting a commercial and an instructor's license in rotorcraft. Many of my students went on to fly for the air force during the Vietnam War. Two others were astronauts, one being Jack Swigert, who served on the Apollo 13 moon flight.

"On board the *Hornet* I made the acquaintance of a chief aviation machinist's mate, Charles Granvill Meserve. When I returned to Laguna Beach after leaving the air force, I found out that his sister, Barbara, lived there. I arranged to say hello . . . and it was love at first sight. We were married in Santa Ana on the fourteenth day of July 1947, and have been together ever since.

"I consider the Doolittle Raid the second most important event of my life. The most important was my marriage, fifty-three years ago, and it will ever be so. Although many adverse circumstances have befallen Barbara and me over the past half-century, I would not trade one moment of our shared life and love for all the treasures of the world.

"My life today revolves around my wife, who suffers from heart problems and diabetes, and has begun to lose her short-term memory. This, we have been told, is the onset of Alzheimer's. I am her sole caregiver."

MAJ. GEN. DAVID M. "DAVEY" JONES: "In 1964 I got orders to NASA headquarters in D.C., when they were just exploding. The Gemini Project was just coming in, Apollo was in its genesis, and NASA was expanding rapidly. I was deputy associate administrator for [the] Manned Space Flight Program. Damned if I know what that meant, but I had a good parking place! Then things got real interesting, by golly. In 1964 I got orders to Cape Canaveral, the AF test range in Florida where the Kennedy Space Center is located.

"On launch, the Apollo spacecraft circled the Earth, and then they were sent into translunar trajectory over the Indian Ocean. At that point there was no radar coverage and instrument communication, so the air force had eight Boeing 707s called ARIA [advanced research and instrumented aircraft] with an eight-foot radar dish in the nose—a great big bulbous nose—for the communications. They would fly out of Australia, the West Coast, Florida, Africa, and sometimes South America, whatever the orbit might be. We positioned airplanes where the spacecraft would go into lunar trajectory, and the aircraft would then pass all the information on the burn to Houston.

"I'd go to Houston for the recovery. When the astronauts came home for reentry into the Pacific, they'd enter a blackout period where there is no communications at all, and again we'd put an airplane under the position where they'd come out of the blackout. So our plane was the first one to hear, not only the voices, but the instrumentation from the astronauts reporting on the conditions. Pretty damn interesting, and that was my last assignment.

"At the time of the raid on Tokyo, and after it was over, none of us paid any attention to it. We were lucky to get home, we all went back to war, and we never thought a thing about it. As the years go by we are still amazed at the interest people have. But of course now, we're getting kind of scarce."

COL. JAMES "HERB" MACIA: "I returned to Tucson and became a reserve officer in 1946. Recalled in 1951, I attended a specialized school and went to Europe, where there was a large buildup. I served as staff planning officer, assigned to the Air Force's European command. Promoted to colonel, I became involved with the Lockheed U-2 and early satellite reconnaissance programs. After serving with the Strategic Air Command as director of intelligence, Second Air Force, I was assigned to the Air Force Security Service. I completed my military career as deputy chief of staff, operations; commander of the European Security Region; and chief of staff. I was the last Doolittle Raider to remain on active duty, retiring in 1973."

Herb "retired" by working into his seventies as the business manager at Assumption Seminary in San Antonio. After the death of his wife, Mary Alice, Herb moved to Arlington, Virginia.

ELLEN LAWSON: "In the last years of his life, TED was in a great deal of pain and required pain-killing medication, but his mind was still as bright as ever. He was limited in what he could do, though, because every time he moved he was in pain. He thought amputees just had to suffer but in fact it turned out he'd broken his back, which for many years we didn't know. He had one operation, which worked fine for about five years, but then we were flying with these friends down into Mexico, and sitting too long and all that, and it started in again. He had another back operation by a navy doctor, and that operation was not a success. He required a lot of transfusions, and never regained his health.

"After four years at Lake Arrowhead, we moved up to Northern California, where it was closer to the hunting and fishing. As a family we loved to go duck hunting, and Ted was able to get in some flying. Here we get the snow all around us.

"On January 19, 1992, Ted had a pulmonary aneurysm and died. He was interred at Chico Cemetery Mausoleum in Chico, California.

"Today, I still live on our acre of walnut trees. And I just finished the harvest: It went well, in spite of the winds and the rain. All I can think is: Finished!"

ACKNOWLEDGMENTS

I'd like to humbly thank Rick Kot, an editor who went far beyond the call of professional duty in kicking rot; Jennifer Rudolph Walsh, my tank-outside, heart-of-platinum inside agent of dreams; Mark Siegel for his prompt and accurate transcription services; and Elisa Petrini and John McFarland for their editorial acumen.

I am in great debt, for their heroic assistance in research, to the remarkable staff of the greatest library in the world, the New York Public; Raymond Teichman and Robert Parks, archivists, the Franklin D. Roosevelt Library, Hyde Park, New York; Kate Flaherty, Still Picture Division, National Archives and Records Administration, College Park, Maryland; Rebecca Rice and Jim Holberg, the Filson Club Historical Society, Louisville, Kentucky; and Les Stehmer and Edwin Lazo of Automated Data Solutions for their wizardry in microfiche.

Working on this book taught me many things, including the fact that the United States Air Force produces the greatest guys and gals in the world. I cannot praise enough Yvonne Kinkaid, U.S. Office of Air Force History, Bolling Air Force Base, Washington, D.C.; Lynn Gamma, archivist of the Air Force, Joseph D. Caver, archivist, and Essie Roberts, archive technician, Air Force Historical Research Agency, Maxwell Air Force Base, Alabama; and for last-minute aid in covert research, Tony Strotman, M.Sgt., USAF (Ret.).

My biggest salute has to go to the surviving men and women—as generous in their eighties as they were brave in their twenties—of this story. Though many of them don't like being called heroes, well, dammit, in my book, you are:

William L. Birch
Robert C. Bourgeois
William M. Bower
Clayton J. Campbell
Richard E. Cole
Mary Davenport and Julie Fierman
Jacob D. DeShazer

Justine Emmens
Thomas C. Griffin
Dick Hamada
George Hammond
Nolan and Julia Herndon
Everett W. Holstrom
Travis Hoover
Joseph Jackson
David M. Jones
Frank and Betty Kappeler
Richard and Rosemary Knobloch
Ellen Lawson
Tung-Sheng Liu
Harry C. McCool
Chase J. Nielsen
Henry A. Potter
Hilda Wildner
M. E. York

HISTORY RUNS AWAY . . .

page

xii   "**Higgins was the man who won the war for us**" R. W. Apple, Jr., "Flashin' Those Dreamy Eyes Way Down Yonder," *New York Times,* November 24, 2000.

xiii **Twelve hundred World War II vets are dying every day** Tina Kelley citing Department of Veterans Affairs statistics in "Amid the Relics of Combat, Veterans Recall Flights and Flak and Friends," *New York Times,* December 3, 2000; and Irvin Molotsky, "Panel Backs World War II Memorial on Mall in Washington," *New York Times,* July 21, 2000. The VA believes that over five million American WWII vets are alive as of December 2000.

VOLUNTEERS

page

3   **Though they were Army Air Corps men** Though the United States Army Air Corps officially became the United States Army Air Forces on June 20, 1941, it took more than a year before the term AAF would reach general usage, perhaps because the service continued to refer to its subordinate organization that trained men and supplied air-specific matériel as the AAC until July 2, 1942. Even in posters released after that date, Brigadier General Doolittle can be seen urging would-be recruits to join the Army Air Corps, and most servicemen considered themselves AAC for at least the first seven months of World War II. In part to honor their memories, I've followed that convention here, with AAC as the general name until July 2, 1942, and AAF as the official name throughout and thereafter.

3   **"stooging around, going from A to B"** author interview, request for anonymity.

3   **"It was Christmas Eve 1941"** *et. seq.* author interviews, Mr. Hammond, 2/21/01, and Mr. Holstrom, 11/26/00.

5   **The entire country was in fact already in a state of panic** David Fromkin, *In the Time of the Americans* (New York: Alfred A. Knopf, 1995); Mike Wright, *What They Didn't Teach You About World War II* (Novato, Calif.: Presidio Press, 1998); Robert Leckie, *Delivered from Evil: The Saga of World War II* (New York: Harper & Row, 1987).

6   **"We got the call to report to base"** Dr. James C. Hasdorff, "Interview of Colonel James H. Macia," United States Air Force Oral History Program, July 15–16, 1987, Air Force Historical Research Agency, Maxwell Air Force Base, Ala.; and Dr.

James C. Hasdorff, "Interview of Major General David M. Jones," United States Air Force Oral History Program, January 13–14, 1987, Air Force Historical Research Agency, Maxwell Air Force Base, Ala.

6   **The decade's first army recruits** Fromkin; Wright.

6   **"get out or get dead"** John C. McManus, *Deadly Sky: The American Combat Airman in World War II* (Novato, Calif.: Presidio Press, 2000), p. 44.

7   **Even the B-25s flown by the men of the Seventeenth Bomb Group** Norman L. Avery, *B-25 Mitchell: The Magnificent Medium* (St. Paul, Minn.: Phalanx Publishing Co., Ltd., 1992); Joe Baugher, "American Military Aircraft Encyclopedia," *Elevon: Aviation on the Internet,* http://www.csd.uwo.ca/~pettypi/elevon/baugher_us/b025i.html.

7   **"These planes had absolutely"** Tina Kelley citing AAF ball gunner Chick Berger.

7   **"Once you fired your guns"** Dr. James C. Hasdorff, "Interview of Chief Master Sergeant Bert M. Jordan," United States Air Force Oral History Program, June 15, 1988, Air Force Historical Research Agency, Maxwell Air Force Base, Ala.

7   **"The bottom turret was very complicated"** Lowell Thomas and Edward Jablonski, *Doolittle: A Biography* (New York: Doubleday, 1976), p. 163.

8   **"The B-25 was a really superior airplane"** Lt. Travis Hoover, "Personal Report," Chungking, China, May 15, 1942; and Capt. Ted W. Lawson, *Thirty Seconds over Tokyo* (New York: Random House and Cutchogue, N.Y.: Buccaneer Books, 1943), p. 7.

8   **"We took about fifteen airplanes to Minneapolis"** author interview, Mr. Jones, 11/21/00.

9   *Dangerous* **is a pretty bad word** author interview, Mr. Bourgeois, 10/17/00.

9   **"One day our ROTC group"** Dr. James C. Hasdorff, "Interview of Brig. Gen. Richard A. Knobloch," United States Air Force Oral History Program, July 13–14, 1987, Air Force Historical Research Agency, Maxwell Air Force Base, Ala.

10   **"One night I was on guard duty"** Hasdorff, Jordan.

10   **"A sergeant called me"** Dr. James C. Hasdorff, "Interview of Reverend Jacob D. DeShazer," United States Air Force Oral History Program, October 10, 1989, Air Force Historical Research Agency, Maxwell Air Force Base, Ala.

10   **had them transferred to Eglin Field** *et seq.* For further details of the Doolittle Raid, see Greg DeHart, writer and producer, Roger Mudd, narrator, *One Hour over Tokyo,* History Channel, May 26, 2001; Carroll V. Glines, *The Doolittle Raid* (New York: Orion Books, 1988), *Doolittle's Tokyo Raiders* (Princeton, N.J.: D. Van Nostrand Company, 1964), and *Four Came Home* (Missoula, Mont.: Pictorial Histories Publishing Co., 1981); James M. Merrill, *Target Tokyo: The Halsey-Doolittle Raid* (Chicago: Rand McNally & Co., 1964); Charles Messenger, producer, *True Action Adventures: Bolt from the Blue: The Doolittle Raid,* History Channel, April 18, 2001; Edward Oxford, "Against All Odds," *American History,* August 1997; and Duane Schultz, *The Doolittle Raid* (New York: St. Martin's Press, 1988).

10   **"The reason Eglin was chosen"** Dr. James C. Hasdorff, "Interview of Col. Edward J. York," United States Air Force Oral History Program, San Antonio,

Texas, July 23, 1984, Air Force Historical Research Agency, Maxwell Air Force Base, Ala.

10   "For secrecy's sake, we ate separately" author interview, Mr. Kappeler, 2/11/01.

11   "you won't need them where you're going" Lawson, p. 31.

11   "In the 25, if an enemy fighter comes up" Dr. James C. Hasdorff, "Interview of Lieutenant Colonel Horace E. Crouch," United States Air Force Oral History Program, April 1989, Air Force Historical Research Agency, Maxwell Air Force Base, Ala.

11   "I don't know whom they scared most" Lt. Col. Robert G. Emmens, *Guests of the Kremlin* (New York: Macmillan Company, 1949), p. 35.

11   "Special five-hundred-pound demolition bombs" Brig. Gen. James H. Doolittle, "Report of the Aerial Bombing of Japan, 5 June 1942," Air Force Historical Research Agency, Maxwell Air Force Base, Ala.

11   "We had Bendix turrets" Hasdorff, York.

12   The Norden bombsight was America's biggest secret weapon Don Sherman, "The Secret Weapon," *Air & Space,* March 1995, pp. 78–87; John H. Lienhard, "Norden's Bombsight," *Engines of Ingenuity,* University of Houston, http://www.uh.edu/engines/epi1004.htm.

13   In the computer's stead sat a cheap sliding gauge Col. C. Ross Greening, *Not As Briefed* (Pullman: Washington State University Press, 2001).

13   The four men loaded up into a Billy H. L. Miller, "Training the Doolittle Fliers," from *The Pacific War Remembered: An Oral History Collection,* J. T. Mason, Jr., ed. (Annapolis, Md.: Naval Institute Press, 1986).

14   "drop the landing flaps" Merrill, p. 28.

14   "At around four or five hundred feet" author interview, Mr. Holstrom, 11/26/00.

14   "You'd go to power and turn things loose" author interview, Mr. Jones, 11/21/00.

15   "In those days, we figured" Greening, *Not As Briefed,* p. 16.

15   "Some pilots were doing a lot of crazy things" Dr. James C. Hasdorff, "Interview of Capt. Charles J. Ozuk, Jr.," United States Air Force Oral History Program, July 1989, Air Force Historical Research Agency, Maxwell Air Force Base, Ala.

15   "We did low flying" Hasdorff, DeShazer.

16   "laid one of the *Duck*'s one-hundred-pound eggs" Lawson, p. 27.

16   "A lot of the turret's electrical connections" Hasdorff, Crouch.

16   "So much work had to be done on the turrets" Doolittle, "Report."

16   "A certain amount of training was devoted" Greening, *Not As Briefed.*

17   "Our planes were in the air" Lawson, p. 29.

17   "The record number of 'firsts' we were attempting" Greening, *Not As Briefed.*

17   "Most of the wives showed up" Hasdorff, Jones.

17   "After everybody was transferred out of Oregon to Columbia" author interview, Mrs. Lawson, 12/4/00.

18   "The biggest rumor I heard" author interview, Mr. Birch, 12/12/00.

18   "At night, back in barracks" Lawson, p. 23.

18   "The officers bunked in one giant room" author interview, Mr. Kappeler, 2/11/01.

19 "We were young" Kate Callen, United Press International, "Key WWII Mission Recalled; Doolittle's Raiders Reunite in Torrance," *Los Angeles Times,* April 18, 1987.

19 "I was fairly well convinced" Glines, *The Doolittle Raid,* p. 111, citing response to questionnaire, U.S. Office of Air Force History, undated reference.

20 As something of a joke Eric Larrabee, *Commander in Chief: Franklin Delano Roosevelt, His Lieutenants and Their War* (New York: Harper & Row, 1987), p. 222.

20 "Suddenly, in the air above me" Curtis LeMay, *Mission with LeMay* (Garden City, N.Y.: Doubleday, 1965), pp. 13–14.

20 "My mother tells me" Hasdorff, Knobloch.

20 "speed and accuracy of perception" McManus, p. 239.

20 "learning how to handle a basic airplane" McManus, p. 239.

21 "I had one little girl that used to come out" Hasdorff, Knobloch.

21 "In 1938 I was working at a little library" author interview, Mrs. Lawson, 12/4/00.

21 "I was chucking a thirty-six-dollar-a-week job" Lawson, p. 5.

22 "Batavia is a very small town" Hasdorff, York.

23 "I started out in horses" author interview, Mr. Jones, 11/21/00.

24 "I grew up outside Beaver, Oklahoma" author interview, Mr. McCool, 10/21/00.

24 "When I got through high school in 1931" Hasdorff, DeShazer.

25 "My responsibility was to see" author interview, Mr. Birch, 12/12/00.

26 "Today we're in a new level of civilization" Hasdorff, Crouch.

26 "The feeling that we would never be accepted" Hasdorff, Macia.

26 "You're flying with a crew" Kelley.

26 "These men hung together" McManus, p. 360.

26 "We were whipped into shape" Schultz, p. 54, citing response to questionnaire, U.S. Office of Air Force History, October 27, 1971.

27 "I was sent on down to Miami" author interview, Mr. Hammond, 2/21/01.

27 With their six tubes shooting a mix *et seq.* For the full details of the Nazi U-boat attack on the North American coastline, see Michael Gannon, *Operation Drumbeat* (New York: HarperCollins, 1990).

28 "I cannot describe the feeling with words" Gannon, p. 231, citing Reinhard Hardegen, *"Auf Gefechtsstationen!" U-Boote im Einsatz gegen England und Amerika* (Leipzig: Boreas-Verlag, 1943).

29 "All the vacationers had seen" cited by David M. Kennedy in "Victory at Sea," *Atlantic Monthly,* March 1999.

29 On February 23 at ten o'clock eastern time Doris Kearns Goodwin, *No Ordinary Time* (New York: Simon & Schuster, 1994), p. 319.

29 "drivers had pulled over" Saul Bellow, *It All Adds Up* (New York: Viking, 1994), pp. 28–29.

30 "My fellow Americans" Franklin D. Roosevelt, "Address of the President Broadcast over a Nationwide and Worldwide Radio Hookup on the Occasion of the 210th Anniversary of George Washington's Birthday, February 23, 1942 at 10.00 P.M., E.W.T.," Franklin Delano Roosevelt Library, Hyde Park, N.Y.

"THE MAN WHO CAN NEVER STAND STILL"

page

32   "We're in for something *really* big" Schultz, p. 58.

32   "Of course he was a legend" Hasdorff, Macia.

32   "It didn't take but two minutes" Hasdorff, Jones.

32   "My name's Doolittle" citing Merrill, p. 27; Schultz, p. 58; and Elizabeth Mullener, "30 Seconds over Tokyo," *New Orleans Times-Picayune*, April 18, 2000.

33   "Within five minutes, we were his" Schultz, p. 61.

33   Jimmy Doolittle was arguably the most dynamic For a more in-depth look at the life of this amazing figure, see *Biography: Jimmy Doolittle: King of the Sky*, Arts & Entertainment Television Networks, 1996; Lt. Col. Sue Baker (AFMC Public Affairs Individual Mobilization Augmentee), "Remembering Granddad Doolittle," *AFMC Public Affairs*, February 1998; Lieutenant Colonel Burch, Major Fogelman, and Captain Tate, "Interview: Gen. James H. Doolittle," United States Air Force Oral History Program, September 26, 1971; Gen. James H. "Jimmy" Doolittle with Carroll V. Glines, *I Could Never Be So Lucky Again* (New York: Bantam, 1991); Carroll V. Glines, *Jimmy Doolittle: Daredevil Aviator and Scientist* (New York: Macmillan, 1972); Mac Laddon, "Interview with Lt. General Doolittle," *Reuben Fleet*, San Diego, August 14, 1970; Kenneth W. Leish, "The Reminiscences of James Harold Doolittle," Aviation Project Collection, Columbia University Oral History Research Office, 1960; Quentin Reynolds, *The Amazing Mr. Doolittle* (New York: Appleton-Century-Crofts, 1953); Lowell Thomas and Edward Jablonski, *Doolittle: A Biography* (New York: Doubleday, 1976); and William R. Wilson, "Jimmy Doolittle Reminisces," *American History*, July/August 1997.

34   "We were just three" Doolittle, *I Could Never*, p. 15.

35   "At the age of five" Doolittle, *I Could Never*, p. 21.

35   "We had many dogs running loose in town" Doolittle, *I Could Never*, p. 23.

35   "In the winter of 1909–1910" Burch, Fogelman, and Tate.

36   "Joe was a nice little girl" Wilson.

37   "I tried to think of any advantages" Wilson.

37   Even those with broad piloting experience today For details on the remarkable history of aviation, see Tom Crouch, "The Thrill of Invention," *Air & Space*, April/May 1998; Heiner Emde, illustrated by Carlo Demand, *Conquerors of the Air* (New York: Viking Press, 1968); Stephen Ives, producer and director, "Lindbergh," *The American Experience*, WGBH-Boston, 1999; Donald S. Lopez, *Aviation: A Smithsonian Guide* (New York: Macmillan, 1995); Isaac Mizrahi, producer, *Chasing the Sun*, KCET (Community Television of Southern California), July 2, 2001; and Robert Wohl, "Aviation's Belle Époque," *Air & Space*, April/May 1996.

37   "held onto each other's hand[s]" Lopez, citing a Kitty Hawk lifeguard.

38   "They done it!" Lopez.

38   "Many thought air mail just next to suicide" airmail pilot Dean Smith, cited in Mizrahi.

39 "When you're up there, you're God" cited in Ives.

39 "like a sex maniac in a whorehouse" Lauren Kessler, *The Happy Bottom Riding Club: The Life and Times of Pancho Barnes* (New York: Random House, 2000).

39 "A poor pilot is not necessarily a dangerous pilot" Thomas and Jablonski, *Doolittle*, p. 34.

39 "A crack-up was not always serious" Doolittle, *I Could Never*, p. 59.

39 "I was pretty upset" Steve Wilstein, Associated Press, "Jimmy Doolittle Turns 90," *Los Angeles Times*, December 14, 1986.

40 "While I was hedge hopping" Doolittle, *I Could Never*, p. 50.

40 "the man who can never stand still" Glines, *Jimmy Doolittle: Daredevil Aviator*.

40 "Doolittle was a great commander" author interview, Mr. Birch, 12/12/00.

41 "very astute" Hasdorff, Knobloch.

41 "as if controlled by one hand" Thomas and Jablonski, *Doolittle*, p. 50.

42 "As far as I know" Doolittle, *I Could Never*, p. 72.

43 "When I hit" Doolittle, *I Could Never*, p. 73.

43 "A favoring wind was on my quarter" Doolittle, *I Could Never*, p. 74.

45 "On May 23, 1926, the Chilean pilots" Doolittle, *I Could Never*, p. 115.

46 "On the ground we had a small beacon" Burch, Fogelman, and Tate.

47 "Her beer-making skills made our home" Doolittle, *I Could Never*, p. 136.

48 "Anything that stalls at a hundred knots" citing Delmar Benjamin in Phil Scott, "Something Gold, Something New," *Air & Space*, February/March 1995.

48 "Recognizing that this airplane would be extremely hot to handle" Doolittle, *I Could Never*, p. 181.

48 "It was an uncomfortable flight" Thomas and Jablonski, *Doolittle*, p. 138.

49 "I was sent up to Detroit" Burch, Fogelman, and Tate.

SHIP

page

50 "They shook us out of the sack" Hasdorff, Crouch.

50 "those who were left behind at Eglin" Maj. Harry Johnson, Jr., Adjutant, "B25-B Special Project," handwritten and undated notes for army file, Air Force Historical Research Agency, Maxwell Air Force Base, Ala.

50 "When Ted took off for California" author interview, Mrs. Lawson, 12/4/00.

50 "so low we could look up at the telegraph wires" Lawson, p. 31.

50 "When we got to Texas and New Mexico" Hasdorff, DeShazer.

50 "We played funny little games" Merrill, p. 18.

51 "That's where I was raised" Cindy Hayostek, "Exploits of a Doolittle Raider," *Military History*, March 1996.

51 "On our flight from Eglin to Sacramento" author interview, Mr. Birch, 12/12/00.

52 "One incident was typical" Doolittle, *I Could Never*, p. 253.

52 "We just happened to find out" Schultz, p. 82.

53 "a bunch of stuck-up SOBs" author interview, Mr. Bourgeois, 10/17/00.

53 "Just a minute, Colonel. You will have to give us a detailed report" Merrill, p. 36.

53   "'General, it occurred to me'" Doolittle, *I Could Never,* p. 248.

54   "McClure had a movie camera" Lawson, p. 32.

55   The USS *Hornet*'s deck For the full details on the history of *Hornet,* see Lisle A. Rose, *The Ship That Held the Line* (Annapolis, Md.: Naval Institute Press, 1995); and Dwayne Miles, "USS *Hornet* CV-8 statistics," http://www.usshornetclub. com, May 26, 2001.

57   The chain-smoking, sunburned Mitscher Rose, p. 7.

58   marine sergeant George Royce Merrill, p. 37.

58   "strained and defensive" Greening, *Not As Briefed.*

58   "the marine personnel in particular" Hasdorff, Crouch.

59   "Old Bill Miles and I" Hasdorff, Crouch.

59   "The navy fliers were very interested" Lawson, p. 35.

59   "We were all drinking very freely" Hasdorff, Macia.

59   "I remember lots of things" author interview, request for anonymity.

60   "More than once, it crossed my mind" Schultz, p. 90.

60   Men looking for a quieter time Merrill, p. 39.

60   "Next morning, I had an early breakfast" Doolittle, *I Could Never,* p. 257.

60   "May good luck and success be with you" Schultz, p. 90.

61   "My heart sank" Doolittle, *I Could Never,* p. 261.

61   "If there's any of you who don't want to go" Helena Pasquarella, "Moorpark Man Recalls a Fateful Flight over Japan During WWII," *Los Angeles Times,* July 22, 1993.

61   "When Doolittle revealed what the mission was" author interview, request for anonymity.

61   "They told us over the loudspeaker" Hayostek.

61   "The sailors I saw" Merrill, p. 41.

61   "America had never seen darker days" Doolittle, *I Could Never,* p. 2.

62   "From that time on, the navy could not do" Hasdorff, Crouch.

62   "My roommate on the *Hornet,* Gus Wildhelm" author interview, Mr. Jones, 11/21/00.

62   "There was a sergeant" Hasdorff, Knobloch.

62   "As we passed under the great Golden Gate Bridge" Sgt. George E. Larkin, Jr., "Personal Diary, October 18, 1942," Filson Club Historical Society, Louisville, Ky.

62   "At that time you almost have to have lived it" Hasdorff, York.

64   "The *Hornet*'s 'Chicago pianos,'" Lawson, p. 43.

64   "The late call to stations was sounded" Lawson, p. 41.

64   "We found out soon enough" author interview, request for anonymity.

65   "Fortunately, after about twenty minutes" Glines, *The Doolittle Raid,* p. 96, citing Joseph W. Manske, response to questionnaire from Air Force Office of Information, March 28, 1957.

65   "They issued us sextants" Hasdorff, Ozuk.

65   "Pork and beans" Hayostek.

65   "I began to wonder how many more days" C. Hoyt Watson, *The Amazing Story of Sergeant Jacob DeShazer* (Winona Lake, Ind.: Life and Light Press, 1950;

reprinted as *DeShazer,* Coquitlam, British Columbia: Galaxy Communications, 1991), p. 13.

65 "We couldn't convince ourselves" Lawson, p. 41.

66 "Well, Hank, how does it look to you?" Merrill, p. 93.

66 "I've done everything I can" Merrill, p. 95.

66 "simply to look at the feet" Schultz, p. 99.

67 "I think our initial reaction" Schultz, p. 100, citing Stephen Jurika, interview, United States Naval Institute, March 17, 1976.

67 "the pilots were a carefree bunch" Schultz, p. 54, citing "The Doolittle Raid," Public Affairs Department, CBS News, 1950.

67 "I felt that if Lieutenant Jurika" Schultz, p. 100.

67 "At one point during Eglin" author interview, Mr. Jones, 11/21/00.

68 "I never got seasick on the *Hornet*" author interview, Mr. Birch, 12/12/00.

68 "We found that practically all of the machine guns" Capt. John M. Wisdom, Assistant Chief of Air Staff, Intelligence, "Interview with B-25 Crew That Bombed Tokyo and Was Interned by the Russians," June 3, 1943.

69 "The navy was standing watch" Hasdorff, Jones.

69 "Believe it or not, there was a billiard table" author interview, request for anonymity.

69 "Not being a gambler" Doolittle, *I Could Never,* p. 269.

69 "Doc White was putting out whiskey" author interview, Mr. Bourgeois, 10/17/00.

69 "if they were captured dropping bombs on Japan" Schultz, p. 103.

70 The commander replied Glines, *The Doolittle Raid,* p. 61.

DAI NIPPON TEIKOKU

page

71 the world's most astounding military power For more on the history of Japan's involvement in the Great East Asia War, see Herbert P. Bix, *Hirohito and the Making of Modern Japan* (New York: HarperCollins, 2000); Haruko Taya Cook and Theodore F. Cook, *Japan at War: An Oral History* (New York: New Press, 1992); John Costello, *The Pacific War* (New York: Rawson, Wade, 1981); William Craig, *The Fall of Japan* (New York: Dial, 1967); Gavan Daws, *Prisoners of the Japanese* (New York: William Morrow/Quill, 1994); John W. Dower, *Embracing Defeat: Japan in the Wake of World War II* (New York: W. W. Norton and Company, 1999); John W. Dower, *War Without Mercy: Race and Power in the Pacific War* (New York: Pantheon, 1986); James F. Dunnigan and Albert A. Nofi, *Victory at Sea* (New York: William Morrow, 1995); Richard B. Frank, *Downfall: The End of the Imperial Japanese Empire* (New York: Random House, 1999); Frank Gibney, *Senso: The Japanese Remember the Pacific War: Letters to the Editor of Asahi Shimbun,* translated by Beth Cary (Armonk, N.Y., and London: M. E. Sharpe, 1995); Joseph C. Grew, *Ten Years in Japan* (New York: Simon & Schuster, 1944); Grace P. Hayes, *The History of the Joint Chiefs of Staff in World War II: The War Against Japan* (Annapolis, Md.: Naval Institute Press, 1982); Edwin P. Hoyt, *Japan's War: The Great Pacific Conflict,*

1853–1952 (New York: McGraw-Hill, 1986); Samuel Hynes, Anne Matthews, Nancy Caldwell Sorel, and Roger J. Spiller, advisory board, *Reporting World War II* (New York: Library of America, 1995); Saburo Ienaga, *The Pacific War: 1931–1945* (New York: Pantheon, 1978); Robert Leckie, *Delivered from Evil: The Saga of World War II* (New York: Harper & Row, 1987); Walter Lord, *Day of Infamy* (New York: Henry Holt, 1957); Military Intelligence Service, War Department, "Japanese Land Operations from Japanese Sources, December 8, 1941 to June 8, 1942," *Campaign Study #3,* November 18, 1942, Air Force Historical Research Agency, Maxwell Air Force Base, Ala.; J. D. Potter, *Yamamoto: The Man Who Menaced America* (New York: Viking, 1965); Gordon W. Prange, *At Dawn We Slept: The Untold Story of Pearl Harbor* (New York: McGraw-Hill, 1981); Gordon W. Prange, with Donald M. Goldstein and Katherine V. Dillon, *God's Samurai* (McLean, Va.: Brassey's Inc., 1990); Hampton Sides, *Ghost Soldiers* (New York: Doubleday, 2001); Ronald H. Spector, *Eagle Against the Sun* (New York: Free Press, 1984); and John Toland, *Infamy* (New York: Doubleday, 1982), and *The Rising Sun* (New York: Random House, 1970).

73   **Over the next eight years** Sangmie Choie Shellstede, ed., *Comfort Women Speak* (New York: Holmes & Meier, 2000).

73   **"At the last stage of their training"** Cook and Cook, p. 37.

74   **During *Nanjin Datusha*** For details see Iris Chang, *The Rape of Nanking* (New York: Basic Books, 1997).

74   **"Few know that soldiers impaled babies on bayonets"** Chang, citing Japanese veteran Nagatomi Hakudo in Joanna Pitman, "Repentance," *New Republic,* February 10, 1992.

75   **Japan's attack on Pearl Harbor** Toland, *The Rising Sun,* p. 190, and *Infamy,* p. 250.

75   **"in case the enemy's main fleet is berthed at Pearl Harbor"** Toland, *Infamy,* p. 251.

75   **Considered by both Japanese and Americans** Costello, p. 281.

76   **his most authoritative Japanese biography** referring to Hiroyuki Agawa, *The Reluctant Admiral: Yamamoto and the Imperial Navy* (Tokyo: Kodansha International, 1979).

76   **"a major calamity for the world"** Larrabee, p. 364.

76   **The American secretary of state, Cordell Hull** Kenneth S. Davis, *FDR, The War President: 1940–1943* (New York: Random House, 2000), p. 315.

76   **"If war eventuates with Japan"** Prange, *At Dawn We Slept,* p. 45.

77   **March 1941: Yoshikawa Takeo** Costello, p. 84.

77   **"if we begin on November 3"** Costello, p. 98.

78   **Nicknamed *Tako* (octopus)** Prange, Goldstein, and Dillon, *God's Samurai,* p. 3.

78   **The subordinates actually in charge** Spector, p. 68.

78   **"the Army Air Corps units"** Costello, p. 651.

78   **"it is terribly important"** Fromkin, p. 432.

79   **"It all looks too precise"** Toland, *Infamy,* pp. 14 and 258.

79   **decodes a cable from Tokyo** Spector, p. 94.

79   **"the purpose of a war with the United States"** Costello, p. 113.

80   **The Japanese liner *Taiyo Maru*** Spector, p. 81.

80 "I'm praying to the gods" Spector, p. 81.

80 "on the brink of chaos" Spector, p. 83.

81 "Our aim is to blanket the whole area" Spector, p. 85.

81 "on a monthly basis for civilian needs," "no glimmer for hope," "in the hands of you and Knox," and "Japan may attack the Burma Road" Costello, p. 120.

82 A new employee, Mrs. Dorothy Edgars Spector, p. 87.

82 "I address myself to Your Majesty at this moment" Franklin Roosevelt, "Telegram of December 6, 1941 to H.I.M. Hirohito," Franklin Delano Roosevelt Library, Hyde Park, N.Y.

83 "This means war" Davis, p. 338.

83 "Meditation on inevitable death" citing Tsunetomo Yamamoto, *Hagakure,* in Hoyt, *Japan's War.*

84 "Just what significance the hour set" Kennedy, "Victory at Sea."

84 "In the predawn darkness of 7 December" Mitsuo Fuchida and Masatake Okumiya, *Midway: The Battle That Doomed Japan* (Annapolis, Md.: United States Naval Institute, 1955), p. 24.

85 "not to worry about it" Spector, p. 3.

85 "Hurrah for the English!" Fuchida and Okumiya, p. 121.

86 "Presently the harbor itself became visible" Fuchida and Okumiya, p. 24.

87 "We're going to have an air show!" Lord, p. 89.

88 "As we closed in" Fuchida and Okumiya, p. 24.

89 "slowly and stately . . . as if she were tired" Lord, p. 189.

90 "as white as his uniform" and "I wish it had killed me" Toland, *Infamy,* p. 11.

90 "A warm feeling came with the realization" Costello, p. 139.

91 "Before we're through with 'em" Costello, p. 141.

91 now replaced by panic spreading across the island Lord, p. 227.

92 "said that he had already been in touch" Joseph C. Grew, "Telegram to Cordell Hull," (dated 12/8/41, received 12/10/41, 6:23 A.M.), Franklin Delano Roosevelt Library, Hyde Park, N.Y.

92 "It is almost certain that the U.S." citing Rear Adm. Ugaki in Glines, *The Doolittle Raid,* p. 10.

92 "Japanese cities, being made of wood and paper" Agawa, p. 127.

92 *"Across the sea, corpses in the water"* Spector, p. 7.

92 "It was obvious to me" Costello, p. 145.

92 "I was sure the American Fleet had scored a great victory" Toland, *Infamy,* p. 14.

94 "The fruits of victory" Costello, p. 214.

94 "I could feel my face go white" PBS.org, "MacArthur," *The American Experience,* 2001, http://www.pbs.org/wgbh/amex/macarthur.

THE DREAMER, PARALYZED

page

96 For thirteen years For details on the upper echelons of the United States government in World War II, see Stephen E. Ambrose, *The Supreme Commander: The*

War Years of General Dwight D. Eisenhower (Garden City, N.Y.: Doubleday, 1970); Henry H. Arnold, *Global Mission* (New York: Harper & Row, 1949); Arthur Bryant, *Triumph in the West, 1943–1946* (London: Macmillan, 1959); Kenneth S. Davis, *FDR, The War President: 1940–1943* (New York: Random House, 2000); David Fromkin, *In the Time of the Americans* (New York: Alfred A. Knopf, 1995); Doris Kearns Goodwin, *No Ordinary Time* (New York: Simon & Schuster, 1994); Joseph C. Grew, *Ten Years in Japan* (New York: Simon & Schuster, 1944); Grace P. Hayes, *The History of the Joint Chiefs of Staff in World War II: The War Against Japan* (Annapolis, Md.: Naval Institute Press, 1982); Ernest J. King and Walter Muir Whitehill, *Fleet Admiral King: A Naval Record* (New York: W. W. Norton, 1952); Eric Larrabee, *Commander in Chief: Franklin Delano Roosevelt, His Lieutenants and Their War* (New York: Harper & Row, 1987); Robert W. Love, Jr., *The Chiefs of Naval Operations* (Annapolis, Md.: Naval Institute Press, 1980); David McCullough, *Truman* (New York: Simon & Schuster, 1992); Ted Morgan, *FDR* (New York: Simon & Schuster, 1986); PBS.org, "Eleanor Roosevelt," *The American Experience,* 2001, http://www.pbs.org/wgbh/amex/eleanor/filmmore/transcript/transcript2.html; Forrest C. Pogue, *George C. Marshall,* Vol. 2, *Ordeal and Hope* (New York: Viking, 1966); Robert E. Sherwood, *Roosevelt and Hopkins* (New York: Harper & Brothers, 1948); and Barbara W. Tuchman, *Stilwell and the American Experience in China* (New York: Macmillan, 1971).

96   During the day men and women would meet Goodwin, p. 22.

97   At the age of fifteen Larrabee, p. 3.

97   He'd also refer to the navy as "us" Larrabee, p. 142.

97   "If you run into troubles" Davis, p. 7.

97   "At no time during his presidency" Davis, p. 321.

97   17 percent of the nation Goodwin, p. 42.

98   A U.S. poll from the summer of 1940 Goodwin, p. 70.

98   After the fall of France Fromkin, p. 386.

98   "It's a terrible thing" David Grubin and WGBH Boston, "FDR," *The American Experience* (PBS Video, 1994).

98   the president had commissioned Goodwin, p. 272.

99   only two include a wheelchair Grubin and WGBH Boston.

99   "How did it happen?" Grubin and WGBH Boston.

99   "Now it is impossible for us to lose the war" Costello, p. 181.

99   As of 1940 the United States stood fourteenth Goodwin, p. 23.

99   "against Europe's total war" cited in Goodwin, p. 52.

100   in testimony before Sen. Harry S. Truman Fromkin, p. 450.

100   "He would talk over something informally" Goodwin, p. 24.

100   "was very much like chasing a vagrant beam of sunshine" Larrabee, p. 644.

101   "I didn't feel I could sleep at ease" PBS.org, "MacArthur."

101   King would additionally wonder Gannon, p. 168.

101   "Lord how I need him" PBS.org, "MacArthur."

101   "tall, spare and taut" Gannon, p. 168.

101   "He is one of the most even-tempered men in the Navy" Larrabee, p. 155.

101   "his weaknesses were other men's wives" Larrabee, p. 155.

101   At meetings of the Joint Chiefs Thomas M. Coffey, *Hap: The Story of the U.S. Air Force and the Man Who Built It* (New York: Viking Press, 1982), p. 260.

102   "The Army thought the Navy was patrolling" Hynes et al., p. 298, citing Raymond Clapper, *Watching the World* (New York: McGraw-Hill, 1944). The results of the Roberts Commission can be found in Harry L. Hopkins, "Report from the Commission created by Executive Order 'to ascertain and report the facts relating to the attack made by Japanese armed forces upon the Territory of Hawaii on December 7, 1941,'" January 24, 1942, Harry L. Hopkins papers, Franklin Delano Roosevelt Library, Hyde Park, N.Y.

102–103   "seems to have forgotten that his record in Manila" PBS.org, "MacArthur."

103   "That's the way we talked while we were wooing her" Costello, p. 150.

103   "the whole organization belongs to the days of George Washington" Costello, p. 178.

103   In September 1938 Roosevelt, who understood German Sherwood, p. 100.

103   Hap took his first flying lesson in 1911 from Al Welsh Arnold, *Global Mission,* p. 19.

104   "he operates at 2,000 RPMs" Coffey, p. 113.

104   "maybe you can't do it" Coffey, p. 256.

104   "headstrong, often tactless" Coffey, p. 11.

104   "defied description by usual categories" Coffey, p. 120, citing senior air corps staff officer Maj. Laurence Kuter.

104   "I tried to give Arnold all the power I could" Larrabee, p. 221, citing Forrest C. Pogue, *George C. Marshall,* Vol. 2, p. 44.

105   "we could convince the mass of Japanese" Henry H. Arnold, "8.2, Doolittle Raid," personal collection of papers donated to the Air Force Archives by Murray Green, including relevant Eisenhower papers, roll 43812, Army Historical Research Agency, Maxwell Air Force Base, Ala.

105   On December 23, 1940, the president had signed off Dunnigan and Nofi, p. 253; and Reynolds, p. 175.

105   "the Flying Tigers were really a rough bunch" Hasdorff, Macia.

106   "What we have got to do, Henry" Tuchman, p. 280, citing John M. Bloom, *From the Morgenthau Diaries* (Boston: Houghton-Mifflin, 1959–67), pp. 366–67.

106   "Immediately after the attack on Hawaii" Arnold, "8.2, Doolittle Raid," citing *Stimson Diaries,* Sun, Dec 14, 1941.

106   "find ways and means of carrying home to Japan proper" Reynolds, p. 175.

107   "pet project" Arnold, *Global Mission,* pp. 298–99.

107   FDR had urged his lieutenants Arnold, "8.2, Doolittle Raid."

108   "If the Army has some plane" Reynolds, pp. 171–72.

109   "I started right away" Schultz, p. 14, citing D. B. Duncan, "Secret Planning for the Tokyo Raid," J. T. Mason, ed., *The Pacific War Remembered.*

109   "Go see General Arnold about it," Schultz, p. 14.

109   On Christmas Eve the general had been chatting Arnold, *Global Mission*, p. 276.

110   "anything that Doolittle wants, help him get" Arnold, "8.2, Doolittle Raid," interview of Gen. Charles F. Cabell, July 30, 1969.

110   "I was given by Hap Arnold" Mac Laddon, "Interview with Lt. General Doolittle," *Reuben Fleet*, San Diego, 14 Aug 70.

111   "it would take a few months" Arnold, "Memorandum of White House Meeting, January 28, 1942" in "8.2, Doolittle Raid."

111   "I feel that the plan which is now in progress" Arnold, "Memorandum for the President, Janaury 28, 1942" in "8.2, Doolittle Raid."

111   On February 2, in a cold and foggy dawn Rose, pp. 38–42.

LIFTOFF

page

113   Halsey's transmission on the tenth Glines, *The Doolittle Raid*, p. 61.

114   Two in particular, sent as advance patrol Merrill, p. 52.

115   An early newspaper typo Wright, p. 271.

115   "an aggressive, feisty leader" Doolittle, *I Could Never*, p. 251.

115   "If the Japanese navy had had a half-dozen Halseys" Prange, Goldstein, and Dillon, p. 118.

115   "We were tremendously excited" Alvin Kernan, *Crossing the Line: A Bluejacket's World War II Odyssey* (Annapolis, Md.: Naval Institute Press, 1994), pp. 31–46.

116   During one especially wild ride Lawson, p. 42.

116   "We fueled at sea" Kernan, pp. 31–46.

116   "Reuters, British news agency, has announced" Schultz, p. 110.

117   in fact Hap Arnold did have two other missions in the works author interview, Tony Strotman, webmaster, 341st Bomb Group Web Tribute (http://www. 341stbombgroup.org) and 308th Bomb Group on the Web (http://www. 308thbombgroup.org), 7/25/01; "Letter from Brigadier General Merian C. Cooper, May 22, 1970" in Arnold, "8.2, Doolittle Raid"; and James W. Walker, group historian, and Robert J. Giordano, web coordinator, "376th Heavy Bombardment Group, Inc. Veterans Association," http://www.376hbgva.com/history.htm.

117   In 1908 a group of American ships had visited Tokyo Bay Rose, p. 64.

118   How much did FDR know about Special Aviation Project #1 Arnold, "8.2, Doolittle Raid" and *Global Mission*, pp. 298–99; and King and Whitehill, p. 376.

119   "Practically all our lookouts were youngsters" cited in Stan Cohen, *Destination: Tokyo* (Missoula, Mont.: Pictorial Histories Publishing Company, 1983).

120   "This was real warfare" Schultz, p. 120.

120   "There were heavy swells" Stephen Jurika interviewed by Paul B. Ryan, March 4, 1976, *U.S. Naval Institute Oral History Transcripts*, Annapolis, Md.

120   "I remember thinking that it was a very curious way" and "*Nashville*'s gunnery was disgraceful" Kernan, pp. 31–46.

121   "Yes, they are beautiful" Schultz, p. 121.

121   "We knew that the pilots really didn't have" Schultz, p. 123.

121   "cold chills were running up and down my spine" Greening, *Not As Briefed,* p. 22.

121   "Doolittle called us all on the deck" Helena Pasquarella, "Moorpark Man Recalls a Fateful Flight over Japan During WWII," *Los Angeles Times,* July 22, 1993.

122   "When we get to Chungking" Doolittle, *I Could Never,* p. 273.

122   "The night before, we pretty well understood" Hasdorff, Macia.

122   "This was zero weather conditions. Zero" Hayostek.

122–23   "I had Mercator charts" Hasdorff, Ozuk.

123   "Will you-all do a fellow a big favor" Lawson, p. 52.

123   "We knew the odds against us" Glines, *Doolittle's Tokyo Raiders,* p. 140.

123   "We were further away than we anticipated being" Hasdorff, Knobloch.

123   "We had done a lot of preflighting" author interview, Mr. Jones, 11/21/00.

124   "the sums I arrived at" Lawson, p. 51.

124   Copilots checked the tire pressure First Motion Picture Unit, Army Air Forces/War Department, *How to Fly the B-25,* Official Training Film TFI-3360, 1944.

125   "if there are any problems with your craft" Hasdorff, Crouch.

125   "A rough sea such as the one in front of us" Doolittle, *I Could Never,* p. 5.

125   "You knew how long it would take them" Schultz, p. 128.

126   "He won't make it!" and "With full flaps" Lawson, p. 55.

126   "Confident," "We were particularly confident" and "It'd be a pretty bad feeling" *One Hour over Tokyo.*

126   "I doubt if one man expected to return alive" S. Sgt. Robert Fishel, " 'Some Will Be Heroes, Some Will Be Angels,' Doolittle Said to Fliers on Tokyo Raid; Keesler Major in Party," *Keesler Field News* (Mississippi), May 27, 1943.

126   "with yards to spare" and "A real strong gust of wind" author interview, Mr. Hoover, 5/20/01.

127   "The weather was not good" author interview, Mr. Jones, 11/21/00.

127   "I was on the line now" Lawson, p. 56.

127   "Imagine our feeling" Schultz, p. 132.

128   "With only one exception, takeoffs were dangerous" Rose, p. 70, citing the *Hornet* War Diary.

128   "The ship shuddered under the strain" Emmens, p. 3.

128   "The sea was rough" Lt. Kenneth E. Reddy, "Personal Diaries, 4/6/42–5/9/42."

128   "You'd think the later airplanes" Hasdorff, Knobloch.

129   "When we left the ship" Hayostek.

130   "We had blocks behind" Hasdorff, DeShazer.

130   "Psychologically that was a pretty big shock to us" Dr. James C. Hasdorff, "Interview of Lt. Col. Robert L. Hite," United States Air Force Oral History Program, Enid, Okla., December 15–17, 1982, Air Force Historical Research Agency, Maxwell Air Force Base, Ala.

130   "I thought, 'Should I tell the pilot?' " Hasdorff, DeShazer.

130   "one of the most courageous deeds in military history" John L. Frisbee, contributing ed., "First over Tokyo," *Air Force Magazine,* April 1989, vol. 72, no. 4.

BOMB

page
132 "I kept the clean nose of the *Ruptured Duck*" Lawson, pp. 59–61.
132 The U.S. Rubber Company of Indiana Doolittle, "Report of the Aerial Bombing of Japan, 5 June 1942."
133 "We were over six hundred miles when we launched" author interview, Mr. Jones, 11/21/00.
133 "I got the crew together and presented my plan" Schultz, citing Harold F. Watson, response to questionnaire, Air Force Office of Information, March 28, 1957.
133 "At about eleven o'clock we" Emmens, p. 5.
134 "From the takeoff until I got to land" author interview, Mr. McCool, 11/29/00.
134 "The navigator was now the key man" Reddy.
134 "They lack only one thing" Hynes et al., p. 636, citing John Steinbeck, "Fear of Death as Green Troops Sail to Invasion," *New York Herald Tribune,* October 3, 1943.
134 "Naturally, not knowing what it was going to be like" Brendan Gill, "Young Man Behind Plexiglas: Profile of an American Bombardier," *The New Yorker,* August 12, 1944, citing 1st Lt. Joseph Theodore "Ted" Hallock.
135 "I knew once I got to Tokyo" Hasdorff, Ozuk.
135 "The Boss and I took turns at flying" Glines, *The Doolittle Raid,* p. 81, citing Richard E. Cole, response to questionnaire, Air Force Office of Information, March 28, 1957.
137 "I swung very quickly around" Doolittle, *I Could Never,* p. 9.
137 "It looks real, doesn't it?" Cohen.
138 "Flak is very deceptive" Hasdorff, Macia.
138 "They're missing us by a mile, Paul" Merrill, p. 79.
138 "I kept Paul Leonard advised of enemy aircraft" Glines, *The Doolittle Raid,* p. 81, citing Richard E. Cole, response to questionnaire, Air Force Office of Information, March 28, 1957.
138 "They bothered us" and "They probably think," Merrill, p. 79.
139 "The concussion was so hard" author interview, Mr. Hoover, 5/20/01.
140 "entirely unsatisfactory. Operating the turret for twelve hours" and "It is impossible to quickly shift" Doolittle, "Report of the Aerial Bombing of Japan, 5 June 1942."
142 "I made a turn so we could see" Capt. J. Pinkney, "Untitled After-Action Interviews," Chungking, China—Headquarters, Army Air Forces, Washington, D.C., June 15, 1942, Air Force Historical Research Agency, Maxwell Air Force Base, Ala.
142 "caught a fleeting glimpse of a playground" Lawson, p. 62.
143 "I was almost on the first of our objectives" Lawson, p. 66.
143 "It was just impossible for me to believe" Lawson, p. 70.
144 "Hell, I'd seen lots of Jap laundry calendars" Emmens, p. 9.

144   "After flying for about thirty minutes" Hasdorff, York.

144   "Suddenly Ski pulled up to about fifteen hundred feet" Emmens, p. 11.

144   "I wasn't going through this thing without firing that gun" Schultz, p. 154.

144   "people would think there was some secret reason" author interview, Mrs. Emmens, 10/10/00.

145   "majestic deliberation" Col. A. W. Brock, Jr., Deputy Assisant Chief of Air Staff, Intelligence, "Memorandum for the Commanding General, Army Ground Forces," October 2, 1943, Air Force Historical Research Agency, Maxwell Air Force Base, Ala.

145   "a nice sunshiny day with overcast antiaircraft fire" and "We were surprised and shocked" Schultz, p. 156.

145   "Come on you bastards" Merrill, p. 89.

145   "what I saw was four streams of tracer bullets" Schultz, p. 158.

146   "I encountered heavy AA fire over my target" Richard O. Joyce, 1st Lt., Air Corps, 0-401770, "Report of Tokyo Raid, Airplane #40-2250," Chungking, China, May 2, 1942.

146   "laying an unbroken carpet of fire" Brock.

146   "I increased power" Joyce.

146   "I had my machine gun in the lower nozzle" Hasdorff, Crouch.

147   "I heard the copilot's voice over the interphone" Larkin.

148   "It came from Hawaii!" Merrill, p. 80.

148   "Enemy plane!" Merrill, p. 92.

149   "Most of the people did not believe it" Glines, *The Doolittle Raid*, p. 143, citing undated statements made to intelligence officers.

149   "The bombing of Tokyo and several other cities" Saburo Sakai, *Samurai* (New York: E. P. Dutton, 1958), pp. 148–49.

149   "We heard a lot of planes overhead" Grew, *Ten Years in Japan*, p. 526.

149   "Our fondest wish had come true" Tom Bernard, "Japs Were Jumpy After Tokyo Raid," *Stars and Stripes*, April 27, 1943.

149   "many of the people were killed by machine gun bullets" John G. Norris, "Doolittle Pledges New Tokyo Raids," *Washington Post*, April 23, 1943.

149   "When I heard the alarm I ran to the roof" Staff, "'Worst' Feared for Tokyo Fliers by Neutral Diplomats in Japan," *New York Times*, April 24, 1943.

150   "Our targets were the docks, oil refineries, and warehouses" author interview, Mr. Birch, 12/12/00.

150   "On the way to the target in Yokohama" Jack D. Stovall, ed., *Tales of the Marauders* (Cordova, Tenn.: Wings of Courage Press, 1994).

150   "After crossing Kasumigaura lake" Col. Merian C. Cooper, Assistant Chief of Air Staff, Intelligence, "The Doolittle Air Raid on Japan Known as First Special Aviation Project"; "Report on Doolittle raid on Tokyo, 18 April 1942, with collection of interviews, messages and maps"; "Reports on B-25 Aircraft"; "Assessment of Damage, Tokyo Raid"; "Report and Analysis on Tokyo Raid"; and "Interviews with Pilots and Air Crews Conducted After the Raid," Air Force Historical Research Agency, Maxwell Air Force Base, Ala.

151   "They were very trim, silver planes" Reddy.

151   "We were right on course toward a large refinery" author interview, Mr. Birch, 12/12/00.

151   "When our bombs dropped" Cooper.

152   "We sighted several small fishing craft" author interview, Mr. Birch, 12/12/00.

152   "Here I got what was perhaps my greatest scare" Reddy.

152   "I remembered that I had the impression" Schultz, p. 166.

152   "sparks were seen to fly from the building and transformers" Pinkney.

153   "I had a little camera" Hasdorff, Knobloch.

153   "Everybody out!" Merrill, p. 92.

154   "It became necessary to bear to the northwest" Cooper.

155   "We were making a complete turn" Watson, p. 20.

155   "We skimmed along down a valley" Watson, p. 21.

156   "The Japs chased us all the way home, of course" Schultz, p. 216.

156   "an interception of [Doolittle's] pathfinding plane" Brock.

157   "A large fleet of enemy bombers" Schultz, p. 172.

157   "The nightmare of the Japanese militarists" Merrill, p. 102.

157   "Chinese newspapers reported" Brock.

158   "The cowardly raiders purposefully avoided industrial centers" and "the damage caused was very slight" Merrill, p. 102.

158   "the enemy's daring enterprise" and "The few enemy planes that did manage" Schultz, p. 172.

158   After the war MacArthur's occupying forces Merrill, p. 102.

158   "the material loss to the United States was $3,200,000" Brock.

158   *"Was the 18th of April in forty-two"* Merrill, p. 101.

159   "Aboard the carrier *Hornet*" Charles R. Greening, Colonel, USAF, *The First Joint Action,* "A monograph submitted to the Faculty of the Armed Forces Staff College, Norfolk, Virginia, Fourth Class," 21 December 1948.

160   "JAPAN REPORTS TOKYO" cited in Schultz, p. 203.

160   "US WARPLANES RAIN BOMBS" *One Hour over Tokyo.*

CRASH

page

161   "We turned west over the China Sea" Doolittle, *I Could Never,* p. 9.

161   "We had looked at the target and weather information" author interview, Mr. Jones, 11/21/00.

162   At that time China was a country that no American who hadn't been there could ever possibly hope to understand For details on the history of China in World War II, see especially Eric Larrabee, *Commander in Chief: Franklin Delano Roosevelt, His Lieutenants and Their War* (New York: Harper & Row, 1987); Barbara W. Tuchman, *Stilwell and the American Experience in China* (New York: Macmillan, 1971); William B. Allmon, "Successor to the Flying Tigers: THE CATF," *Aviation History,* March 1997; Daniel Ford, *Flying Tigers* (Washington, D.C.: Smithsonian Institution

Press, 1991); Fei Hu Films, *The Story of the Flying Tigers,* Chinese Public Television, 1998; and Saburo Ienaga, *The Pacific War: 1931–1945* (New York: Pantheon, 1978).

163   "if such conception is seriously held" Tuchman, p. 284.

163   he was used to the idea of dictatorships Larrabee, p. 540.

164   one military historian quipped Jack Fischer, "Vinegar Joe's Problem," *Harper's Magazine,* December 1944.

164   "I am just scribbling to keep from biting the radiator" Tuchman, p. 36, citing Joseph W. Stilwell and Theodore H. White, ed., *The Stilwell Papers* (New York: DaCapo, 1991).

165   "We stayed in the worst shit-holes you could imagine" Colin Heaton, "Black Sheep Leader," *Aviation History,* May 2001.

165   "By 10 March, Rangoon had to be fired and evacuated" Brock.

167   "On 18 April, Alexander made another attempt" Brock.

168   "We tried to contact the field at Chuchow" Doolittle, *I Could Never,* p. 9.

168   "The signal for which they listened did not come" Brock.

169   "At about a quarter to five" Emmens, p. 15.

169   "It didn't seem a good idea" Emmens, p. 15.

170   "The door opened abruptly" Emmens, p. 25.

171   "When we went to bed that night" Hasdorff, York.

172   "The general has asked me to tell you" Emmens, p. 39.

173   "I dove out head first" Glines, *The Doolittle Raid,* p. 81, citing Richard E. Cole, response to questionnaire, Air Force Office of Information, March 28, 1957.

173   "We hit the China Coast just below Ningpo" Hoover.

173   "I started to look for a place to land" author interview, Mr. Hoover, 5/20/01.

174   "grabbed a box of cigars and candy bars" Merrill, p. 113.

174   "Direct westerly course taken on 29th parallel" Capt. David M. Jones, "Narrative Report," Chungking, China, May 18, 1942.

174   "Our last fixed point was the southern tip of Kyushu" author interview, Mr. Jones, 11/21/00.

175   "My bailout was a very frightening experience" Jones, *Narrative Report.*

175   "You blow that hatch and you go out through that black hole" author interview, Mr. Jones, 11/21/00.

175   "With no visibility downward or upward," Glines, *The Doolittle Raid,* p. 115, citing Thomas C. Griffin, response to questionnaire, Air Force Office of Information, March 17, 1957.

177   "The weather was just stinking from the ground up" Hasdorff, Crouch.

177   "I figure that we will be out of gas" and "Thanks for a swell ride!" Schultz, p. 120.

177   "They simply told us back in those days" Hasdorff, Crouch.

177   "I left the engines of the ship running" Joyce.

178   made "the situation seem even more ominous and unreal" Greening, *Not As Briefed,* p. 36.

178   "All our reserve tanks were drained to the last drop" Reddy.

179   "We wished each other luck" author interview, Mr. Birch, 12/12/00.

179 "I was the third person to leave the plane" Stovall.

180 "One engine was sputtering" Mullener.

180 "None of us had ever jumped from a plane" Hasdorff, Knobloch.

180 "I went third" Hasdorff, Macia.

182 "After landing, we had to destroy the plane" author interview, Mr. Hoover, 5/20/01.

183 "It's hard and embarrassing to speak of love for a plane" Lawson, p. 74.

184 "Is that you, McClure?" Schultz, p. 126.

185 "Goddamn, you're really bashed open!" Lawson, p. 78.

185 "I vaguely reached up to my mouth and felt it" Lawson, p. 77.

185 "I was lucky" Cpl. David Thatcher, "Personal Report," Chungking, China, May 15, 1942.

187 "When I warmed up a bit" Lawson, p. 82.

ESCAPE

page

191 "Crawled about twenty feet downhill" Schultz, p. 180.

191 "Suddenly a tree limb brushed my feet" Glines, *The Doolittle Raid,* p. 81, citing Richard E. Cole, response to questionnaire, Air Force Office of Information, March 28, 1957.

191 "I stood up, unhurt" Doolittle, *I Could Never,* p. 10.

192 "We contacted a Chinese farmer" author interview, Mr. Hoover, 5/20/01.

193 "In July 1937" author interview, Mr. Liu, 5/23/01.

194 "After about a week we got to Chuhsien" author interview, Mr. Liu, 5/23/01.

195 "I swung between them like a butchered hog" and "About two hundred tough-looking, sinister men" Lawson, pp. 96–98.

196 "I was pretty high up in the mountains" Hasdorff, Ozuk.

197 "About this time the brush parted" Glines, *The Doolittle Raid,* p. 90, citing Jacob E. Manch, response to questionnaire, Air Force Office of Information, March 28, 1957.

198 "he landed on extremely rough terrain" Doolittle, "Report of the Aerial Bombing of Japan, 5 June 1942."

198 "The next morning, April nineteenth" author interview, Mr. McCool, 11/29/00.

199 "When they searched Lieutenant McCool and found his .45" Hasdorff, Jordan.

199 "Soon after, Brick Holstrom and Lucien Youngblood arrived" author interview, Mr. McCool, 11/29/00.

200 "At first light it wasn't raining" author interview, Mr. Jones, 11/21/00.

201 "Suddenly a Chinese officer appeared in the doorway" Glines, *The Doolittle Raid,* p. 117, citing James N. Parker, response to questionnaire, Air Force Office of Information, March 27, 1957.

202 "I came out of the clouds" Hasdorff, Crouch.

202 "My stiffness and soreness had intensified during the night" Reddy.

203 "I cut a scarf out of my chute for a souvenir" author interview, Mr. Birch, 12/12/00.

204 "On the way we walked through many small villages" author interview, Mr. Kappeler, 2/11/01.

205 "When I bailed out in China" Hayostek.

205 "When I walked in" author interview, Mr. Bourgeois, 10/17/00.

205 "I came down in a rice paddy" Hasdorff, Knobloch.

206 "They didn't have lines like they did in France" Hasdorff, Knobloch.

206 "There was this Chinese band" *One Hour over Tokyo.*

206 "Eventually I came across Staff Sgt. Jake Eierman" Hasdorff, Macia.

207 "I was never so glad to see anyone in my life" Glines, *The Doolittle Raid,* p. 132, citing John Hilger's personal diary.

208 "The Chinese took us up to Chuhsien" Hasdorff, Macia.

208 "The officer, surrounded by about a dozen armed soldiers" Doolittle, *I Could Never,* p. 11.

209 "I was taken to the place where the boss was located" Richard E. Cole, response to questionnaire, Air Force Office of Information, March 28, 1957.

209 "I encountered four Chinese men armed with rifles" Cooper, "The Doolittle Air Raid on Japan Known as First Special Aviation Project."

209 "Paul Leonard and I went to the crash site" Doolittle, *I Could Never,* p. 12.

211 "I'm sure he had never seen a white man before" Margaret Yarwood Lamb, *Going It Alone: Mary Andrews—Missionary to China, 1938–1951* (Calgary, Canada: Aquila Books, 1995).

211 "You were having a nightmare" Lawson, p. 105.

214 "'Pretty good.' He poked around my lower leg" Lawson, p. 117.

214 "During the first song I halfheartedly mumbled the words" Staff, "She Nursed Raiders of 'Shangri-La,'" *Daily Telegraph* (Sydney, Australia), May 7, 1956.

215 "While we were hiding in the cabin of a boat" Doolittle, *I Could Never,* p. 277.

216 "Mr. President, you remember the novel of James Hilton" Samuel I. Rosenman, *Working with Roosevelt* (New York: Harper & Row), 1952.

217 "Mission to bomb Tokyo has been accomplished" Cooper, "The Doolittle Air Raid on Japan Known as First Special Aviation Project."

217 "From the standpoint of damage" Gen. Henry H. Arnold, "Memorandum for the President," April 23, 1942, Franklin Delano Roosevelt Library, Hyde Park, N.Y.

218 "they have thousands and thousands of workers under them" and "We hadn't noticed a loudspeaker" Emmens, p. 46.

219 "'How would you like to look forward to'" Emmens, p. 54.

219 Eisenhower and Arnold drafted a reply Arnold, "8.2, Doolittle Raid," p. 265.

220 "All [of the interned Americans] have received courteous and generous treatment" Brock.

220 "Doc was scissoring dead flesh" Lawson, p. 120.

222 "4/20/42: We got to Chuchow (Chuhsien)" Reddy.

226 "to destroy the air bases" Schultz, p. 239, citing D. Bergamini, *Japan's Imperial Conspiracy* (New York: William Morrow, 1971).

226 "the Japanese began their advance upon Chuchow" Brock.

227 "We fed the Americans and carried them to safety" Schultz, p. 241, citing the Reverend Charles Meeus in *Reader's Digest,* May 1944.

227 "From some of the villagers who had managed to escape death" Schultz, p. 239, citing Father George Yager and bishop Charles Quinn in the *New York Times,* May 26, 1943.

227 "These Japanese troops slaughtered" Brock.

228 "Headquarters spokesmen sarcastically pooh-poohed" Fuchida and Okumiya, p. 63.

230 "Don't take it out on me" and "Completely unknown to me," Doolittle, *I Could Never,* p. 286.

232 "It certainly was fine for you" Franklin Delano Roosevelt Library, Hyde Park, N.Y.

232 "I am pleased to report" Mullener.

233 "The raid had three advantages" Leish.

233 "One airplane, badly crashed" Brock.

233 "Hallmark's crew bailed out near the coast" Brock.

234 "Attempts to ransom prisoners" Brock.

SEIZED

page

235 **The extraordinary chain** For more details on the history of the Japanese-held Raiders, see Carroll V. Glines, *Four Came Home* (Missoula, Mont.: Pictorial Histories Publishing Company, 1981).

236 "Farrow said over the interphone" Hasdorff, DeShazer.

237 "There seemed to be the quietest quiet coming down" Hasdorff, Hite.

237 "Stand up, or me shoot" Glines, *The Doolittle Raid,* p. 101, citing undated manuscript furnished by Nielsen.

238–39 "I could see inside their mud houses" and "You are in the hands of the Japanese" Watson, p. 23.

240 "Where are the other two men?" Glines, *The Doolittle Raid,* p. 101, citing undated manuscript furnished by Nielsen.

240 "In the morning when the chickens were crowing" Hasdorff, Hite.

241 "They put us into cells" Hasdorff, Hite.

241 "Everyone going out swore" author interview, request for anonymity.

241 "Bear in mind the fact that to be captured" cited in Costello, p. 216.

242 "One of the officers, using lots of slang" Watson, p. 25.

244 "I personally severed more than forty heads" cited in Cook and Cook.

244 "I'd sit there, cold" Hasdorff, DeShazer.

245 "My arms were bound to the back of a chair" testimony of Chase Nielsen, United States Military Commission, Shanghai, China, February 27, 1946.

246 "We are the Knights of *Bushido*" Merrill, p. 155.

247 "Their scale has five notes" Lawson, p. 148.

247 "looked like a turret" Lawson, p. 129.

247 "We stayed at the hospital" Cooper.

247 "Before we left the grounds of the little hospital" Lawson, p. 134.

247 "After I was in bed" Lawson, p. 145.

248   "It was tough that night, trying to sleep" Lawson, p. 136.

248   "The springs of that truck just weren't springs" Lawson, p. 142.

249   "In their bewilderingly casual way" Lawson, p. 154.

249   " 'You think it was worthwhile' " Lawson, p. 170.

250   " 'We were sort of orphans for a while' " Hasdorff, Knobloch.

250   "With a bunch of the other guys" author interview, Mr. McCool, 11/29/00.

251   "On the sixteenth [of May 1942]" author interview, Mr. Birch, 12/12/00.

252   As the Doolittle Raiders were thrown For details on the battle of Midway, see especially James F. Dunnigan and Albert A. Nofi, *Victory at Sea* (New York: William Morrow, 1995); Mitsuo Fuchida and Masatake Okumiya, *Midway: The Battle That Doomed Japan* (Annapolis, Md.: United States Naval Institute, 1955); Frank Gibney, *Senso: The Japanese Remember the Pacific War: Letters to the Editor of Asahi Shimbun,* translated by Beth Cary (Armonk, N.Y., and London: M. E. Sharpe, 1995); Edwin P. Hoyt, *Japan's War: The Great Pacific Conflict, 1853–1952* (New York: McGraw-Hill, 1986); Saburo Ienaga, *The Pacific War: 1931–1945* (New York: Pantheon, 1978); David M. Kennedy, "Victory at Sea," *Atlantic Monthly,* March 1999; Eric Larrabee, *Commander in Chief: Franklin Delano Roosevelt, His Lieutenants and Their War* (New York: Harper & Row, 1987); William C. Mann, "Battle of Midway Rewritten from Grave," *Ottawa Citizen,* August 29, 1999; Lisle A. Rose, *The Ship That Held the Line* (Annapolis, Md.: Naval Institute Press, 1995); and Ronald H. Spector, *Eagle Against the Sun* (New York: Free Press, 1984).

254   "come in from the northwest on bearing 325 degrees" Larrabee, p. 359.

255   "we figured by golly if they could do it" Rose, p. 130.

255   "[A]bout one hour after the planes had departed" Rose, p. 160, citing John B. Lundstrom, *The First Team: Pacific Naval Air Combat from Pearl Harbor to Midway* (Annapolis, Md.: Naval Institute Press, 1984).

256   "Sight what appears to be ten enemy surface ships" Larrabee, p. 362.

256   "We had by this time undergone" cited in Larrabee, p. 371.

258   "Zeros were coming in on us in a stream from astern" Spector, p. 177, citing "Reminisces of Vice Admiral James E. Thach," U.S. Naval Historical Center, pp. 245–52.

258   "curved white slashes on a blue carpet" Larrabee, p. 374, citing Clayton D. James, "Torpedo Squadron Eight," *Life* magazine, April 31, 1942, pp. 70–80.

258   "At that instant a lookout screamed" Fuchida and Okumiya, p. 158.

259   "the closest squeak and the greatest victory" cited in Kennedy.

259   In June 1942 Imperial Japanese Navy *I-25* William H. Langenberg, "Japan Bombs the West Coast," *Aviation History,* November 1998.

260   "I had talked to some of the boys about Ellen" Lawson, p. 175.

261   "[O]ne of the boys let out a surprised sound" Lawson, p. 176.

261   "This is better than Moscow" Emmens, p. 85.

261   "We learned from the attaché" Hasdorff, York.

262   "What about the rest of the boys" Emmens, p. 85.

262 "Food and cigarette shortages were quite common now" Emmens, p. 104.

263 "Our November food ration was even worse" Emmens, p. 176.

263 "contrary to international law" Schultz, p. 261, citing *International Military Tribunal, Far East*, pp. 14600, 14662–64, 27904–6, 28873, and 38621–22, National Archives and Records Administration.

264 "After leaving Nagoya, I do not quite remember the place" Glines, *Four Came Home*, pp. 116–19.

265 "the coal soot from the train ride" Watson, p. 30.

265 "In the bottom part of the hotel they had made bamboo cells" Hasdorff, Hite.

266 "The way you determine that [you had] beriberi" Hasdorff, Hite.

266 "Everyone could tell when they were going to die" Daws, p. 121.

266 "One day Lieutenant Hallmark passed out" Watson, p. 33.

266 "I helped Dean Hallmark" Hasdorff, Hite.

267 "Any individual who commits any or all of the following acts" Schultz, citing *International Military Tribunal, Far East*, pp. 14662–64.

DEATH

page

268 "Ross Greening's wife, Dot, and I moved to Myrtle Beach" author interview, Mrs. Lawson, 12/4/00.

268 "On my way to Walter Reed" Lawson, p. 179.

268 "Doolittle came in" Lawson, p. 180.

269 "Because of Ted's mother being sick" author interview, Mrs. Lawson, 12/4/00.

269 "You'll never know how relieved I am" Lawson, p. 181.

269 "Ted arrived today" J. H. Doolittle, Brigadier General, U.S. Army, "Letter to Mrs. Ellen A. Lawson," June 17, 1942. Ellen Lawson private papers.

270 "I'm glad to know the truth" Lawson, p. 182.

270 "What if you aren't in top condition" Lawson, p. 183.

270 "I was sitting in my room a day or two later" Lawson, p. 184.

271 "He was thin" and "McClure was there" author interview, Mrs. Lawson, 12/4/00.

271 "The second amputation was as bad as the first one" Lawson, p. 185.

272 "General Arnold called me to his office" Burch, Fogelman, and Tate.

273 "the blackest day in history" Leckie, p. 437.

273 "I was assigned to a new squadron of B-25s" author interview, Mr. Hoover, 5/20/01.

274 "The next thing I knew" author interview, Mr. Jones, 11/21/00.

274 "I had to go into Youks-les-Bains, Algeria" Doolittle, *I Could Never*, p. 334.

275 "There were six of us from the Doolittle group" Hasdorff, Macia.

276 "I led five raids, the last on Bizerte" author interview, Mr. Jones, 11/21/00; also see Paul Brickhill, *The Great Escape* (New York: W. W. Norton, 1950).

278 "On July 17, 1943, Col. Ross Greening, based in Marrakech" Greening, *Not As Briefed*.

280 "Word came out that we were evadees" Hasdorff, Knobloch.

280 "After some missions over Sicily and Italy" author interview, Mr. Hoover, 5/20/01.

281 "They announced, in Japanese, our so-called sentence" Hasdorff, Hite.

281 "Since I had known of the humane nature of the Emperor" and "I believe the verdict issued by the chief prosecutor" cited in Watson, p. 36.

282 "I hardly know what to say" All these letters, which would serve as evidence in the 1946 War Crimes Tribunals, are cited in Oxford.

282 "Your lives were very short" Schultz, citing testimony at War Crimes Trials, Shanghai, China, 1946, *International Military Tribunal, Far East,* pp. 27904–6.

283 After two months of shore leave For further details on Guadalcanal and the death of CV-8, see Costello; Dunnigan and Nofti; Larrabee; Rose; and Spector.

283 "Duty is a heavy burden" cited in Dunnigan and Nofti, p. 186.

284 "pitiless, . . . amalgamated hell" Rose, p. 235.

284–85 "I remember [the torpedo planes] coming in" and "felt as though the ship was a rat" Rose, p. 244.

285 "It was the middle of winter" Emmens, p. 197.

286 "It was the twenty-fifth of March" Emmens, p. 219.

287 "The other occupant of Ski's compartment" Emmens, p. 234.

289 "Bob Emmens and I differ on this" Hasdorff, York.

289 "The tribunal finds the defendants guilty" Schultz, citing *International Military Tribunal, Far East,* p. 14600.

289 "I had expected to be executed" Watson, p. 37.

290 "If the Americans win the war you are to be shot" Hasdorff, Hite.

292 "I believe it was in the month of November" Hasdorff, Hite.

293 "They opened all our cell doors" Hasdorff, Hite.

294 "We toasted those who couldn't be with us" Doolittle, *I Could Never,* p. 343.

295 "I believed now that the war was entirely lost" Prange, Goldstein, and Dillon, p. 91.

295 Lanphier and Barber would spend the rest of their lives Richard Goldstein, "Rex T. Barber, Pilot Who Downed Yamamoto, Dies at 84," *New York Times,* August 1, 2001.

295 "Isn't there someplace where we can strike the United States?" Bix, p. 466.

295 "It is with a feeling of deepest horror" Franklin Delano Roosevelt, radio address to the nation, April 21, 1943.

295 "JAPAN'S BARBAROUS ACT" "News of the Week," *New York Times,* April 25, 1943.

295 "the cruel, inhuman and beastlike American pilots" cited in Oxford.

296 "In violation of every rule of military procedure" and "she crumbled and begged for mercy" John G. Norris, "Doolittle Pledges New Tokyo Raids," *Washington Post,* April 23, 1943.

296 "I wonder if, and hope and pray" and "The Japanese just can't be so heartless" Staff, "Parents of Fliers Doubt Execution," *New York Times,* April 23, 1943.

297 "some of Doolittle's companions" Staff, "Threat to Fliers," *New York Times,* April 22, 1943.

METAMORPHOSIS
page
298 "Our hearts sank as we slowed to a stop" Emmens, p. 240.
299 "Ski and I were assigned to the job" Emmens, p. 245.
299 "All our meetings with Kolya were clandestine" Emmens, p. 251.
299 "He has actually been in contact with a guy" Emmens, p. 255.
300 "he increased his gait until he was right behind him" Emmens, p. 256.
302 "I asked to write a letter to the prison governor" Hasdorff, Hite.
302 "I don't know—what an atheist is" Hasdorff, DeShazer.
303 "It was the first time that I had ever" Hasdorff, Hite.
303 "Before I knew what was going to happen" Watson, p. 49.
304 "Lord, though I am far from home" Watson, p. 49.
304 "The pain in my foot was severe" Watson, p. 50.
305 "One morning he opened the slot" Hasdorff, DeShazer.
306 In the decades between the wars For details on the history of high-altitude strategic bombing, see Brian Todd Carey, "Operation Pointblank: Evolution of Allied Air Doctrine," *World War II,* May 2001.
307 "We were told that after twenty-five" Gill.
308 "Abdul says that we are to be ready to go" Emmens, p. 264.
308 "experiencing an exhilaration which I found difficult to conceal" Emmens, p. 267.
309 "A third individual appeared out of the darkness" Emmens, p. 274.
310 "There was animated conversation" Emmens, p. 278.
311 "It was about twelve-thirty when we started" Emmens, p. 283.
312 "We made a quick turn into the place" Emmens, p. 286.
313 "I lay down on a real bed" Emmens, p. 289.
314 "I'll tell you one thing, Herndon" Jeff Wilkinson, "Doolittle Crewman Says Plane Ordered to Fly to Soviet Union," *The State* (Columbia, S.C.), June 3, 2001.
314 The task would be assigned to B-29s For the history of LeMay's firebombing of Japan, see Larrabee, p. 584.
315 "I heard the huzzle-huzzle of something falling" Larrabee, p. 619, citing George Martin, "Black Snow and Leaping Tigers," *Harper's Magazine,* February 1946.
316 "the hundred million," to die "like shattered jewels" Dower, p. 22.
317 "Before he got out of the hospital" author interview, Mrs. Lawson, 12/4/00.
318 "no efforts to persuade him to the contrary" Arnold, "8.2, Doolittle Raid."
318 "Ted decided he next wanted to get out of the country" author interview, Mrs. Lawson, 12/4/00.
319 "By March, Ted had to return to the hospital at Walter Reed" author interview, Mrs. Lawson, 12/4/00.
320 "[E]xcept for a thoroughly tactful and touching romance woven through the film" Bosley Crowther, "Thirty Seconds over Tokyo," *New York Times,* November 16, 1944.

320   "We were in love, but I don't know if we were in *that* kind of love" author inter-
       view, Mrs. Lawson, 12/4/00.

320   "Not only is it a timely saga of our war in the Pacific" Abel, "Thirty Seconds
       over Tokyo," *Variety*, November 15, 1944 [writer's first name unattributed].

320   the first major Hollywood production discussed in detail in Martin F. Norden,
       "Resexualization of the Disabled War Hero in 'Thirty Seconds over Tokyo,'" *Jour-
       nal of Popular Film and Television*, June 1, 1995.

322   "I still kept going over the verses in the Bible that I had memorized" Watson, p. 60.

324   "start praying. . . . I asked, 'What shall I pray about?'" Watson, p. 63.

324   "We had a little signal" Hasdorff, Hite.

324   "Despite the fact that it was broad daylight in our cabin" William L. Laurence,
       "Atomic Bombing of Nagasaki Told by Flight Member," *New York Times*, Septem-
       ber 9, 1945.

PEACE

page
326   "I could not help wondering what would happen" Watson, p. 65.

327   "did not turn in Japan's favor" Dower, *Embracing Defeat*, p. 33.

328   "it is my earnest hope and indeed the hope of all mankind" Craig, pp. 299–301.

328   "Here is the victor announcing the verdict" Toshikazu Kase, *Journey to the Mis-
       souri* (New Haven, Conn.: Yale University Press, 1950), pp. 7–8.

328   "Our people . . . knew how to advance" Dower, *Embracing Defeat*, p. 290.

328   In the spring of 1941, when his thoughts were turning For the history of the
       OSS and CIA, see especially Michael Warner, CIA History Staff, "The Office
       of Strategic Services," CIA Publications, May 2000, http://www.cia.gov/cia/
       publications/oss/index.htm.

329   "Both of my parents were born in Hiroshima, Japan" author interview, Mr.
       Hamada, 8/15/01.

331   "Several enemy fighter planes taxied" author interview, Mr. Hamada, 8/15/01.

332   "Everyone came to look at us" Watson, p. 66.

333   "We were in that hotel" Hasdorff, DeShazer.

334   His paranoia increased For the details of George Barr's last days as a POW, see
       Capt. George Barr, "Rough draft of a story by Captain George Barr, pertinent to
       the trials in Shanghai of those Japanese officials held responsible for the execution
       of three Doolittle fliers who participated in the raid on Tokyo," March 30, 1946,
       in the papers of James Harold Doolittle, Library of Congress, Washington, D.C.

334   "I guess our people learned a lot about prisoners of war" Hasdorff, Hite.

335   "I was in uniform, wearing my wings" McManus, p. 369.

335   "After the war ended, these men had time to think" author interview, request for
       anonymity.

335   "One thing I've noticed in the interviews I've done" Dr. Gerald Levine, inter-
       viewed by Aaron Elson, Veterans Administration Hospital, East Orange, N.J., in
       Jimmy Doolittle and Me, http://www.tankbooks.com/ptsd.htm.

336   "How was the best way to let God use me?" Hasdorff, DeShazer.

338   "George had been orphaned at six months of age" Doolittle, *I Could Never,* p. 459.

341   The Shanghai trial was one of over 2,200 legal proceedings For details see Robert Barr Smith, "Justice Under the Sun: Japanese War Crimes Trials," *World War II,* September 1996.

342   "Because Japanese soldiers killed my parents" Prange, Goldstein, and Dillon, p. 202.

343   "How steady, so beautiful, and so useful it was" Prange, Goldstein, and Dillon, p. 190.

343   "We got in to Yokohama" Hasdorff, DeShazer.

345   "I stayed in the service" author interview, Mr. Jones, 11/21/00.

346   "I received orders to go to Tampa" author interview, Mr. McCool, 11/29/00.

346   "There was a lot of Lend-Lease money" author interview, Mr. Liu, 5/23/01.

346   "Ted Laban came" Hasdorff, York.

346   "Some would say we raised hell at that Miami reunion" Doolittle, *I Could Never,* p. 508.

347   "I never missed it a speck" Wilson.

348   "It was like having the sun come up" Prange, Goldstein, and Dillon, p. 212.

348   "I am Fuchida Mitsuo" Prange, Goldstein, and Dillon, p. 214.

349   "Fuchida had two women" Hasdorff, DeShazer.

349   "In 1948, the Raiders decided to have a reunion in Minneapolis" author interview, Mr. Liu, 5/23/01.

349   "We have held a reunion every year since" Doolittle, *I Could Never,* p. 508.

350   "In 1959, the reunion was held in Tucson" Hasdorff, Macia.

351   "I think that the only reason" Heaton.

352   "I wonder why the hell" Charles McCarthy, "Raiders Reunion," *Fresno Bee,* May 11, 2001.

352   "They are like sons to me, that group of boys" and "The guys that I have known on the Doolittle Raiders" *One Hour over Tokyo.*

CODA

page

354   "The building shuddered, realigned itself" John Tauranac, *The Empire State Building* (New York: Scribner, 1995), and William Roberts, "July 28, 1945—Plane Hits Building—Woman Survives 75-Story Fall," *Elevator World,* March 1, 1996.

355   In its Strategic Master Plan Jack Hitt, "Battlefield Space," *New York Times Magazine,* August 5, 2001.

357   "You did the right thing" Richard Rongstad, "Pearl Harbor Pilot to Tibbets: 'You Did the Right Thing,'" *Sun Tzu's Newswire,* September 20, 1998.

359   "were not provided necessary and critical intelligence" and "the intelligence available to Admiral Kimmel and General Short" Neal Thompson, "Son Fights

to Redeem His Father from the Blame for Pearl Harbor; Edward Kimmel Argues That Admiral Was Made a Scapegoat for Disaster," *Baltimore Sun,* December 7, 1999, and Kevin Baker, "The Guilt Dogging the Greatest Generation," *New York Times,* November 12, 2000.

359 **"Even if one admits"** cited in Prange, *At Dawn We Slept,* p. 841.

360 **"The Commission examined 127 witnesses"** Hopkins.

361 **"tricked, provoked, incited, cajoled, or coerced"** Prange, *At Dawn We Slept,* p. 677.

361 **Any tourist visiting Japan today** For details on the contemporary Japanese relationship with its World War II history, see especially Howard W. French, "Japan's Resurgent Far Right Tinkers with History," *New York Times,* March 25, 2001; Howard W. French, "Shrine Visit and a Textbook Weigh on Koizumi's Future," *New York Times,* August 12, 2001; Thomas L. Friedman, "Under the Volcano," *New York Times,* September 29, 2000; Karl Taro Greenfield, *Speed Tribes: Days and Nights with Japan's Next Generation* (New York: HarperCollins, 1994); Ed Jacob, "The Quirky Japan Homepage," http://www3.tky.3web.ne.jp/~edjacob, March 1, 2001; Nigel Lloyd, "Cloud Over the Empire of the Sun," *The Times* (London), July 29, 1995; Peter Maas, "They Should Have Their Day in Court," *Parade,* June 17, 2001; David McNeill, "An Unwelcome Visit from the Uyoku," *New Statesman,* February 26, 2001; John Nathan, "Tokyo Story," *The New Yorker,* April 9, 2001; Murray Sayle, "A Dynasty Falters," *The New Yorker,* June 12, 2000; Murray Sayle, "The Kamikazes Rise Again," *Atlantic Monthly,* March 2001; and Geraldine Sherma, "Japan's War Heroes Have Their Shrine," *Toronto Globe and Mail,* December 7, 1991.

365 **"After the war, the CIA requested my services"** author interview, Mr. Hamada, 8/15/01.

365 **"where the president's plane flies out of"** Hasdorff, Knobloch.

366 **"I retired in 1978"** author interview, Mr. Liu, 5/23/01.

367 **"After the raid, five of us reported to a B-26 Group"** letter from Mr. Griffin, 8/15/00.

367 **"After the war, I continued on in the service"** author interview, Mr. Holstrom, 11/26/00.

368 **"After Chungking, I was one of the fourteen"** letter from Mr. Cole, 9/3/00.

368 **"After the war was over"** author interview, Mr. Hoover, 5/20/01.

368 **"I got 'bit by the education bug'"** author interview, Mr. McCool, 11/29/00.

369 **"In Los Angeles they gave me a decoration ceremony"** author interview, Mr. Birch, 12/12/00.

369 **"In 1964 I got orders to NASA headquarters in D.C."** author interview, Mr. Jones, 11/21/00.

371 **"I returned to Tucson"** Hasdorff, Macia.

371 **"In the last years of his life"** author interview, Mrs. Lawson, 12/4/00.

SOURCES

"Air Power Historian, Volume IV, Number 4, 10-01-1957." Air Force Historical Research Agency, Maxwell Air Force Base, Ala.

Allmon, William B. "Successor to the Flying Tigers: THE CATF." *Aviation History*, Mar. 1997.

Ambrose, Stephen E. *The Supreme Commander: The War Years of General Dwight D. Eisenhower*. Garden City, N.Y.: Doubleday, 1970.

The American Experience: Eleanor Roosevelt. http://www.pbs.org/wgbh/amex/eleanor/filmmore/transcript/transcript2.html, 2001.

The American Experience: FDR. Produced by David Grubin and WGBH Boston. PBS Video, 1994.

The American Experience: Lindbergh. Produced and directed by Stephen Ives. WGBH Boston, 1999.

The American Experience: MacArthur. http://www.pbs.org/wgbh/amex/macarthur, 2001.

Ammer, Christine. "Fighting Words." *Military History*, Winter 2001.

Andrews, Mary. Letter to Dean Davenport, July 6, 1994.

Apple, R. W., Jr. "Flashin' Those Dreamy Eyes Way Down Yonder." *New York Times*, Nov. 24, 2000.

"Army Air Forces in the War Against Japan, 01-01-43." *Army Air Forces Historical Studies No. 34*, Air Force Historical Research Agency, Maxwell Air Force Base, Ala.

Arnold, Henry H. "8.2, Doolittle Raid" (personal collection of papers donated to the Air Force Archives by Murray Green, including relevant Eisenhower papers). Air Force Historical Research Agency, Maxwell Air Force Base, Ala.

———. "Biennial Report (1 Jul 39 to 30 Jun 41) of the Chief of Staff of the United States Army to the Secretary of War, 1941, Army Air Forces/Director of Intelligence Service, Informational Intelligence Summary (Special) No. 20." Air Force Historical Research Agency, Maxwell Air Force Base, Ala.

———. *Global Mission*. New York: Harper & Row, 1949.

———. "Memorandum for the President." Jan. 28, 1942, Franklin Delano Roosevelt Library, Hyde Park, N.Y.

———. "Memorandum for the President." Apr. 23, 1942, Franklin Delano Roosevelt Library, Hyde Park, N.Y.

———. "Memorandum for the President." May 3, 1942, Franklin Delano Roosevelt Library, Hyde Park, N.Y.

————. "Memorandum of White House Meeting, January 4, 1942." Air Force Historical Research Agency, Maxwell Air Force Base, Ala.

"Assistant Chief of Air Staff Intelligence, 06-03-1943." (Document contains interview with crew of B-25 aircraft that participated in Lt. Col. James H. Doolittle raid— 18 Apr. 42 bombing of Tokyo, Japan—and flew afterwards to Russia and internment.) Air Force Historical Research Agency, Maxwell Air Force Base, Ala.

Associated Press. "Sunken German U-Boat Found in Gulf of Mexico." *New York Times,* June 9, 2001.

————. "Toast to Victory," *Air Force Times,* May 4, 1998.

Avery, Norman L. *B-25 Mitchell: The Magnificent Medium.* St. Paul, Minn.: Phalanx Publishing Co., Ltd., 1992.

Baker, Kevin. "The Guilt Dogging the Greatest Generation." *New York Times,* Nov. 12, 2000.

Baker, Lt. Col. Sue. (AFMC Public Affairs Individual Mobilization Augmentee). "Remembering Granddad Doolittle." *AFMC Public Affairs,* Feb. 1998.

Barr, Capt. George. "Rough draft of a story by Captain George Barr, pertinent to the trials in Shanghai of those Japanese officials held responsible for the execution of three Doolittle fliers who participated in the raid on Tokyo." Mar. 30, 1946, in the papers of James Harold Doolittle, Manuscript Division, Library of Congress, Washington, D.C.

Barry, Rick. "Doolittle Raiders Gather for 54th Anniversary; Respect for the 23 Warriors Bridges More Than One Generation Gap." *Tampa Tribune,* Apr. 21, 1996.

————. "Doolittle Raiders to Toast Comrades; Veterans Carry on Annual Tradition After Historic WWII Raid on Tokyo." *Tampa Tribune,* Apr. 19, 1996.

Baugher, Joe. *Elevon: Aviation on the Internet.* "American Military Aircraft Encyclopedia." http://www.csd.uwo.ca/~pettypi/elevon/baugher_us/b025i.html.

Bernard, Tom. "Japs Were Jumpy After Tokyo Raid." *Stars and Stripes,* Apr. 27, 1943.

Bier, Jerry. "Recalling the Raiders." *Fresno Bee,* May 13, 2001.

Biography: Franklin D. Roosevelt, The War Years. Arts & Entertainment Television Networks. 57 min. 1994.

Biography: Jimmy Doolittle: King of the Sky. Arts & Entertainment Television Networks. 57 min. 1996.

Bix, Herbert P. *Hirohito and the Making of Modern Japan.* New York: HarperCollins, 2000.

Bone, James. "Air Ace Wins Honour of Yamamoto Kill." *The Times* (London), Apr. 1, 1997.

Boyce, Lt. Col. Ward. Taped Interview with Lt. Col. Jasper J. Harrington. U.S. Air Force Oral History Interview, Mar. 28, 1981, Air Force Historical Research Agency, Maxwell Air Force Base, Ala.

Boyne, Walter J. "The Sky Was the Limit." *Washington Post,* July 28, 1991.

Bradley, Tom. "Ethnic Narcissism and Infertility in Japan." *FrontPageMagazine.com,* Jan. 2, 2001.

Brickhill, Paul. *The Great Escape.* New York: W. W. Norton and Company, 1950.

Brock, Col. A. W., Jr. (Deputy Assistant Chief of Air Staff, Intelligence). Memorandum for the Commanding General, Army Ground Forces. Oct. 2, 1943, Air Force Historical Research Agency, Maxwell Air Force Base, Ala.

Bryant, Arthur. *Triumph in the West, 1943–1946.* London: Macmillan, 1959.

Buell, Harold L. "The Hornets and Their Heroic Men." © 1992, The USS Hornet Club, Inc. http://www.usshornetclub.com.

Burch, Lieutenant Colonel, Major Fogelman, and Captain Tate. "Interview: Gen. James H. Doolittle." United States Air Force Oral History Program, Sept. 26, 1971.

Buruma, Ian. "My Enemy's Enemy Is My Friend." *The Independent* (London), May 1, 1995.

Bush, George H. "Remarks at the Presentation Ceremony for the Presidential Medal of Freedom." White House, July 6, 1989.

Callen, Kate (United Press International). "Key WWII Mission Recalled; Doolittle's Raiders Reunite in Torrance." *Los Angeles Times,* Apr. 18, 1987.

Carey, Brian Todd. "Operation Pointblank: Evolution of Allied Air Doctrine." *World War II,* May 2001.

Carr, Edward Hallet. *What Is History?* New York: Alfred A. Knopf, 1961.

Carter, K. C., and R. Mueller. "Combat Chronology, Army Air Forces in World War II," 09-15-1945. Albert F. Simpson Historical Research Center and the Office of Air Force History, Air Force Historical Research Agency, Maxwell Air Force Base, Ala.

Chang, Iris. *The Rape of Nanking.* New York: Basic Books, 1997.

Chasing the Sun. Produced by Isaac Mizrahi. KCET (Community Television of Southern California), July 2, 2001.

Civil Air Patrol, *Cadet Leadership: 2000 and Beyond.* Vol. 1, 1999, Maxwell Air Force Base, Ala.

Coffey, Thomas M. *Hap: The Story of the U.S. Air Force and the Man Who Built It.* New York: Viking, 1982.

Cohen, Stan. *Destination: Tokyo.* Missoula, Mont.: Pictorial Histories Publishing Company, 1983.

"Columbia Journal; Doolittle Raiders Recall 30 Seconds in History." *New York Times,* Apr. 14, 1992.

Cook, Haruko Taya, and Theodore F. Cook. *Japan at War: An Oral History.* New York: New Press, 1992.

Cooper, Col. Merian C. (Assistant Chief of Air Staff, Intelligence). "The Doolittle Air Raid on Japan Known as First Special Aviation Project"; "Report on Doolittle raid on Tokyo, 18 April 1942, with collection of interviews, messages and maps"; "Reports on B-25 Aircraft"; "Assessment of Damage, Tokyo Raid"; "Report and Analysis on Tokyo Raid"; and "Interviews with Pilots and Air Crews Conducted After the Raid." Air Force Historical Research Agency, Maxwell Air Force Base, Ala.

Cooper, Brig. Gen. Merian C. Letter re: Doolittle, Haynes, Halverson, May 22, 1970, from Henry H. Arnold, "8.2, Doolittle Raid" (personal collection of papers donated to the Air Force Archives by Murray Green), Air Force Historical Research Agency, Maxwell Air Force Base, Ala.

Copp, DeWitt S. *Forged in Fire: Strategy and Decisions in the Air War over Europe.* Garden City, N.Y.: Doubleday, 1982.

Costello, John. *The Pacific War.* New York: Rawson, Wade, 1981.

Craig, William. *The Fall of Japan.* New York: Dial, 1967.

Crouch, Tom. "The Thrill of Invention." *Air & Space,* Apr./May 1998.

Davis, Kenneth S. *FDR, The War President: 1940–1943.* New York: Random House, 2000.

Daws, Gavan. *Prisoners of the Japanese.* New York: William Morrow/Quill, 1994.

DeFao, Janine. "Island Makeover; Folks Feared the Navy's Departure Would Sink Alameda." *San Francisco Chronicle,* Dec. 17, 1999.

Demler, Marvin C. Personal papers collection, 01-01-1943–01-01-1944. Air Force Historical Research Agency, Maxwell Air Force Base, Ala.

Doolittle, Gen. James H. "Jimmy," with Carroll V. Glines. *I Could Never Be So Lucky Again.* New York: Bantam Books, 1991.

Doolittle, Lt. Col. James H. Memorandum to the Chief Commanding General Army Air Forces, Subject: B25B Special Project (handwritten, n.d.). Air Force Historical Research Agency, Maxwell Air Force Base, Ala.

Doolittle, Brig. Gen. James H. Letter to Mrs. Ellen A. Lawson. June 17, 1942. Ellen Lawson private papers.

———. Report of the Aerial Bombing of Japan, 5 June 1942. Air Force Historical Research Agency, Maxwell Air Force Base, Ala.

Dower, John W. *Embracing Defeat: Japan in the Wake of World War II.* New York: W. W. Norton and Company, 1999.

———. *War Without Mercy: Race and Power in the Pacific War.* New York: Pantheon, 1986.

Duncan, D. B. "Secret Planning for the Tokyo Raid." In J. T. Mason, ed., *The Pacific War Remembered: An Oral History Collection.* Annapolis, Md.: Naval Institute Press, 1986.

Dunne, John Gregory. "The American Raj." *The New Yorker,* May 7, 2001.

Dunnigan, James F., and Albert A. Nofi. *Victory at Sea.* New York: William Morrow, 1995.

88th Communications Group Web Team, U.S. Air Force Museum, Wright-Patterson Air Force Base, Ohio. http://www.wpafb.af.mil/, Jan. 14, 2002.

Elder, Sean. "The Sappiest Generation." *Salon,* July 31, 2000.

Elson, Aaron. Interview with Dr. Gerald Levine, Veterans Administration Hospital, East Orange, N.J. In *Jimmy Doolittle and Me,* http://www.tankbooks.com/ptsd.htm.

Emde, Heiner. *Conquerors of the Air.* New York: Viking Press, 1968.

Emmens, Lt. Col. Robert G. *Guests of the Kremlin.* New York: Macmillan Company, 1949.

Falkenberg, Jim. "Finding Forgiveness at Pearl Harbor." Columbus, Ohio: Bible Literature International, 2001.

Fallows, James. "Around the World in Eighty Megabytes." *Atlantic Monthly,* Mar. 2001.

———. "Freedom of the Skies." *Atlantic Monthly,* June 2001.

Finnegan, William. "The Poison Keeper." *The New Yorker,* Jan. 15, 2001.

Fischer, Jack. "Vinegar Joe's Problem." *Harper's Magazine,* Dec. 1944.

Fishel, Staff Sgt. Robert. "'Some Will Be Heroes, Some Will Be Angels,' Doolittle Said to Fliers on Tokyo Raid; Keesler Major in Party." *Keesler Field News* (Mississippi), May 27, 1943.

Ford, Daniel. *Flying Tigers.* Washington, D.C.: Smithsonian Institution Press, 1991.

———, ed. *Glen Edwards: The Diary of a Bomber Pilot.* Washington, D.C.: Smithsonian Institution Press, 1998.

Frank, Richard B. *Downfall: The End of the Imperial Japanese Empire.* New York: Random House, 1999.

French, Howard W. "Japan's Resurgent Far Right Tinkers with History." *New York Times,* Mar. 25, 2001.

———. "Shrine Visit and a Textbook Weigh on Koizumi's Future." *New York Times,* Aug. 12, 2001.

Friedman, Thomas L. "Under the Volcano." *New York Times,* Sept. 29, 2000.

Frisbee, John L. "First over Tokyo." *Air Force Magazine* 72, no. 4 (Apr. 1989).

Fromkin, David. *In the Time of the Americans.* New York: Alfred A. Knopf, 1995.

Fuchida, Mitsuo, and Masatake Okumiya. *Midway: The Battle That Doomed Japan.* Annapolis, Md.: United States Naval Institute, 1955.

Gannon, Michael. *Operation Drumbeat.* New York: HarperCollins, 1990.

Gendler, Neal. "Minnesotan Will Seek Only Intact B-25 from Doolittle's Tokyo Raid." *Minneapolis Star Tribune,* Feb. 27, 1993.

Geyer, Georgie Anne. "When 'Failure' Becomes 'Success.'" *New Orleans Times-Picayune,* Apr. 25, 1996.

Gibney, Frank. *Senso: The Japanese Remember the Pacific War: Letters to the Editor of Asahi Shimbun,* translated by Beth Cary. Armonk, N.Y., and London: M. E. Sharpe, 1995.

Gibney, Jim. "Chinese Honored for Aiding U.S. Fliers." *Denver Post,* Mar. 19, 1992.

Gill, Brendan. "Young Man Behind Plexiglas: Profile of an American Bombardier." *The New Yorker,* Aug. 12, 1944.

Glines, Carroll V. "Air Power Visionary Billy Mitchell." *Aviation History,* Sept. 1997.

———. "American Ingenuity Behind Barbed Wire." *Friends Journal,* Spring 2001.

———. *The Doolittle Raid.* New York: Orion Books, 1988.

———. *Doolittle's Tokyo Raiders.* Princeton, N.J.: D. Van Nostrand Company, 1964.

———. *Four Came Home.* Missoula, Mont.: Pictorial Histories Publishing Company, 1981.

———. *Jimmy Doolittle: Daredevil Aviator and Scientist.* New York: Macmillan, 1972.

———. "Strike Against Japan." *Aviation History,* Mar. 1998.

Goldstein, Richard. "Rex T. Barber, Pilot Who Downed Yamamoto, Dies at 84." *New York Times,* Aug. 1, 2001.

Goodwin, Doris Kearns. *No Ordinary Time.* New York: Simon & Schuster, 1994.

Gray, Capt. Robert M. "Participation in the Doolittle Raid on Tokyo 04-18-1942." Research Studies Institute, Air Force Historical Research Agency, Maxwell Air Force Base, Ala.

Greenfield, Karl Taro. *Speed Tribes: Days and Nights with Japan's Next Generation.* New York: HarperCollins, 1994.

Greening, Col. C. Ross. *The First Joint Action.* Monograph submitted to the Faculty of the Armed Forces Staff College, Norfolk, Va., Fourth Class, Dec. 21, 1948.

———. *Not As Briefed.* St. Paul, Minn.: Brown Bigelow, 1945.

———. *Not As Briefed.* Pullman: Washington State University Press, 2001.

Greer, Judith. "Did FDR Know?" *Salon,* June 14, 2001.

Grew, Joseph C. Telegram to Cordell Hull (dated 12/8/41, received 12/10/41, 6:23 A.M.). Franklin Delano Roosevelt Library, Hyde Park, N.Y.

———. *Ten Years in Japan.* New York: Simon & Schuster, 1944.

Grout, Carole. "Local Vets Played Big Roles in WWII." *New Orleans Times-Picayune,* Aug. 27, 1995.

Hailey, Foster. *Pacific Battle Line.* New York: Macmillan Company, 1944.

Hasdorff, Dr. James C. "Interview of Brig. Gen. Richard A. Knobloch." United States Air Force Oral History Program, July 13–14, 1987, Air Force Historical Research Agency, Maxwell Air Force Base, Ala.

———. "Interview of Captain Charles J. Ozuk, Jr." United States Air Force Oral History Program, July 1989, Air Force Historical Research Agency, Maxwell Air Force Base, Ala.

———. "Interview of Chief Master Sergeant Bert M. Jordan." United States Air Force Oral History Program, June 15, 1988, Air Force Historical Research Agency, Maxwell Air Force Base, Ala.

———. "Interview of Col. Edward J. York." United States Air Force Oral History Program, San Antonio, Texas, July 23, 1984, Air Force Historical Research Agency, Maxwell Air Force Base, Ala.

———. "Interview of Colonel James H. Macia." United States Air Force Oral History Program, July 15–16, 1987, Air Force Historical Research Agency, Maxwell Air Force Base, Ala.

———. "Interview of Lieutenant Colonel Horace E. Crouch." United States Air Force Oral History Program, Apr. 1989, Air Force Historical Research Agency, Maxwell Air Force Base, Ala.

———. "Interview of Lt. Col. Robert L. Hite." United States Air Force Oral History Program, Enid, Okla., Dec. 15–17, 1982, Air Force Historical Research Agency, Maxwell Air Force Base, Ala.

———. "Interview of Major General David M. Jones." United States Air Force Oral History Program, Jan. 13–14, 1987, Air Force Historical Research Agency, Maxwell Air Force Base, Ala.

———. "Interview of Reverend Jacob D. DeShazer." United States Air Force Oral History Program, Oct. 10, 1989, Air Force Historical Research Agency, Maxwell Air Force Base, Ala.

Hayes, Grace P. *The History of the Joint Chiefs of Staff in World War II: The War Against Japan.* Annapolis, Md.: Naval Institute Press, 1982.

Hayostek, Cindy. "Exploits of a Doolittle Raider." *Military History,* Mar. 1996.

Heaton, Colin. "Black Sheep Leader." *Aviation History,* May 2001.

Hilger, Maj. John A. "Report of Airplane No. 40-2297." Chungking, China, May 2, 1942.

Hitt, Jack. "Battlefield Space." *New York Times Magazine,* Aug. 5, 2001.

Hoffman, Bruce. "One-Alarm Fire." *Atlantic Monthly,* Dec. 2001.

Holstrom, Lt. Everett W. "Personal Report," Chungking, China, May 14, 1942.

Hoover, Lt. Travis. "Personal Report," Chungking, China, May 15, 1942.

Hopkins, Harry L. "Report from the Commission created by Executive Order 'to ascertain and report the facts relating to the attack made by Japanese armed forces upon the Territory of Hawaii on December 7, 1941.'" January 24, 1942, Harry L. Hopkins papers, Franklin Delano Roosevelt Library, Hyde Park, N.Y.

How to Fly the B-25 (Official Training Film TFI-3360). First Motion Picture Unit, Army Air Forces/War Department. 33 min. 1944.

Hoyt, Edwin P. *Japan's War: The Great Pacific Conflict, 1853–1952.* New York: McGraw-Hill, 1986.

Hull, Cordell. Department of State Memorandum of Conversation, December 5, 1941. Franklin Delano Roosevelt Library, Hyde Park, N.Y.

Hynes, Samuel, Anne Matthews, Nancy Caldwell Sorel, and Roger J. Spiller (Advisory Board). *Reporting World War II.* New York: Library of America, 1995.

Ienaga, Saburo. *The Pacific War: 1931–1945.* New York: Pantheon, 1978.

Jackson, Robert. *Bomber! Famous Bomber Missions of World War II.* New York: St. Martin's Press, 1980.

Jacob, Ed. "The Quirky Japan Homepage." http://www3.tky.3web.ne.jp/~edjacob, Mar. 1, 2001.

Johnson, Maj. Harry, Jr. (Adjutant). "B25-B Special Project." Handwritten and undated notes for army file, Air Force Historical Research Agency, Maxwell Air Force Base, Ala.

Jones, Capt. David M. "Narrative Report," Chungking, China, May 18, 1942.

Joyce, Richard O. (1st Lt., Air Corps, 0-401770). "Report of Tokyo Raid, Airplane #40-2250," Chungking, China, May 2, 1942.

Kase, Toshikazu. *Journey to the Missouri.* New Haven, Conn.: Yale University Press, 1950.

Kelley, Tina. "Amid the Relics of Combat, Veterans Recall Flights and Flak and Friends." *New York Times,* Dec. 3, 2000.

Kennedy, David M. "Victory at Sea." *Atlantic Monthly,* Mar. 1999.

Kennedy, Edward. "Patton Struck Soldier in Hospital, Was Castigated by Eisenhower." *St. Louis Post-Dispatch,* Nov. 23, 1943.

Kernan, Alvin. *Crossing the Line: A Bluejacket's World War II Odyssey.* Annapolis, Md.: Naval Institute Press, 1994.

Kessler, Lauren. *The Happy Bottom Riding Club: The Life and Times of Pancho Barnes.* New York: Random House, 2000.

King, Ernest J., and Walter Muir Whitehill. *Fleet Admiral King: A Naval Record.* New York: W. W. Norton and Company, 1952.

Krakauer, John. *Into the Wild.* New York: Villard, 1996.

Krebs, Albin. "James Doolittle, 96, Pioneer Aviator Who Led First Raid on Japan, Dies." *New York Times,* Sept. 29, 1993.

Laddon, Mac. "Interview with Lt. General Doolittle." *Reuben Fleet,* San Diego, Aug. 14, 1970.

Lamb, Margaret Yarwood. *Going It Alone: Mary Andrews—Missionary to China, 1938–1951.* Calgary, Canada: Aquila Books, 1995.

Langenberg, William H. "Japan Bombs the West Coast." *Aviation History,* Nov. 1998.

Larkin, Sgt. George E., Jr. "Personal Diary, October 18, 1942." Filson Club Historical Society, Louisville, Ky.

Larrabee, Eric. *Commander in Chief: Franklin Delano Roosevelt, His Lieutenants and Their War.* New York: Harper & Row, 1987.

Laurence, William L. "Atomic Bombing of Nagasaki Told by Flight Member." *New York Times,* Sept. 9, 1945.

Lawrenson, Helen. "Damn the Torpedoes!" *Harper's Magazine,* July 1942.

Lawson, Capt. Ted W. *Thirty Seconds over Tokyo.* New York: Random House and Cutchogue, N.Y.: Buccaneer Books, 1943.

Leckie, Robert. *Delivered from Evil: The Saga of World War II.* New York: Harper & Row, 1987.

Lehrer, Jim. "Character Above All: An Exploration of Presidential Leadership." *The News Hour.* PBS, http://www.pbs.org/newshour/character/essays/roosevelt.html.

Leish, Kenneth W. "The Reminiscences of James Harold Doolittle." Aviation Project Collection, Columbia University Oral History Research Office, 1960.

LeMay, Curtis. *Mission with LeMay.* Garden City, N.Y.: Doubleday, 1965.

Liebling, A. J. "The Foamy Fields." *The New Yorker,* Mar. 20, Apr. 3, 10, 17, 1943.

Lienhard, John H. "Norden's Bombsight." *Engines of Ingenuity.* University of Houston, http://www.uh.edu/engines/epi1004.htm.

Life. Editors of. *Our Finest Hour: Voices of the World War II Generation.* Des Moines, Iowa: Life Books, 2000.

Lindbergh, Charles A. *The Wartime Journals of Charles A. Lindbergh.* New York: Harcourt Brace Jovanovich, 1970.

Lloyd, Nigel. "Cloud over the Empire of the Sun." *The Times* (London), July 29, 1995.

Lopez, Donald S. *Aviation: A Smithsonian Guide.* New York: Macmillan, 1995.

Lord, Walter. *Day of Infamy.* New York: Henry Holt, 1957.

Love, Robert W., Jr. *The Chiefs of Naval Operations.* Annapolis, Md.: Naval Institute Press, 1980.

Lowman, David D. *Magic: The Untold Story of U.S. Intelligence and the Evacuation of Japanese Residents from the West Coast During WWII.* www.athenapressinc.com, 2001.

Maas, Peter. "They Should Have Their Day in Court." *Parade,* June 17, 2001.

McCarthy, Charles. "Raiders Reunion." *Fresno Bee,* May 11, 2001.

McCullough, David. *Truman.* New York: Simon & Schuster, 1992.

McManus, John C. *Deadly Sky: The American Combat Airman in World War II.* Novato, Calif.: Presidio Press, 2000.

McNeill, David. "An Unwelcome Visit from the Uyoku." *New Statesman,* Feb. 26, 2001.

Mann, Carl. *Lightning in the Sky: The Story of Jimmy Doolittle.* New York: Robert McBride & Co., 1943.

Mann, William C. "Battle of Midway Rewritten from Grave." *Ottawa Citizen,* Aug. 29, 1999.

Marcus, Jon. "Far and Away." *Condé Nast Traveler,* July 2000.

Marshall, George. *Biennial Report of the Chief of Staff of the United States Army to the Secretary of War.* July 1, 1939, to June 30, 1941. Washington, D.C.: Government Printing Office, 1941.

Marshall, S. L. A. (Chief of Military History, Department of the Army). "Tokyo Raid" (n.d.), Air Force Historical Research Agency, Maxwell Air Force Base, Ala.

Martin, George. "Black Snow and Leaping Tigers." *Harper's Magazine,* Feb. 1946.

"Material About Tokyo Raid." (Includes Tokyo critique, paraphrase of incoming messages from special file, and comments and suggestions made by members of Doolittle mission of 18 Apr. 42 concerning aircraft and equipment.) Air Force Historical Research Agency, Maxwell Air Force Base, Ala.

Matheny, Dave. "Search Is on for Chunk of Aluminum, and Rest of '42 Doolittle Raid Remains." *Minneapolis Star Tribune,* Apr. 22, 1994.

The Merck Manual. Whitehouse Station, N.J.: Merck & Co., Inc., 2001.

Merrill, James M. *Target Tokyo: The Halsey-Doolittle Raid.* Chicago: Rand McNally & Co., 1964.

Miles, Dwayne. "USS *Hornet* CV-8 statistics." http://www.usshornetclub.com, May 26, 2001.

Military Intelligence Service, War Department. "Japanese Land Operations from Japanese Sources, December 8, 1941 to June 8, 1942." *Campaign Study #3,* Nov. 18, 1942, Air Force Historical Research Agency, Maxwell Air Force Base, Ala.

Miller, H. L. "Training the Doolittle Fliers." In J. T. Mason, Jr., ed., *The Pacific War Remembered: An Oral History Collection.* Annapolis, Md.: Naval Institute Press, 1986.

"Miscellaneous Special Studies." (Includes assessment of damage from Tokyo Raid.) Jan. 1, 1944, Army Air Forces Historical Division, Air Force Historical Research Agency, Maxwell Air Force Base, Ala.

Mitscher, Marc A. "Report of Action, April 18, 1942, USS *Hornet.* " U.S. Naval Historical Center, Annapolis, Md.

Molotsky, Irvin. "Panel Backs World War II Memorial on Mall in Washington." *New York Times,* July 21, 2000.

Morgan, Ted. *FDR.* New York: Simon & Schuster, 1986.

Morgenthau, Henry. "Memorandum for the President re: Bank of Japan." Dec. 3, 1941, Franklin Delano Roosevelt Library, Hyde Park, N.Y.

Morrison, Bob. "The Last Hurrah?" *Herald Tribune* (Sarasota, Florida), Apr. 11, 1998.

Mullener, Elizabeth. "30 Seconds over Tokyo." *New Orleans Times-Picayune,* Apr. 18, 2000.

Nathan, John. "Tokyo Story." *The New Yorker,* Apr. 9, 2001.

Norris, John G. "Doolittle Pledges New Tokyo Raids." *Washington Post,* Apr. 23, 1943.

O'Dwyer, William J. "From Tokyo to Stalag Luft I." *Flight Journal,* Oct. 1999.

Ohira, Rod. "Fate Entwines Lives Since Pearl Attack, Doolittle Raid." *Honolulu Advertiser,* May 20, 2001.

One Hour over Tokyo. Written and produced by Greg DeHart. Narrated by Roger Mudd. History Channel. 57 min. May 26, 2001.

Oxford, Edward. "Against All Odds." *American History,* Aug. 1997.

Pae, Peter. "In Arlington, Full Honors for a Sky-Blazing Hero; Hundreds Attend Funeral of Gen. Jimmy Doolittle." *Washington Post,* Oct. 2, 1993.

"Parents of Fliers Doubt Execution." *New York Times,* Apr. 23, 1943.

Pasquarella, Helena. "Moorpark Man Recalls a Fateful Flight over Japan During WWII." *Los Angeles Times,* July 22, 1993.

Pinkney, Capt. J. "Untitled After-Action Interviews," Chungking, China—Headquarters, Army Air Forces, Washington, D.C., June 15, 1942, Air Force Historical Research Agency, Maxwell Air Force Base, Ala.

Pogue, Forrest C. *George C. Marshall.* Vol. 2, *Ordeal and Hope.* New York: Viking, 1966.

Potter, J. D. *Yamamoto: The Man Who Menaced America.* New York: Viking, 1965.

Prange, Gordon W. *At Dawn We Slept: The Untold Story of Pearl Harbor.* New York: McGraw-Hill, 1981.

Prange, Gordon W., with Donald M. Goldstein and Katherine V. Dillon. *God's Samurai.* McLean, Va.: Brassey's, Inc., 1990.

Pye, Michael. "A Tapestry of Traditions: Japan's Religions." *Erdman's Handbook to the World's Religions.* Grand Rapids, Mich.: William B. Erdmans, 1994.

Pyle, Ernie. *Last Chapter.* New York: Henry Holt and Company, 1945.

Reddy, Lt. Kenneth E. "Personal Diaries, 4/6/42–5/9/42." Courtesy Kenneth Reddy.

Reynolds, Quentin. *The Amazing Mr. Doolittle.* New York: Appleton-Century-Crofts, 1953.

Riddle, Lyn. "For Doolittle's Men, It's Party Time Again." *Los Angeles Times,* Apr. 16, 1992.

Roberts, William. "July 28, 1945—Plane Hits [Empire State] Building—Woman Survives 75-Story Fall." *Elevator World,* Mar. 1, 1996.

Rongstad, Richard. "Pearl Harbor Pilot to Tibbets: 'You Did the Right Thing.'" Sun Tzu's Newswire, Sept. 20, 1998.

Roosevelt, Franklin D. "Address of the President Broadcast over a Nationwide and Worldwide Radio Hookup on the Occasion of the 210th Anniversary of George Washington's Birthday, February 23, 1942, at 10.00 P.M., E.W.T." Franklin Delano Roosevelt Library, Hyde Park, N.Y.

———. "Telegram of December 6, 1941, to H.I.M. Hirohito." Franklin Delano Roosevelt Library, Hyde Park, N.Y.

Rose, Lisle A. *The Ship That Held the Line.* Annapolis, Md.: Naval Institute Press, 1995.

Rosenman, Samuel I. *Working with Roosevelt.* New York: Harper & Row, 1952.

Ryan, Paul B. Interview with Stephen Jurika, March 4, 1976. *U.S. Naval Institute Oral Transcripts.* Annapolis, Md.

Sakai, Saburo. *Samurai.* New York: E. P. Dutton, 1958.

Sayle, Murray. "A Dynasty Falters." *The New Yorker,* June 12, 2000.

———. "The Kamikazes Rise Again." *Atlantic Monthly,* Mar. 2001.

Schnaufer, Jeff. "Legend Flying High." *Los Angeles Times,* Apr. 17, 1994.

Schultz, Duane. *The Doolittle Raid.* New York: St. Martin's Press, 1988.

Scott, Phil. "Something Gold, Something New." *Air & Space,* Feb./Mar. 1995.

Shellstede, Sangmie Choie, ed. *Comfort Women Speak.* New York: Holmes & Meier, 2000.

"She Nursed Raiders of 'Shangri-La.'" *Daily Telegraph* (Sydney, Australia), May 7, 1956.

Sherma, Geraldine. "Japan's War Heroes Have Their Shrine." *Toronto Globe and Mail,* Dec. 7, 1991.

Sherman, Don. "The Secret Weapon." *Air & Space,* March 1995.

Sherwood, Robert E. *Roosevelt and Hopkins.* New York: Harper & Brothers, 1948.

Sides, Hampton. *Ghost Soldiers.* New York: Doubleday, 2001.

Silcox, Marilyn. "Colonel Davenport: Memories Relived." *Gulf Defender,* Dec. 5, 1986.

Sledge, E. B. *With the Old Breed at Peleliu and Okinawa.* Novato, Calif.: Presidio Press, 1981.

Smith, Lt. Donald G. "Personal Report," Chungking, China, May 14, 1942.

Smith, Robert Barr. "Justice Under the Sun: Japanese War Crimes Trials." *World War II,* Sept. 1996.

Spector, Ronald H. *Eagle Against the Sun.* New York: Free Press, 1984.

Steinbeck, John. "Fear of Death as Green Troops Sail to Invasion." *New York Herald Tribune,* Oct. 3, 1943.

Stilwell, Gen. Joseph. "Incoming Message From: Chungking To: Agwar For Ammisca, Attn Sec War and Chief Staff." Apr. 1, 1942, Franklin Delano Roosevelt Library, Hyde Park, N.Y.

The Story of the Flying Tigers. Fei Hu Films, Chinese Public Television, 1998.

Stovall, Jack D., ed. *Tales of the Marauders.* Cordova, Tenn.: Wings of Courage Press, 1994.

Switzer, John. "USS *Hornet* Was Stung by Storms, Enemy Fire." *Columbus Dispatch,* Nov. 11, 1999.

Tanaka, Yuki. *Hidden Horrors: Japanese War Crimes in World War II.* Boulder, Colo.: Westview Press, 1996.

Tauranac, John. *The Empire State Building.* New York: Scribner, 1995.

Taylan, Justin (webmaster). "Pacific Wrecks Database." http://www.pacificwrecks.com/history/USAAF/3-42.html.

Taylor, Chris, Nicko Goncharoff, Mason Florence, and Christian Rawthorn. *Japan—A Travel Survival Book.* Hawthorn, Australia: Lonely Planet, 1997.

Terkel, Studs. *"The Good War": An Oral History of World War II.* New York: New Press, 1984.

Thach, Vice Adm. James E. "Reminiscences" (n.d.). U.S. Naval Historical Center, Annapolis, Md.

Thatcher, Cpl. David. "Personal Report." Chungking, China, May 15, 1942.

Thomas, Lowell, and Edward Jablonski. *Doolittle: A Biography.* New York: Doubleday, 1976.

Thompson, Neal. "Son Fights to Redeem His Father from the Blame for Pearl Harbor; Edward Kimmel Argues That Admiral Was Made a Scapegoat for Disaster." *Baltimore Sun,* Dec. 7, 1999.

"Threat to Fliers." *New York Times,* Apr. 22, 1943.

Toland, John. *Infamy.* New York: Doubleday, 1982.

———. *The Rising Sun.* New York: Random House, 1970.

Tolischus, Otto D. *Tokyo Record.* New York: Harcourt, Brace & World, 1943.

True Action Adventures: Bolt from the Blue: The Doolittle Raid. Produced by Charles Messenger. History Channel, Apr. 18, 2001.

Tubbs, Vincent. "Wide Awake on an Island Beachhead." *Baltimore Afro-American,* Feb. 12, 1944.

Tuchman, Barbara W. *Stilwell and the American Experience in China.* New York: Macmillan, 1971.

USS *Hornet* Museum website. http://www.uss-hornet.org.

Van Deerlin, Lionel. "Who Really Shot Down Admiral Yamamoto?" *San Diego Union-Tribune,* Mar. 20, 1996.

Wakley, Ralph. "Doolittle Raiders: Son Recalls Famous Dad." Associated Presss Newswires, Apr. 14, 200.

Walker, James W., group historian, and Robert J. Giordano, web coordinator. "376th Heavy Bombardment Group, Inc. Veterans Association." http://www.376hbgva.com/history.htm.

War Department. "Newspaper Clippings, 04-18-42." Air Force Historical Research Agency, Maxwell Air Force Base, Ala.

Ward, Geoffrey C. *A First-Class Temperament: The Emergence of Franklin Roosevelt.* New York: Harper & Row, 1989.

Warner, Michael. "The Creation of the Central Intelligence Group." *Studies in Intelligence,* Fall 1995.

Warner, Michael, and CIA History Staff. "The Office of Strategic Services." CIA Publications, May 2000, http://www.cia.gov/cia/publications/oss/index.htm.

Watson, C. Hoyt. *The Amazing Story of Sergeant Jacob DeShazer.* Winona Lake, Ind.: Life and Light Press, 1950. Reprinted as *DeShazer.* Coquitlam, British Columbia: Galaxy Communications, 1991.

Webster's American Military Biographies. New York: Merriam Co., 1978.

Weiner, Eric. "All About/Avionics; American Electronics Companies Still Rule the Cockpit." *New York Times,* Feb. 18, 1990.

Weiss, Jeffrey. "Flier's Log: UTD Library Gains Famed Aviator Doolittle's Papers." *Dallas Morning News,* Feb. 24, 1995.

Weitzner, Pete. "'Chasing Ghosts' Trails a WWII Mystery to Russia." *Orange County Register,* May, 18, 1997.

White, T. H. "Greatest Show on Earth." *Life,* Nov. 9, 1942.

Wilder, Ross R. "Response to Questionnaire." Air Force Office of Information, Mar. 27, 1957, Air Force Historical Research Agency, Maxwell Air Force Base, Ala.

Wilkinson, Jeff. "Doolittle Crewman Says Plane Ordered to Fly to Soviet Union." *The State* (Columbia, S.C.), June 3, 2001.

Williams, Jack. "'Jack' Fitzgerald Jr.; Devised Short Takeoffs." *San Diego Union-Tribune,* Mar. 7, 2000.

———. "Maj. Griffith Williams, 78; Flew on Doolittle's Tokyo Raid." *San Diego Union-Tribune,* Aug. 25, 1998.

Wilson, William R. "Jimmy Doolittle Reminisces." *American History,* July/Aug. 1997.

Wilstein, Steve (Associated Press). "Jimmy Doolittle Turns 90." *Los Angeles Times,* Dec. 14, 1986.

Wisdom, Capt. John M., assistant chief of air staff, Intelligence. "Interview with B-25 Crew That Bombed Tokyo and Was Interned by the Russians." June 3, 1943, Air Force Historical Research Agency, Maxwell Air Force Base, Ala.

Wohl, Robert. "Aviation's Belle Époque." *Air & Space,* Apr./May 1996.

World War II Air Commando Association. "WWII Air Commando," Apr. 30, 1992, Air Force Historical Research Agency, Maxwell Air Force Base, Ala.

"'Worst' Feared for Tokyo Fliers by Neutral Diplomats in Japan." *New York Times,* Apr. 24, 1943.

Wright, Mike. *What They Didn't Teach You About World War II.* Novato, Calif.: Presidio Press, 1998.

PERMISSIONS

Gen. James H. Doolittle, with Carroll V. Glines, *I Could Never Be So Lucky Again,* copyright © 1991 by the John P. Doolittle Family Trust. Used by permission of Bantam Books, a division of Random House, Inc.

Lt. Col. Robert G. Emmens, *Guests of the Kremlin,* New York: The Macmillan Company, 1949, used by permission of Justine M. Emmens.

Cindy Hayostek, "Exploits of a Doolittle Raider," *Military History,* Mar. 1996, with permission of Primedia Special Interest Publications (History Group), copyright © 1996 *Military History* magazine.

Sgt. George Elmer Larkin, Jr., 1918–1942, "Papers." Courtesy Filson Club Historical Society, Louisville, Ky.

Capt. Ted W. Lawson, *Thirty Seconds over Tokyo,* New York: Random House, 1943, used by permission of Ellen Lawson and the three Lawson children.

Lt. Kenneth E. Reddy, "Personal Diaries, 4/6/42–5/9/42." Courtesy Kenneth Reddy.

C. Hoyt Watson, *The Amazing Story of Sergeant Jacob DeShazer,* Winona Lake, Indiana: Life and Light Press, 1950; reprinted as *DeShazer,* Coquitlam, British Columbia: Galaxy Communications, 1991, courtesy Reverend Jacob DeShazer.

INDEX

"Accelerations in Flight" (Doolittle), 4
Aerodrome, 37
Aguila, Task Force, 117, 226
Aichi D3A, 78
Air Force, U.S., xi, 355, 356
Air Group 8, U.S., 285
Air Medal, 4
Air Transport Command (AC), 251
Aito, 156
Akagi, 77, 94, 156, 258–59
Akers, Frank, 67
Akihito, crown prince of Japan, 328
Alameda Naval Station, 54–55, 355
Aleutian Islands, 253
Alexander, E. H., 167, 168
Ambrose, Stephen, xii
American History, xi
Anderson, Lieutenant Commander, 114–15
Anderson, USS, 285
Andrews, Adolphus "Dolly," 28
Andrews, Mary, 212, 213, 221
Antares, USS, 84
Arashi, 257
Arcadia Conference, 103
Arizona, USS, 85, 86, 88–89, 90, 99, 361
Armour Company, 42
Army Air Corps, U.S., 19–20
    aviation training in, 23–24
    Flying Tigers merged into, 164
    hierarchy in, 26
    naming of airplanes in, 51
    recruits in, 19–21
Army Aircraft Warning Service Information Center, 85
Army General Classification Test, 20
Arndt, R. W., 256
Arnold, Chuck, 350
Arnold, Henry H. "Hap," 49, 53, 60, 78, 88, 103, 107, 109–10, 117, 118, 160, 162, 217, 219, 229–32, 273, 296, 306, 307, 314, 318

background of, 103
FDR and, 104–5, 111
King and, 101–2
Marshall and, 104
postwar career of, 356
Raiders decorated by, 271–72
refueling sites issue and, 162–65, 66
Arram, Abdul, 300–302, 308–11, 313
Asaeda Shigeharu, 77
Astor, Vincent, 29
At Dawn We Slept (Prange), 5
Atlantic Fleet, U.S., 358
Australia, 94, 95, 102, 229, 330
aviation:
    Doolittle's achievements in, 41–43, 44, 46–47
    early development of, 37–39
    in post–World War I era, 41

B-58 Test Force, 345
Backus, E. N., 167, 168
Bain, Edwin V., xvii, 153, 154, 275
Balch, USS, 56
Baltimore, USS, 85
Barber, Rex T., 294–95
Barnes, Pancho, 39
Barr, George, xviii, 129, 233, 236, 240–42, 244, 264, 281, 291, 317, 322, 332–34, 337–39, 341
Bataan, 93, 95
Bataan (film), 319
Bat Out of Hell, see plane sixteen
Battleship Row, 77, 78, 85, 88–89, 369
Belgium, 49, 99
Bellow, Saul, 29–30
Bell P-39 Aircobra, 6
Benham, USS, 56
Berger, Chick, 7
Best Years of Our Lives, The (film), 320–21
Biden, Joe, 359
Birch, Barbara, 370
Birch, John M., 215–16

Birch, William L., xiv, xvii, 18, 19, 25–26, 40–41, 51, 68, 150, 151–52, 179, 203–4, 251–52, 369–70
Bissell, Clayton, 164, 216, 223–25, 252
Bissell, Wayne Max, xvi, 201
Bither, Waldo J., xvii, 152, 180
Bitter, Gustav, 149, 315–16
Blanken, John, 85
Blanton, Thadd Harrison, xvii, 62, 124
Bloch, Claude C., 84
Boeing B-17 Flying Fortress, 7, 87, 88, 100, 256
Boeing B-29 Superfortress, 365
Bogart, Larry, 58
Bombardier's Oath, 12
Bomber Squadron 3, U.S., 156
Bomber Squadron 6, U.S., 257
Borneo, 77, 94, 95
Bourgeois, Betty, 363
Bourgeois, Robert C., xvii, 9, 61, 65, 69, 122, 129, 153, 180, 205, 206, 363
Bower, Lorraine, 363
Bower, William M., xvii, 26, 50–51, 152, 350, 363
Boyington, Gregory "Pappy," 165, 351
Bradley, Omar, 100
Braemer, Fred Anthony, xv, 135, 137, 138, 173, 209–10
Brereton, Lewis, 91, 93
Brotherhood of the Skies, 26
Brown, Joe E., 350
Bryant, H. L., 82
Buchanan, Daniel, 330
Buck, Pearl S., 162, 163
Bunker Hill, USS, 305
Burma, 71, 74, 77, 79, 164–65, 227, 251, 330
Burma Road, 163, 251
Burwell, Harvey, 40, 41
Bush, George W., 355
Butler, J. C., 156
Bywater, Hector E., 75, 81

California, USS, 85, 89
Cambodia, 74
Campbell, Clayton J., xvii, 152, 205, 206, 363
Campbell, Mary, 363
Campbell, R. K., 156
Capra, Frank, 36
Carpenter, Edmund, 330
Cavalry Journal, 99
Central Intelligence Agency (CIA), 356, 359, 365
Central Tokyo Steel Mills, 142

Cerf, Bennett, 318
Charlie (Jai Fu Chang), 187–88, 213
Chemical Warfare Service, U.S., 11
Chen, Dr., 212, 221, 247, 248
Chennault, Claire, 105–6, 117, 131, 164–65, 226, 252, 329
Chiang Kai-shek, 74, 106, 157, 160, 162, 163, 225, 357
  refueling sites issue and, 164–65
Chiang Kai-shek, Madame, 162, 225, 357
Chicago Tribune, 82
Chihaya Masataka, 359
Chikuma, 84, 256
China, Nationalist, 63, 68, 71, 99
  Japan's "rape" of, 73–74
  U.S. perception of, 162–63
China, Republic of (Taiwan), 357
China National Aviation, 92
Churchill, Winston, 96, 103, 111, 273
Cimarron, USS, 56, 60, 115
Civil Air Patrol, 28
Civilian Aviation Program, 24
Clapper, Raymond, 102
Clark, Mark, 273
Clever, Robert Stevenson, xvi, 123, 132, 143, 183, 184–85, 187–88, 195, 214, 247, 275, 295
Cline, Clair, 280
Coast Guard Auxiliary, U.S., 28–29
Cole, Martha, 368
Cole, Richard E., xii, xv, 126, 135, 138, 173, 191, 209, 232, 368
Columbus Evening Dispatch, 160
Communication Ministry, Japanese, 158
Congress, U.S., 92, 104, 105, 356, 359, 361
Considine, Bob, 318
Consolidated B-24 Liberator, 49, 117, 280
Conway, Tod, 87
Cooper, Merian C., 117, 314
Coral Sea, USS, 358
Corregidor, 93, 94
Covell, Peggy, 342–43, 347, 348
Creehan, Pat, 122
Crouch, Horace Ellis, xvii, 11, 16, 26, 50, 57, 58–59, 62, 123, 146–47, 177, 202, 364
Crouch, Macia, 364
Crowther, Bosley, 320
Cummings, Bob, 350
Cunningham, William S., 329, 331–32
Curry, Duncan, 89
Curtiss, USS, 85
Curtiss P-1 Hawk, 44–45, 48
Curtiss P-40 Warhawk, 105

Dalton, John, 356
Daniels, Josephine, *see* Doolittle, Josephine
    Daniels
Dani-Yang, 201
Dauntless, USS, 108
Davenport, Dean, xvi, 54, 132, 143, 183,
    185–87, 195, 211–12, 247, 321, 364
Davenport, Mary, 364
Davis, Kenneth S., 97
D-Day, *see* Overlord, Operation
Defense Department, U.S., 356, 359
de Gaulle, Charles, 273
De Havilland, D. H., 4, 42
De Havilland, Geoffrey, 42
DeMille, Cecil B., 40, 317
Depression, Great, 19
DeShazer, Florence Matheny, 336–37, 343,
    345, 364
DeShazer, Jacob Daniel, xviii, 15, 50, 65, 120,
    123, 135, 233, 236, 317, 357
  background of, 24–25
  in bombing of Japan, 154–55
  captured by Japanese, 238–39
  essay on imprisonment by, 343–44, 364
  Fuchida and, 348–49, 357
  in launch from *Hornet*, 129–30
  liberation of, 332–33
  marriage of, 336–37
  in missionary service, 343–45, 348–49, 364
  as POW, 242–44, 264–66, 289, 291, 293,
    302, 305–6, 317, 322–24, 326
  religious conversion of, 302, 303–4
  volunteers for raid, 10
Destination Tokyo (film), 320
Detachment 101, U.S., 330
Detroit, USS, 85
Dieter, William J., xvi, 233, 235–38, 239, 295
Dill, John, 103
Distinguished Flying Cross, 43, 244, 272, 280,
    369
Dobashi Midori, 148
Dönitz, Karl, 27
Donovan, William J., 328–29, 359
Doolittle, Frank, 34, 35, 36
Doolittle, James H., xv, 32–47, 52, 58, 65–66,
    67, 69, 70, 116, 117, 118, 155, 160, 161,
    167, 168, 198, 229, 238, 242, 270, 274,
    296, 297, 314, 318, 320
  annual reunions and, 346–47, 349–50,
    352
  aviation records and achievements of,
    41–43, 44, 46–47
  background and career of, 33–36, 39–46

  in bailout from plane one, 172–73, 191–92
  Barr and, 338–40
  in bombing run over Japan, 137–38, 141
  broken ankles of, 45–46, 191
  childhood of, 34–35
  in China after bailout, 208–10, 215,
    225–26
  death of, 363
  described, 35, 40
  DFC awarded to, 43
  in 8th Air Force, 307
  Eisenhower's antipathy toward, 272–73
  fame of, 40, 43–44, 48
  FDR's welcome-home plan for, 229–32
  first raid report of, 217
  Halsey described by, 115
  introduced to Seventeenth Bomb Group,
    32–33
  at Japanese surrender, 327
  knighted, 308
  on last night ashore, 60
  in launch from *Hornet*, 125–26
  Lawson visited by, 268–69
  marriage of, 39
  Marshall's phone conversation with, 61
  Medal of Honor awarded to, 230–32
  as mission leader, 53–54, 110–11
  at MIT, 44, 46
  in Overlord, 308
  personality of, 34, 40–41
  President's Medal of Freedom awarded to,
    363
  promoted to brigadier general, 225
  raid as viewed by, 232–33
  Raiders decorated by, 271–72
  raid's first anniversary and, 294
  retirement of, 347
  17th Bomb Group briefed by, 61
  in 12th Air Force, 272–73, 274, 294
  university education of, 36–37
  in World War I, 37, 39–41, 49
Doolittle, James H., Jr., 47, 231
Doolittle, James H., III, 363
Doolittle, John, 47, 231, 363
Doolittle, Josephine Daniels "Joe," 36, 39, 42,
    47, 60, 229, 231–32, 352, 363
  signed tablecloth of, 47
Doolittle, Rosa Ceremah Shephard, 34, 35, 36
Doolittle Raid:
  annual reunions of, 346–47, 349–53
  approach to Japan in, 131–36
  bombing runs in, 136–48
  briefings for, 61, 66–67, 69–70

Doolittle Raid (*cont.*)
  captures in, 235–67
  Chiang's reaction to, 227
  Doolittle's first report on, 217
  Doolittle's leadership in, 53–54, 110–11
  Doolittle's perception of, 232–33
  effects of bombings in, 148–50, 158
  FDR's knowledge of, 118
  as film subject, 318–21
  final leave before, 59–60
  first anniversary of, 294
  fuel shortage in, 131–33
  initial idea for, 105, 106–7
  Japanese announcements of, 157–58, 216,
    218–19
  launch from *Hornet* for, 121–30
  Lawson's memoir about, 21, 318
  Low's proposal of, 108–9
  maps used in, 67–68
  onset of, 60–61
  refueling issue in, 162–67
  reprisals and punishments for, 226–28,
    259–60, 268–97, 321
  rescue attempts in, 233–34
  secrecy and, 53, 56, 110, 111
  surprise in, 135–36, 150, 155
  targets of, 63
  training for, 15–18, 50
  in U.S. media, 160, 216–18
  volunteers for, 8–10
  War Department's official communique on,
    295, 318
  Yamamoto's reaction to, 228–29
  see also specific planes and crew members
Doolittle Raiders Association Scholarship
    Fund, 350
dos Remedios, Caesar Luis, 290, 341
Douglas A-20, 87
Douglas B-18, 23, 87
Douglas B-23 Dragon, 109
Douglas DB-7, 106
Douglas Devastator, 57, 255, 256
Douglas SBD-3 Dauntless, 255, 283
Douhet, Giulio, 306, 307
Drumbeat (Paukenschlag), Operation, 27–28,
    29, 260, 360
Duncan, Donald "Wu," 108–9, 110, 111, 112,
    114, 162
Duquette, Omer Adelard, xvii, 252, 295
Dutch East Indies, 74, 78, 81, 95, 99, 102
Dykema, Mrs. T. J., 232

Eaker, Ira, 306–7
Eastern Sea Frontier, 28, 29

Edgars, Dorothy, 82
Eglin Field, Fla., 10–11, 13–14, 17
  today, 355
Eierman, Jacob, xvii, 154, 206–7
Eighth Air Force, U.S., 306–7, 308
Eighth Fleet, U.S., 358
Eisenhower, Dwight D., xii-xiii, 33, 100, 101,
    102, 218, 276
  Doolittle disliked by, 272–73
Electric Machinery Works, 154
Ellet, USS, 56
Elliott, George, Jr., 85
Emmens, Justine, 364
Emmens, Robert G., xvi, 11, 128, 133, 144,
    169–71, 218, 262, 263, 285–89,
    298–300, 308–14, 354, 364
Empire State Building, 354
England, Bessie, 212, 221
England, Frank, 212–13, 214, 246–47
Enigma, 253
Enola Gay, 357
Enterprise, USS, 56, 91, 108, 305
  at Midway, 254–55, 257, 259
  nuclear-powered reincarnation of, 355
  Pearl Harbor attack and, 78, 81–82, 90
  at Santa Cruz Islands, 283–85
  in Task Force 16, 113, 115–16, 119–21,
    156–57
Essex, USS, 305
European Recovery Program (Marshall Plan),
    357
Europe-first strategy, 105

Faktor, Leland D., xv, 174, 198, 215–16, 295
Fanning, USS, 56
Farrow, William G., xviii, 123, 129, 135, 155,
    233, 236, 242, 264, 280–83, 289,
    295–97, 344
Fast Carrier Task Force 58, U.S., 357
Federal Bureau of Investigation (FBI), 79, 93
Fenno, F. W., Jr., 114
Fickle Finger of Fate, see plane twelve
"fifth column," 87
Fifth Fleet, Japanese, 120
Firefly, Project, 321
First Air Fleet, Japanese, 77–78, 306
Fitzgerald, John E., 112, 356
Fitzhugh, Dottie, 365
Fitzhugh, William N., xv, 173, 181, 349, 365
Fitzmaurice, Donald E., xvi, 233, 235–38,
    239, 295, 296
Five Daring Acrobats, 41
Fletcher, Frank "Jack," 254
Flood, Charles, 86

Flying Tigers (American Volunteer Group), 105–6, 164, 358
Fokker Dr-I triplane, 37
Foley, Francis Drake, 284, 285
Forbis, James, 85
Ford, John, 124
Foreign Ministry, Japanese, 80
Forsythe, John, 320
Forty-seventh Bomb Group, U.S., 345
Forty-ninth Air Division, U.S., 345
France, 49, 98, 99, 273
Free French, 273
Free Methodist Church, 343
Friedman, William M., xiii
Fuchida, Joe, 357
Fuchida Mitsuo, 94, 295
    death of, 357
    DeShazer and, 348–49, 357
    on effect of Doolittle Raid, 228
    on Japanese naval leadership, 115
    at Japanese surrender, 327
    at Midway, 256, 258–59
    in Pearl Harbor attack, 77–78, 83, 84, 86, 88, 90–91
    in Philippine Sea battle, 306
    religious conversion of, 342–43, 347–49
Fujita Nobuo, 260
Fusco, PFC, 87

Gaines, Jesse, 87
Gallagher, T. A., 157
Gardner, Melvin J., xvii, 51, 151, 178, 203–4, 252, 295
Garfield, John, 320
Gay, George, 255–57, 259
Gee-Bee Sportster R-1, 47–48
Genda Minoru, 78
Geneva Conventions, 148
George VI, king of England, 308
Georges, Col., 166
Germany, Imperial, 71–72
Germany, Nazi, 28, 65, 74, 76, 78, 98, 99, 102, 103, 306, 314, 341
Gibbons, Hubert B., 119, 120
Gilbert, Patty, 17–18
Glines, Carroll V., 40, 366
Gobeo, Frank, 86
Good Earth, The (Buck), 163
Goodwin, Phillip, 35
Grant, Cary, 320
Gray, Robert Manning, xv, 51, 134–35, 139, 174, 260, 276, 295, 320
Grayling, USS, 257
Grayson, USS, 56, 60

Great Britain, 28, 71, 76, 79, 95, 98, 99, 227
Great Depression, 19
Greater East Asia Coprosperity Sphere, 95
Great Escape, xii, 277
Great Pacific War, The (Bywater), 75
Green Hornet, see plane six
Greening, Charles Ross, xvii, 6, 13, 15, 16, 17, 19, 25, 51, 58, 118, 121, 125, 150–52, 159, 178, 179–80, 202–3, 204, 252, 260, 274, 275, 278–80, 364
Greening, Dot, 268, 278, 364
Grew, Joseph, 80, 82, 92, 149
Griffin, Esther, 367
Griffin, Thomas Carson, xvi, 60, 67–68, 145, 175, 201–2, 275, 367
Grumman F4F-4 Wildcat, 57, 255, 283
Grumman F6F Hellcat, 305
Grumman TBF Avenger, 283
Guadalcanal, Battle of, 283, 294
Guam, 72, 77, 82, 91, 95, 110
Gulfamerica, S.S., 29
Gulf War, 355
Guy Named Joe, A (film), 364
Gwin, USS, 56, 60

Hagakure (*The Book of the Samurai*) (Yamamoto), 83
Haguro, 156
Hale, Alan, 320
Hallmark, Dean Edward, xvi, 142, 232, 235–40, 246, 264–67, 280–83, 289, 295–97, 344
Hallock, Ted, 307
Halpro Project, 117, 226
Halsey, William F. "Bill," 56, 90–91, 113–15, 117–19, 121, 125, 156, 167, 254, 283, 327, 358
Halverson, Harry E., 117
Hamada, Dick, 329–31, 332, 365
Hamada, Irene, 365
Hammond, George, 3–5, 27
Hancock, USS, 358
Handler, Frank, 86
Hardegen, Reinhard, 28, 29
Hari Kari-er, see plane eleven
Harmon, Millard F., Jr., 54
Hata Itsura, 281–82
Hata Shunroku, 267
Haw Haw, Lady, 157
Hawks, Howard, 318
Haynes, Caleb V., 117
Hearst, William Randolph, 42
Helena, USS, 85, 86
Hell's Angels, 358

Hemingway, Ernest, 29
Herndon, Julia, 365
Herndon, Nolan A., xii, xvi, 133, 143–4, 169, 171, 287, 299, 313, 314, 365
Higgins, Andrew Jackson, xii
Hilger, John A., xvii, 51, 53, 153–54, 181, 207, 260, 268, 346
Hill, Max, 149
Hilton, James, 216
Hirohito, emperor of Japan, 63, 71, 78, 94, 226, 281, 295, 328, 362
  death of, 363
  Pearl Harbor attack and, 79–80, 82
  war blame issue and, 341–42
  war's end announced by, 326–27
Hiryu, 77, 94, 156, 259
Hite, Portia, 365
Hite, Robert L., xviii, 129, 130, 233, 236–37, 240–42, 264–67, 280–81, 290–92, 302–3, 305, 324, 332, 333, 334–35, 336, 339, 340, 341, 352, 365
Hitler, Adolf, 27, 49, 74, 99
Hiyo, 306
Ho Chi Minh, 329
Holstrom, Everett W., xv, 3–4, 10, 24, 114, 140, 141, 198–99, 260, 352, 367
Holstrom, Hattie, 352, 367
Hong Kong, 71, 74, 81, 92, 93–94, 95
Hong Kong Clipper, 92
Honjo Seikichi, 148
Hoover, Herbert, 97
Hoover, J. Edgar, 79
Hoover, Travis, xv, 8, 126, 138–39, 173, 181–82, 192–93, 195, 273–74, 280, 346, 349, 365, 368
Hope, Bob, 68, 350
Hopkins, Harry, 82–83, 99
Hornet, USS, 60–61, 113, 107–8, 119–20, 159, 295, 319
  aircraft of, 57
  B-25 aircraft tested on, 111–12
  crew of, 56–57
  described, 55
  interservice rivalry on, 58–59
  at Midway, 254–57, 259
  naming of, 56
  new version of, 305, 316, 355
  raid launched from, 121–30
  17th Bomb Group loaded on, 57–58
  sunk, 283–85
Horton, Edwin Weston, Jr., xvii, 146, 147, 177, 202
Howe, Task Force, 56, 113, 115

Hull, Cordell, 76, 80, 81, 84, 93, 105–6, 361
Hypo (Op-20-G), 252–53, 294

I-25, 259–60
Ickes, Harold, 78
Iida Minoru, 148
Illustrious, HMS, 75
Imperial Japanese Navy, 75, 306
Indonesia, 71, 79, 95
Influence of Sea Power Upon History, The (Mahan), 96, 254
International Military Tribunal for the Far East, 281, 341–42
Intrepid, USS, 305
Iran, xii
Ishii Shiro, 227
Italy, 76, 99, 102, 279, 294, 341
"I Was a Prisoner of Japan" (DeShazer), 343–44, 347, 364
Iwata, Mrs., 148
Iwo Jima, Battle of, 314

Jacot, Nestor, 330, 332
Jai Fu Chang, *see* Charlie
James H. Doolittle Military Aviation Library, 363
Japan, xii, 28, 65, 68, 99, 162, 305
  atomic bombing of, 324–25
  bacterial warfare waged by, 227–28
  in China, 73–74
  firebombing of, 315–16
  modern history of, 71–73
  pan-Pacific campaign of, 74–75, 78, 92–95
  picket boat warning system of, 119–21, 156–57
  surrender of, 326–28
  uyoku cult in, 361–62
  see also Pearl Harbor attack
Japan Advertiser, 158
Japanese Diesel Manufacturing Company, 158
Japanese Steel Corporation Factory Number One, 158
Japan Special Steel Company, 146
Jarman, Fontaine, Jr., 330, 333
Java, 77, 94
Jessel, George, 350
Jimmu, emperor of Japan, 80
JOAK, 157–58
John Birch Society, 216
Johnson, Harry, Jr., 50, 126
Johnson, "Singing Boy," 250–51
Johnson, Van, 320

Joint Chiefs of Staff, U.S., 100, 101, 102, 124, 329, 355
Joint Committee on the Investigation of the Pearl Harbor Attack, 361
Jones, Aden Earl, xv, 139, 174
Jones, David M., xvi, 6, 8–9, 13–14, 17, 22–23, 32, 62, 67–69, 123, 127, 133, 141–42, 143, 161–62, 174–75, 200, 204, 215, 249, 274, 275, 277, 280, 345–46, 370–71
Jones, USS, 112
Jordan, Bert M., xv, 7, 10, 140, 199, 365
Joyce, Richard Outcalt, xvii, 146, 147, 155, 177–78, 260
Jurika, Stephen, 58, 66–67, 69–70, 120, 125, 157, 186, 285

Kaga, 77, 94, 257, 258
Kappeler, Frank Albert, xvii, 10–11, 18–19, 60, 134, 150, 178, 179, 204, 252, 365
Kawasaki Aircraft Factory, 154
Kawasaki Ki.61 Type 3, 151
Kawasaki Truck and Tank plant, 145
Kaze Toshikazu, 327–28
Kempeitai, 243–46, 264–65, 322, 342
Kennedy, John F., xi
Kennedy, Joseph, 98
Kernan, Alvin, 115, 116, 120
Kimi (Fuchida's mistress), 347
Kimmel, Edward, 359
Kimmel, Husband, 76, 81, 84, 88, 90, 359, 360–61
King, David, 89
King, Ernest J., 28, 29, 60, 76, 100, 107–8, 109, 110, 111, 117, 118, 160, 273, 306, 356, 360
  Arnold and, 101–2
Kinkaid, Thomas, 283
Knobloch, Richard A., xvii, 9, 20, 41, 62, 123, 128–29, 152–53, 180, 205–6, 250, 280, 365–66
Knobloch, Rosemary Rice, 9
Knox, Frank, 76, 81, 88, 99, 100, 101, 117, 361
Kobayashi Yoshinori, 362
Kolya (Russian agent), 288, 298, 299–300, 308–9, 313
Konoye Fumimaro, 80
Korean War, 336, 350, 365
Korn, Donald L., 86
Kramer, Alvin, 82, 83–84
Kratovil (copilot), 261
Kumano Tatsuo, 242

Kurilchyk, Richard, 354
Kwangtung Army, Japanese, 73, 74

Laban, Theodore H., xvi, 287, 299, 313, 346
Lamarr, Hedy, 319–20
Landsdowne, USS, 327
Langley, Samuel D., 37
Lanphier, Thomas, Jr., 294–95
Laos, 74
Larkin, George Elmer, Jr., xvii, 62, 147, 177, 251–52, 276
Laurence, Bill, 324–25
Laurey (sailor), 117
Lawson, Ann, 319
Lawson, Ellen, 17–18, 21–22, 50, 69, 184, 260–61, 268–72, 317–18, 320, 321, 371–72
Lawson, Mayme, 268
Lawson, Ted W., xvi, 8, 14, 16, 17, 18, 50, 54, 59, 64, 65, 69, 126, 232
  as author of filmed book on raid, 21, 317–21
  background of, 21–22
  in bombing run over Japan, 142–43
  in China after plane crash, 195–96, 211–14, 220–22, 230, 247–50, 260–61
  in crash landing, 183–88
  Doolittle's visit with, 268–71
  Ellen's reunion with, 270–72
  in launch from *Hornet*, 124, 127, 132
  leg amputated, 220–22
  postwar career of, 371–72
Layton, Ed, 254
League of Nations, 73
Leiland, Major, 252
LeMay, Curtis "Iron Ass," 20, 314–15, 316, 368–69
Lend-Lease, 104, 106, 163, 227
Leonard, Paul John, xv, 135, 138, 191, 209–10, 215, 274–75, 295
LeRoy, Mervin, 319
Lexington, USS, 66, 78, 82, 113, 305
Liberal Democratic Party, Japanese, 362
Library of Congress, 5
Life, 261
Lilienthal, Otto, 37
Lindbergh, Charles A., 20, 32
Ling, Captain, 239, 240
Lockheed Hudson, 106
Lockheed P-38 Lightning, 6, 274, 294, 307
Loew's Incorporated, 318
Los Angeles Times, 5

Lost Horizon (Hilton), 216
Lovelace, Sergeant, 14, 272
Low, Francis "Frog," 107–10, 162, 356
Luce, Clare Boothe, 365
Luce, Henry, 162
Lucky Thirteen, see plane thirteen
Ludlow, USS, 112
Luftwaffe, 308
Luxembourg, 49

MacArthur, Douglas, 33, 88, 93, 94, 102, 158,
   250, 272, 314, 327, 328, 329, 330, 341,
   342, 359–60
McCarthy, James F., 112
McClure, Charles L., xvi, 18, 32, 54, 59–60,
   61, 183, 184–88, 195, 214, 247, 271
McCluskey, Wade, 257–58
McCool, Harry C., xi, xv, 24, 134, 140–41,
   198–99, 250–51, 346, 368–69
McElroy, Agnes, 366
McElroy, Edgar E., xvii, 152–53, 205–6, 249,
   366
McGurl, Eugene Francis, xvi, 174, 222, 295
Macia, James Herbert, Jr., xvii, 6, 26, 32, 51,
   59, 105, 122, 137, 154, 180–81, 206–8,
   275–76, 280, 350, 371
Macia, Mary Alice, 122, 371
McKinney, Glenn, 232
MacLeish, Archibald, 5
Magic, 252–53, 259
Magpie, Operation, 330–31
Mahan, Alfred Thayer, 97, 254, 308
Malaya, 74, 77, 78, 79, 82, 85, 94, 95
Manch, Jacob Earle, xv, 18–19, 123, 134–35,
   139–40, 174, 197–98
Manchukuo, 72
Manchuria, 72
Manske, Joseph W., xvi, 64–65, 175
Mao Zedong, 74, 163, 164, 357
Marco Polo Bridge incident, 73
"Marianas Turkey Shoot," 306
Marshall, George C., 60, 61, 81, 83, 84, 94,
   97, 98, 102, 106, 107, 117, 160, 162,
   217, 224, 230–32, 259, 273, 329
   Arnold and, 104
   and Chinese Civil War, 356–57
   Doolittle's phone conversation with, 61
   FDR's relationship with, 100–101
   Nobel Prize awarded to, 357
   refueling site issue and, 162–65
Marshall Plan (European Recovery Program),
   357
Martin, Glenn, 100
Martin B-26 Marauder, 109, 274, 346, 365

Maryland, USS, 85, 89, 90
Mason, Charles P., 283, 284
Matsuhigecho oil warehouse, 154
Maya, 156
Medal of Honor, 230–32, 351
Meder, Robert John, xvi, 233, 235, 237–38,
   240, 246, 264, 290–93, 296, 302, 303,
   305, 322–23, 341, 344
Meiji, emperor of Japan, 79
Meiji Restoration, 71
Meredith, USS, 56, 60, 116
Meserve, Charles Granvill, 370
MGM, 318, 319–20, 364
Midway, Battle of, 252–59
   breaking of Japanese codes and, 252–53
   Doolittle Raid and, 229, 254
   Japanese losses in, 259
Midway atoll, 229
   today, 358
Mike (Mikhail Constantinovich Schmaring),
   218, 262–63
Mike, Task Force, 56, 113, 115
Miles, Bill, 59
Military Ordinance Number Four, Japanese,
   267
Miller, Doris, 90
Miller, Henry, 13, 14, 58, 63–64, 65–66, 121,
   128, 358
Miller, Lieutenant, 157, 233
Miller, Richard Ewing, xv, 138–39, 194, 275,
   295
Missouri, USS, 327
Mitchell, Billy, 41, 306, 307
Mitchum, Robert, 320
Mitscher, Marc Andrew "Pete," 57, 58, 60, 61,
   111, 112, 113, 117, 122, 128, 156, 157,
   254, 283, 357–58
Mitscher, USS, 358
Mitsubishi A6M (Zero), 57, 78, 100, 256,
   257, 294, 305
Mitsubishi Aircraft Works, 154
Mitsubishi G4M, 78
Mitsubishi Heavy Industrial Corporation,
   158
Molter, Albert, 89
Monssen, 56, 60
Morgenthau, Henry, 5, 106
Morison, Samuel Eliot, 101
Moysey, Frank, 149
Muniz Lavalle, Ramon, 149–50
Musashi, 254
Mustin, USS, 285
Myers, Richard, 355
Myoko, 156

Nachi, 156
Nagato, 228
Nagoya Aircraft Factory, 158
Nagoya Castle, 154
Nagoya Second Temporary Army Hospital, 158
Nagumo Chuichi, 81, 84, 90, 91, 253, 255–56, 283
Nakajima B5N, 78
Nashville, USS, 56, 60, 120
National Aeronautics and Space Administration (NASA), xii, 44, 370
National Air and Space Museum, 47
National Hemp and Dressing Company, 158
National Security Act (1947), 356
Nation's Hero!, A, 232
Nautilus, USS, 257
Naval Cryptographic Section, 82
Navy Department, U.S., 28, 29, 117, 329
Netherlands, 49, 72, 79, 99
Nevada, USS, 85, 86, 89, 90
New Deal, 97
New Guinea, 95, 102, 294
Newsweek, 81
New York Herald Tribune, 81
New York Times, 81, 160, 227, 295, 296, 320, 351
Nichi Nichi, 158
Nichols, Ray, 330, 331–32
Nielsen, Chase Jay, xvi, 142, 233, 235–36, 237, 240, 245–46, 264–65, 291, 293, 296, 302, 322, 332, 333, 336, 339, 341, 365, 366
Nielsen, Phyllis, 366
Nimitz, Chester, 102, 117, 250, 253, 254–55, 305, 314, 329, 356, 358
Niswander (pilot), 261
Nitto Maru, 120–21, 135, 155, 156, 167
Nixon, Richard, 359
Nomura, Mr., 153
Norden bombsight, 12–13, 15
North American Aviation, 350, 354
North American B-25 Mitchell, 7, 109, 131, 352
    armament of, 7–8
    in Empire State Building crash, 354
    flaws of, 7–8
    modifications of, 11–13, 17
    takeoff techniques of, 13–14
    tested on *Hornet,* 111–12
    training in, 15–17
North American P-51 Mustang, 354
North American X-15, 354

Northampton, USS, 56
Not As Briefed (Greening), 364
Novey, Jack, 335
Noyes, Walt, 39
Number One, Operation, 75, 77, 91

O'Donnell, Rosie, 88
Office of Strategic Services (OSS), 163, 328–29, 330, 333, 359
Office of War Information, 319
Ogura Oil Refining Plant, 152
oil, 76
Okada Ryuhei, 340–41
Okasaki Hospital, 148
Okinawa, Battle of, 314, 363
Oklahoma, USS, 85, 89, 90
On War (Kobayashi), 362
Ordnance Department, U.S. Navy, 57
Osborne, Edgar G. "Ozzie," 125, 127, 129
Outerbridge, William, 84
Overlord, Operation, 101, 273, 308, 329
Ozuk, Charles John, Jr., xv, 15, 65, 122–23, 135, 139, 174, 196–97, 222, 275, 366
Ozuk, Georgian, 366

Parker, James N., xvi, 201
Patton, George S., 33, 100, 272
Pearl Harbor attack, 3, 5–6, 27–28, 72, 75–91, 105, 110
    conspiracy theory of, 359–61
    execution of, 86–91
    Hirohito and, 79–80, 82
    inspiration for, 75
    Japanese organization and forces in, 77–78, 79
    oil issue and, 76
    onset of, 84–86
    panic in aftermath of, 91
    U.S. deployments in, 85–86
    U.S. sightings in, 84–85
    warnings of, 76–77, 79, 81, 84, 360–61
Peck, Otto, 6
Penguin, USS, 91
Pennsylvania, USS, 85, 89
Perkins, Frances, 92
Perkins, Mahlon, 330, 331
Perry, Matthew, 71, 327
Pétain, Henri, 273
Philippine Clipper, 92
Philippines, 72, 77, 78, 79, 81, 82, 91, 92–93, 94, 95, 102, 110, 228, 329, 359–60
plane one:
    in approach to Japan, 134–35
    in bombing run over Japan, 137–38, 141

plane one (*cont.*)
  crew in bailout from, 172–73
  crew roster of, xv
  fate of crew of, 191, 208–10, 215
  in launch from *Hornet,* 125–26
  see also Doolittle, James H.
plane two, 173
  in approach to Japan, 134
  in bombing run over Japan, 138–39,
    141
  crash landing of, 181–82
  crew roster of, xv
  fate of crew of, 192–95
  in launch from *Hornet,* 126
plane three (*Whiskey Pete*), 51
  in approach to Japan, 134
  in bombing run over Japan, 139, 143
  crew in bailout from, 174
  crew roster of, xv
  fate of crew of, 196–98
plane four:
  in approach to Japan, 134
  in bombing run over Japan, 140–41
  crew roster of, xv
  fate of crew of, 198–200, 250–51
plane five:
  in bombing run over Japan, 141–42,
    143
  crew in bailout from, 174–75
  crew roster of, xvi
  fate of crew of, 200–201, 215–16, 249
  in launch from *Hornet,* 127
plane six (*Green Hornet*), 51, 140, 142, 339
  crash landing of, 235–36
  crew of, as POWs, 237–40, 245–46,
    264–65, 281, 290–93, 302–5, 316–17,
    321–24, 332–36
  crew roster of, xvi
plane seven (*Ruptured Duck*):
  in approach to Japan, 132
  in bombing run over Japan, 142–43
  crash landing of, 183–88
  crew roster of, xvi
  fate of crew of, 195–96, 211–15, 220–22,
    247–50, 260–61
  found wreckage of, 272
  insignia of, 14
  in launch from *Hornet,* 127
  see also Lawson, Ted W.
plane eight:
  in approach to Japan, 133
  in bombing run over Japan, 143–44
  crew in escape from Soviet Union, 298–302,
    308–14

crew of, interned in Soviet Union, 172,
    218–20, 261–63, 285–89, 295
  crew roster of, xvi
  in landing in Soviet Union, 169–72
  in launch from *Hornet,* 128
plane nine (*Whirling Dervish*), 51
  in approach to Japan, 132–33
  in bombing run over Japan, 145–46
  crew in bailout from, 175–76
  crew roster of, xvi
  fate of crew of, 201–2
plane ten:
  in bombing run over Japan, 146–47,
    155–56
  crew in bailout from, 176–78
  crew roster of, xvii
  fate of crew of, 202, 251–52
plane eleven (*Hari Kari-er*), 19, 25, 134, 260
  in bombing run over Japan, 150–52
  crew in bailout from, 178–80
  crew roster of, xvii
  fate of crew of, 202–4, 222–26, 251–52
  insignia of, 51
  in launch from *Hornet,* 128–29
plane twelve (*Fickle Finger of Fate*), 51, 180,
    252
  in bombing run over Japan, 152
  crew roster of, xvii
plane thirteen (*Lucky Thirteen*):
  in bombing run over Japan, 152–53
  crew in bailout from, 180
  crew roster of, xvii
  fate of crew of, 205–6, 249, 250
plane fourteen:
  in bombing run over Japan, 153–54
  crew in bailout from, 180–81
  crew roster of, xvii
  fate of crew of, 206–8
plane fifteen:
  in bombing run over Japan, 154
  crash landing of, 182–83
  crew roster of, xviii
  fate of crew of, 210–11, 213–15
  in launch from *Hornet,* 129
plane sixteen (*Bat Out of Hell*), 51, 65, 123,
    339
  in bombing run over Japan, 154–55
  crew in bailout from, 236–37
  crew of, as POWs, 238–44, 264–67,
    280–83, 289–93, 302–5, 316–17,
    321–24, 332–36
  crew roster of, xviii
  found wreckage of, 272
  in launch from *Hornet,* 129–30

Platte, USS, 116
Pocket Testament League, 348
Pohl, David W., xvi, 68, 287, 299, 310, 313
Poland, 49, 72
Popov, Dusko (Tricycle), 79, 93
Popular Mechanics, 36
Portal, Charles, 109–10
Portugal, 99
Potter, Henry A., xv, 126, 135, 138, 161, 209–10, 352, 366
Pound, Dudley, 29
Pound, William R., xvii, 180
Powhatten, USS, 327
Prange, Gordon, 5
precision bombing strategy, 12, 306–7, 314–15
Pressler, Red, 86
Prince of Wales, HMS, 94
Princeton, USS, 358
Pulitzer Trophy, 44
Purple Heart, The (film), 320
Pu Yi, 72

Qing Dynasty, 72
Quigley (sailor), 117

Radio Japan, 216
Radio Tokyo, 116
Radney, Douglas V., xv
Raiders' Memorial, 350
Raid of the Fire Wind, 316
Raleigh, USS, 85, 86
Ramapo, USS, 89
Randall, G. D., 157
Ranger, USS, 358
Reddy, Kenneth E., xvii, 13, 128, 134, 151, 152, 178, 202–3, 222–26, 276, 295
Reluctant Admiral, The (Agawa), 76
Republic P-47 Thunderbolt, 307
Repulse, HMS, 94
Richter, Melvin, 330
Richtofen, Manfred von, 37
Rickenbacker, Eddie, 32, 48
Ring, Stanhope, 158
Roberts Commission, 102, 360
Rochefort, Joseph J., 252–53, 358
Rockwell International, 354–55
Rodgers, Calbraith Perry, 42
Rommel, Erwin, 274
Roosevelt, Eleanor, 319
Roosevelt, Franklin D., 5, 29–31, 94, 106, 107, 110, 198, 227, 251, 259, 273, 297
    Arnold and, 104–5, 111
    background of, 97–98, 162

death of, 355–56
described, 96
disability of, 98–99
Doolittle Raid knowledge of, 118
executions announcement and, 295–96
Marshall's relationship with, 100–101
OSS and, 328
Pearl Harbor attack reaction of, 93, 97, 99
Pearl Harbor conspiracy theory and, 359, 361
Shangri-La speech of, 216–17
U.S.-Japanese relations and, 73, 78, 80, 81–83
"welcome home plan" of, 229–32
Roosevelt, Sara Delano, 98, 216
Rosenbaum, Tutelee, 60
Rosenman, Sam, 216
Roth, William, 359
Roundup, Operation, 273
Royal Air Force, 306
Royal Navy, 29, 356
Royce, George, 58
Ruptured Duck, see plane seven
Russia, Imperial, 72

Sabine, USS, 56
St. Louis, USS, 85
Salt Lake City, USS, 56
San Francisco, USS, 85
Santa Cruz Islands, 283
Saratoga, USS, 66
Sawada Shigeru, 340–41
Saylor, Edward Joseph, xviii, 367
Saylor, Lorraine, 367
Schmaring, Mikhail Constantinovich (Mike), 218, 262–63
Schoenbeck, Ernst Von, 45
Schuirmann, R. E., 163
Scott, Eldred V., xvi, 132, 145–46, 201
Scott, Robert Lee, Jr., 117
Second American Volunteer Group, 106
Sessler, Anna Bell, 367
Sessler, Howard Albert, xviii, 19, 60, 61, 121–22, 154, 367
Sevareid, Eric, 163
Seventeenth Bombardment Group, U.S.:
    aircraft flown by, 7–8
    Doolittle's briefing of, 61
    Doolittle's introduction to, 32–33
    Drumbeat Operation and, 27–29
    equipment of, 52–53
    Japanese submarine destroyed by, 4
    loaded onto *Hornet,* 57–58
    naming of airplanes in, 51

Seventeenth Bombardment Group (*cont.*)
  origin of, 23
  Pearl Harbor attack and, 5–6
  recruits and volunteers of, 19–27
  in transfer from Oregon, 3–5
  in transfer to Alameda, 54–55
  in transfer to California, 50–51
Seventh Air Force, U.S., 94
Shangri-La, USS, 217
Shell Oil, 48–49
Shokaku, 94, 156, 283–84, 306
Short, Leslie Vernon, 90
Short, Walter, 78, 84, 87, 359, 360–61
Sicily, 294
Signal Corps, U.S., 37
Silver Star, 186, 280
Sims, Jack A., xvii, 60, 275–76
Singapore, 71, 74, 77, 81, 82, 84, 85,
  94, 95
Sledgehammer, Operation, 273
Smith, Donald G., xviii, 14, 129, 154, 182,
  210, 260, 275, 295
Smith, William F., Jr., 354
Smithsonian Institution, 47
Smyth, Mrs., 248
Soong, T. V., 162, 217, 333
Soryu, 77, 94, 156, 257, 258
Soucek, Apollo, 66
Soviet Union, xii, 144, 164, 342
  German invasion of, 74
  plane eight's crew in escape from, 298–302,
    308–14
  plane eight's crew interned in, 169–72,
    218–20, 261–63, 285–89, 295
Spaatz, Carl "Tooey," 294
Spain, 99
Spatz, Harold A., xviii, 65, 129, 155, 233, 242,
  264–65, 281–83, 289, 295–97, 344
Special Aviation Project #1, *see* Doolittle Raid
Special Ops (SO), 329
Spencer, Evelyn, 232
Spruance, Ray, 254, 255
Stalag Luft I, 279–80
Stalag Luft III, 275, 277
Stalin, Joseph, 164, 165, 286, 298
Standley, William, 219–20, 263
Stark, Harold "Betty," 81, 83, 84, 100, 101,
  359
State Department, U.S., 80, 220, 295–96, 329
Steinbeck, John, 134
Stephens, Robert J., xv, 141
Stern, General, 172
Stilwell, Joseph, 33, 160, 164, 166, 216, 226,
  227, 234, 327

Stilwell Papers (Stilwell), 164
Stimson, Henry L., 76, 81, 100, 107, 329,
  361
Stork, J. Royden, xvii, 147, 177
Strategic Air Command, U.S., 369
*Study of Strategy and Tactics in Operations
  Against the United States*, 75
Sugiyama Hajime, 263, 281, 295, 328
Sumatra, 94, 95
Sumner, M., 232
Supermarine Spitfire, 307
Sutherland, John, 120
Sutherland, Richard K., 91
Suzuki Kikujiro, 148
Swan, USS, 85
Sweden, 99
Swigert, Jack, 370
Switzerland, 99

Taiho, 306
Taiyo Maru, 80
Takada Teruhiki, 321
Takahashi, General, 331
Takamatsu, prince of Japan, 78, 345
Takao, 156
Tangier, USS, 85
Taranto attack, 75, 109–10
task force, standard size of, 55–56
Task Force 16, U.S., 56, 62, 167, 356
  en route to launch area, 114–18
  Japanese discovery of, 119–21
  Japanese knowledge of, 113
  Japanese pursuit of, 156–57
Task Force 17, U.S., 283
Tatsuta Sotojiro, 282, 289, 340–41
Tauranac, John, 354
Taylor, Thomas, 85
Tennessee, USS, 85, 90
Tenth Fleet, U.S., 356
Thach, James E., 258
Thailand, 77, 85
Thatcher, David J., xvi, 132, 142–43, 183–88,
  195, 215, 275, 295, 319, 320
Thaxter, Phyllis, 318
Third Air Force, U.S., 345
Thirteenth Army Military Court, Japanese, 281
Thirty-fourth Attack Squadron, U.S., 23
Thirty Seconds over Tokyo (film), 318–21, 364
Thirty Seconds over Tokyo (Lawson), 21, 318
Thompson Trophy, 47–48
Thresher, USS, 109, 114–15, 159, 320
Thumb, Ensign, 59
Tibbets, Paul, 357
Time, 81, 99, 162

Togo Shigenori, 82, 92
Tojo Hideki, 74, 80, 81, 92, 263, 281, 342, 362
Tokyo Gas and Electric Engineering Company, 145
Tominaga Shozo, 73
Tone, 84
Tong, T. T., 223
Tora! Tora! Tora! (film), 369
Torch, Operation, 110, 273, 294, 329
torpedoes, 57
    Japanese, 77, 99
Torpedo Squadron Eight, U.S., 57, 255, 256–57, 259
Towns, Mrs. Charles A., 338–39
Tracy, Spencer, 320
Tripartite Pact, 76
Trout, USS, 109, 114–15, 159, 320
Truelove, Denver Vernon, xvi, 64, 141–42
Truk, Battle of, 57
Truman, Harry S., 100, 328, 356, 359
Trumbo, Dalton, 318, 319
Tsuji Masanobu, 77
Tully, Grace, 216
Tung-Sheng Liu, 193–95, 346, 349, 366
Tunisia, 294
Turing, Alan M., xiii
Tuteur, Werner, 337
Twelfth Air Force, U.S., 272–73, 274, 294
Twentieth Century–Fox, 320
Tyler, Kermit, 85

U-123, 29
U-boats, 27–28, 29, 305
Ugaki Matome, 121
Unit 731, Japanese, 227, 342, 359
Uno Shintaro, 244
Uokosuka E14Y1 floatplane, 260
U.S. Rubber Company, 132
Uyenoshita Steel Works #2, 154
uyoku cult, 361–62

Valparaiso Inn, 17–18
Van Marter, John O., 3
Variety, 320
Vichy France, 273
Vietnam, 74
Vietnam War, 334, 336, 350, 355, 369, 370
Vincennes, USS, 56, 60, 119
Vin Fiz, 42
Vormstein (sailor), 117

Wagner, Glenn, 348
Wake Island, 77, 82, 91–92, 94, 95, 107, 110, 329

Wako Yusei, 340–41
Waldron, John C., 255, 256
Walker, Robert, 319, 320
Wall, Bob, 129–30
Ward, USS, 84
War Department, U.S., 28, 67, 104, 105, 156, 160, 230, 318, 329, 364
Warner, Jack, 318
War of 1812, 254
Washington Post, 102
Wasp, USS, 305
Watson, Edwin "Pa," 100
Watson, Harold Francis, xvi, 133, 145, 176, 201, 268, 271, 272
Watson-Watt, Robert Alexander, xiii
Wells, Florence, 153
Well-Well (interpreter), 244
West Virginia, USS, 85, 89, 90
Whirling Dervish, see plane nine
Whiskey Pete, see plane three
White, Thomas Robert, xviii, 69, 154, 182–83, 185, 211, 213–15, 220–22, 247–48, 295
Why We Fight (film), 36
Widhelm, Gus, 62, 159
Wilder, Rodney R. "Hoss," xvi, 3–4, 200, 260
Wildner, Carl Richard, xv, 123, 134, 138, 173, 181, 194, 349
Williams, Adam Ray, xvii, 206, 352
Williams, Griffith Paul, xviii, 182, 210, 275
Williams, P. D., 116
Wilson, Woodrow, 97
Wiseman, O. B., 119
Wong, Captain, 206
Wong (partisan), 239–40
World War I, 39, 65, 97
World War II, xiii, 336, 355
    Japanese surrender in, 326–28
    onset of, 5–6, 72
    strategic bombing in, 306–7, 314–15
    U.S. unpreparedness in, 99–100, 103
Wright, Orville, 37–38
Wright, Wilbur, 37–38
Wright-Patterson Air Force Museum, 350

Yamaguchi Hiroichi, 149
Yamamoto Isoroku, 306, 362
    background of, 75–76
    death of, 294–95
    Doolittle Raid as viewed by, 228–29
    Midway operation and, 253–54, 255, 256, 259
    Pearl Harbor attack and, 77, 81, 155

Yamamoto Tsunetomo, 83
Yamato, 254
Yokohama Manufacturing Company, 158
York, Edward J., xvi, 8–9, 10, 11–12, 13, 19,
    22, 52–53, 57, 128, 133, 144, 169, 171,
    219, 261–62, 285–89, 299–301, 308,
    311–14, 346, 354, 365, 367
York, M. E., 367
Yorktown, USS, 78, 254, 255, 257–59, 305
Yoshida Katsuzo, 148

Yoshikawa Takeo, 77
Youngblood, Lucien Nevelson, xv, 140, 141,
    199
Yuzawa Michio, 158

Z, Operation, *see also* Pearl Harbor attack
Zero (fighter), *see* Mitsubishi A6M
Zimbalist, Sam, 318–19
Zuiho, 283–84
Zuikaku, 94, 156, 283